PENGUIN BOOKS

# THE EAGLE UNBOWED

Halik Kochanski read Modern History at Balliol College, Oxford and then completed a PhD at King's College London. She has taught at both King's College London and University College London and presented papers to a number of military history conferences. She has written a number of articles and is the author of *Sir Garnet Wolseley: Victorian Hero* (1999). She is a Fellow of the Royal Historical Society. She has been a member of the councils of the Army Records Society and Society for Army Historical Research and remains a member of both societies. She is also a member of the British Commission for Military History and the Institute for Historical Research. She is currently a judge for the Templer Medal book prize.

# HALIK KOCHANSKI

# The Eagle Unbowed

*Poland and the Poles in the
Second World War*

PENGUIN BOOKS

PENGUIN BOOKS

Published by the Penguin Group
Penguin Books Ltd, 80 Strand, London WC2R ORL, England
Penguin Group (USA) Inc., 375 Hudson Street, New York, New York 10014, USA
Penguin Group (Canada), 90 Eglinton Avenue East, Suite 700, Toronto, Ontario, Canada M4P 2Y3
(a division of Pearson Penguin Canada Inc.)
Penguin Ireland, 25 St Stephen's Green, Dublin 2, Ireland (a division of Penguin Books Ltd)
Penguin Group (Australia), 707 Collins Street, Melbourne, Victoria 3008, Australia
(a division of Pearson Australia Group Pty Ltd)
Penguin Books India Pvt Ltd, 11 Community Centre, Panchsheel Park, New Delhi – 110 017, India
Penguin Group (NZ), 67 Apollo Drive, Rosedale, Auckland 0632, New Zealand
(a division of Pearson New Zealand Ltd)
Penguin Books (South Africa) (Pty) Ltd, Block D, Rosebank Office Park,
181 Jan Smuts Avenue, Parktown North, Gauteng 2193, South Africa

Penguin Books Ltd, Registered Offices: 80 Strand, London WC2R ORL, England

www.penguin.com

First published by Allen Lane 2012
Published in Penguin Books 2013
001

Copyright © Halik Kochanski, 2012

The moral right of the author has been asserted

Typeset by Jouve (UK), Milton Keynes
Printed in Great Britain by Clays Ltd, St Ives plc

A CIP catalogue record for this book is available from the British Library

ISBN: 978-1-846-14358-8

www.greenpenguin.co.uk

*To my parents – Stanisław Kochański and Teresa Kicińska*

# Contents

# List of Illustrations

# List of Maps

# Acknowledgements

I am grateful to the following for allowing me to examine and quote from archival material in their collections: Dr Andrzej Suchcitz, Keeper of Archives, Polish Institute and Sikorski Museum; The Trustees of the Imperial War Museum; The Trustees of the Polish Underground Study Movement Trust; The Trustees of the British Library; The National Archives; Yale University, The Avalon Project; the Keith Sword collection at the UCL School of Slavonic and East European Studies Library; and the permission of A. P. Watt on behalf of The Executors of the Estate of Jocelyn Herbert, M. T. Perkins and Polly M. V. R Perkins to reproduce the poem 'Unreasonable' by A. P. Herbert.

I wish to thank all those who were prepared to share their personal memories with me or those of their parents, and to help me to track down obscure material and in the translation of complex documents: especially Nina Reich, Marzena Reich, Anna Banach, Renia Achmatow-icz, Krzysia Machoń, Anna Skoweska, Iwona Sierzputowska, Yarema Bogaychuk, Olga Vasilivna, Elżbieta Lester, Kazimierz Janowski, Kasia Litak, Jedrzej Kozak and Miko Giedroyć. My gratitude also goes to Igor and Ania Korczagin, who were my wonderful guides to Lwów and Stanisławów, and to Nadia Cikaylo-Zuzuk for showing me around the family home, now a children's library in Tłumacz.

I also received a great deal of advice, support and encouragement while writing this book. I am grateful to my brother Martin who read endless drafts of the manuscript; for the advice of Professor Anita Prażmowska at the London School of Economics; for the support of my agent Robert Dudley; for the wise, pertinent and constructive comments of my editor Simon Winder; and to Hubert Zawadzki, who reviewed the entire manuscript. Any errors that remain are, of course, my own.

# Abbreviations

| | | |
|---|---|---|
| AK | *Armia Krajowa* | Home Army |
| AL | *Armia Ludowa* | People's Army |
| BCH | *Bataliony Chłopskie* | Peasant Battalions |
| CIGS | Chief of Imperial General Staff | |
| DP | Displaced Person | |
| GL | *Gwarda Ludowa* | People's Guard |
| IRC | International Red Cross | |
| KNP | *Komitet Narodowy Polski* | Polish National Committee |
| KOP | *Korpus Ochrony Pogranicza* | Border Protection Corps |
| KPP | *Komunistyczna Partia Polski* | Polish Communist Party |
| KRM | *Krajowa Rada Ministrów* | National Council of Ministers |
| KRN | *Krajowa Rada Narodowa* | National Council for the Homeland |
| NIE | *Niepodległość* | Independence |
| NKVD | *Narodnyy komissariat vnutrennikh del* | People's Commissariat of Internal Affairs |
| NSZ | *Narodowe Siły Zbrojne* | National Armed Units |
| OSS | Office of Strategic Services | |
| OUN | *Orhanizatsiia Ukrains'kykh Natsionalistiv* | Organisation of Ukrainian Nationalists |
| OWI | Office of War Information | |
| OZN | *Obóz Zjednoczenia Narodowego* | Camp of National Unity |
| PKN | *Polski Komitet Narodowy* | Polish National Committee |

| | | |
|---|---|---|
| PKWN | *Polski Komitet Wyzwolenia Narodowgo* | Polish Committee of National Liberation |
| PPR | *Polska Partia Robotnicza* | Polish Workers' Party |
| PPS | *Polska Partia Socjalistyczna* | Polish Socialist Party |
| PRC | *Polski Korpus Przysposobienia i Rozmieszczenia* | Polish Resettlement Corps |
| RGO | *Rada Główna Opiekuńcza* | Central Welfare Council |
| RJN | *Rada Jedności Narodowej* | Council of National Unity |
| RONA | *Russaya Osvobodityelnaya Narodnaya Armya* | Russian National Liberation Army |
| SL | *Stronnictwo Ludowe* | Peasant Alliance |
| SN | *Stronnictwo Narodowe* | National Alliance |
| SOE | Special Operations Executive | |
| SP | *Stronnictwo Pracy* | Labour Alliance |
| TRJN | *Tymczasowy Rząd Jedności Narodowej* | Provisional Government of National Unity |
| UB | *Urząd Bezpieczeństwa* | Security Office |
| UNRRA | United Nations Relief and Rehabilitation Administration | |
| UPA | *Ukrains'ka Povstans'ka Armiia* | Ukrainian Insurrectionist Army |
| WiN | *Wolnośc i Niezawislość* | Freedom and Independence |
| ŻOB | *Żydowska Organizacja Bojowa* | Jewish Fighting Organisation |
| ZOW | *Związek Organizacji Wojskowej* | Union of Military Organisation |
| ZPP | *Związek Patriotów Polskich* | Union of Polish Patriots |
| ZWZ | *Związek Walki Zbrojnej* | Union for Armed Struggle |

# Definitions of Poland and the Poles

Who are the Poles? The 1931 census recorded the total population of Poland as 32,000,000. Of these, 22,000,000 were ethnic Poles; 4,500,000 were Ukrainians; 3,000,000 were Jews; 1,000,000 were Belorussians; 750,000 were Germans; and the remainder were classified as 'locals'. These were all Polish citizens and will be considered as such throughout this book. At times it will be necessary to point out the ethnicity of certain Poles. For example, the treachery of the ethnic German Polish citizens; the civil war against ethnic Poles waged by the ethnic Ukrainian Polish citizens; and the debates over which pre-war Polish citizens the Soviet authorities would permit to join the Polish Army in the Soviet Union. In general the term Jew has been used as a shorthand for Polish Jew, especially in the chapter on the Holocaust. Modern Poland, after the extermination of the Jews and the post-war redrawing of its frontiers, is a homogeneous country, 97 per cent ethnic Polish. But during the period covered by this book Poland's population was ethnically heterogeneous and many of her citizens from the national minorities felt themselves to be Polish citizens and were prepared to fight and die under the Polish flag. The Polish war cemetery at Monte Cassino demonstrates this: in one corner there are crooked crosses marking the graves of those Poles of Uniate or Eastern Orthodox faith and, diametrically opposite, the graves of Polish Jews, marked by a Star of David.

Where is Poland? For the purposes of this book 'Poland' is taken to represent the territory of the pre-war Second Polish Republic. Because of Poland's post-war move to the west the names of certain cities have since changed. For example, the Polish city of Stanisławów is now the city of Ivano-Frankivsk in Ukraine, and the city of Breslau, formerly in Germany, is now Wrocław in Poland. The first mention of each place where the name has changed has the modern name in round brackets.

The shifting of the Polish frontiers and the alteration to the composition of Poland's population have occasionally made the provision of accurate statistics extremely difficult. Where there are different statistics, the debates over the numbers have been summarised.

# Guide to Polish Pronunciation

It is difficult to read a book without at least imagining how the names of the places and people in it might be pronounced. Here is a guide to the pronunciation of Polish that will let you read this book with comfort. It is more approximate than a phrasebook or textbook would be; even so, the result will be comprehensible to a Pole.

Polish is a lot easier to pronounce than it looks. For some reason English-speakers panic at the sight of so many consonants – and yet English and not Polish has a nine-letter word with only one vowel ('strengths'), and it is English and not Polish that has a place-name with six consecutive consonants ('Knightsbridge'). It is all a matter of familiarity.

### Stress

Every Polish word in this book has the stress on its penultimate syllable.

### The vowels

**a** as in 'but', **e** as in 'bet', **i** as in 'beat', **o** as in 'bot', **u** = **ó** as in 'put', **y** as in 'bit'.

**ę** is a more nasal e: **Kęty** sounds like 'Kenty'.

**ą** is a nasal vowel: **stąp** sounds like 'stomp'.

### The consonants

**w** is a 'v' sound and **ł** sounds like English 'w'.

**ch** and **h** sound the same as 'h'.

**j** sounds like the 'y' in 'yet'.

**c** is pronounced as 'ts'.

**ń** sounds like Spanish 'ñ' or like the first consonant in 'unused'. Coming before a consonant it is a little different: the middle syllable of Kochański rhymes with 'wine'.

**sz** and **cz** are like 'shop' and 'chop', so **szcz** should be no more frightening than 'pushchair'.

rz = ż is like the z in 'pleasure'.

ś, ć and ź are higher-pitched versions of sz, cz, rz/ż (think of 'sheet' versus 'shoot'). The distinction is hard for English-speakers to manage but you will be comprehensible if you ignore it. In front of the letter i, the letters s, c and z are pronounced as if they were ś, ć and ź.

## The ends of words

A voiced consonant at the end of a word becomes unvoiced: for example, b becomes 'p' and d becomes 't'. Thus bóg (god) and buk (beech tree) are both pronounced like 'book'.

1. The Second Polish Republic, 1922–1939

# *Preface*

Every post-war generation learns about its parents' war from two sources – the public (that is, books, school, TV) and the private: the parents themselves. As the daughter of Polish parents, born and educated in Britain it was strange that my parents' own reticence about what they went through during the Second World War was matched by a curious editing out of most of the Polish experience from the history I was taught. Only towards the end of his life, badgered by his children, did our father tell us his story. My first introduction to the experiences of Poles during the war came from the novel *The Silver Sword* by Ian Serraillier, which appeared to me simply to be an exciting story of children struggling to survive in German-occupied Warsaw. Through *Soldier Bear* by Geoffrey Morgan and Wiesław Lasocki, I was also introduced to Wojtek, the Syrian bear cub adopted by the Polish 22nd Artillery Supply Company during their time in the Middle East, who was enlisted as a private in the Polish II Corps and served alongside it in Italy, carrying ammunition cases and shells in return for beer and lit cigarettes.[1]

Later on my interest in military history led me to examine the Second World War in detail and I soon realised that there were numerous 'histories' of the war. The most prevalent was the Anglo-American view that the Second World War was a 'good' war, fought to liberate Europe from the evil forces of Nazi Germany. The emphasis given to this commonly held assumption is that the Second World War was somehow a justifiable conflict, in contrast to the First World War, which was nothing more than a dynastic struggle that blighted the lives of a generation. Hence there has been an emphasis on using the liberation of German concentration camps by the western allies, such as Bergen-Belsen, Dachau and Buchenwald, to justify the entire war as expunging Nazism and re-establishing Europe as a normal, liberated place.

Poland just does not fit into this almost 'comfortable' picture of the Second World War. The German occupation of Poland from September

1939 to January 1945 demonstrates the application of Nazi policies at their most extreme. The Poles, as *Untermenschen*, had value to the Germans only to the extent to which their labour could be exploited. They had no place in the grandiose Nazi schemes for the creation of German *Lebensraum* in the east and, once their labour ceased to be of value, they were to be exterminated through starvation. The Polish Jews were considered to have no value at all and thus became the first category of *Untermenschen* to be exterminated, rapidly and with industrial efficiency, at the killing centres of Chełmno, Sobibor, Bełżec, Majdanek, Auschwitz and Treblinka on the pre-war territory of the Second Polish Republic. The facts of the German occupation of Poland are known and widely accepted. But it is less generally known, or indeed accepted, that the Poles also suffered greatly at the hands of the Soviets, both during the first occupation from September 1939 to June 1941, and again when they re-entered Poland at the beginning of 1944 and in the years to follow.

Despite the huge historiography of the Second World War, the history of Poland and the Poles during the period remains largely unknown. The whole history of the Polish experience continues to be obscure and is often misunderstood largely because it has been treated in parts, and not as a whole. There are studies of Poland under German occupation, and of Poland under Soviet occupation, both in 1939–1941 and from 1944 onwards. There are also many personal narratives of experiences of deportation, exile and escape from the Soviet Union. The participation of the Poles in the allied war effort has also been written about – notably the Polish contribution to the breaking of the Enigma code, Polish pilots in the Battle of Britain and the Polish capture of the monastery at Monte Cassino – but there is no study in English of the communist 1st Polish Army and its contribution to the German defeat on the Eastern Front. Then, of course, there is the vast literature of the Holocaust. Many of these studies have much to commend them, but they all suffer from one fundamental weakness: by treating one aspect of the Polish experience of the Second World War, misconceptions abound precisely because the whole experience is not under examination.

When the Poles do appear in much of the historiography of the Second World War, myths, misconceptions and subtle distortions tend to abound. Perhaps the most pervasive myth is that of Polish cavalry charging at German tanks during the September 1939 campaign: an image born of a single incident when a successful Polish cavalry charge at a German infantry unit turned to carnage on the arrival of a German armoured unit. Perfect material for the German minister of propaganda, Jozef Goebbels, to use to demonstrate the backwardness of the Poles, but material that has become disseminated and accepted through the use of German newsreel footage in programmes such as the iconic series *The World at War*, produced in the 1970s when German film footage was the only material available to the producers. There has been a tendency to view the Poles as a brave people ruled by fools, an opinion voiced by Winston Churchill in the first volume of his *The Second World War*: 'It is a mystery and tragedy of European history that a people capable of every heroic virtue, gifted, valiant, charming, as individuals, should repeatedly show such inveterate faults in almost every aspect of their governmental life.'[2] Poland probably had no more than the average number of bad politicians and generals, and the extremely challenging strategic situation in 1939 and lack of options once the country had been devoured by its neighbours suggest that the actions of Polish politicians should be considered more fairly.

The Poles are also viewed without sympathy because of their attitude towards the Soviet leader Josef Stalin. During the war the British and American public had been subjected to a skilful propaganda campaign designed to cultivate the image of Stalin as 'Uncle Joe': the man whose armies were bearing the brunt of the fighting in the war, thereby saving British and American casualties. But for the Poles Stalin was the man who stole their homes, deported them deep into the Soviet Union and murdered the Polish officer corps and intelligentsia. To reward Stalin for the efforts of his armies, Churchill and Roosevelt effectively gave away half of pre-war Poland to Stalin and did little to prevent him from imposing communism. This is the crux of the Polish belief that Poland was betrayed. As the British ambassador to the Polish Government, Owen O'Malley, wrote: 'This difference of view between the Poles and their allies was natural, for Poland is situated next door to the jungle where the gorillas and rattlesnakes live, and the Poles thought they knew much more about the nature and behaviour of these animals than Mr Churchill and Mr Roosevelt.'[3] To add insult to injury, this betrayal continued into the Cold War years as the Soviet crime at Katyń in 1940 was covered up by successive British and American governments.

There is an uncomfortable degree of truth to the Polish complaints.

Stalin was appeased during the war by the western leaders but for very good reasons. What the Poles did not and do not understand is that the psychological trauma of the First World War led to a natural reluctance in 1939 on the part of the French and the British to sustain anything like the same level of casualties only twenty years later. The British themselves accepted the truth of this uncomfortable reality. General Sir Alan Brooke was disparaging in his comments in his diary berating the poor fighting performance of British commanders in the early campaigns of the war, questioning whether Britain had in fact lost an entire generation of leaders in the First World War.[4] One can only imagine the depth of chagrin felt by Churchill when Stalin baited him at the Kremlin in August 1942: 'You British are afraid of fighting. You should not think the Germans are supermen. You will have to fight sooner or later. You cannot win a war without fighting.'[5] Churchill himself recognised that the British performance in the desert against a very limited German-Italian force bore little resemblance to the Soviet effort against the bulk of Hitler's land forces. He noted the reluctance to take casualties and the consequent slow advances, commenting in November 1942: 'I never meant the Anglo-American Army to be stuck in North Africa. It is a spring-board and not a sofa.'[6]

Of course the British did fight the Germans, first winning the battle of the Atlantic, a prerequisite for the launching of the Second Front, and then in Italy and Northern Europe, and contributed to Germany's defeat through the controversial strategic bombing campaign against Germany. But none of this helped the Poles. As France was falling in June 1940, the Polish prime minister and commander-in-chief, Władysław Sikorski, visited London and learnt from government ministers there the appalling level of British unpreparedness for war. The fall of France and the absence of the land forces of the western allies from the European continent for over three years meant that the liberation of Poland would be delivered by the forces of the Soviet Union. The reluctance at the time by the Poles to accept this unpalatable reality led to tragedies such as the Warsaw Uprising. For the Poles the First World War had come close to being a 'good war': the defeat and collapse of the three countries which had partitioned her territory led to the restoration of Poland's independence. The Second World War in contrast was nothing but a catastrophe. At its end Poland became the only allied country to be abandoned behind the Iron Curtain.

The Poles are all too frequently dismissed as unrepentant anti-semites who stood back as the Germans exterminated the Jews on Polish territory. István Deák has noted that the sides in the debate have become disturbingly polarised. Some Jews claim that the Poles not only supported the extermination of the Jews but did nothing to help them, even assisting the Germans by betraying the Jews hiding in their midst. In response there are the extreme nationalist Polish claims that the Jews did not deserve to be saved, because of their strong support for communism before the war and during the 1939–41 Soviet occupation of the eastern provinces and also the pro-Soviet actions of Jews after 1944. This is the crux of the Polish anti-semitism versus *żydo-komuna* ('Jewish communist') debate. In an interview on his eightieth birthday in 1988, Simon Wiesenthal summarised his approach to the debate: 'Just as I, as a Jew, do not want to shoulder responsibility for the Jewish communists, I cannot blame 36 million Poles for those thousands of *szmalcownicy* [blackmailers who preyed on the Jews].'[7] A historian, Richard Lukas, has commented: 'It seems that we are confronted by double-standard scholarship; canons of objectivity are abandoned when the subject concerns the relationship of Poles to Jews during the war. If a more objective view prevailed in the historiography on the Holocaust, there would be less said about Polish anti-Semitism and more about the great tragedy that overwhelmed Polish Christians at the time of the German occupation of Poland.'[8] This book will therefore seek to place the Holocaust of the Polish Jews within the context of German policy in Poland at the time.

The reality is that there were Polish anti-semites who betrayed Jews to the Germans, and, indeed, a few who participated in the killings, but there were many Poles who did all they could to save the Jews. Only in Poland was concealment of or the rendering of assistance to a Jew punishable by death, and yet only in Poland was an organisation established specifically to care for the Jews in hiding, *Żegota*. It is true that Jews were prominent among the Polish collaborators during the first Soviet occupation of Poland. It is also true that Jewish Poles were disproportionately represented among the political officers of the communist Polish armies and in the post-war government and security services. Yet Polish Jews also suffered under the Soviet occupation and shared the vicissitudes and hardships of exile in the Soviet Union. However, all this is overshadowed by the fact that the Polish Jews were the 'unequal victims' in Poland in the Second World War. Six million Poles died during the conflict. Although half were Christian Poles and half were Jewish Poles, those Jews represented 90 per cent of the pre-war Jewish population of Poland. Yet as Deák has concluded: 'the unholy competition for claiming primacy in suffering continues'.[9]

The history of Poland and the Poles in the Second World War has also been overshadowed by the political debates of the subsequent Cold War. In communist Poland, blatant historical untruths were published. The efforts of those Poles who fought in the Polish armies in the west were denigrated and their achievements minimised. Leading Polish commanders, such as General Władysław Anders, were deprived of their Polish citizenship and became the personal victims of a distorted history. In contrast, the achievements of the Polish armies fighting alongside the Soviets were lauded. The Polish Underground Army (*Armia Krajowa*) was especially vilified: branded as fascists, its members were arrested and imprisoned immediately after the war. The only Polish resistance acknowledged was that of the far smaller *Armia Ludowa*, which owed its allegiance to the communist Poles. Discussion of Katyń was forbidden unless the direct lie of German culpability was followed. The deportations to the Soviet Union were known but little talked about. They could not be denied entirely because important Polish communist figures, such as General Wojciech Jaruzelski, had themselves been deported. The Holocaust was not recognised as a unique catastrophic event but was subsumed within the general history of Polish losses during the war. In private, naturally, families would share their experiences of the war and so educate their children with a more accurate narrative.

The end of communism has permitted a revisiting of the history of the Second World War with the opening of the Soviet archives and the records held by the NKVD.* For example, the archives show that at Yalta Stalin was absolutely determined to ensure his control over Poland and that there was little chance that western diplomacy would have been able to change that.[10] Yet there are still many blank pages and empty folders with regards to Stalin's policy towards Poland and towards the Warsaw Uprising.[11] It also appears that the revelations emerging from the archives have unsettled the Russians. In 2009 the

---

* Forerunner of the better-known KGB.

Russian president, Dmitri Medvedev, set up a History Commission whose object is to 'defend Russia against falsifiers of history and those who would deny the Soviet contribution to the victory in the Second World War'. The Soviet archives are now less easily accessible in the 2010s than they were in the 1990s.

So what was the Polish experience of the Second World War? It was different from that of any other country. Poland was under occupation by foreign armies from the first day of the war to the last. During September 1939, Poland was invaded by both Germany and the Soviet Union; they partitioned Polish territory between them. Part of Poland was annexed by Nazi Germany, and her eastern provinces were incorporated into the Soviet Union. In June 1941, Germany invaded the Soviet Union and by the end of that month occupied the entire territory of pre-war Poland. This German occupation lasted until the beginning of 1944 when the Soviet armies again crossed the pre-war Polish-Soviet frontier. Yet the position of this frontier had been changed at the Teheran conference by the Big Three – Britain, the United States and the Soviet Union – without the agreement of the Polish Government-in-Exile, resident in London. In July 1944, the Soviet armies crossed the Bug river, the new Polish-Soviet frontier, and for the remainder of that year Poland was once more jointly occupied by the Germans and Soviets. Only in January–February 1945 was the whole of Poland liberated from German occupation. But this did not bring real liberation to Poland, because the country was now under Soviet occupation and administered by a Soviet-sponsored Polish provisional government. The end of the war in May 1945 saw a Poland with no government recognised by the Big Three and without its frontiers settled. Subsequent international negotiations and fraudulent domestic elections resulted in a Poland moved about 125 miles to the west and under communist governmental control.

Poland not only emerged from the Second World War with new frontiers and a new form of government but also with a greatly changed population. In 1939 Poland was a heterogeneous country with significant national minorities of Ukrainians, Belorussians, Lithuanians, Germans and Jews, but in 1945 Poland became a homogeneous country. Poland, which had been the largest home in Europe for Jews before the war, bore witness to the German extermination of Polish and European Jewry on her soil. The loss of Poland's pre-war eastern provinces to the Soviet Union removed most of the Ukrainian, Lithuanian and Belorussian national minorities, and most of the remainder were expelled in the years immediately after the end of the war. To the west and north the expansion of Poland into former German territories included the expulsion of the German population. Millions more Poles were now to be found outside Poland, as members of the Polish armed forces who had fought alongside the western allies, as refugees who had fled the German and then Soviet occupation, as deportees taken to the Soviet Union during the war and awaiting repatriation, and finally as a great mass of displaced persons who had been forcibly relocated to Germany during the war.

Not only was the Polish experience of the war unique, but so was the reaction of the Poles. No other country formed four different armies. The first, created out of the remnants of the defeated Polish Army of the September 1939 campaign, fought in France in 1940, the Western Desert, Normandy, and at Arnhem. The second army, the II Corps, was formed from the Polish citizens who were deported to the Soviet Union in 1940 and 1941, and then released under the terms of the Sikorski–Maisky agreement after the Soviet Union had joined the Allies. This corps fought in the Italian campaign, notably at Monte Cassino. The third Polish army, confusingly known as the 1st Polish Army, was later formed in the Soviet Union under the aegis of the Polish communists and fought on the Eastern Front. The fourth army was in Poland itself: the Home Army, *Armia Krajowa* (AK), which is best known for the Warsaw Uprising in 1944. Poland also formed a government-in-exile, first in France and then, in 1940, in London. This government was recognised as the legitimate government of Poland by all the Allies until January 1945, when the Soviet Union switched its favour to the communist-dominated Lublin Committee. The activities of the Polish Government-in-Exile were mirrored within Poland with the formation of an Underground Government. This not only contained representatives of all the major Polish political parties, but also created a fully-functioning skeleton civilian administration, ready to take over the country on its liberation from the German occupation.

This book is not a personal family narrative, but the things that members of my family went through help to illustrate the myriad of Polish experiences in the Second World War, covering practically everything apart from the Holocaust itself – occupation, imprisonment, deportation, starvation, forced labour, living in hiding, service in the *Armia Krajowa* and the Underground Government, fighting in both the communist Polish Army and the II Corps; the bizarre combination of fighting the Germans one week and volunteering for work in Germany the next; fleeing Poland to become a refugee in Switzerland; being shipped to Britain to form a new life there; and being repatriated to western Poland from exile in the Soviet Union and from their homes in the former eastern provinces of Poland. Their experiences, and those of many others in this book, illustrate the extreme stresses of Polish life during the war, the critical decisions that had to be taken, the terrible role of sheer chance, the consequences of their actions and the results. What they all have in common is the simple desire to survive under the most difficult circumstances.

This book is not a nationalistic study. It will not seek to defend either Polish government policy or the actions of individuals unquestioningly. The aim is to present the most complete picture of the Poles and Poland in the Second World War to date. In order to achieve this, I have had to weave my way through an extremely complex historiography. I have first tried to present the facts and the arguments as they were seen at the time and only then referred to later debates – both because Polish history has too often been seen through the distorting lenses of politics or ideology and because at crucial points in the story the main participants were acting on extremely incomplete information. The aim is not to offend, not to demean, but to inform, to challenge long-held preconceptions and to inspire new debates on what is an extremely varied, complex and interesting subject.

# I

# The Rebirth of Poland

Poland had once been a great country, and the largest in Europe. In 966 King Mieszko I accepted Christianity for himself and for his country, not from the Orthodox Church which would have linked Poland closely with Russia, nor from the German missionaries which might have made Poland a part of Germania, but Christianity was accepted directly from papal envoys. This was an important step for Poland: it meant that her religion tied her closely to western Europe, while by remaining outside the Holy Roman Empire she asserted her independence. Poland played a major role in the geopolitics of eastern Europe. The Polish and Lithuanian victory at the battle of Grunwald in 1410 put a halt to the advance of the Teutonic Knights into eastern Europe, and in 1683 the Polish king, Jan Sobieski, commanded the armies before the gates of Vienna in a battle that saved Christian Europe from the infidel Turks.

In 1385 Poland united herself with Lithuania as two countries sharing the same monarch, a commonwealth of two nations, which at its height stretched from the Baltic to the Black Sea. The Polish-Lithuanian Commonwealth was multi-ethnic: Polish, Lithuanian, Belorussian, German, Armenian, Kashub, Jewish, Tartar, and many other minorities. It was also multi-religious: Roman Catholic, Protestant, Uniate Catholic, Eastern Orthodox, Jewish and Muslim. Indeed, three-quarters of world Jewry lived in Poland, welcomed there by Poland's kings at a time when they were persecuted elsewhere. Education and learning were valued: in 1364 one of the oldest universities in Europe, the Jagiellonian University in Kraków, was opened. Poland's constitution in the eighteenth century was the most liberal in Europe. Under it the monarch, often a foreigner, was elected. Beneath him there was a democracy of nobles (*szlachta*), any one of whom could exercise the *Liberum Veto* and end a session of the *Sejm*, Poland's parliament, though this was rarely done.[1]

Poland was surrounded by the increasingly centralised and expansionist states of Russia, Austria and Prussia, and towards the end of the eighteenth century these powers partitioned Poland three times. The First Partition took place in 1772 and Poland lost 30 per cent of her territory and 35 per cent of her population to the three countries. The remainder of the Polish state remained nominally independent and in 1791 produced the first written constitution in Europe, whose clauses included the abolition of the *Liberum Veto*. The date of its proclamation, 3 May, would remain a day of celebration in Poland. This modern constitution was insufficient to save Poland from the attention of her rapacious neighbours: indeed, it may have even provoked them, because a year later the Second Partition saw Prussia making gains in Silesia and Pomerania, and Russia advancing further west into Poland. Finally, in 1795, the Third Partition wiped Poland from the map. European statesmen were preoccupied by the events in Revolutionary France and barely noticed the demise of Poland. Only some enlightened commentators voiced their opinions: for example, Edmund Burke described the partitions as a 'very great breach in the modern political system in Europe'. A decade later it was unsurprising that many Poles should look with favour upon the one man, Napoleon Bonaparte, who appeared to be capable of rearranging the states of Europe. In 1812, about 98,000 Poles marched with the *Grande Armée* into Russia hoping to regain independence for their country. After Napoleon's defeat, the statesmen of Europe met in Vienna to reconstruct Europe. Poland was discussed, but the restoration of her independence was a minor consideration. Instead of reconstituting Poland as an independent state, the Congress of Vienna created 'Congress Poland', a tiny state covering less than 50,000 square miles and with a population of 3,300,000. This had a considerable degree of autonomy but was considered to be under the suzerainty of Russia, with the tsar as king of Poland. To the south, the former capital, Kraków, was turned into a republic.[2] The rest of Poland remained under Austrian, Russian and Prussian control.

The Poles did not accept their fate without a fight. In 1794 there had been a national uprising under Tadeusz Kościuszko, which was ended after defeat by the Russian Army at the battle of Maciejowice. In 1830 a group of minor nobles staged another revolt and attempted to assassinate the Russian Grand Duke Constantine in Warsaw. In February 1831, the Russian Army invaded Congress Poland and by the end of the year had suppressed the uprising. In 1848–9 there were widespread revolutions across Europe and the Poles staged their own in the Austrian and Prussian partitions, again without success. In January 1863, a more widespread uprising began and the brutality of its suppression by Russian forces drew gasps of horror from western politicians. Their attention, however, was focused on the Civil War engulfing the United States, and so they did nothing. This uprising was the last. Many members of the nobility who had taken part were exiled to Siberia and had their estates confiscated by the Russian authorities. The majority of the Polish population reached a measure of accommodation with their occupiers.

Throughout the nineteenth century the Poles still saw themselves as Poles: a nation deprived of a country, an experience that would be repeated during the Second World War. To outsiders the Poles were seen as helpless and hopeless romantics:

> To the average inhabitant of Western Europe, the history of Poland is a yawning chasm whose edges are obscured by the overhang of accepted commonplaces – that the Poles are a romantic people, good at fighting, riding, dancing and drinking, pathologically incapable of organisation or stable self-government, condemned by geography and their own ineptitude to be the victims of history.[3]

The Poles themselves subscribed to similar notions with a deep yearning for the glories of the past as expressed in Adam Mickiewicz's poem *Pan Tadeusz* (1834) and in the novels of Henryk Sienkiewicz (1846–1916). More pertinent to the history of Poland in the Second World War were the central position the concept of a national uprising came to occupy in Polish military strategy and the ingrained western view of Poles as a nation incapable of governing themselves.

In August 1914, the Poles found themselves thrust into an incongruous position when two of the partitioning powers, Germany and Austria-Hungary, were at war with the third, Russia, with Poles fighting in all three armies. To begin with, Polish representatives in the three parliaments all continued their policy of accommodation and made declarations of loyalty to their overlords. All three partitioning countries acknowledged the fact that the Poles wanted the restoration of their independence, and each held out the prospect as an inducement to secure Polish cooperation in their war efforts. The Russians, ruling over the largest portion of Polish territory, made the first bid when, on 14 August 1914, their commander-in-chief, Grand Duke Nikolai, issued a proclamation to the Poles referring to the 'resurrection of the Polish nation and its fraternal union with all Russia'. This suggested a return to something akin to Congress Poland, a measure of autonomy under Russian suzerainty, rather than to full independence. Russian opinions, however, became irrelevant during the course of 1915 as the armies of the Central Powers mounted successful offensives and by the end of the year were in control of all of the lands of Congress Poland. The Central Powers needed more manpower after the offensives of 1916, and so in November 1916 Austria and Germany issued a declaration in Warsaw promising a restoration of Poland's independence. A leading Polish politician Roman Dmowski believed that this bid for the loyalty of the Poles, 'did more than anything else to indicate to European statesmen the international importance of the Polish question ... It was a powerful incentive to occupy themselves seriously with the question.' After the February 1917 revolution in Russia and the abdication of the tsar, the Russian Provisional Government made a counter-bid for Polish support with a promise to create an independent Polish state 'comprising all the lands where the Polish people constitute the majority of the population [which would be] united with Russia by a free military alliance'.[4]

From the beginning, the Poles were divided over which side offered the best prospects for the independence of Poland, and what steps should be taken to achieve it. One view was expounded by the socialist politician Józef Piłsudski, who saw Russia as Poland's principal enemy but also believed that the Poles themselves should take steps to win their own independence rather than merely wait to be helped by a cynical Great Power sponsor. Accordingly, on 6 August 1914, he led an armed unit from Kraków and marched across the Austrian-Russian border towards Kielce aiming to reach Warsaw. His attempt to foment a national revolution in Poland failed, through apathy and confusion, and his forces were defeated by the Russian Army near Kielce. Piłsudski then turned to the Austrians, who welcomed his support. They allowed him to raise his own troops, which would operate under Austrian command. Ultimately he formed an army of around 20,000 men: the legend of the Piłsudski Legions was born and would grow during the interwar years.

An alternative view to Piłsudski's was expounded by Roman

Dmowski, the founder of the National Democratic Party, who saw Germany as Poland's principal enemy. In 1914 he formed the Polish National Committee (*Komitet Narodowy Polski*), which advocated cooperation with Russia. In 1916 the committee moved to Switzerland and thence to Paris, where it hoped to win the hearts and minds of the Entente statesmen for the cause of Polish independence. Working alongside him was the internationally renowned Polish pianist Ignacy Paderewski. In late 1915 Paderewski travelled to the still neutral United States to champion the cause of Polish independence. The friendship he formed with President Woodrow Wilson's foreign policy adviser, Colonel Edward House, was instrumental in the fruition of this aim. In January 1917, Wilson made his 'Peace Without Victory' speech in which he announced that: 'Statesmen everywhere are agreed that there should be a united, independent and autonomous Poland.'

Like Piłsudski, Paderewski wanted Poles to be seen to have contributed towards the restoration of their own independence. In March 1917, a month before the United States entered the war, he approached Colonel House with a proposal for the formation of a Polish army to be recruited from immigrant Poles which, after training in Canada, would be despatched to fight on the Western Front. The Russian Provisional Government was hostile to the idea, fearing that the Germans and Austrians would retaliate by mobilising the around 800,000 Poles available to them into their armies. This could then turn the tide of fortune against Russia on the Eastern Front. But, in October 1917, the United States War Department announced that Poles in America who were not naturalised Americans could enlist in the new Polish Army, the so-called Blue Army (*Błękitna Armia*), named for their blue French Army uniforms. Eventually 24,000 Polish-Americans were despatched to France where they fought in the final campaigns on the Western Front in the Champagne region under the command of General Józef Haller.

Events now began to move in Poland's favour: in April 1917, the United States had declared war on Germany and in November 1917, the Bolsheviks overthrew the Provisional Government in Russia. The Bolsheviks too promised Poland full independence after the war. The response of the Central Powers was to ensure the loyalty of the Polish troops operating in their armies. The German and Austrian military authorities demanded that the Legionnaires take an oath of allegiance to the German and Austrian emperors, but Piłsudski himself refused and was imprisoned in the fortress of Magdeburg until 10 November 1918. Those Legionnaires who were not disarmed joined the illegal Polish military organisation *Polska Organizacja Wojskowa* (POW), run by a former member of Piłsudski's staff and the future commander-in-chief of the Polish Army, Edward Rydz-Śmigły. It engaged in sabotage in the rear of the German and Austrian armies.

The Entente Powers responded differently. The British and French governments now recognised the Polish National Committee 'as unofficial representatives of the Polish nation'. The committee was chaired by Dmowski, and on it Paderewski represented the United States, Ladislas Sobański, Britain, and Count Constantine Skirmunt, Italy. Of greatest importance was Wilson's Fourteen Points, issued on 8 January 1918, in which Point Thirteen read: 'An independent Polish state should be erected which should include the territories inhabited by indisputably Polish populations, which should be assured a free and secure access to the sea, and whose political and economic independence and territorial integrity should be guaranteed by international covenant.'[5]

The First World War ended suddenly on 11 November 1918 when an armistice was signed between the Entente Powers and Germany. It brought immediate peace to western Europe but, in contrast, the unexpected end to the war found eastern Europe in turmoil and the Poles caught unprepared. The Treaty of Brest-Litovsk on 3 March 1918, which had taken Russia out of the war, had left the Central Powers in control of all Polish territories, but now the terms of the armistice required the Germans and Austrians to vacate the region. The Polish National Committee made a successful request to the victorious powers that the Germans and Austrians be permitted to remain in place until a new Polish government was ready to take control. This step was deemed necessary because another treaty, also signed at Brest-Litovsk (Brześć), of 9 February 1918 had signed over control of the eastern half of the Austrian province of Galicia to the newly formed Ukrainian People's Republic. The Poles claimed East Galicia for themselves. The Bolsheviks were in Wilno (Vilnius), the city Piłsudski wanted to be in the new Poland. Poland actually did not have a government at all at the time of the armistice. Although Dmowski's National Committee in Paris was recognised as the official representative body of Poland by the Entente

Powers, events in Poland posed a challenge to its authority. A socialist government under Ignacy Daszyński had been formed in Lublin and had declared the existence of the Polish republic, and a separate Polish committee in Kraków claimed to rule western Galicia. Then on 10 November, Piłsudski arrived in Warsaw and entered into negotiations with Daszyński. The two men agreed that Piłsudski would be the head of the new independent Polish state and Daszyński would be its first prime minister. The latter was soon replaced by Jędrzej Moraczewski. On 16 November, Piłsudski announced the independence of Poland to the world. The Entente was uncertain on how to treat the two challengers – Piłsudski and Dmowski – for the leadership of Poland and left them alone to settle matters between themselves. At the end of 1918, Paderewski returned to Poland and acted as an arbiter.[6]

Piłsudski and Dmowski had very different opinions on the future shape of Poland. Piłsudski looked back to the period of the multinational Polish Commonwealth and had a vision of a future federation of nationalities within the new Polish state. This would include the Ukrainians, Belorussians and Lithuanians in Kresy, the eastern borderlands of Poland. These national minorities would not be forced to become Poles but would be welcomed into the Polish fold while retaining their own national identities. The result would be a powerful Polish state capable of defending itself against its mortal enemy, Russia. But Dmowski had a very different vision. As a National Democrat, he advocated the supremacy of the Poles. He wanted the frontiers of Poland drawn to include as few of the national minorities as possible, and those who remained within Poland to be assimilated and educated to become true Poles. Dmowski's programme was to be used by the Polish delegation to the peace conference that opened at Versailles in January 1919. Piłsudski, however, was not prepared to wait upon decisions made in Paris and resorted to the use of arms to settle Poland's future in the east. Even before the peace conference opened he had seized Lwów (L'viv) on 21 November 1918 from the Ukrainian armed bands (*Sitchovi Striltsi*), using a hastily constituted force of Poles. The Poles then endured a siege by the Ukrainians, and the defence of Lwów by poorly armed forces, mainly of youths (some of them as young as nine) and women, entered into Polish folklore. The battle for Lwów is a controversial issue between Ukraine and Poland which still resonates today. After the Second World War, when Lwów was allocated to the Ukraine, the graves of the Polish soldiers in the Lychakivskiy cemetery were destroyed.* Since independence, Ukraine has begun restoring these graves but has omitted the inscription for the medal awarded 'for the defence of Lwów' from them.[7]

The statesmen who gathered at Versailles had met to decide the terms of peace with Germany but their discussion ranged over many subjects. The shape of a reconstructed Poland preoccupied the four men responsible for the main decisions for some considerable time and each – Woodrow Wilson for the United States, David Lloyd George for Britain, Georges Clemenceau for France and Vittorio Orlando for Italy – approached the question from a different standpoint. Their decisions had to be taken in the absence of Russia, then embroiled in a vicious civil war. Two overriding principles operated in consideration of the future of Poland: the right of self-determination for national groups and the need for the new state to be economically and strategically viable in the long term. It would soon become apparent that the two principles were difficult to reconcile. The decisions reached would have profound implications throughout the Second World War.

In the first place, Poland had few easily defined borders. The south at least was simple because the Carpathian mountains suggested a natural frontier. The Baltic sea in the north suggested another natural one, but the whole of the coastline was occupied by East and West Prussia. East Prussia was a region indisputably German, while West Prussia had a mixed population of German and Polish ethnicity. Wilson had promised the Poles free access to the sea, a measure deemed essential to Poland's economic independence. For this to become a reality, difficult decisions would have to be taken regarding the size of a Polish Corridor through German territory. In the period of the partitions the German population had spilled southwards from East Prussia and eastwards from Silesia, which had not been Polish since the fourteenth century. The result was a mixed Polish and German population in Silesia and in West Prussia and Poznania. It was soon apparent that wherever the Polish-German frontier was drawn, substantial numbers of Poles and Germans would be left outside their native countries. The situation was even worse in the east. Wilno and its surrounding countryside was inhabited mainly

* The monuments and victory arches were partly demolished, and some of the graveyard complex was used as a motor repair shop.

by Poles and Jews, and so the Poles claimed it for themselves. Yet the newly independent state of Lithuania coveted the city as its capital. To the south, Lwów was a Polish intellectual and social island in an ocean of Ukrainian peasants. The Ukrainians had never possessed an independent state. Their land had been split along the Dnieper river between the Russian Empire and the Polish-Lithuanian Commonwealth until the end of the eighteenth century when, after the partition of Poland, the whole territory became part of the Russian Empire. During the later nineteenth and early twentieth centuries, a Ukrainian intelligentsia had emerged with a sense of nationalism and these people hoped that the statesmen at Versailles would allow them too to take advantage of the collapse of Russia and establish an independent Ukraine that would include eastern Galicia and its principal city, Lwów.

The French delegation was most popular with the Poles. France feared that German militarism would arise again and with the collapse of Russia, her ally since 1892, wanted to see a powerful Poland to act as a guardian against German expansionism. Therefore the French foreign ministry produced a memorandum outlining a large Poland, a country which would include Upper Silesia, Poznania, the lower Vistula area of West Prussia and parts of Pomerania and East Prussia. French policy on Poland's eastern frontier was less clearly defined: if the Bolsheviks should gain the upper hand, then the further east Poland's frontier lay, the further away the danger of Bolshevism stayed from the rest of Europe. If, however, the Bolsheviks were defeated, then France wanted to renew her alliance with Russia and did not want to have caused ill feeling by having supported Poland's aims in the east.[8]

Lloyd George's position was the most complex of the four. As a Protestant he was alarmed by the prospect that Protestant Germans might be ruled by Roman Catholic Poles; as a Welshman, for whom Welsh was his mother tongue, he was in favour of self-determination for national minorities, but as the prime minister of Britain he was alarmed by what a broad application of self-determination could mean for the future of the British Empire, especially at the time when Ireland was agitating for independence; and finally, as a statesman, he feared that a large Poland would be the cause of future conflicts. His opinions were influenced by Lewis Namier, a naturalised and assimilated Polish Jew, who had been born Ludwik Niemirowski and had emigrated to Britain in 1906. Namier bore no love for the country of his birth and was out of sympathy with its claims to be a Great Power in the east. The Poles saw Lloyd George as the principal opponent of their attempts to rebuild a great country. It appeared to them that he was doing everything he could to thwart their nationalist ambitions. Lloyd George responded sharply: '[Poland] has won her freedom, not by her own exertions, but by the blood of others; and not only has she no gratitude, but she says she loses faith in the people who won her freedom.'[9] The British Government was determined that Poland should be created as the Entente Powers thought fit and that the Poles should have no say in the matter. Just before the armistice was announced, the Foreign Office sent a note to the Polish National Committee stating that the British Government 'would view with serious displeasure any military or other action of the Polish Government in East Galicia or elsewhere, of a nature to prejudice or forestall the decisions of the Peace Conference'. Orlando for Italy had no strong feelings on Poland and swayed between Clemenceau's position and that held by Lloyd George. Wilson was the most idealistic of the four men and often took on the role of arbiter.[10]

The drawing of Poland's frontier with Germany was devolved to the Polish Commission, chaired by Jules Cambon, a former French ambassador in Berlin. Its other members were General Lerond, Baron Degrand, Sir William Tyrell, the Marquis della Torretta and R. H. Lord, a professor from Harvard with a deep knowledge of partitioned Poland. The challenge facing them was to decide between two options on how Poland was to have free access to the sea. The first, which Lloyd George favoured, was the internationalisation of the Vistula, which flowed through Warsaw and central Poland before reaching the Baltic at the Bay of Danzig. This solution would leave Poland permanently at Germany's mercy regarding her access to the sea since the banks of the Vistula would remain in German hands. The second option was to ensure Poland's economic independence through the creation of a Polish Corridor through German territory. The disadvantage of this solution was that the Corridor would cut off the 1,600,000 Germans in East Prussia from the rest of Germany and another 2,000,000 Germans would be left in Poland.

The Polish Commission presented its first report on 12 March 1919, and it granted the Poles everything they could have hoped for. Its recommendations were that a Polish Corridor should be created that would adopt a rather strange shape so as to include the whole of the Vistula and the main railway to the coast within Polish territory; the city at the mouth of the Vistula, Danzig (Gdańsk), would be given to Poland; Upper Silesia with its rich industrial resources was also allocated to Poland.[11]

The report was discussed by the Council of Ten at Versailles a week later. Lloyd George felt that the Poles were gaining far too much at the expense of Germany and demanded that the commission reconsider its report. After the commissioners returned it to the council unchanged, Lloyd George issued his famous Fontainebleau memorandum on 25 March in which he said:

> The proposal of the Polish Commission that we should place 2,100,000 Germans under the control of a people which is of a different religion and which has never proved its capacity for stable self-government throughout its history must, in my judgement, lead sooner or later to a new war in the East of Europe.

In particular Lloyd George opposed the designation of Danzig, a city almost entirely populated by Germans, to Poland. He was also appalled by the assignment of Upper Silesia to Poland. His last argument was given strong support when the Germans, having seen the draft treaty, complained that the loss of Upper Silesia would reduce their ability to meet reparation payments, more so since they were also losing control of the mines in the Saar region to France. Lloyd George proposed instead to make Danzig a Free City under the control of the League of Nations with guarantees of free access to the port facilities for the Poles. He also suggested the use of a new tool, the plebiscite or referendum, in areas where the population was mixed, such as Marienwerder and Allenstein on the edges of the Corridor and Upper Silesia, so that the population could decide to which country they wanted to belong.[12] Clemenceau objected to the idea of plebiscites but Wilson, the eternal arbiter, ruled in favour.

The western frontier of Poland was finally settled over the following two years. Article 104 of the Treaty of Versailles charged the allies with the negotiation of a treaty concerning the governance of Danzig, which would include the Free City within the customs frontier of Poland and would guarantee the Poles free use of the transport, port and communications facilities in the city. After long and difficult negotiations, the Free City of Danzig was finally born on 15 November 1920 and a High Commissioner of the League of Nations appointed. The plebiscites in Marienwerder and Allenstein were held in July 1920 and resulted in a vast majority vote in favour of inclusion within the borders of East Prussia.

The future of Upper Silesia proved to be far more problematic and led to a split between Britain and France. Both countries favoured considering the destiny of the province as a whole, but the challenge facing them was that the ownership of the mines and most of the urban population of the industrial cities were German, whereas the Poles had a clear majority in the rural districts. Indeed, much of the population viewed itself as Silesian rather than Polish or German. The French drew a frontier that would include the entire industrial triangle of Tarnowitz–Gleiwitz–Kattowitz in Poland; the British argued equally strongly that the entire triangle should go to Germany. The Poles themselves staged uprisings in Upper Silesia in August 1919 and August 1920, aiming at overthrowing the German administration in the region. Both were suppressed with the help of Entente troops, although the French were noticeably sympathetic towards the Polish insurrectionists. These troops were in Upper Silesia to ensure a fair vote in the plebiscite scheduled for March 1921. Article 88 of the Treaty of Versailles had laid out its terms but had been poorly worded, leading to a lengthy dispute over who had voting rights: the Poles claimed that the vote should go only to those living in Upper Silesia at the time of the plebiscite, but the Germans demanded the inclusion of all those who had been born there, a measure designed to swing the vote in their favour. The Entente Powers agreed with the German argument but the plebiscite settled nothing. The Germans had a 60 per cent majority overall, almost entirely concentrated in the industrial areas. The Poles then staged a third uprising in May 1921, which was again suppressed by Entente troops. Finally, the League of Nations resolved the issue in the way that it had been determined to avoid: it split the province. The Poles gained some of the industrial region centred around Kattowitz (Katowice) but most of the industrial areas went to Germany, including Gleiwitz (Gliwice). Then the frontier turned again giving Poland the industrial towns of Tarnowitz (Tarnowskie Góry) and Lublinitz (Lubliniec) to the north of the industrial triangle. The Wirth government in Germany resigned in disgust, and the Poles accepted the League of Nations' decision in October 1921 with a distinct lack of enthusiasm.[13]

A by-product of the Versailles conference was the Minorities Treaty. All the countries in eastern Europe were required to sign it, an acknowledgement by the statesmen at Versailles that however the frontiers were drawn a significant number of national minorities would remain outside their native countries. In the Polish case the news from the east of attacks on Jews caught in the crossfire of clashes between Poles and Ukrainians horrified those at the conference. The Jewish lobby at Versailles had begun by requesting the creation of an autonomous Jewish state within Poland but, when that was rejected, demanded safeguards against what they claimed to be rampant Polish anti-semitism. Dmowski unwittingly fuelled the argument for a Minorities Treaty through his own ardent nationalism and no less strident anti-semitism, which won him few friends in Paris. He made no secret of the fact that he regarded the national minorities as aliens.

The treaty compelled its signatories to ensure 'full and complete protection of life and liberty to all inhabitants ... without distinction of birth, nationality, language, race or religion'. The members of these minorities would have the right to appeal directly to the League of Nations for the redress of any grievances. The treaty was seen as an insult by the Poles, as an unwarranted interference in their own national affairs. It was also viewed as unfair since there were more Poles left in Germany than Germans left in Poland, but the former had no legal redress. In 1934, when the Soviet Union was about to be admitted to the League of Nations, the Polish Government realised that the Minorities Treaty would give the Soviets a great opportunity for using allegations of breaches to foment Ukrainian and Belorussian nationalism against Polish interests. It therefore declared that Poland would no longer be bound by the treaty.[14]

It was in the east that the differences between Polish ambitions and Entente policy would diverge most sharply. The Poles were extremely emotional when it came to considering the borderlands, Kresy. As soon as it became clear in 1918 that Poland would indeed be an independent country again, they viewed their possession of the region as a reassertion of the greatness of their nationhood, a throwback to the time of the great Polish-Lithuanian Commonwealth. Few Poles believed that Poland could, or indeed should, regain her 1772 frontier, but in his memorandum to the Great Powers of 26 March 1917, Dmowski spelt out the case for the inclusion of East Galicia and the western parts of the Ukraine and Belorussia. There was a sound economic reason for the possession of East Galicia, which had been part of the Austrian partition: the province contained important oil deposits around Drohobycz (Drohobych) and many other mineral resources. The Entente Powers were, however, reluctant to allocate Kresy to Poland, because of the principle of self-determination: the Poles there were outnumbered by the Ukrainians, Lithuanians and Belorussians. Lithuania was already an independent country, and the Entente Powers had no remit at the Versailles Conference to settle its frontier with Poland. The problem lay with the Ukrainians and Belorussians. Neither had any history of independence, but Ukrainian nationalism was well advanced and had been supported by Austria on the eve of her defeat. Belorussian nationalism was less advanced and given scant consideration by the Great Powers since the region was viewed as too poor economically to sustain an independent existence.

The Commission on Polish Affairs despatched a mission to Kresy to attempt to determine the ethnic make-up of the population and where its loyalties lay. It found the task more complex than expected: for example, when one peasant was asked what his nationality was he replied simply, 'I am a Catholic of these parts.' Various solutions for East Galicia were considered: a division of the territory between Poland and the Ukraine, a plebiscite or a 25-year mandate for Poland. The commission traced two possible frontiers in its report of 17 June 1919: the line ran from the Dvina river on the Russian-Latvian border down the Zbrucz river. The problem came when the frontier hit East Galicia, and two options were suggested. Line A assigned Lwów, Drohobycz and the oilfields to the Ukraine, while Line B left them in Poland. This was the origin of what would become known as the Curzon Line.[15]

Fear of Bolshevism ultimately helped to settle the fate of Kresy. In 1918 and 1919 the Entente Powers had armies in Russia safeguarding their national interests while the civil war between the White Russian armies and the Bolshevik-Soviet Red Army continued. Poland began to be seen as an important bulwark against the union of Bolshevism in Russia with the communist revolutionaries in Europe. This was a very real concern: in January 1919 the Spartacist uprising began in Berlin; in March Béla Kun, a communist, seized power in Hungary; and in June a

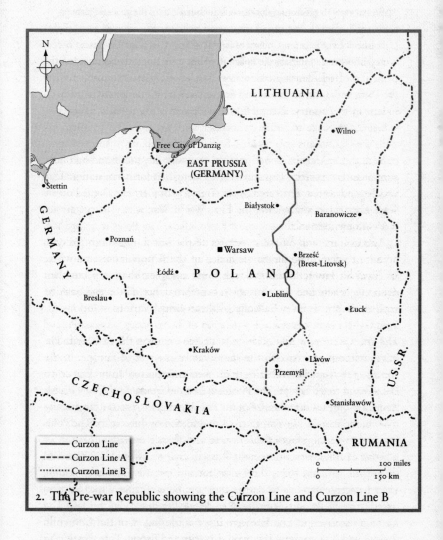

2. The Pre-war Republic showing the Curzon Line and Curzon Line B

Slovak Soviet Republic was declared. Consequently on 25 June 1919, it was announced:

> With a view to protecting the persons and property of the peaceful popula-
> tion of Eastern Galicia against the dangers to which they are exposed by the
> Bolsheviks, the Supreme Council of the Allied and Associated Powers decided
> to authorise the forces of the Polish Republic to pursue their operations as
> far as the river Zbruch (which separates Galicia from East Ukraine).
>
> This authorisation does not, in any way, affect the decisions to be taken
> later by the Supreme Council for the settlement of the political status of
> Galicia.[16]

Indeed, the Supreme Council refused to assign East Galicia to Poland permanently until the Russian Government had been consulted. This vacillation was demonstrated by the Treaty of St Germain, signed on 10 September 1919 and ending the First World War with Austria, which made no mention of the future of East Galicia. The Poles were furious, as Adrian Carton de Wiart, a member of the British mission in Poland, noted. At a ball held at the residence of the British representative in Warsaw, Sir Horace Rumbold, the Poles enjoyed the dinner but then deliberately snubbed their host by refusing to dance. The evening ended with a pro-British Pole challenging an anti-British Pole to a duel.[17]

The Poles were now in a position to decide events in the east for them-selves without reference to the statesmen of the rest of Europe. In the spring of 1919, Haller's army had been transported from France to Poland and together with the Piłsudski Legions made up the new Polish Army. This meant that the size of the Polish Army increased dramatically from 6,000 men in November 1918 to 900,000 by July 1920. The Poles received mixed messages from Britain and France over the question of whether Polish intervention in the Russian civil war would be welcomed or not. In January 1920, the Polish foreign minister, Stanisław Patek, visited Entente capitals to gather their opinions. France appeared pre-pared to grant Poland a free hand to decide her destiny in the east. The messages received in London were more confusing. Winston Churchill, the minister for war and the main instigator of Entente intervention in Russia, gave the impression that Britain would welcome Polish interven-tion against the Soviets, but Lloyd George explicitly warned Patek:

If Poland insisted on retaining within Poland areas which were indisputably Russian according to the principles generally applied by the Peace Conference and if the Bolshevik Government refused peace on this ground and attacked Poland in order to recover Russian districts for Russia it would be very difficult, if not impossible, for the British Government to get public opinion to support military and financial outlay in these circumstances.[18]

Piłsudski saw Russia's descent into civil war as an opportunity for Poland. He knew that it was not in Poland's interests to see a victory for the Whites since the Provisional Government had only offered limited independence to Poland. Nevertheless, he formed an alliance with the Ukrainian nationalist Symon Petlura by which Poland, in return for the Ukrainian recognition of Polish sovereignty over East Galicia, would recognise Ukrainian sovereignty over territory that had belonged to the former Polish Commonwealth in 1772. Then both forces attacked the Soviets, and on 8 May 1920, the Polish forces under General Rydz-Śmigły entered Kiev.

In January 1920, the Soviet Government had offered peace terms to the Poles which would have given Poland a frontier well to the east of what was to be the Curzon Line, but this had been rejected by Poland on French advice. This offer had been made because the Soviets feared that the Polish forces might join those of General Anton Denikin and mount a joint attack on the Red Army. Now in the spring of 1920, the Soviets felt stronger and in May they launched an offensive against Poland. To the north, the army under General Mikhail Tukhachevsky attacked the northern flank and the Poles were forced to retreat, abandoning Wilno and the province of Białystok. To the south, the Soviet Army under General Yegorov Budienny forced the Poles to retreat to Lwów. Poland appealed to the Entente Powers for help but their appeal was both ignored by governments and refused by organised labour. The Comintern called on the workers of all countries to oppose aid for Poland; Belgium banned the sale of arms and food to Poland; Germany declared neutrality and forbade the transit of armaments across its territory; and the German dock workers in the Free City of Danzig refused to unload shipments for Poland. In Britain Ernest Bevin and other left-wingers organised a 'Hands Off Russia' campaign. Czechoslovakia not only refused to allow the passage of armaments but also took the opportunity to seize the disputed region of Austrian Silesia around Teschen for itself. A group of American pilots, however, decided to assist the Poles and offered their services to Paderewski, and seventeen American pilots led by Major Cedric Fauntleroy joined the 3rd Fighter Squadron in Lwów, which was renamed the Kościuszko Squadron. Three Americans died in combat and a plaque celebrating their exploits was erected in the Lychakivskiy cemetery in Lwów.

In July 1920, the Entente Powers met at Spa to discuss German coal shipments. The Polish foreign minister, Władysław Grabski, came to ask them for help. Lloyd George castigated the Poles for provoking the war, and demanded that they withdraw 150 miles westwards and renounce claims to Wilno and East Galicia. If the Poles agreed, then if the Soviets advanced further, 'the British Government and their Allies would be bound to help Poland with all the means at their disposal'. Grabski turned in vain to the French: Clemenceau had been clearly in favour of a strong Poland but his successor as prime minister, Alexandre Millerand, was content to let Lloyd George take the lead in negotiations. The United States had by this time retreated into neutrality after the Senate had rejected the Treaty of Versailles and membership of the League of Nations. On 10 July, the beleaguered Grabski agreed to Lloyd George's terms. The Poles were to withdraw to the line laid out by the Polish Commission in June 1919 and the Soviets were to halt 50 miles east of it. The future of East Galicia would be decided by the next allied conference, scheduled to take place in London. Then a step was taken which would have enormous repercussions during the Second World War. According to the instructions sent from Spa to the Foreign Office in London, Grabski had agreed to a demarcation line based on Line B, whereby Lwów would remain in Poland. The telegram sent from the Foreign Office to Moscow, however, used Line A. It had been redrafted by someone in the Foreign Office, almost certainly Lewis Namier. (Because Lord Curzon was the foreign secretary at the time the line stipulated became known as the Curzon Line although he actually had no role in drafting it.)

The Poles felt that the allies had held them to ransom at Spa and were deeply unhappy about the poor terms that Grabski had obtained for them. The Soviets saved the situation by rejecting Lloyd George's plan. On 20 July they made a counter-proposal offering Poland a boundary 'to the east of the frontier marked out by the imperialists of London and

Paris'. The offer was made while the Soviets were preparing for a renewed offensive, which opened on 1 August when the five Soviet armies under Tukhachevsky captured Brest-Litovsk (Brześć), advanced to the north of Warsaw and cut the railway communications between Warsaw and Danzig. The allies did little: the British mission headed by Lord Edgar D'Abernon only left London on 21 July, preceded by a French mission led by Jules Jusserand but, most importantly, including General Maxime Weygand. Negotiations for an armistice opened between the Soviets and the Poles but the terms offered by the Soviets were draconian, amounting to the reduction of Poland to little more than a satellite. On 10 August, Lloyd George informed Parliament that in his opinion the Poles had provoked the Soviets and that the 'Soviets were entitled to demand from Poland guarantees that would render impossible any similar attack in the future.' Lord D'Abernon, in contrast, felt that: 'These terms were so extravagant that I cannot conceive any Polish government taking them into consideration.' The French Government urged the Poles to stand fast.

Then came the so-called 'Miracle of the Vistula'. The Soviets had arrived at the gates of Warsaw in early August and the entire Polish population was mobilised to meet them. Weygand was on hand to offer advice to Piłsudski. A gap had appeared between Tukhachevsky's army and the army led by Budienny, and this was where the Poles attacked on 16 August. Later there would be a dispute over who was responsible for the successful plan. The National Democrats wished to downplay Piłsudski's role for political reasons and attributed the victory to Weygand.* The French general himself wrote: 'this victory is a Polish victory, carried out by Polish generals in accordance with the Polish operational plan'. Two generals who would feature during the Second World War, Kazimierz Sosnkowski and Władysław Sikorski, played important roles in the fighting. The future commander of the Polish II Corps, Władysław Anders, was wounded fighting the Soviets. With the pressure on Warsaw relieved, the Poles continued on the offensive, defeating the Soviet armies at Komarów-Zamość and Lwów and at the Niemen river. Lord D'Abernon doubted, 'if in the whole course of history an invading army was involved in a more complete catastrophe'. The Soviets withdrew from Wilno and left the Lithuanians in control. On 9 October, General

---

* Weygand was awarded the *Virtuti Militari*, Poland's highest military medal.

Lucjan Żeligowski with 15,000 locally recruited troops seized the city for Poland.

The Poles and Soviets met at Riga in neutral Latvia to negotiate a peace settlement, and on 8 March 1921, the Treaty of Riga was signed. The so-called Riga Line became the new frontier of Poland. Poland abandoned her claim to about half the territory of the former Polish Commonwealth, but her sovereignty over the former Russian provinces of Wilno, Wołyń and part of Polesie and over East Galicia was confirmed.* The Polish representative in London, Prince Eustace Sapieha, asked Curzon whether the British Government would guarantee the Riga Line and received the ominous reply: 'If the Bolsheviks at any future date crossed the frontier now about to be laid down, would it be regarded by the Great Powers as an act of hostility against them? I thought it most unlikely that they would accept any such obligation.' On 15 March 1923, the Conference of the Ambassadors recognised the Riga Line as Poland's eastern frontier. It is significant that at this time Lloyd George, who had done so much to hinder the settlement of Poland's frontiers, was no longer in power.[19]

Lord D'Abernon described the battle for Warsaw as 'the eighteenth decisive battle in the world', and its international significance should not be forgotten. In October 1920, Vladimir Lenin spoke in Moscow of the war: 'If Poland had become Soviet, if the Warsaw workers had received from Russia the help they expected and welcomed, the Versailles Treaty would have been shattered, and the entire international system built up by the victors would have been destroyed.' Leon Trotsky went further in 1923, when he acknowledged that had Poland become a Russian satellite, then the world revolution he so desired could have extended into Germany in the wake of the crisis caused by the occupation of the Ruhr by French troops and the catastrophic collapse of the economy. Indeed, the Soviets had built up their military strength during the Ruhr crisis with the intention of overrunning Poland should a general war break out. Finally, in 1924, a resolution was passed at the congress of the Comintern which called for the incorporation of the territories Russia had lost to Poland after the Polish-Soviet War into the new Soviet Union. Now, however, the Soviet Union abandoned the cause of world revolution, temporarily at least, and adopted the New

* East Galicia consisted of three Polish provinces: Lwów, Stanisławów and Tarnopol.

Economic Plan and pressed for rapid industrialisation. Stalin never forgave the Poles for the defeat they had inflicted. Indeed for him, as the political commissar who had accompanied Budienny's armies, revenge became a personal issue.[20]

The Polish-Soviet War had an enormous effect within Poland. It reminded the Poles that the Russians, whether tsarist or Soviet, brought repression and subjugation, with the result that the Polish Communist Party (*Komunistyczna Partia Polski*, KPP) found few supporters except in the ethnic minorities. The Riga Line had abandoned 1,000,000 Poles in the Soviet Union but it also meant that about one-third of the population of Poland was not ethnically Polish. The war glorified the position of the army within Polish society but had in some ways a detrimental effect on the future development of the armed forces. The cavalry had proved the most valuable arm and its success then contributed to the failure of the Polish armed forces during the interwar years to recognise fully the enormous impact that mechanisation would have on the conduct of future wars. The successful outcome of this war led the Poles to believe that Poland had fulfilled 'her traditionally self-perceived role as Europe's last bastion of civilised, Christian values against the barbaric, Asiatic east – meaning Russia'.[21] Furthermore she had achieved this victory alone, abandoned by Britain and France, and this led the Poles to believe that Poland was a great country that could stand alone against the might of her neighbours.

Poland had suffered a fiery rebirth. In the early years of the Second Republic, Poland had fought six wars to secure her frontiers: against Germany for Poznania in 1918 and in Upper Silesia in 1919–21; against the Ukrainian nationalists for Lwów and East Galicia in 1918–19; against the Czechs for Teschen in 1919–20; against the Lithuanians for Wilno in 1918 and 1920; and the major war against Soviet Russia in 1919–21. Now, in 1921, the Poles were finally left alone to settle their own future. The history of the Second Republic was to prove to be one of mixed fortunes. As one historian has described it:

> The Promised Land is always something of a disappointment to those who have viewed it from afar. The Poles had dreamed of it so long that it was inevitable they would find the new condition wanting. They had associated every problem and evil with the unnatural state of captivity. The sudden

removal of this only revealed that the problems and blemishes were within themselves. And all the pent-up aspirations released from this captivity rapidly came into collision with one another. The Poles had dreamed of their Arcadia individually, and had to live in it collectively.[22]

The Poles had to rebuild their country after over a century of partitions and after their territory had been one of the main battlegrounds of the Eastern Front in the First World War. Victory over Soviet Russia had ostensibly united the country but, as will be seen, the inclusion within her frontiers of such a high proportion of members of national minorities was to prove a fundamental weakness.

The First World War and its aftermath had caused immense damage within Poland, and about 450,000 Poles had been killed and 900,000 wounded, fighting in four different armies. In the opinion of one American visitor, R. T. Buell, 'except for Belgium, Poland had suffered greater devastation than any other European nation'. Nearly 2,000,000 buildings had been destroyed and 11,000,000 acres of agricultural land ruined. As the Russians retreated they had stripped Poland of industrial equipment and plant. The German occupation led to the confiscation of all resources of use to the German war effort and the imposition of high delivery quotas. The Germans had also deliberately wrecked the textile and steel industries so that they would no longer be able to compete with German industries. Yet at Versailles it was decided that neither Poland nor Czechoslovakia was entitled to any reparations from Germany, on the grounds: 'Poland had nominally been at war against us even though it had been against the will of the Polish people.' Consequently the ability of Poland to rise from the ashes would depend largely on its ability to attract foreign investment.[23]

The effects of the partitions also had to be undone. At the end of the war there were at least six different major currencies circulating in Poland, and the situation was only rectified in 1924 with the issue of the new Polish złoty. The railway system had been developed to facilitate communications between the partitioning powers and their respective capitals. Consequently, there was no direct railway link between Warsaw, formerly in the Russian partition, and Poznań, only 170 miles away but formerly in the German partition; nor, more crucially, between the centre of the country and the sea. There were also four different legal codes in use: those of the three partitioning powers in addition to the

Napoleonic Code in the area of old Congress Poland. Each country had imposed its own taxation system on Poland, with differing degrees of direct and indirect taxation. Polish industry and trade had also been operating to the benefit of the partitioning powers, and now that the German and Russian economies lay in ruins Poland needed to find new outlets for her trade. Seventy per cent of the population worked in agriculture and most of them lived on the poverty line. Indeed, it was estimated that there was a surplus agricultural population of over 4,000,000 peasants. There had been a period of rapid industrialisation at the end of the nineteenth century with the growth of the textile industry in Łódź and a metallurgical industry in the Dąbrowa Basin, but the oil and mineral resources in Kresy had not yet been fully exploited.[24]

In March 1921, Poland adopted a new constitution based on that of the French Third Republic. The Polish parliament was divided into two houses: the *Sejm*, elected by proportional representation by all citizens aged over 21, and the Senate, elected by citizens aged over 30. The president was elected for seven years and had no power of veto over legislation. He could issue decrees but only with the counter-signature of the prime minister and the minister in whose sphere of responsibility the subject of the decree lay. The country was divided into seventeen provinces or voivodeships (*wojewódstwa*), which were then subdivided into districts. The judiciary was independent and the constitution guaranteed freedom of speech, conscience, belief, assembly and of the press.

Both the Polish constitution and that of the French Third Republic contained a fundamental flaw: the system of proportional representation led to a large number of small parties, which meant that every government had to rule through a coalition. For example, in 1925 there were 92 registered political parties, 32 of which had elected representatives in the *Sejm*. In 1920 the leader of the Peasant Party, Wincenty Witos, formed an all-party coalition to govern Poland at the height of the crisis caused by the war with Soviet Russia, but it collapsed in September 1921 after the crisis was over, and thereafter it proved impossible to form a stable government. There were fourteen different governments in the period up to May 1926. A similar situation prevailed in the French Third Republic, where between 1920 and 1930 there were fifteen different governments and ten prime ministers.

French government, however, remained stable because France had a strong civil service, which continued to run the country while the politicians squabbled. As a result of the partitions, Poland had few experienced politicians or civil servants. In the German partition, Poles were able to be elected to the *Reichsrat* and had their own parliamentary club. They were not, however, permitted a role in the civil service, and the central administration had remained in German hands. The Russians had not trusted the Poles with any function within local administration after the 1863 uprising and had embarked on a policy of intense russification. Only after the 1905 revolution in Russia were Polish deputies elected to the *Duma* and Poles allowed to form social associations used to train Polish administrators. The Austrians had been much kinder to the Poles. After the *Ausgleich*, the union between Austria and Hungary in 1867, a Polish Land Parliament and Land Government had been established in Lwów. Poles were able to join the Austro-Hungarian civil service and most local administrators in Galicia were Polish. Poles were also able to enter the Austrian parliament and even become ministers. The twin pressures on Poland, of the necessity to create a governing class and to industrialise, led to a rapid growth in education. In 1918 it was estimated that nearly 40 per cent of the population was illiterate, mainly in Kresy. Compulsory primary education for seven years was introduced and a great expansion of secondary education began. The numbers attending universities also increased, and many of the universities, including those in Kraków, Warsaw, Lwów, Poznań and Wilno, were highly regarded at home and abroad.[25]

The Polish economy was weak from the start and inflation was rampant. Poland was unable to attract a significant amount of foreign investment, and any loans granted were normally on a short-term basis with their renewal dependent on the state of the world economy. Agrarian reform was begun in 1919 with the ambition of breaking up the large estates and distributing the land to the peasants, but the process met with limited success. The fact was that no amount of agrarian reform could solve the problem of the excess agricultural population and the only immediate practical solution lay in emigration. Between 1920 and 1929 nearly 1,250,000 people emigrated, mostly to the United States or to France and Belgium. Polish industry had a reputation for strikes and inefficiency which weakened its ability to attract foreign loans. Germany launched a tariff war against Poland in 1925, which damaged the Polish economy since half of her trade was with Germany. Poland was extremely badly affected when the Depression hit Europe at the start of the 1930s. The Polish Government was as helpless in the face of the collapse of the international economy as other governments worldwide. Unemployment soared and government expenditure was drastically cut. Only Germany, Austria and Czechoslovakia in Europe suffered a higher degree of industrial decline than Poland. In the mid-1930s the world economy began to improve and with it the Polish economy. Unemployment began to fall and living standards rose, but Poland still lagged behind her competitors in terms of output. Steps towards greater industrialisation were taken with the creation of the government-sponsored Central Industrial Region between Kielce and Kraków. In order to ensure that Germany could never strangle Polish sea-borne trade, in 1924 the Poles began dredging a new port at Gdynia, adjacent to Danzig, and by 1938 it was the busiest port in the Baltic.[26]

The Polish economy needed the encouragement of a strong government, but Poland failed to produce one. No one party was strong enough to form a stable government, and the coalitions that were formed proved argumentative rather than constructive. In May 1926 there was a crisis when the Polish National Bank refused to grant the government a further loan. Piłsudski then staged a *coup d'état* by marching into Warsaw at the head of a few battalions of troops and demanding the resignation of the government. The president, Stanisław Wojciechowski, ordered the army to crush the coup, but few regiments moved to support him and the railwaymen refused to move the trains containing the troops loyal to the government. After three days of street fighting and the death of 379 people, the president resigned. The *Sejm* offered Piłsudski the presidency but he declined because his motive for the coup had not been power for himself but the creation of a strong government. Ignacy Mościcki became the new, and indeed the final, president of the Second Republic. The new regime became known as the *Sanacja* (Cleansing or Health) and was a political bloc representing a broad range of political interests, united only in the desire for strong government and a stable economy. The *Sanacja* also stood for ending the corruption endemic in Polish institutions, and the civil service and army were purged. The freedom of the press was gradually curtailed, and politicians and soldiers who opposed the regime suffered for their beliefs. Sikorski, for example, fell out with Piłsudski, was placed on the reserve list in 1928 and then spent the next four years abroad. On the eve of the 1930 elections, Piłsudski had the leaders of the main opposition socialist and peasant parties, such as Witos, arrested and imprisoned in the fortress of Brześć. Dmowski's National Alliance party, *Stronnictwo Narodowe* (SN), won the majority of votes in the 1930 elections, but Dmowski himself had no love for the *Sanacja* regime, and mounted an anti-semitic campaign to discredit Jewish advisers to the president, before retiring from politics in 1937.[27]

In May 1935 Piłsudski died and was buried in the crypt of Wawel Cathedral in Kraków in the company of Polish kings. His heart was taken to Wilno and buried with the body of his mother. From the time of his coup to his death Piłsudski had exercised an enormous influence over Polish politics and, despite its authoritarian undertones, the *Sanacja* Government had been more stable than those preceding the coup and had overseen an improvement in the economy. After his death, though, Polish politics became even more authoritarian as power became concentrated in the hands of three men: the president, Mościcki, the head of the armed forces, Rydz-Śmigły, and the foreign minister, Józef Beck. These three men would be collectively responsible for the near-disastrous situation Poland found itself in when war broke out in 1939. Their powers were confirmed by the new constitution, promulgated in 1935, which gave far more power to the number of president, further reduced the role of the *Sejm* and increased the number of issues that could be dealt with by presidential decree. The 1935 elections were boycotted by a number of parties but the government formed a Camp of National Unity (*Obóz Zjednoczenia Narodowego*, OZN), which included the National Democrats. Their ruling principles were centralism, the importance of the army, the supremacy of the Roman Catholic Church and a rejection of separateness of the national minorities.

Many prominent opposition leaders fled abroad, and in 1936 some, including Witos and Sikorski, met at Paderewski's house in Morges, Switzerland, and founded the Morges Front as a centre-right opposition. The weak Polish Communist Party (KPP) was crushed by the government. Some leaders were imprisoned. Others fled to the Soviet Union, where they were killed during the Great Terror: the KPP itself was disbanded on Stalin's orders in 1938. Those communists, such as Edward Ochab, Marceli Nowotko, Paweł Finder and Alfred Lampe, who would emerge during the Second World War, survived Stalin's purges solely because the Polish Government had imprisoned them.

When the war broke out, the 1935 constitution was still in operation, and it is ironic that the Polish Government-in-Exile, which contained many opposition leaders who despised that constitution, was forced to continue its use in order to maintain continuity between the pre-war and wartime Polish governments.[28]

A chronic problem for the Second Republic was the status of the national minorities, which often undermined the domestic stability of Poland and also alienated potential allies. The first point to note about them is their sheer numbers. The 1931 census figures reveal that out of the total population of Poland of 31,915,900, there were: 22,102,723 Poles, 4,441,000 Ukrainians, 2,822,501 Jews, 989,900 Belorussians, 741,000 Germans and 707,100 'locals'.* Of these the Poles, Jews and Germans were spread out among all the Polish voivodeships. The Ukrainians were dominant in Kresy, particularly in the Wołyń, Stanisławów and Lwów voivodeships; the Belorussians were concentrated in Nowogródek; and the 'locals' in Polesie. The national minorities had their own religions, which encouraged them to feel separate from strongly Roman Catholic Poland. The Germans were predominantly Protestant; the Ukrainians were split between the Uniate Church, which used the Eastern Catholic rite, and the Russian Orthodox Church, to which most Belorussians also belonged. Then of course there were the Jews, whose Judaism ranged from the ultra-orthodox Hasidic rite, which promoted the separateness of Jews, to more moderate forms that allowed for a degree of assimilation.

It is also important to note the economic distribution of the minorities. The Germans in the west dominated the industry and factory ownership of the region and therefore much of its wealth. In the east the Ukrainians and Belorussians were primarily employed in agriculture. The Jews were a largely urban population, and the 1921 census recorded that three-quarters of the Jews lived in towns and cities whereas only 22 per cent of ethnic Poles did so. The economic distribution of the Jews was extremely wide, ranging from extreme poverty in the *shtetls* of Kresy to dominance in artisanship and the crafts, with a high representation in trade and the professions such as law and medicine. The ethnic Poles were also engaged in a wide range of economic activities, but a

---

* People with little sense of national identity, mostly illiterate Belorussian peasants.

broad generalisation can be made that they suffered from an anti-industrial and anti-urban outlook. This was encouraged by conservative groups and by the Roman Catholic Church and was extremely damaging. Modern Poland needed to industrialise, and leaving this in the hands of the Germans and Jews was both short-sighted and created anger during the years of the Depression. The Polish concentration on agriculture, an activity which engaged 70 per cent of the Poles, condemned many of them to a life of poverty and caused them to resent the success of the tradesmen, industrialists and professionals, activities open to them but which they had allowed to become dominated by others. Attempts by Catholic Poles to improve their economic standing through professional education led to clashes with those Polish Jews who were also working their way up from the poverty of the *shtetls* and would lead to hostility between the two groups.[29]

During the 1920s the Polish Government pursued policies in Kresy that were contradictory. In accordance with the terms of the Minorities Treaty, the minorities were allowed to be taught in their own language in primary schools and had their own press and social and welfare associations. Although the Ukrainians boycotted the 1921 census and the November 1922 elections, later in the 1920s there were Ukrainian representatives in the *Sejm*. The Uniate Church was for the most part allowed to operate freely, but in contrast the Orthodox Church was subject to some restrictions. Many Ukrainians still harboured resentment against the Polish state for having wrecked their chances of independence. These feelings were fostered by the Soviets, who, in the early 1920s, encouraged Ukrainian nationalism.

The Polish Government also pursued a policy designed to polonise Kresy. Between 1919 and 1926 about 9,000 former privates and NCOs in Piłsudski's Legions were given grants of land, especially in the Nowogródek and Wołyń voivodeships. During this period about 143,000 hectares were distributed to these so-called military colonists (*osadnicy*), who were often armed by the government. One historian has described the reaction of the Ukrainians and Belorussians: 'For the most part, these colonists were regarded by the local population, who had expected to receive the land, as squatters, thieves and enemies of the people.'[30] The national minorities also resented the fact that only about two-thirds of the colonists actually farmed their own land, while the remainder rented it out to the local peasants. Furthermore, the large Russian estates were passed largely intact to their new Polish owners. Given the nature of rural poverty in the region, where over two-thirds of the buildings lacked sewers, water pipes, electricity and gas, the resentment of the Ukrainians and Belorussians is understandable.[31]

The Ukrainians were radicalised by the intrusion of Poles into what they considered their land. In January 1929, a congress was held in Vienna where the Ukrainian Military Organisation, led by Evgeni Konovalets, combined with smaller Ukrainian groups and took the name Organisation of Ukrainian Nationalists (*Orhanizatsiia Ukrains'kykh Natsionalistiv*, OUN). The OUN resolved that: 'Only the complete removal of all occupiers from Ukrainian lands will allow for the general development of the Ukrainian Nation within its own state.' The Soviets, who were now suppressing Ukrainian nationalism on their side of the border, provided no support, but the Germans stepped in with encouragement, money and training for the Ukrainians.

The OUN embarked on a terror campaign in Kresy, attacking symbols of the Polish state and communication facilities, such as telegraph lines and railways. They also were responsible for the assassination of opponents of Ukrainian nationalism, regardless of nationality. The list of those murdered in the OUN campaign of 1929–30 include 35 Ukrainians, 25 Poles, 1 Jew and 1 Russian, and even those working towards Polish-Ukrainian reconciliation, such as the Interior Minister Bronisław Pieracki, and Tadeusz Hołówko, were murdered. The Polish Government reacted sharply. Piłsudski held the villages near places where sabotage had occurred collectively responsible, Polish cavalry units were billeted on them, fines levied, beatings handed out to opponents and nearly 2,000 Ukrainians were arrested. In 1933 and 1934, violence surged again and in response the Poles established a prison camp at Bereza near Brześć which became notorious for its brutal regime. The legacy of bitterness between the Ukrainians and Poles exploded during the Second World War. The history of that time is still very much alive in Ukraine to this day: Poles are now made welcome in western Ukraine, formerly East Galicia, but in the town library in Tłumacz where the author was conducting interviews in 2009, there was a prominent display of books on the Polish terror campaign of the 1930s. In contrast, Belorussian nationalism was far less developed than that of the Ukrainians and, although the Belorussians undoubtedly resented the influx of military colonists on to their land, no violent clashes occurred between the two sides.[32]

In the years immediately after the rebirth of independent Poland, around 575,000 Germans emigrated from the provinces of Poznań and West Prussia, which had formed the Prussian and then German sections of the partition. In this partition the policy pursued, most notably by Otto von Bismarck, had been to ensure that much of the agricultural land was consolidated into large estates owned by Germans. Polish efforts at land reform deliberately targeted these German estates, breaking up 68 per cent of these in contrast to only 11 per cent of the large Polish estates. The German industrial workers in Upper Silesia were discriminated against and suffered a high level of unemployment. The Germans were in general quietly hostile to the Polish state, forming their own associations sponsored by Weimar Germany, which engaged in anti-Polish propaganda and agitation. The situation changed after 1933 when Hitler came to power in Germany. The German minority now became enthusiastic Nazis but, unlike the Sudeten Germans, did not form a political party to further their aims. Instead they received funds from Germany and carefully began to develop what would become an effective fifth column in 1939, armed and ready to assist the German armed forces and to point out to the invading Germans those Poles who should be targeted.[33]

The Polish state in the interwar period included nearly 3,000,000 Jews, over 1,000,000 in Kresy, much of which had been part of the Russian Pale of Jewish Settlement.* Eighty per cent of Polish Jewry were unassimilated and so looked different from the Poles: 'the dark, motley crowd, Jews in their traditional garb, with beards and side-locks, in "kaftans", in skull-caps, in black hats'. These Jews spoke Yiddish, and a prominent Jew, the Nobel Laureate Isaac Bashevis Singer, later wrote: 'Rarely did a Jew think it necessary to learn Polish, rarely was a Jew interested in Polish history or politics.'[34] Their orthodoxy with the *tzaddikum*, *yeshivoth* and Torah institutions emphasised their 'otherness' from the Poles. During the nineteenth century there had been a movement towards Jewish assimilation, the abandonment of the traditional

---

* This was the only area of the Russian Empire where the Jews were permitted permanent residency and was established by Catherine the Great in 1791.

Jewish garb and even, in some cases, conversion to Christianity. Yet in interwar Poland the assimilationist movement began to decline because: 'The stronger Polish nationalism grew, the more the Jewish community stressed its Jewish nationality, and the higher rose the wall separating both nationalist feelings.'[35] The Zionist leader Ze'ev Jabotinsky wrote in 1937: 'We formed the ghettos ourselves, voluntarily, for the same reason for which the Europeans in Shanghai establish their separate quarter, to be able to live together in their own way.'[36] The result was that Poles and Jews each considered non-Poles and non-Jews as 'the other', and both 'distrusted those of their own kind who tried to strike up a relationship with "the others", and there was always that underlying fear of losing substance'.[37] Nevertheless, a rich Jewish culture developed in Polish cities and flourished during the Second Republic, especially in Warsaw. The Poles also viewed the Jews as disloyal to the Polish state. During Poland's difficult rebirth, the Jews in western Poland had voted in the plebiscites for incorporation into Germany and many continued to speak German at home. In the east some Jews had fought with the Lithuanians against the Poles over the possession of Wilno and with the Bolsheviks in the Polish-Soviet War. This led to the birth of the tragic spectre that would haunt Polish-Jewish relations during the Second World War and beyond – *żydo-komuna* – the communist Jew. Added to this was the growth of Zionism, encouraged by the 1917 Balfour Declaration, which called for the establishment of a Jewish homeland in Palestine. Zionism tended to deter the Jews from loyalty to and involvement in the new Polish state.

The National Democrats who dominated Polish governments until Piłsudski's coup were anti-semitic in that they wanted 'Poland for the Poles'. To this end Jewish emigration was encouraged, and between 1921 and 1931 around 400,000 Jews left Poland, mostly for the United States and Palestine. Anti-semitism became overt and more vociferous during the 1930s as the Depression hit Poland. Economic rivalry between the Poles and Jews grew as Poles resented Jewish domination of trade and industry and called for a boycott of Jewish shops. The emerging Polish middle class resented the predominance of Jews in the professions and called for the imposition of a *numerus clausus* to restrict the number of Jews attending Polish universities, some of which notoriously created so-called 'ghetto benches' to separate the Jews from the Poles in lecture halls. Opportunities for emigration began to dry up as the British and Americans imposed quotas for immigration to Palestine and the United States, giving priority to German and Austrian Jews. The Polish delegate at the League of Nations urged the British to accept more Polish Jews, and the Polish Government encouraged the Zionist movement. It even provided training facilities for the *Irgun* and *Hagana*, the two organisations in Palestine preparing for armed rebellion against the British authorities. The Polish foreign minister, Beck, approached the French Popular Front government to explore the possibility of Jewish emigration to the French colony of Madagascar: a special delegation which included Jews was despatched there to investigate conditions.

Jewish emigration was a policy supported by a broad range of parties for motives that could be placed anywhere on the spectrum from anti-semitism to Zionism. Only the insignificant far right advocated the actual expulsion of Jews. A consensus that Poland contained too many Jews resulted in the passing of a new law on state citizenship in March 1938. It withdrew Polish citizenship from Poles who had resided outside the country for over five years and was deliberately aimed at preventing the 20,000 Polish Jews who lived in Austria from returning to Poland after the *Anschluss*. Similarly in October 1938, when around 17,000 Polish Jews living in Germany were rounded up and expelled into Poland without their possessions, the Polish Government refused to admit the 5,000 who had been outside Poland for over five years. These stateless Jews were forced to live in a special camp near Zbąszyń on the border and were cared for by Jewish agencies. Germany only stopped the expulsion of Jews at the end of October when the Polish Government threatened to deport German citizens from Poland. Polish anti-semitism, however, was not a prelude to the policy of extermination pursued by the Germans during the war. Indeed, some of the most prominent anti-semites of the interwar period were among the first to condemn the Holocaust and to call for action to save Jewish lives.[38]

It cannot be claimed that the Polish Second Republic was a great success. It had, after all, been born suddenly after the collapse of the three partitioning powers, and its frontiers drawn by the statesmen at Versailles and by the sword. On the positive side the Second Republic did succeed in undoing much of the damage caused by the partitions and by 1939 had rationalised the currency and legal system and built up a Polish civil service. Great strides had been taken in education and limited progress made towards industrialisation and agrarian reform. Interwar Europe was a very unsettled place and the Polish Second Republic needs to be seen in this context. Parliamentary democracy may have failed after only eight years but even the excesses of the *Sanacja* regime in the mid- to late-1930s never approached those being committed in the Soviet Union where the Great Famine and Great Terror victimised millions, nor did Polish anti-semitism ever move towards aping the Nuremberg Laws and other anti-Jewish actions being undertaken within Germany. There were, however, also many failures. Of these the most important, when considering the impact that policies followed during the Second Republic would have on Poland during the Second World War, was the failure to bring about a reconciliation between the national minorities and the Polish state and between the Poles and the Jews. Poland's frontiers followed the vision laid out by Piłsudski, including within them the national minorities, but the policies that alienated these minorities from the Polish republic followed the vision of the highly nationalistic Dmowski. One is forced to agree with the comment: 'If the Second Republic had not been foully murdered in 1939 by external agents, there is little doubt that it would soon have sickened from internal causes.'[39] Then, when the foreign policy of Poland is added to the equation, it is possible to see how and why the western powers became disillusioned with the country they had created at Versailles and as the structure of the whole Versailles settlement began to unravel they began to pursue a policy of appeasement.

# 2

# Polish Foreign Policy, 1920–1939

Among the 'new' countries of eastern Europe, Poland occupied an unenviable position. As the largest country in the region, she aspired to Great Power status yet was too weak economically and militarily to fulfil such a role. Sandwiched between two weakened but yet potentially powerful countries, Germany and the Soviet Union, Poland struggled to find a satisfactory and long-lasting way to ensure her security. Poland's rebirth had been a difficult struggle and had left her largely surrounded by hostile neighbours: only Rumania, with which Poland had a treaty of friendship, and Latvia were on good terms. Germany was angered by the existence of the Polish Corridor which separated East Prussia from the rest of the Reich. The Soviets had been thwarted in their ambition to spread world revolution through their defeat in the Polish-Soviet War. The Lithuanians were outraged by the Polish seizure of Wilno, the city the Lithuanians coveted as their capital. The Poles themselves were furious with the Czechs for having taken the opportunity of the distraction of the Polish-Soviet War to seize the majority of the Duchy of Teschen, including areas where the Poles were in a clear majority.

Poland was restored as an independent country at the time of the prostration of the countries which had partitioned her during the eighteenth century. Two of them, Germany and the Soviet Union, were united in their hatred of this new Polish state. In 1922 their representatives met at Rapallo in Italy, and signed a treaty by which they renounced territorial claims against each other. The rationale behind this treaty, however, eerily foreshadows the 1939 Molotov–Ribbentrop Pact. As the head of the German Army, General Hans von Seeckt explained to the chancellor, Joseph Wirth:

When we speak of Poland, we come to the kernel of the eastern problem. Poland's existence is intolerable and incompatible with Germany's vital interests. It must disappear, and will disappear through its own weakness and through Russia with our aid . . . The attainment of this objective must be one of the firmest guiding principles of German policy, as it is capable of achievement – but only through Russia or with her help. A return to the frontier of 1914 should be the basis of agreement between Russia and Germany.[1]

Throughout the interwar period, the German foreign ministry followed a strongly anti-Polish line. This policy reflected the sentiments of German statesmen even before Hitler came to power. For example, in August 1930, a minister without portfolio, Gottfried Treviranus, spoke emotionally in front of the Reichstag: 'In the depth of our souls we remember the torn land of the Vistula, the bleeding wound on the eastern border, this crippled split in the Reich's lungs', and added an ominous warning: 'Frontiers of injustice will not withstand the right of the nation and the national will to live.'[2]

If Poland was to withstand the expansionist plans of her two neighbours, she needed allies. On the face of it the defensive alliance signed with France in 1921 afforded some degree of security, but it was deeply flawed. In the first place, the French viewed the alliance as only one part of its policy of constructing a 'Little Entente' of the 'new' countries in the east to act as a counterweight against the resurgence of German power. Indeed, the creation of the 'Little Entente' can be seen as a purely temporary measure, necessary only because France's former long-standing ally, Russia, was in disarray. Secondly, the French worked hard to befriend Czechoslovakia, efforts which the Polish diplomats deplored. But the fundamental weakness of the alliance was over what could be considered a *casus belli*, a reason for war. The treaty clearly stated that an unprovoked attack on the territory of one country by Germany would be a pretext for a declaration of war by the other. This meant, for example, that any German attack on the Polish Corridor would bring the alliance into play. But what of Danzig? It was by no means clear whether a German attack on Danzig and its reabsorption into the Reich would be a *casus belli* because the situation was complicated by Danzig being a League of Nations city. It seemed most likely that the French would demand that the matter be referred to the League of Nations for settlement. Certainly they would not attack Germany.[3]

French policy towards Danzig was shared by the British: in 1925 the foreign secretary, Austen Chamberlain, made public his opinion that 'no British Government will or ever can risk the bones of a British Grenadier' for Danzig.[4] Polish concern about the trustworthiness of its western ally was reinforced by the 1925 Treaty of Locarno.[5] It guaranteed Germany's western frontiers but deliberately excluded her eastern ones, thereby suggesting that these might be subject to future negotiation, probably at Poland's expense, with the blessing of the Great Powers.

While France and Britain were most concerned about the resurgence of Germany, Poland's attention was firmly fixed eastwards, towards the Soviet Union. The Poles found it difficult to forget that the Soviets had reached the gates of Warsaw in 1920 and nearly crushed their independence only two years after it had been restored. The Treaty of Riga had left the populations in the east split between the two countries: Poland had a large minority of Ukrainians, as well as a significant number of Belorussians and a smaller minority of Lithuanians, whereas over 1,000,000 Poles were left in the Soviet Union. Throughout the 1920s, each country engaged in a significant amount of espionage against the other. Both used Ukrainian nationalism as a tool in their policy. In 1924 the Comintern's 5th Congress passed a resolution calling for the incorporation of East Galicia into the Soviet Union, and the Soviets flooded the eastern provinces of Poland with literature inciting the national minorities to rise up against their Polish rulers. The Poles retaliated by sending numerous spies across the frontier and training Ukrainian military units for action in the Soviet Ukraine. They also created a Border Protection Corps (*Korpus Ochrony Pogranicza*, KOP).[6]

Given the undoubted hostility between Poland and the Soviet Union, it may seem surprising that in 1932 the two countries signed a treaty of non-aggression. The rationale behind the treaty was the weakness of both. The Soviet Union was engaged in a massive programme of collectivisation which led to famine, especially in the Ukraine. Polish border guards were besieged by starving Ukrainian peasants seeking refuge in Poland and begging the Poles to come to the rescue of the Ukraine. Poland was in no position to intervene militarily in the Soviet Union, nor did she ever plan to do so. Indeed, she only ever had purely defensive plans against a Soviet invasion. But Stalin did not know this, and had actually convinced himself that the Polish spies, now mostly captured, were evidence of Polish aggressive plans. Thus the non-aggression treaty suited both parties. The Soviet Union gained most from the treaty. Despite appeals by its own Ukrainian population, Poland did not publicise its extensive knowledge of the man-made famine in the Soviet Union lest this be seen as an unfriendly act. The result was that the Soviet Union continued to be viewed by the international community as a country that should be wooed back into the fold. In 1933 the United States extended diplomatic recognition to the Soviet Union, and in 1934 the Soviet Union joined the League of Nations. The Polish failure to publicise the catastrophic consequences of forced collectivisation had extremely serious consequences for Poland. It meant that when international efforts were being made before the war, and indeed during the war, to woo Stalin, the reluctance of the Poles to accede to this policy was seen as unreasonable obstruction and not as a defence against the justifiable fear of the consequences of an extension of Soviet power westwards.[7]

In January 1933, Adolf Hitler came to power in Germany with the avowed policy of overturning the provisions of the Treaty of Versailles. Poland's worst nightmare had come true and she now had powerful and hostile neighbours to the east and west. Polish foreign policy during the 1930s has been subject to criticism, largely because of the diplomacy of her foreign minister Colonel Józef Beck, who was appointed to his post in 1933 and remained in place until Poland's defeat in 1939. Beck himself justified his policy in his memoirs, written while in internment in Rumania during the war:

> Polish policy rests on the following elements: it follows from our geographical position as well as from the experiences of our history that the problems to which we must attach decisive importance are those posed by the relations with our two great neighbours, Germany and Russia. It is therefore to these problems that we must devote the greatest part of our political activity and of our modest means of action. History teaches us: 1) that the greatest catastrophe of which our nation has ever been victim has been the result of concerted action by these two Powers, and 2) that in this desperate situation there was not to be found any Power in the world to bring us assistance . . . Another conclusion which imposes itself is that the policy of Warsaw should never be dependent upon Moscow or Berlin.[8]

This policy was open to misinterpretation, seen often as being too pro-German and anti-Soviet. Beck's pursuit of an independent foreign policy led to isolation and opprobrium, until at last, in March 1939, a form of redemption was attained with the announcement of the British guarantee to Poland.

The non-aggression treaty with the Soviet Union had drawn no international comment but the signature of a non-aggression treaty with Germany in January 1934 drew fierce criticism. For example, in his memoirs, the former Czech president Eduard Beneš claimed that: 'It increased the tension between France and Poland, caused fresh tension between ourselves and Poland and between the Soviet Union and Poland. In addition, it accelerated the already patent withdrawal of France from the whole of Central Europe.'[9] Beneš clearly believed that the pact had led directly to the 1938 Munich crisis. Yet from the Polish point of view it can be argued that the treaty was a high point of Beck's diplomacy, and a necessary reaction to existing events. French weakness was already evident. In 1933, after Germany had left the League of Nations and the Disarmament Conference, Piłsudski had used private contacts in Paris to sound out the French on the prospects of opposing Hitler in some form, short of a preventative war. He learned that the French were too weak to take any action.[10] He was also suspicious of the motives behind the plans for the formation of a Four Power Pact of Italy, Germany, France and Britain, which he suspected might be detrimental to Polish interests. There was also evidence of increased anti-Polish propaganda in Germany and aggressive posturing. The Nazis dominated the Senate in Danzig and unilaterally repudiated the harbour police agreement, at Poland's expense. The Poles responded by reinforcing their tiny garrison on the spit of land adjacent to Danzig, Westerplatte. This action led to international condemnation for the Poles while the German provocation was overlooked. Piłsudski urged his ambassador in Berlin, Józef Lipski, to negotiate an agreement with Germany.[11]

Hitler was willing to override the objections of the German foreign ministry and negotiate with Poland quite simply because he wanted to secure Germany's eastern flank while the country was rearming. The negotiations led to the settlement of various outstanding issues between the two countries. Germany had been financing Ukrainian nationalists in Poland to undermine Polish authority and it was agreed that this would end. This volte-face was immediately tested when after assassinating Bronisław Pieracki, the Polish minister of the interior, the

Ukrainian nationalist Mykola Lebed fled to Germany using a new passport issued by the German legation in Danzig. The Gestapo agreed to arrest him but then put obstacles in the way of his extradition to Poland. Ultimately Lebed was returned to Poland, where he was tried and sentenced to death; this sentence was later commuted to life imprisonment and the Germans released him during their occupation of Poland.[12] The second benefit of the treaty was that it ended the nine-year-long tariff war between Germany and Poland, which had been damaging to the economies of both countries. The third issue to be settled was the treatment of the national minorities. Poland had abandoned the Minorities Treaty in 1934 because of fears of how the Soviet Union might manipulate it now that it was a member of the League. This effectively left the German minority in Poland as unprotected as the Polish minority in Germany always had been. Ultimately no agreement was reached on this issue because of the problem of Danzig. Hitler's policy towards the Free City fluctuated wildly: he was perfectly capable of demanding the inclusion of Danzig within the Reich one moment, and then ordering the Nazi leader in Danzig, Albert Forster, to limit his anti-Polish agitation the next. At present, in 1934, it suited his purpose not to unsettle the Poles too much while he turned his attention towards rearmament, the militarisation of the Rhineland and the *Anschluss* with Austria.[13]

The Polish-German non-aggression pact did not damage Poland's relations with the Soviet Union nor with France. Beck visited Moscow in February 1934 and received a warm welcome. France had already demonstrated her preoccupation with her own security by beginning the construction of the Maginot Line in 1930. Indeed, it is possible to claim that France had already abandoned eastern Europe and preferred to see Poland and other eastern countries as within the Soviet Union's defensive realm. This policy is best illustrated by the sponsorship of an 'Eastern Locarno' by the French foreign minister, Louis Barthou, which saw the Soviet Union as the defender of eastern Europe. While Czechoslovakia warmly supported the proposal, Poland did not, and the proposal was quietly dropped after Barthou's assassination and his replacement by Pierre Laval. Further evidence of the important and favourable position that the Soviet Union held in the eyes of powers other than Poland is supplied by the signature of two alliances in May 1935: between France and the Soviet Union, and between Czechoslovakia and the Soviet Union. Far from shifting into the German camp as

Poland's detractors have suggested, Beck was actually willing to act to prevent German revisionism. In March 1936, when Germany reoccupied the Rhineland, Beck informed the French ambassador in Warsaw, Leon Noël, that if France were to fight Germany then Poland would fulfil her treaty obligations and attack Germany. The French foreign minister, Pierre-Étienne Flandin, did not even inform the French cabinet of this offer. It was clear, in any case, that France was not prepared to resist Germany's deliberate breach of the Versailles Treaty without British support and this was not forthcoming. In March 1938, the *Anschluss*, the union of Austria and Germany, took place. This deliberate breach of the Versailles Treaty was ignored by the Great Powers. Britain and France appeared to be determined to appease Hitler and, in such circumstances, Poland had to find her own way to security.[14]

It is Beck's conduct over the Czech crisis that has led to the most opprobrium. At worst, Poland was viewed as a German collaborator in the dismemberment of Czechoslovakia: at best, as an opportunist power. There can be no doubt that Beck was hostile to Czechoslovakia. In August 1938, his instructions to Lipski included the statement that, 'We do not believe that this country is capable of existing', and in September, 'We consider the Czechoslovak Republic to be an artificial creation.'[15] But this does not mean that Beck was prepared to connive at Hitler's dismemberment of it, rather the evidence points to his policy being one of independently advancing the rights for the Poles in Teschen whenever Germany sought more rights for the Sudenten Germans. Hitler was content to see Prague squeezed between two jaws of a vice and encouraged the Poles, but did not seek collaboration with them. Some voices in Warsaw urged Beck to leave negotiations over Teschen until the Sudetenland question had been settled, but he forged ahead regardless. When, at Berchtesgarten, Neville Chamberlain and Hitler agreed to solve the Sudetenland question through a plebiscite, Poland requested the same treatment for Teschen. Then on 19 September, Britain and France decided that the Czechs should cede the Sudetenland to Germany, so Poland similarly demanded the cession of Teschen. The Great Powers were not interested in the Polish demands, and Hitler knew this. At the Godesburg meeting, he raised the question of the Polish and Hungarian minorities in Czechoslovakia, not at the request of those governments, but solely to raise the level of threat behind his demands.

The result was that Chamberlain returned from the Munich conference on 29 September boasting of having secured 'peace in our time' and the Sudetenland was ceded to Germany. Accordingly, on 30 September, Poland delivered an ultimatum to Czechoslovakia demanding the Czech evacuation of Teschen. The Czechs did not comply, and between 2 and 13 October Polish troops and civil authorities occupied Teschen.[16]

The Munich crisis was the apogee of appeasement. Britain and France were not prepared to go to war to save Czechoslovakia. Nor was Poland. The Polish ambassador in Paris, Juliusz Łukasiewicz, told the French Government that if a war with Germany broke out because of French military assistance to Czechoslovakia, then the Franco-Polish alliance might not necessarily be applied. The Soviet Union warned Poland that any attack on Czechoslovakia would lead to a denunciation of the Polish-Soviet non-aggression pact, and backed up its warning by mobilising its armies along Poland's eastern frontier. The Soviet Union later claimed that it was the only country that was prepared to intervene to save Czechoslovakia, but in fact was waiting to see what France would do. If France did not act, then the Soviet Union would do nothing. In any case the Soviets could not actually do anything unless Poland and Rumania granted the Red Army passage to reach Czechoslovakia. The Poles naturally were not forthcoming, not trusting the Soviets to leave once invited on to Polish territory, and not believing that the Soviet Union was in reality any more prepared to go to war over Czechoslovakia than were Britain and France.[17]

Poland emerged from the Munich crisis with its reputation badly damaged because of the seizure of Teschen. Anthony Eden wrote in his diary: 'I left Raczyński [Polish ambassador in London] in no doubt as to what I thought of present Polish behaviour, and in mitigation he maintained that once we had legalised Germany's seizure of Sudetenland, Poland could hardly be blamed.' Eden had to concede that Raczyński had a point.[18] In his memoirs, Raczyński set out the extent of Poland's isolation after Munich: 'Parliament and the press treat us with restraint, but the atmosphere has become cold and hostile. This is true at the Foreign Office also. From the public I have been receiving both anonymous and signed letters of bitter reproach, insult or derision. The chief political leaders avoid meeting me.' Even personal friends such as Samuel Hoare and Winston Churchill ignored him.[19]

\*

On 24 October 1938, the Polish ambassador in Berlin, Lipski, was invited to what he expected to be a routine meeting with German foreign minister, Joachim von Ribbentrop. To his shock he learnt that Poland had become the next target of Hitler's aggression. Ribbentrop presented Lipski with a list of German demands: the return of Danzig and the construction of an extraterritorial motorway and railway across the Corridor. Poland was offered an extension of the non-aggression pact for a further twenty-five years, various other minor concessions, and was invited to join the Anti-Comintern Pact.

Poland quite simply could not agree to the German demands. At Versailles it had been agreed that Poland should have free access to the sea, and this was why the predominantly German port of Danzig had been made a Free City, with guarantees for Polish trade, and rights for the German population. The Polish Corridor had been created specifically to give Poland access through her own territory to Danzig. The Poles recognised the danger implicit in Ribbentrop's demands: if they agreed to the return of Danzig to the Reich, then there was a real danger that the entire Polish Corridor would lose its rationale and become the next target for German expansion. As the 1930s had progressed the authority of the League of Nations had declined through its failure to construct firm policies towards the Japanese invasion of Manchuria and the Italian invasion of Abyssinia. Therefore it seemed that the days of free cities like Danzig, guaranteed by the League of Nations, were numbered. Poland could not rely on Britain and France for help over Danzig, given the readiness of both countries to appease Hitler. Nor could they agree to give up Danzig since that would mean that the majority of Polish trade would become subject to the whims of the Germans, allowing them to strangle the country they despised by economic means. The Polish response, made on 31 October, reflected these fears, proposing a bilateral Polish-German agreement to 'guarantee the existence of the Free City of Danzig so as to assure the freedom of national and cultural life to its German minority and also guarantee all Polish rights'. Beck refused to consider joining the Anti-Comintern Pact because this would put an end to his careful balancing act between Germany and the Soviet Union.[20]

Isolated from the western powers after Munich, Poland now had to look for allies elsewhere. One possibility was Lithuania, a country with which Poland had historic links prior to the partitions of Poland, and with which diplomatic relations had been restored in March 1938. However, Lithuania resented the high-handed manner in which the Polish Government had demanded the restoration of relations in response to an incident on the frontier during which a Polish soldier had been killed by a Lithuanian border patrol. The Lithuanians were also still smarting from the loss of Wilno, and, furthermore, were warned by the Soviet Union, which considered the Baltic States as within its sphere of interest, not to become too close to Poland.

Hungary, a country with which Poland historically had had good relations dating back to medieval times, was a more likely candidate. Poland wooed Hungary by offering her political – but not military – support if Hungary took over the region of Sub-Carpatho-Ruthenia, which Hungary had possessed until the Treaty of Trianon had assigned it to Czechoslovakia. This impoverished region contained a very mixed population with different nationalist aspirations. Germany hoped that by encouraging the Czech Government to grant it self-government, an upsurge in Ukrainian nationalism would serve Germany's eastern policy by weakening both Poland and the Soviet Union. Poland, on the other hand, hoped that the takeover of the province by Hungary, which would give them a common frontier, would prevent German advances.

Beck also sought Rumanian collaboration by suggesting that Rumania should take over the easternmost part of the region, which had a sizeable Rumanian population. Rumania declined for a number of reasons: she did not want to antagonise her ally Czechoslovakia by participating in its further dismemberment, and Rumania did not want to strengthen Hungary in case the latter, now more powerful, should begin to agitate for the return of Transylvania. The deciding factor, however, in Beck's ultimate failure to gain Rumanian and Hungarian support was German economic, diplomatic and military strength. The First Vienna Award in November 1938 by Germany and Italy gave Sub-Carpatho-Ruthenia to Hungary, drawing her closer to German policy in eastern Europe. Hungary also joined the Anti-Comintern Pact. Rumania also began to move closer to Germany with the negotiations of long-term and wide-ranging agreements whereby Germany would buy the majority of Rumanian exports and assist in the exploitation of her natural resources, especially oil.[21]

Thus by the start of 1939 Polish foreign policy was in tatters and German demands were growing more menacing. Poland was diplomatically isolated, and her attempts to woo Hungary and Rumania were viewed as evidence of further collusion with German plans in eastern Europe. Indeed, it has been suggested that during this period 'Britain feared a German-Polish deal whereby Poland was either drawn into the German orbit or persuaded to adopt a policy of benevolent neutrality towards Germany.'[22] Yet in Poland events were viewed differently. She was trying to reach a bilateral agreement with Germany over Danzig, but German responses and demands were becoming more aggressive, and Poland had good reason to fear that the city's future might be settled by the Great Powers seeking to appease Hitler. On 9 December, the head of the Foreign Office Central Department, William Strang, informed Raczyński of Halifax's intention to withdraw the League's protection from Danzig by the middle of January 1939. Beck managed to get this decision postponed, yet the pro-German conduct of the British as Rapporteurs to the League of Nations in Danzig made him fearful for the future.[23]

So why was Poland's diplomatic isolation brought to a close in March 1939 when the British prime minister, Neville Chamberlain, announced the British guarantee to Poland? The answer lies in the events of that month, which seemed to leave the policy of appeasement in ruins. German troops entered Prague, and Slovakia was given autonomy guaranteed by a German treaty of protection. Hitler wrested the port of Memel from Lithuania, thereby extending German influence in the Baltic. This move caused considerable alarm among the politicians in Warsaw, who undeniably drew parallels between Memel's former status as a city under international protection until the Lithuanians had seized it in 1923, and Danzig. At the same time, further alarm was raised in Polish circles when Hungary, despite now having a common border with Poland as Poland had long wanted, appeared to be leaning clearly towards the German camp, as demonstrated by the news that the Hungarian Government was prepared to allow German troops passage across its territory on the way to the Rumanian oilfields. Hitler had broken the agreement he had made at Munich with Chamberlain six months earlier. Germany was now quite clearly assuming a dominant position in eastern Europe and securing access to vital raw materials. This in turn would make Britain's principal weapon against Germany – blockade – worthless.[24]

Rumania's rich resources, particularly of oil, made her attractive to Germany: an interest which concerned Britain and France. So, when, on 17 March, the Rumanian minister in London, Viorl Tilea, asked the foreign secretary, Lord Halifax, for a British loan to finance rearmament and for British support to create a bloc of Poland, Rumania, Greece, Turkey and Yugoslavia against German advances he met with a warm reception. During a conversation between Beck and the French premier, Edouard Daladier, on the following day, Beck's request for French support for Poland should Germany seize Danzig was judged acceptable on the condition that Poland extended the 1931 Polish-Rumanian treaty of mutual support against the Soviet Union to cover German aggression as well. As the French foreign minister, Georges Bonnet, told Halifax on 21 March, Poland was the only country in a position to offer real and immediate assistance to Rumania.[25]

Beck, however, was not convinced that the Rumanian plan for a large bloc against Germany was feasible since too many of the countries involved had territorial disputes with each other. Nor did he react any more favourably to a British proposal made by the British ambassador in Warsaw, Sir Howard Kennard, to him, and by Halifax to Raczyński, that Poland should join Britain, France, Yugoslavia, Turkey, Greece, Rumania and the Soviet Union in issuing a joint declaration of their intention to oppose any further German aggression in south-east Europe, in the form of consultation and not necessarily military action. To Beck this proposal appeared to be the last gasp of appeasement and, moreover, he resented the inclusion of the Soviet Union. Instead, Beck proposed a bilateral Polish-British agreement. This would be linked to a Polish declaration of the resoluteness of its policy and a definition of the limit to the concessions Poland was prepared to offer Germany over Danzig.[26]

The British Government believed that it had to act to stop German aggression in the east. Lord Halifax considered: 'We had to make a choice between Poland and the Soviet Union; it seemed clear that Poland would give greater value.' On the afternoon of 30 March, Chamberlain, Halifax and the permanent under secretary at the Foreign Office, Sir Alexander Cadogan, sat down to draft a reply to a parliamentary question to be posed the next day, asking what the British Government would do if Germany attacked Poland.[27] On the afternoon of 31 March, Chamberlain stunned the House of Commons with his response:

I now have to inform the House that during that period, in the event of any action which clearly threatened Polish independence, and which the Polish Government accordingly consider it vital to resist with their national forces, His Majesty's Government would feel themselves bound at once to lend the Polish Government all support in their power. They have given the Polish Government an assurance to this effect.[28]

This guarantee has been described as: 'An emotional response by British politicians to the rapid progress of German aggression in March 1939 ... To the Poles it served the purpose of adding a card in a game of bluff against Germany – a game in which the Poles felt themselves to be increasingly in a weak position.'[29] Or as extraordinary because it meant: 'The decision for war or peace was entrusted to another country and, in effect, was placed in the hands of a man who was not trusted in London or Paris.'[30]

Cadogan wrote in his diary that Britain hoped to gain a reciprocal guarantee with Poland to ensure that Germany would have to fight on two fronts:

We have been told that this is essential. Germany is unable at the moment to embark on a war on two fronts. If she were free to expand eastward and to obtain control of the resources of central and Eastern Europe, she might then be strong enough to turn upon the Western countries with overwhelming strength.[31]

Beck visited London on 3 April and he and Raczyński had meetings with Halifax, who stressed to Raczyński that the fate of Danzig should not be allowed to escalate into conflict and urged the Poles to remain open to new German proposals. Raczyński replied that, by stressing negotiations, 'the British government exhibits its ignorance of the actual state of affairs'. Beck remained determined to solve the question of Danzig directly with Germany.[32] He did not trust the British: the break-up of Czechoslovakia was an example of how Hitler was prepared to dismember a country piece by piece once he had received international approval for the first step. In Beck's opinion the British guarantee was 'the last preventative move, or otherwise a decisive action to assure a powerful ally for our country should Germany not want to withdraw from the aggressive plans against us'.[33] He believed that Czechoslovakia had been dismembered because it had been weak, had not made it clear to Hitler that it would fight to retain its territorial integrity, and had tamely allowed the international community to decide its fate. Poland was different, she would fight, and she now had the guarantee of a major power to back her up. Beck told the *Sejm* on 5 May that although Poland wanted peace, she did not believe in peace at any price and was prepared to fight: 'There is only one thing in the life of men, nations and states which is without price, and that is honour.'[34]

This was a brave statement given that Poland was now virtually surrounded by Germany and by countries within the German sphere of influence. Whereas the Poles had gained confidence from the British guarantee, Hitler had been greatly angered by it: on 3 April, he ordered his military leaders to prepare for war against Poland, and on 28 April he abrogated the Polish-German non-aggression pact and the 1935 Anglo-German naval agreement. The American ambassador to Warsaw, Anthony Drexel Biddle, was told by a leading official of the Danzig Senate: 'Danzig and the Corridor represented only a part of the question in Germany's mind vis-à-vis Poland – there was Upper Silesia as well, and even the matter of Poznań.'[35] In fact Hitler wanted much more: on 23 May, he stated that with Poland there would be war and no such peaceful solution as had been made over Czechoslovakia since 'Danzig is not the subject of the dispute at all. It is a question of expanding our living space in the East, of securing food supplies, and of settling the Baltic problem.'[36] Nevertheless, talks continued between Poland and Germany throughout the summer.[37]

When the British guarantee was announced in Parliament, a number of politicians immediately voiced their opinion that the guarantee was largely pointless unless the Soviet Union was also a guarantor of Poland. For example Lloyd George said:

> If we are going in without the help of Russia we are walking into a trap . . .
> If Russia has not been brought into this matter because of certain feelings
> the Poles have that they do not want the Russian there, it is for us to declare
> the conditions, and unless the Poles are prepared to accept the only condi-
> tions with which we can successfully help them, the responsibility must be
> theirs.

This opinion echoed that of Churchill, who said that, 'To stop here with a guarantee to Poland would be to halt in No-man's Land under fire of both trench lines and without the shelter of either.'[38] But Poland had good reasons for not cooperating with the Soviet Union. On 7 May, the Polish ambassador in Moscow, Wacław Grzybowski, held talks with the Soviet foreign minister, Vyacheslav Molotov. In return for signing an agreement with Britain and France, the Soviet Union wanted Poland to grant the right for Soviet troops to pass through Polish territory, the end of the Polish-Rumanian alliance, and the limitation of Britain's guarantee to Poland to cover only Poland's western frontier with Germany. Knowledge of these talks determined Beck's stance throughout the period of Anglo-French approaches to the Soviet Union.[39] He firmly believed that once on Polish territory the Soviet troops would never leave again, suspecting 'that Marshal Kliment Voroshilov was attempting today to reach in a peaceful manner what he had attempted to obtain by force of arms in 1920'. Beck told the French ambassador to Poland, Leon Noël: 'Nothing assures us that, once they are installed in the eastern parts of our country, the Russians will participate effectively in the war.' He concluded that cooperation with the Soviet Union was 'a new partition which we are asked to sign; if we are to be partitioned, we shall at least defend ourselves'.[40]

Ultimately Anglo-French negotiations with the Soviet Union failed not because of Polish intransigence but because the Soviets saw Germany as a more valuable ally. Britain and France did not realise that the Soviets were conducting negotiations with Germany at the same time as they were holding talks with them, but the Poles did. The Polish military attaché in Moscow was aware that the Soviets seeking transit visas across Poland were high-ranking military officers.[41] On 23 August, the Molotov–Ribbentrop Pact was signed and in a secret protocol the Fourth Partition of Poland was agreed upon.

Poland believed that Britain and France were the two most powerful allies that she could have hoped to gain. After all, Britain had a powerful navy and France had a large, modernised army. But the political guarantee to Poland would be largely meaningless unless she could secure commitments of economic and military assistance. In May 1939, military negotiations took place in Paris between Polish and French officers. Poland sent high-ranking army, navy and air force officers under the minister for war, General Tadeusz Kasprzycki, and the French party was led by the supreme commander designate, General Maurice Gamelin, backed by the commander-in-chief of the army, General Alphonse

Georges, and the chiefs of staff of the navy and air force. The military agreement signed on 19 May committed France to start immediate air operations against Germany and a limited ground offensive on the third day after mobilisation, to be followed by a major offensive with the bulk of her troops on the fifteenth day. During this time Poland would wage only a defensive campaign. The air agreement signed on 27 May also stipulated that three French bomber squadrons would be despatched to Poland and that a special air mission under General Paul Armengaud would be sent to Poland to command the squadrons and to coordinate their efforts with the Polish Air Force. The French promised to consider Germany as the principal enemy should Italy also declare war. These agreements appeared to bode extremely well for Poland: she seemed to have gained the firm commitment of an ally with a large, well-trained army. Yet simultaneously political negotiations were being carried out. These did not run smoothly because Poland wanted a German occupation of Danzig to be a *casus belli* while the French, following the British lead, did not. It was only on 4 September, the day after France had declared war on Germany and three days after German forces had entered Poland, that this now worthless political agreement was signed.[42]

However, although it was unknown to the Poles then, it now appears clear that the French never had any intention of mounting an offensive against Germany. Even during the Munich crisis General Georges had told the French cabinet that an offensive against the German defences on the Siegfried Line was impossible. In the middle of July 1939, General Gamelin spoke privately to Lord Gort, the British Chief of Imperial General Staff (CIGS), and confided to him: 'we have every interest in the war's beginning in the east and becoming a general conflict only little by little. We shall thus have the time necessary to put on a war footing all Franco-British forces.'[43] The British politicians knew of the French unwillingness to fight too: Churchill learnt of the French plans for a strictly limited offensive from meeting Georges and other senior French officers during a visit to France in August. General Edmund Ironside, the inspector-general of overseas forces, noted in his diary: 'The French have lied to the Poles in saying that they are going to attack. There is no idea of it.'[44]

The British chiefs of staff had informed Chamberlain, even before the British guarantee to Poland was given, that Britain could offer no practicable help to Poland in the event of a German attack. In May 1939, a British military mission arrived in Warsaw to discuss war plans with the Poles. The relative low ranks of its members should have been a warning of the British lack of commitment. The mission was led by Lieutenant-Colonel Emilius Clayton. He had been Britain's first military attaché to Poland after the First World War and knew the country and the Poles, but he was brought out of retirement and raised to the rank of brigadier specially to lead the mission. The other British officers were a naval captain and a Royal Air Force (RAF) group captain. The talks revealed that Britain would give no military or naval support to Poland. Because the Baltic would be easily dominated by the German Navy it was proposed to send three Polish destroyers to Britain on the outbreak of war to aid the British naval effort against Germany. The air discussions were more fruitful: the RAF would bomb German military targets, and Clayton further intimated that if the Germans bombed Polish civilian installations then the RAF would bomb Germany at will. Although the Polish military liked Clayton on a personal level, they had hoped to meet someone more senior who could reveal Britain's war plans, and therefore they were delighted when General Ironside visited Poland in July. Yet Ironside had been despatched by the War Office to 'obtain better information than we had hitherto been able to obtain as to the direction in which Marshal Edward Śmigły-Rydz's mind was moving'.* After discussing the state of Poland's forces, Ironside was convinced that the 'Poles were strong enough to resist' and that 'you might take Poznania in a couple of months, but you couldn't overrun the whole country in a couple of months'. Back in Britain more promises were made to the Poles. On 3 August, Air Vice-Marshal A. Boyle wrote to Lieutenant-Colonel Bogdan Kwieciński, the Polish military attaché, 'to ask the Polish defence authorities for their permission and assistance in preparing an advanced base in Poland, from which bombers of the British Metropolitan bomber force could operate temporarily in the event of war, and in laying down stocks of materiel and equipment in Poland, which would be essential for this purpose'. The plans were detailed and would take a month to put into effect once Polish permission had been received. But Poland did not have a month left.[45]

Poland was a desperately poor country, so another method by which

* Usually Rydz-Śmigły.

Britain and France could assist her was in the form of loans for domestic rearmament and for the purchase of armaments abroad. Under the terms of the 1936 Franco-Polish loan agreement France could grant Poland export credits up to the value of 430,000,000 francs. Yet as the military and political negotiations dragged on through the summer of 1939, it became clear to the Poles that France was unwilling to sell its armaments to the Poles or to grant loans for Poland to build up its own defence industry. The British were equally unhelpful, giving Poland only £8,000,000 in export credits under humiliating terms. Poland placed orders for military hardware immediately but found few sellers. Indeed, as the Labour MP Hugh Dalton told the House of Commons:

> Nothing has been arranged whereby Poland can obtain purchasing power to obtain from other countries, including the United States and the Scandinavian countries, arms and equipment which she cannot obtain from us, not because we cannot supply them, but because all that we are producing we require ourselves.[46]

Both Britain and France were preparing for a long war for which economic strength would be crucial, and were also naturally prioritising their own security requirements. Consequently France was unwilling to sell any equipment to Poland, and Britain only offered 100 Fairey Battle light bombers and fourteen Hurricane fighters. After the war began Britain gave Poland another 5,500,000 złoty in cash credits.[47]

Beck had made it quite clear to the world that Poland would fight to defend her soil against German encroachments. The question as yet unanswered was whether Poland actually *could* do so. Geographically Poland was a difficult country to defend, with only a few natural barriers. On her eastern border, the impenetrable Pripet marshes formed a natural defensive barrier that would at least force an invading enemy to split its forces. To the south, the Carpathian mountains provided a natural frontier with Czechoslovakia. There were, however, no natural barriers between Polish and German territory either in Upper Silesia, East Prussia or along the Corridor. The three great rivers, the Narew, Vistula and San, flowing from south to north across Poland, were the only natural obstacles on the wide plains of Poland, which provided ideal tank territory, and the deep forests could be bypassed by armour.[48]

The Polish armed forces were commanded by Marshal Rydz-Śmigły. The French ambassador in Warsaw, Leon Noël, described him as:

> Honest, upright and at the same time not lacking in finesse, cultivated, possessing, for example, a deep knowledge of the Napoleonic era, he was far from being without merits, but Piłsudski's favour and events laid upon him responsibilities which he certainly did not seek and for which he was not prepared.[49]

On paper at least, the Polish Army was reasonably strong: on 1 September 1939, Poland had about 1,000,000 men organised in 37 infantry divisions, 11 cavalry brigades and 2 armoured brigades plus artillery, and there were another 1,000,000 men in the reserve. Lieutenant-Colonel Edward Sword, the British military attaché in Warsaw, realised that Poland's 'comparative poverty is directly responsible for the material inferiority of her air force and limits the equipment of land forces, particularly as far as artillery and mechanisation are concerned'.[50] In 1938–9 over 1 billion złoty had been spent on Poland's armed forces, a significant proportion of the national budget. This was a sum that Poland could ill-afford and which was partly raised by 'voluntary' donations of a portion of their salaries by army officers and public servants. Even schoolchildren were asked to donate their sweet money towards buying armaments.* To put Poland's spending in context: the figure was about 10 per cent of the Luftwaffe's budget for 1939 and fifty times less than Germany's defence spending as a whole.[51]

Poland's relative poverty also had a detrimental effect on the fighting abilities of the army. The conscripts lacked technical training with modern weapons, although the non-commissioned officers and junior officers were better trained. Poland's meagre industrial resources meant that her armaments were of a mixture of Polish, French, Russian, Czech and British manufacture. There was an overall shortage of light and heavy machine guns. There were over 300 medium and light tanks in the motorised armoured brigades and a further 500 light reconnaissance tanks, or 'tankettes', were attached to infantry divisions and brigades. Since independence Poland had greatly improved her road network and as a result the number of lorries had increased. Nevertheless, although the army needed 12,000 lorries for transport, there were

---

* The submarine purchased was *Orzeł*.

only 6,000 in the whole of Poland by 1937. As a result the infantry, like much of the German Army, was still largely dependent on horse-drawn transport. The signals units were well equipped with telephones, but their radios had been purchased from the French after the First World War and were obsolete.[52]

Mobility had been a feature of the Eastern Front during much of the First World War and during the Polish-Soviet War, and hence Piłsudski and his followers in the Polish general staff viewed the cavalry as an important component in the armed forces. As in Britain, the cavalry was seen as the elite force and most of the officers came from the aristocracy and wealthy landowning gentry. Poland did recognise that the days of the cavalry charge had passed. The principal role of the cavalry was now to be reconnaissance and not offensive action. In case they had to fight to defend themselves then they were armed with rifles, pistols and machine guns and trained to fight dismounted like mounted infantry-men. Poland was in the process of forming armoured units but her poverty delayed this. Despite all this, it has to be said that the Polish armed forces underestimated the extent to which armoured formations had changed the nature of warfare. In 1937 Major-General Władysław Anders held a field exercise with the Nowogródzka Cavalry Brigade in which a large cavalry formation was ordered to defend itself against attack by a large armoured group. The results alarmed him and provided an ominous portent of what would happen in 1939. The officers showed that they had little idea of how to mount a defensive operation in the face of armour. They also appeared to have failed to carry out a basic requirement of the cavalry or indeed of any armed group: adequate reconnaissance of the terrain.[53]

Poland never managed to develop a true military doctrine of its own. Polish operational doctrine, such as it was, was based on mobility. But this was mobility at the speed of cavalry troops and not of the mechanised formations of the German Army. The senior officers had learned their trade as junior officers in the armies of Russia, Germany and Austro-Hungary. Between the wars French military doctrine had been closely studied and copied. Sword's reports to London hinted at the impact this had: 'as far as training is concerned, the Army possibly suffers from a certain conflict between French and German doctrine, together with a lack of appreciation of the power of modern weapons'. While he had little doubt as to the powers of leadership of the senior officers nor of the powers of endurance of the rank and file, he noted that there appeared to be a demonstrable failure to understand or comprehend the speed with which Panzer formations could advance.[54]

In 1932 Poland established a native aeronautical industry by bringing existing aircraft factories into government ownership and by constructing a Czech Škoda engine plant on Polish soil. The fighters produced by the Polish Aircraft Works, PZL, were modern: indeed, when its production began in 1934 the P-11 was the most modern fighter in the world. Its successor, the P-24, was better armed and faster and earned Poland valuable foreign currency with its export to Rumania, Greece, Bulgaria and Turkey. Therein lay the problem caused by Poland's poverty. On the eve of the war the P-24 was still being exported, forcing the Polish Air Force to rely on the by-now-obsolete P-7 and P-11 fighters. In real terms this meant that Polish fighters were capable of only 300 kph against the Messerschmitt 109 with 407 kph, and also the Messerschmitt could fly higher and was better armed. Added to that, the Poles only had 392 combat planes against the Luftwaffe's 1,941 fighters. Only in bombers was the Polish Air Force comparable to the Luftwaffe. The Łoś bomber was faster and carried a heavier bomb load than the Heinkel HE-111. The Polish Government had purchased 160 Morane 406 fighters from France and 100 Fairey Battle light bombers from Britain, but none arrived before the war. The role of the air force units, part of the army and navy, was to support the army groups to which they were attached. Reserve airfields were constructed to prevent the air force being bombed out of existence on the outbreak of hostilities, but supplies of spare parts and aviation fuel were not concentrated there and were vulnerable to destruction by German bombers.[55]

Between 1920 and 1936 Polish military planners had concentrated exclusively on defence against invasion from the east by the Soviet Union. Consequently, Poland built fixed defences in the east while the main supply centres were built in the west, out of reach of an invading Soviet army. In 1936, following the announcement of conscription in Germany, Rydz-Śmigły ordered the preparation of plans for defence against German attacks from the north and west. Basically these plans envisaged a rerun of 1914: the main German thrust would come from East Prussia and Pomerania, with a subsidiary attack to the south-west through Silesia. The Polish defence plan aimed at preventing the two main attacking forces from joining up and mounting a joint attack on Warsaw. Polish forces also aimed to keep the Germans out of Polish Silesia, so as to protect Poland's main industrial areas. The planners also sounded a warning alarm: against Poland's 37 infantry divisions and 11 cavalry brigades the Germans would probably despatch 70 of their one hundred divisions. Polish defence plans were altered radically by the events of March 1939 when, as a result of the dismemberment of Czechoslovakia, Poland now had to defend a total of 1,000 miles of frontier against Germany. Plan Z (*Zachód*) moved the axis of Polish defence to the south-west where it was now thought the main German attack would be made. This late change in plans had a detrimental effect. Commanding officers were called to Warsaw to be briefed individually on the tasks for their sector, but they were given little idea of what their neighbouring units would be doing. In fact one senior officer, Lieutenant-Colonel Stanisław Mosser, chief of staff of Army Poznań, shared his commander's plans with his neighbouring commanders and was disciplined and removed from his post. Supply dumps were to have been moved east of the Vistula but little had been done about this.[56]

Plan Z was known to Poland's western allies: indeed, even the American ambassador in Warsaw knew the details. Plan Z envisaged: 'When circumstances made it advisable, [order a] gradual retirement of the main body of Polish troops under the cover of delayed action to a main defensive position along the line of the Narew, Bug, Vistula and San rivers.' This was to be a holding action while the British and French attacked in the west, and the Polish planners hoped 'to be able to keep intact a central reserve for use in a counter-offensive especially if the Germans start drawing troops from the east to reinforce the west'.[57] The Poles were under the impression that the British and French understood their plan and the absolute necessity of mounting an effective offensive in the west within the previously agreed time period, but as indicated above, neither of Poland's allies had any intention of mounting an offensive. 'The idea that Britain and France could complacently plan on the assumption that Poland would succumb to a German attack, without being galvanised into action, simply did not enter into Polish calculations.'[58]

A British military mission under the energetic and eccentric Polonophile General Carton de Wiart arrived in Poland on 24 August, and the French mission led by the elderly General Louis-Augustin-Joseph

Faury arrived on 23 August. Their purpose was to give moral rather than real support to the Poles. The mission leaders pointed out one fundamental weakness of Plan Z – the intention to defend the whole of western Poland. For example, Carton de Wiart urged Rydz-Śmigły to withdraw the troops from the frontier so that they would not be overrun, but he 'held the view that if he retired at all, he would be accused of cowardice'. There were two other reasons why it was seen as essential to defend the western frontier. First, if the Poles did not defend Polish Pomerania and the Poznań region then, if Hitler ordered a halt to offensive operations once German troops had occupied these areas and taken Danzig, the chance existed that the British and French would place immense pressure on the Poles to end the fighting. Indeed, Hitler was so convinced that neither Britain nor France wanted to go to war for former German territory that his reasoning was along the lines: 'The isolation of Poland will be all the more easily maintained, even after the outbreak of hostilities, if we succeed in starting the war with sudden, heavy blows and in gaining rapid success.' The second reason was economic. Despite great strides having been taken between the wars in the construction of the Central Industrial Region which straddled the Vistula, Poland's economic strength, such as it was, largely depended on the resources of Silesia. Therefore, Poland had to concentrate her strength on defending this area against the expected main German attack, and the anticipated attacks in the north were now viewed as less important. In fact, confusion reigned on the eve of the war as troops were moved into and then withdrawn from the Corridor, because on the one hand Poland wanted to defend all her territory, but on the other hand troops in the Corridor would be on a suicide mission sandwiched between the pincers of two advancing German armies.[59]

Throughout August the Germans increased their pressure on Poland. It now became clearer that Germany would not be satisfied just with the return of Danzig to the Reich and the extraterritorial motorway and railway, but demanded also the return of the portion of Poland that had formed the German partition. Polish customs officers in Danzig were subjected to attacks by the Nazis. German press and radio thundered about the alleged mistreatment of Germans in Poland. The British ambassador in Berlin, Sir Neville Henderson, was inclined to believe the stories, convinced that Polish intransigence was about to bring Britain and France into a conflict with Germany, while Sir Howard Kennard, the British ambassador to Warsaw, investigated some of the German claims and 'found that these allegations were characterised by exaggerations, if not complete falsification', and made this clear in his telegrams to London.[60] Hitler was becoming increasingly determined to separate Poland from her western allies, and the British Government was attempting to find some way to prevent the Polish-German dispute from becoming a war. In line with the British guarantee and subsequent talks, on 25 August, an Anglo-Polish alliance was signed in London stipulating: 'Should one of the Contracting Powers become engaged in hostilities with a European Power in consequence of aggression by the latter ... the other Contracting Power will at once give the Contracting Power engaged in hostilities all the support and assistance in its power.'[61]

The signature of this alliance should have convinced the Poles and indeed Hitler that Britain was sincere in her intentions. However, as Raczyński noted: 'The ink had scarcely dried on it when Lord Halifax started unfolding to me fresh ideas for a compromise with Germany!'[62] Three days before the invasion of Poland Chamberlain told Hermann Goering's special envoy, Birger Dahlerus, that the Poles would concede Danzig, subject to the retention of certain Polish rights, and would allow the extraterritorial link across the Corridor subject to international guarantees. The Poles were not informed that Chamberlain was conceding what the Poles had refused. Had they known, then it would have confirmed to the Polish Government that Britain was prepared to begin the process of dismembering Poland as it had done at Munich in the case of Czechoslovakia. It is therefore also not surprising that Hitler did not believe that Britain would really go to war with Germany over Poland.[63]

The Poles were well aware of the build-up of German troops on their frontier during August 1939. The Wehrmacht could be mobilised completely without a public announcement of general mobilisation. The Polish mobilisation plan, Plan W, envisaged that only 75 per cent of the infantry and the whole of the cavalry could be secretly mobilised. The timing was therefore crucial, but British and French diplomats pressurised the Polish Government to delay mobilisation while they sought a peaceful solution to the Polish-German problem. On 24 August, orders were sent off for a secret mobilisation. As far as Jan Karski, a second lieutenant in the artillery, was concerned, it was secret only in so far as there were no posters or public announcements. When he arrived at Warsaw station to join the train to take him to his depot, he noted that 'it looked as though every man in Warsaw were there'. On the night of 25–26 August, German and Slovak troops attacked the Jabłonka railway tunnel in the Carpathians. This attack, premature only because Hitler had postponed the invasion of Poland originally planned for 26 August, was repelled, but it was one of an alarming series of German border incursions. Rydz-Śmigły now urgently needed to order a general mobilisation and prepared the relevant orders to be issued on 29 August, but British and French pressure again forced him to cancel these plans and on 27 August he issued more secret mobilisation orders and ordered his army commanders to their headquarters. Eventually the Polish Government lost patience with its allies and on 30 August ordered a general mobilisation to begin on the following day. On the 29th Hitler had demanded the arrival in Berlin by 30 August of a Polish emissary with full powers to make the required concessions. On 31 August, he refused to see Lipski, who had not been granted the necessary powers by the Polish Government. Instead, Ribbentrop read out the list of demands to Henderson so fast that he could not take notes: he was not allowed to read the document.[64]

On the evening of 31 August, German radio reported that Polish soldiers had attacked the German radio station at Gleiwitz (Gliwice) in Upper Silesia and killed several Germans. In fact the attackers were SS soldiers dressed in Polish Army uniforms and the 'victims' were concentration camp inmates who had been killed earlier. On 1 September, Germany launched its invasion of Poland. The delays to Polish mobilisation meant that not all reservists had reached their depots, and many of those who had arrived had not received their equipment and weapons. In all, 10 Polish divisions were unprepared for the onslaught that was about to hit them.

# 3

# The September 1939 Campaign

At 4.45 a.m. on 1 September 1939, the pre-Dreadnought German battleship *Schleswig-Holstein* opened fire against the small Polish military depot on Westerplatte in Danzig. Orderly Sergeant Józef Lopaniuk was on duty when he heard what he first assumed to be thunder but quickly recognised as artillery fire. After consulting his major, he sounded the alarm. Warrant Officer Władysław Baran recalled: 'The air rocked. Fountains of sand, stones and smoke rose up. Shattered trunks and branches of trees, pieces of human bodies and weapons flew in the air. The deafening thunder of explosions was interrupted from time to time by the shrill screams of the dying.'[1] Simultaneously the SS launched an attack on the Polish post-office workers in Danzig, who resisted strongly and declined a German appeal for their surrender. When the fighting forced them to take refuge in the basement of the post office, the Germans poured petrol into the building and set it alight. As the suffocating Poles emerged to surrender the SS shot them. The *Daily Telegraph* correspondent Clare Hollingworth happened to be in Katowice in Polish Upper Silesia when she saw the German forces advancing across the frontier and the Luftwaffe flying overhead.

> I grabbed the telephone, reached the *Telegraph* correspondent in Warsaw and told him my news. I heard later that he rang straight through to the Polish Foreign Office, who had no word of the attack. The *Telegraph* was not only the first paper to hear that Poland was at war – it had, too, the odd privilege of informing the Polish Government itself.[2]

In London the Polish ambassador, Edward Raczyński, visited the foreign secretary, Lord Halifax, to beg for immediate help. General Ironside was informed of the German attack by Winston Churchill. When

**Legend:**
→ German advances commencing 1 September 1939
→ Soviet advances commencing 17 September 1939

3. The German and Soviet Invasions of Poland

Ironside reached the War Office he discovered that they knew nothing about it. The CIGS, Lord Gort, did not believe the news but told the secretary of state for war, Leslie Hore-Belisha, who went to Downing Street to inform Chamberlain.[3] In Poland 'the outbreak of war was no surprise to anybody and many greeted it with jubilation, expecting a swift and easy victory. The nation was conditioned by propaganda, spread by the media, of German weakness and the strength of the Polish-French-British alliance.'[4] The radio announcement of the outbreak of war was followed by the playing of the national anthem and Chopin's *Polonaise in A Major*.[5]

The German ground attack heralded a new form of warfare: *Blitzkrieg*, or lightning war. Rather than advancing along broad fronts as in previous wars, the Germans concentrated their forces into highly mobile armoured columns that smashed into Poland from three directions simultaneously. In the north-west, the German Army Group North, under General Fedor von Bock, was split into two forces. The Fourth Army under General Günther von Kluge launched an attack from German Pomerania with the aim of cutting the Corridor, thereby isolating Polish forces on the coast, and then joining the Third Army, under General Georg von Küchler, which was attacking from East Prussia, for a joint drive on Warsaw. The Polish Army Pomorze, under General Władysław Bortnowski, was not defending the Corridor in strength because it realised that this would be futile; instead, his troops were based on the Brda river. Army Modlin, commanded by General Emil Krukowicz-Przedrzymirski, fortified the Mława against the anticipated advance of the German Third Army. But the main weight of the German attack was further south. Army Group South, under General Gerd von Rundstedt, received the highest number of Panzers in any German formation. The Eighth Army under General Johannes Blaskowitz and the Tenth under General Walter von Reichenau launched their attack on the Łódź–Kraków triangle. This was defended by Army Łódź under General Juliusz Rómmel and Army Kraków under General Antoni Szylling. In the south-west, the Fourteenth Army under General Wilhelm List attacked Army Kraków.[6]

The second new aspect of *Blitzkrieg* was the ruthless application of air power by the Luftwaffe. Civilians had been bombed during the Spanish Civil War, notably at Guernica, but on nothing like the scale inflicted by the Germans in Poland. Wieluń, a farming town 60 miles east of Breslau, had the dubious honour of becoming the first town in Poland to be flattened by German bombs. The hospital, school, churches and shops were all bombed and over 1,600 people, 10 per cent of the town's population, were killed on the first day of the war. Polish armoured trains, effective against the Panzers, proved of limited utility as the Luftwaffe destroyed the railways.[7] Everywhere towns were bombed, refugee columns strafed, passenger trains bombed and their fleeing passengers machine-gunned. Nothing seemed to escape the force of the Luftwaffe. General Carton de Wiart wrote later: 'And with the first deliberate bombing of civilians, I saw the very face of war change – bereft of romance, its glory shorn, no longer the soldier setting forth into battle, but the women and children buried under it.'[8] The strength of the Luftwaffe awed the Poles: one child observed, 'You couldn't even see the sky. I just couldn't believe how they had built so many planes.' Civilians were strafed from the air on the road. A Polish report stated that: 'Along the Warsaw-Kutno road during the entire month of September, mounds of decomposing cadavers were to be seen, consisting for the most part of women and children.'[9] Ryszard Zolski, working in an ambulance unit, witnessed hospitals, ambulances and ambulance trains being bombed despite being marked prominently with a red cross.[10] The Germans might have attempted to justify the bombing of towns ahead of their advance on military grounds but this does not explain why towns well to the east of the Vistula were bombed early on. For example, Stanisławów (Ivano-Frankivsk), in the far south-east of Poland, was first bombed on 8 September and then subjected to ten more raids in the following week. Stanisław Kochański had a lucky escape. Watching the bombing raids from the attic of his family's house through binoculars, he was forcibly dragged out of the attic by his father just before bombs fell around the house, shattering windows, dislodging roof tiles and leaving shell fragments lodged in the walls.[11] On 10 September, Warsaw became the first European capital to be subjected to bombing raids: there were twelve on that day alone.

Concentrated too near the frontier, Polish defences were quickly overwhelmed in many areas, and General Heinz Guderian was delighted by the speed with which his Panzers crossed the Corridor. The Brda river defences were bypassed by German armour, leaving the road open for a rapid drive southwards. Army Modlin did, however, succeed in slowing the advance of the Third Army at the Mława, forcing the

Panzers to wait for their infantry to catch up before renewing the attack. In the south, where Polish planners had hoped to make a stand to defend Poland's industrial region, Polish defences were overwhelmed by the combination of German armour and air power.[12] Jan Karski was a lieutenant in the Mounted Artillery Division stationed at Oświęcim on 1 September when the Luftwaffe bombed their camp and then the Panzers advanced and fired at the ruins: 'The extent of the death, destruction and disorganisation this combined fire caused in three short hours was incredible. By the time our wits were sufficiently collected even to survey the situation, it was apparent that we were in no position to offer any serious resistance.' Karski and his colleagues in Army Kraków began to retreat, a phenomenon that was becoming familiar to most of the Polish Army.[13]

The Poles did not, however, retreat without a fight. A fierce battle took place in the village of Mokra, north of Częstochowa, on the line dividing Army Kraków and Army Łódź. During this battle the Volhynian Cavalry Brigade charged at German infantry and successfully scattered them before the Germans massacred the cavalry with their machine guns and artillery. Further north, the Polish 18th Uhlan Regiment of the Pomorze Cavalry Brigade was ordered to attack the flank of the German 20th Motorised Division in order to cover the retreat of the Polish infantry. The Uhlans' adjutant, Captain Godlewski, queried the order to charge and was told by his commanding officer, Colonel Kazimierz Mastalerz, 'Young man, I'm quite aware what it is like to carry out an impossible order.' With sabres drawn, the 250 men charged at the German infantry, who fled. At this point a column of armoured cars and tanks came upon the scene and fired at the cavalry, killing half of them in minutes. This is the incident that gave rise to the German propaganda, much repeated since, that Polish cavalry had charged at German tanks.[14]

On 2 September, Army Pomorze was still withdrawing from the Corridor under intense German pressure. It attempted to mount a defence on the Ossa river near the city of Grudziądz, but at this critical juncture Polish commanders made a significant error. For no apparent reason the Poles decided to swap the positions of the two divisions defending the main road. In the resultant chaos, as troops became entangled and communications broke down, the commander of the Polish 16th Division, Colonel Stanisław Świtalski, panicked and ordered a retreat to the south-west. Although he was promptly sacked, the Poles did not recover in time to mount a firm defence of Grudziądz. The Luftwaffe bombarded the Polish troops and once the planes had finished their work and the smoke cleared:

> In front of us appeared a blood-chilling sight. Bodies were strewn across the road, and the horses who were killed were still in harness . . . In a nearby field lay the scattered remains of equipment and vehicles . . . The trenches were full of slain soldiers . . . There were so few soldiers left alive that in reality the 34th and 55th Infantry Regiments had ceased to exist as individual units.[15]

The Polish defences on the Mława were eventually bypassed by the Germans and by late afternoon Army Modlin began to retreat to the line of the Vistula. Further south, the situation was even more serious, as the Germans had succeeded in forcing a breach between Army Kraków and Army Łódź, forcing both armies to retreat. Karski wrote that by the end of that day, 'we are now no longer an army, a detachment, or a battery, but individuals wandering collectively towards some wholly indefinite goal'. In fact Army Kraków did recover in time to mount a significant defence line before Kraków and prevent the German attacks from forcing a breach between Army Kraków and Army Karpaty under General Kazimierz Fabrycy to its east. On the central front, Army Poznań, under General Tadeusz Kutrzeba, had still not come into the battle but was forced to retreat towards Kutno because of the retreat of neighbouring Army Łódź and Army Pomorze.[16]

Sunday 3 September is remembered in Britain as the day she declared war on Germany: when at 11 a.m. the ponderous tones of Chamberlain were heard on the radio announcing the start of the hostilities. Later that day in Parliament the deputy leader of the Labour Party, Arthur Greenwood, spoke: 'Poland we greet as a comrade whom we shall not desert. To her we say, "Our hearts are with you, and, with our hearts, all our power, until the angel of peace returns to our midst".'[17] In Paris the Polish ambassador, Juliusz Łukasiewicz, struggled to get the French to honour their alliance obligations. The French Government prevaricated, stating that it needed to recall the Chamber of Deputies before a decision could be taken, and then waiting for Italy either to respond to an appeal for neutrality or to intervene diplomatically to stop the German war against Poland. Łukasiewicz recorded that during those first three days in September: 'Our ally France took a definitely defensive stand and was much more concerned with its relations with Rome than with the needs of our war situation, which already demanded immediate air action in the west.'[18] At last, on the afternoon of 3 September, France declared war on Germany. In Warsaw crowds had been watching the British and French embassies ever since the German attack. Finally the news they had been waiting for came: 'This announcement was followed by the playing of the three national anthems, British, French and Polish. It was received by everybody with enthusiasm. In a few minutes all the streets were decorated by flags of the three nations.' The British ambassador, Sir Howard Kennard, and the military attaché Colonel Edward Sword were greeted by loud cheers when they appeared on the balcony of the British embassy.[19] The *Chicago Tribune* correspondent William Shirer was in Berlin and noted of the crowd: 'They listened attentively to the announcement. When it was finished, there was not a murmur. They just stood there. Stunned.'[20] Ribbentrop had convinced Hitler that Britain would not declare war over Poland. His belief was shared by many Germans who had not expected that a local war against Poland would become a world war.

The Poles urgently needed not just British hearts but British and French power, because by the end of the first week Polish forces were being pushed back on all fronts. Army Modlin was withdrawing to the fortress city of Modlin and Army Pomorze was moving southwards towards Warsaw. The most critical sector was the breach between Army Łódź and Army Kraków near Piotrków. The Polish reserve, Army Prusy, under General Stefan Dąb-Biernacki, was still being mobilised when the high command decided that the situation at Piotrków justified the risk of putting the under-strength reserve into action, and on 5 September, it encountered the German 1st Panzer Division and lost the battle for Piotrków. A notable feature of this battle was that this was the first major encounter between Polish and German armoured units. The Polish 2nd Light Tank Battalion destroyed 17 German tanks, 2 self-propelled guns and 14 armoured cars with the loss of only 2 tanks. Despite this Polish commanders had little idea of how to use armour and any fleeting opportunity to exploit this success was lost. On the evening of 5 September, the commander-in-chief Marshal Rydz-Śmigły ordered Army Kraków, Army Prusy, Army Poznań and Army Łódź to begin withdrawing to defensive positions behind the Vistula and Dunajec rivers, thereby abandoning western Poland. Army Poznań and Army Łódź were then ordered to join with a part of Army Modlin to form a new Army Lublin under General Tadeusz Piskor to defend the northern approaches to Warsaw. Army Kraków and Army Karpaty were ordered to form a new Army Małopolska under General Kazimierz Sosnkowski, which first attempted to defend the Dunajec river but soon began withdrawing further east to the San river.[21] These retreats were in accordance with the Polish defence plan: a withdrawal to the major rivers. But the Polish military planners could not have taken the weather into account, and General Carton de Wiart had noted on the eve of the war: 'The country west of the Vistula was terrain admirably suited to tanks at any time, but now, after a long, long spell of drought, even rivers were no longer obstacles, and I did not see how the Poles could possibly stand up to the Germans in country so favourable to the attacker.'[22] A Polish colonel reflected on how even the rivers of central Poland proved to be no barrier to German armour: 'The rivers were all dried up; the San was a trickling rivulet which artillery and caterpillars could ford where they wished.'[23]

The situation at the end of the first week was critical and action was urgently needed in the west in order to reduce the pressure on Poland. Throughout the September campaign, the Polish Government and high command misled the population into believing that the British and French were engaging the Germans in the west. It was inconceivable to the Poles that their two powerful allies would do nothing active to assist Poland in her hour of need. British and French inactivity equally amazed the Germans, and ample evidence emerged at the 1946 Nuremberg trials of the weakness of the German army in the west in 1939. General Alfred Jodl told the tribunal: 'If we did not collapse already in 1939 that was due only to the fact that during the Polish campaign the approximately 110 French and British divisions in the west were completely inactive against the 23 German divisions.' General Wilhelm Keitel revealed: 'We soldiers had always expected an attack by France during the Polish campaign, and were very surprised that nothing happened . . . A French attack would have encountered only a German military screen, not a real defence.' The Germans believed that by using their 2,300 tanks when all German tanks were in the east, the French could have easily crossed the Rhine and entered the Ruhr, which would have caused the Germans great difficulties.[24] The French did make a brief incursion into Germany, crossing into the Saar at three points on 7 September. Łukasiewicz was, however, alarmed to hear: 'It was clear that the war had not yet started there. In an attempt to avert or postpone it, the German troops had not only not initiated any aggressive action but had not returned the fire of the French artillery; rather they had hung signs over their trenches stating that they did not wish to fight France.'[25] The French were only too keen to take the Germans at their word and withdrew from the Saar. The Nazi propaganda minister, Jozef Goebbels, wrote in his diary: 'The French withdrawal is more than astonishing; it is completely incomprehensible.'[26]

The simple fact was that neither the British nor the French government nor their military chiefs had any will to prosecute a war with Germany at this stage. Indeed, it is possible to sum up allied policy as moving from a reluctance to take any action in support of Poland that might lead to German retaliation against them, to one of deluding themselves that there was nothing they could do in any case because their armed forces were not ready for war, to the final justification that there was no point in taking any action because Poland was being so rapidly overrun. For example, the British blamed the French for not using their powerful army and air force to aid Poland, whereas the French responded by emphasising Britain's general lack of preparedness for war. By 8 September, the argument was being used that the situation in Poland was so desperate that there was no point in bombing Germany or launching a ground offensive. At the first meeting of the Anglo-French Supreme War Council on 13 September, Chamberlain and Édouard Daladier congratulated themselves on not having undertaken operations against Germany. Chamberlain stressed: 'there was no hurry as time was on our side'. Halifax explained to Raczyński that Britain was planning for a three-year war and nothing would be gained by taking premature offensive action. Ironside regretted allied inactivity, recording in his diary on 29 September 1939: 'Militarily we should have gone all out against the Germans the minute he invaded Poland . . . We did not . . . We thought completely defensively and of ourselves. We had to subordinate our strategy to that of the French . . . We missed a great opportunity.'[27]

Neither Britain nor France wanted to be the first country to bomb Germany, fearing immediate German retaliation on their cities and civilians, yet that bombing was what the Poles wanted most of all. On 5 September, Raczyński received an appeal from Warsaw: 'The Polish Air Force appeals to the Command of the Royal Air Force for immediate action by British bombers against German aerodromes and industrial areas within the range of the Royal Air Force, in order to relieve the situation in Poland.'[28] The British response was for the air ministry to write a memorandum for the British ambassador in Poland, Kennard, who was embarrassed by RAF inactivity:

> Since the immutable aim of the Allies is the ultimate defeat of Germany, without which the fate of Poland is permanently sealed, it would obviously be militarily unsound and to the disadvantage of all, including Poland, to undertake at any moment operations unlikely at that time to achieve effective results, merely for the sake of a gesture. When the opportunity offers, we shall strike with all our force, with the object of defeating Germany and thus restoring Polish freedom.[29]

Instead the RAF bombed the German fleet at Wilhemshaven and Brunsbüttel and dropped propaganda leaflets over Germany. The British Government thought that this would demoralise the German population. Arguments were put forward against the bombing of German industry on the grounds that it was in private ownership. General Gamelin explained French inaction on the grounds: 'the French air force could not undertake the bombing of German military objectives without the participation of the British, who had the overwhelming majority of Allied bombing power at their disposal'.[30]

There were other ways in which Britain and France could assist Poland: namely, through the supply of armaments and financial aid. General Mieczysław Norwid-Neugebauer arrived in London on 8 September with a shopping list of armaments urgently needed by the Polish Army. Primarily the list comprised fighters and bombers but also included an assortment of infantry weapons, ammunition and transport. These requests were backed by the support of a member of the British military mission in Poland, Captain Davis, but the British were not prepared to give Poland any of their meagre supplies of war materiel. Norwid-Neugebauer only obtained 15,000 Hotchkiss guns and 15–20,000,000 rounds of ammunition – in any case the supplies would not arrive for six months. Supplies already purchased by Poland from Britain and France before the war now failed to arrive because the

Rumanians would not allow the French ship to unload her cargo in Constanţa. Financial aid was, however, more forthcoming. Loans were made to Poland to purchase armaments from the Soviet Union: the British loan was £5,000,000 and the French 6,000,000 francs. On 6 September the Cabinet learnt of an agreement whereby 'a large deposit of gold at present held by the Bank of England on the Bank of International Settlements' account will in future be held by the Bank of England for the account of a Polish bank in Warsaw'. This was aimed at depriving the Germans of the opportunity to seize Polish gold in the same way that they had seized Czech gold deposits in March. The Polish Government did, in fact, succeed in smuggling 325,000,000 złoty in gold from the Polish bank into Rumania when it crossed into that country. This was then transported to France and, when France was attacked, to French North Africa, where it became trapped and unavailable to the Poles until the Allies seized the region from the Vichy French forces in 1942.[31]

Poland was left to fight alone. By the end of the first week the Poles could only attempt to slow the German advance, but could not stop it. Everywhere the Polish retreat was hampered by the flight of civilians eastwards clogging up the roads. Fela Wiernikówna was in Łódź and watched the refugees from the western border region flee: 'Cars, women with children in pushchairs and in their arms, men with bundles. Among them the peasants drove their cattle. The voices of the cows and goats mingled with the tears of the children.'[32] A hospital administrator Zygmunt Klukowski struggled to move his military hospital nearer to the Rumanian border because of the refugees: 'This whole mass of people, seized with panic, were going ahead, without knowing where or why, and without any knowledge of where the exodus would end.'[33] Others decided to stay at home because: 'There is no front and no rear area, the danger is everywhere, nowhere to go, because what is here is everywhere.'[34]

The German advance was greatly facilitated by the conduct of the ethnic Germans in Poland, the *Volksdeutsche*. As Clare Hollingworth put it, 'Invasion is simplified when one has such good friends in the country invaded.'[35] Many of these ethnic Germans were armed and had secretly received military training in Germany before the war. Polish soldiers and civilians were appalled by the disloyalty demonstrated by their German neighbours. A document recovered from a downed German plane revealed that this disloyalty was deliberately encouraged by the Germans, who hoped that *Volksdeutsche* reservists in the Polish Army would refuse to go to their stations on mobilisation and that those that did would desert at the first opportunity and join the German forces. Ethnic Germans were also encouraged to assist by conducting guerrilla warfare in the Polish rear. They would make themselves known to the German troops 'by means of signs of recognition and passwords'.[36] The German policy was successful: Private Wilhelm Prüller noted in his diary on 17 September: 'two Polish soldiers of German *Volksdeutsche* ancestry are fighting with us; they came to us voluntarily and are the best of *Kameraden*'.[37]

The Polish authorities were aware that the ethnic Germans might prove disloyal in the event of war and had prepared lists of suspect Germans before the war. As soon as the German armies crossed the frontier, 10–15,000 ethnic Germans were arrested and force marched towards Kutno. On the way they were attacked by Poles and it has been estimated that around 2,000 were killed. The invading Germans also knew whom they wanted to arrest: prior to the war the Nazis had drawn up a *Sondersfahndungsbuch*, Wanted Persons' List, of those Poles who had been identified by the *Volksdeutsche* as likely to oppose the imposition of Nazi rule. Heading this were the intelligentsia and government officials, but also included were Polish participants in the interwar uprisings in Silesia. The policy of German terror began on 4 September in Katowice, when the German security police murdered 250 Poles. Jews were also targeted, particularly in Będzin, Katowice and Sosnowiec. Feelings ran especially high in Bydgoszcz (German: Bromberg) where there was a large ethnic German population, who began shooting at Polish soldiers and even attacked a Polish priest. On the afternoon of 3 September, the Polish Army marched out of Bydgoszcz amid cries from the Polish population: 'Don't abandon us, because the Germans will murder us all here!' The local Polish defence unit turned on the Germans and killed between 700 and 1,000 ethnic Germans. When the Wehrmacht entered the city it was quick to take revenge. Between 6 and 13 September, 5,000 Poles were killed in the neighbourhood of Bydgoszcz and 1,200 in the city alone.[38]

On 7 September the great battle on the Westerplatte finally came to an end. The Polish military depot, with fewer than 200 defenders, had been persistently bombarded from the sea and bombed by the Luft-waffe. After two days the commander of the Westerplatte, Major Henryk Sucharski, lost his mind and ordered a surrender. He was strapped to his bunk by his mutinying soldiers and the defence was continued by his deputy, Captain Franciszek Dobrowski.[39] The German bombardment caused enormous damage as 'enemy artillery fire literally ploughed the land'. One defender wrote: 'The barracks are unrecognisable after all the damage. In the cellar, soldiers lie along the walls, overly tired, the wounded on stretchers. The only light comes from a candle. Hygiene is beneath contempt, the air is awful.' Then on 7 September, a German shell hit the ammunition store and the order was issued: 'If anyone is still alive out there, go and surrender.' Bernard Rygielski recalled:

> The German commander asked about the size of the group. He did not want to believe that we were just so few, he had thought that there were 2000 of us. Then he called out: Attention!, saluted, and then spoke to us. After reassuring us that we were safe, he recalled Verdun, and told his soldiers that we should be seen as an example of how a few men could hold off an opponent. He handed back Major Henryk Sucharski his sword.[40]

The German soldiers showed their respect for the defenders, standing to attention and saluting them as they marched into captivity. The Germans lost over 300 men in the fighting for the Westerplatte whereas the Poles lost 15. By 19 September, the situation in Danzig was sufficiently secure for Adolf Hitler to visit the city, now reabsorbed into the Reich. The German population greeted him with jubilation.

Army Łódź fought hard around the city of its name; Army Prusy fought valiantly near Radom, and Army Kraków managed to escape across the Vistula despite the Germans having crossed the river at Szcz-ucin ahead of them. In the north, Special Operational Group Narew under General Czesław Młot-Fijałkowski attempted to resist German attacks across the Narew and at the same time form a new defence line on the river Bug in eastern Poland. Guderian noticed the weakness of Polish forces in north-eastern Poland and obtained permission to switch his advance south-eastwards to conquer eastern Poland instead of join-ing the general movement on Warsaw. The advance of his Panzer units led to the fall of Wizna, opening the road to Brześć and the rest of east-ern Poland, which was still largely undefended.[41]

At this critical juncture the Polish high command failed its army. On 7 September, Rydz-Śmigły moved the high command from Warsaw to Brześć. Communications had not been fully prepared there and effective control over the armies was all but lost just when the new defence lines were under preparation. Sometimes field commanders received one set of orders from Warsaw, where the chief of staff, General Wacław Stachiewicz, had remained, and another from Brześć – neither of which necessarily accurately reflected the situation in the front line. General Stanisław Sosabowski's memoirs ably attest to the chaos caused by conflicting and misleading orders and the eventual breakdown in communications. Rydz-Śmigły's flight had been preceded by the exodus of the government and administration from Warsaw on 4 September, and the departure of the Ministry for Foreign Affairs and the diplomatic corps on 5 September for Nałęczów and Kazimierz, near Lublin. At each stage German radio based in Breslau broadcast the new location of the diplomats. On 7 September, the government began its eastward trek, first to Łuck, then to Krzemieniec, before reaching the Rumanian frontier at the town of Kuty on 14 September.[42]

Just as Rydz-Śmigły was abandoning Warsaw for Brześć, an opportunity arose for a Polish counteroffensive by Army Poznań. Led by the most imaginative of the Polish commanders, General Tadeusz Kutrzeba, this attack aimed to disrupt the left flank of the German advance on Warsaw and retake Łęczyca and Piątek, relieve the pressure on Army Łódź, and allow time for the defences of Warsaw to be strengthened. The Bzura valley north of Łódź was the strongest Polish position remaining – the Poles had a threefold advantage in infantry and a twofold advantage in artillery – and there were no German Panzers in the area. The initial attack on 9 September met with some success and on 10 September, the Germans were in retreat having lost 1,500 men taken prisoner of war by the Poles from the 30th Infantry Division alone. Captain Christian Kinder of the German 26th Infantry Regiment noticed that his troops 'were shaken by the superior power of the enemy, [and] were beginning to be resigned to defeat'. The German response was immediate and the 1st and 4th Panzer Divisions were diverted westwards from the outskirts of Warsaw to assist the German counterattack. Most of the Tenth Army was brought into the battle as well as 800 tanks and 300 bombers.[43]

Kutrzeba had been too optimistic in launching his attack. His Order of the Day for 11 September read: 'The enemy is in retreat. He is withdrawing from the Warsaw area and is encircled by us. In his rear our fellow countrymen form rebellious groups. Revolt throughout the Poznań region. Forward to total victory!' Stirring words indeed: but they did not reflect the truth. While Kutrzeba had 9 infantry divisions and 2 cavalry brigades, totalling 150,000 men, they were not in a condition to fight. Discipline had broken down in many units as a result of the constant retreat, and other units were exhausted. For example, the 26th Infantry Division had just fought hard for four days west of Bydgoszcz. Kutrzeba's plan also depended on Army Łódź being able to tie down the Germans while the Bzura offensive took place, but this army was a broken one and could not contribute to the battle. By the night of 12 September, it was clear that the offensive had failed and that the German lines had been bent in some places but broken nowhere. Kutrzeba admitted defeat: 'We were encircled, and the noose around our necks would tighten day by day, if Warsaw did not come to our aid.' Far from aiding the retreat of Army Pomorze to Warsaw, Kutrzeba now needed its aid to extract his forces from the Bzura front.[44]

The only hope left to the Polish troops was to retreat towards Warsaw through a narrow twelve-mile wide gap between the Vistula and the main road to Warsaw. This area was covered by the forest of Kampinos, dense woods interspersed with bogs, marshes and the tributaries of two rivers. According to Kutrzeba, the forest became the 'grave of the Army of Poznań'. The Germans dropped 328,000 kg of bombs on the Bzura front and Kampinos forest on 17 September alone. These ferocious air attacks broke the Polish armies. A German officer, Captain Johann Graf von Kielmann, noted their effects: 'The captured Poles are driven half-insane by fear and throw themselves on the ground – even in captivity – whenever there's the sound of an aircraft engine from somewhere.' German artillery pounded the forest relentlessly.[45]

Lieutenant-Colonel Klemens Rudnicki, commanding the 9th Lancers, witnessed Polish units wandering the forest desperately seeking an escape. The Poles were short of food, ammunition and arms – and above all lacked maps of the region. Consequently, Captain Z. Szacherski of the 7th Mounted Light Infantry recorded:

There were dead Germans everywhere, on the road and in the ruined buildings. I gave my men orders to go through the Germans' map and trouser pockets in the faint hope of finding the maps which we needed so desperately. At last our search was rewarded: we found a map of the Brochów-Sochaczew area in the pocket of a dead NCO. For us, it was the most valuable booty of the entire war.

He then planned the escape of his troops from the forest. They had to cross a 1¼-mile stretch of open, flat ground to reach the cover of the next village and the Germans had the road covered by artillery:

I drew my sabre and gave the command: 'Squadron follow on at the gallop!' And to the accompaniment of the low thunder of the guns, we raced off like the wind. I glanced to my left. In the distance I could see the steep far bank of the Vistula, dominating the entire region; it was from there that the German artillery was firing. We had put about 200m[etres] behind us when the Germans intercepted the road with their firing, sending up a formidable barrage in front of the village of Czeczotki as we approached.

I looked over my shoulder: the 17th Regiment was spread out as if on a parade ground, keeping its regulation distances in exemplary fashion. Close behind me at the head of the column were the regimental colours; ahead of me, a formidable screen of fire – a booming, moving wall of sand, dust, flames and iron. The regiment was steadily drawing nearer to this thunderous barrier. Though the horses were tired, the pitch of nervous tension induced the weaker beasts to keep up the tempo and the entire cavalcade careered directly at the screen of fire. We were nearly in their range – another 200 metres, another 150, and already scraps of shrapnel were whistling round our heads, with sand spurting into our eyes at every explosion. Then, suddenly, all was quiet. At the very same moment that we stared death right in the face, the Germans had ceased firing. Confused and disconcerted, we disappeared into the village and the cover of the trees.[46]

No reason has been discovered why the German artillery stopped firing at that moment. Szacherski and Rudnicki were among the soldiers who escaped the German noose and reached the temporary sanctuary of Warsaw: on 17 September so did Kutrzeba and his staff. The Germans captured 180,000 Polish troops and a huge amount of Polish materiel. At least 17,000 Poles had died in the battle, and German losses were also heavy with 8,000 dead and 4,000 captured.[47]

The first German Panzers had reached the outskirts of Warsaw on 8 September. The defence of the outskirts was being organised by the Warsaw Defence Command under General Walerian Czuma. The energetic mayor, Stefan Starzyński, roused the population of the city to help, sending all fit men out to dig anti-tank ditches. Over 150,000 people responded, both men and women, of all ages and all religious denominations. Makeshift barricades were constructed from overturned trams, removal vans and furniture, and they stopped the advance of the 35th Panzer Regiment in the suburbs of Ochota and Rakowiec. The next German attack was made by the 4th Panzer Division with assistance from the infantry. A German soldier later wrote: 'Terrible fire descended upon us. They fired from the roofs, threw burning oil lamps, even burning beds down onto the panzers. Within a short time everything was in flames.' Units from the German Third Army attacked through Praga, the eastern suburb of Warsaw, on 15 September but were heavily defeated. The Germans withdrew to try again later with reinforcements.[48]

The Polish defence plan *Zachód* had envisaged an organised Polish retreat to eastern Poland, where the forces would regroup and launch a counteroffensive when the western allies had attacked in the west. The retreat lacked organisation. This was partly due to constant pressure from the German ground and air forces, but partly also due to the collapse of the Polish communications network, which meant that the high command had little idea of what was going on at the front. The new Army Group South, to be made up of Army Kraków and Army Małopolska and commanded by General Kazimierz Sosnkowski, was ordered to go to the defence of Lwów, but the two armies were prevented from joining forces by the German 2nd Panzer and 4th Light Division. On 18 September, Army Kraków launched a counterattack at Tomaszów Lubelski but by 20 September was overwhelmed and forced to surrender. Other forces attempted to reach Lwów, which had been under siege by the German 1st Mountain Division since the 12th. The forest of Janów, twelve miles north of Lwów, became the main battleground. The Polish corps chronicler wrote:

> The forest as a refuge and escape, the forest as a trap and ambush, the forest
> of darkness and thicket, as guardian angel and defender, the upturned tree
> trunks as our enemies, which creep around, move around, leap out, which
> are front and back, in a word the forest is the ally of the defenders.[49]

The *Volksdeutsche* and local Ukrainian-Polish citizens assisted the Germans by revealing some of the Polish positions, thereby ensuring that the German artillery would be accurate. Polish casualties were very high from artillery fire, and when the infantry and Panzers attacked the surrounded Poles, the Polish soldiers were ordered to break out of the forest in small units and to seek refuge in Lwów.

On 17 September 1939, the Soviet Union invaded Poland. This had serious implications for the defence of Lwów from the Germans, which had been entrusted to General Władysław Langner, who had 4 battalions and 12 artillery guns. On 18 September, a German plane dropped a canister into the city which contained a Polish flag and a letter from the German command:

> The Germans expressed their admiration of the valour of the defence, emphasised the fact that further resistance would be impossible, declared that soldierly honour had been satisfied, and proposed that the city should be surrendered, promising to leave the officers their arms.[50]

The Poles declined the offer and the battle continued. On 20 September, the Germans were ordered to cease firing on Lwów because the Red Army was entering the city. Under the erroneous impression that the Soviets were allies, Langner's chief of staff, Colonel Kazimierz Ryziński, met the Soviet commander, Colonel Ivanov, and surrendered Lwów to the Red Army. Similar confusion existed in the fortress of Brześć. Just as the Poles were about to surrender to the Germans, Guderian was informed that the Red Army was about to advance. The German withdrawal was so rapid 'that we could not even move all our wounded or recover our damaged tanks'. On 22 September, Guderian met the Soviet Colonel Semyon Krivoshein to hand over the city. This was an important moment for both Germany and the Soviet Union. The last time representatives of the two countries had met in Brześć was to sign the humiliating Treaty of Brest-Litovsk which took Russia out of the First World War in 1917. Now the meeting was to be the first step in the Fourth Partition of Poland.[51]

Poland's multi-ethnicity provided the Soviet Union with its excuse to invade eastern Poland. In the early hours of the morning of 17 September, Poland's ambassador in Moscow, Wacław Grzybowski, was handed a note by the Soviet foreign minister, Molotov, which he refused to accept. The note, which was then copied to all the ambassadors in Moscow, attempted to justify the actions of the Soviet Union:

> The Polish Government has disintegrated and no longer shows any sign of life. This means that the Polish state and its Government have, in point of fact, ceased to exist . . . Left to her own devices and bereft of leadership Poland has become a suitable field for all manner of hazards and surprises which may constitute a threat to the USSR. For these reasons the Soviet Government, which has hitherto been neutral, cannot any longer preserve a neutral attitude towards these facts.
>
> The Soviet Government also cannot view with indifference the fact that kindred Ukrainian and Belorussian people, who live on Polish territory and who are at the mercy of fate, should be left defenceless.[52]

This was exactly the same argument the Russians had used in 1795 to justify the Third Partition of Poland.[53]

The Soviet invasion delighted the Germans. As early as 3 September, the German foreign minister, von Ribbentrop, had sent a telegram to the German ambassador in Moscow, Count Friedrich Werner von Schulenburg, asking him to warn Molotov that Germany 'would naturally, however, for military reasons, have to continue to take action against such Polish forces as are at that time located in Polish territory belonging to the Russian sphere of influence'. On 10 September, Molotov replied to Schulenburg that the Soviet Union would soon invade eastern Poland on the pretext of offering protection to the Ukrainians and Belorussians living there. The Soviet Union was anxious not to appear as an aggressor.[54] It was not clear about the terms of the British and French alliance with Poland, and did not want to run the risk of becoming embroiled in a war with those two countries. Indeed, the Soviets even attempted to persuade the Polish Government, then sheltering in Kuty on the Polish-Romanian frontier, to invite the Soviets into Poland as a protecting power. The Soviet ambassador to Poland, Nikolai Sharonov, approached the American ambassador, Drexel Biddle, asking him to talk to the Polish foreign minister, Beck, on the subject. Biddle told the Russian ambassador to talk to Beck directly, which he did, and Beck refused even to consider such a request.[55]

Jock Colville, assistant private secretary to Neville Chamberlain, wrote in his diary on 17 September: 'the announcement by which the

Soviet Government attempted to justify their act of unparalleled greed and immorality is without doubt the most revolting document that modern history has produced'.[56] In London Raczyński pressed the British Government to lodge a protest in Moscow at the Soviet action, but it reminded him that a secret protocol to the Anglo-Polish treaty of 25 August 1939 stipulated that it applied only to Germany, and that consequently there was no obligation on Britain to declare war on the Soviet Union. The British ambassador in Moscow, Sir William Seeds, was consulted and replied, 'I do not myself see what advantage war with the Soviet Union would be to us, though it would please me personally to declare it on Mr Molotov.'[57] Instead, Chamberlain made a statement in the House of Commons: 'His Majesty's Government has learned with indignation and horror of the action taken by the Government of the USSR in invading Polish territory', but added that the action was not unexpected.[58] The Soviet occupation of eastern Poland immediately became a politically controversial issue. On 24 September, an article by Lloyd George appeared in the *Sunday Express*, entitled 'What is Stalin up to?', which justified the invasion on the grounds that the Soviet Union was only occupying territory in which the ethnic Poles constituted a minority. Raczyński sent a letter to *The Times* countering Lloyd George's arguments: *The Times* declined to publish it so Raczyński had 300 copies printed privately and distributed to prominent politicians and journalists.[59] On 26 October, Halifax went even further when he informed the House of Lords:

> It is perhaps, as a matter of historical interest, worth recalling that the action of the Soviet Government has been to advance the boundary to what was substantially the boundary recommended at the time of the Versailles Conference by the noble Marquess who used to lead the House, Lord Curzon, who was then Foreign Secretary.[60]

This statement led to a protest from Raczyński. Britain simply had neither the means nor the will to attack the Soviet Union. The British Government, only a few days into the war, already recognised the fact that would prove enormously damaging to the Polish cause: Britain needed the power of the Soviet Union to defeat Germany and was convinced that the German-Soviet alliance was only a temporary measure.

On 17 September, the Polish president, Ignacy Mościcki, and the senior members of his government crossed into Rumania. As soon as they had reached their sanctuary, the commander of the Polish Army, Rydz-Śmigły, and his staff followed. His deputy chief of staff, Colonel Józef Jaklicz, was impressed 'by how calm and composed he was, despite having taken the difficult decision to abandon Poland'.[61] Others were far less favourably impressed. Carton de Wiart noted: 'Śmigły-Rydz will never be forgiven by the vast majority of Poles for his decision to desert his Army, and although I know that he was not the right man to be in command of the Polish forces, it had never occurred to me that he would throw aside his responsibilities in a hysterical rush to save his own skin.'[62] The outrage was caused by the fact that the Poles were still fighting the Germans and Warsaw had not yet fallen. There was also the question of how to react to the Soviet invasion since no orders had been given. On 20 September, Rydz-Śmigły made a final broadcast to the Polish armed forces in which he stressed that the bulk of the Polish Army was engaged in fighting the Germans and that 'in this situation it is my duty to avoid pointless bloodshed by fighting the Bolsheviks'.[63] The Soviets had not been invited into Poland but now it was a case of 'to save what can be saved', and the plan was to withdraw as many troops as possible to Rumania and Hungary from where they should make their way to France and form a new Polish army.[64]

Deprived of guidance from their high command, the Polish troops did not know how to react to the Soviet invasion. It was an invasion in force: two Soviet fronts, the Belorussian Front under the command of General Vasily Kuznetsov and the Ukrainian Front under the command of General Semen Timoshenko, crossed the frontier with 24 infantry divisions, 15 cavalry divisions, 2 tank corps and several tank brigades, and advanced towards the line pre-agreed with the Germans. The appearance of the Red Army cavalry appalled the Poles: 'Instead of saddles they covered horses with blankets. Horses would fall under the riders, exhausted from tiredness. They were so thin that it was fearsome to look at them.'[65] The Soviet soldiers were hungry and approached local villages begging for food. The Poles had no idea whether the Red Army were aggressors or had crossed the frontier as allies against the Germans. Indeed, it appears that many Soviet soldiers were also unclear.[66]

The Polish frontier was lightly held by units of the KOP, whose commander, General Wilhelm Orlik-Rückemann,* received no orders from

---

* Despite his Germanic name, Orlik-Rückemann was a Pole.

the high command or the government, but decided to fight: 'The security guards and the KOP ... at first defended themselves doggedly.
Bolshevik forces advanced incessantly. At the watchtowers of Mołotków
and Brzezina the Bolsheviks used machine guns in a hard fought
battle.'[67] Near Juryszany in the province of Wilno, a KOP cavalry patrol
encountered a large group of Soviet cavalry and made a brief charge
before heading for the cover of the nearby woods. In Grodno (Hrodna)
a makeshift local defence force was hastily put together from the remnants of troops retreating from Wilno and included a number of boy
scouts. It defeated the first Soviet attack on 20 September: the army used
its remaining weapons against the advancing tanks, while the boy scouts
darted between the tanks throwing Molotov cocktails. Ten Soviet tanks
were destroyed that day before the local defence force was overwhelmed
on the 21st.[68] Twelve more Soviet tanks were destroyed by the 101st
Reserve Cavalry at Kodziowce near the Lithuanian border. A two-day
battle was fought in the triangle formed by the villages of Borowicze
(Borovychi), Hruziatyń (Gruziatyn) and Nawów, and the Soviets lost
over 200 men before forcing the Poles to surrender. In all, Molotov
reported to the Supreme Soviet on 31 October that the Red Army had
lost 737 men killed and 1,862 wounded. Polish losses are unknown.[69]

Most Polish troops heeded the orders of Rydz-Śmigły and fled for the
relative safety of Rumania, Hungary and Lithuania. Others, however,
had no choice but to surrender to the Soviets. In Lwów some junior officers gathered under the windows of the room where the staff were
awaiting the Soviet representatives and shouted: 'Shame on those who
sold Poland to the Bolsheviks! Treason!' Some soldiers took the opportunity of the wait before the formal surrender to render their weapons
useless and dispose of emblems of rank. This last action proved important because the first question the Soviet soldiers asked was, 'Who are
the officers?' The Poles did not betray them and, unknown to all the
soldiers then, this instinct to conceal rank would save many lives. When
the Pińsk river flotilla surrendered to the Soviets, the officers were
marched away from their men. Shots were heard and the men learnt
that their officers had been killed by the Soviets despite having surrendered in good faith.[70]

Molotov's note of 17 September had also contained the statement
that 'Warsaw as the capital of Poland no longer exists', but this was

premature. After the rebuff in the suburbs of Warsaw on 8 September, German plans for the defeat of Warsaw changed. Surrounded by Panzers and infantry divisions, the city was now to be bombarded and bombed into submission before the ground troops would advance. The Germans amassed over 1,000 artillery pieces and 13 infantry divisions for the battle. Rydz-Śmigły had entrusted the overall defence to General Rómmel, ordering him to hold Warsaw 'as long as there is sufficient ammunition and food'. The aim was to buy time for Poland until her allies launched an offensive in the west. Rómmel called upon the population to be steadfast by deliberately lying to them when he stated that the Germans were already withdrawing from Poland to fight in the west. He refused to meet the German delegate who wanted to discuss the unconditional surrender of Warsaw. The Germans made their position clear: 'Refusing the German offer of surrender merely means unnecessary bloodshed from which the population cannot be spared as Warsaw will be treated as a fortress.' On Hitler's direct orders Warsaw was to be starved into submission. Polish requests to evacuate the civilian population were refused but on 22 September there was an hour-long ceasefire to allow around 1,000 foreign nationals time to escape.[71]

From 22 September, Warsaw was subjected to an endless artillery bombardment and run of bombing attacks. The pianist Władysław Szpilman recalled:

> The corpses of people and horses killed by shrapnel lay about the streets, whole areas of the city were in flames, and now that the municipal waterworks had been damaged by artillery and bombs no attempts could be made to extinguish the fires. Playing in the studio was dangerous too. The German artillery was shelling all the most important places in the city, and as soon as a broadcaster began announcing a programme German batteries opened fire on the broadcasting centre.[72]

The mayor, Stefan Starzyński, made a final broadcast just before the power station was put out of action, in which he praised the resoluteness of the population of Warsaw: 'And as I speak to you now, through the window I see, enveloped by clouds of smoke, reddened by flames, a wonderful, indestructible, great, fighting Warsaw in all its glory.' He finished by calling for revenge on Berlin. Many civilians did not hear his broadcast, as they were sheltering in basements: 'We do not know what is happening outside, we do not even know what is happening across the street.' On 25 September, the Germans escalated the number of bombing raids on the city centre, bombing until thick clouds of smoke concealed the targets, and at the peak 200 fires raged unchecked. A doctor, Ludwik Hirszfeld, thought that the scene must look like the end of the world. About 40,000 civilians were killed during the German artillery and air bombardment of the city.[73]

Not only was Warsaw being flattened by artillery and bombs and on fire but the population was now beginning to starve. At the beginning of the war the mayor had urged citizens not to hoard food and they had obeyed him. Now, at the end of September, there was little food left and the number of people to be fed had increased dramatically with the reinforcement of the Warsaw garrison. Troops rushing to the aid of Warsaw were appalled by the sight of the city. General Sosabowski described the state of the capital:

> I had seen death and destruction in many forms, but never had I seen such mass destruction, which had hit everyone, regardless of innocence or guilt. Gone were the proud buildings of churches, museums and art galleries; statues of famous men who had fought for our freedom lay smashed to pieces at the bases of their plinths, or stood decapitated and shell-scarred. The parks, created for their natural beauty and for the happy sounds of laughing, playing children, were empty and torn, the lawns dotted with the bare mounds of hurried graves. Trees, tossed into the air with the violence of explosion, lay with exposed roots, as if they had been plucked by a giant hand and negligently thrown aside.
>
> Almost the only noise on this morning was the rumble of bricks as walls, weakened by bombs, finally subsided. The smoke of burning houses pillared into a windless sky and the smell of putrefaction lingered in the nostrils.[74]

On the morning of 27 September, acting on Rómmel's orders, General Kutrzeba surrendered Warsaw and the Germans entered the following day. The shock to the soldiers who had wanted to continue fighting was tremendous:

> We listened silently to these grim words; there were no questions or comments. Our minds recognised the inevitability of capitulation, but our feelings could not be reconciled to it. Was this to be the end? It was as though one had had a heavy blow on the head and was overcome by some mental paralysis.[75]

On 30 September, 140,000 Polish troops marched out of Warsaw into captivity: 'The few civilians we passed gazed woodenly at us, without praise or condemnation.' The Polish defenders were treated with respect by the Wehrmacht. General Kutrzeba and his chief of staff, Colonel Aleksander Pragłowski, were besieged by a pack of photographers wanting to record the fall of Warsaw for German propaganda. They were then sent to POW camps for the rest of the war. Starzyński had a less happy fate: he was arrested by the Gestapo and imprisoned in several different locations. His ultimate fate is unclear but it is generally accepted that he was shot at Dachau concentration camp.[76]

Eighteen miles north-west of Warsaw the fortress of Modlin was still holding out. It had been a fortress since Napoleonic times, comprised of a citadel surrounded by ten forts, and had been improved by the subsequent Russian occupiers and again by the Poles, who had added strong anti-aircraft defences. The Germans recognised the seriousness of the task ahead of them and by late September had gathered 4 infantry divisions and a Panzer division to attack the city. On the night of 27–28 September, the Germans sent a Polish major through their lines to inform the defenders, under the command of Brigadier Wiktor Thommée, that Warsaw had surrendered. On the following day, a white flag was seen flying above the citadel but the forts continued to resist German attacks. Two forts had fallen by the time Thommée surrendered on 29 September. The Germans captured nearly 24,000 Poles.[77]

The German campaign in Poland was not yet over and there was still fighting on the Baltic coast. Danzig had been captured and the port of Gdynia fell on 14 September. Polish defences were now concentrated on the Hela peninsula, a narrow spit of land, 20 miles long and a few hundred yards wide, stretching into the bay of Danzig. It was defended by about 2,000 men under the command of the head of the Polish admiralty, Vice-Admiral Józef Unrug. The Hela peninsula was remorselessly bombarded from the sea by the *Schleswig-Holstein* and *Schlesein* and bombed by the Luftwaffe, but German infantry had to attack to force its surrender on 1 October.[78]

General Franciszek Kleeberg provided the final act. He commanded Special Operational Group Polesie, and by incorporating into it the remnants of Special Operational Group Narew and various other units, he had at least 17,000 men under his command. They fought a series of actions against the Red Army near Milanów, inflicting over 100 casualties on the Red Army. Kleeberg then turned his attention towards the Germans. Realising that his ad-hoc force had little chance of reaching the capital, he planned to raid the main Polish Army arsenal near Dęblin and seize enough weapons and ammunition to wage guerrilla warfare. At Kock, however, his force ran into the German 14th Corps, and after fierce fighting and high casualties, Kleeberg and around 16,000 soldiers surrendered on 6 October.[79] The Polish campaign was now over.

Poland's losses in the September campaign were high: 66,300 soldiers and airmen were killed and 133,700 were wounded; 694,000 soldiers were captured by the Germans and 240,000 by the Soviets. Unlike the Soviet Union, Germany was a signatory to the Geneva Convention governing the treatment of prisoners of war, but there were numerous instances of Polish POWs being shot by the Wehrmacht during the campaign, the worst atrocity being the execution of 300 men near Radom. Two main temporary camps were established at Rawa Mazowiecka and Sojki, where the Poles were forced to sleep in the open air and received no medical attention. The Wehrmacht attempted to shift blame for the atrocities on to the SS and Gestapo. For example, the surrendering Polish officers at Modlin had been promised parole after their surrender but found themselves in captivity. When General Thommée protested to a German general he received a disingenuous reply: 'Herr General is wrong: the German Generals gave you their word as soldiers and have kept it; you and the entire gallant garrison of Modlin were released, and if you were then arrested by the police and detained by the police as prisoners, you must understand that the police and politics are above the army.'[80] This conversation took place in Colditz, a camp run by the Wehrmacht. Only around 85,000 Polish soldiers and airmen managed to escape to neighbouring countries. Equipment losses were almost total. The notable exception was the 10th Cavalry Armoured Brigade, mobilised too late to take much part in the campaign, which crossed into Hungary with its tanks. One hundred aircraft were flown to Rumania, where the pilots were interned. The German losses were far lower: 10,572 men killed, 30,322 wounded and 3,409 missing.[81]

The Polish Air Force was too small and too outdated to prevent German air superiority. Contrary to German reports it was not wiped out on the ground on the first day of the war, for it had already been dispersed to its secondary airfields scattered throughout Poland, and all that the Germans hit were training and sporting aircraft. Indeed the only Polish military aircraft destroyed by the Luftwaffe on the ground were 17 Karaś bombers on 14–15 September at the Hutniki airfield. Given the obsolescence of the Polish fighters, they did surprisingly well against the Luftwaffe. At 7 a.m. on 1 September, Lieutenant Władysław Gnyś shot down 2 Dornier 17 Bombers, the first Polish Air Force kills of the war. During the first week, Polish fighters accounted for 105 German planes, the majority having been shot down by the units defending Warsaw.[82] One Polish pilot later described the air war in Poland:

> The superior manoeuvrability of our machines was obvious. We beat them hollow whenever they appeared even in overwhelming numbers to accept a combat. But in pursuit – we had to bite our fingers. They were miles ahead in speed and firepower. Their bursts of two cannon and four machine guns sounded like thunder in June. Our machines could only bark pitifully with their two machine guns.[83]

The ability was there, the will was there, but the technology was lacking. Polish losses were exceptionally high and by 6 September the air force had lost 50 per cent of their planes. The high command then ordered the survivors to fly east beyond the Vistula. This was a disastrous decision because preparations had not been made to receive them and there were no spare parts and little fuel. German air attacks on the roads meant that the ground crews struggled to make their way eastwards. On 17 September, the Polish Air Force shot down a Dornier bomber and a Soviet fighter and then obeyed orders to fly to Rumania. There they hoped to find the French and British planes promised to them. The Rumanians, however, had forbidden the French ship to unload the Morane fighters at Constanța, and a British ship carrying Fairey Battle bombers turned for home at Gibraltar.[84]

Both types of Polish bombers, Karaś and Łoś, were too poorly armoured to be able to fly safely at low levels to bomb German formations accurately. They did, however, do their best and met with some success. During the critical battle in the Piotrków sector in the first week, they repeatedly bombed the German forces, and on 4 September, the Germans reported that Polish bombs had destroyed or badly damaged 28 per cent of the 4th Armoured Division. Out of a total bomber force of 154 the Poles lost 38 planes.[85]

The Polish Navy had little impact on the September campaign. The destroyers *Wicher* and *Gryf* laid mines off the Hela peninsula and on 3 September exchanged fire with the German destroyers *Lebrecht Maas* and *Wolfgang Zenker*, damaging the latter and forcing both to be withdrawn. The Luftwaffe then sank both Polish destroyers and 3 minesweepers. The submarines had no impact because the Germans sent few merchant ships into Polish waters. The lack of fuel and supplies forced the submarines to leave Poland. The *Ryś*, *Żbik* and *Sęp* reached Sweden, where they were interned; the *Wilk* sailed directly to Britain. The *Orzeł* had been interned in Estonia, disarmed and put under guard, but the crew managed to overcome the guard and sail for Britain without any charts or navigation equipment; it was hunted by both the German and Soviet navies but managed to escape the Baltic. The submarines then joined the Royal Navy and were stationed at Dundee. Arrangements had been made for 3 Polish destroyers, *Grom*, *Błyskawica* and *Burza*, to sail to Britain on the outbreak of war; they left Poland on 31 August and joined the Royal Navy at Rosyth.[86]

A commission was established by the Polish Government-in-Exile in France to investigate the reasons behind Poland's defeat. Prominent members of the opposition were quick to blame the *Sanacja* Government. General Władysław Sikorski had fallen out with the ruling military clique and at the outbreak of war had been living on his estate in semi-retirement. He had offered his services, which were declined. In France he orchestrated a witch-hunt against those who had overlooked him. The first stage of this assessment was drawn to a close by the German attack on France in May 1940. In June 1940, after fighting for little longer than the Poles, the French Army surrendered and 1,900,000 soldiers were made prisoners of war. This total was nearly twice the size of the Polish Army in the September campaign.[87] The French and British air forces were vastly more modern than the Polish, yet one analysis of the French campaign has argued that an approximate calculation of enemy losses per day of campaigning per allied plane demonstrates that the Poles had fought considerably more effectively in September 1939 than the Allies did in May–June 1940.[88] Equally, during the first month of the Barbarossa campaign in June 1941, the German Army conquered Soviet territory far exceeding the size of Poland. It was clear that the lessons of the Polish campaign had not been learned by those countries liable to be attacked by Germany. Yet two extremely detailed and able reports by western observers had been produced, by the American ambassador, Drexel Biddle, and by the head of the British military mission, Carton de Wiart, but both were ignored.[89] Indeed, Peter Wilkinson, a member of the British mission, later said: 'Really the terrifying thing was that the very able despatch of De Wiart . . . describing the lessons from the Polish campaign was pigeon-holed entirely by the War Office.'[90] In February 1940, Sikorski had given a lecture to the French leaders on 'The Most Important Experiences and Conclusions of the 1939 Campaign'. He also met Gamelin and Weygand on several occasions and urged the French Army to form strong armoured formations. His advice was ignored.[91]

The first lesson was that valour was not enough against a well-armed enemy. There was no doubt about the bravery of the Polish soldiers. Germans recalled seeing how the Poles would man an anti-tank gun firing at the Panzers and as each man was killed, another would take his place until all were dead. One German soldier wrote:

> Before any attack the Poles give three cheers – each one a long drawn out cry that sounds like animals baying for blood. Although they are absolutely suicidal in the face of our fast-firing machine guns I must admit that to stand and watch as those long lines of infantry come storming forward is quite unnerving.[92]

General Albert Kesselring, commanding Luftwaffe operations in Poland, wrote later: 'It is a tribute both to the Polish High Command and to our own achievement that the Polish forces had enormous fighting spirit and in spite of the disorganisation of control and communications were able to strike effectively at our points of main effort.'[93] General Ernst von Kab stated:

> The Polish soldier was tough and fought fiercely, yet at the same time had modest needs and demanded little in the way of supplies. These virtues were typical of Polish soldiers wherever we encountered them . . . whether they were a group of survivors holding out for days on end without food and ammunition in great forests or swamps . . . or surrounded Polish cavalry detachments often breaking through with reckless courage, or even simple infantrymen who dug themselves in before some village, defended their position until each of them in turn was killed in his rifleman's pit, and stopped fighting only when life ended.[94]

When the Polish infantry had parity with or superiority over the German infantry, they did inflict high casualties on the Wehrmacht. Carton de Wiart reported to London: 'the German of 1939 is not the German of 1914'. The Germans themselves concluded that their infantry had not performed as well as expected and needed further training.[95]

The Polish campaign also highlighted major weaknesses in the structure of command which the Poles had copied from the French Army. There was a unanimous belief that the Polish high command, particularly Rydz-Śmigły and his chief of staff, General Stachiewicz, had failed the country. The system of command was over-centralised and Rydz-Śmigły was in direct command of 7 armies and 1 independent operational group, and at the same time he was expected to formulate new defence plans. This burden was obviously too much for one man. Rydz-Śmigły's departure from Warsaw hit morale badly, and it was also a disastrous decision, for at Brześć he lacked the communication structure essential to maintain control over the Polish war effort, and increasingly the orders he issued bore little resemblance to the situation on the ground. Other Polish commanders were also criticised. Stachiewicz managed to escape from internment in Rumania and finally reached London in 1943, but he was not made welcome there by the Polish armed forces and was given no further employment. Fabrycy reached the Middle East but was only given a minor role in the Polish division formed there. Dąb-Biernacki was condemned for having abandoned his army to surrender without him and was not employed again. Commanders of smaller Polish units or those commanding armies towards the end of the campaign, such as Sosnkowski and General Wincenty Kowalski, fared better and were employed in the newly formed Polish Army in France. The majority of Polish generals spent the remainder of the war as POWs in Germany, and 10 became POWs of the Soviets.

Foreign commentators focused on the Germans' use of their Panzers. Ironside wrote in his diary: 'Gamelin said that the chief lesson to be learnt from the Polish campaign was the penetrative power of the speedy, and hard-hitting German armoured formations and the close co-operation of their Air Force.'[96] Gamelin failed to notice an important aspect to the German use of armour: the Panzers could advance through thick forests, so their progress on 1 September through the Tuchola forest in Pomerania foreshadowed their advance through the Ardennes. The Germans learnt their own lessons from the campaign. For all of the impact that the Panzers had made on the Polish forces, they too showed alarming weaknesses. Twenty-five per cent of the Mark I and Mark II tanks were destroyed in Poland along with 40 per cent of the Mark IIIs and 30 per cent of the much vaunted Mark IVs.[97] Breakdowns were the most common cause of loss but the Polish anti-tank guns, the best weapon in the Polish armoury, had also played an important role. It was clear to the German high command that improvements in equipment and training were essential before mounting an offensive against the better-armed western allies.

It was widely recognised that the September campaign proved that cavalry had no place in modern warfare. Rudnicki has analysed the performance of the Polish cavalry and concluded that the main problems were that horses could not travel as fast as armoured columns, and were particularly vulnerable to bombing and shellfire. When in combat, the fighting strength of the troop was reduced by the number of men needed to hold the horses.[98] Polish cavalry charges against tanks are the most enduring myth of the Polish campaign, and as has been shown above the German propaganda campaign against the Poles exploited one incident when Polish cavalry, having scattered the German infantry, accidentally encountered German tanks. Occasionally, out of the desperate need to break out of an encirclement such as in the Kampinos forest, individual cavalrymen did charge individual tanks: 'The idea was to ride to the tank, hop on it, lift the flap and throw a hand grenade in. This was sometimes successful, but inevitably suicidal.'[99]

What is less well known is that the German Army also used cavalry in the September campaign. The German First Cavalry Brigade, with a strength of 6,200 men and 4,200 horses, operated on the eastern flank of the Third Army advancing into Poland from East Prussia. Towards the end of the campaign the Nowogródzka Cavalry Brigade was attacking the German 8th Infantry Division when it was in turn attacked by German cavalrymen:

> Drawn sabres flashed over the heads of the German cavalrymen as the bulk of their force veered ponderously down from the high ground with growing momentum. Clearly the Germans, with their heavy warhorses, were simply aiming to run down their enemies in a headlong downhill gallop. But the Poles saw a chance in the manoeuvrability of their lighter mounts.[100]

The battle was fought mostly with sabres. The German cavalry then retreated uphill and were pursued by the Poles into the forest, where the German infantry opened fire on them with machine guns.

Arguably the most significant contribution to the swift German victory was the ruthless application of German air power, which drew no distinction between military and civilian targets. There was, however, a noticeable reluctance in Britain and France to believe the reports from Poland about the deliberate targeting of civilians by the Luftwaffe. On the first day of the war Kraków, Łódź, Gdynia, Brześć and Grodno were among the first cities in Poland to be bombed. The British and French governments urged the Polish Government not to retaliate against targets in Germany so as not to 'provoke' Hitler. Even after the German high command openly announced on 13 September its intention 'to bomb and shell open towns, villages and hamlets in Poland, in order to crush resistance by the civilian population', the British Government was not prepared to believe this. The *Daily Telegraph* correspondent Clare Hollingworth was bombed and machine-gunned as she fled eastwards and was horrified to discover on her return to Britain that the BBC had not broadcast her reports of the deliberate targeting of civilians. It was only when Kennard and Biddle, having reached Rumania, reported 'the bombardment of the entirely undefended village [Krzemieniec] in which the foreign missions accredited to Poland were at the time accommodated' that Polish accounts were believed.[101] The bombing of Warsaw foreshadowed the Blitz. First the waterworks were deliberately targeted, putting the pumps out of action, before incendiary bombs were dropped on the city.

When the Polish president, Ignacy Mościcki, and the government officials crossed the frontier into Rumania on 17 September, they had done so with the verbal assurances of the Rumanian Government that they would be given assistance to reach the Rumanian port of Constanţa. The French ambassador to Poland, Leon Noël, had informed the Poles that France would grant them hospitality. The Rumanian Government, however, was under intense pressure from Hitler to renege on the deal. One government official, Eugeniuz Kwiatkowski, noted the result: 'They divide us. The President is to be placed near Bacau, government ministers and the Marshal [Rydz-Śmigły] will be sent to Craiova, near the Bulgarian border. Officials will be scattered all over the place, the army interned, equipment taken. It would have been better to have evacuated to Hungary.'[102] Indeed, Biddle sent a despatch to the secretary of state stating:

> While Marshal's internment is covered by Hague Convention of 1907, I am aware of no precedent for the internment of the Government of a belligerent country if that Government seeks transit through a neutral country. If therefore my assumption is correct in this regard Rumania's internment of Polish Government officials would represent a violation of international law.[103]

Neither the British nor the French government made any great efforts to persuade the Rumanian Government to release the interned Polish ministers. The president felt that he had no alternative but to resign so that a Polish government-in-exile could be established in France.* His efforts to do so were hampered by the Rumanians banning direct communications between the ministers, which was circumvented by Colonel Beck's wife acting as liaison and conducting the necessary negotiations.[104]

The establishment of a Polish government-in-exile was possible because the 'constitution took into account the needs and possibilities of wartime, and contained no prescription which would render impossible the existence and functioning of state authority outside the frontiers of the country'.[105] Mościcki nominated the Polish ambassador in Italy, General Bolesław Wieniawa-Długoszowski, as his successor, but on 26 September, in an act that came as 'a complete bombshell' to the British Government, the French Government refused to recognise him.[106] The Polish ambassador in Paris, Juliusz Łukasiewicz, met the Polish ambassador in London, Raczyński, to discuss alternatives. It was felt that Ignacy Paderewski was too ill to take office, and the whereabouts of the preferred candidate, General Sosnkowski, were unknown; therefore, they settled on Władysław Raczkiewicz as the most suitable. Having been a former president of the Senate and currently chairman of the Organisation for Poles Abroad, he was seen as politically neutral and

---

* In December 1939, Mościcki was released and allowed to move to Switzerland where he remained for the rest of the war. Beck died in internment in Rumania in June 1944. Rydz-Śmigły escaped from Rumania in December 1940 and returned to Poland via Hungary and Slovakia to serve in the AK. He died in Warsaw in 1941 and was buried under his alias 'Adam Zawisza'; a new tombstone with his correct name was erected in 1994.

unlikely to offend either the members of the *Sanacja* regime or the representatives of the opposition. He was also accepted by the allied governments and was duly sworn into office. General Sikorski had accompanied Noël on his return to Paris on 24 September. Łukasiewicz, in charge in Paris until a new president was appointed, did not know what to do with Sikorski but soon gave him command of the Polish Army re-forming in France. After becoming president, Raczkiewicz appointed Sikorski as prime minister and then, on 7 November, as commander-in-chief. On 9 December, a National Council of twenty-two representatives of Polish political parties was established. The new government was based in Angers, on the Loire, 190 miles from Paris.[107]

Sikorski's government was weak from the start. The pre-war opposition members, including Sikorski, clashed with those members of the *Sanacja* regime who had escaped from Rumania. The result disgusted Polish soldiers who wanted a united and strong government to lead them:

> Taking into account that the war was still in progress and that our main goal was to fight for Poland's freedom, it was necessary to end the disputes, halt the internal bickering, and unite in a common effort. Unfortunately, none of the parties was willing to do so. The followers of Józef Piłsudski refused to cease their political intrigues and even formed a few clandestine groups.[108]

One of the leading intriguers was Łukasiewicz, whose supporters alleged he was being treated as a leper by Sikorski despite having worked so hard to get French support for Poland during the September campaign and despite his responsibility for the establishment of the Polish Government-in-Exile in France. The result was that Łukasiewicz left the foreign service in November 1939, and after the Polish Government moved to London, became a founder of the League for Poland's Independence, which was highly critical of Sikorski, especially with regard to his policy towards the Soviet Union. Foreign observers also noted the weaknesses of the new Polish Government.[109] For example, Lewis Namier wrote a lengthy memorandum in November 1939 on the Polish Government for R. A. Butler, the parliamentary under secretary for foreign affairs, claiming that Sikorski had made his government larger than necessary because he felt the need to represent every shade of political opinion. Worse still: 'The first selection was in some cases rather haphazard – a man of the second rank was included in the government because he was available, and because no one could say whether a more representative member of that party had been, or could be, able to escape from Poland.'[110]

In November the Polish cabinet produced a memorandum on the aims of the new Polish Government. It was to lead the fight for the restoration of Poland's independence through its command of the new Polish Army, through coordinated action with Poland's allies, Britain and France, and through the establishment of a resistance in Poland. The government would also care for the Polish refugees, and would make plans for the future political, social and economic systems of a new Poland.[111] In late November Sikorski and the foreign minister, August Zaleski, travelled to Britain for what was supposed to be a two-day visit but which was extended at the request of the British to a week. There they met Chamberlain, Halifax, General Ironside and King George VI and returned to France full of optimism regarding future diplomatic and military cooperation with Britain. General Sosnkowski had reached France in October, having first escaped to Hungary from Soviet-occupied Poland. In November Sikorski appointed him the minister responsible for the Polish resistance, and soon afterwards Sosnkowski issued his first set of guidelines on its structure and aims. These guidelines were entrusted to the courier Jan Karski to take back to Poland.[112] The Polish Government was securely established in France, a new Polish army was being built, but in Poland the population was being subjected to catastrophic twin occupations by Germany and by the Soviet Union, and urgently needed guidance on how to cope with Rydz-Śmigły's prediction: 'Germany will destroy our body, Russia will destroy our soul.'[113]

# 4

## The German and Soviet Occupation of Poland to June 1941

At the beginning of October 1939, Poland was a totally shattered country: after a month of fighting, a modern European state with 32,000,000 citizens, occupying an area of nearly 150,000 square miles, had quite simply ceased to exist. Now both occupiers sought to impose two alien systems – Nazism and Communism – on the entire Polish population. The people were scattered: the POWs were being marched into either Germany or the Soviet Union; soldiers and airmen were making their way into Rumania and Hungary; and the bombing had created a vast mass of refugees who had abandoned their homes in the face of the German advance and now had to find their way back if they could – or if they had ended up in the Soviet zone, then they had to create a new life there.

Everywhere people could see the consequences of the war: 'Every city, town and railway station showed the effects of bombing and shelling. The skeletons of buildings and depots projected stiffly from piles of debris. Whole blocks were cluttered with tangled and inextricable ruins.' There were mass graves of soldiers who had died in the fighting and of civilians who had been deliberately targeted by the bombing. In Warsaw one-fifth of housing had been badly damaged or destroyed:

> Warsaw was a shocking ruin of its former self; the disaster that had befallen
> it exceeded in magnitude my direct anticipation. The gay metropolis had
> disappeared. The handsome buildings, the theatres, the cafés, the flowers,
> the cheerful, noisy, familiar Warsaw had vanished as utterly as if it had
> never existed . . . The inhabitants were worn, tired, and disconsolate.[1]

The future leader of the Underground Government, Stefan Korboński, noted that 'what gave Warsaw its new look was the noisy shapes in grey-green uniforms, barking their every word and roaming the streets

N

DANZIG
(annexed by
Germany,
September
1939)

LITHUANIA

R. Neman

•Wilno

EAST
PRUSSIA

DANZIG-
WEST
PRUSSIA

•Stettin

POMERANIA

Białystok •

WESTERN
BELORUSSIA

U.S.S.R.

Poznań•

R. Vistula

WARTHEGAU

R. Warta

•Warsaw

Łódź•

P O L A N D

G E R M A N Y

LOWER SILESIA

•Lublin

R. Bug

SUDETENLAND

UPPER SILESIA

Kraków•

Oświęcim (Auschwitz)•

WESTERN
UKRAINE

•Lwów

R. Dniester

SLOVAKIA

Stanisławów•

HUNGARY

Frontier of Poland, August 1939

Division of German and Soviet spheres of interest by
the Molotov-Ribbentrop Pact, 23 August 1939

Annexed by Germany, October 1939

General Government, established October 1939

Frontier of Reichgauen (with names)

Annexed to the USSR, November 1939

Transferred by the USSR to Lithuania, October 1939

Transferred by Germany to Slovakia, November 1939

0          100 miles

0          150 km

4. The Division of Poland Between Germany and the Soviet Union

and open spaces of the City'.[2] Swastikas appeared on all the main buildings. People were stopped randomly on the street, their papers scrutinised and parcels examined. Former soldiers concealed their appearance by dressing like office workers, while the office workers themselves, with legitimate documentation, could walk freely. Jewish shops had the Star of David painted on them to identify them as Jewish enterprises and to discourage the Poles from entering. The best restaurants and cafes in every city were taken over by the Germans for their exclusive use.

The Fourth Partition of Poland had been agreed between Von Ribbentrop and Molotov in a secret protocol to the Soviet-German treaty of friendship on 23 August 1939. The demarcation line ran along the Pisa, Narew, Vistula and San rivers. Hitler had not drawn up firm plans for the governance of Poland prior to the German invasion and had toyed with the idea of retaining a small rump Polish state. The Soviets, however, were strongly opposed to such a concept and urged Hitler to join with them in totally extinguishing the 'bastard of Versailles'. Through the new Soviet-German treaty of friendship signed on 28 September 1939, the Soviets withdrew from central Poland to behind the Bug in exchange for a recognition of Soviet interests in Lithuania. The new demarcation line followed the Curzon Line in most aspects. The German zone comprised 72,800 square miles of Polish territory, inhabited by 20,000,000 Poles. The Soviet zone comprised 77,720 square miles, inhabited by 12,000,000 Polish citizens, and this region contained prime agricultural land and much of Poland's natural resources, such as oil. Hitler then annexed Danzig and the Polish provinces of Poznań, Pomorze and Łódź, which were now divided between two *Reichgauen*, Danzig-West Prussia and Warthegau, and then incorporated into the Reich. Polish Upper Silesia was also annexed. All these regions were particularly rich in industry, agriculture and coal. The annexed areas did not correspond with the old German partition; indeed, the frontier of the Reich now extended between 95 and 125 miles to the east of the 1914 frontier. The newly created *Reichsgau* of Danzig-West Prussia was to be governed by Albert Forster, the former Nazi Gauleiter in Danzig, and the Warthegau by Arthur Greiser, the former president of the Senate in Danzig. Both men were ardent Nazis. The remaining portion of the German-occupied zone was renamed the General Government (*Generalgouvernement*), and Hitler appointed as its governor the Nazi lawyer Hans Frank, who established his government in Wawel Castle in Kraków.[3] On 25 October 1939, the German Army handed over authority over Poland to the civilian administrators.

The Germans had already established precedents for the government of occupied territories. The protectorate of Bohemia-Moravia retained a president, a government, an administration and a small militia, but its freedom was restricted by the overlordship exercised by the Reich protector, Konstantin von Neurath. Slovakia also had its own government, led by the Catholic priest Father Jozef Tiso, which was internationally recognised as independent but in practice was subject to a strong German advisory presence. The previous German military occupation of Poland, between 1915 and 1918, had been relatively benign. General-Governor Hans von Beseler had governed through a council of Polish notables. In 1939, therefore, the Polish elite expected to 'follow a set of harsh but civilised rules and bend them to their own advantage' as they had done before.[4]

At the start the Germans did indeed search for collaborators. Wincenty Witos, leader of the Peasant Party and a former prime minister, was offered, but declined, his release from Gestapo imprisonment in exchange for becoming prime minister in a collaborationist government. The Germans obtained the release of Prince Janusz Radziwiłł from the Soviet-occupied zone and suggested that he form a Polish government subservient to the Reich, but he declined. In October 1939, an activist in the pre-war Polish fascist party, *Obóz Narodowo-Radykalny* (National Radical Camp), Andrzej Świetlicki approached the Germans with some fellow-travellers offering collaboration. Professor Władysław Studnicki was another potential collaborator: intensely anti-Soviet, he was in favour of German-Polish collaboration against the Soviet Union. In December 1939, he wrote a memorandum to the German Government criticising the brutal German conduct in Poland on the grounds that it undermined hopes for united action against the Soviet Union. He presented this memorandum to Josef Goebbels when he visited Berlin in January 1940 and was promptly interned in Babelsberg. After his return to Poland in summer 1940, he continued to press for German-Polish collaboration for the rest of the war. By April 1940, Hitler had forbidden the German military commanders to hold further talks with Poles about any degree of independence. During the war Poland was very proud of its record in never having had a 'Quisling', but the reason was 'not because a sufficiently prominent person could not be persuaded to cooperate, but because the Germans had no interest in granting the Poles authority'.[5]

Nazi ideology demanded the total subjugation of Poland and erasure of all evidence of her statehood. Heinrich Himmler advocated that 'all Poles will disappear from the world . . . It is essential that the great German people should consider it as its major task to destroy all Poles.' Frank spoke of the new role of the Poles as 'the slaves of the Greater German Reich'.[6] Poland was to be plundered and then economically exploited in the service of the Reich. Polish culture was to be erased and Poland turned into an 'intellectual desert', with access to education severely restricted. Frank demanded:

> The whole Polish system of information must be dismantled. The Poles are not to be allowed wireless sets; they are to be left nothing else – there is to be no press which might express any opinions. In principle, they are to have no theatres, cinemas or cabarets, so as not to dangle before their eyes what they have lost.[7]

The future role for Poland was to be a 'giant reservoir of labour' for the Reich. All these policies would be put into effect by a ruthless application of terror. Walls of houses were covered with German notices and orders, and two phrases made a repeated appearance: 'strictly forbidden' and 'on the penalty of death'. An early example of German terror occurred in November 1939 when around 100 Poles were executed in Wawer, near Warsaw, in reprisal for the assassination of two German policemen.[8] Red posters would appear in the streets displaying the photographs of 'Polish bandits', yet, as Frank told a journalist from *Völkischer Beobachter*, there was a contrast between German policy in Poland and that in the Bohemian-Moravian Protectorate: 'There were large red posters in Prague announcing that today seven Czechs had been shot. I said to myself: if I wanted to hang a poster for every seven Poles that were shot, then all the forests in Poland would not suffice in order to produce the paper necessary for such posters.'[9]

The sheer scale of what the Germans were attempting to impose on Poland only became clear gradually. The war had delayed the start of the school and university academic year, and it was assumed that when hostilities ceased education would restart. A professor at the

Jagiellonian University in Kraków, Stanisław Urbańczyk, wrote on 19 October:

> The Senate resolved, with one vote against, that lectures should begin. Provisional enrolments first, followed by the quiet opening of the university. A quiet opening, rather than a ceremonial one with the traditional procession of professors from the church of St Anne, so as to avoid having to invite the German authorities. Instead there was simply a service held in the church of St Anne, at which the [national] hymn 'Boże, coś Polskę' was for the first time sung with the changed chorus: 'Lord, give us back our homeland and our freedom!'[10]

On 6 November 1939, the SS arrested 183 professors from the Jagiellonian University and 168 of them were sent to Sachsenhausen concentration camp.[11] Most schools did not reopen after the war began, and in May 1940 Himmler determined German policy on education:

> For the non-German population of the East, there must be no higher school than the fourth grade of elementary school. The sole goal of this schooling is to teach them simple arithmetic, nothing above the number 500, writing one's name, and the doctrine that it is divine law to obey the Germans . . . I do not think that reading is desirable.[12]

Accordingly, all Polish secondary schools and universities remained closed. The Poles reacted swiftly to this last decree: in autumn 1939, the Secret Teachers' Organisation was founded in Warsaw to provide an underground secondary education for thousands of Polish schoolchildren, ultimately throughout Poland. Similarly, the University of Warsaw went underground. Children toured the cities and towns, visiting their teachers at their homes or in secret locations. They sat exams and received cryptic messages such as: 'I was very interested in what you had to say', to exchange for proper educational certificates after the war.[13]

The Germans attempted to destroy or steal all symbols of Polish culture. Frank ordered that all works of art that had belonged to the Polish state as well as noted private collections should be confiscated, or as he expressed it, 'safeguarded'. The Polish Government in London kept extensive records during the war on the looted art treasures of Poland, and the catalogue lists 511 works. Among these spoils were paintings by Canaletto, Raphael's *Portrait of a Youth*, Rembrandt's *Landscape*, Leonardo da Vinci's *Lady with Ermine*, and the great reredos by Wit

Stwosz from St Mary's Church in Kraków.[14] Some of these pieces were earmarked for Hitler's planned gallery in Linz, but others were looted by German officials for themselves, including Frank. Indeed, after the war American troops found a Leonardo, a Rembrandt, a fourteenth-century Madonna and artifacts from churches in Kraków in Frank's house in Bavaria. Monuments to Tadeusz Kościuszko, leader of the 1794 Polish uprising against Russia, were destroyed in Kraków, Łódź and Poznań, as well as those commemorating the battle of Grunwald in 1410, when Polish-Lithuanian forces had stopped the expansion of the Teutonic Knights. Museums, art galleries, publishing houses, theatres and any outlet for public entertainment were closed. The Poles, as slaves of the Germans, were deemed to have no requirement for culture or entertainment.[15]

The economic exploitation of Poland began with the seizure of Poland's industrial resources and supply of raw materials. Factories were dismantled, and large quantities of iron and steel, precious metals, chemicals and oil taken to Germany before the end of 1939. Then German policy changed as it was realised that it was more efficient for Polish industry and workers to remain *in situ* serving the Reich, and an office of the Four Year Plan was opened in Kraków under General Bührman. Under its auspices policies were put in place to intensify agricultural and industrial production, and to introduce rationing. Agriculture was reorganised: large landed estates were treated as separate economic units and placed under direct German control, and all villages were ordered to give the Germans a fixed quota of their produce. By February 1941, the *Treuhandstelle Ost* had taken control of 85,246 industrial concerns and 121,120 commercial businesses from the Poles. Many more businesses had been transferred to private German ownership. By May 1941, the Germans had counted and registered the entire population, their animals, property, commerce and industry, which would enable them to exploit further Poland's resources in the future.[16]

The impact on the Polish population was immediate and catastrophic. The złoty was undervalued in relation to the mark to enable Germany to buy goods cheaply. The Germans seized control of the Bank of Poland and withdrew all large denomination notes from circulation. All Polish money was later replaced by German-issued złoty banknotes which no one trusted. Rampant inflation robbed the Poles of their savings. Taxes were raised. In January 1940, the Germans even began confiscating warm clothing from the Poles: 'Yesterday the German police took all sheepskin coats from passing villagers and left them only in their jackets.' By April 1940, the only unrationed items were potatoes, barley and sauerkraut. Conditions were worst in the cities where the food supplies were extremely low. Poles were entitled to 609 calories per day, the Jews to 503, in contrast to the Germans, who obtained 2,600. The result was near famine and consequently, in early 1940, the Reich Agriculture Minister for the Four Year Plan, Herbert Backe, was forced to provide Frank with at least 10,000 tons of bread grain per month. In April 135,000 tons of grain were sent from Germany to the General Government to see the cities through to the next harvest. Frank had no interest in preventing famine in the cities on humanitarian grounds but he did fear a resurgence of resistance should the people starve, just when German forces were occupied in western Europe. The black market flourished. Much of the German-imported grain went to the Catholic Poles, because as Frank admitted regarding the Jews, 'Whether or not they get any fodder to eat is the least thing I am concerned about.' By the end of 1940, average Polish rations had risen to 938 calories whereas those of the Jews had declined to 369.[17]

Zygmunt Klukowski, superintendent of the hospital in Szczebrzeszyn, noted in his diary in May 1940: 'The Germans are trying to destroy our most valuable asset, our youth.'[18] They did this in two ways: by depriving the young of an education and by deporting them as slave labourers to Germany. Unemployment in Poland had been high before the war with an estimated surplus of 4,000,000 agricultural workers. Germany, on the other hand, suffered from a shortage of agricultural workers, and before the war there had been an agreement between the two countries which facilitated the employment of 60,000 Poles to help with the 1938 harvest. Because of the tradition of working in Germany and because of rampant inflation in Poland and higher unemployment, by the spring of 1940, around 20,000 Poles had volunteered to work in Germany. In January 1940, however, Backe had demanded that Frank should send him 1,000,000 Poles from the General Government, 750,000 of whom would be agricultural labourers, and half of these women. The substantial shortfall in volunteers meant that the Germans would have to resort to compulsion to fill the quotas.[19]

The circumstances under which the Poles worked in Germany had changed. Instead of being treated as equals as in the pre-war years,

Himmler's decree on Polish labour in March 1940 made it clear that Poles were now to be treated as slaves. They were forced to wear a violet letter 'P' on their clothing, and were forbidden to attend church services and places of entertainment, use public transport or have sexual relations with Germans. The Poles wrote home advising others not to volunteer to work in Germany. Backe therefore asked that the Wehrmacht be given authority 'to cause, by force, the necessary number of workers to be transported to Germany', and in April the conscription of all non-Jewish Poles was extended to cover all those aged between 14 and 25. The Poles did all they could to evade the mass round-ups for labour; many spent each night sleeping at a different location or, in the summer, sleeping outside, while others found employment in the organs of local government, where Polish participation was restricted to the lower grades only. The latter was not to assist the Germans, but simply because a certificate of such employment gave exemption from labour in Germany. Others bought or borrowed the Jewish white-and-blue armband or yellow star, since the Germans did not want Jews to come to Germany.[20]

The Wehrmacht had responsibility for 694,000 Polish POWs by the end of hostilities. The 30,000 officers were sent to Oflags in Germany: the generals and staff first to Hohnstein and then Königstein, and the majority of officers to Murnau or Gross Born (Borne Sulinowo). Conditions were poor in these camps until the spring of 1940, when Red Cross parcels began to arrive. The 664,000 rank and file, however, were scattered through numerous camps in occupied Poland and in Germany, surviving the bitterly cold winter of 1939–40 in tents, while engaged in the construction of the rows of huts which would soon be used to house French and British POWs. In direct contravention of the Geneva Convention governing the treatment of POWs, in November 1939, the German foreign ministry informed the Swedish legation in Berlin that because the Polish state no longer existed, it considered Sweden's mandate as the protecting power of Polish POWs to have lapsed.[21]

In the spring of 1940, these men were compulsorily released from their POW status and became slave workers – principally in German agriculture but also in road building and other hard-labour projects. The POWs were subject to the same draconian restrictions as the Polish civilians. There is evidence, however, that some Germans were reluctant to treat Polish soldiers as badly as the authorities wanted. A report by the German Social Democratic Party in exile noted: 'The behaviour of the population in its contacts with Polish POWs is a matter of serious concern to the regime ... The Nazis are doing all they can to prevent contact between the German population and the Polish prisoners. Nonetheless, relations between the local residents and the Polish prisoners are becoming closer.'[22] The Polish POWs were, however, inadequately housed, ill-fed and overworked. Those who became sick were sent back to Poland where the Polish welfare agencies cared for them. Countess Karolina Lanckorońska in Kraków was caring for the returning POWs, and when she asked an officer for permission for the Poles to pray together on Christmas Eve, they had the following exchange: '"But they'll start praying for Poland's freedom." "I promise that they won't do it out loud." At that point, the man I was talking to – a former Austrian army captain – burst out laughing', and permission was granted.[23]

The fate of the 60,000 Jewish Polish POWs was far worse. They were segregated on arrival at the POW camps and given the hardest work to do. They also received such low rations that by the spring of 1940, 25,000 of them were dead. The remainder were then, like the Christian Poles, deprived of their POW status but, unlike the Christian Poles, they were sent back to Poland. A Christian POW Zbigniew Stypułkowski watched:

> Their hopes rose when the Germans started to send loads of Jewish POWs to Poland. For public works – it was claimed, to the ghetto – as it turned out later on. Apparently the German Armed Forces did not want to assume responsibility for the mass murder of POWs and discharged them as prisoners. They were to be dealt with by the German civilian authorities.[24]

Many did not even make it back home but were murdered on the way, notably 350 near Parczew. The remainder were crammed into the ghettos that the Germans had already established in Poland.

The impact of the German occupation did not fall equally on all Polish citizens. The Poles with German ancestry, the *Volksdeutsche*, benefited hugely. They had in many cases assisted with the German invasion and had been responsible for some of the worst atrocities during the conflict, and formed themselves into a civilian militia, the *Volkdeutscher Selbstschutz*. The Poles were appalled by the conduct of their Polish neighbours: 'people from our town, Poles' who in the German presence 'suddenly heard the call of their German blood! Mostly they were scum: even jailbirds, card-sharps, thieves, petty (and not so petty!) crooks'. Some of the Polish Germans even joined the SS. Frank established a *Sonderdienst* of the *Volksdeutsche* to work with local administrators to enforce labour service and the collection of the harvest. Their local knowledge made it far harder for the Polish peasants to evade the German demands. A decree was promulgated establishing four categories of Poles eligible for Germanisation: the *Volksliste*. The first two categories covered those who had proved themselves to be of German descent through their active work in the 'ethnic struggle', and those who, despite their passivity, had satisfactorily demonstrated their German origins. Both categories were immediately eligible for conscription into the Wehrmacht but a concession was made to allow for previous service in the Polish Army. The third category covered 'persons of German descent' who had 'developed connections with Polish nationality', to whom German citizenship was only granted conditionally. Men in this category were often forced to sign the *Volksliste*: 'My brother was going to be taken to one of these local concentration camps unless he signed a paper. He decided to sign because he felt he'd die in the camps and his parents would not be treated any better.' In late 1941, the men from this category were conscripted into the Wehrmacht. The final category were those of German descent who insisted that they were Poles and whom the Germans therefore regarded as renegades.[25]

The impact of the ideology behind the creation of the *Volksliste* was greatest in the regions annexed to the Reich, Danzig-West Prussia and the Warthegau, where there were over 10,000,000 Poles and only 600,000 Germans. The Germans dictated that this area of prime agricultural land and industry was to be inhabited only by *Volksdeutsche*, so ethnic Germans from eastern Poland occupied by the Soviets, the Baltic provinces, Bessarabia, Bukovina and Dobruja were to be brought there, and all the Jews and the majority of Poles, apart from a reservoir of slave labour, were to be expelled into the General Government. One historian of the process has concluded:

Well before the decision to pursue the Final Solution had been made and well before the first Jewish transports rolled to Chelmo and Belzec in the winter of 1941–1942, the National Socialists had, through trial and error, mastered the 'science' of human round-ups, the expropriation of property, and the shipment of human cargo en masse to the East. Without this valuable experience . . . it is safe to assume that the Nazis' war of annihilation against the Jews of Europe would not have gone as smoothly and swiftly as it did.[26]

Over the winter of 1939–40, the deportations began as the Poles were herded into unheated cattle trucks to be transported into the General Government. Mrs J.K., living in Gdynia, recalled that the German police gave her a few hours to leave and told her 'that not only must I be ready, but that the flat must be swept, the plates and dishes washed and the keys left in the cupboards so that the Germans who were to live in my house should have no trouble'.[27] Others were ordered to leave welcoming bouquets of flowers. In some towns families were given twenty minutes in which to pack, and 'during this time the electric light was switched off for the whole block, so that families could not find the things they wanted to take with them'. The Polish deportees were allowed to take between 45 and 100 pounds of luggage from the houses that they had lived in perhaps for their entire lives. The trains would stop at railway sidings along the way to dispose of frozen corpses, a large number of which were those of children.[28]

No preparations had been made in the General Government for the deportees' reception, and Frank demanded that a temporary halt be called to the deportations to allow his officials to resettle the homeless Poles. In 1942, when a new wave of deportations was in process within the General Government, Frank reminded his government ministers of the situation back in 1939–40:

> You remember those terrible months in which day after day goods trains, loaded with people, poured into the General Government; some wagons were filled to overflowing with corpses. That was terrible when every District Chief, every County and Town Chief, had his hands full of work from early morning to night to deal with this flood of elements which had become undesirable in the Reich and which they wanted to get rid of quickly.[29]

The deportations resumed in the spring of 1940, and by the end of the year, 305,000 Christian Poles had been deported from their homes in addition to nearly 1,000,000 Jews, who were sent to the Łódź ghetto.

The economic effect of the deportations from the annexed lands was not what the Germans had expected, and the incoming *Volksdeutsche* did not impress the local Nazi officials. Most were farmers, and inefficient farmers at that, using outdated agricultural methods. The towns of the annexed regions were depopulated, especially by the expulsion of the Jews, but few of the *Volksdeutsche* had commercial or industrial experience. After the expulsion of the Poles, a Swedish journalist visiting Gdynia, now renamed Gotenhafen, felt that the more appropriate name would be Totenhafen: the port was dead because the machinery had been dismantled and sent to Germany. In a report issued at the end of 1940, the Reich Agriculture Ministry noted that the Poles were not planting their fields with crops for the new season because they did not expect to be there to harvest them and that this would have serious consequences for the food supply in the Reich and General Government. The Gauleiter of Danzig-West Prussia, Albert Forster, was aware of the problem and stopped the expulsions after only 17,000 Baltic Germans, mostly farmers with their families, had arrived to take the place of 130,000 Poles. He also admitted a large number of Poles from the third category on to the *Volksliste*. In the Warthegau, the Gauleiter, Arthur Greiser, who was an even greater supporter of Germanisation and deportations than Forster, was also forced to relent on the expulsions, because the Poles ran the railway system and he needed their cooperation to keep the trains running. The Germans were appalled to discover that many of the incoming *Volksdeutsche* did not know German, and language lessons had to be organised before they could receive their new homes. Most had expected to be able to live in the old Reich and were not keen on occupying farms in regions still inhabited largely by Poles. Consequently, although by January 1941, over 500,000 *Volksdeutsche* had been rehoused, the majority were still living in SS-run transit camps.

Germanisation continued regardless. The major cities in the region were renamed: Łódź became Litzmannstadt, and Rzeszów, Reichshof. When Jan Karski visited Poznań, now known as Posen, he noted: 'The city with the finest historical tradition in all Poland was now, to all appearances, a typical German community. Every sign on stores and banks and institutions was in German. The street names were in German. German newspapers were being hawked on the corners.' Only German was being spoken in public and the remaining Poles were allowed to live only in the suburbs. The Poles had to adapt quickly to their new status as German slaves.[30] The experiences of Zygmunt Szkopiak's family illustrate German policy at this time. His father owned a farm near Bydgoszcz and, until the SS arrived, had had good relations with the local Germans. Now a German neighbour seized the farm and allowed the family to live in one room and to work in return for minimum rations. In mid-1940, the Szkopiaks were informed that they could now rent their own farm from their German neighbour. In August 1941, German policy changed again, and the family was deported to Austria to work as slave labour on a farm in Carinthia.[31] This experience seems not to have been unusual.

German policy towards the Polish Ukrainians was full of paradoxes. On the one hand, they viewed the Ukrainians as *Untermenschen* on the same level as the Poles, but on the other, they saw some benefit in treating the Ukrainians better. Frank explained his policy to his government officials:

> Although he would not permit the creation of a great national common organisation of the people of the Ukraine, it might nevertheless be possible to found a kind of self-help and welfare organisation for a great number of Ukrainians. For the rest it was recommended that the principle, 'Divide et impera' be subscribed to in the General Government.[32]

The Ukrainians were permitted to keep their national institutions, and separate Ukrainian schools were allowed to remain open. They also had their own welfare agency, *Ukraiźnyi Dopomogowyi Komitetji*. Whereas the Catholic Church was persecuted throughout Poland, the Uniate and Russian Orthodox Churches were not. That 30,000 Ukrainians voluntarily crossed from the Soviet zone to live under German occupation suggests that they viewed it more favourably than the Soviet occupation despite the fact that in the Soviet zone the Ukrainians were now united under one government. The Ukrainian peasantry, however, suffered equally with the Poles, being subject to the same draconian quotas for the delivery of agricultural produce to the Germans. After the German invasion of the Soviet Union, the gulf between the German policies towards the Poles and the Ukrainians would widen considerably.[33]

There were an estimated 2,000,000 Jews in German-occupied Poland and for the Germans this was their first contact with a great mass of largely unassimilated Jews, whose distinctive clothing, long beards and ringlets made them easily identifiable. Indeed, there were 400,000 Jews living in Warsaw alone, more than had lived in the whole of Germany in 1933. The Polish Jews were aware of the Nuremberg Laws and the effect that *Kristallnacht* had had on Jews in Germany.[34] During the first week of the war, over 250,000 Jews fled eastwards into what would become the Soviet-occupied zone. The remainder suffered sporadic violence and murder at the hands of the Germans during the actual hostilities. For example, in Leżajsk the Jewish men were ordered by the Germans to set fire to their own synagogue and to dance in a circle around the burning building. In the first part of their occupation, the German policy towards the Jews focused on five areas: identification, registration, expropriation, exploitation and concentration. In the General Government all Jews over the age of ten had to wear a white armband with a blue Star of David; in Warthegau they wore a yellow star. The Jews had to register their businesses, property and all other assets, such as cash, jewellery, antiques and gold. In some areas Jewish shops were allowed to stay open; in others they were closed and expropriated by the Germans. A report of the government delegate, the Polish Government-in-Exile's representative in Poland, for the last few months of 1939 summarised German policy as 'harassment of the Jews, suppression of their political, economic and cultural role, accompanied by sustained although unsuccessful attempts to secure the participation of the Polish masses, and to convince the latter that the struggle against Jewry serves their interests'.[35]

The Germans forced the Jews to govern themselves through the establishment of a *Judenrat* in every town where there was a substantial Jewish population. Adam Czerniaków was appointed president of the *Judenrat* in Warsaw. Chaim Kaplan believed that 'the President is a decent man. But the people around him are the dregs of humanity'.[36] Indeed, throughout Poland the Jews condemned the activities of their so-called leaders or representatives: 'Despite the *Judenrat*'s involuntary role in carrying out Nazi orders, most Jews found their conduct indefensible, especially abhorrent was their discriminatory and inequitable treatment of many Jews in matters of housing and forced labour, which was always demeaning.' The conduct of the *Judenrat* over the issue of forced labour was regarded as most offensive to poor Jews who noted: 'the work was not only unpleasant, but it was painful as well as one was usually beaten and battered. These rich Jews often hired poorer

Jews as their substitutes.'[37] Jews were first set to work clearing the rubble and damage created by the war. Gradually a network of labour camps was established throughout Poland where Jews were engaged in undertaking drainage projects, the building of barracks for the Germans and the construction of military facilities for the German armed forces.

The Germans explored various possibilities for dealing with the Jewish 'problem'. The first project was to create a Jewish reservation in the Lublin region. Around 45,000 Jews were sent there from Polish territory now annexed to the Reich and from Germany and the Protectorate. An SS officer addressed them on their arrival in November 1939: 'There are no dwellings. There are no houses. If you build, there will be a roof over your heads. There is no water; the wells all around carry disease. There is cholera, dysentery and typhoid. If you bore and find water, you will have water.'[38] The result was an extremely high mortality rate and in March 1940 the transports ceased. The next project was to encourage Jews to cross into the Soviet zone, and to this end a camp was established near the demarcation line close to Bełżec. In early 1940, Jan Karski visited the site and wrote a report for the Polish Government-in-Exile:

> An enormous proportion walked and slept under the open sky. Very many people were without proper clothing or other covering. While one group slept, the other waited its turn, so that outer garments could be lent to one another. Those who waited jumped and ran around so as not to freeze . . . All are frozen, in despair, unable to think, hungry – a herd of harassed beasts, not people. This has being going on for weeks.[39]

The main crossing point between the two occupation zones for those Poles returning to their pre-war homes was in the town of Przemyśl and the dilemma facing the Jews was apparent there. Columns of Jews fleeing German cruelty met columns of Jews fleeing Soviet poverty, each group beseeching the other to turn back. The Germans even toyed with the idea of creating a Jewish reservation on the island of Madagascar, but British naval power precluded the exercise of that option, which was hardly more than a fantasy in any event. Finally, it was decided to concentrate Jews into ghettos where their numbers could be eroded through overwork and starvation.

The first ghetto was established in Piotrków Trybunalski in October

1939 and eventually approximately 400 more were created. According to the historian Raul Hilberg:

> The ghetto was a captive city-state in which territorial confinement was combined with absolute subjugation to German authority. With the creation of the ghettos, the Jewish community of Poland was no longer an integrated whole. Each ghetto was on its own, thrown into sudden isolation, with a multiplicity of internal problems and a reliance on the outside world for basic sustenance.
>
> Fundamental to the very idea of the ghetto was the sheer segregation of its residents. Personal contacts across the boundary were sharply curtailed or severed altogether, leaving in the main only mechanical channels of communication: some telephone lines, banking connections, and post offices for the dispatch and receipt of letters and parcels. Physically the ghetto inhabitant was henceforth incarcerated. Even in a large ghetto he stood never more than a few minutes' walk from a wall or fence. He still had to wear the star, and at night, during curfew hours, he was forced to remain in his apartment house.[40]

Work on the Warsaw ghetto was begun in October 1940 in the working-class quarter of the city: 113,000 Poles had to be ejected from their homes and 138,000 Jews moved in. Emanuel Ringelblum wrote in his diary on 13 October: 'Today was a horrifying day; the sight of Jews moving their old rags and bedding made a horrible impression. Though forbidden to move their furniture, some Jews did it. There were cases of vehicles containing furniture being stopped or taken away.'[41] In the middle of November, the Germans combed the city and collected up 11,130 Jews who had not moved into the ghetto. The ghetto was then sealed: it was surrounded by ten-feet high walls with fifteen entry points. In the beginning it formed the shape of a 'T', but the shape would alter as streets were added or subtracted as the population of the ghetto changed.

The Łódź ghetto was established in February 1940 in a slum area, Bałuty. It already contained 62,000 Jews, and 100,000 Jews from the surrounding areas were brought in, as well as 60,000 Jews from Germany. The president of the *Judenrat* there was Chaim Rumkowski. There were 60,000 Jews in Kraków, and Frank ordered that the historic city centre should be *Judenfrei* by the start of November 1940. The first part of their dislocation was voluntary, the 23,000 Jews who left before the middle of August could move with their belongings to anywhere in the General Government, but after that the Germans began a policy of expulsions of 20,000 Jews to other ghettos, before creating a closed ghetto in the nearby Podgórze district of the city.[42]

The determining factors for survival in the ghetto became wealth and contacts. Smuggling flourished and was carried out mostly by small children, who found it easier to escape through narrow gaps in the wall or wire. They ran a great risk of punishment from the Jewish police inside the ghetto and the German authorities outside if caught. In the Warsaw ghetto, the Jews from outside the city, who had been forbidden to bring any property with them, suffered the most:

> Such was the misery that people died of hunger in the streets. Every morning, about 4–5 a.m., funeral carts collected a dozen or more corpses on the street that had been covered with a sheet of paper and weighed down with a few rocks . . . Cart after cart filled with nude corpses would move through the streets.[43]

By February 1941, Ringelblum could note in his diary: 'Almost daily people are falling down dead or unconscious in the middle of the street. It no longer makes so direct an impression.' Jews slipped away from work parties outside the ghetto in search of food. 'Polish-Jewish economic relations were very much alive in spite of the constant obstacles and hindrances created by the invaders, and trade continued with the ghetto.'[44] Poles also risked their lives to get food to the starving Jews: 'A Christian was killed today . . . for throwing a sack of bread over the wall.'[45] Some smuggling was well-organised, as Jarosław Iwaszkiewicz discovered when he rode the tram that passed through the ghetto: 'The tram driver keeps a few parcels near him and looking out for the people – known only to him – drops his load while slowing down at bends. The parcels are immediately caught with a skilled and greedy hand and quickly disappear into the black crowd.'[46]

Opportunities for escape and smuggling were limited in the Łódź ghetto because it was totally cut off from the Christian neighbourhoods. Some Polish customers did send food parcels to the Jewish merchants with whom they had done business before the war. The wealthy who could get parcels sent to them from outside did not suffer, nor did those who worked in the *Judenrat*, nor did the Jewish police and their families. The Germans themselves noted the contrast between the poverty and filth of the ghetto and the businesslike luxury of the Jewish headquarters.[47] Starvation reduced the numbers in the ghetto only for the Germans to cram in more Jews as they closed the smaller ghettos and transported more Jews from Germany to Poland. However, the process of decimating the Jewish population through starvation and overwork was not progressing fast enough to satisfy the Germans and so they began to examine possibilities for a 'final solution' to the Jewish problem.

The ultimate fate of the Jews is well known, and after the German invasion of the Soviet Union, the Jews would become the principal target. In the first part of the German occupation, however, the Poles were the main victims of the German policy of terror. The General Government was a place 'in which poverty, fear, terror and hunger held indisputable sway'.[48] The Germans resorted to three principal methods of terror. The first was the practice of taking hostages from among the elite to ensure the good behaviour of the rest of the population. For example, the schoolteacher or the village head was taken in the villages of Poland during the autumn of 1940 to ensure that the peasants delivered their grain quota. When posters celebrating Poland's Independence Day, 11 November, appeared on houses in Kraków in 1939, Frank ordered that one man should be taken from each house displaying the posters and shot, while the chief of the SS and higher police, Otto Wächter, took 120 hostages against any outward display of Poland's independence.[49] A year later prominent citizens were taken hostage in Warsaw to ensure that the city remained quiet on Independence Day.[50] Indeed, hostages were taken so frequently that the superintendent of the hospital in Szczebrzeszyn, Zygmunt Klukowski, made preparations: 'I have my small suitcase packed and ready near my bed, in event of arrest. At night my shoes and suit are ready, so I can dress quickly.'[51]

The second method was the *łapanka*, the mass round-up. Blocks would be encircled and then everyone caught inside arrested. In June 1940, the Germans rounded up 20,000 Warsaw citizens, and all men aged under 40 were sent for forced labour in Germany, while all women between 17 and 25 were sent to East Prussia as agricultural labourers. Stefan Korboński was caught in a round-up in September 1940, when the entire Staszic housing estate in Warsaw was surrounded and everyone taken on trucks to the former Polish Light Horse barracks near Łazienki: 'Walking to the front of the crowd I passed a cross-section of Warsaw:

workmen, merchants, artisans, intellectuals; all were standing the knowing what to expect.' Employees of the public utilities, such as electricity stations and waterworks, were quickly released. The remainder had their papers examined and then were taken to the riding school:

> There was strict discipline there. Hundreds of men were lying on the sawdust that covered the turf. No one was allowed to stand up. In the wide gangway SS men marched up and down with whips in their hands, which they used unsparingly. On the side-galleries other SS men had machine guns at the ready.[52]

Around 1,500 men remained there for four days after which about 300 were released, including Stefan Korboński, and the remainder sent to labour or concentration camps.

Imprisonment, often followed by execution, was the third terror method pursued by the Germans. Pawiak prison in Warsaw was used by the German Security Police for brutal interrogations and the Gestapo had its main headquarters at Alje Szucha. The final destination of many Poles was the village of Palmiry on the road from Warsaw to Modlin:

> This desolate spot among the woods was selected by the Gestapo in Warsaw as an execution site. A clearing in the wood was enlarged by cutting down the trees around it. Before each execution a pit of the required size was dug in the sandy ground, usually in the form of a ditch about 3 metres deep. The victims were brought from Warsaw by lorry ... The blindfolded victims were led to the clearing. There they were lined up on the edge of the pit and machine-gunned.[53]

In spring 1940, the former Polish artillery barracks at Oświęcim were reopened as the new concentration camp of Auschwitz, situated in the Polish part of Upper Silesia which had now been incorporated into German Upper Silesia. One of the early inmates was Jan Komski, who had been caught by the Germans in Slovakia when he was trying to get to France to join the Polish Army. Put on a train back to Poland, he arrived in Kraków 'where we were greeted with German expressions of jubilation' because Paris had just surrendered. He was sent to Auschwitz and witnessed the construction and extension of the camp complex:

> The camp expanded rapidly. The Germans added eight new buildings. The size of the camp grew through depopulation and confiscations. The first

to suffer were the workers who lived in railroad huts in the vicinity of the tobacco building. They were driven out. Similarly, the inhabitants of Zasole, another district close to the camp, were affected.[54]

Until the German invasion of the Soviet Union and the launch of the Final Solution, the majority of prisoners at Auschwitz were Polish Christians: there were 18,000 of them in 1941.[55]

The Poles put up a strong resistance to the German policies, which led to an escalation in German terror. In March 1940, Frank informed his government ministers:

> Generally we have to take into account the ever increasing resistance in the circles of the intelligentsia, clergy and former officers. Resistance against our rule in this country has already assumed organised forms. The least attempt on the part of the Poles to any action would have led to a general settling of accounts with the Polish community with the object of its final annihilation. In this event, I would not hesitate to introduce a reign of terror with all its consequences. I have issued an order to arrest several hundred members of secret organisations for three months, so as to prevent anything happening in the nearest future. The last words of the Führer before my departure were: 'Take care to keep absolute peace there. I shall not tolerate anything that disturbs the peace in the East'. This I shall endeavour to do.[56]

After discussions with the heads of the German police, Friedrich-Wilhelm Krüger and Bruno Streckenbach, Frank ordered the beginning of *Außerordentliche Befriedungsaktion*, Aktion AB, the effective extermination of much of the Polish intelligentsia. Timing was key because on 10 May 1940 Hitler launched the attack in the west, and as Frank commented: 'It is obvious that as long as this land was in the limelight throughout the world, we were deprived of the chance of undertaking anything on a large-scale', but now that the world was distracted the murderous process could begin.[57] In Warsaw Pawiak prison was virtually emptied and the victims taken to Palmiry; in Kraków prisoners were taken to nearby Krzesawice and shot; those held in Lublin castle met the same fate outside the city; and a sandy area near Częstochowa became the graveyard for groups taken from there and from Radom. In all it has been estimated that about 3,000 members of the Polish intelligentsia were murdered and a further 30,000 were arrested and imprisoned.

Aktion AB effectively deprived Poland of many of the leaders who could have provided guidance and leadership through the even darker days that would follow. Separate German attacks deprived the Poles of a vital source of comfort, their religion, as thousands of priests were arrested and imprisoned. It has been estimated that around 2,800 Polish priests and monks out of a total of about 18,000 were killed and 4,000 were imprisoned: 846 Polish priests died in Dachau alone.[58]

In his evidence at the Nuremberg trials, Frank admitted: 'It was the resistance movement, which started from the very first day and was supported by our enemies, which presented the most difficult problem I had to cope with.'[59] When addressing his government officials on the need to start Aktion AB, he claimed:

> One could deduct from ample indications and acts that resistance movement of the Poles, organised on a large scale, existed in the country and that we were standing on the very brink of considerable and violent events. Thousands of Poles were already enrolled and armed in secret societies and were being incited in the most rebellious manner to commit every kind of outrage.[60]

Frank was right: the resistance did begin almost immediately. The first resistance movement, the Polish Victory Service (*Służba Zwycięstwu Polski*), was established before the surrender of Warsaw by General Rómmel, who appointed General Michał Karaszewicz-Tokarzewski as its first commander 'with the task of continuing the struggle for independence and the integrity of the frontiers in their entirety'.[61] The Germans granted Warsaw a 48-hour window for the Poles to gather together all their weapons and lay them out in designated squares but young Poles frantically went round the squares gathering these weapons and taking them to the main hospital. There they were cleaned and oiled, wrapped in oilskins and buried at the bottom of the graves prepared for the dying patients in the hospital. As one participant in this operation, Alexander Maisner, noted: 'This entire operation was properly organised (i.e. the weapons were all listed as were their hidden whereabouts) by the nascent Polish underground army.'[62] The early period of the Polish resistance is characterised by the springing up of around a hundred groups, each formed by men who knew and trusted each other, for example, the Secret Polish Army, the Military

Organisation of the Wolves, the Union of Reserve Officers and the Union of Non-Commissioned Officers.[63]

Sikorski was opposed to Karaszewicz-Tokarzewski, who had been a member of the Piłsudski camp and was therefore linked to the now discredited *Sanacja* regime. He also needed to impose his personal authority and that of his government over Poland from outside the country. So, in November 1939, Sikorski established the *Związek Walki Zbrojnej* (ZWZ), Union for Armed Struggle, as the military resistance movement in Poland and appointed General Kazimierz Sosnkowski as its overall commander-in-chief with General Stefan Rowecki as commander-in-chief in occupied Poland. Karaszewicz-Tokarzewski was then despatched, with Klemens Rudnicki as his chief of staff, to establish the resistance in the Soviet-occupied zone. All of Poland was to be divided into districts and within them cells would be formed on a pyramid system whereby each member of a cell of five only knew the other four; each would then separately and secretly recruit five more members and so on.[64]

The purpose of the resistance was set out in Instruction No. 1 on 4 December 1939: 'Preparations [should be made] for an armed uprising at the rear of the armies of occupation, to occur at the moment of entry of regular Polish forces into the country', but the population was urged to be patient since premature action 'would in no way be proportionate to the repression that it would necessarily bring down on the country, giving the occupant an excuse for the ruthless extermination of the Poles'. Further guidelines followed in April 1940, advocating sabotage and diversionary operations and the repression of collaborators, who would be shot if found guilty. The fall of France shocked the Polish population and because it was obvious that the war would now be a long one, new plans were required. In November 1940, instructions were sent to Rowecki ordering him to concentrate on preparations for future action when the timing was opportune, but in the meantime to attack the German communications system, particularly the railways.[65] Sikorski had already established an important contact in London: in October 1939, he met General Colin Gubbins, who would shortly become involved in establishing the Special Operations Executive (SOE), which would become responsible for supplying arms to the occupied countries. By the beginning of April 1940, the British War Office had supplied the Poles with 4 wireless transmitters, 1,390 revolvers, 1,000 lbs of high explosive, 500 assorted incendiary bombs and fuses, carried from France via Italy, Yugoslavia and Hungary by Polish couriers. The underground launched attacks on trains carrying goods from the Soviet Union to Germany, and provided the British with evidence of the German build-up for Operation Barbarossa.[66]

The emphasis of the Union for Armed Struggle was on preventing sporadic outbursts of resistance, such as the murder of a German settler in the village of Józefów, Lublin province, for which the German reprisals involved the round-up of Poles from 6 nearby villages and the execution of at least 100. Impromptu acts of defiance such as the establishment of shrines on the mass graves from the September 1939 campaign were, however, smiled upon. For example, the events in Krasnobród on All Saints' Day, 1 November 1940:

In their local cemetery approximately 300 soldiers and officers of the 1939 campaign are buried. On their graves 180 wreaths were laid, with uncounted numbers of candles. Two large red and white Polish flags were installed, one with the Polish white eagle. By the large graves of the unknown soldiers, which were covered with battle helmets, one sparkling clean rifle with a belt and cartridge pouch was placed. Many white and red lamps were lit. A second rifle was placed on the grave of Maj. Gluchowski.

The cemetery was crowded. Never before had so many people attended services. Most of the people were assembled around the military graves. All of this was in front of the German terrorists and made a colossal impression. That evening the local priest removed the flags and the Polish police took one of the carbines. The other one is still on the grave of Maj. Gluchowski.[67]

The killing of Gestapo men and Polish informers was sanctioned, but otherwise the resistance was preoccupied with the recruitment, organisation and training of armed units, the maintenance of morale, and the care of families of the men who were killed or arrested, and above all letting the population 'realise that somewhere there was someone who cared'. Finance came in part from Britain, but was also supplied by local landowners.[68]

When Karski returned to Poland from his first trip as a courier to the Polish Government, he brought with him instructions for the creation of a complete underground state. The initial plans drawn up in April

1940 were for the establishment of three government delegates for Poland: for the General Government, the German-annexed regions and for the Soviet-occupied zone. After the fall of France the structure was revised so that one delegate, Cyryl Ratajski, was appointed for the whole of Poland. Working under him were three representatives of political parties: Kazimierz Pużak for the Socialists (PPS); Aleksander Dębski for the National Party; Stefan Korboński for the Peasant Party; while Rowecki represented the underground army.[69]

The establishment of the underground state was complicated by the desire for each political party in Poland to maintain its own communications with its representatives outside the country. This led to a major argument between Sosnkowski and the minister for the interior, Stanisław Kot, over radio communications, and conflict within the resistance in Poland as various emissaries and couriers competed to use the few relatively secure routes out of the country. Nonetheless, over the next few years the Underground Government extended its sphere of operations into every aspect of governmental activity in Poland to become in effect a 'government in waiting'. It provided advice to the population on the extent of cooperation allowed between Poles and Germans – official contact was only permitted in areas relating to relief, medicine and charity, and no personal, social or cultural contacts. This was somewhat idealistic because there were many areas in which the Poles and Germans had to work closely together. For example, although the Germans retained all the higher administrative posts, they needed the Poles to fill the lower administrative levels and the Poles needed the jobs in order to survive and feed their families. The matter of policing was complex because, whereas the SS, Gestapo and German police took over most aspects of crime-fighting, as well as adding a long list of new crimes, a Polish police force was needed to combat common crimes such as theft. This necessity for cooperation, if not actual collaboration, often compromised the participants' moral position and as German terror increased, the police in particular would be challenged by the demands made of them.[70]

The resistance and Underground Government flourished in the General Government but met with more limited success in the annexed territories and in the Soviet-occupied zone, where the Poles were extremely vulnerable to betrayal by members of the local ethnic minorities. In the region annexed to the Reich, the *Volksdeutsche* used their extensive local knowledge to uncover clandestine activities among the Poles. The situation was vastly worse in Soviet-occupied Poland:

> The mainspring of Soviet police tactics was their efforts to spread mutual distrust among the population. The result was that while German methods unified and strengthened the nation, those of the Soviet weakened and split it. In the Russian zone, even old friends never revealed their political feelings to each other and everyone was the prey of suspicions.[71]

The extension of an organised resistance into the Soviet zone was completely stopped when Rudnicki was arrested almost immediately after arriving. He was sent to Siberia, and it emerged in late 1941 that he might have been betrayed by the head of the Lwów district of the resistance, Colonel Emil Macieliński, who had been forced to become an informant for the Soviet secret police, the NKVD. Jan Karski visited Lwów before making a trip to the Polish Government and was given a message by a law professor to take back to Sikorski:

> There is one thing you must understand and tell the men in Warsaw. Conditions here are very different, indeed. For one thing, the Gestapo and GPU [Soviet Secret Police] are two entirely different organisations. The men of the Russian secret police are more clever and better trained. Their police methods are superior. They are less crude, more scientific and systematic. Many of the ruses and practices which work well in Warsaw will not do at all in Lwów. Very often the various branches of the underground cannot take the risk of contacting each other because of the difficulty of eluding the GPU agents and even knowing who they are.[72]

The resistance faced an additional problem: as part of the German-Soviet treaty of friendship the two countries agreed to exchange information on 'Polish agitation that affects the territory of the other country', and several meetings were held between the Gestapo and the NKVD. This collusion between the two enemies meant that resistance members could not flee one zone for another and then re-establish operations in the new one, since they would be arrested as soon as their details had been sent to the appropriate authorities.[73]

The Soviet Union broadcast to the world that its forces had invaded eastern Poland on 17 September 1939 to rescue their fellow Ukrainians and Belorussians from the oppression they had suffered at the hands of the now fleeing Polish Government. In fact, as a Soviet journalist wrote at the time: 'it is an event which must completely change the conditions of existence, the whole framework of life'.[74] Beneath the Soviet rhetoric of rescue from persecution lay a more sinister purpose: the imposition of a 'revolution from abroad' entailing the complete destruction of all previous political, economic and social structures, which would bring eastern Poland, already a poor area, down to the level of impoverishment of the Soviet Union.

The Soviets deliberately unleashed a reign of terror against the Polish population in Kresy, but at the beginning it was terror by proxy. During their invasion the Soviets dropped leaflets urging the local Ukrainians and Belorussians to rise up and rob and murder their Polish neighbours. Local prisons were opened and criminals released to engage in attacks on the Poles. Local militia units were established to hunt down Polish officers, local government officials and the *osadnicy*, the hated Polish military settlers. Retreating Polish units were attacked by armed bands and isolated soldiers seeking their units were stripped, beaten and left to find their way home naked. The Ukrainian nationalist organisation, OUN, championed the violence and its units were responsible for the murder of about 600 Poles.[75] The Poles resisted. In Stanisławów on the evening of 19 September as the last Polish units left the town, a rumour spread that the Ukrainians would attack that night. Polish youths too young for the army gathered together to defend the town but the only people who appeared the next day belonged to the vanguard of the Red Army.[76] Henryk N. wrote that the military settlers of Śmigłowo organised a resistance group and when they saw the Ukrainians 'approaching they pulled out who knows where from rifles going back to the [1863] uprising and even a machine gun and they started peppering the Ukrainians'.[77] Not all violence against the Poles was carried out by the locals. Elizabeth Piekarski recalled how she, then fourteen years old, and her nine-year-old sister were ordered by Polish communists, who were not local, to witness the execution of 42 local inhabitants who were viewed as intellectuals and rich people, and 2 Orthodox priests, outside the gates of the Piekarski estate. She and her sister were put against a wall and threatened with execution. The communists then went on to pillage the house and rob the estate farm of its livestock.[78] Such murders and seizures of land and livestock were common throughout eastern Poland. Many of those officers and administrators at risk went into hiding:

Leon Kochański, deputy head of the Stanisławów province, left his family and hid with his brother Franciszek in the remote town of Bolechów (Bolekhov) in the Carpathian mountains. His son, Zbigniew, a Polish cavalry officer, fled to the house of his uncle Czesław Tuzinkiewicz in Białohorszcze, near Lwów.[79]

The Polish administration of Kresy had been heavy-handed in the 1930s, so it is not entirely surprising that the arrival of the Red Army was seen by the non-ethnic Poles as a blessing:

> It was the rule rather than the exception for villages and towns to greet Red Army units with the traditional symbols of hospitality ... a loaf of bread and a measure of salt; flowers thrown at passing soldiers; 'Triumphal arches' hastily erected across the road, as on a festive day, or, in communities better informed politically, a display of red banners (easily prepared by cutting the white strip off the Polish flag). Sometimes Ukrainian national colours were flown by the cheering population.[80]

The Ukrainians and Belorussians welcomed the end of Polish rule and the opportunity to realise their nationalist aspirations through unification with their Soviet Ukrainian and Belorussian brothers. The Lithuanians were grateful to the Soviets for allocating Wilno to their country on 10 October 1939 despite the fact that they were in a minority in the city. The presence of a large number of Jews in the welcoming crowds shocked the Poles and contributed towards strengthening the existing anti-semitic beliefs that some held. What the Poles did not analyse at the time was exactly which Jews welcomed the arrival of the Soviet authorities. Later investigations have suggested that many of the Jews who greeted and later collaborated with the Soviets were not pre-war residents of Kresy but came from the estimated 300,000 to 400,000 refugees from German-occupied Poland. The initial joyous reaction to the arrival of the Soviets is immediately understandable on the grounds of gratitude that the Red Army would protect them from the Germans. As one Jew wrote: 'Who cared about Communism? Who paid any attention to theoretical problems of national economy, when one faced an immediate danger to life?' Nevertheless there were local politically aware Jews who greeted the Soviets and were favourably disposed towards communism, and along with many Ukrainians, Belorussians and Lithuanians, they would become enthusiastic collaborators with the Soviet authorities in their anti-Polish activities and would fill the posts in the local administration that the Poles were forced to relinquish.[81]

In fact the Soviets exaggerated the extent of anti-Polish sentiment held by the non-ethnic Polish population of Kresy. There is evidence to show that members of the ethnic minorities helped their Polish neighbours: 'in spite of repressions against them the local people helped us as best they could'.[82] Property stolen from the Poles in the opening weeks of the occupation was often surreptitiously returned to its rightful owners. When prominent Poles were arrested, the locals often went to their aid. For example, following the arrest of Bronisław Wawrzkowicz's father by the local militia:

> My young brother Marian and I went to the nearby hamlet with the idea of collecting as many signatures as possible from the local Ukrainians with whom we had previously lived in complete amity. After four hours we returned very happy having not only 40 signatures but also a letter written by the eldest man in the hamlet which gave father a very complimentary character.[83]

Their father was released. Again, Stanisław Kujawiński was arrested by the Soviets in Grodno but a Jewish taxi driver successfully begged the Soviets to release him.[84] When Leon Kochański, arrested in May 1940, was put on trial in Stanisławów a year later, so much evidence was gathered from local Ukrainians and Jews to show that he had carried out his duties without any bias against the ethnic minorities that he was acquitted.[85] Members of the ethnic minorities also warned their Polish neighbours of imminent Soviet action against them. For example, Feliks Gradkowski remembered: 'The Jewish committee, to which part of the *osada* was entrusted, forbade the Ukrainians to harm us, indeed they helped us as much as they could, for example, pre-warning my father to sell what he could, as they knew of the plans to move us on in the near future.'[86] Or Adela Konradczyńska-Piorkowska who wrote of a Ukrainian, now in local government, who 'was a man my father employed for ploughing. Because my father had helped him and his large family during hard times, he now came to our aid, warning my father twice against being transported.'[87]

The strongest evidence of negative feeling towards the new authorities emerged during the political revolution imposed in Kresy by the Soviets. The OUN wanted not incorporation into the Soviet Ukraine but independence for the Ukraine, and as this was not the Soviet plan, the most prominent nationalist leaders were arrested. Leading Polish politicians were arrested too, including a former prime minister, Leon Kozłowski, and Stanisław Grabski. Elections to the assemblies of the newly created provinces of Western Ukraine and Western Belorussia were set for 22 October 1939.[88] The Poles in Lwów considered boycotting the elections but 'direct threats were made against anyone who considered not voting. People were told that they will be dismissed from work, arrested, or sent to Siberia if they did not.'[89] They were also informed that the turnout for the elections had been predetermined at 99.2 per cent regardless of what the actual turnout was. The candidates were mainly Soviet citizens from the Soviet Union and included some senior officers in the Red Army. A voting booth was erected in each polling station but its use was actively and threateningly discouraged. Voters were given instructions on where to place their cross and had to show their ballot paper to an election official after it had been filled in. In Brody when a Soviet officer asked a voter to read the ballot papers to him, the election committee members 'turned pale and were terrified, because the papers were covered in words in Polish and Ukrainian making insults at the authorities'. After a while the Soviet officer burst out laughing and cried out that the Poles had behaved 'exactly like us'. He then ordered the election committee to burn the ballot papers and signed a sheet giving the turnout as 99.2 per cent and the names of the candidates placed in order of their importance.[90] In his correspondence and meetings with Churchill and Roosevelt, Stalin later used the results of these fraudulent elections as justification for his demand to retain the former provinces of eastern Poland within the frontiers of the Soviet Union.

A wave of arrests followed the elections. The ethnic minorities realised that the Soviets were no longer interested in winning their support and certainly did not approve of their aspirations for national independence. Indeed one Pole, Henryk, wrote that after the elections, 'You no longer saw hordes of Ukrainians with red bands on their arms and rifles and proudly and haughtily strutting around town. They didn't spit any more when they saw a Pole and with pity they nodded their heads in mutual understanding.'[91] The suspicions were confirmed when the national assemblies met and in a matter of days voted to request the Soviet Union to incorporate the provinces of Western Ukraine and Western Belorussia into the Soviet Union. One member of the assembly for Western Ukraine, a Ukrainian lawyer named Vinnechenko, voted against incorporation, and was arrested and sentenced to eight years in the Gulag. The Soviet Union accepted the provinces' wishes on 1 and 2 November 1939.[92]

On 29 November 1939, a Soviet decree was published giving Soviet citizenship to the population living in Kresy. It covered all Polish citizens resident in Kresy on the night of 1–2 November; those who had lived in Wilno; and people who had arrived in the Soviet zone on the basis of the 16 November citizen-exchange agreement with Germany. Refusal to accept Soviet citizenship meant no job and therefore no means of survival.[93] The only Polish citizens who actually had a choice were the Jewish refugees. Given what we now know about the fate of the Jews under German occupation, it may seem surprising that many Jews opted to return to the General Government. The head of the Ukrainian Communist Party, Nikita Khrushchev, noted in his memoirs:

> There are long lines standing outside of the place where people register for permission to return to Polish territory. When I took a closer look, I was shocked to see that most of the people in line were members of the Jewish population. They were bribing the Gestapo agents to let them leave as soon as possible to return to their original homes.[94]

Not all Jews were accepted, since the Germans were of course themselves encouraging the Jews to leave. Moshe Kleinbaum expressed the dilemma faced by the Jewish refugees: 'Until now we had been sentenced to death, but now our sentence has been converted to life imprisonment.'[95] The population of Kresy, regardless of ethnicity, soon found out that even accepting the Soviet passport did not guarantee freedom of action because, if the Soviets put the so-called Paragraph 11 on a person's papers, this forbade him or her from living in a town or city or within 60 miles of the frontier. The Soviets also conscripted all males born between 1890 and 1921 (around 210,000), promising them that they would serve in Polish units under Polish command and would only be used in the event of a war with Germany. No such independent Polish units were created.[96]

Once the political revolution had been completed, the Soviet authorities concentrated on the social and economic revolution. They instituted a policy of dismantling all visible signs of the Polish state. Memorials were torn down, and the Polish eagle removed from signs and monuments. Propaganda posters appeared everywhere. Witold T. saw one in Łuck (Lutsk) that caused him great offence: 'One of them particularly stuck in my mind, it showed a white eagle with a four-cornered Polish soldier's cap on its head and clawing at the back of a handcuffed worker. A bolshevik soldier was sticking a bayonet into the eagle. The background was a map of Poland.'[97] Huge posters of Soviet leaders were erected on the sides of buildings and in the schools. Loudspeakers were installed in the streets, broadcasting Soviet propaganda from early morning to late at night. Mobile film projectors toured towns and villages showing propaganda films of life in the Soviet Union. Cyrillic script was introduced in Western Belorussia. The Ukrainian and Belorussian social institutions that had been closed by the Polish Government in the 1930s were reopened. In Lithuania the Polish Stefan Batory University and Polish social institutions were closed.[98]

The Soviets made educational change one of the linchpins of their social revolution. All private and religious schools were abolished. In their place was put a programme of four-year elementary schools, to be followed by seven-year 'incomplete' secondary schools in the countryside and ten-year ones in the towns. The teaching of religion, history, geography and Latin was banned and the textbooks removed from school libraries and burnt. The language of instruction was changed to Ukrainian or Belorussian: teachers were sent on courses to learn the languages, the Soviet syllabus and the principles of Marxist-Leninism.[99] The students and teachers often responded badly to the changes. Witold T. recalled of his school in Łuck:

> The school attitude to meetings was 'simply hostile' as our communist teacher complained, we hooted at the meetings, we didn't want to join the cheering, we didn't sing the 'International', so they wanted to close the school, because they considered it a hotbed of 'counterrevolution'. Arrests among the students and teachers dampened the outer signs of our beliefs (we had to stop saying prayers aloud before lessons) but aside from that they achieved nothing else.[100]

Some teachers tried to limit the impact of the new regime. One student, B. M. Trybuchowski, wrote of his mother, who was a teacher: 'whenever she taught her pupils the Soviet national anthem, she deliberately omitted the second verse which proclaims "No God, no Tsar, no hero". As you might expect she was reported and, as a consequence, was threatened with imprisonment.'[101] Universities were less affected, although young men no longer attended lectures, as many had been conscripted into the Red Army. Certain departments were abolished at Lwów University, such as law and humanities, and new ones were created to teach the new subjects of Darwinism, Leninism and Stalinism. Even where subjects were not removed, the personnel teaching them were changed. When Anna Kochańska started her studies of Polish philology at Lwów University in September 1940, she was taught by Polish professors but these were replaced gradually by Ukrainian ones from Kiev. University study was popular under Soviet rule because it was free and each student received a stipend of 100 roubles.[102]

The Poles sought comfort from their trials through religion, although both occupying forces hit out at the Catholic Church. The partition of Poland caused chaos in the Church organisation with archbishoprics being split by the border. The Germans tried to Germanise the Church in the annexed lands by imprisoning many of the clergy and forbidding the use of Polish, even for confession. In the General Government, clergy were persecuted and many ended up in concentration camps. The Soviets persecuted religious belief in their zone through the application of such a punitive level of taxation that many churches were forced to close.[103] Some did remain open: for example, the church in Białohorszcze run by Father Tuzinkiewicz, whose parishioners were mainly the workers on the Lwów trams.[104] The Carmelite convent in Lwów was turned into an old people's home, and only four nuns were allowed to remain as servants to the occupants. Jews suffered as badly as the Catholics and had to continue their religious practices in private. Zeev recalled of his father, a rabbi: 'During the daytime, older children came and with covered windows Father taught them from sacred books. In the evening, older citizens came, and they sat together with my father over the books.' The rabbi was often questioned by the NKVD.[105]

The Soviets wrecked the economy of eastern Poland. From the start they were amazed by its wealth. One soldier, Georgy Dragunov, noted:

We saw that people were much better off . . . We saw beautifully furnished houses – even peasant houses. [Even] the poorest people were better off than our people – their furniture was polished . . . Each poor peasant had no less than two horses and every household had three or four cows and a lot of poultry.[106]

The houses in the towns of Poland had electricity, which was not the case in Soviet Belorussia or Ukraine. The Soviets responded to Polish wealth by stealing belongings, livestock and produce. They also emptied the shops of goods which had never been seen in such quantities in the Soviet Union. This could lead to such odd incidents as the sight of a Soviet soldier buying twenty boxes of something simply because he could and then being disappointed when he started eating the contents: 'it didn't taste good to him. Only later he found out it was toothpaste.'[107] Certainly the food in the shops was better than Red Army rations: one soldier dropped some of his food in the road and 'the family dog sniffed it and rejected it. The soldier called him a capitalistic dog.'[108] More seriously, the emptying of the shops led to real economic hardship for the inhabitants of eastern Poland. Of 8,500 shops in Lwów, 6,400 were sold out of everything and then closed. Unable to restock their shops, thousands of shopkeepers were effectively bankrupted by the Soviet invasion. This hit the Jewish population especially hard since so many were shopkeepers. The Soviets only imported into the region some inferior soap, salt, matches, tobacco and herrings.[109]

The rouble was introduced as legal tender on parity with the złoty, when before the war the purchasing power of the złoty had been nine times greater. This action not only enabled the Soviets to buy up the contents of the shops cheaply, but also impoverished the entire population of eastern Poland as their cash assets virtually vanished overnight. Added to this, bank balances of over 300 złoty were blocked, the banks were nationalised and the safe deposits opened and their contents confiscated. Everyone was heavily taxed. The workers lost their savings and in many cases their jobs too. Those still in work were introduced to the Soviet practice of imposing arbitrary quotas on output. Many factories and even government buildings were completely dismantled and the machinery, furniture and fittings sent back to the Soviet Union. For example, virtually all of the Białystok textile industry was sent east. Polish oil, foodstuffs, wood and cattle were shipped to Germany as part of the Soviet-German economic agreement. There was widespread unemployment and endemic poverty; bartering skills became essential for survival.[110]

The agricultural and social revolution had an equally devastating effect on the entire population of Kresy. At the start of the occupation the peasants had been encouraged to steal land from the Polish landowners, and village committees were established to reallocate the land.

In January 1940, however, the Soviets changed their policy and began to collectivise the land into large units and impose a high degree of state control over the peasants. By the spring of 1941 there were over 9,000 kolkhozy (collective farms) in Western Belorussia and nearly 3,000 in Western Ukraine.[111] All animals and possessions were listed and could not be sold or transferred without permission. Many better-off Poles were evicted from their homes or allowed to live in only a small part of them. Anna Levitska recalled how her family's villa was appropriated by Red Army officers: 'They took over the furniture and all the other things which meant that everything was now theirs ... It was a small house which had five rooms – they occupied four of the rooms ... We no longer had any right to any of it ... Even the clothes ...'[112] The Kochański family had fled their house in Stanisławów after bombs had fallen nearby and taken shelter with their grandmother Emilia Tuzinkiewicz in nearby Tłumacz (Tlumach). Unable to return to Stanisławów because Red Army pilots had taken over their house, they were then evicted by a Pole named Makarewicz, and the family of eleven had to move into a house with two small rooms and a kitchen.[113] The Soviets delighted in their new-found wealth and status and their conduct provided some humour for the beleaguered Poles, such as the sight of Russian women going to the theatre wearing Polish nightdresses or stories of Soviet soldiers washing in the bowls of lavatories and wondering out loud why the water ran so fast.[114]

In the Soviet Union there was a maxim: 'there are only three categories of people: those who were in prison, those who are in prison, and those who will be in prison'. Stalin's Great Terror had hit the Polish population in Soviet Ukraine and Belorussia in 1937 with extreme brutality: nearly 20,000 Poles in Soviet Belorussia were arrested and of these nearly 18,000 were shot; in Soviet Ukraine around 56,000 Poles were arrested, of whom over 47,000 were shot. The remainder were despatched to exile in Kazakhstan. This hostile Soviet policy was now extended into Kresy. Local government officials, lawyers, policemen, and political and social activists were arrested, interrogated and frequently sentenced to death; indeed, it has been estimated that about 10 per cent of all adult males were in prison at one time or another.[115] Interrogations focused on examining the arrestees' lives since 1920. Many were sentenced for merely having taken an active role in Poland when she was an independent, sovereign country. Franciszek Kochański was arrested, convicted and sentenced to serve in a labour camp in the Urals solely because he had worked for the Polish State Railway.[116] Others were arrested for their activities since the war had begun: Alexander Maisner, who had fled the German zone and was arrested trying to cross into Lithuania, was charged with having entered the country illegally, not having an identity card and trying to leave the country illegally. He was sentenced to eight years in the Gulag.[117]

The conditions in the prisons were appalling with starvation rations, great overcrowding and frequent brutal interrogations. For example, the prison at Brześć had a capacity of 2,680 prisoners but housed 3,807. A prisoner in Lwów recalled:

> Every night they call out some of the condemned: some of them are given hard labour for life, others are taken into the cellars where the executioners carry out the death sentence with a shot in the back of the skull. If you stay in the death cell for a month it gives you hope that your sentence will be changed.[118]

So keen were the Soviets to destroy Polish statehood that even when the Germans launched operation Barbarossa, the Soviets continued to murder their prisoners: it has been estimated that all 150,000 prisoners on 22 June 1941 were either killed on the spot or moved east and then often killed. No attempt was made to evacuate the prisons of Lwów, and the shooting of prisoners there continued until 28 June when the NKVD finally fled the advancing Germans: there were so many bodies in the Brygidki and Zamarstynów prisons that the cellars were not opened because of the fear of epidemics.[119] No attempt was made to evacuate prisoners from Dubno; they were shot. Władysław Grzebyk noticed: 'Indeed the man in charge of this atrocity . . . was so engrossed in what he was up to that he did not manage to flee in time, was caught up by a German vanguard in Pantalia and, along with a number of his companions, was killed on the spot.'[120]

The Soviet authorities had responsibility for around 240,000 Polish POWs. These vastly exceeded the number the NKVD administrative machinery could deal with. From the moment of their surrender, the officers had been separated from their men and many shot out of hand. Those who survived this culling suffered a different fate from that of the soldiers, who were confined in impromptu camps established throughout Kresy and Soviet Ukraine. Conditions were appalling: in the camp at Podliszki Małe near Lwów, around 2,000 Polish POWs were housed in cowsheds; in Jaryczów Stary, they lived in pigsties; at the Żytnia camp, there were no washing facilities for the first six months. At the beginning of October 1939, around 42,400 ethnic Ukrainian and Belorussian Polish soldiers were released and permitted to return to their homes. After the conclusion of the German-Soviet agreement on population exchanges, the Soviets despatched nearly 42,942 Polish soldiers to German-occupied Poland and received 13,757 in return. Polish Jews made unsuccessful petitions to the Soviets not to be returned to their homes in the German zone. The Soviets forced 25,000 POWs to work on the Nowogród–Wolyński–Lwów road, others were sent to Pechora to build a railway, and labour camps were established in the Soviet Union at Rovensk, Krivoi Rog (Kryvyi Rih), Yeleno-Karakub and Zaporozh'e, where the POWs worked in the mines and in the metallurgical industry.

In October 1939, the Polish officers, government officials, and police and prison guards were despatched to three camps in the Soviet Union: Starobel'sk, about 130 miles south of Kharkov; Ostashkov, about 105 miles west of Kalinin (Tver); and Kozel'sk, about 155 miles southeast of Smolensk. The highest-ranking officers were sent to Starobel'sk to live in an old monastery where there was a lack of sleeping space and little food and water: on 1 April 1940, the camp population was 3,893 POWs. Conditions were similar at Kozel'sk where on 1 April 1940 the headcount was 4,599 officers, of whom about half were reserve officers; the camp at Ostashkov contained a mixture of 6,300 officers and policemen, housed in the former Nil Hermitage.

The NKVD interrogated all the officers, seeking out those who had a positive opinion of the Soviet Union, but noting that the majority were strongly anti-Soviet. Those who responded favourably to Soviet overtures, such as Colonel Zygmunt Berling and sixty others, were separated from their fellows and ultimately sent to live in luxurious conditions in Moscow until Stalin came to a decision on what to do with them.[121] The general anti-Soviet sentiments of the majority sealed their fate: on 5 March 1940, the head of the NKVD, Lavrenty Beria, sent a memorandum to Stalin outlining the extent of the 'counter-revolutionary' opinions of the Polish officers in the camps and highlighting reports of 'counter-revolutionary' activity in Kresy led by former officers, policemen and gendarmes. He recommended that these 'hardened, irremediable enemies of Soviet power' should be subjected to a new interrogation by a troika of three NKVD officers, Vsevolod Merkulov, Bogdan Kobulov and Leonid Bashtakov. The memorandum supplied the figures of 14,700 Polish officers, officials, landowners, police, intelligence agents, gendarmes, settlers and prison guards in the POW camps, and 11,000 Poles currently in prisons in Kresy. It made clear that the fate of those hostile to the Soviet Union would be execution: Stalin clearly indicated his assent to Beria's proposals.[122]

Much has been written about why Stalin ordered the massacres of the Polish officers and officials. Why murder them when if they had been imprisoned in the Gulag they would have died at the typical rate of about 20 per cent a year? Several theories have been put forward. One is that the NKVD was already struggling with such a high number of POWs and was now expecting to receive a large number of Finnish POWs. Another theory is that, despite Sikorski considering the possibility of forming a Polish army in the Soviet Union in case of war with Germany, he had taken the anti-Soviet step of giving permission for a Polish brigade to join the planned Anglo-French expeditionary force to assist Finland in its war against the Soviet Union. Since all attempts to re-educate the Polish officers had largely failed, it is also possible that Stalin and the NKVD feared the effect of despatching such high numbers of recalcitrant prisoners into the Gulag system. Another suggestion is that the murder of prominent Poles in the Soviet Union was linked with the German Aktion AB against the Polish elite in German-occupied Poland. There had been meetings between the Gestapo and NKVD, notably in Lwów in October 1939, and later in Berlin between Heinrich Himmler and Beria's deputy, Merkulov. Stalin therefore knew what the Germans were doing.[123] What is certain, however, is that the world was distracted at this time by events in western Europe.

The troika re-interrogated all the officers, offering them the tantalising prospect of being able to return to their homes. Merkulov reported to Beria on the results:

> The majority of officers coming from the German territories do not wish to go to the Polish land occupied by Germany, but want to go to neutral countries such as France where they would volunteer for the French army and fight against Germany, then turn against the Soviet Union and restore

Poland from the Oder to the Dnieper. Some officers dream of finding themselves in Romania, then joining the Weygand army and forming an armed detachment against the Soviet Union ... The soldiers whose families live in the Ukraine and Belorussia showed panic and fear of going home. They explained the reason for this fear of returning home in the following way: 'Here in the camp we're sitting quietly under the care of the NKVD and camp authorities, and as POWs no one can touch us. At home we won't be POWs anymore and as citizens of the Soviet Union, we'll be under its law. They can arrest us there, send us to prison because every one of us has committed some offence against the Soviet Union.'[124]

The executions of the Polish officers began in early April and continued until late May 1940.

The prisoners from Starobel'sk were taken by train in groups of 100–200 to Kharkov where they were held in the NKVD prison. Two men who were separated from their colleagues survived: Józef Czapski, who would devote much energy after the 1941 Sikorski–Maisky pact in searching for the officers, and Bronisław Młynarski. The prisoners from Ostashkov were taken to the NKVD prison at Kalinin. They thought they were going home and so a band played as they marched out of the camps. However, as one of the NKVD soldiers responsible for the killings described the process in the 1990s: the men were led individually into a soundproofed cell and 'two men held [the prisoner's] arms and a third shot him in the base of the skull'. The prisoners from Kozel'sk were taken by rail in batches of several hundred to Gniazdovo station and then by bus to the edge of the Katyń forest, where they were shot before being buried in mass graves. A number resisted, attested by the fact that when their bodies were discovered in 1943, some soldiers had their hands tied behind their backs, coats secured over their heads and bayonet wounds. One female Polish pilot, Janina Dowbor, was also killed at Katyń. Concurrent with these murders of Polish officers, the NKVD were executing their Polish prisoners in NKVD prisons in Kiev, Kharkov and Kerson: around 18,632 prisoners died in this bloodletting, of whom 10,658 were ethnic Poles, and their burial sites are still being discovered.[125] The final transport from Kozel'sk on 12 May 1940 was sent to a camp at Yukhnov, and these prisoners survived. Among them was a professor from the Stefan Batory University in Wilno, Stanisław Swianiewicz, who would later write about his experiences.[126]

The Soviet authorities concluded by early 1940 that there were broad swathes of the Polish citizenry in Kresy who were irredeemably hostile to the Soviet ideology, and consequently, in February 1940, they launched the first of four mass deportations of what they perceived to be the hostile elements, deep into the interior of the Soviet Union. The first group to be deported were the controversial *osadnicy* who were seen as the oppressors of the Ukrainian and Belorussian majority. Along with them travelled other representatives of Polish state control: policemen and foresters. In April 1940, the families of those officers imprisoned in the Soviet Union and in Poland, in hiding or abroad were also deported. In June 1940, it was the turn of the refugees from German-occupied Poland who had refused to accept Soviet passports, of whom around 30 per cent were Polish Jews. Finally, in June 1941, even as German bombs were falling on them, the Soviets deported the Polish citizens from Lithuania and the other Baltic States together with those omitted from the earlier deportations.[127]

As soon as the Soviet authorities were in place, they had begun the process of identifying every single person in Kresy, and classifying them by age, sex, ethnicity, religion, occupation, relationships and home ownership. These lists facilitated the deportation process and meant that it progressed so fast that most people were caught totally unprepared, particularly because no one knew the criteria for selection. The Soviets used the same methods for all the deportations: a group of three men, usually an NKVD officer, a militiaman and a Red Army soldier, would arrive at the house of the victims in the middle of the night. The family would be given between thirty minutes and two hours to pack up to 220 pounds of possessions and food per person. Sometimes people were taken with only what they could wear or carry with them. As Janina Żebrowski-Bulmahn wrote later, 'How do you pack a whole way of life into a trunk? How do you decide in a few short moments what is important to carry to a life you do not know?'[128] The answer was that few Poles had any clear idea about what to pack but a number received help from friendly neighbours. For example, Ryszard Rzepczyński recalled:

Some Ukrainian women from the village who knew what was happening came to our house and asked my mother for some sacks. When they were given some they took an axe and set about chopping the heads off our ducks and chickens. They filled two sacks with the birds with their feathers still on. Then they put them on our two sledges.[129]

These two sacks fed the whole wagon of deportees. Many Soviet soldiers helped the families by advising them on what to take, for example, axes or a sewing machine and, on occasions, doing the packing themselves for their victims. Occasionally children had to pack for their traumatised parents: Kazimierz Dobrowolski's mother was ill so he did the packing and when they arrived in Kazakhstan they found that among the items he had packed were his French dictionary, a recipe book and some Christmas decorations.[130]

The ignorance of the criteria for selection for deportation shook the entire population of Kresy. One child noted of the February deportation that it: 'made an enormous impression on even the most pro-communist groups. They started expressing their dislike of bolshevism openly, in spite of repression.' Resistance to deportation began to appear. Ten-year-old Janusz K. was staying with his grandparents when the NKVD came for them in April 1940 and recalled: 'The people of the village [Ukrainians] attacked the car and a struggle with rifle butts began. They did not want to let us go, they snatched me away by force and hid me in an attic.' He was then reunited with his mother, but they were both transported in the June 1940 deportation.[131] Others tried to hide vulnerable family members: Anna Mineyko successfully concealed her five-month-old baby and told the NKVD that she only had two children and her baby had died.[132] Few resorted to such drastic measures as Janka Tuzinkiewicz. The NKVD arrived to collect the Kochański and Tuzinkiewicz families, which included the mother and her sister Janka, six children, and the children's grandmother. Janka declared that her mother would not be taken except over her dead body:

> She was serious about this threat and a great argument broke out. Fearing that she might lose the battle and wanting to give herself more courage, Aunt Janka grabbed a bottle of vodka and, to put it figuratively, started pouring it into herself. One of the Soviets took the bottle away from her but it was too late. Not used to alcohol and suffering from a serious heart condition, she quickly lost consciousness.[133]

The NKVD panicked and sent one of the children for a doctor, who revived Janka. Her mother was left behind and not deported. The family then managed to convince the authorities that the baby, Marta, who had a rash on her face, had scarlet fever – a disease greatly feared by the Soviets – so she was left behind in the custody of her grandmother.

After packing, deportees were driven to the local station and loaded into cattle wagons for the journey east. Stefania Buczak-Zarzycka wrote of the scene:

> We could see the aged, the pregnant, the infirm, even those on stretchers, and crying babies all being forcibly herded into carriages for animal transportation. In the confusion, families were divided and we could see people begging the Russians to allow them to remain as family units. I could almost physically see and touch terror, panic, despair and I thought that I could only be witnessing the end of the world.[134]

The February deportees suffered the most: an estimated 10 per cent died, mostly from the cold. Some wagons had an ample supply of fuel, which heated one end of the wagon but left the other end so cold that people's hair froze to the sides of the wagons; others had too little, and bunks had to be torn up for fuel. Hardly any food was handed out, just occasional watery soup and a piece of bread. Overcrowding was common to all the transports, with people having to stand and lie down in turn, which was alleviated slightly when they were moved to the wider Russian-gauge trains at the frontier. Births took place, although few newborn babies survived. Flat cars at the ends of the trains were used to carry corpses to the next large town or city, where they were left at the trackside awaiting burial in an unknown location. On crossing the frontier 'singing broke out you could hear from the front to the back end of the train the national anthem'. For all their singing, the deportees were filled with despair as they headed towards an unknown destination and future.[135]

# 5

# Exile in the Soviet Union

Exile to remote regions of the Russian Empire was not an unknown phenomenon for the Poles. After the unsuccessful uprisings against the Russians in the nineteenth century, they had been exiled to Siberia, including ancestors of some of the deportees now crossing the frontier into the Soviet Union. But these earlier exiles had known the reasons, while those deportees of 1940 and 1941 did not know where they were going, for how long or even why. Nearly two-thirds of them originated from parts of Poland which, prior to 1918, had been in the Russian Empire, and these people had either their own or their parents' recollections of Russian unpredictability, inefficiency and ruthlessness, and had some idea of their future treatment and standard of living. But for the 38 per cent who came from East Galicia, which had been part of the Austro-Hungarian Empire, or who were refugees from western Poland, there was little knowledge of what lay ahead.

Many deportees later wrote or spoke about their growing sense of alienation from everything familiar as they neared and then crossed the Ural mountains, the traditional border between European and Asiatic Russia. Whether it was the dark, forbidding and apparently impenetrable forests of Siberia and north European Russia, where even during the summer the sun struggled to penetrate, or the endless featureless flat steppe stretching bleakly to the horizon in Kazakhstan, nothing seemed familiar to the Poles. Their experiences during the months under the Soviet occupation had already shaken them and they had been further mentally and physically weakened by their appalling journeys in the cattle trucks taking them further and further away from home. The Soviet attitude towards life and work was encapsulated in the statement, *u nas kto ne rabotaet tot i ne kushaet* ('here, if you don't work, you don't eat'), and a major shock for the Poles was that this was the actual truth. Exile in the Soviet Union would prove to be one seemingly endless battle for survival.

Apart from the civilian deportees whose experiences will be covered in this chapter, there were 196,000 Polish POWs who were now working in labour camps; 210,000 Polish citizens who had been conscripted into the Red Army, and another 250,000 who had been arrested and sentenced to hard labour in the Gulag; and an unknown number of Polish citizens who had volunteered to work in the Soviet Union.[1] Immediately after the war statistics were produced on the number of civilian deportees: a report by the ministry of justice for the Polish Government-in-Exile gave a figure of 980,000; the authors of the history of the Polish Armed Forces, *Polskie Siły Zbrojne*, estimated that between 1,050,000 and 1,200,000 Polish citizens had been deported.[2] These numbers have formed the basis for the calculations of later historians, among whom there was a general agreement that 220,000 civilians were deported in February 1940; 320,000 in April 1940; 240,000 in June 1940; and 200,000–300,000 in June 1941. The total of around 1,000,000 civilian deportees was used for many years,[3] but recent research using the Soviet archives has challenged this. Using the NKVD's own records for the deportations, a study in 1997 concluded that 140,000 were deported in February 1940; 60,000 in April 1940; 80,000 in June 1940; and 40,000 in June 1941. This total of 320,000, still substantial, was accepted by another study published in 2000 where the authors gave a range of 309,000–327,000.[4]

This enormous reduction needs explanation, is open to challenge and arguably needs still further research. In June 1941, the Soviet authorities admitted that there were 387,982 Polish citizens being held in the Soviet Union. But whom did they consider to be Polish citizens? Several points need to be taken into consideration. First, the Soviets classified the entire population in its zone of occupation in Poland according to ethnicity: Polish, Ukrainian, Belorussian and Jewish, so it is possible that the NKVD numbers only cover those whom the Soviets considered to be ethnic Poles. Secondly, it should be remembered that in November 1939 the people of Kresy were ordered to relinquish their Polish citizenship and to become Soviet citizens, but there was a reluctance to do so especially by the refugees from German-occupied Poland, and it is entirely possible that the Soviet figures are low because they counted only those deportees who had not taken up the Soviet passports and therefore still carried their Polish ones. Thirdly, it is necessary to consider the mortality rate: exact figures cannot be produced, because the Soviets did not keep such statistics, but it is thought that around 30 per cent of the deportees, prisoners and POWs died per year, which fits with the normal 'wastage' within the Gulag system. Lastly, the low overall Soviet numbers are all the more puzzling because they do not accord with the Soviet authorities' own orders in 1940–41. For example, Beria's directive on the April 1940 deportation gives an estimate of 75,000 to 100,000 civilians to be deported: far higher than the 60,000 in the NKVD records used in recent research. Scholars are still examining the Soviet archives, and after more demographic studies and research into the statistics of later repatriations, the number of civilian deportees is being revised upwards again. Although these do not approach those published by the Polish Government-in-Exile, it now seems likely that there were at least 500,000 Polish citizens deported in 1940–41,[5] and of these ethnic Poles were 52 per cent; Jews about 30 per cent; and Ukrainians and Belorussians about 18 per cent. These will all be considered Poles in this chapter.

The deportees from eastern Poland were exiled to remote regions of northern European Russia, to Siberia and to a broad swathe of northern Kazakhstan, stretching as far as the Siberian border and the frontier with Mongolia. Each deportation had a different classification according to Soviet law, which defined its location, the living conditions and, consequently, the chances of survival of each group.

The first exiles, seized in February 1940, were treated in a similar style to the *kulaks*, the wealthy peasants deported by Stalin at the start of the Great Terror. They were designated as 'special settlers' (*spetspereselentsky-osadniki*) in special settlements of between 100 and 150 families, living far from populated areas and under the direct supervision of the NKVD. These settlements were in north European Russia, particularly the Arkhangel'sk district and the Komi ASSR, and Siberia, especially the Sverdlovsk, Omsk, Tobolsk, Novosibirsk and Krasnoyarsk districts. There were large numbers of peasants and forest workers in this deportation, and, used to hard work, they had a relatively higher survival rate than many of the later deportees.

The April 1940 deportees were primarily women and children who had been condemned to exile under the same Article 59 of the Soviet Criminal Code which had condemned Soviet women to the Gulag during the Great Terror: as a 'member of the family of a traitor to the Fatherland'. These women and children were guilty of belonging to a family where the men had previously been arrested by the NKVD, were in hiding, were prisoners of war or had fled abroad. Classified as 'administrative exiles' (*administrativno-vysslanye*), they were distributed in six provinces of Kazakhstan: Aktyubinsk, Kustanai, Petropavlovsk, Akmolinsk, Pavlodar and Semipalatinsk. Survival rates were low, and relatively few escaped the Soviet Union following the amnesty in 1941.

Classified as 'special settlers-refugees' (*spetspereselentsky-bezhentsy*), the June 1940 deportation contained whole families – Polish, Ukrainian, Belorussian and above all Jewish – who had fled German-occupied Poland for the Soviet zone: many of them had refused to accept Soviet passports and were therefore seen as politically suspect. They were sent to Siberia and the north European Russian regions of Sverdlovsk, Chkalov, Yakutsk, Arkhangel'sk and the Mari ASSR, and lived in NKVD-supervised settlements. Few of these deportees were allowed to leave the Soviet Union after the amnesty so relatively little is known about their fate. Their survival rate is, however, likely to have been relatively low because, as refugees, they possessed little money and had few belongings to barter for food.

The final deportation from eastern Poland was part of the major Soviet ethnic cleansing programme in the territories most recently incorporated into the Soviet Union: northern Bukovina, Bessarabia and the Baltic States. It took place in June 1941 on the eve of the German invasion of the Soviet Union, and the last trains were leaving eastern Poland as German bombs were dropping. The Poles taken were mainly refugees who had escaped from eastern Poland into Lithuania after the Soviet invasion: classified as 'exiled settlers' (*ssyl'no-poselentsky*), they were theoretically given the rights of free Soviet citizens, allowed to choose their place of work and where to live. On arrival in the Soviet Union, however, the men were separated from their families and sent to labour camps in the Sverdlovsk region, and their families were settled in Altayski Kray with some sent as far as the Aktyubinsk district of Kazakhstan. Again, little is known of their survival rate because relatively few qualified, under Soviet terms, for the amnesty.[6]

It would be impossible to overstate the sense of culture shock endured by the Poles on their arrival in the Soviet Union. The February 1940 deportees travelled to their work camps in the depths of winter, through deep snowdrifts far into the seemingly endless forests. One man wrote of his camp:

> All around the horizon stretched the dark wall of the forest. The paths through the camp zone were made of two planks laid side by side; they were swept every day by the priests, who cleared away the snow with large wooden shovels . . . outside the kitchen stood a queue of ragged shadows, in fur caps with flaps over their ears, their feet and legs wrapped in rags and tied about with string.[7]

In contrast, the deportees sent to Siberia in summer 1940 found the sight of the forest reassuring and familiar: 'Even severely exhausted and afraid, we found it hard to resist the charm of this forest with its heavy scent of resins, its lichens and bracken, its candle-straight spruce, its pines with golden trunks, its white birches.'[8] In contrast, those sent to Kazakhstan entered a totally unfamiliar landscape where 'the steppe rolls away on all sides like a sea. Not a tree or a shrub breaks it vertically anywhere. There is almost no life. A few mournful birds pass rarely overhead.'[9] Nina Kochańska later said: 'Our first contact with this terrible reality and the first part of our stay in this land, forgotten by both God and men and avoided from afar by civilisation, whose poverty and primitiveness peered out from every corner, was shocking.'[10] In the featureless steppe there was no shelter from the burning sun during the summer. Everywhere clouds of mosquitoes made life miserable for everyone.

The most pressing requirement for all the deportees was to find accommodation. In this respect, those in Siberia had some advantage over those sent to Kazakhstan, for they had the labour camps which had been built by earlier victims of Stalin's purges and ethnic cleansing. The Milewski family, for example, arrived at Kokornaya village, 185 miles south-east of Arkhangel'sk, and were assigned a room in a barracks that had been built in 1933 by Ukrainian *kulaks* who had simply been left in the middle of the forest to fend for themselves. Yet even living in the barracks was a world away from the deportees' previous life in Poland. There was great overcrowding, for a room measured approximately 13 × 23 feet and each family was supposed to fit in, regardless of size. The Milewski family numbered eleven men, women and children. The head of the NKVD, Beria had stipulated that each individual was entitled to at least 32 square feet of living space, but this appeared to be impossible to achieve. The barracks were crudely constructed from logs cut in the forests and inadequately insulated by stuffing moss in the cracks. Inadequate heat was provided by a tiny wood-burning stove in each room, though at least there was a plentiful supply of fuel. There was, however, no electricity or running water, which meant that hygiene became a major problem and outbreaks of typhus, caused by the ideal breeding conditions for lice, were common and devastating. Bedbugs also made the lives of the deportees a misery. The NKVD viewed any attempts to improve the standard of the barracks as bourgeois behaviour, and sometimes moved such enterprising deportees to another location and forced them to start again from scratch.[11]

In Kazakhstan the women and children were forced to fend for themselves. It was not unusual for the Poles to be driven from the railway station and deposited in a village or small town with no instructions. They were shocked by the living conditions in Kazakhstan. Nina Kochańska recalled on her arrival at Dawidówka in Kustanai province: 'The people ran out to meet us. I wondered where they lived, because all around us and as far as the horizon, I could not see any houses. There was only something which looked like shabby cowsheds or stables.'[12] These turned out to be huts made of clay with bare earthen floors and no furniture, their new homes for the foreseeable future. The huts were constructed by cutting strips of turf from the steppe into bricks and laying them to form the walls. Thin planks were placed on top of the turf walls the whole length of the hut, on which poles and branches were placed to make the roof. Finally the roof, walls and floor would be smeared on both sides with clay mixed with animal dung to create a waterproof film. These huts would only last two or three years before needing to be rebuilt. They were breeding grounds for every type of insect and teemed with earwigs, woodlice, fleas, bedbugs and, of course, the ever-present lice. As in Siberia, the NKVD viewed any attempt to improve the huts as suspicious behaviour. One woman who had spent hours collecting fragments of glass and attaching them to pieces of rag which she then stuck together to glaze a window was told by the NKVD that the Poles 'had to atone for the lives which Polish workers had been made to live', and not live well themselves.[13]

Kazakhstan was a poor region. The Kazakhs had traditionally been a nomadic people, moving on when the food ran out. During Stalin's great collectivisation of agriculture in the 1930s, they had been forced to settle in collective farms, kolkhozy. The Poles were now supposed to find a place for themselves in these kolkhozy or starve to death. Their reception on arrival varied. If the kolkhoz had achieved its state targets and had food to spare, then they received a relatively warm welcome. But if a kolkhoz had suffered a poor harvest and was behind in paying its dues to the state, then the last thing it needed was an influx of hungry women and children. On arrival in one poor town in eastern Kazakhstan, Zdzisława Kawencka and the other exhausted women and children were subjected to a kind of slave auction by the kolkhoz managers, who selected those who they believed would become the best workers. Those with young children were left to the end because no one wanted them, yet they were forbidden to leave the area to which the NKVD had brought them.[14]

The Poles also had to persuade the local people either to allow them to rent a hut for themselves, or to absorb them into the existing primitive accommodation. In many cases families had to be split up. The Kochański family numbered seven: their aunt found room with another Polish deportee, their mother and the two youngest children slept in one hut. The remaining three children shared a straw mattress on the floor of another hut. In the morning their landlady would open the door and allow a pig to run in to wake them up: the pig then spent the day sleeping on the children's mattress. The lack of furniture was a difficulty which could not easily be remedied since wood was scarce on the steppe. The Poles had to make the best of what they had brought with them. Beds were made by laying large suitcases filled with straw on stones; seven-year-old Krzysia Kochańska slept in the large wicker basket which had carried the family's belongings from Poland.[15]

Many of the settlements in Kazakhstan lay a long distance from a river and so all the inhabitants had to rely on wells for water. This limited water supply naturally reduced the level of hygiene. Furthermore, as soon as any soap brought from Poland had run out white clay had to be used as a replacement. For those settlements near a river, washing was not a problem except that the livestock used the same water to drink from and bathe in. The lack of privacy was an embarrassment to many. Tadeusz Pieczko recorded how they obtained permission from the kolkhoz manager to build a bathhouse and a latrine. The local people never used the bathhouse and were fascinated by the latrine since they could see no reason for not using the same running water from which they took their drinking water for their bodily requirements.[16]

Whereas the forests of Siberia provided the deportees with ample fuel for heating their barracks, it was very different in Kazakhstan. There the lack of trees meant that Poles had to gain a quick affection for *kiziak* (dried animal manure). *Kiziak* features largely in their written accounts, particularly of the children. They all learned to follow the cows and quickly gather up their waste, which was laid in the sun and dried before being stored for the winter. When burnt, *kiziak* gave out little flame but great heat and, in temperatures that could drop to −50 °C (−58 °F), this was a lifesaver. Indeed, some Poles' main work on the kolkhoz was gathering and storing *kiziak*, which was also used to waterproof the primitive living accommodations. For those who did not have access to *kiziak* during the first winter, other means of heating the huts had to be found. The Kochański family were not given an allocation of *kiziak* but, on the advice of the kolkhoz manager, Stanisław spent days going far into the steppe where there was a dried-up lake overgrown with osier, cutting and then transporting sheaves back to Dawidówka. Unfortunately osier burns very quickly and towards the end of the winter, the family had to restrict the lighting of the stove to alternate days.[17]

Having found somewhere to live, the Poles now needed to obtain work in order to eat. The deportees taken in the February and June 1940 deportations and sent to the north of Russia and to Siberia were tasked, by Resolution 2122-617ss of the Soviet of People's Commissars of 29 December 1939, with 'clearing forests in regions belonging to the People's Commissariat of Forestry of the USSR'.[18] Work assignments were handed out to everyone aged 16 and above. In practice children as young as 10 also had to work. This mainly involved felling trees, sawing branches and hauling timber. This work was carried out throughout the year, even in the winter when the temperature fell to −70 °C (−94 °F) and there was little daylight. The only seasonal change came in the late spring with the thaw that enabled the timber to be floated down the rivers. The younger children, aged 10 or 11, had to work in the saw-mills. Stanisław K. was only 11 years old and yet was expected to carry boards 40 feet long and 2 inches thick. Lucjan Królikowski described the workday:

We left for work around seven in the morning to the accompaniment of a clanking on a piece of steel rail. We returned at six or seven in the evening. At lunchtime, the guards brought us our meals in a large, defective thermos sliding on wooden runners ... The work was hard, all the harder since very few of us had had any experience at it. In addition, we could not rest at night because of the bedbugs.[19]

Other Poles were sent to work in the mines, where they often had to work twelve-hour shifts standing in freezing cold water. Some, including children, were sent to build a railway, and a 14-year-old girl recalled:

We were taken to lay railway track. The ground was frozen as hard as stone. You dug the best you could with a pick and shovel and loaded the earth onto a wagon. All day you worked like that, and at night we came back to a sort of cafe where we were given soup, if we were lucky. If not we got the 400 grams [14 ounces] bread ration. The soup was made of fish heads boiled in clear water. After this 'meal' we went back to the barracks to sleep on the floor.[20]

Rations were allocated only to those who worked and, furthermore, their level was determined by the percentage of the 'norm', or quota, they achieved. The most productive workers received 2½ pounds of bread per day and the less successful 1¾ pounds: children who worked received 11 ounces. In addition, they would sometimes get a thin, watery flour soup. The deportees supplemented their rations by picking mushrooms and berries in the forests. Since the rations allocated were barely sufficient to maintain life in a sedentary person and certainly not sufficient to maintain the life of someone engaged in hard labour, the deportees began to starve slowly. Those too young, too old or too sick to work were entirely dependent on handouts from the meagre food of their family members. First old people and small children died, along with those deportees with no family members or close friends to share rations with them.[21]

The position of the so-called 'free settlers' in kolkhozy in Kazakhstan was rather different. They received no work assignments but they were expected to work to earn the right to share in the produce of the kolkhoz. By this means they accumulated workdays which would, at a later date, be translated into entitlements to food. It should be remembered that for the most part there were few men among the exiles, especially in Kazakhstan: they were enduring their own version of hell in the Gulag or in POW camps. Before the war few women in Poland had ever worked to support themselves or their families; they stayed at home bringing up the children. Consequently, a theme that runs through many accounts is the effort children and young adults made to earn sufficient entitlement to food so that the mothers did not need to work.[22]

The work on the kolkhozy in Kazakhstan was seasonal. Spring would be heralded by parties going out into the steppe to search for pieces of agricultural machinery that had been left out over the winter, since no one had taken the responsibility of noting their location. Then the ploughing season would begin, with oxen or tractors. The Poles had no prior experience of using oxen, and several accounts recorded how the beasts were frequently uncooperative until spoken to with Russian and Kazakh swearwords. The tractor crews were viewed as the elite: housed and fed better than the other workers, it was a job coveted by the Poles. Stanisław Kochański taught himself to drive a tractor and was soon working far out in the steppe ploughing and sowing the wheat. Kazimierz Dobrowolski remembered that the grass on the steppe was very tough and care had to be taken to prevent the plough from getting blocked. The area expected to be turned per day was unachievable even if the crews worked late into the night. Kochański recorded how he was advised by a fellow driver to plough to the correct depth on the outside of the field, but then to raise the height of the plough slightly in the middle of the field so that it only scratched the surface. This enabled him to get the work done more quickly, and there was little chance of detection since no Russian overseer was likely to want to get his boots muddy inspecting the whole field.[23]

As the wheat was growing, teams of women would be sent out into the fields to do the weeding. The fields were plagued with wormwood, which grew very quickly, so needed to be weeded three times in each growing season. The work was very hard, involving going along the rows of growing wheat bent double, in heat up to 50 °C (122 °F), pulling out the tough wormwood. It was very bitter and wiping a sweaty face with one's hand would lead to a feeling of being on fire. The women often took breaks from their work, and leaving a few to keep watch for the mounted overseer, the others would lie on the ground and sleep. There was no shade so the water in the metal container left with them would heat, and the hot water did little to quench the raging thirst of the workers.[24]

At harvest time, the entire kolkhoz would move on to the steppe to gather the wheat and cut the hay, working long into the night. It was absolutely vital for survival to have a good harvest since the state would take a fixed amount of wheat, and if the kolkhoz did not grow more than this, its population would starve during the winter. Even mothers with small children left them behind in the kolkhoz and joined the harvesters. The quota was impossible to achieve: the norm for tying bundles of hay was 500 per day and Weronika Hołowak wrote later that she could manage 90. The norm for transporting the hay was 12 carts per day, but even with great effort only 7 or 8 were manageable. Kazimierz Dobrowolski learned to cheat by loading fewer heaps of hay on to each cart, arranging them to look as though it was full. Care had to be taken by the workers not to fall into the hollow centre and give the game away. While the harvest was in progress children, Polish, Russian and Kazakh, were organised into a crèche. In theory the responsibility of looking after these children was a better job than harvesting all day and night, but in practice, as Józefa Kochańska discovered, looking after babies and tiny children in a virtually unventilated room was in itself unpleasant since no soap was available for washing the nappies, only water.[25]

After the harvest the grain had to be winnowed, and cleaned of wormwood, which would leave a bitter taste. This was very hard and dusty work and was done at night. The women worked in teams of three: one would turn the handle of the winnowing machine, the second pour the grain into it using a heavy iron bucket, and the third would use a wooden spade to remove the clean grain and throw it into a heap. The last job was the lightest, but the women would take turns on each. Later the grain had to be carried to the storehouse, which again was very heavy work using iron buckets; it was also dangerous because care had to be taken not to get buried in the tons of grain and suffocated.[26]

In September the potato harvest would begin. Again this involved working bent double and was back-breaking. By then the weather was colder and it was often raining. The potatoes had to be collected and placed into large chests, made from thick planks of wood with iron handles and hinges. When the chests were full, two people could just about manage to lift one. The best potatoes were sent to the state.[27]

Some kolkhozy operated as dairy farms. In the summer the Poles would be sent far out into the steppe to guard the cattle. First, they had to build their own temporary shelters: 'the only accommodation available was a *scherbak* (a shed plaited from wicker). Small green leaves still sprouted on the canes; the shed was plaited all in one piece and the roof was curved.' Naturally all *kiziak* was carefully gathered up to make fuel for the winter. The cows had to be milked and the Poles were taught how to do this. One Polish woman began by washing the udder but was told by the Russian overseer that this was idiotic behaviour and 'so Polish' that she abandoned the hygienic practice. Soviet logic again stunned the Poles: an overseer 'explained to us that in the Soviet Union the amount of milk a cow gives had been established somewhere . . . and the milkmaid who hands in less than her quota has to be fined'.[28] At the end of the summer the kolkhoz would be thrown into disarray by preparations for the vet's inspection of the cattle. No attention was paid to the state of the cows or the cowsheds: instead, vast stocks of vodka were accumulated as a bribe. The Poles were given very little milk or other dairy products even if they worked on a dairy farm. Sometimes the whole produce of the farm was reserved for the Germans, this still being the period of the Nazi-Soviet Pact.[29]

One Polish woman had a rude awakening to the Soviet system of working, when she and her fellow women were told to dig over and shift an enormous pile of *kiziak*. Despite the dung being frozen below the surface, they were given no picks to break it up, and their shovels were made of heavy wood and iron.

> When the sun got high, the ice melted, and the workers were then knee-deep in sticky, stinking, ice-cold dung . . . After a few days, the pile became quite fluid and the women simply churned about in the brown swamp during shifts lasting eight hours, doing nothing to it that was of any use at all. This state of things, though quite obvious, was permitted by the overseer, who did nothing to remedy it and merely saw that the women remained there and kept moving.[30]

The logic behind forcing these women to continue to try to shift dung when it had become liquid was lost on them: it was simply make-work.

In eastern Kazakhstan the main building material was clay. Elizabeth Piekarski recorded the process of making bricks. The clay was dug out from the riverbanks. Large holes were then dug, into which were put the clay, water from the river, together with harsh grass from the steppe and animal dung. Then a dozen people would get into the hole and stir the mixture with their legs, getting scratches and wounds from the grass, which often became infected – there were no medicines. After the mixture had been created, it was poured into large wooden frames to dry into bricks. Russian men did the actual construction of the kolkhoz buildings and the Poles struggled to lift the very heavy bricks above their heads to pass to them. Elsewhere Polish women were employed in brick factories and were again given unachievable norms. Cecylia Czajkowska was expected to produce 500 bricks a day, and another woman had to carry and load 1,000 bricks into the oven during her shift. The Poles then had remove the hot bricks from the oven without any protective clothing.[31]

Other factories that employed the Poles included one called Siesiomojka, where Helena F. and other women worked for eleven-hour shifts sorting and cleaning lamb's wool; the norm was 7 tons per shift, which was unachievable.[32] Nina Kochańska was sent with another Polish girl to a factory called Sienopunkt which produced big bales of compressed straw for the army:

> A machine driven by an internal combustion engine was placed by a stack. Straw was thrown into the machine which then compressed it, cut it into big blocks, tied wire around the blocks and threw them out onto a weighing machine. There was a minimum required weight for such a block. If it was less than the required weight, one had to cut the wire and throw the straw back into the machine. So the output was then less ... We were too weak for this sort of work. Even with the best intentions, we put too little straw, which first had to be hacked out of the packed stack with a pitchfork, into the machine.[33]

They were threatened with court action on a charge of sabotage, which absolutely terrified them, but were saved by the 1941 amnesty which released the Poles from their servitude.

The Poles were also employed on projects of strategic interest to the Soviet Union. In eastern Kazakhstan the Soviets were building a road towards the Chinese-Mongolian frontier, and every kolkhoz had to supply a work crew to build a section. Kazimierz Dobrowolski recorded how the first task was to build shelters for themselves. They were expected to dig channels 2 feet deep along the side of the road and then, on the road itself, the norm was to remove 9 cubic yards of soil per day per person (10 tons). On the first day each man managed about 4 cubic yards, but they soon learnt to cheat by scraping a thinner layer of top-soil off a wider area, and thus avoided a charge of sabotage. They spent three weeks working on their section of the road before returning to their kolkhoz. The Soviets were also building a railway across northern Kazakhstan from Akmolinsk to Kartaly, and Poles were again used. Soviet inefficiency soon became apparent. Stanisław Kochański recalled that work on the railway began before the ground was unfrozen, so that they were laying sleepers and rails on to the permafrost. When the thaw was complete the railway sagged, and the whole process had to be restarted in the summer of 1941. Stanisław Kujawiński, working on the same railway, remembered that their overseer was a Tartar and friendly towards the Poles. He would often put down a figure higher than the true one so that the Poles got paid more. The work by the Poles on the railway terminated abruptly when the news of the amnesty reached them. They just dropped their tools and set off back towards their families or towards where they thought a Polish army was being collected.[34]

The Soviet methods of working shocked the Poles. Despite Stalin's great drive for industrialisation and collectivisation in agriculture, the tools the Poles were expected to use were often primitive and ineffective, and the work was often organised very inefficiently. It appeared that what counted was the appearance of work rather than the actual result. The norms set were rarely achievable. Therefore, in order to give the appearance of having met them, cheating, bribery and corruption became the usual practice. The Poles soon learned how to cheat the system, as it became clear that the overseer was only interested in being able to convince his superior that the work norm had been achieved. Broadly speaking the men were more successful in achieving their targets than the women, not only because they were more used to hard work but also because they were better at bribing their overseers. With little experience of work the Polish women's conscientiousness could often be their downfall. As one man, Jan Lipiński, wrote: 'The norm was possible to fulfil and very easily so. You simply had to slip a few roubles into the hands of the foreman.' Having a sympathetic overseer could make all the difference: Kazimierz Biliński worked under a Soviet brigade leader of Polish origin who was prepared to write down 125 per cent when the Pole concerned had only actually achieved 25 per cent. Yet this system of cheating and bribery was only successful if the overseer was not caught himself. A friend of Eugenia Pavlovna obtained a job as an assistant to the petrol pump attendant. Her manager would often give her a can of kerosene to use for lighting. This arrangement worked well until he was arrested and she lost her job.[35]

The Poles could also obtain better working conditions because of their generally higher level of education. Stanisław Kochański was lodging with a lorry driver who complained that he could not drive long distances because the lights on his lorry were not working. Stanisław read the manual and, following the wiring diagram, identified the loose wire, connected it and restored the lights. News of his success spread and people started bringing their broken tractors and lorries to him to be fixed. Often the problems were simple: for example, a broken cable which had been tied together with a piece of string. The Russians wondered why this did not work and thought Stanisław a genius for reconnecting it properly. Mindful of the danger of being charged with sabotage if he failed to fix something, he refused to undertake any work which involved taking a part of the tractor to bits. His success led to a suggestion that he should get a job at the tractor service station where he would get paid in roubles, an obviously attractive proposition because he had a mother, aunt and four sisters to support. He approached the local NKVD man for permission, but was refused. When he asked why, he was staggered by the response: 'when they think they have learnt everything they can from you, someone will denounce you and accuse you of sabotage, and I will have to arrest you and the saboteur would go free'. The NKVD man only gave Stanisław this helpful warning because he was in love with his aunt, Janka.[36]

Not only was the work extremely hard but the Poles received little reward for their efforts. In Kazakhstan the staple diet was again bread, when available, and soup, plus a few potatoes. The supply of food was very dependent on the productivity of the whole kolkhoz since the state always took its due. Few deportees in the Soviet Union ate any meat at all between leaving Poland and joining the Anders army. Meat would have provided the protein that was essential for survival when carrying out heavy work in an inhospitable climate. It also forms a major part of the Polish diet, so this lack was felt particularly keenly. Stanisław Kochański had no regrets about the time he and the headmaster of the kolkhoz school stole a sheep one winter in the middle of the night when the Poles had been reduced to living on a few potatoes. They got away with the theft and the loss was blamed on the wolves. They acknowledge that this injection of protein almost certainly enabled them and their families to survive the winter. However, eating meat after a long gap and with weakened digestive systems could have a dire effect. Kazimierz Dobrowolski recalled how he was given some beef to eat and had to go outside into the −30 °C (−22 °F) frost five or six times during the following night as a result. Elsewhere, a horse was slaughtered when it died after getting severe colic from eating wet alfalfa, and the meat went off quickly, giving severe food poisoning to the Poles who ate it.[37]

The lack of vitamins and protein had a catastrophic effect on their health. Snow blindness and night blindness were common. In one camp the situation was remedied only when the Soviets delivered a supply of cod liver oil. Many Poles suffered from oedema, which is usual with extreme starvation. This started with the eyelids and the soles of the feet before spreading to other parts of the body. The lack of vitamins also meant that skin infections such as scabies became common and would often develop into ulcers. Any cuts or bruises sustained during work would not heal.

Health care was rudimentary throughout the Soviet Union and especially in the areas to which the exiles were sent. Life was considered cheap and people were forced to work unless the doctor, presuming there was one, agreed that their fever was over 40 °C (104 °F). A woman who contracted pleurisy would have had to walk 8 miles to see the doctor to be excused work: it was therefore less effort to attempt to work. Death or injury to the breadwinner could spell disaster for the family members. When Stanisław R.'s father was hit by a large stone in the mine where he was working, his head and back were injured. The doctor first dismissed him as a malingerer and threatened to reduce his pay by a quarter for six months. When it became clear that the man needed to go to hospital the family were given no rations during his two-week absence. Andrzej W., an 11-year-old boy working on the railway in Siberia, got pleurisy and was admitted to hospital and operated on. There were no medicines, antiseptics or painkillers available so he had to endure the agony of having his side cut open to allow 1½ quarts of pus to drain. He was ill for nine months and later X-rays showed that his lungs had 'almost completely rotted'. Elsewhere 13-year-old Helena F. took her sick brother to hospital only to find that although the ward was full of children with tuberculosis and dysentery, everyone was given medicine with the same spoon. She refused to allow him to be treated and he died shortly afterwards. It has been estimated that nearly 20 per cent of the children among the exiles from eastern Poland died.[38]

The Poles learned to use ancient remedies to cure sickness and injuries. The Siberian forests were a source of rudimentary medicines. Boiling pine and spruce needles and then drinking the brew could ward off scurvy; boiled willow bark and twigs were a substitute for aspirin; and bilberry twigs helped cure diarrhoea. When Stanisław Kochański suffered frostbite on his big toe which festered to the bone, a local person told the family that the best cure was cow's bile applied on a compress with a linen cloth. They had to wait for a cow fall sick and be slaughtered but the homespun remedy worked. Anna Mineyko fell, was cut deeply and broke her leg, and it was saved from gangrene when an old local woman applied a hot brew of dung ash to the wound.[39]

Among the 'free settlers' in Kazakhstan the death rate was between 10 and 15 per cent annually: the old and the children died first. In Siberia there were many deaths from pneumonia and regular, devastating typhus epidemics. In Jeglec in the Arkhangel'sk region, from a settlement of 450 people, 150 died. To add to the trauma of losing a loved one was the difficulty of giving them a decent burial. One mother had to carry her dead son 6 miles back to the kolkhoz from the hospital in the middle of the night during a storm. There was no wood available for coffins in Kazakhstan, and even in Siberia, where wood was plentiful, planks had to be stolen. There are many tales of Poles having to beg locals for the use of a horse and cart to take the dead person out into the steppe or forest for burial and then again beg for the use of a pick so as to dig a grave in the frozen ground since, inevitably, most deaths took place during the hard and long winters.[40]

The climate in eastern Poland is hot summers and very cold winters. Yet nothing prepared the Poles for the extreme weather conditions in the Soviet Union, and few had adequate warm clothing or skis to help them to survive the winter. The snow started in the second half of October and did not clear completely until early May. In Siberia the deportees were forced to work in the forests and mines throughout the winter despite the short hours of daylight and the freezing temperatures. In Kazakhstan the work largely ceased over the winter, because the steppe, short of many landmarks in the summer, became totally featureless and it was easy to lose one's bearings. Transport was by oxen-, horse- or in eastern Kazakhstan, camel-driven sledges. Camels have weak knees and cannot get out of snowdrifts easily, so rules of the road had to be worked out. The camel had the right of way along the narrow paths cut through the snowdrifts. If a cart pulled by a horse or oxen came the other way, it would have to drive off into the snowdrift to allow the camel to pass. The most frightening aspect of the winter months was the *buran* (blizzard). Then the huts would become buried up to the roofs in snow, and the people would be trapped inside unable to push the door open. When a *buran* hit a village, anyone who could get out would then dig a tunnel through the snow to a neighbouring hut, and thus the whole village would be gradually freed from its frozen prison. There was always the danger that an outlying place might be overlooked, which is why some exiles moved into less salubrious quarters, but closer to the village, during the winter.[41]

So how did the Poles survive? Relations with the local people or prisoners who had arrived earlier were a vital determinant. Some Poles encountered fellow Poles in the camps: those who had been victims of Stalin's Great Terror. More commonly, they met Ukrainians who had been exiled during the Great Terror. Lucjan Królikowski was appalled by what he learnt from the earlier exiles:

> We were terrified that we might not get out of this place at all. This fear was all the greater because of the passive resignation of the local people, who were convinced that no one was ever permitted to leave the taiga . . . It was impossible to listen to such stories without a cold fear in one's heart. Were we meant never to enjoy freedom again? We were not, after all, criminals; we had never stolen from anybody. In fact, all our own possessions had been stolen from us.[42]

Relations between Poles and Ukrainians had fluctuated greatly during the period of independent Poland and consequently, when the Poles arrived in settlements in Siberia and north European Russia, they experienced different kinds of welcome. Often they were received as fellow deportees, treated with kindness and sympathy, and this helped them to adapt to their drastically changed circumstances. But some Ukrainians joined the Russians in persecuting the Poles, depriving them of any sort of physical or mental comfort in their exile. The most extreme example comes from a transport of Poles by ship to labour camps in the Kolyma region, when the Polish women, along with those from the Baltic States, were subjected to gang rape by the Russian prisoners.[43]

The NKVD ignored, or more probably actively encouraged, rivalry between different nationalities among the deportees. The Poles were presented to the locals as Polish gentry and therefore 'bourgeois oppressors' of the Polish working man, who needed to be taught a lesson. This did not usually arouse the dislike of the locals, but rather their interest and even their sympathy. Despite the damage caused to their clothing by the long and crowded journey into exile, the Poles were still clearly better dressed than the local population and this made them stand out. This might also provide an object lesson to the locals that capitalism enabled a person to own more worldly goods than could be dreamt of under communism. The NKVD recognised that the appearance of the Poles was itself a disruptive influence. Ursula Sowińska arrived at a Siberian labour camp still well dressed, and aroused the initial hatred of the Russian women in the barracks. Appalled by their poverty she shared her belongings with them and became their favourite: 'None of them ever addressed me as Comrade . . . Instead they called me Barishnia, which means "young lady". But soon I was removed from their side as a destructive and undisciplined element.'[44]

The Poles generally have recorded little of their impressions of the native Kazakhs and much of what they have passed on is derogatory. For example, the Kazakhs 'were very short with bow legs and dressed in sheepskins – very ugly-looking', or 'the Kazakhs were repulsively ugly and very unfriendly'. Other Poles realised that there were reasons for the hostility of the Kazakhs as they had only recently been forced to adopt a different lifestyle and to become farmers. Already resentful, the Kazakhs now found that they were going to have to share the kolkhozy with Europeans. Indeed, sometimes the Kazakhs and Uzbeks were hostile towards the Poles at the start because they saw no difference between them and the Russians who had forced them into kolkhozy. As Adam R., a 13-year-old child, recorded: 'They made no difference between us and the Russians and they took it out on us in any way they could, for the Bolsheviks (NKVD) having taken their grain and cattle and for deporting their sons for work.' Only after the Poles made the initial approach and made it clear that they came from Lukistan, as the locals called Poland, and had not chosen to come to Kazakhstan, did relations improve. Friendships were sometimes created between the Poles and

Kazakhs. Stanisław Kochański became very popular with the tractor drivers in Kazakhstan for his curious tales of life in Poland. Eugenia Pavlovna remembered being taken on a long trip to a river by a Kazakh vet to where there were birds and trees, a more familiar landscape than the steppe. Hanna Ryżewska's two children became friendly with local Kyrgyz people and learnt what they thought was an essential skill: to express contempt or astonishment one must spit through clenched teeth like a camel, and the further you spat the greater the emphasis. One Kyrgyz offered to buy 10-year-old Danusia Ryżewska as a wife for his son in exchange for four sheep and two sacks of dried apricots.[45]

Bartering was the most common method for obtaining more food, particularly protein. The Siberian diary of the Milewski family details the trades that they made and their growing sense of alarm as their goods began to run out and starvation loomed. The Poles were perceived as being very wealthy because of the quality of their belongings and in Kazakhstan the local population coveted them. A plain shirt or bed sheets were rare commodities costing more than a month's wages, and therefore a Pole could exchange what was to her a common item for food. One woman traded pieces of plain ribbon, used in Poland for tying pairs of sheets together, to a Kazakh woman and received in return some eggs and a glass of flour. There was, however, always the inherent danger that the NKVD might view bartering as speculation and at times the locals were too frightened to trade with the Poles. Making use of goods brought from Poland and existing household skills could also earn the Poles money and food. Eugenia Pavlovna made clothes from things brought from Poland, including a black ball gown which was cannibalised in all kinds of ways to make or enhance clothes for the locals. The Kazakhs were particularly fond of embroidery, and some Poles could earn a little money or food by embroidering head scarves and petticoats.[46]

Others were reduced to begging and stealing food in order to survive. Hard labour on very little food killed many breadwinners, leaving the older children with the responsibility for their younger siblings. Twelve-year-old Danuta G. recalled that when her mother was too ill to work and her brother too young to work: 'I went from cottage to cottage and sang and so I brought something home.' The problem of begging children increased as the exile continued and more parents died. Other Poles resorted to theft. This could be merely taking opportunities at their place of work: Max Reich worked in a pasta factory in eastern Kazakhstan and stole pasta to feed himself and his family; working near a field of melons provided other Poles with a welcome supplement to their meagre and limited diet. One woman stole mangolds, normally cattle food, and put them to good use. When boiled, they produced a sweet syrupy water which could be used to give a taste to the thin porridge that was their staple diet. The mangold leaves could be dried and smoked as a substitute for tobacco. Thefts also took place between the exiles: someone cut a hole in the wall of Eugenia Pavlovna's hut and stole some clothing which was then probably used for barter with the locals. One young boy, Alfred P., concluded his account of his time in exile: 'I didn't learn anything good from this trouble except stealing.'[47]

One factor that helped the Poles to survive was that contact between the exiles and Soviet-occupied eastern Poland was restored in the late summer of 1940. Apart from the psychological impact of communicating with their loved ones at home, the immediate benefit to the exiles was the arrival of parcels. These could weigh no more than 17 pounds, but they not only supplied much-needed clothing, medicines, money and food but also goods which could be bartered for food. One exile in Kazakhstan wrote of the locals: 'tea was what they coveted more than anything and, very fortunately, we had a little in our baggage, and later some began to arrive in parcels from Lwów'. Sometimes the Soviets would ban the sending of parcels from certain localities in eastern Poland; for example, in autumn and winter of 1940 no parcels could be sent from Lwów or Tarnopol. Resourceful relatives then hired people to take their parcels to other towns where the restrictions were not in force, but in general the parcel service ran well. During the winter no parcels reached one settlement in eastern Kazakhstan, situated on the other side of a range of mountains from the railway station, because of the deep snow, but when the spring came, the by-then starving Poles received three parcels in one month. The occasional dishonest postman stole parcels for his own use, and Zdzisław Jagodziński recorded how a particular man was caught red-handed several times. Other postmen were more honest: the Kochański family were told that money had been sent from Poland for them but that the postman had spent it himself because of urgent need; he promised to repay the family in the future and did so, every rouble. For those deportees who had been refugees from German-occupied Poland prior to their transport east, there were often no relatives to send them parcels; once their money had run out, survival was a desperate struggle.[48]

Life in exile was a psychological struggle as much as a physical one. There are no statistics for the level of mental breakdown among the exiles, and while suicides were not unknown, little reference is made to them. Elizabeth Piekarski recorded that her mother had a complete mental breakdown and her hands would not stop shaking but nevertheless she was expected to continue working: the kindness of her kolkhoz manager obtained her a job in the kitchens where the work was easier. Another woman has given a clear record of how she and her fellow exiles stayed sane:

> My own mind tended more and more to take refuge in fantasies. I did not want to think about reality. I thought constantly of the past and repeated over and over to myself things learnt long before; books read, people met and known, pictures and places seen. When any of us talked together, we always chose these same subjects. Of the present, none of us desired to talk. It was altogether too difficult.[49]

Krzysia Kochańska was seven years old at the time and was so traumatised by her exile in Kazakhstan that she has few memories of it other than sitting on the basket brought from Poland, in which she slept at night, clutching her doll and staring out into space. The same postal service that brought parcels essential for survival could also add to the mental anguish, for letters from Poland often brought news of the arrests of family members. Or there could be no news at all: a letter sent home might just be returned many weeks later to the sender with no explanation. This happened with family members of Polish officers taken to the prison camps of Kozel'sk, Starobel'sk and Ostashkov, and shot by the NKVD in April and May 1940.[50]

The Poles were a deeply religious people and sought to take comfort from their beliefs in these hellish conditions. The Soviet occupation of eastern Poland had given the Poles an introduction to their attitude towards religion: churches had been closed or heavily taxed, yet there were still priests available and church services were possible. In exile, however, there were few priests and therefore limited access to religious ceremonies. The NKVD tore off crucifixes from around people's necks and smashed all religious pictures, prayers were forbidden and people subject to punishment if found praying. Stanisław K. was in a Soviet orphanage and was locked in a lavatory and given no food for two days when he was caught. Yet even the NKVD and local Party members could be unpredictable about religion. One camp director asked the Poles to pray for his sick son and, when the son died, asked them to say prayers and sing hymns at the burial. He could not do so himself because he was a strict communist. Anna Mineyko recalled an interesting illustration of the Soviet attitude towards religion:

> Kyryllo, our overseer, went away for a few days as his wife, Natasha, gave birth to her third son. Natasha came to us asking if the 'old holy woman' (my mother) would christen her child . . . She said that she believed in God, but her husband did not, and that if he found out he would denounce her to the Party. But when Kyryllo came home, he came ashamed and cap in hand to ask my mother the same favour, requesting that we should not tell his unbelieving wife![51]

When Anna was seen praying by an old Kazakh woman, who was a Muslim, she was warned that she could be denounced, but then the Muslim admitted that she also prayed. The Jews in exile shared the same appalling conditions as the other deportees, and were also denied the comfort of their religious beliefs. Zeev F. recalled how his father, a rabbi, organised prayers in the barracks at Yom Kippur: 'soon the NKVD men appeared and arrested him. During the trial he was not punished but it was put in his record that he is a religious offender.'[52]

In Poland, Christmas was a time of great celebration. On Christmas Eve extended families would gather together and, as soon as the first star appeared, sit down to a twelve-course meatless meal. Then the church bells would ring and they would all travel to Midnight Mass. Life in Siberia and Kazakhstan provided a stark contrast. The 24th and 25th of December were considered normal workdays by the Soviets, but the Poles did what they could to avoid working on them. For weeks before, goods were bartered so that some sort of Christmas meal could be created. The Milewski family had half a pint of milk and a spoonful of butter. They made *makojki* from the wheat flour and had a barley soup and sauerkraut with mushrooms and potatoes. Siberia's one small benefit was it could at least readily provide the exiles with Christmas trees but there were no decorations available, so cotton wool was used. The Dobrowolski family in Kazakhstan had a more meagre meal of flour porridge, an onion and a few potatoes. They also used colourful bits of rag to decorate the house and table. The effort his mother and sister had made moved Kazimierz Dobrowolski to tears when he saw it on his return from work. The NKVD may have tried to force the Poles to work at Christmas and have denied them the comfort of their religion but even they knew when to give up: in Siberia the manager kept coming to Apolinary H.'s family hut to stop the carol singers but eventually gave up when they refused to stop singing even when he threatened to take away their bread rations.[53]

Easter was also a very important religious festival in Poland. Again the extended family would gather together to celebrate and to attend several religious services. The dining table would be heaped with meat dishes, pies and roasts, and many types of puddings. The priest would come to the houses of the well-off to bless the Easter food, while the poorer would take theirs to the church for him to bless. In exile none of this was possible. In Siberia, having arrived with the February 1940 deportation, the Milewski family still had enough belongings to barter for food to add to their supplies brought from Poland in order to have a substantial meal, which included bacon, eggs and cakes, but by 1941 the situation was very different. Food resources were almost totally exhausted after the long winter and there appears to have been no attempt to hoard enough for a celebration. In fact, Easter 1941 does not feature at all in the written or oral accounts of exile. In contrast, the great communist 1 May celebrations were definitely noted, not least because in the Siberian camps the Poles got two or three days off work; in return they were supposed to listen to communist speeches and view communist films. Two days later the Poles attempted to celebrate Polish Constitution Day, which was very much frowned upon by the NKVD; nevertheless groups of Poles gathered together to recite the rosary and to pray for salvation from their godless wilderness.[54]

To send a child to school or not was a question many parents faced. In favour of going to school was the continuation of education and also the fact that at school the children were given a slice of bread each day. Since the Poles, particularly the children, were facing starvation this was an important consideration. Renia Kochańska recalled how her teacher would give out slices of bread and then watch the children as they ate them. Whenever a child dropped a crumb, the starving teacher would bend down and pick the crumb up off the floor and eat it.[55] On the other hand, attendance at school meant further exposure to communist propaganda. The deportees were taught in Russian, which in many cases they had to learn from scratch. They also followed the Soviet curriculum, as they had been doing during the Soviet occupation of Poland. This extract gives a flavour of what they were taught about Glasgow:

> A large industrial centre in Scotland. The population consists of 95 per cent exploited proletarians and five per cent of bloodsucker-bourgeois. Every evening the bourgeois drive in their limousines, bespattering with mud the proletarians who look for the leavings of food in the gutters and dustbins. And every morning the police remove from the streets a dozen or so corpses of proletarians who had died of hunger.[56]

Along with other Russian children they sat exams and obtained certificates, and, the Poles having on the whole been used to a higher standard of education, found the work very easy.

Attendance at school could also cause other problems, both accidental and deliberate, with serious consequences. Vala Miron sat her exams, which went well until her Russian oral. Asked a question about Stalin, 'through a difficulty in pronunciation I accidentally said "Louse Comrade Stalin"'. The examiners turned pale with fury and that night her father was summoned to see the NKVD. He managed to convince them that it had been a genuine mistake in his daughter's pronunciation: in Russian *Voshch* means a leader, while *Vosh*, which sounds very similar, is a louse. However, on 1 May in Siberia, as recalled by Stefania Buczak-Zarzycka, another Polish girl deliberately provoked the Soviet authorities. Every member of the class was given a sweet and a biscuit, and the teacher announced that 'Father Stalin loves all children without prejudice.' A Russian girl then sang 'Papa Stalin gives us sweets, the whole world loves him.' Whereupon a Polish girl stood up and said, 'Papa Stalin gives us soap, because all lice have wings.' Dragged off to the headmaster's office for questioning whether her parents had taught her this, she replied that she was a poetess and had written the verse herself; nevertheless, her father was sentenced to six months in a hard labour camp. Similarly, the fathers of children who drew a pair of spectacles on a portrait of Stalin and an angel at Christmas were also sentenced to six months. Some children were educated at home: one family had a Polish recipe book and used it to teach the youngest child to read and write, which made them all feel very hungry.[57]

The NKVD were omnipotent in Siberia and Kazakhstan. Non-commissioned officers were the labour camp overseers and the Poles were always under threat. The kolkhoz managers, if not actually members of the NKVD, were in close contact with them and ready to punish Poles and, indeed the other nationalities, for any infraction. Any relatively minor misdemeanour could lead to imprisonment: one man received a sentence of ten years' hard labour for criticising Stalin when drunk, another was imprisoned for several months for singing a religious song. The most common and most frightening contacts between the NKVD and Poles came at night when, usually between 2 and 3 a.m., NKVD officers would come into the huts to question the Poles and 'each time we were put through the same round of questions', which always centred on the whereabouts of the men of the family who had escaped arrest in Poland. The experiences of the Kochański family are probably typical of such interrogations. After many visits, one officer finally suggested that the mother should write to the prosecutor's office in Stanisławów supplying the address where her husband and son were hiding, and then the NKVD might consider allowing the family to return to Poland. The family discussed this offer but told the NKVD that the missing family members were in Lwów and that they had no address for them. (In fact, at the time, Leon Kochański was in NKVD custody in Stanisławów but the NKVD in Kazakhstan were unaware of this.)[58]

Escape from exile was almost unheard of. Maria Borkowska-Witkowska, swept into the river when rolling logs in Siberia, was rescued by an escaped prisoner, but she did not know whether he was Polish, Russian or some other nationality. In Kazakhstan 'the absence of roads or of any other communities, the impossibility of anywhere procuring food, the infinite expanses of desert and the hostility of the natives, made any ideas of escape perfectly futile', but such circumstances did not stop Eugenia Pavlovna from trying. She had the advantage of having lived for a number of years in Russia and spoke Russian with a Moscow accent, and she had enough jewellery to be able to bribe the necessary people to get a travel permit. She was, however, betrayed by a Russian woman in Troitsk before she even got the permit. Fortunately for her, the local NKVD man was not interested in deportees and she escaped punishment.[59]

The Polish and British governments were aware of the deportations from Poland but had little idea of the conditions in exile. But everything changed suddenly when on 22 June 1941 Germany launched its invasion of the Soviet Union. This event, cataclysmic for millions, proved to be salvation for the Polish exiles. It is no exaggeration to say that it saved the lives of many of the Poles in Siberia and Kazakhstan. Following an intense period of negotiations presided over by the British, the Sikorski–Maisky agreement was signed on 30 July, and among its provisions an amnesty was granted to all the Poles who had been exiled to the Soviet Union in 1940 and 1941, freeing them from their camps and kolkhozy. Furthermore, a Polish army was to be formed in the Soviet Union. News of the amnesty filtered slowly to the deportees, and everywhere the news was greeted with jubilation. Teresa Lipkowska recorded their reaction: 'When we received the news of the conclusion of the Polish-Soviet Treaty and of the formation of the Polish Army, an indescribable enthusiasm was visible on every face. The people began embracing each other, crying and singing.' Liberty appeared to be within reach.[60] But their sufferings had not yet ended. As the Poles travelled south to join the Polish Army, a humanitarian crisis unfolded. They were already so weakened by disease and starvation that they continued dying on reaching the Polish camps. It has been estimated as a very rough figure that altogether between 15 and 20 per cent of the Poles deported from eastern Poland had died by the end of 1941.

# 6

## Escape from the Soviet Union

The launch of Operation Barbarossa was one of the turning points of the Second World War, the 'invasion too far' that would lead to Germany's ultimate defeat four years later. On the evening of 22 June 1941, Churchill made a radio broadcast in which he welcomed the Soviet Union as an ally in the war against Germany and pledged 'any technical or economic assistance which is in our power, and which is likely to be of service to them'.[1] On 23 June, Sikorski broadcast to Poland and stated that the Polish Government was 'entitled to assume that in these circumstances Russia will cancel the Pact of 1939. That should logically bring us back to the position governed by the Treaty concluded in Riga on 13 March 1921.' He also made an emotional appeal:

> For the love of their country, their freedom and honour, thousands of Polish men and women, including 300,000 war prisoners, are still suffering in Russian prisons. Should it not be deemed right and honest to restore these people to their liberty?[2]

The Polish ambassador to the United States, Jan Ciechanowski, discussed these speeches with Sumner Welles, the undersecretary of state, and felt personally that Churchill should have demanded the end of the Fourth Partition of Poland before pledging assistance to the Soviet Union. He wrote that Welles largely agreed with him, suggesting that 'it would have been better for all concerned if some time had been allowed to elapse and the Soviets had applied to the British government for help and support'.[3] It was certainly frustrating that at the one moment Britain could credibly have bargained with the Soviet Union over Poland's future, and other issues, no attempt was made to do so. The Soviet reaction to Sikorski was immediate: *Izvestia* criticised him for daring to raise the question of the frontier. Thus the stage was set for negotiations to begin in London between Sikorski and the Soviet ambassador, Ivan Maisky, under the watchful eye of the Foreign Office. In Moscow there were also discussions on the Polish question between Stalin and the British ambassador there, Sir Stafford Cripps.

Before considering these negotiations, it is worth examining British and Polish policy towards the Soviet Union during the period of the Molotov–Ribbentrop Pact. British policy is perhaps the easiest to define. Chamberlain had rebuked the Soviet Government for its invasion of Poland but refused to go so far as lodging an official protest. The British ambassador in Moscow, Sir William Seeds, was not withdrawn, but was recalled to London in protest at the Soviet invasion of Finland. In the meantime he was able to report to London on the conditions in Soviet-occupied eastern Poland and on the deportations. Kennard, the former British ambassador in Poland, provided further information.[4] Britain was not at war with the Soviet Union and so did not see the need to publicise Soviet atrocities in Poland, even while it was prepared to voice its disapproval of those by the Nazis. Britain appeared to view the Nazi-Soviet alliance as temporary: sooner or later Hitler would turn on the Soviet Union and Britain would then want the Soviet Union as an ally against Germany. Cripps was appointed ambassador to Moscow on 31 May 1940 to try to bring about an improvement in the relations between Britain and the Soviet Union, but he met with limited success until the German invasion.[5]

The Polish position was far more complex. The Polish Government considered itself at war with the Soviet Union as well as with Germany. On 3 February 1940, it had lodged a protest with the allied and neutral governments about the Soviet policy of conscripting Poles into the Red Army.[6] Yet Sikorski saw some benefit in opening some form of contact with the Soviet Union, by possibly asking the British Government for assistance since Cripps was about to leave for Moscow. Sikorski also held the view that the present alliance between Germany and the Soviet Union was likely to be only temporary. His principal concern was that the Soviet Union should refrain from making further deportations from Poland and should cease its reign of terror there. But what he had to offer the Soviet Union is far more obscure.

Shortly after his arrival in London in June 1940, Sikorski asked Stefan Litauer, head of the Polish news agency in London, to prepare a memorandum on the Polish Government's future policy towards the Soviet Union which he planned to show to Churchill. It was shown to the Polish ambassador in Britain, Raczyński, and Józef Retinger, who was variously described as an *éminence grise* and an arch-intriguer. Both men were appalled by the memorandum and hastily redrafted it. This version was not shown to Churchill but was certainly discussed with Halifax. A proposal contained in both was for the creation of a Polish army of around 300,000 men to be formed in the Soviet Union for use in a war against Germany. The differences between the two memoranda and the other draft material produced at the time centre on the future Polish-Soviet frontier. It is not clear whether Sikorski was determined to defend the Riga Line at all costs on the grounds that it had been settled through negotiations between the Polish and Soviet governments in 1921, or whether he was open to making some concessions. In light of the later dispute over Poland's eastern frontier, it should be stressed that Sikorski never appears to have considered the Curzon Line as the future border, but was only willing to compromise to the extent of conceding most of Polesie, eastern Wołyń and Podole, areas of little economic value to Poland. His efforts in 1940 to reach a rapprochement with the Soviet Union were effectively ended almost as soon as they began. The arrival in London of the Polish cabinet ministers, including the staunchly anti-Soviet foreign minister, August Zaleski, led to a serious government crisis in July 1940 over the issue.[7]

Sikorski continued to develop his policy towards the Soviet Union, cautiously trying to manoeuvre between different factions and viewpoints. As evidence mounted up that Germany was about to invade the Soviet Union, in June 1941 Sikorski expounded his government's policy in a conversation with Cripps, then on leave in London, telling Cripps that he 'saw no reason why Poland should not assist Russia in the event of the outbreak of war against Germany, after an adequate change in their relations'. He had added that the principle to be adopted by the Polish cabinet was that 'the first and main enemy of Poland is Germany, and that, should full Polish sovereignty be recognised within her pre-war frontiers, cooperation between Poland and the Soviet Union would be possible'.[8]

The stakes were therefore high when Sikorski and Maisky met on 5 July 1941 to discuss the conditions required for a resumption of diplomatic relations between Poland and the Soviet Union. Soviet armies were reeling under the German onslaught and had been largely driven off the Polish territory they had occupied. Both the British and the Poles feared that the Soviets would be unable to withstand German pressure and might conclude a separate peace. For Sikorski, this would mean a lost opportunity to rescue the Poles trapped in the Soviet Union; for the British, Soviet power was deemed essential for the ultimate defeat of Germany, and consequently they exerted pressure on Sikorski to make compromises and conclude a quick settlement. For the Soviets, a treaty with the Poles would be little more than good public relations, a means to show to the world that the Soviet Union was a friendly power, a worthy recipient of military aid, and did not harbour expansionist intentions towards its neighbours.

Sikorski immediately attempted to gain a tactical advantage for the first meeting by proposing that Maisky meet him at the Polish headquarters at the Rubens Hotel and gave the precise time. Alexander Cadogan, permanent under secretary at the Foreign Office thought this request 'odd' and smoothed ruffled feathers by suggesting that the two men meet instead on 'neutral' ground at his office.[9] At this first meeting Sikorski made the Polish position clear: the Soviet Government must denounce the treaties with Germany which had partitioned Poland in 1939, and must accept the resumption of normal diplomatic relations between the two countries and the appointment of a Polish ambassador in Moscow. Poland in return would collaborate in the common fight against Germany, and a Polish army would be formed on Soviet soil or be transported elsewhere if that was deemed desirable. In addition, all Polish military and political prisoners were to be freed. Zaleski attempted to up the stakes by telling Maisky the bizarre lie that the Germans were proposing the formation of a puppet government in Poland and offering 'a most considerable extension of their eastern boundaries'.[10] This veiled threat had not been approved by Sikorski, and Zaleski was excluded from further negotiations.

At a second meeting, on 11 July, in the presence of the British foreign secretary, Anthony Eden, the battle lines were clearly drawn. Sikorski wanted the immediate release of all Polish POWs because these men would form the backbone of his new Polish army in the Soviet Union. His figures of 180,000 rank and file and 10,000 officers were based on information released by the Soviet authorities in 1940. Maisky disputed these numbers and argued that there were only 20,000 Polish POWs, claiming that the Soviet authorities had released the majority from POW camps and they were now scattered throughout the Soviet Union in labour camps. He agreed that the Poles who had been or were still POWs would be released immediately after the signature of an agreement with Sikorski. Maisky disputed Sikorski's demand for recognition of the Riga Line, citing the results of the 1939 elections and plebiscites in eastern Poland, but he realised that the negotiations could break down totally over this issue and so offered to postpone its final settlement until later. Eden attempted to reassure the Poles that it was safe to proceed with the frontier question unsettled, by confirming the British Government's position that any territorial changes made during the war would not be recognised.[11] Sikorski was prepared to accept British assurances over the frontier and to continue the negotiations if the subject of the release of Polish civilian deportees and political prisoners was settled, but this too was a major hurdle which nearly ended the negotiations. Maisky argued that if 'after Russia occupied Polish territory one Pole had committed a political crime for which he had been sentenced', he could see no grounds for his release now. Maisky was in a difficult position: to agree to the release of the civilian deportees and political prisoners would be to admit that the Soviet occupation of eastern Poland had been an illegal act. Sikorski's position was that these Poles 'could only be regarded as having committed political crimes because they remained Polish citizens', and for him not to demand their release would be tantamount to accepting that the Soviet authorities had the right to judge and condemn Polish citizens. Eden, worried that the negotiations might collapse, suggested that the question of Polish prisoners should be postponed until after diplomatic relations had been resumed, but neither the Poles nor the Soviets were prepared to delay on this issue.[12]

The talks were often close to stalemate. There were delays while Maisky communicated with Moscow, and poor telegraph communications meant that it often took two days to get a reply as Stalin was preoccupied with Soviet defence efforts against the German onslaught. The Foreign Office encountered similar difficulties in communicating with Cripps, who was trying to help the negotiations by direct contact with Stalin and Molotov. Sikorski was also painfully aware of discontent and suspicion within his own government: there was a particularly stormy cabinet meeting on 15 July while he was in Scotland explaining the proposed pact to the Polish Army in training there. Sikorski's intelligence chief, Colonel Leon Mitkiewicz, noted in his diary:

> The opposition group around General Sosnkowski and Foreign Minister Zaleski as well as President Raczkiewicz's entourage, including the President himself, represent the view that an understanding with Russia is *in principle* necessary *in our present conditions*; but, there is no need to press the issue, we should wait until Russia herself offers us favourable terms: boundaries according to the Treaty of Riga.[13]

On 21 July, Sikorski promised not to sign any treaty unless the Soviets agreed to the Polish position, especially with regard to the political prisoners. At the cabinet meeting on 25 July, when it was clear that Stalin would not agree to the Polish points, Sikorski indicated that he would sign. Three cabinet ministers promptly resigned: Zaleski, General Sosnkowski, the deputy president, and Marian Seyda, the justice minister and leader of the right-wing National Democrats.[14] Raczkiewicz denied Sikorski the powers to sign the agreement, so Retinger approached the British for advice, and the Foreign Office came up with a solution:

> It was decided that since the treaty between Russia and Britain had been signed only by the British ambassador in Moscow and Molotov, similarly it would not be necessary for this agreement to bear the President's signature, all the more so as the Foreign Office had been informed that Maisky was not going to ask for an exchange of credentials and powers, seeing that he was dealing with the head of the Government.[15]

Then to everyone's surprise Cripps achieved a breakthrough, when on 27 July, he met Stalin and Molotov, and as he recorded in his diary: 'The thing that I was really pleased about was that I persuaded him [Stalin] to grant an immediate amnesty to every Polish citizen detained in this country.'[16] Sikorski was now ready to sign the treaty.

On 30 July, the Polish-Soviet agreement, also known as the Sikorski–Maisky pact, was signed. Churchill's private secretary, Jock Colville, wrote: 'It was signed against a background of spotlights and a foreground of cameramen by the P.M., Eden, Sikorski and Maisky, while the bust of the Younger Pitt looked down, rather disapprovingly I thought.'[17] The terms were: the Soviet Union 'recognises the Soviet-German Treaties of 1939 as to territorial changes in Poland as having lost their validity'; diplomatic relations were to be restored along with an exchange of ambassadors; a Polish army would be formed on Soviet soil under a commander appointed by the Polish Government in agreement with the Soviet Government; and, in a protocol, an amnesty* was granted to 'all Polish citizens now detained on Soviet territory'.[18] Eden gave Sikorski credit for the agreement: 'our part was only patient diplomacy tinged with anxiety for what the future must hold for the Poles as the weaker partner'.[19] Maisky claimed credit for the Soviet Union: 'I will only say that they were very difficult negotiations, and that several times they were on the verge of rupture. However, the insistence and flexibility of the Soviet government in the long run overcame all obstacles.'[20] Raczyński felt that the agreement had been concluded as a result of British and American pressure on both the Poles and Soviets,[21] but Sikorski denied that he had bowed to British pressure, and indeed argued that he had forced Eden to take part in the negotiations.[22] The reaction from the political parties in Poland was one of cautious approval: most parties were still clearly hostile to the Soviet Union and uneasy about the lack of a specific and firm agreement on the eastern frontier.[23]

The Sikorski–Maisky pact was followed by other important agreements. On 12 August, the Presidium of the Supreme Council of the USSR issued a decree stating: 'An amnesty is granted to all Polish citizens on Soviet territory at present deprived of their freedom as prisoners of war or on other adequate grounds.'[24] On 14 August, a Polish-Soviet military agreement was signed by General Zygmunt Szyszko-Bohusz and General Alexander Vassilevsky, establishing a Polish army in the Soviet Union. This would be part of Poland's armed forces and owe allegiance to the Polish Government. While it would be operationally subordinate to the Red Army, it was under the authority of the Polish armed forces in respect to its organisation and personnel. The size of the army was to be dependent on the manpower, equipment and supplies available, but would be at least two divisions. The Polish Army would be a land force only, and former members of and volunteers for the Polish Air Force and Navy would be transported to Britain to join the existing Polish services there. Polish citizens, both men and women, in

---

* The use of 'amnesty' was allegedly an error since the word normally suggests some previous wrongdoing on the part of the person being amnestied. According to Retinger, the word should have been 'release' but was accidentally replaced by 'amnesty' by the Polish diplomat Mr Potulicki who drafted the document.

the Soviet Union could volunteer for the Polish Army. Finally, the Polish Army would not be sent to the front until it was fully ready for action and would not operate in units smaller than a division.[25]

Sikorski appointed his close friend Professor Stanisław Kot as the new Polish ambassador to the Soviet Union, and his confidant Retinger as chargé d'affaires. Both these choices have been described as 'unfortunate'.[26] Kot had no experience of diplomacy and, having been brought up in Austrian-run Galicia, had no knowledge of the Russian language or people. The appointment took Kot himself by surprise: he did not want the job and delayed his departure by six weeks to arrange his affairs. He had to work in close collaboration with Molotov, whom he described as 'wooden and unctuous, constantly repeating the same phrases, always inflexible, he was the incarnation of banality'. More commonly Kot had meetings with Molotov's deputy, Andrei Vyshinsky, the former chief prosecutor in the Moscow show trials during the Great Terror, and as Kot described him:

> In private conversation Vyshinsky was very affable, good-humoured, and fond of a joke. In official conversations he resorted to a wide range of argument and unexpected changes of mood, from good manners, laughter, and jest, through civility and chilly courtesy to petty spite, sarcasm, positive rudeness, cynicism, and brutal attacks.[27]

The relations between the two men fluctuated as Soviet policy itself moved: from initial cooperation, to the usual Soviet policy of obstruction, finally descending into downright hostility. Kot left the Soviet Union in July 1942 and was replaced by Tadeusz Romer. There is plenty of evidence to suggest that the Polish Army in the Soviet Union, with Soviet connivance, generally ignored the embassy.

Sikorski nominated General Władysław Anders as commander of the Polish Army in the Soviet Union. Anders had commanded the Nowogródzka Cavalry Brigade in the September 1939 campaign, during which he had been wounded in clashes with both the German and the Soviet armies. He and his troops had been captured by the Soviets and Anders had been imprisoned in Lwów and then in the Lubyanka in Moscow, and was released on the announcement of the amnesty. Sikorski favoured Anders above the more experienced General Mieczysław Boruta-Spiechowicz and General Michał Karaszewicz-Tokarzewski because, unlike them, he was untainted by collaboration with the *Sanacja* regime. Indeed, Sikorski's determination to distance his government from the pre-war government led him to issue orders that officers of the Piłsudski Legions and some other named officers should be excluded from the new Polish Army, orders which Anders ignored. Anders had been brought up in Russian-controlled Poland and had served in the Russian Army during the First World War, spoke fluent Russian and had a clear understanding of the Russian mentality. The choice was a popular one within the Polish military circles in the Soviet Union. General Szyszko-Bohusz wrote to Retinger in September 1941:

> Of the greatest importance is the personality of General Anders, who has the complete trust equally of Soviets and Poles. Without exaggeration, I can say that he is a central character not only for us but for the Soviets as well. They consider him as someone who could play an extremely important role for them, so they take good care of him. Without exaggeration, I can also say that here no one else can accomplish anything. For example, all the problems with the transfer of our civilian population did not begin to move until Anders came back from Buzuluk to Moscow. What the Polish Embassy could not accomplish in two weeks he did in half a day; and even got the Russians to follow through on their promises. This was not a fault of our Embassy but a manifestation that Soviet authorities trust only Anders, want to talk only with him and accept almost without objection his demands.[28]

Sikorski would soon discover that he had unleashed a powerful challenger to his authority. Anders harboured such hatred for the Soviets and inspired such loyalty from his troops, who shared his opinions, that he would on occasions pursue a line independent from and in conflict with Sikorski's wishes.

A Polish military mission was despatched to the Soviet Union, led by General Szyszko-Bohusz, to work alongside the Soviet military mission to the Polish Army. This was nominally led by General Alexei Panfilov while real power rested with the NKVD representative General Georgi Zhukov (no relation to the Zhukov who would take Berlin). The Poles were also expected to work closely with the British military mission led by General Noel Mason-MacFarlane, and Colonel Leslie Hulls was appointed as British military assistant to Anders.[29] The Soviet and Polish military missions met on 19 August and agreed on the formation of two Polish infantry divisions: the 5th at Tatischevo, to be commanded by General Boruta-Spiechowicz, and the 6th at Totskoye, to be commanded by General Karaszewicz-Tokarzewski. The Polish headquarters would be based at Buzuluk on the Volga river.[30]

Sikorski had plans for the formation of a powerful Polish army in the Soviet Union. Using the figures supplied by the Soviets in 1940, he knew that he should have at his disposal: 10 generals, 52 colonels; 72 lieutenant-colonels; 5,131 regular officers; 4,096 reserve officers, and 181,223 other ranks. The British agreed with his assessment: 'It is believed that the total number of Poles who might eventually become available in Russia is 120,000–150,000.'[31] Neither the Polish nor the British governments had any idea of the fate of the Polish POWs or civilian deportees since they had vanished from sight into the depths of the Soviet Union, but while they accepted that a substantial number might have perished, they anticipated that the two divisions could be easily filled by men who had served in the Polish Army of 1939, creating a force totalling 30,000. The Soviets readily accepted this figure; but what the Poles did not realise until later was that the Soviet authorities expected the Poles to limit the army to 30,000, whereas the Poles expected the freedom to recruit as many divisions as possible. This is why when the Poles announced the formation of the new army, recruitment was thrown open to all Polish citizens who had been resident in Poland on 1 September 1939. The rank and file would be recruited from those born between 1897 and 1923 inclusive, with preference for former soldiers who had been taken as POWs by the Soviets. The officers were to be recruited from those born in 1892 or later, retired and reserve officers, and those mobilised in 1939.[32]

On 5 September, Anders met Kot for the first time and received Sikorski's written instructions on the formation of the Polish Army in the Soviet Union. No mention was made of numbers but the troops were to be deployed only 'after they have attained full combat readiness', and 'I wish in the first place that the troops may be used in a way enabling them to fulfil single-handed a task which would be important from the point of view of the whole war, and secondly that they may cooperate as closely as possible with our British Allies.' Sikorski's strong preference was that the Polish Army should be deployed to defend the oilfields in the Caucasus because that was a 'very important and self-sufficient task' and 'they would have the opportunity of stretching a hand to our British Allies and of fighting side by side with them as well as with the

Russian ally'. He expected that the British would supply the Polish Army with uniforms and equipment. In his instructions to Kot, Sikorski had stressed that by Poles he meant all who had held Polish citizenship in September 1939 and urged Kot to remain firm on this point in negotiations with the Soviets. Sikorski also expected the Soviets to release the Poles they had conscripted into the Red Army.[33]

On 25 August 1941, Jan Szczyrek and Emanuel Freyd were appointed to head the new Polish Welfare Committee, which was tasked with discovering how many Poles were in the Soviet Union and whether they were being released from their camps in accordance with the amnesty. They were to be directed southwards towards a better climate and the Polish Army. Delegates were appointed to head regional and local committees, and 'men of trust' appointed in areas with fewer than fifty Polish families, all of whom would be responsible for ensuring the welfare of those unable to work and for distributing aid received from the International Red Cross.[34] From the third week of September, the Polish authorities were in position to direct the Poles to the army camps: representatives were sent to the key railway stations such as Kuibyshev, Gorki and Novosibirsk.[35]

What the Soviets had offered the Poles under the terms of the Sikorski–Maisky pact and what the Poles were demanding in the practical application of these terms was unprecedented. Never before had such a general amnesty been proclaimed. The Soviets were notoriously suspicious of foreigners and yet now they had agreed to the formation of a foreign army on their soil whose loyalty rested with a foreign government based in London. As if that was not enough, the Soviets were now expected to allow representatives of this foreign power, Polish delegates, complete freedom of movement throughout the Soviet Union. The Soviets did not find it easy: indeed, Colonel Hulls had to wait for over four months for permission to enter the Soviet Union, and his American counterpart was refused a visa.[36] The formation of the Polish Army was also taking place at a time of immense pressure on Soviet resources and infrastructure. The Germans were still advancing on all fronts and the Red Army was taking massive losses. The railway system, weak at the best of times, was subjected to the strain of having to move the Red Army westwards and evacuating factories and workers to the east, as well as coping with the flow of Poles from the north to the south.

*

The reaction of the Poles to the news of the amnesty stunned the Polish and Soviet authorities and caught them totally unprepared for the wholesale movement of all who could leave. Some Poles received the information from the NKVD, while others saw the news published in the Soviet newspapers or heard it broadcast on the radio. In some areas the Poles were called to formal meetings with the NKVD and given special release documents (*adostovierenya*) and food rations and directed to the nearest railway station.[37] Those in labour camps in the most remote Kotlas region heard of the amnesty months later from 'men who, having been taken prisoner by the enemy, managed to escape back to the Soviet side. These men were immediately arrested, we were told, by the Soviets (no doubt as potentially dangerous) and shipped to Kotlas.'[38] Others in the labour camps heard of the amnesty in October but were not released for another month; but in the interim the deportees were entitled to 100 per cent rations regardless of how much work they did.[39] Wherever they were, as soon as the news of the amnesty reached them the Poles moved south 'like a swollen river blindly rushing ahead', desperately seeking recruitment into or at least the protection of the army.[40] Adam Gołębiowski recorded: 'our joy in expectation of a release was irrepressible and incomprehensible to the Russians, depressed, puzzled and those in charge of administration probably concerned that the plans imposed on them by higher authorities will not now be fulfilled in time'. The Gulag authorities realised that they would be unable to fulfil their quotas without Polish manpower.[41]

In many camps in the northernmost parts of the Soviet Union, the Poles needed to make rafts to drift down the rivers to reach the nearest railway. At Yarensk these were made for every family who wanted to leave; the men cut down the trees and 'the women and young children gathered vines which the older children boiled and these were used to bind the logs together'.[42] Others did not travel until the winter and had to make sledges, and 'we found the snow to be so deep that we were up to our armpits at almost every step, and we trudged this way for a whole week' covering a distance of 60 miles.[43] Heartbreaking decisions had to be made: to travel into an unknown future or to wait for the authorities to organise their departure, and sometimes family members had to be left behind because they were too sick to travel. The Poles, intoxicated with their freedom, became very aware of the Russian prisoners left behind:

In two separate places we came across political prisoners in the Gulag . . .
Despite it being winter, they wore only rags, and tatters, their feet bound
in rags, their hands frost-bitten. In conversation one could easily recognise
that these were educated people. What was absolutely certain was, that
none of them would ever emerge from that place, because their sentences
stretched from 30 to 40 years.[44]

There were many examples of these doomed Gulag prisoners giving
the Poles lifts in their lorries to the nearest railway station.

Reaching the nearest station marked for many the beginning of
another nightmare. Wanda Godawa reached Kotlas to discover that the
station was 'awash with Polish families, all hungry, huddling in rags
because of the cold and, like us, anxious to board any goods train
travelling south'.[45] Many Poles record their feelings of frustration and
desperation as train after train, packed with Poles, passed through their
station without stopping. For the most part the NKVD did their best to
facilitate their movement, issuing tickets and directing them to trains
where available, but some Poles did not receive assistance. Anna Belińska
reached a station to find it full of people and no sight of a train:

> My husband searched out the station master to ask what might be done.
> His suggestion was that my husband should determine which people really
> wanted to travel on and collect from them sufficient money to hire an
> engine, trucks and driver. And this is what happened. Those who could
> afford it paid for a place.[46]

Food and water were difficult to obtain and families became separated
as some members left the train to scavenge for supplies and then missed
its departure. For others there were joyful reunions as men located their
families after two years' separation. The train journey was the end for
many as hunger and illness took their toll: 'At each stop the corpses of
dead children were taken off, indeed our entire route was strewn with
the bodies of children.'[47]

Kot claimed that the policy of the embassy was: 'where free settlers
have a roof over their heads and the possibility of at least minimum
earnings, they should not move'. This revealed his ignorance of the true
state of Poles in Kazakhstan. They had been called 'administrative
exiles', and this seems have confused the Polish authorities, who appear
to have thought that they had sufficient means to sustain a reasonable

level of living. In addition the newly freed deportees from the north joined those already in Kazakhstan since April 1940. The Polish authorities ordered the latter deportees to remain on their kolkhozy until the Polish Army was in a position to receive, train and, above all, feed the new recruits.[48] In fact the German invasion of the Soviet Union led to a further deterioration of conditions on the kolkhozy, as every able-bodied Soviet male had been called up for military service, creating more work for the Poles, and the state had raised the quotas so high that little food remained to feed the workers; famine was a real possibility.

The flood of desperate Poles from the frozen north to the warmer climes of Uzbekistan and Kazakhstan led to a humanitarian crisis. There was too little food to sustain them all in the south, and their departure from the work camps in the north was damaging the Soviet war economy. Vyshinsky accordingly asked Kot to put an end to the movement, but Kot said that he was powerless to stop it. Then in November the Soviet authorities moved 45,000 civilian Poles from Uzbekistan to Kazakhstan, where the conditions were marginally better, and stopped revealing the news of the amnesty to those Poles still trapped in labour and POW camps.[49] The new influxes from the north were sent to kolkhozy where they had to work digging irrigation ditches and picking cotton for their food rations. Conditions were dire and in many cases worse than the labour camps they had left. Wiesława Derfel recalled: 'We ate almost anything: hog-weed, lucerne, nettles, sometimes stolen melons and apricots, we even hunted for hedgehogs, lizards and crows.'[50] The civilians were filled with a terrible fear that, scattered throughout Uzbekistan and Kazakhstan, they might be overlooked by the Polish authorities when spring came.

The civilians also found that the Polish delegates could be unhelpful on occasions. Thirteen-year-old Felicja Szalaśny faced a dilemma: her mother died shortly after they reached Uzbekistan, so she went to the Polish delegate at Zyadin and asked for a place at the orphanage, but was told that she was too old and turned away. She then tried to join the Junaks (Oddziały Junaków), the Polish cadet force, but was told that she was too young: 'so I found myself out on the streets, with nowhere to go'. In tears and starving, she was approached by two other delegates, who listened to her story, shared their food with her and found her a place at the orphanage in Zerbulak.[51] In February 1942, the Milewski family finally reached Kuibyshev from Siberia and thought that their travails had ended, but they were wrong: 'I ran to the embassy thinking that I would be welcomed as a hero. But they welcomed us like dogs. We were put in a school: a nest of dirt, disease and starvation. We had to sleep on the floor.'[52]

The state of the POWs staggering into the army camps appalled the witnesses. A Polish deportee Eugenia Pavlovna boarded a train in Kazakhstan full of former soldiers and recorded the shattering impression they made on her:

> What I saw was a collection of skeletons covered in rugs, their feet wrapped in newspaper or dirty cloth, kept in place with pieces of string, although many had nothing on their feet at all. There was not a normal face to be seen. They were either very thin, the colour and texture of yellow parchment, or bloated and shapeless like the face of a drowned man. Their eyes were sunken and either completely lifeless or glowing feverishly. They all looked old and shrivelled although some of them, at least, must have been young.[53]

She was appalled to learn from these men that they were the fittest to leave their prison camps and that many had been too sick to travel. Another witness provided a description of the arrival of the men at the Polish army camps:

> They came exhausted, in rags, impoverished, covered with sores, louse-infected, without hair, having come through typhus, and resembling rather some strange creatures more than human beings. They made their way with the last efforts of their dwindling strength. And it happened on occasion that near the station, or in the yard of the Recruitment Commission, they expired. They died quite simply from exhaustion, from having wasted away, on the very threshold of a new life.[54]

The Polish military authorities suspected that the Soviet authorities were deliberately releasing the sickest men and retaining the fittest for labour, and Kot pressed Vyshinsky repeatedly to speed up the release of the Polish POWs.[55] The Poles who reached the camps brought news of others: nearly 20,000 Poles had been forced to work in the lead mines of Kolyma but only a few hundred were fit enough to attempt the journey south to the army, and out of these only 20 arrived; all the 3,000 Poles who had worked in the lead mines of northern Kamchatka had died of lead poisoning before the amnesty.[56]

Sikorski and Anders were in total agreement on the subject of the recruitment of all Polish nationals, regardless of ethnicity, although Anders would have liked to restrict the recruitment of Jews to a figure commensurate with the percentage of Jews in the pre-war population of Poland. Even at a time of overwhelming crisis, the mentalities of the Second Republic remained intact. The NKVD interfered in the recruitment process through its representatives present in the Polish army camps. One recruit recalled:

> I was seen by a Polish doctor, by a Russian doctor and by an NKVD officer. I was young and healthy and my surname was a typical Polish surname. However, if there was a surname that sounded Ukrainian or Jewish, the NKVD man asked a lot of embarrassing questions. He tried to stop Ukrainians joining the Polish army. The same happened to Jews – if they had a typical Jewish name they had some difficulty. But some of the Ukrainians and Jews were caught trying to pretend they were Poles . . . The Ukrainians looked like Poles, but if they stumbled and made mistakes [in the language] they weren't permitted to join the Polish army.[57]

On 1 December, the Soviets issued a note stating: 'Only the levying of Poles from Western Ukraine and Western Belorussia is permitted. Other nationalities are not to be included in the levy.'[58] The NKVD directed those of Ukrainian, Belorussian and Jewish origin to the Red Army. The failure to recruit a significant number of members of the national minorities into the Polish Army rebounded on the Polish authorities later when the question of its evacuation from the Soviet Union arose. Then it was claimed that the Poles were deliberately hampering the efforts of these people to join the Polish Army, whereas the truth was that the NKVD and the Soviet military authorities were deliberately attempting to restrict the eligibility of Polish citizens to the army for political purposes.

Evidence also emerged that the NKVD was trying to suborn former Polish soldiers and recruits. The Polish authorities were aware of the problem, and in the instructions Kot received from Sikorski, he was advised: 'everything possible must be done to the effect of protecting the Polish troops formed on Soviet territory from the influence of Soviet propaganda'.[59] Many Poles were subjected to pressure to act as NKVD informers and to pass information on the organisation of the Polish army, the embassy and the relief effort.[60] On his release Colonel

Klemens Rudnicki, who had successfully concealed his officer status from the NKVD by adopting a false identity, was asked to sign a statement that he 'would undertake to denounce to the NKVD all persons suspected of activities obnoxious to the Polish or Soviet Governments, or to their common cause'. Rudnicki refused, but he later discovered that many officers and men had signed the declaration and were then blackmailed by the NKVD. These men now tried to change their names or join other garrisons, and some disappeared without trace. The Soviets also bugged the Polish headquarters at Buzuluk; Anders removed the hidden microphones and returned them to the highly embarrassed Soviet liaison officer, Colonel Wołkowyski. But the Soviets repeated the offence when building the new Polish headquarters in Yangiyul in Uzbekistan, and the Poles discovered that all the wires from the microphones led to Wołkowyski's quarters. The Soviet authorities also had a presence at the Polish headquarters: for example, Lieutenant-Colonel Zygmunt Berling, one of the officers who had been granted preferential treatment by the Soviets after responding positively to their overtures. Anders showed great generosity and forgiveness towards these pro-Soviet officers and gave them employment. He also protected them against the hostility of other officers, although he did order Colonel Leopold Okulicki, his chief of staff, to keep a close eye on them.[61] Anders's dilemma was that he did not know whether these men had genuinely converted to communism or had merely pretended in order to secure better living conditions or, indeed, in the light of the probable execution of the bulk of the Polish officer corps, to save their lives.

As former soldiers and new recruits flooded into the Polish camps, Anders became deeply concerned by the low number of officers arriving. Only 300 reported to the Polish authorities after having successfully concealed their officer status from the Soviets. None arrived from the Soviet POW camps at Kozel'sk, Starobel'sk and Ostashkov. Anders instructed Captain Józef Czapski to compile a list of missing officers and to initiate enquiries among the officers and former soldiers reporting in as to their whereabouts.[62] Some senior officers had survived, including men such as Okulicki, who would briefly command the 7th Division before travelling to London for training prior to being transported to Poland to take a leading part in the resistance, and Lieutenant-Colonel Nikodem Sulik, who would command the 5th Division throughout the Italian campaign. The pro-Soviet officers under

Berling, who had been transferred from the Griazovetz POW camp to the so-called 'Bungalow of Bliss', were also released.[63] When Anders and Sikorski met Stalin on 3 December 1941, Sikorski gave Stalin a list of 4,000 missing officers, adding that it was incomplete 'since it contains only names which we were able to take from memory'. Stalin, knowing perfectly well that he had signed the order for the execution of these officers, responded by suggesting that they must have escaped to Manchuria.[64]

For the men who had been in the Red Army, joining the Polish Army was very difficult. Thousands of 19-year-old men from eastern Poland had been conscripted in 1940, but distrusted by their commanders as capitalists, many had been directed to labour battalions or split into small groups within units of the Red Army. Now they had to find some way to leave that army and join the Polish Army. The adventures of Leonidas Kliszewicz illustrate the struggle. He was in a Red Army artillery unit and was sent to the front near Smolensk. On 25 July, there was a meeting of the whole unit, and all soldiers from Poland and the Baltic States were separated from the others and taken to Rostov where, on 31 July, they were told about the formation of a Polish Army. The men were then segregated by ethnic origin: the Poles were sent to work as lumberjacks and foresters through the summer and given no information about the location of the Polish Army, while the ethnic minorities were directed back towards the Red Army. It was only on 1 October that Kliszewicz managed to find his way to Gorki and join the 7th Division camped nearby, but no one knew what to do with him because he had no discharge papers. By the end of December, with the assistance of the Polish civilian authorities, he reached the Polish camp at Tatischevo and was assigned to the 5th Tank Battalion.[65] He had effectively deserted from the Red Army. This story was probably not uncommon. A historian of the Red Army has recorded that desertion rates were high among soldiers from eastern Poland and the Baltic States: for example, 4,000 men from the 26th Army were gone by 6 July.[66] Undoubtedly some of these men may have been genuine deserters, who lacked any desire to die for the Soviet Union or wanted to travel westwards to protect their families from the Germans, but it is equally likely that they continued the fight but under the Polish flag.

The Soviets had an effective method of limiting recruitment to the Polish Army: the supply of food and equipment. Given their view that

30,000 was the upper limit, the Soviets wanted the surplus men directed into production since they had already called-up every able-bodied man into the Red Army.[67] By the end of November 1941, however, the strength of the Polish Army stood at 40,961 men, including 1,965 officers;[68] Kot took up the issue directly with Stalin himself and Stalin agreed to raise the quota to 44,000 rations.[69] This would help, but only to a small degree, because by that time the Polish Army was also feeding over 70,000 civilians who had reached the sanctuary provided by the army, and more were arriving every day.

If the Soviets could not supply the Polish Army, then the Polish authorities hoped that the British and Americans could help. Indeed, Colonel Hulls received orders: 'Your job is to do all you can to help the Russians in the identification and forwarding of all military Supplies arriving by convoy at ARCHANGEL. I want you to pay particular attention to the correct forwarding of all items for the POLES.'[70] On 2 October 1941, an Anglo-American-Polish conference was held at the Moscow residence of the American ambassador, Laurence Steinhardt, to discuss supplies for the Polish Army. The British representative, Lord Beaverbrook, was on a mission to find out what the Soviets wanted the British to supply, and was extremely hostile to Polish requests that they should be allocated supplies separately from the Red Army. The Americans, led by Averell Harriman, were keen for direct supplies to the Poles but Beaverbrook was adamant that they should be given only whatever the Soviets could spare. As Kot reported to Sikorski, the British generals 'declared that Beaverbrook is a fortress which they cannot take by storm, but they will endeavour to outflank it'. Six days later there was another conference, at which Mason-MacFarlane announced that 50,000 complete sets of British equipment were on their way to the Soviet Union for the Polish Army. Beaverbrook allegedly exploded and demanded to know: 'On what basis and who sent them? I know nothing of this.'[71]

The Soviets might have wanted a Polish division to be sent to the front as soon as possible but seemed incapable of providing sufficient uniforms or equipment so that the men and women could be properly trained. Adam Gołębiowski recorded:

> Some of our uniforms were also sent from England, but most were provided by the Russians trying to show their compassion. The variety of these must

have been excavated from very old stores and some of our chaps received
uniforms of imperial Russia and Austrian armies and picturesquely embroi-
dered uniforms of the Hungarian army of the First World War.[72]

British supplies began to arrive and the 5th and 6th divisions received
uniforms. Zdzisława Kawencka was accepted for service in the
Women's Auxiliary Service and went to get her uniform from the
quartermaster. She was given a British men's winter uniform although
she was very small and very thin, and the result was comical: the sleeves
were a foot longer than her arms and the trousers reached her armpits,
held up by braces which had ten knots and by a belt that wrapped
round her twice. She was teased by the soldiers, who commented that
there was a uniform and boots walking round by themselves, yet she
was proud to have joined the army. The women were given rifles and
bayonets and put on guard duty, but there were no bullets.[73] It was clear
that the Polish Army could not be formed into an effective fighting force
until its supply problems had been resolved. This is why as early as
October 1941 the Polish Government had suggested to Eden[74] that if
the Polish Army was moved to the south of the Soviet Union, it would
become easier for the British and Americans to supply it from Iran.*
When Kot saw Stalin in mid-November, he found the Soviet leader
receptive to the idea but wanting to postpone discussion of the details
until Sikorski's visit in December.[75]

Solutions clearly needed to be found to the humanitarian crisis facing
the Poles in the Soviet Union and much hope was placed on Sikorski's
visit. He met Stalin in Moscow, then close to the German front line, on
3 December, and he later commented on this first meeting, at which
Anders and Molotov were also present: 'Stalin received me rather coldly
at first. He seemed to suspect me of being some sort of agent of Churchill. However, when I convinced him that this was not the case, the
atmosphere quickly changed and became more favourable.'[76] There
were many moments of friction. Stalin obviously resented Anders's
charge that the Soviets were not fulfilling the terms of the amnesty and
releasing men for the Polish Army, and he responded to the issue of the

---

* On 25 August 1941, Iran was split into two zones of occupation: the British in the
oil-rich south and the Soviets in the north. This was forced on the Iranian government and
the Shah, Reza Pahlevi, abdicated in favour of his son.

missing officers with bluster and denial, insisting that the officers must have escaped to Manchuria. The discussion on moving the Polish Army to the south or even out of the Soviet Union altogether to Iran was dominated by Stalin's suspicions that the Polish Army did not want to fight alongside the Red Army. He refused to accept the Polish argument that it was not reluctance to fight that was holding the Poles back but that the Soviets had quite simply failed to produce sufficient food and equipment. The men also discussed the recruitment of the ethnic minorities in the light of the recent Soviet decree directing them to the Red Army. At stake here was Sikorski's defence of the pre-war Polish-Soviet frontier, but he weakened his position by declining to discuss that issue over dinner at the Kremlin. His refusal is entirely understandable given the seriousness of the Polish government crisis caused by the signing of the Sikorski–Maisky pact, but it would have profound consequences. The series of meetings ended with a declaration of friendship and mutual assistance signed by Stalin and Sikorski, and the extension of an invitation by Stalin to Sikorski to make a second visit.[77] Stalin appeared to have been impressed by Sikorski and Anders and at the end of December authorised Anders to recruit men for 6 divisions, with a total strength of 96,000, and promised that the rations would be supplied for them.[78]

Sikorski also visited the Polish army camps at Buzuluk and Totskoye, accompanied by his British aide, Victor Cazalet, who recorded his impressions of the 20,000 troops at Totskoye:

> Every man looked half-starved. Their faces were grey, quite a different colour from those of ordinary people. Most of them looked as if they had been frost-bitten. They were living in tents. There were no houses, no wood except that which they pulled down with their own hands, no YMCA huts, no cinemas or shops, no town or village to which they could go . . .
>
> Yet when these men marched by . . . they showed a spirit which was truly remarkable. They thought themselves in heaven after two years in labour camps.[79]

A semblance of normal life had been created at Buzuluk with lectures, concerts and variety shows organised by a group of Polish actors, who had been on tour in the Soviet Union when the war started and had been stranded there, but then had found their way to the camp.[80]

Sikorski only paid brief visits to the camps. He had planned to return to Moscow for more meetings with Stalin but was suffering from severe gastric flu and so left the Soviet Union with his business, arguably, half-finished.

The relocation of the Polish Army took place in January and February 1942. From the point of view of organisation this move was disastrous as it was now spread through Kazakhstan, Kirghizstan and Uzbekistan. The headquarters moved to Yangiyul, south-west of Tashkent; the 5th Infantry Division was in Dzhalyal Abad, almost on the Chinese border; the 6th Infantry Division was in Shachrizyabs (Shahrisabz), near Samarkand in south Uzbekistan; the 7th Infantry Division in Kermine in central Uzbekistan; the 8th Infantry Division in Czok-Pak in Kirghizstan; the 9th Infantry Division was near Ferghana in Uzbekistan; the 10th Infantry Division in Lugovoy in south Kazakhstan; the artillery at Karasu in Tadzhikistan; the Engineers in Vrevskoye in east Uzbekistan; the armoured forces in Otar in west Kirghizstan; and the army depot in Guzar in south Uzbekistan. The poor infrastructure in the region meant that journeys between the camps took days. Communications were also poor as the telephone often worked for only an hour a day, and matters only improved in March when radio communications were established.[81]

The new military camps themselves were primitive. Lugovoy 'consisted of thousands of tents pitched on a wide, muddy, plain, above which towered the Pamir mountains covered with snow'.[82] Hulls alerted the British military mission in Moscow to the Poles' plight:

> The situation as regards food, shelter and hygiene in this part of Russia could hardly be worse, and as a consequence there have been serious epidemics ... Food is the worst feature – 750 grams of black bread and one meal, if it may be so described, a day. The meal consists usually of soup made of rice or meal, and a ration of preserved or salt fish. The latter is omitted if the soup contains meat. Weak tea morning and evening. Once or twice a week there are vegetables in the soup.[83]

The onset of spring and summer led to a rise in the sickness rate in the overcrowded camps. In February 1942, 38.8 per cent of soldiers were sick, but in some areas it was as many as 73.5 per cent. Between February and August, the Polish Army hospitals treated around 49,500 cases of contagious diseases, mostly typhus. Malaria was also common.[84] The sickness rate was exacerbated by the strenuous training regime now in place. One soldier reported:

> Some of the officers were stupid – they thought they could simply recreate the conditions of before the war. They sent soldiers out in training up into the hills in the heat of the day. In one unit the officer in charge was a doctor. He was a marvellous person, the kind you only come across once in a lifetime. He knew, of course, being a doctor that you can't take soldiers for exercise or drill when it was about 35 degrees C. So he allowed people to stay in their tents, going out in the evening when it was cooler. He looked after the food himself and took special responsibility for the sick. The other officers could have done that but didn't.[85]

The problem was that most of the experienced officers had been executed in 1940 and the replacements, some of them from Britain, had little idea of the capabilities of their troops.

The Polish Welfare Committee had little noticeable impact on the state of the civilian deportees until Sikorski's meeting with Stalin in December, when he obtained a loan of 100,000,000 roubles for welfare work from the Soviet Government. This was a major concession by Stalin, who believed that the Polish authorities should fund relief work from their own resources, but Cripps and Sikorski had put it to him that he had a moral obligation to assist the Poles because they were not in the Soviet Union by choice.[86] The loan came none too soon because as the army moved to the south so did the civilians. Dr Wasung wrote to the Polish embassy from Katta Kurgan: 'Here in southern Russia I am witnessing a terrifying martyrdom of the Polish population.'[87] Guzar became 'one of the largest Polish cemeteries in the Soviet Union'.[88] The station at Kermine, the site of a recruiting station, 'was one huge refugee camp'.[89]

> In Kermine the local cinema was turned into the hospital for infectious diseases. Here, without any medicine, any surgical measures and no food other than the occasional piece of black bread, hundreds of men lay on the ground undergoing nightmares. In these conditions thousands died, their shrivelled remains were put into boxes to be taken by six strong men to communal graves, dug at the town's peripheries. Once the ditches were full, the bodies were covered with quick lime and topped with soil.[90]

With the callousness born of an over-familiarity with death, Jerzy Kucięba recalled: 'one of our pastimes in the transit camp was guessing how many dead on any one day would be carried from the hospital in Kermine to the nearby cemetery. On one particular day the coffin which was used to transport the corpses passed my tent forty times.'[91] Hulls alerted the War Office to the condition of the Poles: 'These people – the best elements of a third of the Polish Nation – can only survive if pressure be brought upon Stalin to exercise genuine good will, and real facilities be given to Red Cross workers to reach them.'[92]

From February 1942 onwards, relief work at last started to have some beneficial impact on the Poles. The Polish relief authorities distributed aid that arrived via Iran and Archangel from Britain, the United States, and many other countries, including India, China, Australia and New Zealand. During 1942 the United States alone sent 7,414 tons, despite the shortage of shipping caused by the war with Japan.[93] Most of this was provided under the terms of the Lend-Lease agreement but voluntary American bodies also made an important contribution,[94] including from Jewish organisations (which were on the whole fairly distributed by the Polish delegates).[95] The position of the Polish Jews in the Soviet Union was precarious because under the 1 December decree the Soviet authorities considered them to be Soviet citizens. For example, in December 1941 the NKVD arrested two prominent Polish Jews, Henryk Ehrlich and Victor Alter, at the Polish embassy, accusing them of working for the Germans. Kot agitated for their release but was informed that the two men were considered to be Soviet citizens and therefore of no concern to the Polish embassy.[96]

Schools and orphanages were opened, and at last the Poles had access to religious services organised by the army padres. In Kustanai the orphanage and school were housed in the same building and conditions there were considerably better than on the kolkhozy, with supplies, albeit limited, of vegetables and dairy produce. Elsewhere conditions were not so good. Hanka Swiderska recalled the orphanage near Guzar which was situated 'in a treeless and waterless vicinity, in an old ruined kolkhoz, where snakes, tarantulas, and scorpions ran rampant. Lizards crawled on people, and in the night the mosquitoes did not let people sleep.' The shortage of water and poor food led to outbreaks of dysentery and pellagra, which killed several children. Lucjan Królikowski was responsible for running an orphanage and noted: 'It was an exception if someone handing over an orphan to the nursery remembered his name or knew his age.'[97] By July 1942, there were 129 orphanages,

50 old people's homes, 21 feeding stations and 115 food kitchens in the south of the Soviet Union.[98]

At the beginning of March 1942, the establishment of the Polish Army in the Soviet Union stood at 70,000 men: the 5th and 6th Divisions were full strength, the 7th Division was at half strength, and the remaining three divisions (8th, 9th and 10th) were skeleton forces of between 1,700 to 2,800 soldiers. On 2 February 1942, Anders had met the Soviet military authorities, who demanded that the 5th Division be sent to the front immediately. Anders had good grounds for his refusal: the division consisted of men who had fought in the September 1939 campaign, and while it had its full complement of small arms it had no heavy equipment, nor had it received any training in the use of artillery and other heavy weapons. Anders also knew that it was against Sikorski's explicit orders to despatch a single division to the front. The Soviets claimed that the division would receive the necessary training, and their authorities, angered by Anders's refusal, declared that from 21 March 1942 the Polish Army would receive rations for only 44,000 men. On 18 March, Anders met Stalin and appealed to him to raise the number of rations, and it was agreed that the reduction in rations would be postponed until the end of the month. The surplus 30,000 soldiers would be evacuated to Iran across the Caspian Sea, where the British would supply and equip them before they returned to the Soviet Union to fight alongside the Red Army. Their civilian dependants could be evacuated too.[99] An alternative evacuation route via Ashkhabad and Meshed was also suggested. Stalin appointed Zhukov to be in charge of the Soviet side of the evacuation and on 19 March, Anders appointed Berling to take charge of the Polish side.

Preparations for the reception of the troops had begun at Pahlevi (Bandar Anzali), the port in Iran on the Caspian Sea earmarked as the reception centre, in the middle of February, and a joint Anglo-Polish party arrived with the permission of the Soviet commander in Teheran, necessary because Pahlevi lay within the Soviet zone.[100] The Soviet authorities in Moscow had then ordered the mission back to Teheran.[101] Now, in the middle of March, the evacuation was on and as the British ambassador in Iran, Reader Bullard, wrote to his wife:

Tremendous preparations are being made, mostly by British military authorities but also, according to their means, by the Poles to receive in this country some thousands of Poles who were interned in Russia and are now to join the British forces at home or in the Near East. Apart from Polish troops 500 Polish children are passing through from Russia to India, where they will be looked after. 200 Polish children are to come from Russia to Isfahan, where the CMS [Church Missionary Society] will help to look after them. They will want feeding up, these children; and so will the troops.[102]

The orders for the evacuation were given on 23 March and the first ship left Krasnovodsk in Turkistan on the following day.[103] General Szyszko-Bohusz later wrote:

> The NKVD showed sparkling organisational skill. Trains were made available almost without any delays, even though wagons and locomotives had to be brought from all over the south-eastern regions of the USSR. On the Caspian Sea all the ships of greater or lesser size were mobilised and they managed to avoid creating any kind of serious blockage at Krasnovodsk.[104]

Anders decided that the fittest men and the best-equipped units should remain in the Soviet Union because they were best able to survive. Consequently the 5th, 6th and 7th Divisions and the Engineers and Artillery remained behind apart from their weakest men, while the 8th, 9th and 10th Divisions were completely evacuated.[105] New recruits to the Polish Army, such as Kazimierz Dobrowolski and Stanisław Kochański who had already been enlisted but had been ordered to remain in their kolkhozy in Kazakhstan, were included in the evacuation. In Krasnovodsk the Poles boarded a variety of ships, including oil tankers, which were so crammed with soldiers and civilians that on some there was only one foot separating the deck from the water. The trip across the Caspian, which lasted for anything between 24 hours and 3 days, was desperately uncomfortable: seasickness was compounded by the shortage of water and the lack of toilet facilities, and many were suffering from dysentery.[106] The last ship carrying the Polish Army reached Pahlevi on 5 April. Those permitted to leave recalled: 'When we received this news our joy was boundless. To get out of this cursed land was something that exceeded our wildest dreams.'[107] But they had mixed emotions: family members left behind, dead, missing or only clinging on to life, hoping for a future rescue effort, while they themselves were sailing into an unknown but surely better future. They had no intention of ever returning to the Soviet Union.

When the evacuation staff, made up of Poles, and British and Indian officers and men, arrived at Pahlevi on 25 March, they found the first ship already in the harbour ready to disgorge its cargo of desperate humanity. Ryszard Zolski recalled his arrival:

> Now we could see many Army officers, wearing several kinds of uniform, English, Persian and Polish/English, like mine. They seemed very grim, as they surveyed the cargo of human wreckage being unloaded. Perhaps they were trying to assess what potential was left in us.
>
> Their faces expressed pity, and disgust – that once healthy, stalwart men had been brought to such a state of misery and dejection . . . Spontaneously, I and many hundreds of us, knelt on those golden sands, raising our eyes to heaven, silently thanking God for our safe journey and at last our longed for freedom. Bowing my head, I reverently kissed the sands of Persia – that free land. Emotion was so strong that many of us were weeping from sheer joy. Even some of those who greeted and checked us in, had eyes filled with tears.[108]

The soldiers were immediately separated from the civilians and taken to a camp where they 'had to strip, have a shower, a haircut, be powdered with insecticide and were issued with new tropical uniforms'.[109]

For many civilians getting on a ship was a matter of life and death: some mothers not on the list even threw their babies into the cargo nets of the departing ships in the desperate hope that at least one member of the family might survive. The Polish soldiers tried to help as many families as possible. Irena Szunejko and her mother had a lucky experience: at Tashkent they met a Polish soldier who was searching for his family, which had been deported to Siberia. On hearing that Irena's mother came from the same part of Poland as he did, 'he took her hand and said: "Come with me – you are my sister and you can live." We never saw the man again.'[110] Churchill was appalled at the number of civilian dependants arriving in Iran and telegraphed Eden: 'Are we going to get nothing but women and children? We must have the men.'[111] General Tadeusz Klimecki, Sikorski's chief of staff, telegraphed Anders:

> In view of the great food difficulties in Iran it is necessary to stop absolutely transport of families until agreement is reached with British authorities as it may hamper or restrict military evacuation. How many members of

families have you already evacuated and how many do you intend to evacuate?

Kot sent a similar telegram ordering Anders to be discreet about the evacuation: so many Poles were arriving in the south of the Soviet Union hoping to leave the country that they were exacerbating the already desperate food situation.[112] In total, 31,189 soldiers and 12,408 civilians were evacuated in March–April 1942.[113]

Soviet-Polish relations deteriorated after the first evacuation, and there were arguments about strategy among the Poles. Sikorski still wanted to retain a Polish army in the Soviet Union but Anders was keen to evacuate as many people as possible. The Soviets started to hamper the relief efforts as the Poles began to be viewed as a hostile element. Beginning in July 1942, but greatly increasing towards the end of the year, the Soviets began arresting the Polish delegates and imprisoning them, charged with anything from spying for a foreign country to minor offences. Polish schools and orphanages were also closed and the aid which had been sent from abroad was now withheld.[114] There was also great tension in Polish-Soviet military relations. For example, as Arnold Rymaszewski later related: 'A Russian major came over [to the Polish camp] to persuade the Polish major representing the Polish garrison command to stay with the Russian army. When the Polish major refused, the Russian shot him. The sentry who stood outside the office shot the Russian major.' The Soviets demanded the execution of the Polish sentry, a request denied by the Polish command: 'We were put on red alert. All the ammunition provided for training was put in belts, we slept fully dressed, ready to march to Ashkhabad to get to Iran.' The Soviets backed down.[115] As news of the arrests of delegates and the forced withdrawal of Polish military officers from the main railway junctions spread, Rudnicki recalled:

We decided to offer strong resistance if the Soviets attempted to take us by force, and to hack our way through to Afghanistan or Iran. We even began to prepare for such an emergency. Under the pretext of excursions, we reconnoitred the passes and roads to the Afghan frontier, and studied the possibility of taking over by force the trains running to Ashkhabad en route to the Persian frontier. We reconnoitred the disposition of the nearest Soviet garrisons, and their stores where we could secure the necessary equipment.

Rudnicki acknowledged, however, that 'this secretly designed plan was quite fantastic, and could hardly have been carried out in practice – especially as many soldiers were at the time laid low by malaria'.[116]

Sikorski told the Polish cabinet that the remainder of the Polish Army would only be evacuated from the Soviet Union if it was faced with starvation. On 30 June, Anders briefed Sikorski: 'the food situation grows worse and worse', there was a general lack of medicines, and there were epidemics of malaria, typhus and dysentery. There were about 16,000 civilians near the army and they were suffering the same hardships and dying in large numbers. Sikorski then asked Churchill for assistance in obtaining permission from Stalin for a second evacuation.

Churchill was willing to make this effort because of the strategic situation. That summer Rommel had launched the major offensive in the Western Desert which led to the fall of Tobruk and German troops reaching the Libyan-Egyptian frontier. The Germans had also made great advances in the Soviet Union and threatened the Soviet oil supplies, much as Sikorski and Anders had predicted earlier. Churchill therefore telegraphed Stalin in July:

> I am sure it would be in our common interest, Premier Stalin, to have the three divisions of Poles you so kindly offered join their compatriots in Palestine, where we could arm them fully. These would play a most important part in the future fighting as well as keeping the Turks in good heart by a sense of growing numbers to the southward.

The British were prepared to accept a large number of civilians too, despite the shortage of food in the area. Churchill added a veiled threat: 'If we do not get the Poles we should have to fill their places by drawing on preparations now going forward on a vast scale for Anglo-American mass invasion of the Continent.'[117] Since the opening of this Second Front was Stalin's greatest concern, on 1 August the necessary orders were issued. Nine days later the evacuation of 43,476 soldiers began and was completed on the 31st.[118] The 6th Division was the last to leave and its second in command, Rudnicki, became 'the last embarked Polish soldier in Krasnovodsk to take leave of this inhuman country'.[119] The pro-Soviet Berling chose to remain behind and would later command the 1st Army, the Polish army in the Soviet Union established by the Polish communist committee.[120]

The decision to include more civilians was controversial. The Poles wanted permission to evacuate the soldiers' families and the *Junaks*, together with 50,000 Polish children accompanied by 5,000 mothers or guardians,[121] but the British were concerned about how they would cope with such an influx into a region with limited food resources. Kot stressed to Vyshinsky that he was making this appeal in the knowledge that there were at least 160,000 destitute Polish children in the Soviet Union, so that even with this evacuation less than a third would be saved from an uncertain fate.[122] Vyshinsky argued that the Soviets could not provide sufficient transport, because of the need to evacuate Soviet citizens from the Caucasus and Crimea ahead of the German advance.[123]

The Polish civilians faced heartbreaking choices over whether to apply for a place in the evacuation. Józefa Kochańska and her family were eligible for inclusion because her son Stanisław was in the Polish Army and had left in the March evacuation. She lacked the money to make her own way to Krasnovodsk and hoped that her son would be able to send some, not knowing that he was dangerously ill in a hospital in Teheran. She also hoped that her husband would somehow cross the steppe and rescue her. Consequently she decided to remain in exile with her youngest daughter. An older daughter, Nina, stayed with them although she could have joined the *Junaks* and been evacuated. The two remaining daughters, Lala and Renia, were already in an orphanage in Kustanai since there was no food for them on the kolkhoz. When the decision was taken by the Polish authorities to evacuate all the orphanages, Józefa had to give her permission for them to leave: 'Yes, let them go, maybe they will be saved. Today I cooked the last potatoes, there is nothing else.'[124]

Other civilians did not have any choice. There was a limit to the number and ethnicity of civilians permitted to leave. Teresa Glazer remembered what it was to wait to hear if you had been included:

> The list of people included in this transport was being read out in alphabetical order and since there were more people waiting to get out of Russia than it was possible to include in that transport, you could hear people crying when their letter was finished and the list went on to the next letter of the alphabet.[125]

The Soviet authorities were adamant that only ethnic Poles would be allowed to leave and the NKVD closely checked the documentation of the evacuees. This order also prevented Jews from going: it was not unusual for a member of the NKVD to ask a soldier or civilian to drop his trousers to check for circumcision before allowing the man onto a ship.[126]

The August evacuation took place in more difficult circumstances than the one in March. The weather was extremely hot and the heat forced many Poles to abandon what little luggage they had on the march to the port. The situation in Krasnovodsk was appalling:

> There, without protection from the intense sun and heat, we waited all day to board the ship. Heaven and earth created such intense heat that it became painful to breathe. Instead of a cool sea breeze, our lungs were filled with the foul odour of oil from the Baku oilfields. We could not even reach the water itself because the shoreline and sea were covered in oil.[127]

The NKVD had prevented the sickest Poles from boarding the ships at all, but even so the civilians who were evacuated in August were in a very poor physical condition. The voyage across the Caspian weakened them further and many were 'frequently hardly able to crawl off the ship' at Pahlevi.[128] Zofia Stępek's 13-year-old sister weighed only 55 pounds and had to be carried off the ship, as did Renia Kochańska.[129] The August evacuation consisted of 26,094 civilians. A further 2,694, mostly children, came by road from Ashkhabad in Turkistan to Meshed in Iran.

The evacuation of the Poles was a relief to them and to the Soviets alike. General Szyszko-Bohusz was told by an NKVD officer: 'You will leave, but it will take us twenty years to absorb the mess you have caused by your presence here.'[130] On their arrival in the Soviet Union the Poles had given the appearance of being more wealthy than the majority of Soviet citizens and this could be viewed as a damning indictment of the supposed benefits of communism. For the soldiers the evacuation represented an opportunity to fight to restore Poland's honour and freedom, and for the civilians it was nothing more or less than a chance to live.

The soldiers evacuated from the Soviet Union were sent to camps in Teheran. The journey from Pahlevi through the Elburz mountains made a great impression on the Poles. Lorries and buses had been hired with Iranian drivers who 'drove like demons along the narrow, dangerous mountain roads'. Anders described the journey:

> At first it ran not far from the shore of the Caspian Sea, with wide tilled fields on either side, but then it gradually climbed, passing through

mountain gorges and dense forests, from which it emerged high in the mountains, to wind at a great height along the edge of a precipice, diving, at one place, through a tunnel driven through the rock. The road was open to traffic for only five months of the year: snow-drifts, avalanches and flooded mountain streams made it impassable the rest.[131]

The Poles would sometimes see the carcasses of lorries which had failed to make a bend lying crushed in the ravines. After this frightening but exhilarating part of the journey, the road traversed an almost uninhabited sandy desert. Because Teheran lay in the Soviet zone the soldiers were soon put in lorries and sent on to Qizil Ribat in Iraq. That country was under British occupation and there was a large RAF base at Habbaniya.* Coming the opposite way were American trucks laden with aid for the Soviet Union. Occasional plaques by the roadside reminded the Poles that Alexander the Great and Darius III had passed that way with their armies centuries before.

The troops were first sent to training centres near Mosul and Kirkuk in Iraq. Camping in the desert was miserable:

> During the day we huddled in our tents and roasted like so many chickens in the oven. During the night, we huddled in our tents, freezing and trying to stop our teeth from chattering, an exercise we had foolishly imagined we had left far behind us. For recreation, the environment arranged for us to be plagued with both scorpions and hairy black-widow spiders.[132]

Crossing the desert to the concentration point for the army at Khanaqin in Iraq was uncomfortable and confusing: 'It was so hot, one could scarcely breathe – the perspiration on our faces a nuisance, while the tropical shirts we were wearing stuck to our bodies ... After a few hours driving, we saw a town looming in front of us, and became quite cheerful at the prospect of finding cool shade and water.'[133] The driver laughed and told them that it was a mirage. Relations between the British and Iraqis were poor because the Iraqis blamed the British for food shortages, and they extended this hostility to the Polish soldiers. After reorganisation the Polish Army was transferred to Palestine to camps near Gaza for training.[134]

The soldiers were followed by the *Junaks*, who were sent to Camp

---

* In April 1941, the pro-German former Iraqi prime minister Rashid Ali al-Galiani had attempted a coup and the British had occupied the country.

Barbara, near Ashqelon. General Anders had established the cadet force for boys aged between 14 and 17 on 12 September 1941 in the Soviet Union, to build up a reservoir of trained manpower for the army. When the army was evacuated, a cadet school was established in Palestine to provide schooling and preliminary military training for the boys, who would graduate and enter the cadet officer schools run by the Polish Army for six months before joining their units. The education system was based on the pre-war six-year Polish secondary school curriculum. Military training was provided up to platoon command level. The British Army gave great assistance to the cadet schools: the Medical Corps took responsibility for health care, the Education Corps provided teachers of English, and the army also supplied the physical training instructors. By all accounts the cadets soon regained their health and were lively, exuberantly celebrating their freedom, and constantly up to tricks:

> The cadets discovered that their Arab waiters had a knack for Polish obscenities, and naturally this linguistic sideline was encouraged. Personal animosities among the waiters were stoked in the knowledge that at the height of each quarrel the antagonists would slip into Polish abuse of the most elaborate kind.

Boys who were not suitable as officers attended other cadet schools and received a more technical education and learnt army trades.[135] Young girls were also sent to separate *Junak* (*Ochotniczki*) schools to be prepared to join the Women's Auxiliary Service.

Not all the soldiers evacuated from the Soviet Union remained with the Polish Army in the Middle East. Sikorski had agreed with Stalin that 15,000 soldiers and 3,500 airmen and sailors, out of the existing but growing strength of 70,000, would travel to Britain to expand the Polish forces in Britain. Volunteers were also accepted for the Polish Air Force. The route was normally from Basra in Iraq to Karachi in India to camps in South Africa, to wait until a suitable fast ship or convoy was ready to take the soldiers, sailors and airmen on to Britain. At Camp Haydock near Pietermaritzburg in South Africa:

> Our training continued – daily marches, exercises with various mock-attacks, and as well as having to watch out for the enemy, there were many different types of cactus plants, the leaves of which had very spiteful spikes.

Our dress was designed for the tropics, so that our bare arms and legs were vulnerable. These cacti were a great nuisance to us, but not so dangerous as the many kinds of snakes, and other creepy-crawlies which were quite frightening, unaccustomed as we were to them.[136]

On leave in Cape Town one group of Polish airmen caused a scandal when they followed the sound of music and entered a dance hall for black South Africans:

We bought tickets and went inside. Apart from ourselves, everybody in the room was black. It was obviously a formal event because they were all immaculately turned out in evening dress or ball gowns, though they seemed unconcerned that we were only wearing our uniforms.

Despite our violation of the dress code, we still had a great time dancing with all these black ladies for much of the night until we reluctantly had to drag ourselves back to our billets for a spot of sleep.[137]

The next day all hell broke loose and the Polish airmen were told in no unclear terms that this was a country where whites and blacks did not mix.

The journey to Britain was fraught with danger as German U-boats were active in the Atlantic. Stanisław Kochański had been accepted for training as a bomber pilot but missed his first transport because he had been critically ill with typhus in Teheran. He missed his second transport because he had an arm swathed in bandages after a minor cut had become infected – a frequent problem among evacuees whose immune systems had not yet recovered – and according to the embarkation officer, this meant that he would not be able to swim should the ship be torpedoed. Indeed, the first transport that Kochański should have joined suffered a fate that became both famous and controversial. On 1 September 1942, RMS *Laconia* left Cape Town with 80 civilians, 268 British soldiers, 1,800 Italian POWs and 160 Poles acting as guards. On 12 September, off the west coast of Africa, 'suddenly we felt an enormous blow followed by a horrifying explosion and the ship keeled over almost immediately. Everything started to clatter across from one end to the other, the lights, though, did not go out for a while.' Then a second torpedo hit the ship and the order was issued to abandon ship. The German commander of U-156, which had fired the torpedoes, Werner

Hartenstein, heard the cries of the Italian POWs and began a rescue operation. Other U-boats in the area assisted and towed the lifeboats to a rendezvous with Vichy French ships, including the cruiser *Gloire* from Dakar, which picked up 70 Poles. The U-boats were then forced to break off the rescue operation when attacked by a B-24 Liberator bomber, which led to the controversial order by the German admiral Karl Dönitz for submarines not to rescue survivors from the ships they had torpedoed, soon echoed by a similar order by the United States admiral Chester Nimitz. The rescued Poles were well treated by the French sailors, some of whom had Polish origins and spoke good Polish, and were interned in a camp at Qued-Zem, near Casablanca, and given uniforms of the French Foreign Legion. When the Allies invaded north Africa in November, the Poles sailed again to Britain, arriving on 6 December 1942. Other sailings were safer, though lengthy. Alexander Maisner travelled from Basra to Karachi, then to Durban and Cape Town, followed by crossing the Atlantic to Rio de Janiero, and then sailing to New York before finally recrossing the Atlantic to Glasgow.[138]

The presence of the Polish Army in Palestine brought to the forefront the sensitive question of relations between ethnic Poles and their Jewish countrymen. Only 4,226 Jewish soldiers were evacuated from the Soviet Union, for which Polish anti-semitism has been blamed but the true picture is more complicated. Jews were keen to join the Polish Army in the Soviet Union. Indeed, two Zionist politicians, Miron Sheskin and Mark Kahn, had proposed the formation of a separate Jewish brigade in October 1941, which was supported by Sikorski, who was pro-Zionist. But neither he nor Anders wanted to see a high proportion of Jews in the army when there were so many ethnic Poles desperate to enlist, and Anders issued an order restricting the recruitment of ethnic minorities, including Jews, to 5 per cent of the NCOs and 10 per cent of the rank and file. The NKVD, as has already been noted, limited the numbers of ethnic minorities, including Jews, leaving the Soviet Union. Above all it was the British authorities who were hostile to the inclusion of a high number of Jews in the Polish Army. The Foreign Office, which discussed the issue on numerous occasions, concluded: 'It is in particular desirable that such [Polish] units should contain as low a proportion of Polish nationals of Jewish race, and that in no circumstances should Polish Jews be formed into separate military units within the Polish forces in the Middle East.' The British ambassador to the Polish Government, Sir Cecil Dormer, accordingly sent a memorandum on 30 March 1942 asking the Poles to limit Jewish recruitment because of British interests in Palestine.[139]

When the Polish Army reached Palestine, 3,000 Jews deserted: among them, though not listed as a deserter, was the future Irgun leader Menachem Begin. The British authorities blamed Polish anti-semitism for the desertions, but as one Jewish historian of the II Corps has noted there were few anti-semitic incidents when the corps was in Palestine. In a post-war interview, Anders explained his attitude towards the desertions:

> I believed that the Jews had two loyalties, one towards Palestine, the other towards Poland, and this is why I did not intend to keep them in the Polish Army by force. I issued strict orders not to pursue Jewish soldiers who left the ranks on reaching Palestine. I believe that these Jews, who considered fighting for the independence of Palestine as their first duty, had the right to do so.[140]

Anders's opinion is echoed in the memoirs of soldiers of the Polish Army, who could not blame the Jews, who had been saying 'Next year in Jerusalem' at the conclusion of their Passover and Yom Kippur prayers for centuries, for deciding that this year Jerusalem was just a small step away and taking that step. A Polish Army report summarised the official Polish attitude:

> The Army command has shown maximum restraint over those who have left the ranks of the Polish Army, limiting itself to determining the circumstances of their desertion ... There have only been two cases when the security forces of the Polish Army, and that on the request of the British Army command, took part, indirectly, in tracing deserters. These were found hiding in kibbutzim, in Hulda on the night of 2 to 3 October 1943, and in Ramat Hakovesh on 16 November. Because the real reason for the search, as it soon became known, was to find hidden arms, the Polish authorities avoided participating in such actions in the future.[141]

The Polish Army hindered the British search for deserters by refusing to hand over their photographs to the British military police. When deserters were caught and returned to the Polish Army, they usually were demoted and given short and light punishments. The British also blamed the Poles for the mysterious increase in arms appearing in the *kibbutzim*, and while they were probably correct in suspecting that the source was the Polish Army, they could not prove whether the arms had been donated to the Jews or stolen from the Poles. The 838 Jewish soldiers who remained in the II Corps fought in Italy, where 28 officers and men were killed and 52 wounded.[142]

Polish soldiers sometimes encountered an unwelcome reminder of the Soviet occupation of eastern Poland on meeting people who had been enthusiastic then about the arrival of the Red Army and now were wearing Polish Army uniforms. Edward Wierzbicki had such an encounter:

> It took much for me to stomach the fact that this insect was in Polish military uniform and that he had escaped the 'Soviet Paradise' while so many worthier Poles remained there forgotten ... Yet when I spoke up about this matter and within my criticism suggested there should be stricter verification as to characters enrolling in the Polish Army the only comment I received by way of answer was: 'There will be a military front line and he'll get his chance for rehabilitation.'[143]

It cannot be ascertained how many of those who welcomed the Soviet invasion later escaped from the Soviet Union with the Polish Army but this was surely not the only case. Nina Kochańska found the name of the man who had evicted her family from their house in Poland on the list of those who died at Monte Cassino.[144]

The Polish military authorities had cause to suspect that a small number of officers and NCOs had been subverted by their contact with communism. Berling had deserted from the Polish Army when it was evacuated from the Soviet Union and in July 1943 was court-martialled *in absentia* and found guilty of desertion and sentenced to death. Anders's aide-de-camp, Captain Jerzy Klimkowski, had been suborned by the NKVD while in the Soviet Union and in July 1942 had even offered to arrest Anders. After leaving the Soviet Union with Anders, he himself was arrested and imprisoned; after the war he returned to Poland and smeared Anders's reputation.[145] In February 1944, 6 Poles – 4 officers and 2 NCOs – were court-martialled, and five were found guilty of the charge of 'deliberately acting to the detriment of the Armed Forces of Poland in time of war'. The officers were also found guilty of 'creating an illegal revolutionary organisation, supported by the Palestinian Communist Party', while Lieutenant R. L. Imach and Second Lieutenant S. Szczypiorski were also found guilty of having passed intelligence and codebooks to Soviet officers and both were sentenced to fifteen years in prison. The most senior of the officers, Captain K. Rozen-Zawadzki, was sentenced to life imprisonment. The other two men received shorter sentences. All were imprisoned at Qassasin in Egypt.[146]

Nearly all the soldiers in the Anders army were extremely hostile to the Soviet Union. The British were aware of this and, because the Soviet Union was now an ally, tried every expedient to stop the Poles from openly condemning the Soviet Union. Tadeusz Żukowski recalled that when the army reached Palestine: 'As Russia claimed all those born in eastern Poland as its nationals, we born in eastern Poland were told to erase our birthplaces from our military documents, we were also instructed not to speak ill of the Soviet Union.'[147] Adam Gołębiowski had fond memories of an Royal Army Service Corps officer, Captain Hughes, who was attached to the Polish Army. The Poles did not speak English and Hughes did not speak Polish but 'within a week or two we all discovered what an excellent asset alcohol represents in learning a foreign language and a bottle of whisky a day was essential'. He wrote of Hughes:

[He] was an intelligent man, rather anxious to learn as much as possible about Soviet life, displaying however a very limited knowledge of Russian geography and history. He expected to be posted shortly to [the] British mission in Moscow.

We tried hard to correct his preconceived ideas of a mighty ally, unfortunately, with a typical, exaggerated Polish manner. Therefore our stories and explanations did not seem to impress him very much and in consequence, the more we tried to convince him that [the] Soviet Union represents a reprehensible system, based on cruelty to its own citizens and that its rulers govern in a manner completely opposite to noble ideas of Marx and Engels, our efforts fell on deaf ears.

Now and again he would dismiss our stubborn perorations with a shrug of shoulders and teased us by calling Stalin, 'Good old Uncle Joe', knowing perfectly well that this epitaph would make us see red.[148]

It became clear as time passed that whenever the Soviets issued any statement criticising the Poles and the Poles issued a refutation, the

British Government and military authorities would give publicity to the Soviet argument but gloss over any Polish riposte.

Several memoranda for the War Office written by Colonel Leslie Hulls demonstrate the complexity of Anglo-Polish relations concerning the Polish Army. He had joined Anders in the Soviet Union and seen for himself the appalling appearance of the troops in the Polish Army camps. In July 1942, Hulls expressed his belief that the Polish Government was out of touch with the state of the Polish Army in the Soviet Union, while he believed that the remaining troops could not survive there under the prevailing conditions, and therefore recommended their evacuation. In response to the Soviet charge that the Polish Army had left because it did not want to fight the Germans, Hulls wrote a lengthy memorandum in December 1942 defending it and setting out the precise reasons why the Polish Army had been evacuated. On several occasions he informed his superiors that morale was being detrimentally affected by the lack of further evacuations from the Soviet Union, the lack of news from their families left behind and the way that Poland was being treated in the press:

> If the events which have overtaken them were taking place in an enemy country, the men would have no alternative but to bear with them. But Russia is an Ally, who enjoys from her Allies all the consideration, cooperation and assistance which Britain and the U.S. can give. Yet she is treating Poland but little better than is Germany.

While the Soviets were gearing up for the break in diplomatic relations with the Polish Government which would come in April 1943 after the revelations of the Katyń massacre, they made public attacks on the Polish Army and against Anders personally, and distributed their anti-Polish propaganda throughout the Middle East. Anders and his army felt betrayed because it appeared to them that the British Government would not help. For example, a meeting in Baghdad in May 1943 between Anders and Lieutenant-General Sir Henry Pownall to discuss the impact of the break in Polish-Soviet diplomatic relations was inconclusive. Hulls informed the War Office that the Polish Government was not keeping its army informed of its activities: 'As a result, such confidence as the Polish Govt. may have enjoyed *vis à vis* the Army (by far the greatest part of the Polish population existing in freedom) is rapidly diminishing.'[149] This is why Sikorski visited the Polish Army at its camps throughout the Middle East. He was killed on his return journey to Britain when his plane crashed on take-off from Gibraltar.

When the Polish Army entered Iraq it became part of the British 10th Army commanded by General Sir Henry Maitland Wilson. A British liaison unit led by Brigadier Way, and later by Brigadier Firth, supervised its organisation. The first Polish plan, designed by the chief of staff, Major-General Tadeusz Klimecki, envisioned the creation of two army corps, each consisting of two infantry divisions, and two tank brigades. The British military recommended a different organisation, which the Poles accepted in September 1942, for one army corps consisting of two infantry divisions, an armoured division, an infantry brigade, an artillery division and various supporting units; this became known as the Polish II Corps.[150] In November 1943, the Polish commander-in-chief, General Sosnkowski, visited the II Corps and warned Anders that he had just conferred with Generals Eisenhower and Alexander in Algiers and that they had mooted a plan which would have entailed a complete reorganisation of the II Corps. Anders was greatly upset by this news. The Allies had landed in Italy and were making slow headway up the peninsula, the II Corps was ready to go into battle and Anders was aware that for political reasons it was essential that the Polish Army should start fighting the Germans as soon as possible. The planned reorganisation would have weakened the corps, with the proposed transfer of several thousand men to the Polish Air Force in Britain. Sosnkowski supported Anders, as did General Wilson, who wrote to the War Office opposing the reorganisation and nothing more was heard of the matter.[151]

The British Army supervised the training of the Polish Army in Iraq during 1943 and a close collaboration developed between Pownall and Anders. The Poles had to become accustomed to using British equipment and about 20,000 drivers had to be trained. The principal problem facing the II Corps was its officers, as too few had survived incarceration in the Soviet Union to staff an army corps. So officers were despatched from Britain, selected from among those who had managed to escape from Poland in 1939, but many of them were too old and too set in their ways to adapt to the new requirements of war. Anders dismissed about 1,000 officers, and young cadet-officers were pushed into positions of responsibility above their rank as soon as they left the officer training schools. Training was stepped up when the II Corps was transferred to Gaza in Palestine in the late summer of 1943. In September 1943, the corps held manoeuvres under the command of Major-General Leonard Holmes and watched by General Wilson, and 'took' Mount Sinai, Nazareth and other places. Wilson pronounced himself satisfied that the II Corps was ready for action, and the corps was moved to Egypt to prepare for transfer to the front in Italy. But Anders was depressed by the move to Italy since he was in favour of an attack in the Balkans as being the shorter road back to Poland.[152]

# 7

# Poland's Contribution to the Allied War Effort, 1940–1943

At the end of the September 1939 campaign, Poland had lost an army: 694,000 soldiers had become prisoners of war of the Germans and 240,000 of the Soviets. Yet thousands had obeyed Marshal Rydz-Śmigły's order to seek refuge in neighbouring countries. It was estimated that around 30,000 Polish soldiers and airmen were in Rumania; 40,000 in Hungary; 13,800 in Lithuania; and 1,300 in Latvia. Sikorski told his cabinet in 1939: 'The re-creation of the Polish Army in its greatest size is the most important and essential goal of the Government.' The basic Polish premise was: 'We do not beg for freedom, we fight for freedom.' To achieve this end the Polish Government had two strategic aims. The first was to show the world that although Poland was now under German and Soviet occupation, its armed forces were still active in the war. The second was to gain a place in the Anglo-French Supreme War Council, which would give the Polish Government a say in the allied decision-making process. This was the rationale, explained in a February 1940 memorandum by the Polish chief of staff, Major-General Tadeusz Klimecki, as to why Polish forces should participate in the proposed allied expeditionary force to Finland, which was then under attack by the Soviet Union. He argued: 'Polish units on Finnish territory will offer vital proof that Poland exists and is fighting as part of the allied front . . . The very fact of Poland taking part in allied action will permit us to place unequivocally the issue of Poland's relations with the other two Allies externally and internally.' The Polish Government, however, met with limited success in this.[1]

Under the terms of the Hague Convention, neutral countries were obliged to disarm and intern the Polish forces who entered their territory. Yet the maintenance of the thousands of Polish soldiers and airmen

was prohibitively expensive, and the Rumanian and Hungarian governments either turned a blind eye to their escape or actively assisted them.
In Rumania the Polish embassy worked round the clock to provide
passports for escaping Polish servicemen: 'They were well informed and
enterprising people, scheming, wheeling, dealing, bribing and doing
everything they could to get everybody out of Rumania before the
Germans took over the country.'[2] The British embassy in Bucharest was
also useful. A British diplomat, Robin Hankey, later related how 400
Polish airmen dressed as Jews to escape Rumania and travelled to Britain via Palestine.[3] The Hungarians were even more helpful. The Polish
military attaché in Budapest, Colonel Jan Emisarski-Pindelli, organised
the evacuation office and worked in close collaboration with an official
in the Hungarian Interior Ministry, Józef Antall, and with the Hungarian-Polish Committee for the Care of Refugees. There were three main
escape routes from Hungary and Rumania: from the Black Sea ports of
Constanţa and Balcik and then through the Dardanelles to Syria or
Marseilles; through Yugoslavia or Greece and thence by sea to France;
or overland via Yugoslavia and Italy.[4]

The Hungarian military were particularly welcoming to the Poles
and facilitated their escape. The regiment of the Podolska Cavalry under
Lieutenant-Colonel Gilewski was invited to be the guests of the 3rd
Hungarian Hussar Regiment: 'There, in front of the barracks, the elderly Colonel von Pongratsch was waiting along with his officer corps in
ceremonial array. My regiment was given full honours as it marched on
to the parade ground.'[5] Lieutenant-General Stanisław Maczek was in a
camp in Hungary where the Hungarian commandant played cards with
the Polish officers and deliberately arranged to receive a report on the
status of his guards while doing so, and he recommended that the Polish
officers leave at the rate of no more than 10 men a night, that being the
maximum number he could conceal in his records.[6]

Those troops who had crossed into Lithuania and Latvia generally
had a more difficult time reaching the west. Some made it across the
Baltic to Sweden and Norway with relative ease but the stories of others
attest to their determination and endurance. Antoni Położyński reached
Britain in January 1941 having travelled from Lithuania to Estonia and
then to Finland where he stowed away on a ship bound for New York,
from which he eventually travelled to Britain. Chaim Goldberg reached
the Soviet Union and then travelled to Japan on a forged visa before

reaching Canada where he joined the Polish Army, which had a recruitment office there, and was finally sent to Britain in October 1941.[7]

Poland's contribution to the allied victory in the Second World War began even before the first shot had been fired. The achievement in breaking the codes created by the military German Enigma cipher machine, understanding its operation and building replicas was arguably the greatest contribution that Poland made to the allied war effort, but one that the Polish Government was of course unable to publicise. Without the ability to break the Enigma codes, the Allies would have quite simply lost the battle of the Atlantic, and with that, the war. Yet the other major Polish imput in this field was that her cryptographers kept the secret throughout the war. Had the Polish cryptographers who were captured and questioned by the Gestapo revealed what they knew, then the Germans could have made sufficient changes to block out allied decryption efforts, and thereby the invasion of Europe would have had to be made without this priceless advantage. The details of how Enigma was broken had to be kept secret for some decades after the war had ended, because many countries around the world continued to use Enigma-type ciphers, and British and American intelligence operations would have been hampered if they had changed to something less breakable. The Polish contribution was thus obscure until a book published in Poland in 1967 revealed that the Poles had broken Enigma before the war, and a book in English published in 1974 informed the world that the Allies had been able to read German messages throughout the war.[8]

In January 1929, a commercial Enigma machine was sent to Poland by mistake and the Germans drew attention to the shipment by requesting its immediate return without customs inspection. The machine was secretly examined over a weekend by Ludomir Danilewicz and Antoni Palluth, directors of a Warsaw-based communications company, AVA. Looking like a complex typewriter, the Enigma machine was based on a combination of electrical and mechanical systems with keys, rotors, a plugboard and electrical connections. It was capable of producing a vast number of permutations as the encryption keys could be changed daily. The machine was carefully repacked and returned to Germany. AVA was in close collaboration with Poland's Cipher Bureau, which in turn had close links with the cryptologists working at the Mathematical

Institute in Poznań. Three of its brightest graduates, Marian Rejewski, Henryk Zygalski and Jerzy Różycki, set about trying to discover the secrets of Enigma and how its codes might be broken.[9]

The military version was still more complex, and before the Poles could break its codes they had to know in detail how it worked. They never had access to an actual machine; but Hans Thilo Schmidt, who worked in the German Defence Cipher Office, provided French intelligence with an operator's instruction manual and the key settings for September and October 1932, and the French passed them to the Poles. By the end of the year, the Poles had deduced the internal workings of the military Enigma machine, and over that Christmas Rejewski decrypted a signal sent by the Reichswehr. The AVA company then began manufacturing replica machines and the Poles developed a number of methods for automating the recovery of the keys of intercepted messages, first by means of a card index and then by perforated sheets. In late 1938 they mechanised the process by building a 'bombe', which was effectively the equivalent of six Enigma machines coupled together. This could recover a daily encryption key in about two hours, replacing the manual work of a hundred people. The concept of a bombe would be later developed further at the Government Code and Cipher School at Bletchley Park and the technology behind it was used in the early days of computing.[10]

At the end of 1938, the Germans introduced two new rotor wheels and other refinements. The Poles rapidly deduced all the details of the modifications by analysing the encrypted messages created by the modified machines, but their introduction nevertheless increased the complexity of the daily key recovery by a factor of at least ten. In the summer of 1939, when war looked inevitable, the Polish General Staff decided to share their knowledge with the British and French, who had struggled for years to understand and break Enigma without success. The official British history of intelligence during the war ascribes this decision to the need for more resources to develop the equipment necessary for speedy decryption, but Rejewski claimed:

> It was not [as Harry Hinsley suggested, cryptological] difficulties of ours that prompted us to work with the British and French, but only the deteriorating political situation. If we had had no difficulties at all we would still, or even more so, have shared our achievements with our allies as our contribution to the struggle against Germany.[11]

On 24–25 July the head of the Polish Cipher Bureau, Lieutenant-Colonel Gwido Langer, and his colleague Lieutenant Maksymilian Ciężki hosted a meeting with leading British and French cryptographers in the outskirts of Warsaw. The British representatives, Dillwyn ('Dilly') Knox and Alastair Denniston, and the French representatives, Gustave Bertrand and Henri Braquenié, were shown how to break the code and were given a replica machine each. When the war broke out, the Polish cryptographers destroyed all but two of their machines and fled for the Rumanian border and then travelled to France, reaching there in early October, where they set up operations near the town of Gretz-Armainvilliers, about 25 miles north-east of Paris. There they continued to read Enigma messages, reading 8,440 German messages: over 1,000 on the Norway campaign and about 5,000 on the French campaign. The French would not allow them to travel to Britain but a British cipher expert, Alan Turing, visited them in early 1940.[12]

The fall of France led to the second Polish contribution to Enigma: keeping the secret. The French and Polish cryptographers had fled to Toulouse before the armistice was proclaimed. Their boss, Gustave Bertrand, was in a dilemma: he first evacuated them to Oran in Algeria but then decided that they should return to Vichy France and re-establish the bureau at the Château des Fouzes in Uzès. The British wanted the Poles out of France but Betrand was determined to keep hold of them, and, unbelievably, the Polish Government did not realise what a priceless but extremely vulnerable asset they had in France and made no attempt to help their cryptographers escape. The Polish cryptographers maintained separate communications with the Polish Government, and such a show of independence did not endear them to Betrand. In November 1942, their position became extremely precarious when they learned, probably from the French resistance, that the Allies were about to invade North Africa and that the chances of a German occupation of Vichy France were high. The château was evacuated ahead of the German arrival, but Betrand behaved deplorably by frequently thwarting the attempts made by the Poles to escape the country. Rejewski and Zygalski managed to cross the Pyrenees into Spain, where they were imprisoned. On their release in May 1943, they reached Britain via Portugal, arriving there in July. They were sent to the Polish decryption unit at Stanmore, near London, which had a direct line to the British at Bletchley, and worked on the SS cipher and various lower-grade codes for the remainder of the war.[13]

1. Annual commemoration of Piłsudski's counter-offensive against Russia, Wilno, 14 August 1939

2. Troops from the Warsaw garrison after the surrender, 28 September 1939

3. German troops taking down
Polish government symbols, Gdynia,
September 1939

4. Soviet troops marching through Wilno, September 1939

5. A column of Jews guarded by German soldiers is marched through the streets of Warsaw during the winter of 1940

6. Polish POWs doing reconstruction work in the formerly Polish province of Poznań

7. Sikorski, Zaleski and Raczyński, London, November 1939

8. Polish refugees in Rumania waiting for a bank to open

9. Raczyński, Sikorski, Churchill, Zaleski and Attlee signing the agreement between Poland and the United Kingdom, 1 August 1940

10. Clementine and Winston Churchill and Sikorski in Fife, Scotland inspecting troops of the Polish 1st Rifle Brigade, October 1940

11. Antoni Głowacki (*left*) with a fellow pilot during the Battle of Britain. Głowacki once shot down five German aircraft in one day. He ultimately settled in New Zealand.

12. Polish Army howitzer training exercise, Scotland, May 1941

13. The footbridge connecting the 'Small Ghetto' to the 'Large Ghetto' in Warsaw with Chłodna Street, down the middle of the picture, reserved for Aryans

14. Raid on the Warsaw Ghetto – a photograph found on the body of a German soldier killed on the Eastern Front

15. Polish refugees from the Soviet Union in Iran, November 1942

16. General Sikorski and General Anders, Cairo, July 1943

The other Polish cryptographers underwent appalling suffering. Różycki had been drowned when the ship carrying him and his colleagues back to France from Algeria was sunk. Palluth, Edward Fokczyski, Langer and Ciężki were all captured by the Germans. Palluth and Fokczyski were sent to the Sachsenhausen-Oranienburg concentration camp but fortunately the Germans never realised their valuable secret. Langer was not so lucky: the Gestapo tracked him down in the internment camp at Schloss Eisenberg, near Most, and interrogated him. After the war he gave details of his interrogation:

> I told him that before the war, we conducted tests, and sometimes we did find a solution, but during the war, we didn't manage to decode anything, since the Germans had made changes, which they knew about, just before the war started.

The Germans knew from the decrypted Enigma messages found at the Polish Cipher Bureau that the Poles had broken the code but were prepared to believe Langer's mixture of truth and lies, especially when his story tallied with Ciężki's. Both men survived the war and settled in Britain after their liberation.[14]

By the end of October 1939, 3,842 Polish officers and men, of whom 1,320 were airmen, had escaped from Poland and reached France. This number would in due course reach 43,000 officers and men by June 1940.[15] Even while the fighting had continued in Poland, the Polish ambassador in Paris, Julius Łukasiewicz, issued an appeal to the large community of Poles resident in France:

> The one-half-million-strong Polish emigration will join its ranks, as behoves citizens of the Polish nation, to take an honourable part in liberating their homeland from the yoke of its two age-old foes. Within a few days announcements posted in all communes of the French Republic will call upon you to register; in two weeks you will come before draft boards, and subsequently a good many of you will be called into the ranks of the first Polish division in France. The tens of thousands of men who, for the time being, will remain in French war factories, working for the common cause, will be called up in the coming months to new units of the Polish Army formed beyond the borders of the Republic.[16]

This appeal was repeated by Sikorski's first Order of the Day, issued on

28 September 1939. He was convinced that a Polish army of 120,000 men could be formed in France. But the French and Belgian governments proved unhelpful: both were prepared to allow recruitment to the Polish Army but insisted on exemptions for Poles working in war-related industries. This proviso exempted over 35,000 Polish miners in northern France alone. Volunteers were slow to come forward and by May 1940, the Polish Army numbered 66,953 men, barely half of what Sikorski had envisaged.[17]

The newly re-formed Polish armed forces met with a mixed reaction from their allies. The navy came off best, for under the agreement signed with Britain on 19 November 1939, the Polish Government retained absolute sovereignty over its navy – both ships and personnel – and their ships sailed under the Polish flag, under the command of Polish officers and under the overall command of Admiral Jerzy Świrski. All Polish ships carried a British signals officer for the coding and decoding of signals. The Polish Air Force was very keen to collaborate with Britain after the September campaign rather than remain in France with the Polish Army. The reason given was that the Poles had more familiarity, gained before the war, with British equipment but actually it was that the Poles rated the RAF far higher than the French *Armée de l'Air*. The British insisted that the Poles should be treated on the same lines as Commonwealth troops and swear allegiance to the king, a demand the Poles naturally resented greatly. Also the RAF was initially sceptical about the Poles' flying abilities but soon learned that the Poles found the transfer to Hurricanes easy. There were some minor problems, such as having to remind the Polish pilots to lower their landing gear when coming in to land since the Polish fighters had been fixed-wheel.[18]

The Polish Army in the winter of 1939 anticipated being trained and equipped by the French and fighting alongside them when the Germans turned their attention westwards. Their training camp at Coëtquidan in Brittany had appalling conditions, and Bogdan Grodki noted his impressions on arrival:

> In a dirty, muddy entrance near an inn, barns and pigsties stood in a quadrangle. I looked inside. On the pavement and concrete slabs under the feeding troughs were laid armfuls of hay covered with blankets. Here lived the future soldiers of the Polish Army in dirt and muck.[19]

The Poles referred to the camp as a *koczkodan*, best translated as an old, dirty hag. Conditions did not improve until Sikorski intervened personally. Training proceeded very slowly and most of their equipment dated from the First World War. The French did not appear to value the services of their ally: 'There were no opportunities to make any contact with French officers and they made no effort in that direction themselves unless they had to; they kept aloof and obviously didn't think much of us.'[20] Brigadier-General Stanisław Sosabowski, appointed deputy commander of the 1st Division, believed that his men became infected by the poor morale and ill discipline of the average French soldier. The Poles were blamed for the war and the French appeared to take no interest in learning any lessons about the new German form of warfare from the soldiers of a defeated nation. When Lieutenant Rolski met General Maxime Weygand, commander-in-chief of the French forces in the Middle East, he was questioned about the German tactics: 'He listened attentively, but one could see that he put everything we said through the sieve of his own opinions and only retained the few morsels that fitted in with these.'[21]

The French cannot take all the blame for the unsatisfactory state of affairs, because the Polish Army itself was in considerable disarray. The first historian of the Polish fighting effort noted:

> The Polish army formed in France in the winter of 1939 was probably the queerest lot of men that ever carried rifles and learned attack, defence, taking cover and the other secrets of the infantryman's art. There were in the ranks diplomats, including Mr Lipski, the former Polish ambassador in Berlin, who had carried out many delicate personal negotiations with Hitler and Ribbentrop; there were also Polish miners from the north of France, some of whom had nearly forgotten their native language. Next to boys of seventeen were found university professors of fairly respectable age. There were adventurous volunteers from the Foreign Legion, former legionaries in the Spanish army at Guadalajara, and Polish settlers from Brazil and Peru. Poets, artists and writers made up a small but amusing group. There were priests and there were Jews. There were also many officers, but these were mostly army men of a fairly uniform type, unlike the privates. It was a kind of Noah's Ark collection, with one common feature – they all believed in Poland.[22]

Lipski himself found adaptation to army life somewhat difficult: 'I must admit that the change from my former life as a diplomat was something of a shock. I had to sleep on damp straw in damp, cold barracks, getting up to the sound of the bugle at 5 a.m., eating food from an army kitchen, drilling all day long, and handling heavy machine guns to the accompaniment of an unceasing flow of scathing comment from the sergeant-major.'[23] The Poles were also highly politicised and this caused many problems. Most of the soldiers who had escaped from Poland were officers and were usually loyal to the *Sanacja* regime; they were therefore suspicious of Sikorski's post-mortem of the September campaign, generally a witch-hunt against senior officers blamed for the defeat. The officers also had little in common with their men. The Polish labourers who had been working in France formed the rank and file and were generally left-wing, whereas the senior officers usually held deeply conservative and often right-wing opinions.

Sikorski had hoped to form an army of two corps, each of two infantry divisions, and a large armoured unit, as well as a substantial air force in France, but had to settle for less. On 10 May 1940, when the Germans launched their attack in the west, the Polish order of battle consisted of the 1st Division, 16,000 men, commanded by Major-General Bronisław Duch; the 2nd Division, also 16,000 men, under Major-General Bronisław Prugar-Ketling; the 10th Armoured Cavalry (Mechanised) Brigade, about 5,000 men, of whom only 2,000 were fully trained, under General Maczek. The 3rd Infantry Division, about 8,000 men, under Colonel Tadeusz Zieleniewski, lacked uniforms and weapons, and the 4th Division, with 3,000, under Colonel Rudolf Dreszer, was in the early stages of formation. The best-trained and -equipped Polish formation, the Podole Rifle Brigade under Major-General Zygmunt Szyszko-Bohusz, was away in Norway when the Germans launched their attack on France. The Polish Air Force in France was commanded by Major-General Józef Zając. On paper the establishment seemed reasonably impressive: 1,449 officers, 2,836 NCOs and 2,578 other ranks; but the French had been dilatory in training the Polish pilots on the French Morane and other fighters. Consequently out of the four squadrons created, only one and a half squadrons with a total of 86 aircraft were combat-ready when the Germans attacked.[24]

The Norway campaign in early 1940 was a brief interlude in the Phoney War and one in which the principal allied protagonists, France and Britain, did not cover themselves in glory. The origins of the allied expedition were twofold: to give aid to Finland, which had been invaded by the Soviet Union on 30 November 1939, and to deprive Germany of Swedish iron ore, which it imported for its war industries through the ice-free Norwegian port of Narvik. The Polish Government was keen for its army to be included in the allied expedition because it needed to prove to the world that Poland was still fighting and to gain the recognition from Britain and France that Poland was an ally of value, one which deserved a seat at the Supreme War Council. Political vacillations in Britain and France ensured that an allied expeditionary force was prepared too late to assist Finland, which sued for peace on 6 March. German suspicions regarding allied intentions towards Norway and Sweden – both countries having remained neutral during the First World War – had been aroused, and on 9 April 1940, Germany launched a pre-emptive strike against Denmark and Norway. The Danes capitulated quickly but the Norwegians showed every intention of putting up a fight.

Poland contributed to the Norwegian campaign both at sea and on land. Polish naval units joined the Royal Navy in its attack on the German fleet and during the campaign ten German destroyers were sunk. The Polish Navy lost a destroyer, *Grom*, in the battle, but its submarine *Orzeł* commanded by Captain Jan Grudziński had more luck. On 8 April, it spotted the 9,800-ton German passenger liner *Rio de Janeiro* near Oslofjord, surfaced and ordered it to stop. When the Germans refused to obey, the submarine launched torpedoes and sank the ship. The wreckage revealed that the *Rio de Janeiro* had been carrying German troops for the invasion of Norway. On 14 April 1940, the allied expeditionary force began disembarking at Narvik, which was already in German hands. The Polish Podole Brigade took part in the operations to recapture Narvik, taking first the town of Arkennes across the fjord and on 27–28 May the small town of Beisfjord. In the trenches outside Narvik, the Germans baited the Poles for their readiness to continue the fight, erecting boards with messages such as: 'Why fight for England and her capitalists? The road to Warsaw is free. Cross the Swedish frontier, or throw down arms and cross singly to join us. In accordance with Marshal Piłsudski's will we are building a new Poland with Hitler', or 'The Jews and English are your enemies. The Führer has conquered Holland and is marching on Paris. Your Allies are betraying you. You are fighting for the Jews and the English.' In retaliation the Poles erected a board with a derogatory cartoon of Hitler and the Germans expended much energy on trying to destroy it. The port of Narvik was captured on the night of 28 May, but instead of holding the port and town the allied expeditionary force was ordered to destroy the port facilities and re-embark for France on 8 June because the situation there was critical. The Poles had 97 men killed whereas the Germans lost around 200 men. The Poles received little public recognition for their role, and in 1943 the Polish Ministry of Information published a largely pictorial book, *Polish Troops in Norway*, to put the record straight.[25]

The German attack on the west came as little surprise to the Allies, but its speed and depth shocked them. The German plan was to advance in three army groups: Army Group B, commanded by General von Bock, drove into Holland and northern Belgium. The purpose of this attack was to entice the British and French to advance eastwards into Belgium leaving their right flank exposed. The Poles had unsuccessfully warned the Allies against mounting a defence so far forward, recommending instead that large reserves should be created and the bulk of the armour held back in strong formations. The flank of the allied armies was to be turned by the strongest German force, Army Group A, under General von Rundstedt, which would break through the Ardennes, seize crossings across the Meuse and advance on the French coast, thereby separating the allied armies in the north from the rest of France. The third German force, Army Group C, commanded by General Wilhelm von Leeb, would advance on the Maginot Line and keep the French forces there preoccupied even if it could not break the actual French line. The result was dramatic: in as short a time as it had taken the Germans to defeat the Poles, French and British armies in the north were in total disarray, retreating from the fast-moving and powerful German thrusts. On 26 May, the British began re-embarking their expeditionary force at Dunkirk, and this evacuation ended on 4 June, marking the end of the first phase of the battle for France.

The Polish Army had taken no part in the first phase: they were still undertrained and poorly equipped. On 5 June, the Germans, having brought up their infantry to join the Panzer divisions, now launched the second phase of the battle for France, the drive southwards from the Seine. The French began retreating. General Philippe Pétain now visited Sikorski in Paris and asked him to order the Poles to the front line.

As Sikorski later said: 'How could I refuse; the old man begged me to save France.'[26]

On 26 May, the Polish 1st Division was sent to occupy the Metz sector of the Maginot Line. The haste of the despatch of these troops to the front was obvious to the Poles:

> The men in my platoon were still strangers to me. We had been brought together only a few days earlier, and as yet we had had no opportunity of becoming acquainted. During the last week we had to do work which should have taken months. We were snowed up under bales of new uniforms, new weapons, and motorised equipment, so that we had hardly time to eat, and even less for sleep. We had to learn to drive our brand-new vehicles, which were not yet run in, and to make the acquaintance of the new French sub-machine guns, which we had never seen before.[27]

The 1st Division succeeded in repelling the attack of four German divisions and this prompted Pétain, who had witnessed the battle, to comment to Sikorski: 'if there had only been ten Polish divisions, victory would have been certain'. The division was then asked to cover the French Fourth Army as it retreated from Lorraine, and on 15–16 June it suffered very high casualties in battles in the Isiming–Arwiller sector, along the Munser–Bisping–Azondange line and finally along the Dieuze–Fénétrange line.

The Polish 2nd Division under General Prugar-Ketling was deployed in the region of Belfort near the Swiss border. It took part in battles to hold the bridgeheads over the Saone river to enable the French Army to retreat, and fought in the defence of Montbéliard, in which it sustained and inflicted heavy casualties. The Podole Brigade was rushed back from Norway and landed in Brittany, but was in no condition to be thrust into a chaotic fight: the supply units were missing, there were only between 20 and 40 cartridges per rifle and 200–300 bullets per machine gun, and they had lost all their signalling equipment. Despite this, the brigade was assigned to the defence of the railway junction in Dol, south of St Michel. The 10th Armoured Cavalry Brigade, commanded by General Stanisław Maczek, had received very little training, but now, suddenly, the Poles were given tanks and expected to learn how to drive them. On 13 June, the brigade held off the German attack in the Champaubert–Montmirail region before attacking near Montgivroux. The Poles then followed the French retreat southwards and had a brief skirmish with the Germans around the town of Montbard and seized a crossing over the Burgundy Canal. At this point the division was out of ammunition and petrol, and they destroyed the remaining tanks and other vehicles before beginning the march southwards on foot on 18 June.[28]

The Polish Air Force had a frustrating campaign. Some Polish pilots blamed the faulty tactics employed at the time by both the French Air Force and the RAF, which consisted of flying in a V formation in small groups – which meant that the German fighters always outnumbered them. Furthermore, there was a lack of pre- and post-operative briefings and so no opportunity to disseminate any lessons learnt. The air campaign in France was also limited by the chaos caused by the rapid retreat of the French Army. One Polish pilot, Władysław Chciuk, recorded his experiences on 16 May, when he fought some German Dornier-17s; his plane was shot up and when landing Chciuk hit a tree:

> Belgian rustics showed me to a French infantry unit, where I waited a whole day for transport back to the squadron. None was provided, so I set off walking. After arriving at some French headquarters, I was accompanied across the border. Then, after three days of hitchhiking, horseback, walking, and being arrested twice as a spy I arrived at my airfield. There, I learned from three mechanics left behind to burn abandoned aircraft that my unit had moved to another location – somewhere near Paris. I ordered them to repair one Morane and the next day I flew it to a new base. The airfield's commander, General Weygand, observed my take-off. He wasn't told that my aircraft had defective landing gear, the flaps didn't work, the propeller's pitch couldn't be changed, the aircraft wasn't armed and that I had no parachute ... After landing at Le Bourget, I was told that my *Groupement de Chase* had already moved to Plessis-Belleville, for where I promptly took off.

During May and June, Polish fighter pilots shot down 52 enemy planes and shared 21 more kills with the French. They lost 9 pilots killed.[29]

Historians have recently revisited the battle for France and concluded that the French performance was not as bad as it was viewed at the time. The soldiers fought with determination but were let down by their high command, who lost control of events.[30] Certainly the Poles were not impressed by the French attitude towards the war. One soldier from the 3rd Division noted: 'Motorised columns were not even in retreat, but in disgraceful escape; they threw down their weapons, leaving them behind on the roads, and returned to their homes.'[31] The French high command did little to keep the Poles informed of events and consequently, on 11 June, Sikorski left the Polish headquarters in Paris and travelled east to learn more for himself. Here the duality of his role as prime minister and commander-in-chief was to prove near disastrous; not only did he not find the French high command but he was out of communication with his own government and high command during the most critical phase of the French campaign.[32]

The Polish Government moved southwards when the French Government evacuated Paris and reached a temporary resting place at Libourne, near Bordeaux. The Polish foreign minister, August Zaleski, realised that the French Government had given up the battle and made overtures to the British for the evacuation of his government and the army to Britain. On 17 June, Sikorski finally arrived at Libourne and the next day flew to Britain for consultations with Churchill, leaving Sosnkowski in command of the Polish Army. Sikorski asked Churchill if Britain would continue the war, and received a firm affirmative. The Polish Government embarked on HMS *Arethusa* and travelled to Britain, where on 21 June President Raczkiewicz was welcomed at Paddington station by King George VI. Sikorski visited Churchill in London on 25 June and Jock Colville wrote of the meeting: 'His [Sikorski's] ADC said that the way in which the French ran away was indescribable: they showed no fighting spirit. I hear from all sides that the Poles have been fighting magnificently in France: they seem to be our most formidable allies.'[33]

On 19 June, Sikorski made a radio broadcast ordering all the Poles in France to make their way to the nearest port to await evacuation to Britain. General Duch and the 1st Division were still in contact with the enemy and tangled up in the French retreat: few managed to escape and most became POWs. The 2nd Division was caught on the Swiss border, too far away from any coast, so it crossed into Switzerland, where the Swiss authorities disarmed them and sent them to internment camps. The 11,000 men remained in Switzerland for the rest of the war, while the Polish Government, desperate for trained men, did try to get them released, but without success. Within the Polish community the men of this division later became known as 'the five degrees', since they had nothing to do in Switzerland other than to obtain more education. The 3rd Division was ordered by the French Major-General Louis-Augustin-Joseph Faury to assemble at Vannes to surrender alongside his army; they refused, but most were unable to escape and so were captured. The Podole Brigade, having suffered one debacle in Norway, was also forced to surrender. Polish airmen fared better: many pilots flew directly to England and others to North Africa, and then made their way to Britain by sea.[34]

Elements of the Polish Army struggled to reach the French ports, where, on Churchill's explicit instructions to the Admiralty, the Royal Navy was making every effort to evacuate them. Maczek had 500 men with him and unable to feed such a large body forced them to split into small groups. Remnants of the other divisions were following the same course. The Germans seemed to be everywhere but the French population often warned the Poles of the German presence and advised them on the best route to take. The roads were unsafe and the Michelin road maps Maczek had were of little use for travelling across country. After a march of eighteen days, he finally reached the unoccupied zone where he was relieved to enjoy a normal life: 'being able to go to the cafe for a glass of wine and being able to sleep in a comfortable bed and have a hot bath'. Maczek was effectively stranded in Marseilles and found himself surrounded by Polish soldiers who had somehow acquired civilian clothing but still had the unmistakable bearing of the military. He eventually reached Britain via Morocco and Lisbon.[35]

Elsewhere in France considerable confusion reigned over what the terms of the armistice signed on 22 June meant for the Poles. Article X stipulated that the French Government would cease hostilities immediately; that it would prevent members of the French armed forces from leaving the country; and that it would forbid its citizens from joining foreign armies that were at war with Germany. Nowhere did it mention the Poles explicitly; nevertheless, the French authorities were determined to prevent the Poles from leaving. Two large British transport ships arrived in the ports of Rochefort and La Rochelle on the night of 19 June. Stefan Baluk was trying to leave on a British ship and noted that when some German Dorniers appeared the French anti-aircraft gunners fled for cover. When a Polish officer fired a machine gun at the planes, the French dockworkers begged him to desist and 'not to provoke the Germans'. Polish ships also took part alongside their British counterparts in the operations to evacuate Polish troops from the southern ports of St-Jean-de-Luz and Le Verdon. The French commander at St-Jean-de-Luz tried to stop the embarkation of Polish troops on the night of 24–25 June but was persuaded to turn a blind eye for a few hours; 3,000 men were evacuated.[36] After the campaign was over, Lieutenant-General Sosnkowski wrote a lengthy report for the Polish cabinet that clearly showed how the French Government and high command had hindered the efforts of the Poles to escape from France.[37]

The Polish Army, so painstakingly built up in France, was squandered to facilitate the retreat of the French Army. It suffered 6,000 casualties, including 1,400 killed, and the majority of the troops became POWs or were interned in Switzerland. Only 19,000 soldiers and airmen were evacuated, representing under a quarter of the Polish Army in France at the start of the German invasion. This number could have been higher but many of the recent recruits who had lived in France prior to the war chose to be discharged and return to their homes to protect their families rather than join the Polish troops in an uncertain future in Britain. The historiography of the French campaign barely mentions the existence of, let alone the actions of, the Polish troops, yet in 1940 the French were grateful towards them. Weygand told Maczek: 'I know what you and your brigade have done on the front, how you shielded the French retreat, and I thank you in the name of France', and his unit received 38 *Croix de Guerres* and *Médailles Militaires*.[38] Sikorski had learnt an important lesson from the French campaign: the piecemeal fashion in which the Polish units had been thrown into battle made him determined that, in the future, when the Poles were deployed, they should fight as a clearly identifiable mass of Polish soldiery and not be scattered among allied units.

On 18 June 1940, Churchill told the House of Commons: 'What General Weygand called the "Battle of France" is over. I expect that the battle of Britain is about to begin.'[39] Hitler knew that to launch a successful invasion of Britain the RAF would have to be destroyed first. The Battle of Britain fell into five phases: over the English Channel, 10 July–early August; aerial combat between the RAF and the Luftwaffe, 13–18 August; the German offensive against the RAF airfields, 24 August–6 September; the battle of London, 7–30 September to protect the capital from daylight bombing raids; and, finally, a series of minor raids until 31 October 1940. After the fall of France, the terms under which the Poles served with the RAF were amended, and the oath of allegiance to the British king was dropped. Two Polish fighter squadrons, 302 (Poznań) and 303 (Kościuszko) were formed, although a number of Polish pilots remained flying with their British squadrons. A small Polish fighter command staff was set up within RAF Fighter Command headquarters in Stanmore in 1940. A year later Polish liaison officers were appointed to all bases where Polish pilots were stationed.[40]

The RAF put the Poles through an extremely demanding training schedule. The linguistic barrier was problematic: the pilots were forced to undergo a three-week-long intensive course in the English language, specifically designed to give them the necessary vocabulary for air operations. The group commander of 303 Squadron, Captain Stanley Vincent, also came up with an ingenious solution. He put the Polish fighter pilots on bicycles with radios strapped to their backs and headphones, and sent them pedalling around the airfield in formation so that the Poles soon learnt the English commands. Squadron Leader Ronald Kellett served in 303 Squadron and flew with an English-Polish glossary strapped to his knee. 302 Squadron was made operational on 15 August but was stationed at Leconfield in Yorkshire, outside the main area of the Battle of Britain. Nevertheless, on 19 August, the squadron recorded its first kill when Lieutenant Antoni Ostowicz shot down a Messerschmitt 110.[41]

303 Squadron would become legendary within the RAF. It was stationed at RAF Northolt, near London, and therefore in the centre of the battle. While on a training flight on 30 August, the Poles spotted the Germans and contrary to all orders immediately went to attack. Lieutenant Ludwik Paszkiewicz shot down a Dornier bomber and the RAF concluded from this unconventional action that the Polish squadron was ready to be made operational.[42] The British had harboured doubts about the value of the Poles after the rapid defeat of the Polish Air Force in September 1939, but the Poles had no doubts regarding their own abilities, needing only a modern plane like a Hurricane. The Poles were also viewed as ill-disciplined, reckless and over-keen to fight the Germans, but as the British losses mounted among their inexperienced pilots, they would come to appreciate these qualities in the Polish pilots. A Polish pilot described his first kill:

> I caught up with him easily. He grew in my sights until his whole fuselage filled the mini-circle [of the gun sights]. It was certainly time to fire. I did so quite calmly and was not even excited, rather puzzled and surprised to

find it so easy. Quite different from Poland where you had to scrape and
strain and then instead of getting the bastard, he got you.[43]

The secret to their success was their ability to hold fire until they were
within 100–200 yards of the German plane, whereas the less experienced British pilots started firing at 400 yards. The Polish kills mounted
up and on 27 September 1940, 303 Squadron posted its one hundredth
confirmed kill (but Paszkiewicz was killed too). The Czech pilot Josef
František flew with 303 and was the highest scoring ace in the entire
RAF during the Battle of Britain. He was killed in a crash landing on 8
October 1940.[44]

When the Battle of Britain officially ended on 31 October 1940, the
Poles were acknowledged as having made a contribution that belied
their small numbers. They lost 33 pilots but 34 had become aces – men
who had scored five or more kills. 303 Squadron had downed three
times the RAF average.[45] The Poles received enormous publicity and
gratitude for their daring deeds in the sky. After visiting a Polish squadron in August 1940, the king was heard to remark: 'One cannot help
feeling that if all our Allies had been Poles, the course of the war, up to
now, would have been very different.'[46] The head of Fighter Command,
Sir Hugh Dowding, told Churchill, 'the Poles in our Fighter Squadrons
were very dashing but totally undisciplined'. Churchill in response said:
'one Pole was worth three Frenchmen, Gort and Dowding said nearer
ten!'[47] Having a Polish fighter pilot on one's arm became the height of
fashion for young women in Britain in the summer of 1940, and jealous
RAF pilots sometimes adopted phoney Polish accents to attract girls.
The headmistress of a girls' school ended her speech to the school leav-
ers with the warning: 'And remember, keep away from gin and Polish
airmen.'[48] News of the Polish success in Britain also became widely
known in Poland when the book *Squadron 303* by Arkady Fiedler was
published by the Polish Underground in 1943.[49]

The Polish Government still had one army in the field, flying the Polish
flag. Although France had been the main collection point for Poles
escaping from Poland in 1939, a significant number of men had made
their way to the Middle East, and were organised into the 1st Polish
Independent Carpathian Brigade (1 *Samodzielna Brygada Strzelców
Karpackich*), commanded by Major-General Stanisław Kopański, who

travelled from Paris to take up the command. The brigade was based at Homs in Syria and quartered in castles dating from the time of the Crusades. It formed part of the French Army in the Middle East commanded by General Weygand, and by the time mainland France was defeated, the brigade numbered 4,000 men, trained and equipped by the French. The local French commander, General Eugène-Désité-Antoine Mittelhauser, insisted that the Polish brigade should cease hostilities along with the French forces. Kopański disagreed vociferously and, despite being threatened with arrest, he and his men made their way into British-controlled Palestine with all their equipment. The Poles were secretly aided by General René de Larminat, who would later join the Free French forces in Palestine.[50]

The British, although grateful to receive a fully armed brigade, were somewhat surprised by their arrival, and unsure about what to do with them. They could not be used in the desert campaign launched by General Archibald Wavell in December 1940 because, although the Polish Government had broken off diplomatic relations with Italy, it was not formally at war with Italy. The British respected the Polish desire to take an active part in their operations, though not offensively against Italy. The British also accepted that because of Poland's long-standing relationship with France it would be politically impossible for the Poles to take to the field against the Vichy French in Syria. From mid-January 1941 onwards, the Carpathian Brigade started the process of mechanisation and received training in mountain warfare. It was earmarked to form part of the British expeditionary force to Greece in March 1941. Sikorski strongly supported this because it fitted with his strategy: 'The formation of a new front in the Balkans ... brings us nearer to Poland. It provides conditions for a future offensive on the continent.'[51] However, the departure of the Poles was cancelled at the last minute because the sudden advance of the Afrika Korps under General Erwin Rommel meant that the British needed every trained man in the desert. Instead, the brigade was sent to a fortified camp in Mersa-Matruh, near Alexandria, to protect the approaches to the Nile Delta and also provided troops for twelve POW camps there which housed over 65,000 Italians.[52]

There is no space here to repeat the story of the advances and retreats of the British forces in the Western Desert. Wavell's offensive at the end of 1940 had captured the Libyan port of Tobruk; Rommel's 1941 spring offensive left Tobruk isolated and under siege behind German-Italian lines. In the middle of August, the British commander, General Claude Auchinleck,* informed Kopański that Sikorski, keen to see Polish troops contributing to the war effort, had agreed to a British request to send the Carpathian Brigade to Tobruk. Over ten days, 18–28 August, the brigade, now numbering 288 officers and 4,777 other ranks, was secretly shipped at night from Alexandria, replacing most of the Australian 9th Division.[53]

The fortress of Tobruk was about the size of the Isle of Wight. The perimeter was 31 miles long and the distance from the harbour to the centre was about 9 miles.

> Practically the whole of the Tobruk area was visible to the enemy from one escarpment (hill) or another. Over some parts of it you could not even walk in daylight without being shot at ... The whole area is desert made up of sand and rocks. There is hardly a sign of the faintest scrub. The ground is littered with derelict tanks, aeroplanes and lorries.[54]

Tobruk was defended by the British 70th Division and 32nd Armoured Brigade, a regiment of Indian cavalry, a Czech battalion and various artillery units, totalling 34,113 men all under the command of Lieutenant-General Sir Ronald Scobie.[55]

The Poles were sent to defend the most vulnerable western part of the perimeter, where in May the three Italian divisions along with part of a German division, a total of 33,000 men, had succeeded in making a breach opposite the Medauar Hill. An Australian soldier observed the conduct of the Poles:

> They were Poles, come to Tobruk with the specific intention of killing Germans ... They laughed when I first tried them with my French, in fact they laughed all the time, and they were behaving as if they had a date that very afternoon – with Rommel I think, which made them the oddest of bods.[56]

One Polish officer found a German greatcoat when out on patrol, putting it on he entered the Italian lines, and for two days questioned the Italians about their defences. Then he returned to the Polish lines where he received both thirty days' detention and a decoration for his conduct.[57]

Auchinleck launched Operation Crusader, designed to drive the

---

* Auchinleck had replaced Wavell on 21 June 1941.

Germans back and relieve Tobruk, on 18 November 1941. Initial progress was good and on 21 November, the Tobruk garrison attempted to break out. The newspaper correspondent Alan Moorehead observed the Polish section:

> The Poles broke out of their confinement in Tobruk with the exuberance of Red Indians and now, as their chief of staff said to us with no intention of being funny, 'It makes a nice change for the boys. A very nice change indeed.' It did too. They went into battle as though they were buccaneers boarding a 15th century galleon.[58]

The breakout drew the attacking allied troops 10 miles from the Tobruk perimeter before a German counterattack pushed them back. The allied attack was renewed in December and the siege was broken after the battle of Gazala. Feliks Keidrowski recalled his experiences of an Italian counterattack:

> We were short of ammunition so all 6,000 soldiers had four rounds each. As I was a machine-gun carrier I had 40. The order was not to fire randomly. We stayed in position without shooting facing thousands of advancing Italian soldiers. They were 50–100 yards away from us and still no single shot, our nerves wrecked by the fear of not being able to hold back the Italians, now 50 yards from us still no flare signalling to us 'open fire'. Instead the order went out: 'fix bayonets!' We charged towards them with a roar and all 16,000 Italians got out anything they could wave and surrendered – just like that. We didn't even fire a shot we took them all as prisoners.[59]

The Polish brigade lost 23 men dead and 96 wounded in this battle; its total losses in the Western Desert were 200 killed and 429 wounded. In March 1942, the Carpathian Brigade was withdrawn and sent back to Egypt.[60] Despite heavy demands on manpower as Rommel drove the Allies back to the Egyptian border and the high casualties from the battle of El Alamein, the British Government did not ask the Polish Government to send its troops into the desert again. The focus for the Poles was now to build up a substantial Polish army corps in the Middle East that could be used en masse in the next major allied campaign, using the men recently released from the Soviet Union.

After the fall of France the Polish Government concentrated on building up an army in Britain capable of making a significant contribution to the outcome of the war. No plans had been made by the British Government for the arrival of the Poles in Britain: after all, no one had anticipated the terrible sequence of defeats that summer. The Polish soldiers were welcome, however, since Britain was short of troops and expected Hitler to launch an invasion imminently. Hence at the end of July 1940, Churchill sent a minute to his chief of staff, General Hastings Ismay, urging the chiefs of staff to give the Poles and the Free French priority in the rearmament of the various foreign corps in Britain, even over the Home Guard.[61] In September 1940, on the first anniversary of Britain's declaration of war on Germany, Churchill issued an open letter to the Polish troops:

> On behalf of the Government and people of Great Britain, I am very glad to write this line of welcome to every Polish soldier, sailor or airman who has found his way over to help us fight and win this war . . . we in Great Britain hope that you will find amongst us a happy, if temporary home . . . I know that Polish forces on land and sea and in the air will play a worthy part in achieving this goal.[62]

The terms were quickly settled and the Poles served under the Commonwealth Forces Treaty, which gave the Polish Government the same absolute sovereignty over its army that it already had over its navy. The soldiers were despatched to Scotland to begin building up the First Army Corps. Conditions were poor, particularly the food as General Sosabowski recalled:

> We were even sent British Army cooks. After a few days, by which time the troops were almost on hunger strike, I asked if we could have the raw rations. We were not ungrateful, but my men just could not stomach British food cooked in the British style.

In October 1940, his men were sent to Fife to prepare anti-invasion defences on the east coast. He quickly discovered that local bureaucracy interfered with the construction of defences but 'soon found it was best to meet the farmers, have drinks with them and get the work under way while the papers and forms slowly travelled from department to department'.[63]

The soldiers who had escaped from Poland to Britain were mainly officers: there were too many of them, and their loyalty to Sikorski was suspect. He responded in a controversial manner by retiring many of the most senior officers and allowing a number of young officers to take up contracts with British African colonial troops. To forestall any conspiracy against him, Sikorski also established camps for officers, first in Rothesay on the island of Bute and later on the mainland at Kingleddors and Tinachbrach, which were viewed as little more than penal camps.[64]

Sikorski was optimistic in his plans to rebuild the Polish Army. His original intention was to create an army corps of 4 infantry brigades with a range of support units. The Polish troops who had been evacuated from France would form the nucleus. Sikorski estimated that there were 3,000 Polish nationals in Britain, 170,000 in Canada, an unknown figure but thought to be several thousand in South America, but, above all, around 4,500,000 Polish-Americans of whom 10 per cent were thought to be Polish citizens. Sikorski's plans proved to be wildly overoptimistic. The proposed conscription of Polish nationals living in Britain became the subject of a question in Parliament and was rejected by the British Government. The problem was that many of the Poles had arrived during the 1930s, fleeing the *Sanacja* regime. Some had legally been stripped of their Polish citizenship under the law that deprived Poles of their citizenship if they had spent more than five years outside Poland, and they and the other refugees had no intention of joining the armed forces of such a country and especially not to serve under officers who represented opinions in opposition to their own.[65]

The failure of the recruitment drive in Britain led the new commander of the First Army Corps, Lieutenant-General Marian Kukiel, to conclude that 'new generations, Americans or Canadians with Polish origin, were the only hope, by recruiting volunteers in America, to change the skeletal army into a powerful force'.[66] Poles in the United States had flooded into the Haller army created in France in 1917 to fight under the Polish flag, and so Sikorski and Kukiel had grounds for believing that they would surely do so again. General Haller himself spent the first three months of 1940 in the United States on an unsuccessful mission to recruit Polish nationals. In March 1941, Sikorski visited North America and held meetings with the Canadian prime minister, Mackenzie King, and with the American president, Franklin Delano Roosevelt. The Canadian Government was prepared to permit recruitment for the Polish Army on its soil and would help with organisation and training, with the proviso that Canadian citizens and Poles from the United States would not be enlisted. Roosevelt informed Sikorski that it was illegal under United States law to advocate enlistment in a foreign army. He suggested that a way round the law was to publicise the training camps in Canada. Sikorski visited the main centres of Polish immigration: Chicago, Detroit, Buffalo and New York, making speeches to large audiences. His attitude, however, caused great anger within the Polish-American community when he announced that he did not want their money but their youths to serve in the Polish forces. Sikorski had underestimated how the values of *Polonia* had changed in the United States during the intervening period; the second generation of Polish immigrants felt little for Poland, considering themselves as Americans rather than Poles. As a result the recruitment drive failed and only around 700 men enlisted from North America and 900 from South America. On the other hand, when the United States joined the war in December 1941, young Poles willingly volunteered for the United States armed forces.[67]

Sikorski accordingly had to scale back his plans. Instead of despatching the 4th Brigade to Canada as the officer cadre of the Polish Army recruited in North America, it became the 1st Independent Parachute Brigade (*Pierwsza Samodzielna Brygada Spadochronowa*) with many former officers serving as common soldiers. This brigade was commanded by General Sosabowski. The 2nd Rifle Brigade was turned into the 10th Mechanised Brigade and was commanded by General Maczek.[68]

Given the shortage of troops in Britain it is worthwhile considering why the Polish Parachute Brigade was created. Poland had been one of the pre-war pioneers of military parachuting. After many years of civilian parachuting, it had launched a military programme in 1936 after the Red Army had shown the possible applications through parades and demonstrations. The plan was to create a force of lightly armed troops who would engage in sabotage operations behind enemy lines. The majority of qualified paratroopers had been taken as POWs in 1939, but two key instructors, Lieutenant Jerzy Gorecki and Lieutenant Julian Gebolys, reached Britain and were employed at the RAF parachute training base at Ringway. Polish techniques were so innovative, notably the use of a tower to train men in the correct technique of parachuting, that the British asked the Poles to train parachutists to be dropped in France, Norway, Belgium, Holland and Czechoslovakia. Many within the staff of the Polish and the British forces felt that the Polish Parachute Brigade itself was something of a luxury. Sosabowski wrote: 'I had always felt that my unit was an Army bastard, born out of wedlock, unwanted and with most of the qualities and faults of a love-child – strength, stubbornness and determination.' On 23 September 1941, the unit was granted the title 'The 1st Polish Independent Parachute Brigade' at a parade attended by Polish leaders and British commanders. The Polish Government then authorised Sosabowski to request volunteers from among the Polish troops in Britain. Kukiel, commander of the First Polish Army Corps, sent Sosabowski 100 men who had a long list of misdemeanours, including civil crime, against their names.[69]

The Parachute Brigade remained outside the structure of British command and was to be used exclusively for operations in Poland, to provide well-trained and well-equipped support for a national uprising. At the time of the its creation little thought was given to how this plan could be put into practice. Britain was desperately short of aircraft and operations to Poland entailed great risk. (The subject of support for Poland will be covered in detail in later chapters.) The Parachute Brigade did, however, train the *Cichociemni* ('unseen and silent'), men who were despatched by parachute to Poland to train the *Armia Krajowa* (AK) for operations against the German occupying forces. Strong links with the AK were established and, indeed, women in Warsaw designed and, hiding in the nuns' quarters attached to the Church of the Deaconesses in Theatre Place, created a colour for the brigade:

> The main cloth was in crimson silk; on one side were the national arms of Poland with the eagle and crown and the Warsaw City Coat of Arms; in each corner was a parachute badge. The reverse side depicted Saint Michael the Archangel, patron saint of parachutists; above was the inscription *Warsaw 1939*, and below, expressing the desire of all patriots, the motto *Surge Polonia*.

The standard was consecrated in Warsaw on 3 November 1942, but only reached Britain in 1944 when it was presented to the brigade at an official ceremony on 15 June 1944. It came on the same plane that brought out parts of the V-2 rocket. The emotional importance of such links between the exiles and those trapped in the nightmare of occupied Poland cannot be exaggerated.[70]

The German invasion of the Soviet Union in June 1941 offered the prospect of easing the manpower shortages of the Polish armed forces. The new Polish Army created in the Soviet Union, partly evacuated to Iran, meant that the Polish armed forces might now be in a position to make a notable contribution to the defeat of Germany. The question to be answered was: where should this army be concentrated so as to have the greatest impact? Accordingly, in April 1942, Sikorski convened a meeting in London attended by all his senior commanders. The Polish forces in Britain were represented by the commander of the Polish First Army Corps, Kukiel; the commander of the Polish Parachute Brigade, Sosabowski; the chief of staff, Klimecki; and General Stanisław Ujejski and Admiral Jerzy Świrski, for the air force and navy, respectively. From the Soviet Union came Anders, who was joined by the commander of the Carpathian Brigade, Kopański, in representing the Polish Army outside Britain. This conference was so heated that even the minutes could not be agreed on.[71] The contingent from the Polish Army in Britain naturally wanted the entire Polish Army to be concentrated there because any allied invasion of Europe would be launched from Britain. Kukiel argued that he needed an absolute minimum of 30,000 men to bring his existing units up to full strength and to create a reserve. Ujejski and Świrski also appealed for men to increase their establishments. Opposed to them was Anders, who wanted the entire Polish Army concentrated in the Middle East ready to support allied operations in the Balkans, which offered a shorter route back to Poland. Sikorski's response was: 'It was not possible to say which road to Poland will turn out to be the longest and which the shortest.' He wanted to keep the options open and brokered a compromise which ended up satisfying no one: he proposed that 15,000 troops, later reduced to 8,000, should be sent to Britain from the Middle East as reinforcements. Of these, 5,500 would be allocated to the First Army Corps, but this figure was too low for Kukiel to fill his establishment.[72] Out of these, 300 were sent to the Parachute Brigade, but:

> Many were unfit to be in the army, let alone the Parachute Brigade. Their physical condition after months of starvation and lack of exercise in concentration camps had left them weak and skinny. Bad food had resulted in swollen stomachs, yet they were perpetually hungry. We gave them special rations and extra vitamins and slowly their health improved.[73]

Ujejski argued that he needed 4,000 men just to maintain his current level of strength but received only 1,500. The Navy received 1,000, too few to allow Świrski to take up the British offer of two new destroyers. The remainder of the Polish Army from the Soviet Union was to remain in the Middle East under the command of Anders, but Sikorski hoped that more Polish troops would be recruited in the Soviet Union where they would fight alongside the Soviet forces.

During 1942 a new source of potential recruits appeared: Poles from Upper Silesia and Pomerania who had been conscripted into the Wehrmacht. In June 1942, Captain Alan Graham asked a question in Parliament drawing the attention of the secretary of state for war, Sir John Grigg, to the existence of these estimated 170,000 conscripted soldiers and requesting that 'he will afford every encouragement and facility to such Poles to desert to us' and that they should then be handed over to the Polish authorities. Grigg replied that he was uncertain as to whether any of these Poles were serving in German front-line forces.[74] By 1943 it was clear that they were, when some became POWs in the Western Desert, and the British authorities were helpful about directing them towards the Polish armed forces. As early as 1941 procedures had been established to cope with the small numbers of Polish soldiers reaching Britain after the fall of Poland and France. Then the Foreign Office had asked the Polish Government to give them a list of Polish nationals travelling to Britain from places such as Lisbon, along with a testament to their political reliability. This would prevent the Poles from having to remain in the Royal Patriotic School, the clearing station for foreign nationals entering Britain, before the Polish military collected them. Therefore, in 1942 when the issue of Poles who had served in the Wehrmacht arose, the Polish authorities already had a screening process in place. This was designed to interrogate a POW on whether he had joined the Wehrmacht voluntarily or had been forcibly conscripted, and also on details of his service.[75] In October 1943, questions were asked in Parliament concerning the security vetting of those men now recruited into the Polish Army and their numbers. Grigg confirmed that he was content with the vetting but would not divulge the numbers.[76] In fact they were only in the low hundreds until the Allies regained a foothold on the continent, when they began to rise dramatically.

Sikorski and the Polish commanders could never form a clear strategy, because they were operating in the dark. Without a seat on the Combined Chiefs of Staff in Washington, they had little idea of the future plans of the Allies. After the entry of the Soviet Union and the United States into the war, Poland's value as an ally waned because there were simply too few Polish troops compared to the vast forces the new allies could field. These realities were recognised by the Polish Government after Sikorski's death in July 1943. Kopański, the new chief of staff, wrote a memorandum for the new commander-in-chief, General Sosnkowski, in which he argued that the small size of Poland's army meant that it should abandon its hope of a 'Polish' theatre of operations and simply be satisfied with a more general contribution to the allied war effort, in division strength only if necessary.[77] Kopański's views agreed with those of the Combined Chiefs of Staff. In a directive issued in July 1943 they acknowledged the limitations imposed by the manpower shortage and concluded that Polish forces should not be used in the initial assaults, but would form part of the general reserve to be employed later, wherever and whenever they could make a decisive contribution. It also stated: 'The Polish Parachute Brigade will be reserved for direct action in Poland, but the moment and method of this employment must be governed by the availability of aircraft.'[78]

Poland acknowledged before the outbreak of war that the Polish Navy would be trapped in the Baltic by the far larger German fleet and that its chances of making any useful contribution to the war effort would be minimal. Consequently plans were prepared whereby the Polish destroyers would head for British ports when war seemed imminent. On 30 August 1939 three Polish destroyers – *Błyskawica*, *Grom* and *Burza* – sailed for Leith in Scotland, arriving there on 1 September. The submarine fleet joined them in Britain since submarines would have little chance of success for long in the relatively shallow waters of the Baltic. *Orzeł* was briefly interned in Estonia, and arrived in Britain on 14 October.[79] According to the Admiralty report:

> They only had three requests: to land the sick cook, to replenish their water supplies and to be given breech blocks for their guns. They were then prepared to go to sea forthwith on whatever patrol it pleased the British Navy to employ them.[80]

Poland's merchant fleet also escaped the Baltic. Pre-war legislation had compelled all ship owners to place their vessels at the disposal of the government in the event of war. In late August 1939, the Polish Naval Headquarters warned all ships to head for British, French or neutral ports. As a result virtually the whole of Poland's merchant marine, around 140,000 tons, escaped to contribute to the allied war effort.[81]

Under an auxiliary agreement with Britain, the Polish Government was loaned ships. The destroyer HMS *Garland* was the first to be transferred to the Polish Navy, on 3 May 1940. Further ships were given after the fall of France when French and Belgian ships, abandoned in British ports by their crews who returned home, were turned over to the Polish Navy. These included twelve trawlers, two submarine-chasers and an old French destroyer, *Ouragan*. This last ship was in a poor state of repair and was eventually returned to the Free French Navy on 4 April 1941. In October 1940, the Poles received a new British destroyer, HMS *Nerissa*, which they renamed *Piorun*. Further ships followed, including motor-torpedo boats. On 15 January 1943, the Polish Navy received an old British cruiser, HMS *Dragon*, which it wanted to rename *Lwów*, but, given the sensitivity of relations with the Soviet Union, the British Government threatened to take it back if it was called *Lwów*, so it remained *Dragon*.[82]

There were no operations which could be described as solely 'Polish': rather a consistent contribution to the overall allied war effort. For example, the Polish Navy took part in the invasion of Norway, during which *Grom* was sunk; convoys to Malta, across the Atlantic and to the Soviet Union; the defence of the Western Approaches; and offensive operations such as the Dieppe operation, and the landings in North Africa, Sicily, Italy and Normandy. The only occasion when the Polish Navy received a significant amount of credit for its contribution was for the part played by *Piorun* in the sinking of *Bismarck*. Under the command of Lieutenant-Commander Eugeniusz Plawski, the *Piorun* had been the first ship to spot *Bismarck*, on 25 May 1941, after the last plane following the German ship had returned to *Ark Royal*. The press lauded the Polish crew on its return to port and Plawski received the Distinguished Service Cross.[83]

The first Polish submarine fleet was bedevilled by mechanical problems which limited its usefulness. On 8 April 1940, however, *Orzeł* sank the German transport *Rio de Janeiro*, which was carrying German troops for the invasion of Norway. The *Orzeł* was lost at sea in May 1940. Poland also received submarines from the British, *Sokol* and *Dzik*, and from the United States, *Jastrząb*, which was sunk by a Norwegian destroyer in a 'friendly fire' incident in May 1942 during an Arctic convoy.[84]

Two Polish liners, *Batory* and *Sobieski*, helped in the evacuation of the Polish troops from France in June 1940 before serving as troop ships. The Polish merchant marine took part in the Atlantic and Arctic convoys and lost seventeen ships in the process.[85]

The Polish Navy suffered less from manpower shortages than the other Polish armed services because two training ships, *Iskra* and *Wilia*, had made it into British waters before the outbreak of war and these naval cadets supplied the Polish Navy with its junior officer corps. By November 1944, the Polish naval establishment was 3,545 officers and men and the losses during the war were 431 officers and men. The Polish Navy sank 7 enemy ships and damaged a further 11, sank 2 submarines and damaged a further 9, sank over 80,000 tons of enemy merchant shipping and shot down seventeen German aircraft.[86]

Like the Polish Navy, the Polish Air Force did not make a contribution to the allied war effort that was demonstrably Polish. Their bombers shared in the highs and lows and appalling losses of RAF Bomber Command. In 1940 Polish bombers took part in bombing raids to destroy the German invasion barges being gathered at Calais, Boulogne and Ostend. In March 1941 the Polish bombers made the first of many bombing raids on Berlin,[87] and continued to participate in the strategic bombing of Germany. Bombers were the only aircraft capable of reaching Poland, and in February 1941 Sikorski asked the Air Ministry to release some Polish aircrews from Bomber Command for special duties flights to Poland. This was granted and on 7 November 1941 the first successful flight to Poland was completed, with three instructors and some equipment for the AK dropped.[88] There were continuing tensions between the Poles and the Air Ministry over the use of Polish bomber crews for the strategic bomber offensive because the Poles wanted them for flying supplies to Poland (this debate will be covered in a later chapter).

The British were grateful for the Polish contribution. For example, in 1942, the minister for air, Sir Archibald Sinclair, wrote to Sikorski:

> Polish crews took part in large scale operations in Cologne and Ruhr. The Royal Air Force has learned to admire the valour, tenacity and efficiency of their Polish Allies. In these operations again they here show how admirable is their contribution in support of our common cause to the destruction of the war power of the enemy. We are grateful to you and to Poland for these redoubtable squadrons.[89]

The Polish Air Force suffered from a shortage of manpower and so the number of Polish bomber squadrons remained constant throughout the war. The RAF assisted by turning a blind eye to the fact that they only had 80 per cent of the required ground staff. Reinforcements arrived in Britain from the Poles evacuated from the Soviet Union but these 1,500 men needed to be nursed back to health after the trauma of their imprisonment. The psychological scars were evident too. For example, after one pilot was shot down, his colleagues opened the suitcase he had kept under his bed and found it contained only a set of woollen underwear and a supply of dry biscuits.[90] The 304 Bomber Squadron was part of Coastal Command, spending hours searching the Atlantic and Western Approaches for U-boats. There were also Polish units in Transport Command, operating on the Canada–Britain–Middle East route, and in India and Burma. Women pilots served in the Air Transport Auxiliary Service.[91]

After the success of the Battle of Britain, Polish fighter squadrons continued their form. In 1942 they filled the first three places in a gunnery competition held by the RAF. During the Dieppe operation in August 1942, five Polish fighter squadrons formed a Polish wing commanded by Major Stefan Janus, shooting down 16 German planes, 18 per cent of German aircraft destroyed during this operation. Polish fighter squadrons then joined the RAF Tactical Air Force in 1943, training for close cooperation with the ground forces in the planned invasion of France.[92]

Until the publication in 2005 of the *Report of the Anglo-Polish Historical Commission on Intelligence Co-operation between Poland and Britain During World War II*, relatively little was known about the extent of this cooperation. In Britain the Polish Government re-established its intelligence department, the II Bureau, based on the French *Deuxième Bureau*, under Colonel Leon Mitkiewicz. The AK in Poland operated its own intelligence organisation which reported to London. Under the terms of the Anglo-Polish intelligence agreement of September 1940, the Poles agreed to pass all information they received to the British unless it concerned purely internal Polish affairs. The Poles were in a unique position since their presence as forced labourers or as underground fighters throughout occupied Europe enabled them to gather information to a degree unequalled by any other power. This contribution was quantified in a British report in 1945: it claimed that of the 45,770 intelligence reports from occupied Europe processed by the Allies during the war,

22,047, or 48 per cent, emanated from Polish sources. Wilfred Dunderdale, the report's author, paid tribute to the Poles:

> It will thus be seen that Polish agents worked unceasingly and well in Europe during the last five years, and that they provided, often at great danger to themselves and to their relatives, a vast amount of materials of all kinds on a wide variety of subjects.

The Polish intelligence service grew enormously during the war, from 4 stations with 30 employees and 30 agents to a vast organisation of 8 stations, 2 independent intelligence stations and 33 cells with 1,666 registered agents.[93]

Polish intelligence operated worldwide but was mostly active in Europe. After France fell the former Polish consul at Lille, Aleksander Kawałkowski, remained behind to organise an intelligence and resistance movement from among the Poles living there.[94] The topics covered in the intelligence reports reflected the Allies' anxieties. From France and Switzerland reports were generated on the output of factories producing munitions and armaments for the German war machine. The French Navy was kept under observation at its main base in Toulon. Polish intelligence produced some unique reports: only their agents reported the imminent departure of Rommel's Panzer troops for North Africa at the end of 1940. The British did not believe this, and, consequently, Wavell's desert army was surprised to encounter the *Afrikakorps*.[95] The Poles also had the only allied agent with a network in North Africa, Major Mieczysław Słowikowski, who reported on the attitudes of the Vichy French. The United States consul in Algiers was able to forward his reports to London in his diplomatic pouch because the United States was not at war with Vichy France. Słowikowski warned the Allies that Operation Torch, the invasion of North Africa in November 1942, would encounter French opposition, and he also listed precisely which French regiments were likely to desert to the allied side once the opportunity arose.[96] A Polish woman in the Swiss capital, Berne, served as the link between British intelligence and the anti-Nazi head of the German *Abwehr*, Admiral Wilhelm Canaris.* It also appears that Polish intelligence ran two high-level operatives in the German high command.[97]

---

\* Canaris was arrested by the Gestapo in the aftermath of the July 1944 attempted assassination of Hitler and was executed in April 1945.

The intelligence organisation of the AK had a reach far beyond the borders of Poland. All of its reports were analysed in Poland by the Office of Economic Studies and the Economic Council before summaries were generated for transmission to London. Reports were sent monthly, weekly or sometimes even daily according to the urgency of the material and the demand for it. The reports covered a wide range of intelligence, from the AK's warning of the German build-up for Operation Barbarossa, to, in the spring of 1942, detailed intelligence on the movements of German troops on the Eastern Front, all of which indicated that the main thrust of the German spring offensive would be towards the central Don river and the Caucasus. Thereafter it continued to provide information on the identity of German units, their strength and armaments. The Poles also intercepted 3,000–3,500 letters home from German soldiers and supplied reports, often including direct quotations, summarising the state of their morale.[98]

# 8

# Polish Non-combatants Outside
# Poland, 1939–1945

There were two main waves of Polish civilian refugees during the Second World War: at the beginning of the war, during the German invasion, in several directions, and in 1942, when some who had been deported by the Soviet authorities were evacuated from the Soviet Union. As the German armies swept into Poland during September 1939, Polish civilians fled eastwards and southwards: to the Baltic states of Lithuania, Estonia and Latvia or across the southern frontier, together with the remnants of the Polish Army, to a safe haven in Rumania and Hungary. Although it is likely that around 100,000 civilians fled Poland in 1939 and 1940, many travelled on to another country, so it is difficult to estimate the numbers with any great certainty.[1] For example, many of the refugees who fled to the Baltic States either returned to Poland once the dual occupation of Poland by Germany and the Soviet Union had become a fact, or they remained in the Baltic States. Many of the latter group were later expelled during the great Soviet deportations in 1940 and 1941, and some would become refugees for a second time when they were evacuated from the Soviet Union in 1942. As for those who fled to Rumania and Hungary, some would return to Poland, others would be despatched to Germany as forced labour, while many men of military age would travel westwards to join the Polish Army in France or south to the Middle East to join the Polish Army being formed there. The fall of France in 1940 and the occupation of Vichy France by Germany in 1942 forced the Polish refugees in France to seek security elsewhere. The second great wave of Polish refugees occurred when 42,000 civilians accompanied the Polish Army when it was evacuated from the Soviet Union in the spring and summer of 1942, and after passing through Iran, they would find new temporary homes throughout the world.

*

On 17 September 1939, the Polish Government crossed the frontier into Rumania, accompanied by the remnants of the Polish Army. Chapter 3 described how the government ministers were then interned by the Rumanian authorities, the army disarmed and the soldiers sent to internment camps. From the last weeks of September and for the rest of the year, Polish civilians also fled to Rumania; by the end of October, it was estimated there were 10,000 refugees. The Rumanian authorities had anticipated their arrival and had despatched 25 trains, with bathing and disinfecting facilities, to the frontier, and the Rumanian Red Cross was ready to provide food and drink, but the sheer numbers arriving overwhelmed them. The Poles normally made their own way to Bucharest or sought (and found) shelter in villages throughout the country. The Rumanian Government acted quickly to organise the refugees, establishing 36 provincial centres across the country (but away from the northern frontier), where the Poles were ordered to register, and each adult was given a grant of 100 lei per day and 50 lei per child to pay for their board and lodging. Many of the interned soldiers escaped to join the Polish armies in France and the Middle East, leading to strident protests by the Germans. Fearing a German invasion to seize their oilfields, the Rumanian Government bowed to pressure, and at the end of 1940 an agreement was concluded whereby 1,200 Polish officers and over 50,000 soldiers were transported to Germany as POWs. The officers joined those who had been in POW camps since the defeat of Poland, while the NCOs and rank and file were discharged and used as forced labour. Over 4,000 civilians were also transported from Rumania to Germany and subjected to the same strict rules governing their freedom of movement and labour which were already affecting those Poles who had been sent directly from Poland to work in the Reich. Some civilians fled Rumania for the Middle East or the west, and now more crossed into Hungary, where they received a much warmer welcome.[2]

The most notable feature of the position of the Polish refugees in Hungary was the high level of official cooperation that was developed between the Poles and the Hungarian Government. The regent, Admiral Miklós Horthy, acknowledged Germany's supremacy in Europe and sought and achieved some benefits for Hungary: economic cooperation was developed; Hungary participated in the dismemberment of

Czechoslovakia; and through the First Vienna Award in November 1938, it achieved a common frontier with Poland. Yet Horthy, his prime minister Pál Teleki, and his foreign minister István Csáky, were all adamant that Hungary would remain neutral during the German invasion of Poland and demonstrated the country's independence by refusing permission for German troops to cross Hungarian territory by rail. Hungarian policy stemmed from two factors. First, Hungary had been on the losing side in the First World War and bitterly resented the loss of Transylvania, Slovakia and southern and western territories through the Treaty of Trianon, with the result that in 1939 Hungary was unwilling to alienate the west through too close an alignment with Germany. Secondly, there was the deep sense of alliance between Hungary and Poland, which dated back to the sixteenth century when the Hungarian noble Stefan Batory had been elected king of Poland. Hungary proved its friendship in 1939 by refusing to accept the erasure of Poland from the European map and allowing the Polish legation in Budapest to remain open until German pressure forced its closure in October 1939. But despite this submission, the Hungarian Government extended a warm welcome to Polish civilian and military refugees.

Hungary had disarmed and interned the military refugees when they crossed the border, as the international laws of neutrality required. But around 50,000 Poles were able and, indeed, encouraged to escape to join the newly formed Polish armies (see Chapter 7). By the fall of France, only 20,000 Polish military internees were left, most of them too old or unfit for military service. Their care was supervised by a retired Hungarian colonel, Zoltán Baló, who had been appointed to his post by the defence minister Károly Bartha. Baló worked in close collaboration with the head of the Office of Representatives of Polish Soldiers, Colonel Marian Stiefer, who had served alongside Hungarian soldiers during the First World War. The Polish soldiers resided in camps in south-west Hungary and received allowances from the Hungarian Government. The Germans were outraged and the *Neue Tageblatt* thundered in October 1939: 'we shall no longer tolerate the care that the Hungarians give to this demoralised Polish rabble!' But the German threats were ignored and the Polish soldiers resided in Hungary peacefully until the German invasion of Hungary in March 1944.

As soon as it became apparent that Polish defeat was only a matter of time and that Polish refugees would soon flood through the Verecke, Tatar and Jabłonka passes into Hungary, the Hungarian Government mobilised its frontier troops to receive the soldiers, and in collaboration with the Hungarian Red Cross, to tend to the needs of the civilians. The initial number of civilians was estimated at around 30,000 and they were sent to 47 camps set up, like the military camps, in the south-west of the country. A special department, headed by Jószef Antall, was established within the Hungarian Interior Ministry to care for the Poles through a joint Committee for Help for Polish Refugees (*Komitet Obywatelski do Spraw Opieki nad Polskimi Uchodźcami*), headed by Henryk Sławik. Numerous other associations helped specific groups: the Committee for Youth Affairs supported the education of young Poles, and the Hungarian associations of university professors, doctors and lawyers helped Polish professionals to find jobs or provided them with financial support if they were unable to work. The so-called intellectual elite of scientists, artists, writers, journalists and senior officials received a small daily stipend from the Hungarian Government. Many refugees found employment in Hungary and were given alien citizenship by the Hungarian Government and allowed complete freedom of movement. Those who could not find employment or private lodgings remained in the camps: by 1942 there were only 4,500 people and the number of camps fell to 18, mainly situated around Lake Balaton. The Hungarian Government provided financial assistance for those in the camps, amounts rising in 1943 to match the cost of living. The camps were run by local Hungarian officials or mayors but each had a Polish leader and staff for the day-to-day operations. The Poles were allowed complete freedom to manage their own cultural activities: theatre groups toured the country and the Poles produced their own newspaper, *Wieści Polskie*, of which 500 issues were published during the war.

Official support for cooperation between the Hungarian authorities and the Poles meant that, after the fall of France, Hungary was the only belligerent or neutral country in the whole of Europe where Poles could still receive a secondary school education. The Polish education system operated under Antall's department rather than the education ministry, whose head, Bálint Hóman, was pro-Nazi. A network of primary schools was created near the Polish camps, some so small they had only 10–12 pupils. The teachers were Polish and the pre-war Polish curriculum was followed. A secondary school was opened at Balatonboglár near Lake Balaton, under the headmastership of Hieronim Urban and his successor, Dr Piotr Jędrasik. The teachers were recruited from among the interned army officers and their salaries were paid jointly by the Polish and Hungarian governments. The school had around 300 students, who followed the syllabus of the pre-war Polish *gjmnazja*. Vocational schools were also established: an agricultural school in Bénye; horticulture and telegraph operations in Budapest; bookkeeping and handicrafts in Kestheley; and tailoring in Mad. Approximately 200 Polish students entered Hungarian universities; their entry had been delayed by opposition from Hóman but was permitted at the express demand of Telecki. Because of the language barrier, most studied medicine or technical subjects. There was a general shortage of Polish books in Hungary, especially textbooks and technical manuals, but the Polish Institute in Budapest and the Polish YMCA began a publishing business and produced over 1,000 different books, ranging from fiction to textbooks and dictionaries. Couriers from the Hungarian foreign ministry even distributed some of these books to Polish refugees in other countries, including Bulgaria, Croatia, Greece, Spain, Portugal, Sweden and Italy.

Horthy himself had a personal dislike of Jews and an ambivalent attitude towards the Polish Jewish refugees, but Antall received oral instructions to assist them in 1939. They were offered the opportunity to acquire Hungarian citizenship papers, giving them new names and a Christian identity which was confirmed with a stamp from a Catholic priest, and around 20,000 of them did so. Jews continued to escape from the ghettos in Poland, among them numerous children whose parents had paid for them to be smuggled out into Hungary. In 1941 Hungary entered the war on the German side on what Horthy hoped would be a limited basis, and it participated in the occupation of Poland and in the invasion of the Soviet Union. Initially the flow of Jewish refugees continued, but then government policy changed: those who had accepted Hungarian citizenship were left untouched, but the 14,700 Jews who had arrived since 1939 and not become Hungarian citizens were deported in 1942 into the German-held Ukraine where the Germans shot them. Jewish children, however, were protected and in 1943 a Polish orphanage was established in Vác which had a school attached to it.

Teleki had been determined to keep Hungary neutral but events overtook him (and led to his eventual suicide on 3 April 1941).

Yugoslavia was the catalyst: when a pro-allied *coup d'état* in Belgrade threatened Yugoslavia's membership of the Tripartite Pact with Germany and Italy, which would have left Germany's southern flank open just when preparations were under way for the invasion of the Soviet Union, Germany demanded that Hungary should not only permit the passage of German troops across Hungary but also send its own army to take part in the invasion of Yugoslavia. Telecki resisted but the chief of the Hungarian general staff, General Heinrich Werth, agreed to permit transit of the German army. Telecki was succeeded as prime minister by László Bárdossy and under his premiership Hungary participated in the invasion of the Soviet Union. The unpopularity of the war within Hungary and the increased level of dependence on Germany led Horthy to replace Bárdossy with a more conservative prime minister, Miklós Kálly, in March 1942.

The position of the Polish civilian refugees had not been affected by Hungary's entry into the Second World War but the situation of the military internees was rather more complicated. The Hungarians were well aware that the Poles had established a resistance organisation in Hungary run by Edmund Fietz (or Fietowicz), the representative of the Polish Government. Indeed, Antall provided false papers for Polish couriers crossing Hungary as the link between the resistance in Poland and the Polish Government in London. In 1941 the Germans showed evidence of Fietowicz's activities to the Hungarian authorities and coerced them into arresting him and his collaborators, but Antall and Baló secured the release of most of the Poles and the Kálly government released the remainder. The reason behind this extraordinary behaviour by Germany's ally was the desire to keep channels open between the Hungarian Government and the west. In September 1942, Kálly contacted the Polish resistance through Antall and arranged for Fietowicz to travel to London via Turkey with the message that Hungary wanted to get out of the war. The Polish legation in Ankara then acted as a conduit between the Hungarian and British governments.

After the 2nd Hungarian Army suffered extremely heavy losses in the battles of Stalingrad and Voronezh in early 1943, Hungarian efforts to extract the country from the war took a new turn, with more direct collaboration with the Poles. Colonel Franciszek 'Liszt' Matuszczak was the head of the Polish resistance in the Polish military internment camps and conducted an assessment of the military capabilities of the men in the camps. His conclusion was that around 5,000–6,000 men were fit for service, and plans began to be drawn up for their use in the war. Colonel Jan Korkozowicz now took over command of the Polish troops. Special units were created in the Pesthidegkút camp with the intention that they be used either in Poland, where they would fight alongside the AK, or in the Balkans in support of an Anglo-American invasion. These plans were known to and supported by the Hungarian General Staff, and had the approval of Baló's replacement, Colonel Lorand Utassy; Polish troops were given weapons and ammunition and allowed to carry out exercises on Hungarian army bases. Collaboration was conducted at the highest levels: in November 1943, Colonel Andrzej 'Tokaj' Sapieha held several meetings with General Ferenc Szombathelyi, the Hungarian commander-in-chief. It was apparent from their conversations that the Hungarians were broadly supportive of Polish plans but terrified that the Germans would find out and invade and dismember Hungary. The Germans did indeed find out: a report sent to Berlin at the time stated that there 'exists a Polish resistance unit that has numerous connections with Hungary where they are planning to mount an army of 10,000 men'.

On 19 March 1944, Germany, faced with clear intelligence about Horthy's negotiations with the Allies, invaded Hungary and the situation of the Polish civilian and military refugees was completely changed. The Gestapo moved swiftly against the Polish organisations, arresting the leaders, including Fietowicz. He and his colleagues were tortured and eventually executed in Mauthausen concentration camp in August 1944. Other leaders of refugee organisations were arrested too but Sławik, the president of the Polish Committee, went into hiding, until his wife was caught by the Gestapo, whereupon he gave himself up and was also executed at Mauthausen. In all about 600 Poles were arrested by the end of March 1944. Antall was also arrested and charged by the Germans that he had allowed the Poles to live like 'a state within a state', but the Polish leaders protected him, convincing the Germans that he had known nothing of their activities and so securing his release. The Germans acknowledged that Horthy had guaranteed the Poles their status as refugees and did not dispute it, only demanding that more control be exerted over them and that their freedom of movement be restricted. The school at Balatonboglár was closed and all Polish cultural activities ceased. The powers of the Hungarian-Polish Committee to care for the refugees were effectively ended by the arrest of Sławik. The Polish Government requested that the International Red Cross should take over responsibility for them, and the IRC delegate in Hungary, Frederic Born, did his utmost to protect the Poles, but proved to be largely powerless. Nothing would be done to prevent the deportation of those Polish Jews who lacked Hungarian citizenship papers to their deaths in German-occupied Poland at the same time as the deportation of 475,000 Hungarian Jews.

The situation took a further turn for the worse when the Arrow Cross party came to power in Hungary under Ferenc Szálasi. This fascist-style government had no intention of honouring previous guarantees to the military and civilian refugees, and in October 1944, the new foreign minister, Gábor Kemény, arranged to gather them up and extradite all to Germany. Throughout November Poles were collected and force marched into Germany, and thousands were murdered on the way. Many Poles, however, remained in hiding in Hungary and survived, and after the war they returned to Poland with the assistance of the Soviets or with the help of the Polish committee on repatriation headed by Stanisław Spasiński.[3]

By the end of 1939, between 25,000 and 30,000 Poles had arrived in France, and those of military age joined the Polish Army. The remainder found accommodation and work through the existing Polish population in France, but the fall of France threatened their security: many fled to the unoccupied zone and lived freely under Vichy rule until the German invasion in November 1942. Then some went to Spain, where the authorities imprisoned them in the notorious Miranda prison camp: 450 of them were released in early 1943 after Pope Pius made a plea for their freedom to General Francisco Franco. About 6,000 Polish Jews had reached France and were living in the unoccupied zone, and in September 1942, the Vichy Government began to deport non-French Jews to German-occupied Poland. The Polish Government approached the United States asking the American Government to issue visas to these threatened Jews but their appeal fell on deaf ears. These Polish Jews were deported from France to their deaths.[4]

About 3,000 civilian refugees arrived in Britain with the Polish Army after the fall of France, and most found new homes in London or in

Scotland. These Poles received a warm welcome from the Scots, and in April 1941, a Scottish-Polish Society was founded and chaired by the Earl of Elgin and Kincardine which had nearly 50 branches and around 9,800 members by the end of the war. The society provided entertainment facilities and talks on Polish and Scottish issues. A number of schools were established for the Polish children, most notably at Dunalastair House in Pitlochry, which followed the Polish curriculum and were jointly administered by the Polish Board of Education, part of the Polish Government, and by the Scottish Education Department. The professional education and training of adults was catered for by the establishment of a Polish medical school at Edinburgh University, a Polish agricultural school in Glasgow, a Polish school of architecture in Liverpool, a Polish school of law at Oxford, and various other technical and commercial colleges.[5]

A further concentration of Poles were those men of the 2nd Polish Division who had successfully reached Switzerland and been disarmed and interned. Sikorski wanted them to remain in military readiness to assist in operations on the European mainland when the Allies began their advance. Accordingly the division maintained its organisation as a military unit and carried out training in secret, and the Swiss turned a blind eye to this illegal military activity. Indeed, it suited their plans because Switzerland was under threat of a German invasion and had a military force of only 400,000. The Polish division was included in the Swiss Wahlen plan for the defence of alpine Switzerland, and would be supplied with arms should a German attack occur. The interned soldiers worked in road and bridge construction, and in the forests and mines. Many attended Swiss universities. Polish civilian refugees were also admitted into Switzerland, but only if they could prove that they were of independent financial means and would place no demands for assistance on the Swiss Government. The Polish Government funded those who ran out of money and were unable to find employment. The Swiss, suffering a collapse of the tourist industry during the war, housed the estimated 2,000 Polish refugees in the top hotels throughout the country. As the war was coming to a close in 1945, a new wave of refugees escaped from forced labour in Austria or southern Germany, and again the Swiss demanded that they should make no financial demands on the Swiss Government. Those refugees without funds had to find a sponsor in the existing community of Polish refugees or from family members who had travelled with them.[6]

Wherever the Polish refugees were in Europe, they needed financial means of support. The refugees were encouraged to find employment or to start their own businesses, but opportunities were often limited by linguistic difficulties. The intelligentsia found work in various Polish institutions or on Polish newspapers abroad, and professors could sometimes find employment in foreign universities. Relatively few peasants left Poland, and they could usually find seasonal employment in the agricultural sector. Women with children and the white collar workers found it hardest to gain employment and were therefore largely dependent on charitable donations. Immediately after Poland's defeat, a Polish Relief Fund was established to finance the refugees in Rumania, Hungary and the Baltic States, and the British Treasury made a grant of £100,000. The Polish Government in London provided sufficient finance for the refugees throughout Europe for basic subsistence and some education and cultural activities. The legations of neutral countries were the normal conduits. The Polish Red Cross was also active across the world, providing food, clothing and medicine. Similar activities were also undertaken by the Polish Relief Committee, Caritas, founded in Paris in July 1940 by Father Franciszek Cegiełka. By far the greatest amount of aid came from the United States. By the end of 1939, the Polish American Council had remitted $10,000 to the Commission for Polish Relief, founded by former president Herbert Hoover; the American Red Cross sent another $10,000; and $13,000 was sent to the Polish Government. There were long-running and successful campaigns among the Polish-American community to raise money for Polish refugees, and by the end of the war, the Polish American Council had spent $15,000,000 on assistance for Polish refugees in 23 countries.[7]

The second large wave of Polish refugees, as we have seen, came in 1942, with the evacuation of some of those who had been deported to the Soviet Union. Although this was originally justified as an evacuation of military personnel, large numbers of civilians also came: the first evacuation to Iran in March 1942 included 12,408 Polish civilians; the second, in August 1942, brought another 26,094. A further 2,694 civilians took the overland route from Ashkhabad in Turkestan to Meshed in Iran, and 675 children travelled directly to India. Out of the 40,000 civilians who arrived in Iran, 6,123 joined the Polish Women's Auxiliary Service and a thousand girls went to the female equivalent of the *Junaks*, the *Ochotniczki*. The 1,683 Polish Jews travelled directly to Palestine by sea. This left around 31,740 Polish civilians – the old, the sick, the orphans, and mothers with their families – in need of a new sanctuary.[8]

The civilians, like the soldiers, reached Pahlevi on the Caspian Sea suffering from the effects of the prolonged starvation, hard labour and lack of health care that had characterised their exile in the Soviet Union. Their arrival surprised the British and Indian officers and troops, who had been led to expect only Polish soldiers. Uniforms were at hand to clothe the soldiers, but nothing was available for the civilians until the wife of the counsellor at the British embassy in Teheran, Mrs Holman, organised a vigorous clothes drive and, within three days, clothing and bedding were being rushed to Pahlevi.[9]

None of the evacuation staff had any knowledge or experience of the feeding of starving people. The Poles, unsurprisingly, were desperate to eat as much as they could, often with tragic consequences. The meal most often served in Pahlevi was mutton stew with rice, which was too rich for digestions weakened by long-term starvation. Several hundred Poles, mostly children, died on the beaches from acute dysentery brought on by too much food. Some Poles warned their compatriots against the dangers of over-eating and against a sudden introduction to a rich diet. Renia Kochańska instinctively realised that she could not manage what she was given but, being twelve years old, was too shy to ask for something different, so in order not to appear ungrateful she buried her food in the sand. She had been so weak on her arrival at Pahlevi that a soldier had had to carry her off the ship. Iranian traders made a fortune as the Poles purchased vast quantities of boiled eggs and fruit, which they had not seen since leaving Poland two years earlier.[10]

By the second evacuation, in August, the evacuation staff were far better organised and now comprised 2,517 Polish officers and men; 44 British officers and men; and 339 Indian officers and men.[11] Two camps were established: a dirty camp and a clean camp. All Poles passed through the first, where they were divested of their infested clothing and belongings, washed and disinfected, before passing to the clean camp to await onward transport to Teheran. The few buildings that the evacuation staff had managed to hire in Pahlevi were insufficient, so a vast tented camp grew up on the beaches by the Caspian Sea. A civilian evacuee who arrived on 31 August noted the organisation:

> We were then taken to large tents where each one received a screened-in bed complete with bedding. This was the first time we had slept on a regular bed with a pillow and all the bedding since we had left Poland ... At mealtimes we were directed to an army mess hall and given food twice a day. At first we were given only liquids and bread for a couple of days and were told that many of us would probably come down with dysentery from long periods of hunger.[12]

The health of the evacuees was appalling. Illnesses included typhus, dysentery, pellagra, other fevers and diseases caused by starvation, and respiratory diseases. The August evacuation also brought an upsurge in the number of malaria cases. The peak figure for the sick was on 8 September, when there were 868 Poles in hospital and a further 2,000 recuperating in the convalescent camp. When the Poles departed for Teheran, they left behind 568 graves of their fellow countrymen at Pahlevi.[13]

The unexpected influx of civilian refugees necessitated emergency measures to house them in Teheran. A large machine-gun factory was requisitioned next to the Iranian airfield at Dosha Tappeh, a few miles east of the city. It was capable of housing 5,000 people, although the accommodation was rudimentary: concrete platforms served as beds and the overflow had to sleep on the floor. Adjacent land was leased from the Iranian Government and a tented city grew up, Camp No. 1, and was followed by the creation of four further camps. The Shah had loaned an unfinished orphanage to the British Army, and this was adapted to be a hospital for the Poles. Stanisław Milewski arrived in one of the first transports to Teheran and remembered: 'We were warmly greeted by the Persian people with gifts of food, dates and clothes. We were simply amazed by the sight of smiling people and a bustling city full of open shops and traffic.'[14] His testimony is supported by others who also recall the generous welcome they received in Teheran.

A Polish orphanage was established for 2,600 children and their carers in Isfahan, in the nearby mountains. The orphanage was a 'two-storey building [which] faced the garden, with French windows giving access to a balcony. It stood in the shade of fruit trees and large bushes and there were many beautiful trees including apples, pomegranates and many other trees'. Family members had often become separated by accident at Pahlevi. For example, the sisters Lala and Renia Kochańska were both sent to Isfahan, but arrived at different times and were only reunited when they were about to leave for India. One of the carers at the orphanage recalled the desperation of some women:

> Mothers began to appear [at the orphanage] in search of their children, and these frantic, sometimes disturbed, women often mistook other children to be their own ... We saw or heard of many women whose children had died become so grief-stricken that they claimed small children from the orphanage who were not their own at all. Often the authorities had great difficulty in verifying claims or in tracing these children once they had been taken from the orphanage.

The children mixed with the locals and established good relations with them. One Iranian rented out his motorbike, another taught the boys wrestling, and a local Armenian took a group climbing up Kuh-e Sefid, a mountain over 9,800 feet high: 'We communicated by means of a strange and straightforward language consisting of Russian, English and Persian words.' Schools were also established at Isfahan and in Teheran. The shortage of teachers meant that at Isfahan there would be two weeks of lessons followed by three weeks of holidays.[15]

The Poles quickly made themselves at home in Teheran. In May 1942, a Commission of Education under Piotr Paluch was established, and in time 24 schools were opened to give the children, who had mostly been starved of any schooling in the Soviet Union, an education using Polish textbooks and the Polish curriculum. Schools of tailoring and commerce were set up to give adults a technical education.[16] A report in *The Times* noted: 'Polish notices are seen everywhere; Polish shops have sprung up; and Polish waitresses serve in the cafes and restaurants, where Polish musical and artistic performances have become a regular feature.'[17] The Polish minister in Teheran, Karol Bader, wrote to the Polish foreign minister, Raczyński:

> You should see Teheran today: the streets are full of Poles, including attractive girls in uniform who captivate British officers and the local male population; Polish bands and choirs who have invaded all the bars and hotels; and hordes of peasants with fair hair and light-coloured eyes, who roam around the waste areas outside the town. All this goes to make up the strange historical phenomenon which is called the Polish migration

through Iran. So far, the benefits which it has brought seem from here to be much greater than the disadvantages. Our compatriots have aroused liking as well as sympathy, and have won the hearts of the Persians and British for Poland. What is more, they are doing a great deal for the Allied cause, as the British are coming more and more to realise.

Influx does include some undesirables. Moreover, having escaped from the hell of Bolshevism, the majority's first thought is to enjoy themselves and make the most of life.

Despite all this, they show a striking capacity for rapid regeneration.[18]

Some of the more enterprising Poles moved out of the camps and into Teheran itself, renting whatever accommodation they could find. Their most highly-prized employment was in the Polish administration or in the British or American relief organisations, where they received free food rations.[19]

Yet behind the scenes the Polish presence was causing political difficulties. In August 1941, the Shah of Iran had been forced to abdicate in favour of his son, Mohammad Reza Pahlevi, and Iran was split into two zones of temporary wartime occupation: the British zone in the south and the Soviet zone, including Teheran, in the north. The Soviet occupation was particularly unpopular. The British ambassador, Reader Bullard, noted that the Iranians had been largely indifferent to the Poles on their arrival but suddenly changed to become extremely helpful, and he believed:

The motive may have been partly humanitarian and partly a sensible desire to prevent an epidemic, but I believe it is mainly the result of Schadenfreude at the condition of people who have come here from Russia. One can't help sympathising with them ... if the Persians now find pleasure in helping people they probably consider victims of the Bolsheviks, one can't be surprised. If I saw open signs of this I should try to suppress it, but I don't: I only suspect its existence.[20]

Bullard was supremely aware that negative publicity for the Soviet Union was politically unwise at this critical point of the war. Indeed, the Polish diplomats were not making his job easier: the Polish minister wrote, 'We also have to keep our propaganda going among the Persians – an easy and pleasant task.'[21] It was clear that the Soviets would not allow the Poles to roam freely in Teheran denigrating their country for much longer, and after the first evacuation that Iran could not possibly support such a large number of refugees. In January 1942, even before the evacuations started, there had been riots throughout the Middle East protesting about the shortages of food. With the prospect of a second, larger evacuation (the August group) increasing, the urgent task began of finding new homes for the mass of Polish civilians.

Even before any Poles had left the Soviet Union the plight of Polish children had moved many people. In Britain conversations had taken place between Raczyński and Lord Tweeddale in which the possibility of Polish children being evacuated to India had been discussed. Both Leo Amery, the secretary of state for India, and Lord Linlithgow, the viceroy, were keen to welcome Polish children in India, but pointed out that they would need to be housed in special camps and have separate educational facilities. The numbers would also have to be limited to 5,000 because Indian resources were already being stretched to the limit by the war.[22] Maharajah Jam Saheb Digvijay Sinhji of Nawanagar offered to establish a camp for 500 Polish children close to his summer home in Valivade, near Kolhapur. In March 1942, the weekly Polish magazine in India, *Polska*, published an interview with the maharajah in which he explained his motives:

Deeply moved and distressed by the suffering of the Polish nation, and especially of those who are spending their childhood and youth in the tragic circumstances of this most terrible of wars, I wanted to contribute, and, in some way, improve their lot by offering them refuge in a country which is far away from the ravages of war. Maybe here, in the beautiful hills beside the seashore, the children will be able to recover their health and to forget the ordeal they went through.

The maharajah had become interested in Poland in the early 1920s when he accompanied his uncle, the then maharajah, who was attending the League of Nations in Geneva, where they had met and become the neighbours of Ignacy Paderewski.[23]

In June 1942, Sikorski wrote to Churchill concerning the fate of an estimated 50,000 Polish children still starving in the Soviet Union:

The Polish Government has approached the Governments of countries, who might be of help to us in this matter, (the United States, Canada, South Africa, Egypt, etc.) So far we have received information that thanks to personal interest shown by President Roosevelt, the American Government with the help of the American Red Cross is willing to assume responsibility for a batch of 10,000 of these children who will perhaps find temporary shelter on South African soil . . .

It occurs to me that besides the territory of the Union of South Africa, accommodation might be found in Kenya, Uganda, Tanganyika, Rhodesia and India. It may be that Syria and Palestine could receive some of the children . . .[24]

In June a conference of colonial governors convened in Nairobi and discussed the fate of the Polish civilians. The British minister in Cairo, Richard Casey, cabled the Foreign Office expressing alarm at the potential scale of the refugee problem in the most chilling terms: 'To put matters brutally if these Poles die in Russia the war effort would not be affected. If they [are allowed] to pass into Persia, we, unlike the Russians, will not be able to let them die and our war effort will be gravely impaired.'[25] The result of the conference was a decision to relocate the Poles to various British colonies in Africa. In December 1942, India was encouraged to increase its original offer and agreed to accept an additional 6,000.[26]

The civilians began to be moved from Iran to India during the summer of 1942. Shipping was in short supply because of the war, and there was the danger of attacks by Japanese and German submarines on the sea route to India. There was also a shortage of railway rolling stock in Iran itself to move the civilians to Khorramshahr, so a transit camp was established at Ahvaz, 90 miles from the port. Some children travelled to India overland from Meshed, an extremely dangerous route which crossed Afghanistan. Convoys were under threat of attack by the warring tribes on the Iran–Afghanistan frontier and also by the tribes on the north-west frontier of India: therefore, the Indian drivers and convoy leaders were issued with arms, and at times the convoys were given military escorts. Ten thousand children, half of them orphans and half with their families, settled in India. The Country Club in Karachi was used as a transit camp for those travelling on to their final destinations. Other Polish families and civilians went to Africa: 6,400 to Uganda; 8,000 to Tanganyika (now Tanzania); 5,000 to North and South Rhodesia (now Zambia and Zimbabwe respectively); and 1,500 to Kenya. New Zealand offered a permanent home to 700 Polish orphans, and Mexico offered to take 10,000 adults on the condition that they would work in agriculture. By 1944 only about 8,000 Poles remained in Iran, too old or too sick to make the long journey to a new home. Over 1,000 Poles had died in Teheran as a result of their suffering in the Soviet Union.[27] The St Lazarite Order of monks buried the Polish dead in their cemetery but when that filled up a new Polish cemetery was created.[28]

The Poles enjoyed their sojourn in India, safe from the war and from the depredations they had suffered in the Soviet Union. Two large camps were established for them at Valivade and Balachadi, near Jamnagar, along with other, more temporary settlements at Malir, Bandra and Pan-chgani. The Poles quickly established their own administration. Schools were opened to educate all the children, despite the shortage of teachers, textbooks and equipment. The most advanced female pupils were sent to English convent schools, where 'we were frustrated to the point of tears' by their initial inability to cope with lessons in English.[29] Teen-agers and young adults could study technical subjects. Cultural associations were set up, theatre groups sprang up, and Polish newspa-pers and journals were published. Sports activities were organised and the scouting association flourished. The Maharajah of Nawanagar took a personal interest in the welfare of his own refugee wards. Thirteen-year-old Fredek Burdzy obtained two chicks from a village and soon had a flock of chickens whose eggs supplied the whole camp. The maha-rajah was so impressed by Fredek's enterprise that he gave him two ducklings and five turkey eggs, and Fredek soon had a flock of thirty turkeys. After Fredek had asked why Indian pigs were black, the maha-rajah gave him three European pink pigs. The Polish Government paid the costs of the Polish refugees, using loans received from the British Government. After the war the United Nations Relief and Rehabilita-tion Administration (UNRRA) took over responsibility for the Poles.[30]

British colonies in Africa became the new home for 20,900 Poles, including 3,500 men over the age of military service, over 6,000 women, and 8,000 children of school-age. They were despatched to twenty-three settlements in six countries. There were two camps in Uganda, one deep in the jungle at Masindi and another at Koya on Lake Victoria; five camps in Kenya, at Rongai, Manira, Makindu, Nairobi and Nyali; six camps in Tanganyika, at Tengeru near Mount Kilimanjaro, Kidugala and Ifunda in the mountains, Kigoma, Kondoa and Morogoro; six camps in North Rhodesia, at Abercorn, Bwana M'Kubwa, Fort Jameson,

Livingstone and Lusaka; and four camps in South Rhodesia, at Diggleford, Marandellas, Rusape and Gatooma. Six hundred children were sent to live in former barracks in Oudtshoorn in the Cape region of South Africa. All the camps had British commanders but their administration was Polish. Because most of the refugees from the Soviet Union came from peasant stock, the camp administration was run by the so-called 'Cypriot group', professional people who had fled Poland in 1939 and had travelled from Rumania to Cyprus at the invitation of King George VI.[31] The War Office published a Polish supplement to its standard English-Swahili phrase book.

The Poles found Africa a rather strange and often frightening new experience:

> One day there were shouts and panic and we started to run and hide when we saw a mass of natives armed with spears running noisily into our camp. The situation was saved by the camp commandant who explained to us that this was traditional ceremonial dress and that they wanted to welcome us officially to Africa.

Another girl and her friends were greeted by a 10-foot-long snake when they first entered their barracks. The Poles soon became enchanted by the beauty of the tropical plants and the local wildlife and began to make themselves at home:

> Soon the settlement took on the character of a small town with streets, street signs and even Polish national symbols visible on public buildings and huts. Inside the huts the women expended much energy decorating and personalising their huts into homes with kilims, embroidered cover slips, bedspreads, doilies and floor coverings from stitched bagging materials.

Relations with the British were usually good, but warm friendships between the Poles and the local natives were frowned upon by the colonial administrators. As in India the Poles quickly established schools, their own administration and cultural associations and various businesses.[32] A network of schools was started, run by the Polish Ministry of Religious Affairs, in which the children were taught in Polish and followed the Polish curriculum. English was taught as a second language.[33]

In the Near East, the main Polish presence was military: training camps for soldiers of the Polish Army and schools for the *Junaks*.

Jewish civilian refugees were welcomed and absorbed into the local Jewish community in Palestine. There had been considerable difficulties in getting them out of Iran because, while the Iraqi Government had no control over the military personnel passing through its country, it did ask the British to issue all civilians with transit visas, specifying that no Jews were allowed. Sikorski appears to have made a private arrangement with the Iraqi legation that allowed some Jewish children to transit Iraq dressed in Catholic school uniforms.[34] Several thousand non-Jewish Polish civilians were scattered in camps in Ghazir, Zauk Michael, Ajaltoun and Balodoun in Lebanon, and at Jerusalem, Nazareth, Rehovot, Ain-Karem and Barbara in Palestine. About 5,500 children attended schools there, and a Polish press produced the textbooks needed by their Polish schools and those in Africa and India. About 250 Polish students attended the French Université Saint-Joseph and the American University in Beirut, or were sent to Egypt to attend the technical colleges established there.[35]

Poles were also despatched further afield. On 1 November 1944, 733 orphans with a large team of teachers and administrators arrived at Wellington, en route to a permanent settlement in Pahiatua on North Island, to an enthusiastic welcome by the New Zealanders:

> There were hundreds of smiling Wellington school children waving New Zealand and Polish flags as a gesture of welcome on the platform from which we were to leave for Pahiatua. The singing of the national anthems and gifts of flowers made the occasion even more moving. It was the first direct contact between the children of the two nations, a brief meeting which was to change into a deep and lasting friendship over the years.[36]

The vast continent of Australia did not offer to house any Polish refugees, nor did the United States, although American organisations did provide a great deal of financial and logistical assistance.

The Americans transported 1,500 Poles to Mexico via the United States with the first transport arriving in Mexico on 25 June 1943. It docked near Los Angeles, and the men were sent to a separate quarantine camp from the women and 166 children. Efforts by the local Polish-American community to keep some of the refugees there failed and they were all sent to Santa Rosa, near León in central Mexico. That autumn they were joined by the second transport, which included 408 children. The administration of the hacienda was in Polish hands but was financed through credits issued to the Polish Government by the American Foreign Relief and Rehabilitation Operations. The Americans helped in other ways: the National Council Welfare Conference financed the cultural and sports activities; the Polish American Council funded the purchase of clothing and medicines; and the Polish Felician Sisters from Chicago organised the orphanage and schools.[37]

As the Second World War drew to a close, decisions had to be made regarding the future of these refugees. Chapter 17 will describe the efforts of the UNRRA, who took over the welfare of these refugees from the Polish Government in London, to persuade those scattered victims of Stalin's ethnic cleansing to return home to a Poland under communist rule.

# 9

# The Dark Years: Occupied Poland, 1941–1943

The first period of the German occupation had been characterised by enslavement, destitution, annexation, deportation, an indiscriminate application of terror and the establishment of ghettos for the Jews. Polish hopes that the victory of the western allies might provide an early escape from the German yoke had been dashed when France signed an armistice with Germany in June 1940. The German invasion of the Soviet Union, which started on 22 June 1941 with the entry of German forces into Soviet-occupied Poland, had an enormous impact. The German lines of communication lay across Poland and security became a vital issue for them. Existing German policies of the exploitation of Poland's economic resources and its labour were carried to a new level. The policy of Germanising the east, begun with the annexation of Warthegau, Danzig-West Prussia and Polish Upper Silesia, now led to further 'depolonising' experiments. As German quotas for food and labour from the General Government rose, they were more vigorously enforced, and there was an increase in terror.

As German terror grew in Poland, so did resistance to German rule. In this period the resistance became more organised, with many groups that had sprung up during the first period of the occupation now grouped under the newly formed *Armia Krajowa*, the AK. The Underground Government, the *Delegatura*, extended its influence and scope. During these dark years the Poles faced a struggle for survival in the face of the racial war against them waged by the Germans. The depredations suffered by and the terror inflicted on the Poles would have been the worst event in the Second World War, except that they were overshadowed by an even greater catastrophe, the Holocaust.

*

The German preparations for Operation Barbarossa could not be concealed from the Poles. From the autumn of 1940, Polish and Jewish forced labour began building hospitals, barracks and storage facilities, and over 100 airfields and 50 dispersal strips. A Pole working on an airfield noted the German efforts to camouflage their preparations from prying Soviet planes:

> When the Germans finished the runway they let the grass grow and grazed cattle on it. It looked more like a pasture than an airfield. White clover on the runway provided good grazing. The hangars were constructed by driving tree trunks into the ground. Hanging over this was wire or a green net overlaid with foliage. As leaves dried out they were replaced with fresh.[1]

Road signs for the use of German troops were erected on the roads leading east, and one produced much hilarity among the Poles: in the sign for a dangerous bend – *Gefährliche Kurve* – the second word meant 'whore' in Polish.[2] Above all, the Germans could not their conceal troop movements:

> By day and night, troops were passing through Kraków, equipped with the latest weapons, gleaming uniforms, marvellous horses and huge, shapeless tanks. The whole cavalcade – gigantic, limitless in numbers and scale – rolled on and on, as though it would never end. The procession lasted all day and all night, through the next day and on into the night. One had the impression that it would go on for ever. It streamed out from the railway station, along the Planty Promenade, then disappeared down the Karmelicka and beyond – moving east.[3]

On the first Sunday of June 1941, the Smorczewski family, living in German-occupied Poland close to the German-Soviet demarcation line, went to church as normal. Ralph Smorczewski described what happened next:

> It was not until after Mass, when we emerged into the church cemetery, that we all became aware of some strange goings-on in our park. The continuous roar of numerous heavy engines and the grinding clatter of chains reverberated from the orchard, the lime tree alley and from the park beyond. On entering the orchard through a wooden gate, a horrific sight hit our eyes. The park was full of army vehicles, some moving about, others stationary with their engines still revving. Hurrying home, my eyes travelled in disbelief over tanks, armoured cars, motorcycles with side cars and

other strange looking contraptions, that filled every available space between the trees and amongst the shrubbery.

Soon the Panzer unit departed, 'leaving behind churned up earth, squashed shrubs and broken tree branches'.[4]

Historians of Operation Barbarossa have mostly overlooked the fact that during the first week of the German invasion the battles between the German and Soviet forces were taking place on pre-war Polish territory.[5] Białystok, Grodno, Brześć and Stanisławów, as well as many other places where the Soviet planes were destroyed on the ground, were all formerly Polish airfields. The fortress of Brześć, where the Poles had put up a determined defence against the Germans in September 1939, was now garrisoned by the Soviets and proved as difficult to crack a second time for the Germans despite the Soviet garrison being badly under-strength and ill-equipped. In Lwów there was general panic among the Soviets as the Germans bombed the city, and the Polish and Ukrainian population briefly delighted in the fear displayed by their Soviet oppressors. At the end of June there was a great tank battle in the Łuck–Brody–Równe–Dubno area, which continued for several days until the retreat of adjacent armies forced the Soviets to withdraw across the pre-war frontier. Soviet historians have proudly shown that they did not retreat in total disarray but managed to salvage some of the infrastructure such as locomotives and train carriages and wagons. It should be added, however, that this property was Polish not Soviet, so it merely compounded the misappropriation and dismantling of Poland that had been such a feature of the Soviet occupation.[6]

In the eastern provinces of Poland, now annexed to the Soviet Union, the population had been subjected to Soviet-inspired terror, economic exploitation and deportation. The German invasion of the Soviet Union on 22 June 1941 was greeted with often ill-concealed glee by many Poles. Countess Lanckorońska wrote of the common view:

> We firmly believed that the Germans would beat the Muscovites, after which the Germans, already weakened, would be finished off by the Allies. Then, both our enemies having fallen, Poland would rise between them, morally powerful in the unity and collective harmony imparted to us by this terrible struggle.[7]

The commander of the Polish resistance, General Stefan Grot-Rowecki, informed London that the Poles viewed the invasion favourably because of this hope that the two enemies would destroy each other.[8] Among the non-Jewish population the arrival of the Germans was greeted with a degree of suspicion but also with some relief, as the Soviet terror had affected virtually every sector of the population, and the NKVD had massacred their prisoners in the hours before they fled eastwards. A German officer recorded that when his regiment reached Dubno: 'We could not sleep because there was an awful smell. My regiment was close to a Russian prison and soon we detected the source of the smell. Before leaving the city the Soviet authority had killed all the people in the prison.'[9] In Lwów all the prisoners in the Brygidki jail were massacred: a German soldier and his friends who wanted to visit it did not do so because they 'did not have any gas masks with us so it was impossible to enter the rooms in the cellar or the cells'.[10] The Germans invited the Poles into these prisons to search for their relatives.[11] In the countryside the situation was peaceful once the Germans had passed through: 'There was no police, no authority of any kind. The Poles protected their village, the Ukrainians theirs.'[12]

The Ukrainians greeted the German invasion with the same enthusiasm that they had shown at the Soviet invasion in 1939 and for the same reason. Again they hoped that they would be granted their independence; but the Organisation of Ukrainian Nationalists acted prematurely when, in Lwów at 8 p.m. on 30 June 1941, Yaroslav Stetsko proclaimed the independence of western Ukraine.[13] Ukrainians flocked to help the Germans, providing much of the manpower needed to shoot the Jews, joined German paramilitary formations and wore German uniforms. The independent Ukrainian state was short-lived because, as the governor of the General Government, Hans Frank, declared:

> First of all we should not let the Ukrainians of our District of Galicia believe that we were ready to recognise any independent Ukrainian State within the territories destined for the Greater German Reich ... I see a solution of the Ukrainian problem in this way, that they should, similar to the Poles, remain at our disposal as a working power in the future.[14]

Stetsko and other Ukrainian nationalists, including Stepan Bandera, were arrested by the Germans and sent to Sachsenhausen concentration camp. It was only much later in the war that the Germans encouraged Ukrainian nationalism for their own purposes.

In the early days of the occupation, the German policy appeared to be to allow the Poles to remain in charge of the local administration while the Germans occupied themselves with a 'cleansing action' against 'the Bolsheviks and the Jews', but by the autumn the Germans decided to impose their full authority over their newly captured Polish provinces. East Galicia and the province of Białystok were added to the General Government; the provinces of Wilno, Nowogródek and Polesie were placed in the Reichskommissariat Ostland, governed by Heinrich Lohse; and the province of Wołyń became part of Reichskommissariat Ukraine, governed by Erich Koch. Polish administrators were now replaced by Belorussians, Ukrainians and Lithuanians. The latter two were particularly hostile to their former Polish rulers, with some extremist Lithuanian nationalists openly calling for the creation of Polish ghettos, for Poles to be forced to wear identification badges and for them to have lower food rations than the Lithuanians.[15] The Ukrainian attitude towards the Poles was far worse, and in 1943 it would explode into an orgy of violence, which will be covered in Chapter 12.

During the twin occupations of Poland there had been limited communications between the two zones. As a result 'the people of Lwów knew little about Germany and asked a lot about conditions in the west, of which they knew nothing at all'. Because East Galicia had been part of the Austro-Hungarian Empire before 1918, the population expected a similar type of relatively benign rule to be reimposed, but they were soon to be disillusioned. Soon schoolchildren sang a new rhyme:

| | |
|---|---|
| Żydzi mają nędze, | The Jews have the destitution, |
| Polacy pieniądze, | The Poles have the money, |
| Ukrainicy policji, | The Ukrainians have the police, |
| Niemcy Galicji.[16] | The Germans have Galicia. |

There were mass arrests of the intelligentsia, already decimated by Soviet murders and deportations. For example, the professors of Lwów's Jan Kazimierz University and Polytechnic were arrested and shot on the orders of SS-Hauptsturmführer Hans Krüger. East Galicia was turned into the same educational desert that existed in the rest of the General Government: secondary schools and higher education colleges were closed and their teachers arrested and shot. Theatres, museums and

N

U.S.S.R.

R. Neman

• Wilno

REICHSKOMMISSARIAT
OSTLAND

EAST
PRUSSIA

DANZIG-
WEST
PRUSSIA

• Stettin

BIAŁYSTOK

Białystok •

DISTRICT

R. Vistula

Poznań •

WARTHEGAU

R. Warta

■ Warsaw

Łódź •

G
E
R
M
A
N
Y

LOWER SILESIA

• Lublin

R. Bug

REICHSKOMMISSARIAT
UKRAINE

UPPER SILESIA

• Kraków

G
E
N
E
R
A
L
G
O
V
E
R
N
M
E
N
T

• Lwów

GALICIA DISTRICT

R. Dniester

SLOVAKIA

HUNGARY

5. Poland Post-Barbarossa

0          100 miles
0       150 km

other places of culture were closed and the best of their art taken to Germany. To the indignation of the local population, the Soviet-imposed kolkhozy were not abolished. Indeed, the Reich Agriculture Minister Herbert Backe said that if the Soviets had not imposed them, then the Germans would have had to, because their existence eased the transfer of agricultural property to Germans.[17] Starvation was rife in Lwów: 'There were no shops and the total destruction of economic life brought about by the Bolsheviks was all the more terrible in its consequences because the Germans would neither allow anything to be brought into the city, nor import anything themselves.'[18]

Stanisławów, in the south-east corner of Poland, had a different experience to start with because it was initially occupied by troops from the 2nd Hungarian Army. The Hungarian occupation was benign with a strong humanitarian aspect, and the Hungarians were enormously popular with the Poles. Platoons of Hungarian soldiers would go to Mass in the local churches where they would sing the Polish national song *Boże, coś Polskę*. This had been runner-up in the competition for the Polish national anthem in 1918 and had been later translated into Hungarian as a hymn. The Poles sang in Polish and the Hungarians in Hungarian in perfect amity. The Hungarians did, however, warn the Poles that the situation would soon change. The Olszański family was told: 'Stanisławów will be made part of the General Government, as Lwów already is, so soon the Hungarians will leave and the Germans will come: so go to Hungary now if you can.'[19] Then the situation changed dramatically as, fresh from the murder of the Lwów professors, Krüger made the city his personal fiefdom. Local Ukrainians supplied him with a list of members of the intelligentsia, whom the Gestapo then rounded up and shot.[20]

Life in the General Government for the majority of Polish citizens became one long struggle for survival. The failure of the Wehrmacht to defeat the Soviets quickly meant that the Ukraine, the food basket that the Germans expected to feed the Reich, could not be exploited. Consequently, the General Government was expected to fill the shortfall. Food rationing in the cities was so severe that it was only just above starvation level: the Jews received lower rations and really did starve to death in their ghettos and labour camps. The Germans issued a list of foodstuffs forbidden to Poles, which included veal, pork, all fish, onions and berries.[21] In 1942, when Backe demanded 150,000 tons of grain, a six-fold increase in food exports from the General Government, Frank declared: 'The new levies will be fulfilled exclusively at the expense of the foreign [Polish] population. It must be done cold-bloodedly and without pity.'[22] As a result rations in Warsaw dropped from 552 calories in March 1942 to 468 in April,[23] but even this was not enough, so Himmler ordered that in August 1942 Warsaw should be sealed off from the rest of the General Government to prevent the peasants from selling their produce to the starving city-dwellers.[24] Frank declared a state of emergency from 1 August to 30 November 1942 to 'secure the collection of crops', and German terror in the countryside increased as peasants were shot for not fulfilling their quota.[25] Frank even managed to add a further insult when 'through loudspeakers placed on every street corner, [he] thanked the Polish population for "offering their sugar to the heroic German Army" . . .'[26] The level of rations was so low that it proved counterproductive to the German war effort. The head of German arms production in the General Government, General Schindler, suggested in summer 1942 that ration cards should be limited only to those Poles working in the German interests. Frank's secretary of state, Dr Bühler, confirmed in April 1943:

I can state at this stage that the Polish worker in the General Government is being looked after worse than the foreign workers in Germany, than the worker from the East in the Reich provinces, than the Polish and also the Russian prisoners of war, to say nothing of the consumers' scale of rationing granted to the Czech population in the Protectorate, and to the Polish population in the incorporated Eastern areas. In spite of this the same output is demanded from the Polish population as from that in other regions.[27]

The Poles turned to the black market to survive. Schindler noted that the German armaments industry had to employ at least 20 per cent more workers than necessary because so many of them spent days away from work searching for food. In general the countryside was much better off than the cities, and the peasants would still run the gauntlet of German gendarmes to smuggle food into town and sell it on the black market. Stefan Korboński noted of the peasants: 'They moved like pillars, carrying and transporting by rail or carts tons of foodstuffs in little bags sewn into their underskirts and blouses. Never before have I seen such over-sized busts as in Poland at this time.'[28] Even the Germans were in on the black market. Zbigniew Bokiewicz was a boy scout and heard of a black market operating in Warsaw's freight yards where 'both the German and Polish railwaymen opened wagons of goods at the freight yards, loaded the contents onto trucks, and sold the entire contents as they stood, without letting their purchasers know what they contained'. German drivers would even deliver the goods to storage places.[29] From 1 September 1943, the level of rations in the General Government was increased, which was possible not because the Ukraine had begun to yield its expected riches but because by this time the majority of Polish Jews had been exterminated.[30]

Jobs were hard to find and few of them paid a living wage. One historian has noted the great increase in the numbers of people working in local administration from 122,700 at the beginning of 1941 to 206,300 in the middle of 1943 and cites this as an example of Polish collaboration with the Germans.[31] In fact, it is unknown how many people actually worked in the local administration, because the Underground Government became experts at forging documents to show that the holder worked in an office under German management and was therefore excluded from forced labour. A German economist visited the General Government and reported to Frank that on weekdays in Germany the streets of the cities were empty because everyone was at work but, in contrast, the streets of the General Government were filled with young people, all of whom could show documents proving that they worked for a German-controlled enterprise.[32] By 1943 the Germans had seen through the subterfuge and began to ignore the documents.

Many people lacked the financial resources to live off the black market. The Germans established the Central Welfare Council (*Rada Główna Opiekuńcza*, RGO) to coordinate the relief agencies acting for the Poles, Ukrainians and Jews. Under this umbrella, the Main Welfare Council (*Naczelna Rada Opiekuńcza*), run by Count Adam Roniker, cared for the Poles, although the Polish Red Cross remained independent. The work of the Jewish council under the RGO, the Jewish Self-help Society (*Żydowska Samopomoc Społeczna*), ended with the deportation and extermination of the Jews. These welfare agencies distributed aid received from abroad and helped the poor, children, forced labourers and prisoners.[33] They operated throughout Poland except in the Gestapo-run prison in Stanisławów, where Krüger forbade them access.[34]

Poles and Polish Jews were not the only people suffering. Life for the majority of Soviet prisoners of war marched into the General Government by their German conquerors was short. Zygmunt Klukowski saw columns of them pass through Szczebrzeszyn:

They all looked like skeletons, just shadows of human beings, barely moving. I have never in my life seen anything like this. Men were falling in the street; the stronger ones were carrying others, holding them up by their arms. They looked like starved animals, not like people. They were fighting for scraps of apples in the gutter, not paying attention to the Germans who would beat them with rubber sticks. Some crossed themselves and knelt, begging for food. Soldiers from the convoy beat them without mercy. They not only beat prisoners but also people who stood by and tried to pass along some food.

He believed that 'the entire Polish population, not only the Jews, were very sympathetic to the Russian prisoners'.[35] Massive POW camps were established at Dęblin, Chełm, Siedlce and Zamość for around 500,000 Soviet POWs. Between the end of October 1941 and April 1942 over 85 per cent of them died; Polish peasants attempted to feed them but the Germans shot them and destroyed their villages. The resistance sent reports to London detailing the German treatment of the Soviet POWs.[36]

Wanda Draczyńska summarised the situation in the General Government: 'During the German occupation, there was never a moment when we did not feel threatened. Every time we left home, we never knew whether we would ever see it again.'[37] The principal reason for this was the ever-present threat of the *łapanka*, or round-up for forced labour. An unnamed observer noted:

The wild and ruthless manhunt as exercised everywhere in towns and country, in streets, squares, stations, even in churches, at night in houses, has badly shaken the feeling of security of the inhabitants. Everybody is exposed to the danger, to be seized anywhere and at any time by members of the police, suddenly and unexpectedly, and to be brought into an assembly camp. None of his relatives knows what has happened to him, and only months later one or the other gets news of his fate by a postcard.[38]

Even some sunbathers by the Vistula were seized with not even a chance to gather together their clothes. In the countryside the Germans, assisted by the Polish Blue Police (*Policja Granatowa*), would surround a village and burn it if a sufficient number of labourers did not report for forced labour. At least villagers could hide in the forests to escape the Germans, but this option was not open to city-dwellers. By 1943 there were already nearly 1,000,000 Poles working in the Reich and the labour reserves of the General Government were virtually exhausted. Nevertheless, with the application of even more ruthlessness and by ignoring exemption documents, Frank managed to fill the demands of Fritz Saukel, the German director of labour, for 150,000 Poles in 1943 and 100,000 in 1944.[39] In March 1943, the Germans held a small celebration in Kraków to acknowledge the despatch of the millionth worker to the Reich.[40]

The Poles dreaded being transported there to work because of the rumours of the conditions there. Whereas workers from western Europe enjoyed similar working conditions and rations to the Germans: 'By contrast, the situation of workers from the East ... was characterised by poor diet, low wages, inadequate housing and clothing, excessively long hours, deficient medical care, cheating by German supervisors, abuse and maltreatments, and high mortality.'[41] Draconian regulations had been in force for the Polish workers since 1940, with severe restrictions on their freedom of movement, and the punishment for any infraction was incarceration in a concentration camp or death. Some Germans were brave enough to risk Nazi wrath by still treating the *Untermenschen*, the Poles, well. Katherine Graczyk recalled her relationship with one family:

> On Christmas Eve, I had dinner with them. The windows were covered with tarps. The farmer had to make sure nobody was outside. It was against the law for the Germans to eat with Polish slave labour workers, but they ate Christmas Eve dinner with me anyway. They gave me a Christmas present, too. It was just a rubber apron. That's all they could afford. I appreciated it and I understood the risks they took. They could have gone to prison for such acts of kindness.[42]

At least 130,000 Polish workers died in Germany from maltreatment before conditions started to improve in 1943, when the Germans now began to treat their foreign workers better because they needed the manpower for their armaments factories since the war was turning against them. The death rate was lower than in previous years but still twice that of the German population.[43] Olga Fjodorowna recalled that she and her fellow workers had been reduced to supplementing their diet with 'grasses and leaves ... but they gave us cramps and pains in the heart'. When she was liberated in 1945 she weighed only 68 pounds.[44] Those too sick to work were sent back home and a report on one transport in September 1942 noted:

> There were dead passengers on the returning train. Women on that train gave birth to children that were tossed from the open window during the journey, while people sick with tuberculosis and venereal disease rode in the same coach. The dying lay in freight cars without straw, and one of the dead was ... thrown onto the embankment.[45]

On their return to Poland these people were cared for by the RGO.

Many Poles were sent to camps in the Greater German Reich: Dachau, Mauthausen, Sachsenhausen, Buchenwald and Ravensbrück.[46] Few survived the war. At Ravensbrück, Polish inmates were mainly women who had been sent to work in Germany and had transgressed some draconian regulation. There were also members of the resistance, mainly couriers, who were the most vulnerable members because they had to remain in the same location and were therefore more likely to be caught by the Gestapo.[47] Wanda Półtawska, a young courier imprisoned in Ravensbrück, and other Polish women were selected for the medical experiments led by Professor Karl Gebhardt. These women became known in the camp as 'rabbits' and were subjected to prolonged and agonising experiments involving the injection of bacterial cultures into their bones or muscles and the testing of gas bombs. At least seven Polish women died after operations to remove leg bones, to be used for severely wounded German soldiers. Despite the horrific conditions in the camps, education was continued and many young women, including the surviving 'rabbits', gained their school-leaving certificate, the *Matura*, after passing examinations held by the teachers also imprisoned in the camps.[48]

*Generalplan Ost* was first discussed at the conference of Nazi officials which convened under the chairmanship of SS-Obergruppenführer Reinhard Heydrich at Wannsee in January 1942. The principal purpose of this conference was to discuss the Final Solution of the Jewish problem. But *Generalplan Ost* was more than a plan for the extermination of the Jews. The second version of the plan, produced in

July 1942, envisaged nothing less than the transport of 31,000,000 non-Germans from the General Government and Nazi-occupied western portions of the Soviet Union to Siberia. Himmler explained his policy in the journal *Das Schwarze Korps* in summer 1942: 'Our duty in the East is not Germanisation in the former sense of the term, that is, imposing German language and laws upon the population, but to ensure that only people of pure German blood inhabit the East.'[49] This would take place over a thirty-year period during which the people of these areas would be subjected to a policy of deliberate starvation, so that at least 80 per cent would perish. The territory they vacated would be filled by the introduction of 10,000,000 Germans who would farm the region. The Germans began by clearing the region earmarked for German colonisation of its indigenous Jewish population. The terror accompanying this process, which will be covered fully in Chapter 10, led the Poles to conclude, as Stefan Grot-Rowecki, commander of the reorganised resistance, the AK, reported to London in November 1942: 'after the completion of this action [of destroying the Jews] the Germans will begin to liquidate the Poles in the same fashion'.[50]

The details of *Generalplan Ost* had not been finalised when Himmler ordered the SS and Police Leader of Lublin district, SS-Brigadeführer Otto Globocnik, to begin a trial evacuation of the entire Polish population of the Zamość region. Globocnik was known for his hatred of Poles, 'and for his zeal in carrying out his duties, even in excess of the ones imposed by the Nazi regime'.[51] From November 1942 to March 1943 the Germans cleared the Poles from 116 villages, a total of around 41,000 inhabitants. They were given hardly any notice before their expulsion and allowed to take only what belongings they could carry. A second wave of deportations was begun in spring 1943 with a further 80,000 Poles expelled from 171 villages. In all about 31 per cent of Poles in the Lublin region were deported. Himmler had anticipated importing 50,000 *Volksdeutsche* into the region but could find only 10,000 potential settlers, many of whom could not speak German and had no farming experience. Polish Ukrainians were distributed around the region to protect the *Volksdeutsche*.[52]

The AK ordered the villagers to destroy their properties before leaving, and many either moved in with relatives elsewhere in the General Government or fled to the forests seeking the protection of the AK or partisan units. Indeed, the Germans complained that about 25,000

Poles had fled rather than be resettled. The AK and the partisans attacked the new German settlers, as Frank informed his government in January 1943:

> While the racial Germans had not really been molested previously, several attacks on settlers and cases of arson had occurred since the new settlement. In view of the resettlement in the Zamość county, a large part of the police and gendarmerie which was at the disposal of the district, was being withdrawn from the fight against the bandits. The effect on the neighbouring districts was, furthermore, very bad, and there was occasion for great doubt regarding the spring cultivation.[53]

By May 1943 Frank feared that the 'newly settled areas [were] ... in a state of open rebellion', so that in August 1943, when a delegation from the RGO met him, he 'explained that several low-ranking German officials made big mistakes by enforcing evacuations and that some would be removed from their posts', including Globocnik.[54] The Germans then abandoned the policy of evacuations, but attacks continued on the German settlers and, by April 1944, a substantial number had abandoned the Polish properties they had been given and sought security in a camp in Łódź.[55]

The evacuated Poles were taken to transit camps where, living in appalling conditions, they were segregated into the four categories of the *Volksliste*. Those in the first two categories (1 and 2) were considered candidates for Germanisation according to ancestry or racial characteristics and were sent to Łódź for further examination. Those in the two lowest categories (3 and 4) were deemed unsuitable for Germanisation and were despatched to labour camps. Those seen as politically dangerous were sent to the concentration camps of Auschwitz and Majdanek, where many were gassed on arrival. Men and women aged over 60 were sent to 'retirement villages', formerly populated by Jews, along with others not considered fit for work.[56]

A particular tragedy befell the children from the Lublin region and, indeed, throughout occupied Poland. Frank said: 'When we see a blue-eyed child we are surprised that she is speaking Polish ... I admit that in Poland one can find German racial traits among the people ...' In June 1941, Himmler echoed this:

> I would consider it proper if young children of Polish families with specially good racial characteristics were collected and educated in special children's

homes which must not be too large. The seizure of these children would have to be explained by danger to their health ... Genealogical trees and documents of those children who develop satisfactorily should be procured. After one year, such children should be placed as foster children with childless families of good race.[57]

Under the aegis of the *Lebensborn* programme, the Germans screened Polish children after kidnapping them from Polish orphanages, foster families and even off the street. These children were then sent to children's homes in Poznań, Kalisz, Pruszków, Bruczków or Ludwików and screened further. Those who failed the tests were sent to labour camps in Germany. The records of Auschwitz show the arrival of 39 boys from Zamość in February 1943, all of whom were immediately killed by phenol injections to the heart. Of the approximately 200,000 Polish children kidnapped by the Germans, only between 15 and 20 per cent were returned to Poland after the war.[58]

Poland was unique among all the German-occupied countries in having both a Government-in-Exile in London and an Underground Government in the country itself, the *Delegatura* in Warsaw. The first delegate, Cyryl Ratajski, established 20 government departments, closely related to the pre-war government and civil service, and a system of local delegates. He resigned due to poor health in the summer of 1942 and died soon afterwards. His replacement, Jan Piekałkiewicz, was arrested by the Gestapo in February 1943, and Jan Stanisław Jankowski took over (and survived the German occupation). Jan Nowak, a courier between Poland and Britain, described Jankowski: 'a man of middle height, balding, wearing glasses ... a strong personality, a determined individual, very resolute'.[59] The Underground Government's aims were to maintain the morale of the population through the provision of education and culture; to encourage civil resistance; to undertake propaganda activities; and to prepare for the future. The underground secondary-school education system was established almost from the outset of the occupation, and Warsaw University also reopened in secret. After the German occupation of eastern Poland, the Jan Kazimierz University and Polytechnic in Lwów and the Stefan Batory University in Wilno began operating, and the Jagiellonian University in Kraków also reopened during 1942. In all about 1,000 students were educated in the secret universities. The Underground Government touched all areas of culture: theatre companies put on productions and art exhibitions were staged.[60] German-sponsored cultural events were avoided; for example, part of the Warsaw Philharmonic Orchestra played at the Lardelli Restaurant in Warsaw under the conductor Adolf Dolzycki, who had 'remembered' that he had some German ancestry and signed the *Volksliste*. His performances were therefore shunned by all patriotic Poles.[61]

In December 1942, the *Delegatura* established the Directorate of Civil Resistance under Stefan Korboński.[62] Its duties were varied but primarily consisted of giving advice to the whole Polish population on how it could resist German rule. For example, people were told to ignore all German decrees and contact with the Germans as far as possible. The advice given to professionals included requesting doctors to be prepared to issue false medical certificates so that Poles could avoid forced labour, and asking judges not to send cases from their courts to the German ones. Employers were asked to retain as many staff as possible, again to undermine German efforts to recruit Poles for forced labour in the Reich or into the construction service, the *Baudienst*.[63] Korboński's efforts at fostering passive resistance were effective. When Jan Nowak was stopped in the street by a Gestapo agent on his way from a clandestine meeting, he was asked whom he had been visiting: 'Looking over the German's arm, I could see a small brass plate on the door with the name of a woman dentist. Without hesitation I gave her name and the number of her apartment.' The German rang the bell and asked whether a patient by the name of Jeziorański, Nowak's real name, had just left and the dentist confirmed that he had: 'The unknown woman, whom I had never seen and never would see, had not hesitated for a second. She understood in an instant that someone's life was at stake.'[64]

The Bureau for Information and Propaganda was particularly effective in keeping the Polish population informed of events and policies. The two main publications with the greatest circulation were *Polska Żyje* (*Poland Lives*) and the *Biuletyn Informacyjny* (*Information Bulletin*), which at its height had a print run of 47,000. Complimentary copies were sent to the German governor of Warsaw, Ludwig Fischer. In the Polish archives there are copies of 1,174 different magazines. The Bureau also produced military, technical and educational manuals.[65] The *Delegatura* ran Operation 'N', which produced journals for the Germans with titles such as *Der Soldat* and *Der Hammer*, imitating their style but spreading black propaganda. Copies were distributed all over Poland and even reached the Reich and the Eastern Front.[66] The Poles scored a victory over the Germans when, at short notice, they produced a proclamation announcing that 1 May 1942 was to be a holiday on full pay; even the Germans were taken in to start with and the factories remained shut that day despite frantic German public announcements ordering the workers to the factories.[67] Those Poles who still had access to radios could listen to the radio station ŚWIT,* which was located outside London but pretended to broadcast from within Poland. Every day Korboński would transmit information to London and ŚWIT would then broadcast it back to Poland. This rapid turnaround meant that the news broadcast was current and lent credence to the belief that it was coming from within occupied Poland.[68] It also reassured the Poles that their problems were understood.

In late 1941, the Germans conscripted Poles in class 3 of the *Volksliste*: those with some German ancestry who had previously been regarded as Poles. Dominik Stoltman was one such conscript and wrote later: 'Our only consolation was the news from Polish Radio London telling us that they were aware of the situation in Poland. We were also told that once any volunteer reached the front, they were to cross over. We would then have a chance to join the Polish army to fight our common enemy.'[69] Poles conscripted were encouraged to desert and a stamp shop in Warsaw was the central location for this operation: 'When the coast was clear, the deserters would go into the office at the rear, where their identities would be changed – new clothes, documents, hairstyles – and then go out the back door.'[70] Escaped British POWs were also offered assistance. Initially the hiding of them was undertaken by an impromptu organisation run by Mrs Markowski and Mr Olszewski, but in December 1941 Rowecki received orders from London to organise their concealment and repatriation. The aim was to send the British to Switzerland, and the Polish military attaché in Berne was ordered to render assistance. Unfortunately the escape organisation was penetrated by the Gestapo and many members arrested. British POWs who were recaptured were sent to Colditz or other POW camps. Some British POWs joined the AK: an airman, John Ward, would render great service to the AK through his broadcasts back to London during the Warsaw Uprising.[71]

---

* *Świt* means Dawn.

273

The Polish underground also imitated the style of German decrees satirically. During the winter of 1942, the Germans replaced the plaque on the statue of Copernicus which said that he was a Pole with one that said that he was a German. The Poles took down that plaque and, when the Germans noticed, Fischer issued a proclamation, printed on posters distributed around Warsaw:

> Recently, criminal elements removed the tablet from the Copernicus monument for political reasons. As a reprisal, I order the removal of the Kiliński monument. At the same time, I give full warning that, should similar acts be perpetrated, I shall order the suspension of all food rations for the Polish population of Warsaw for the term of one week.

Kiliński's statue was taken to the vaults of the National Museum; the Poles painted, in tar on the light-coloured walls of the museum: 'People of Warsaw, I am here', signed 'Kiliński'. A week later a poster appeared which imitated Fischer's in format, style and font: 'Recently, criminal elements removed the Kiliński monument for political reasons. As a reprisal, I order the prolongation of winter on the eastern front for the term of two months.' It was signed 'Nicolaus Copernicus', and the winter of 1942–3 did last longer than usual.[72] When the Germans broke the news of the Katyń murders in April 1943, they put up posters inviting a committee to inspect the graves. The Bureau of Information produced a poster that started off with this declaration but then continued:

> In this connection, the General Government has ordered that a parallel excursion be organised to the concentration camp at Auschwitz for a committee of all ethnic groups living in Poland. The excursion is to prove how humanitarian, in comparison with the methods employed by the Bolsheviks, are the devices used to carry out the mass extermination of the Polish people . . .

The posters were so convincing that some German officials pasted them up.[73] A spoof pamphlet circulated with useful phrases for the resistance including: 'Halt! Hands up, face to the ground! Were you a member of the Party, SA or SS? Whoever lies will be shot. We will deal with you as the Germans dealt with us. Hands behind the head, face the wall. Take a shovel and dig a grave!'[74]

\*

The issue of Polish collaboration with the Germans is complex. Jan Gross has suggested that collaboration should be restricted to the political sphere, but Stefan Korboński, as a senior member of the Underground Government, offered a far less restricted definition: 'voluntary cooperation with the enemy to the detriment of country or fellow citizens'.[75] The Polish Government had ordered that the Poles should have as little contact with the German authorities as possible, but this was to prove to be unrealistic. The RGO, for example, was in an extremely difficult position. It was responsible for the welfare of the poor and the shelter of the Poles deported from the annexed regions and ran welfare facilities throughout the General Government. It received finance both from the German occupation authorities and from the Polish Government in London. Therefore, one can assume that its activities should not be construed as collaboration. Yet the German authorities also insisted that the RGO send representatives to stand alongside German authorities at German-sponsored meetings, at which new harsh demands would be placed on the Poles. This demand obviously compromised the RGO and Rowecki for one was unhappy about it.[76] Another example of questionable collaboration was the position of the Polish Red Cross when the graves at Katyń were made public. The Polish Government appears to have taken the view that the Polish Red Cross could be trusted not to collaborate with German propaganda and would undertake independent research on the graves. Accordingly a small Polish technical commission worked on the exhumations at Katyń in the spring and early summer of 1943.[77]

The Underground Government established a system of underground courts to try those Poles accused of collaboration. The most notorious were the Polish Blue Police, who were 'regarded as beyond the pale by the Polish community'. The Germans had reorganised the Polish police at the start of the occupation and the policemen had to take an oath of allegiance to the new regime. Although many refused to do so and lost their jobs, the overwhelming majority took the oath.[78] The newly appointed senior officers were German. The size of the police force increased during the war: from 11,500 in 1942 to about 16,000 in 1943. The police were allowed to carry side arms but, unlike those in the German-occupied countries of western Europe, were not promoted to high ranks. The police existed primarily for the maintenance of law and order, which included checking on train passengers and their luggage, conducting house searches and attempting to stop the black market.[79] They would often attempt to blackmail their victims. The AK kept lists of suspect police officers: 'These contained, apart from proved misconduct, evidence of their standard of living which ascertained whether a dark blue was profiteering from blackmail or extortion.'[80] The principal victims of the Polish Blue Police were the Jews, and this issue will be explored further in Chapter 10. About half the Blue Police collaborated with the AK.[81]

The underground courts tried a variety of crimes. For example, writers and actors who worked with the Germans: the famous film actor Igo Seym worked for German propaganda and was shot; two writers, Czesław Ancerewicz and Józef Mackiewicz, were condemned to death for collaboration but only the former was executed. Over-zealousness in carrying out German decrees was also punished, such as the mayor who, in February 1942, arrested some peasants for possessing bread, on the grounds that they must have acquired it illegally since the mills were closed.[82] Betrayal of members of the AK was taken extremely seriously: one farmer became a Gestapo informer because he was an alcoholic and needed money, and he blackmailed 56 farmers who helped the AK before the AK itself caught up with him and put him on trial.[83] Approximately 10,000 Poles received sentences from the underground courts, but only 200 death sentences were passed and carried out. Minor offences were usually punished by flogging or, in the case of women having sexual relations with Germans, by head shaving. Many people were acquitted or had their cases deferred until the end of the war.[84]

Brigadeführer SS Dr Eberhard Schöngarth stated in April 1943: 'Such an oppression as is being borne by the Polish people has never been borne by any other nation.'[85] The mass labour round-ups, the draconian quotas for foodstuffs, poor rations and the extermination of the Jews all added up to a regime of absolute terror. The sheer scale can be seen through one example: between October 1939 and July 1944 about 100,000 Poles, both Christians and Jews, were interrogated in one prison alone, Pawiak prison in Warsaw, and of these 17,000 were executed and 60,000 were sent to concentration camps. Most executions took place in Palmiry forest on the outskirts of Warsaw but, after the Germans had demolished the ghetto in 1943, around 9,500 people, mostly ethnic Poles, were shot in the ruins.[86] In all the prisons in the General Government, torture and beatings were routine features of interrogation. K. T. Czelny was imprisoned in Rabka because he and his father had offered medical treatment to Jews from the nearby ghetto:

> It was an orgy of sadism and unspeakable cruelty, cynically planned and executed. Their methods ranged from attempts at mild persuasion to brutal beatings and ingenious torture, such as handcuffing the prisoner's hands behind his back and hanging him, by means of a hefty rope threaded through the handcuffs, on the inner door of the interrogation room. After a short while, the excruciating pain in the joints brought unconsciousness. The method used to bring us back was to push a lighted cigarette against either the belly or the genitals.[87]

In Kielce the prison was lorded over by the Gestapo officer Franz Wittek, who all those facing him remember with terror. Marian Skowerski was suspected of being a member of the AK (which he was), and was kept in a cell with twenty-five other men. Each day Wittek would come and stare every man in the eye: then he would decide who was to be taken out and shot, who would be interrogated and tortured further, and who would be released. Skowerski remembered that on the day when he decided that there was no longer any point in being frightened, he was released.[88] In Lwów, the priest Czesław Tuzinkiewicz was summoned to Gestapo headquarters to attest that a parishioner was a good Catholic, and while waiting he witnessed lines of prisoners held against a wall and whipped or beaten about the head if they made the slightest move.[89]

In January 1943, the Polish foreign minister, Edward Raczyński, wrote in a note to the governments of the United Nations: 'Detailed information has been forthcoming in the course of the last weeks regarding a new wave of mass arrests and public executions in numerous parts of the country.'[90] For example, 106 people were hanged publicly in Szopieniec, and in Warsaw 70 people were executed in one street after a warehouse had been set on fire. The German policy of collective reprisals for any act of sabotage or resistance to their authority now increased in scale and was more public. One witness described the process:

> We all knew the big lorry and its special crew; in front there stood a German in a steel helmet, in his hands a big horn. Every few minutes he would blow it in the same fixed manner. On side-benches in the lorry were seated

twelve Germans armed to the teeth. Behind this vehicle was another, smaller one, containing the victims condemned to death. The sound of the horn filled us all with terror. We knew that people were being driven to their deaths. The lorries would stop in the streets with the densest traffic, the hostages would be dragged out to be mown down by machine-gunfire. After the execution the Germans would drive the vehicles back, the horn would sound again and on the pavement would remain the bloody corpses of the victims of German bestiality.[91]

The Germans taped the mouths of the victims because they were angered by their shouts of 'Long Live Poland!' as they prepared to die. The Polish population not only witnessed street executions but also heard tales of life in the concentration camps of Auschwitz I and Majdanek, when handfuls of prisoners were released back into the community.[92] Within the General Government, the Christian Poles in various camps totalled 150,000 in Auschwitz I, 100,000 in Majdanek and 23,000 in Płaszów.[93]

Life outside Warsaw and the large cities was generally easier because peasants could escape into the forests. They became adept at concealing their produce and many actually became richer because of the black market. Nevertheless, over 650 villages were destroyed by the Germans and, like the city-dwellers, the peasants lost thousands of people to forced labour round-ups.[94] Over the course of the occupation, however, the rural areas began to suffer greatly as increased AK action and the presence of Soviet partisans brought draconian German reprisals.

As the German terror increased so did the resistance. On 14 February 1942, Sikorski had reorganised the Polish resistance, changing its name from the ZWZ to AK, under the command of General Stefan Rowecki, code name 'Grot'. His chief of staff was General 'Gregorz' Tadeusz Pełczyński. The new AK had two policies: to extend the reach of its activities into eastern Poland, and to bring all resistance groups under its command. Neither policy was simple to put fully into practice. While the AK did extend its operations into eastern Poland and into the Ukraine, it ran into hostility from Soviet partisans and was at risk of betrayal by Ukrainians, Belorussians and Lithuanians loyal to the Germans. In late 1942, the Germans arrested a number of AK leaders in the eastern provinces and the organisation there had to be rebuilt. For example, in November 1942 Leon Kochański was fortunate to escape arrest, unlike many members of his staff. He then withdrew from underground activity for four months as the organisation was rebuilt and changed his code name.[95] Renewed attempts to penetrate the provinces absorbed into the Reich also met with limited success because of frequent discoveries and betrayal by *Volksdeutsche*. After the arrests of several regional leaders, it was decided to run operations directly from Warsaw. Interestingly enough, the chief of operations in Łódź had the remarkable cover provided by being a *Volksdeutscher* and a member of the Nazi Party, Jan Lipsz 'Anatol'.[96]

On 30 June 1943, disaster hit the AK, when Rowecki was arrested by the Gestapo. He was betrayed by three AK members, Ludwik 'Hanka' Kalkstein, Eugeniusz 'Genes' Świerczewski and Blanka 'Sroka' Kaczorowska, who were in fact informants for the Gestapo.[97] He was taken to Berlin for interrogation. The Polish Government appealed to the British for help. Raczyński approached Eden and Churchill hoping that, at best, Rowecki might be exchanged for the German generals Jürgen von Arnim and Wilhelm von Thoma, or at least be accorded the status of a POW. Churchill was initially in favour but held out little hope that the Germans would take the offer seriously. Eden, however, told the War Cabinet that the legal advisers in the Foreign Office had informed him that under international law, Rowecki was a *franc-tireur* and therefore not eligible to be treated as a POW.[98] Rowecki was replaced as leader of the AK by General Tadeusz Bór-Komorowski ('Bór'). Rowecki was shot in Sachsenhausen concentration camp on the outbreak of the Warsaw Uprising in August 1944.

The AK's strategy of uniting all resistance groups under its command had mixed success. Although many of the smaller units had been ready to accept Rowecki's authority, some of the larger and more politically motivated took longer to convince or did not amalgamate at all. In November 1942, the military wing of the National Party (*Narodowa Organizacja Wojskowa*) accepted incorporation and in July 1943, the military forces of the Peasant Party (*Bataliony Chłopskie*, BCH) were also integrated. The latter were often reluctant to work under the AK because they viewed it as *Panskie Wojsko* – a gentleman's army still closely allied to the *Sanacja* regime. Witold Sągajłło was informed by the local commander of the BCH that there could be no cooperation with him because his staff were all aristocrats and landowners, but Sągajłło took him to meet his staff, where the peasant commander learnt that the AK staff in the area were all second-generation peasants. Sągajłło also took the man around the district, travelling 60 miles in three days, to meet the AK soldiers, whereupon the exhausted peasant leader agreed to let his men be commanded by the AK.[99] The military units of the Communist Party, the People's Army (*Armia Ludowa*, AL), were more closely aligned with the Soviet partisans and remained independent of the AK, although the two armies would sometimes cooperate. Some National Party members did not accept the authority of the AK or the Underground Government, and they formed their own breakaway group, the National Radical Camp (*Obóz Narodowo-Radykalny*), which had its own army, the National Armed Units (*Narodowe Siły Zbrojne*, NSZ), which fought independently from the AK and was known for its anti-semitism. In April 1944, Bór-Komorowski informed London that the reality was that the AK 'was a conglomeration of commanders and detachments, whose attitudes to one another are frequently undisguisedly hostile, and who are held together in a badly frayed thread of formal discipline that may snap at the start of operations'.[100]

The principal focus of the AK was to prepare for a general armed uprising to take place at the most opportune moment when Germany's collapse was evident. During the course of 1942, the emphasis of the resistance was on organisation, sabotage, diversionary operations and preparations for this general uprising. On 9 November 1942, Rowecki issued an order on the policy:

> As to the operation of annihilating the Jews, [carried out] by the occupier, there are signs of disquiet among the Polish public, lest after this operation is completed, the Germans will begin the liquidation of the Poles, in exactly the same manner.
>
> I order self-control and action to calm the public. However, if the Germans do indeed make any attempt of this sort, they will meet with active resistance on our part, without consideration for the fact that the time for our uprising has not yet come. The units under my command will enter armed battle to defend the life of our people. In this battle we will move over from defence to offence by cutting all the enemy channels of transport to the eastern front.[101]

During 1941 and 1942, the AK was responsible for attacks on bridges and railways as far east as Minsk, while Lord Selborne, the head of SOE

(Special Operations Executive), reported that during 1943 the AK had derailed more than 20 trains, damaged 180 locomotives and killed more than 1,000 Germans.[102] There was an ominous indication of the future to these operations: although the western allies were keen to encourage AK activity in support of the Soviet Union, the Soviet reaction was rather different. The AK drew up plans for the simultaneous disruption of all railway lines through Poland to the Eastern Front, along which 85 per cent of all German supplies and manpower were carried. These were transmitted to London, approved by Sikorski and discussed at a meeting between the Polish ambassador in Moscow, Tadeusz Romer, and Stalin. The AK needed the Soviets to state a time when the operation would fit in with their plans but Stalin declined even to give a response.[103]

The AK organised sabotage cells within factories engaged in war production. The shortage of specialists forced the Germans to employ Poles, although the management remained in German hands. Secret groups worked within 37 such factories, sabotaging production where possible but also, very importantly, diverting raw materials, component parts and even finished articles into the AK war chest. Predominantly, this meant facilitating the purchase of ingredients needed for the manufacture of explosives, such as saltpetre and potassium chlorate, by creating false invoices or by ordering large supplies from Germany and diverting the surplus. Sometimes factories producing items for the civilian market also ran a secret operation manufacturing armaments. For example, a factory making padlocks and locks also made tommy guns, a factory making cans for polish also made grenades, and flamethrowers were made in a factory producing fire extinguishers.[104]

There was a substantial resistance organisation within the concentration camps, especially at Auschwitz I. It should be stressed that this resistance existed only in this concentration and labour camp, and had little ability to act in the extermination camp of Auschwitz-Birkenau. The resistance was led by Witold Pilecki, who allowed himself to be arrested in the hope of being sent to Auschwitz, and once there he organised the Union of Military Organisation (*Związek Organizacji Wojskowej*, ZOW). ZOW attempted to alleviate the prisoners' harsh conditions by securing supplies of medicine and food, and by attacking the most brutal kapos (prisoner-supervisors), spies and SS men. Their principal weapon was the use of typhus-infected lice, the supply of which was ample. These would then be placed on the offenders:

> Several SS men infected with typhus died in spite of the fact that they had
> received much better medical attention than prisoners ... Somehow the
> SS guards realised that the most cruel of them were the ones who were
> dying ... There was a general improvement in the treatment of prisoners
> by the SS guards.[105]

The SS became afraid of manhandling the prisoners. Sadistic kapos
were also targeted by having stolen gold and foreign currency smuggled
into their barracks, which led to discovery by the SS and the gassing of
the 'guilty' kapo. As a result: 'The behaviour of all kapos in the main
camp became almost civilised by the end of 1942.'[106] Informers had
their records switched in the hospital so that they were often killed by
the Germans as being too sick to work. ZOW also organised around
600 escapes, of which a third were successful. In May 1942, Stefan
Bielecki and Wincenty Gawron escaped and reached Warsaw, where
they provided the first eyewitness accounts of what was happening in
the whole Auschwitz complex. At the end of April 1943, Pilecki himself
escaped because he believed that his reports from the camp about the
possibilities of an uprising were not being taken seriously by the AK
command. On reaching Warsaw, he learnt that the AK command had
concluded 'that the forces at their disposal were too few and too poorly
armed, that the underground organisation inside the camp was almost
helpless and the SS garrison too numerous and well-equipped', which
was probably only too true.* In April 1944, ZOW helped two Jews,
Rudolf Vrba and Alfred Wetzler, to escape and their detailed 32-page
report on the extermination of the Jews was first broadcast on the BBC
on 15 June 1944.[107]

The resistance extended to the Polish forced labourers in Germany.
In 1942 the German police arrested the leader of this resistance, Leon-
hard Kendzierski, in Stuttgart and under torture he revealed the names
of his colleagues. In April 1944, an AK courier travelled to Cologne

---

* Pilecki served in the Warsaw Uprising. After he was liberated from a POW camp, he
travelled to Italy and joined the Polish II Corps. In October 1945, he returned to Poland
under a false identity and at Anders's request to gather information for the Polish
Government-in-Exile on the arrests of members of the AK by the Soviet and communist
Polish authorities. Pilecki was arrested by the Polish security police in May 1947, repeatedly
tortured before his trial in March 1948, found guilty and executed in May 1948. Pilecki
was rehabilitated in 1990 and posthumously awarded Poland's highest decoration, the
Order of the White Eagle.

with orders for the resistance to organise the forced labourers for action when Germany collapsed. In the meantime they were instructed on methods of industrial sabotage, using such subtle techniques that the sabotaged armaments would pass German inspection. By the second half of 1944, as allied armies closed in on the Reich, the foreign labourers became bolder and there were numerous attacks on German police officers and soldiers and on Nazi Party members.[108]

The AK also took action against the bandits who were preying on the peasants who lived near the forests. These forests were full of people struggling to survive. There were Jews who had fled the ghettos to avoid deportation to the extermination camps: 'We were a terrorised group of young people turned into orphans overnight. Finding each other in this wild, uncaring environment, we realised that history had placed upon us the task of avenging the blood of our people.'[109] Some of these Jews would join the communist resistance, the *Gwarda Ludowa-Armia Ludowa* (GL-AL), a few the AK. After June 1941, there were Soviet soldiers, deserters and escaped POWs, who formed undisciplined bands of men until the arrival of Soviet partisan bands which incorporated them. There were also young Poles who had fled to the forests to avoid being sent as forced labour to the Reich, not all of whom wanted to join the AK and submit to its discipline. All these disparate elements preyed on the local population for food, clothing and money.

Banditry was particularly widespread in the provinces of Lublin, Warsaw and Kraków. Most of these gangs were small and poorly armed but in the area of Lublin province around the village of Piłatka the 'Kiełbasowcy' gang, which consisted of over 60 bandits armed with 40 sub-machine guns and 2 heavy machine guns, terrorised the local peasantry. One victim recalled a visit by the gang:

> They tore up floors, searched the grain storage bins, tore open down quilts and found everything everywhere. They took clothing, shoes, even children's shoes, food, pigs, but most of all they wanted money and vodka. If they didn't find anything they would beat the farmers mercilessly. They were terrible to girls and women.[110]

Banditry was also a problem in the eastern provinces. Father Czesław Tuzinkiewicz, a parish priest in Białochorszcze on the outskirts of Lwów, recalled a visit when the bandits entered a house full of defenceless women but unknown to them a member of the AK was hiding there. He attacked the bandits with an axe, beheading one. The next morning the body lay on the ground but, to prevent identification, the remaining bandits had taken away the severed head of their comrade.[111]

On 31 August 1943, Bór-Komorowski issued Order 116 against banditry to his area, regional and district commanders:

> I instruct all Regional and District Commanders to take action against plundering or subversive-bandit elements where it is necessary.
>
> Each action must be decisive and must aim at suppressing lawlessness. Action should be taken only against groups especially troublesome for the local population and the Command of the Armed Forces in the Homeland; above all against those who murder, rape and rob.
>
> Action should be taken with the aim of liquidating gang leaders and agitators, and not concentrating on the liquidation of entire gangs.[112]

This order has been misinterpreted by some Jewish historians as an order for the AK to eliminate the Jews hiding in the forests by labelling them as bandits, as the Germans did.[113] But Jews were not mentioned in the order at all and only tangentially in Organisation Report 220 to the Polish Government in which Komorowski explained his policy.[114] The Jewish Bund in Poland acknowledged the problem of banditry among some Jews hiding in the forests in a 1943 report to the Bund in London:

> In the forests: certain groups of those who escaped from the ghetto pogroms fled into the forest, by different ways and means, either armed or unarmed, and they continue to live in the woods. Most of them, seeking to survive, have come to form wildcat groups which are looting the countryside, and only a few of them have joined partisan groups operating in the respective regions.[115]

In August 1943, the AK killed 76 Jewish bandits. Further evidence that Komorowski was not calling for the AK to murder the Jews specifically comes in his second order on banditry, issued on 4 November 1943:

> Fight the gangs without regard to the nationality of the criminals or their political or military allegiance; and, therefore, all robber gangs, including those who pretend to carry out military actions, and gangs of this type in our own ranks, should be fought mercilessly, using all possible methods, including the death penalty.[116]

The AK was thereby exhorted to eliminate banditry regardless of the members' ethnic grouping. Some AK commanders argued against the order on the grounds that it had been issued too late: 'Any possibility of getting rid of the bandits had been lost nearly a year before when I was refused permission to set up an independent field force able to deal with this problem. Now, I said, any attempt to get rid of these people would be interpreted as a hostile political action towards the Russians, incompatible with the accepted attitude of the Polish Government towards Russia.' The response from Warsaw was to carry out the order. Most of the bandits caught were tried by the underground military courts and, if found guilty, executed. The AK executed approximately 920 bandits in the period from September 1943 to July 1944.[117]

Before any uprising could take place, the AK needed to undertake the recruitment of soldiers, train them and ensure an adequate supply of equipment. The AK established training schools for its soldiers, NCOs and officers. Zbigniew Bokiewicz took an officers' course in Warsaw: 'Exercises and drills were carried out in private apartments using broom handles in place of rifles.' One of the instructors was a member of the Blue Police.[118] In Lublin, Ralph Smorczewski also received training as an officer: 'This was split into groups of no more than six, which met every few days at addresses chosen by the participants themselves and were never to be repeated twice in succession . . . Members of the group never knew each other's names, all had pseudonyms.'[119] Again they could not train with real rifles. In the rural districts the AK could train better: it was particularly active in the Świętokrzyski mountains near Kielce, in the districts of Radom, Kielce and Lublin, in the forests near Zamość, in provinces of Podole, Wołyń, Białystok and Polesie, and in the districts of Wilno and Nowogródek.[120] Wacław Milewski trained in the Świętokryski mountains:

> On Friday after work, we all set out on the long march to the mountains. About dusk, we reached a village where our weapons were hidden, and we then marched throughout the night, arriving at the summit of the Holy Cross Mountains at dawn. There full-scale training took place. We participated in drills of all kinds and even shot our weapons in a rifle range. On Sunday the entire unit went to Mass. We stood in ranks in front of the church and generally behaved as though there was no German army in

Poland. As far as I remember, the Germans never seemed to make their presence felt.[121]

The troops marched back on Sunday evening and on Monday returned to work as normal.

Training was often provided by Polish officers and men parachuted into Poland from Britain. These *Cichociemni* – 'unseen and silent' – were trained in Britain by SOE. The first drop of two agents, Captain Józef 'Zbik' Zabielski and Major Stanisław 'Kostka' Krzymowski, took place on the night of 15–16 February 1941. Around 600 *Cichociemni* were trained but only 316 were parachuted into Poland by the end of 1944, because of the difficulties of air transport. Witold Sągajłło's AK group received two *Cichociemni* near Ozarow in the Świętokryskie district and was shocked by their lack of training: 'The briefing of the two officers was appalling. Before being sent to Warsaw they had to be coached on how to behave. Yardley perfumes and English cigarettes had to be confiscated, clothing checked for labels, etc.' Most, however, were better prepared and their skills would be put to great use when Operation *Burza* was launched in 1944, the Polish uprising to assist the Soviet advance into Poland.[122]

The difficulties in supplying arms and other supplies to the AK were enormous. Until the Allies landed in Italy, there were two only possible air routes to Poland. The first was over the North Sea, Denmark and the altic before crossing the coast between Danzig and Kolberg (Kołobrzeg), a distance of 800 miles to Pomerania and 1,000 miles to Warsaw district; the second route, over Sweden, was 120–160 miles longer. The only plane with a sufficient range and suitable for airdrops was the Halifax, which, when fitted with extra fuel tanks, had a range of under 2,175 miles. This left little room for navigational errors and reduced the payload from 4,200 lbs to 2,400 lbs. Indeed, on the first operation, on the night of 7 November 1941, the plane ran out of fuel on its return journey and was forced to land in Sweden, where the plane and its crew were interned. Such lengthy flights could only be undertaken during the winter months when the nights were long, but the weather was also worse then and often forced the cancellation of flights. In all there were only about 20 nights a year possible for flights to Poland during 1942 and 1943.[123] This meant that the Polish 138 Special Duties Squadron was not solely devoted to flights to Poland but was

also expected to drop supplies to resistance movements in other countries. Between February 1941 and October 1943, the AK had expected
SOE to provide them with 210 flights bringing 300 tons of war materiel. Instead there were only 72 flights dropping 65 tons.[124] Matters
improved slightly when in October 1943 the Special Duties Squadron,
now renumbered 1586, began operating from Brindisi in Italy and was
supplied with 3 American B-24 Liberators to augment its 3 Halifaxes.
Between April and July 1944, there were 174 successful sorties to
Poland and 114 men and 219 tons of supplies were dropped.[125] The
supplies provided were far too little to equip the 4,000 platoons of
the AK. Arms were also dug up from where they had been buried after the
September 1939 campaign, although many were too rusty to be used
again. The Germans and their Ukrainian and Lithuanian auxiliaries
could sometimes be blackmailed or persuaded into selling arms to the
AK.[126]

The tragedy of the AK's strategy was that it was allowed the freedom
to develop its plans for a general uprising, following the instructions
from the Polish Government, but was in total ignorance regarding the
lack of political willpower and ability by the western allies to devote
sufficient resources to ensure an adequate supply of armaments to the
AK. The Polish Government approached the British requesting, if not
actually demanding, more supply flights to Poland and the allocation of
suitable aircraft to the Polish special duties squadron. When the British
failed to respond, Sikorski turned to the Americans, raising the matter
of the allocation of B-24 Liberators during his meetings with Roosevelt.
Sikorski ignored warnings from the CIGS, General Alanbrooke, that
the 'physical problem of transporting materials for secret armies in
Eastern Europe is insuperable'. In late June 1943, the Polish Government made another appeal to the Combined Chiefs of Staff in
Washington. General Sosnkowski informed Alanbrooke that 'six
hundred trips by air until April 1944 will be necessary for the most
indispensable needs of the Secret Army in Poland'. Sosnkowski, Sikorski and his successor, Stanisław Mikołajczyk, were all aware that the
western allies would not undertake such supplies, and they appear to
have thought that the reason for refusal was political. Indeed, there is
a great deal of evidence to suggest that the Combined Chiefs felt that
Poland fell within the Soviet sphere of operations and this affected their
willingness to authorise an increase in the number of flights. But even

if the political goodwill had existed there would still have been the insoluble problem that sufficient air resources did not.[127]

The AK initially followed a deliberate policy of shying away from direct confrontation with the Germans, because of the impact of German reprisals on the innocent Polish population. But as German terror increased during 1943, the AK turned to more aggressive forms of resistance and launched a policy of assassinations. Jan Nowak summarised the reasons:

> Because of the constant escalation of repression, terror lost its power to terrorise. People simply stopped being afraid because they had nothing much to lose. The mass extermination of the Jews and the liquidation of the ghetto seemed to be the turning point. The rest of the population began to realise that their turn would come next.[128]

The SS and Police Leader for Radom reported a jump in the number of violent attacks on German officials from 105 in April 1942 to over 1,000 in May 1943. In April 1943, an assassination attempt was made on Chief of Police and SS in the General Government, Friedrich-Wilhelm Krüger. In May 1943, Globocnik advised Frank not to visit Lublin, because no guarantee could be made for his security, and in February 1944, there was an unsuccessful attempt to assassinate Frank when a bomb was detonated under the train carrying him from Kraków to Lwów. In February 1944, the Gestapo chief in Warsaw, SS Brigadeführer Franz Kutschera, was shot dead in broad daylight in Warsaw. The response of the Germans was to increase their terrorisation of the Poles. After the assassination of Kutschera, Hitler ordered that a quota of hostages should be taken from every town in the General Government and hanged in public. Sągajłło described the events in one town: 'The next day, a battalion of SS with armoured cars and personnel carriers entered Ostrowiec and during the night thirty-five people were taken at random from their homes and thrown into the town prison.' Mass arrests were made in Warsaw, Radom and Lublin, and, in April 1944, Frank's government was informed that a total of 5,475 people had been arrested on political grounds. More worryingly for the Germans and tragically for the AK, the Germans had also seized over 20,000 weapons, 75,000 bombs, 32,000 pounds of explosives and a great amount of other explosive material.[129]

The delay in the change of strategy had serious consequences for the Polish Government in London and its representatives in Poland, the AK and the Underground Government. Poles determined to oppose the Germans by any means possible became tempted by the activities of the partisans and the communist-inspired AL. Bór-Komorowski understood this:

> German terror was one of the main reasons why partisan fighting was steadily on the increase in those years. Young people threatened with arrest, rescued prisoners, and terrorised peasants fled into the forests. Individuals who could not stand the nervous strain of continual terror and persecution and hoped to live a fuller life in open warfare or those who wished to revenge their next of kin, tortured and murdered – all these reinforced our partisan forces.[130]

In the years after the German invasion of the Soviet Union, Soviet partisan bands had developed and increased their activities in the General Government, posing a significant threat to the authority of the AK and bringing down harsh reprisals on the Polish population. As will be described more fully in Chapter 12, the presence of Soviet partisans, Jewish partisans, the AL, the AK and the NSZ in the forests of Poland led to armed clashes between different units and created a climate of uncertainty just as the Soviet armies began to approach the pre-war Polish frontier. As one resistance fighter described the situation: 'It was difficult to find out which villages we could trust. Some villages supported the AK, some the left-wing AL. There were also partisan groups, such as the BCH (*Bataliony Chłopskie*), formed by farmers, some of whom were left wing, some right.'[131]

The Underground Government was also not as unified as some of its supporters would have liked to claim. The alliance of the four parties – the Polish Socialist Party (*Polska Partia Socjalistyczna*, PPS), the Peasant Alliance (*Stronnictwo Ludowe*, SL), the National Alliance (*Stronnictwo Narodowe*, SN) and the Labour Alliance (*Stronnictwo Pracy*, SP) – who formed the Underground Government was very fragile. They saw each other as rivals and their preoccupation with the need to define 'their own identity for the contest which would take place after the war was a powerful determining factor in actions taken during the course of the war'.[132] The most powerful challenge to the authority of the Polish Government and Underground Government would, however, come from outside for, after the break in diplomatic relations with the Polish Government, the Soviets had begun to sponsor the political and military activities of the communist Poles in the Soviet Union. On the diplomatic front too, the Polish Government was losing the battle for its voice to be heard and for its opinions to be considered seriously by the British and American governments. At the end of 1943, the German armies were in clear retreat and the arrival of the Soviet armies on the pre-war Polish frontier would open a new and terrible chapter for the Poles. German terror policies showed no signs of abating. As Frank remarked in January 1944: 'As far as I am concerned the Poles and Ukrainians and their like may be chopped into small pieces. Let it be, what should be.'[133]

# IO

# The Holocaust, 1941–1943

During the height of the German occupation of Poland, 1941 to 1943, the Poles were reduced to living in conditions of abject poverty and subjected to a systematic German policy of terror. Yet, for all the sufferings of the Christian Poles during this period, they were not being subjected to the unprecedented policy of calculated and deliberate extermination that the Polish Jews faced. Between June 1941 and the end of 1943, 90 per cent of Polish Jewry died – by gas at purpose-built extermination camps, by mass shootings in eastern Poland, and through starvation and shootings in the ghettos. The sheer speed of the Holocaust was in itself deeply shocking as many thousands died each day with honed Germanic efficiency, and this speed overwhelmed the Jews and Poles alike, making an effective response virtually impossible. It was also a policy difficult to comprehend: why in the midst of a world war would a supposedly civilised nation embark on the mass murder of a people, many of whom were capable of work, solely on the grounds of their race? The Jews, the Poles, the world outside, could not comprehend the logic of the policy, and their disbelief and consequent inaction made the job of the Germans easier. Nor could the Jews easily escape their fate: unlike the small number of Danish Jews, they had no neutral country a few miles away prepared to receive them. The principal phase of the Holocaust, in 1942, took place at the height of German power, at the time when German armies were driving deeper into the Soviet Union and the western allies were in retreat in the Western Desert and all across the Far East, and therefore there was no chance of outside intervention.

When the Germans invaded Soviet-occupied Poland, they entered a territory in which 1,350,000 Jews had lived before the war, mainly concentrated in the cities, including Lwów, Wilno and Białystok. Some had fled east as the Soviets had retreated, and some had been deported by the Soviets deep into the Soviet Union: the exact numbers are unknown but it is certain that the vast majority were still in their homes when the Germans arrived. The *Einsatzgruppen* which accompanied the Wehrmacht into Kresy deliberately encouraged or even organised pogroms against the local Jewish population. The Ukrainians needed little encouragement: in Lwów a witness, Philip Friedman, noted: 'The mobs were on the rampage, the howls of the killers mingled with the screams of the victims, and the slaughter in the streets continued.'[1] Felix Landau, a German soldier, saw Jews leaving the main prison in Lwów:

> The Ukrainians had taken some Jews up to the former GPU citadel. These Jews had apparently helped the GPU persecute the Ukrainians and the Germans. They had rounded up 800 Jews there, who were supposed to be shot by us tomorrow. They had now released them.
>
> We continued along the road, there were hundreds of Jews walking along the street with blood pouring down their faces, holes in their heads, their hands broken and their eyes hanging out of their sockets. They were covered in blood.[2]

In Drohobycz the Germans stood back and 'let the Ukrainians run wild and start the first pogrom'.[3] In some cases ethnic Poles also assisted in the murders of local Jews. In Jedwabne, 40 miles from Białystok where the Germans had already murdered over 2,000 Jews, a minority of ethnic Poles turned on their Jewish neighbours and murdered over 300, though some say 1,000 were killed there. Jedwabne was not a spontaneous pogrom but a massacre deliberately encouraged by the Germans and one in which many of the perpetrators were not, as has been alleged, neighbours of the Jews, but had come from nearby villages to take part. One possible motive for taking part in the pogroms could have been revenge against the perceived prominence of the Jews in the Soviet administration.[4]

In general the Germans were disappointed with the results, because once the initial chaos and viciousness unleashed by the Soviet defeat had worn off, the population of Kresy seemed unwilling to continue in German-sponsored 'spontaneous' massacres. Indeed, the report by

*Einsatzgruppe* B from Belorussia in early August 1941 gives probably the most accurate representation of the situation: 'In addition, as we have found in Minsk and the former Polish areas, there is no real anti-semitism here. It is true that the population feels hate and fury towards the Jews and approves of the German actions . . . however, it is incapable of taking the initiative into its own hands in dealing with the Jews.'[5]

By November 1941, the Germans had stamped their authority over Kresy and two policies towards the Jews had emerged: confinement into ghettos and a programme of mass shootings. The two policies ran side by side with no particular logic to them. The shootings were begun by the Germans but soon continued with the assistance of Ukrainian, Belorussian and Lithuanian auxiliaries recruited specially for the purpose. Every town with a Jewish presence had a ghetto established. These were normally no more than a few buildings and some ground surrounded by barbed wire and guarded by a few Germans and local auxiliaries. The sheer number of Jews to be processed caused problems. In Słonim, Gebeitskommissar Gerhard Erren reported that because there were 25,000 Jews in the area, he did not have the manpower nor the barbed wire available to establish a ghetto.

> I thus immediately began preparations for a large-scale action . . . The Jews were then registered accurately according to number, age and profession and all craftsmen and workers with qualifications were singled out and given passes and separate accommodation to distinguish them from the other Jews.

By the end of November 1941, the numbers in Słonim had been reduced to 7,000.[6] Mass murders took place throughout Kresy; for example, in Stanisławów alone 20,000 Jews were killed in October 1941.[7] Throughout 1941 and into early 1942 the shootings continued, and the number of victims has been estimated at around 300,000. Sometimes the Germans utilised facilities created by the previous occupiers. The Soviets had dug a fuel base for a planned airfield in the Ponary Hills: 'They dug enormous holes and paved them with stone. The "caverns" were from forty-five to sixty feet in diameter and up to twenty-five feet deep.' The SS took advantage of these ready-made graves and the nearby railway station to kill 70,000 Jews, mainly from Lithuania but also other places: even from as far away as France.[8]

The Jews in the ghettos of Kresy were poorly guarded and had ample opportunities for escape. Yet many did not attempt this, because the Soviets had given no publicity to the nature of anti-Jewish measures already in operation in the General Government, and so they lacked the sure and terrible knowledge to flee. A German report noted in July 1941:

> The Jews are remarkably ill-informed about our attitude toward them. They do not know how Jews are treated in Germany, or for that matter in Warsaw . . . Even if they do not think that under German administration they will have equal rights with the Russians, they believe, nevertheless, that we shall leave them in peace if they mind their own business and work diligently.[9]

Some did escape successfully and took to the forests, where the Germans hunted them down. Others received assistance. The Hungarians were the first Axis force to occupy Stanisławów, warned the Jews of the fate that would befall them and offered them help to reach the Hungarian border where they would receive new documents giving them ethnic Polish names that did not reflect their Jewish origins. The Committee of Polish Citizens in Hungary raised an outcry over this because the Hungarians had given too many Jews the only Polish surnames they knew, 'Mickiewicz' or 'Piłsudski', which was about as likely as giving all British émigrés the surnames 'Shakespeare' and 'Churchill'. The matter was settled by the Poles providing the Hungarians with a longer list of plausible Polish surnames.[10] The Jews who took up the offer were not, however, usually the native Stanisławów inhabitants but refugees from other areas or other countries such as Czechoslovakia, who had had experience of German conduct. The Hungarian record on the Jews is not untarnished: the Jews from Sub-Carpathian Ruthenia were not offered Hungarian citizenship when Hungary occupied the region but were expelled into German-occupied Ukraine where they perished at Kamianets-Podilskyi.[11]

Life in the ghettos continued to be one long struggle for survival. As the rations for the Christian Poles fell to barely subsistence levels, the negligible rations allocated to the Jews condemned them to a slow death from starvation. Indeed, it has been estimated that 100,000 Jews, or about 20 per cent of the Jews in the ghettos, died before the deportations even began, mostly from starvation.[12] They survived through the work of their welfare agency, *Żydowska Samopomoc Społeczna*, which operated under the auspices of the German-sponsored RGO throughout Poland and distributed aid sent from abroad,[13] but its operations ceased after the major deportations. The smuggling of food into the ghetto assumed an ever-increasing importance: in December 1941, the head of the *Judenrat*, Adam Czerniaków, recorded in his diary the calculation: 'we received legally 1,800,000 złotys' worth of food in the ghetto monthly, and illegally 70–80,000,000 złotys' worth'.[14]

Even though the Warsaw ghetto had been sealed in October 1940, trade continued between the Jews and the Poles. One inmate, Danny Falkner, wrote that the large number of Jewish artisans meant: 'They were now all concentrated in the ghetto and the Poles were deprived of their products: leather goods, woodworks, tailoring. So a two-way traffic developed: raw materials were being smuggled into the ghetto and ready-made articles smuggled out. By these activities people managed to make a living.'[15] The Lower Court had two entrances: the gate on Ulica Leszno opened into the ghetto and the one on Ulica Ogrodowa into the Polish section. Both gates were guarded but the Poles and Jews could arrange to meet there to trade food for finished articles:

Therefore parcels and bundles changed hands inside the building and certain elegant Aryan women accustomed to their old dressmakers and tailors made appointments just there. An obliging usher let the back room be used for trying on overcoats and dresses, top-boots, girdles and brassieres in exchange for a few złoty.

The courthouse was also a meeting place for those couples separated by religion. Abraham Lewin recorded in his diary:

Someone who has been witness to these reunions described them to me. There is in these meetings an overflowing of human tragedy and suffering. A Christian woman comes and kisses her Jewish husband. She brings him a small parcel of food. They talk for a few minutes, move away to one side, kiss again and separate. He back to the ghetto and she to the Aryan part of Warsaw.[16]

One enterprising Jew even managed to keep a cow hidden in the ghetto, and milk was sold in return for fodder and cash. When a German owner of a factory in the ghetto found out, he provided an official ration for the cow.[17]

The Jews in the ghettos were a mixture: 'There were orthodox Jews, assimilated Jews, a few Zionists and Socialists, and even some baptised Jews.'[18] According to the statistics compiled by the *Judenrat* in Warsaw in 1941, there were 1,540 Catholics, 148 Protestants, 30 Orthodox Christians and 43 members of other non-Jewish religions.[19] Three churches remained within the confines of the Warsaw ghetto to cater for those Christians who were considered Jewish under the Nuremberg Laws: they 'wore armlets with the Star of David and prayed to Jesus Christ'. Father Marceli Godlewski remained in his church of All Saints in the ghetto to care for his Catholic Jewish parishioners.[20] Many Jews felt sympathy for these 'Christian' Jews who had often not even realised that they had Jewish ancestry until the Germans informed them of the fact.[21] They did not know the Jewish customs or the Yiddish language, and 'their suffering took on a different quality. For us it was an inevitable adjunct of our heritage; for them it was an additional burden, an unrelieved trauma. The only privilege which remained to them was to leave the whirlpool of the ghetto for the quiet Catholic cemetery on the Aryan side.'[22] The languages used were also diverse: most Jews spoke Yiddish but many assimilated Jews preferred to communicate in Polish or German; adherents of Zionism also started to use Hebrew.

The Germans extended their use of Jewish forced labour and established vast work camps such as the one at Izbica Lubelska, midway between Lublin and Bełżec. The outsourcing of Jewish labour to local landowners and farmers gave the Poles the opportunity to provide assistance. For example, the family of Ralph Smorczewski took the maximum quota of Jews allowed: 'They had to appear working in the fields and on the farms to convince the Germans that they were properly employed, but all this was fictitious. The main purpose was to give them proper food and decent living conditions.'[23] The Kiciński family 'employed' Jews for the same reason. But the Jews needed to do some semblance of work to survive: Mieczysław Kiciński urged the Jews to give the impression of doing work in case the Germans checked up on them, but they were not working when the Germans paid a surprise visit and they were taken away to be shot.[24] In Stanisławów, Leon Kochański, who was working for the Underground Government, put a large number of Jews on the payroll of the sawmill where he was employed as an accountant, specifically to keep them out of harm's way.[25] As the Final Solution began the purpose of the labour camps

**Legend:**
- ⊙ Concentration/extermination camp
- ○ Extermination camp
- ▽ Major concentration camp
- □ Main city with ghetto
- 1939 Polish border

LITHUANIA

*R. Neman*

□ Kaunas        □ Wilno

Stutthof ▽

EAST
PRUSSIA

▽ Soldau

U.S.S.R.

□ Białystok        • Słonim

▽ Potulice        ○ Treblinka

*R. Vistula*

Chełmno ○

*R. Warta*        □ Warsaw        *R. Bug*

Łódź □

○ Sobibór

Lublin
□⊙
Majdanek        Trawniki

▽ Gross-Rosen        ▽ Izbica Lubelska

○ Bełżec

Auschwitz ⊙        □ Kraków

▽ Płaszów        Zasław        Janów ▽        □ Lwów

▽

*R. Dniester*

SLOVAKIA        Stanisławów •

HUNGARY

0 ——— 100 miles
0 ——— 150 km

N

6. Principal Extermination and Concentration Camps

changed. For example, Izbica Lubelska became a holding camp for the Jews until the gas chambers of Bełżec were ready to receive them. Other labour camps became concentration camps, utilising the last dregs of the Jews' ability to work in industries geared towards the German war effort before despatching them to be exterminated when they were no longer capable of work. Examples include Janów near Lwów, Plaszów near Kraków and Poniatów and Trawniki in the Lublin province.[26]

However desperate the situation was in the ghettos and forced labour camps, however many Jews were shot and deposited in mass unmarked graves in Kresy, nothing could have prepared the Polish Jews for the unprecedented operation the Germans would launch in 1942 – *Endlösung* – the Final Solution, the extermination of virtually all Polish Jews. The origins of the German decision are too complex to be repeated here. Probably the most important conference on the subject of the destruction of European Jewry was held at Wannsee, on the outskirts of Berlin, on 20 January 1942. The extermination of the Jews would begin in Poland since that was the region with the greatest concentration of Jews, with Polish Jews as the very first victims. The representative from the General Government, Jozef Bühler, stated:

> Jews should be removed from the domain of the General Government as fast as possible, because it is precisely here that the Jew constitutes a substantial danger as carrier of epidemics and also because his continued black market activities create constant disorder in the economic structure of the country. Moreover, the majority of the two and a half million Jews involved were not capable of work.[27]

The Germans had already experimented with methods of carrying out large-scale exterminations. They had used gas vans to kill mentally deficient patients in East Prussia and, at Auschwitz, had carried out an experiment in a rigged-up gas chamber to kill 250 Poles and 600 Soviet prisoners of war with the industrial pesticide Zyklon-B.[28]

The first death camp, Chełmno, had been operating gas vans before the Wannsee conference convened. The camp had begun life as a labour camp and was situated 9 miles from the town of Koło, which was on the main railway line between Łódź and Poznań, with a spur line leading to the camp. The local inhabitants were expelled, which is why, according to the post-war compendium of German crimes in Poland, 'only a very few people in Poland ever knew of its existence'. The camp was a deserted manor house. The Jews were told that they were being sent to Germany to work but, after having undressed in the house, they were put into trucks in groups of 50 to 70 and gassed with exhaust fumes. The victims were 100,000 of the 450,000 Jews in the Warthegau. The Gauleiter, Arthur Greiser, had specifically asked Himmler for permission to kill them because the Łódź ghetto was so overcrowded and these Jews were unfit for work. The gassing operation began on 8 December 1941 and continued until March 1943. It was used again in June–July 1944 to help speed up the liquidation of the Łódź ghetto. There were only two or three survivors from this camp.[29]

Chełmno had begun life as a labour camp and then became an extermination camp but, as a result of the decision to exterminate the Jews taken at Wannsee, the construction of purpose-built extermination camps began at Bełżec, Sobibor and Treblinka. Bełżec was situated 47 miles north of Lwów on a main railway line but again with a spur to the camp. The camp itself was extraordinarily small, being about 300 yards long and containing three gas chambers into which carbon monoxide would be pumped. Bełżec began operating in March 1942. In May 1942 two further camps were opened. Sobibor was situated 50 miles east of Lublin and again was small: the Jews had to walk along a 100-yard-long 'Road to Heaven' from the undressing stations to the gas chambers. Treblinka also began operating in May 1942. It was situated near Małkinia Górna, halfway between Warsaw and Białystok, and at the beginning there were only three gas chambers, but this was soon increased to thirteen. With the facilities ready Himmler issued the orders on 19 July 1942: 'that the resettlement of the entire Jewish population of the General Government be carried out and completed by 31 December. From 31 December 1942, no persons of Jewish origin may remain within the General Government, unless they are in collection camps in Warsaw, Kraków, Częstochowa, Radom and Lublin.' The extermination of the Polish Jews was known as Operation Reinhard, named after the recently assassinated Reinhard Heydrich.[30]

The extermination camps were brutally efficient: on arrival under 2 per cent of the Jews were selected to work on retrieving the dead from the gas chambers and burying them. About 600,000 Jews died at Bełżec – the majority of Jews in the whole of Galicia and in the Lublin district – before it ceased operation at the end of 1942. Sobibor accounted for 250,000 Polish Jews and Jews from all over Europe before it closed following an uprising by the *Sonderkommando* in October 1943. The largest number of Polish Jews were exterminated at Treblinka, around 900,000 of them taken from Warsaw and the Warsaw region.[31] Because these were extermination camps there were by definition few survivors: an estimated 110 Jews from the four extermination camps, most at Treblinka.[32] This is why much of the knowledge of the killing process comes from the evidence of the Treblinka survivors. The Soviet war correspondent Vasily Grossman interviewed them and local Poles when the Soviet armies overran the site in early 1945.[33] The commission on German crimes in Poland took evidence from thirteen Jews who had escaped during a revolt in Treblinka in August 1943.[34] One of these, Jankiel Wiernik, wrote a short work, 'One Year in Treblinka', which was published in Polish in May 1944 and smuggled out of Poland to the Polish Government in London. He described the arrival of the Jews at Treblinka:

> They took us into the camp yard, which was flanked by barracks on either side. There were two large posters with big signs bearing instructions to surrender all gold, silver, and diamonds, cash and other valuables under penalty of death. All the while Ukrainian guards stood on the roofs of the barracks, their machine guns at the ready.

The men and women were separated and taken to the gas chambers. There carbon monoxide was pumped in after the doors had been sealed and the 'speed at which death overcame the helpless victims depended on the quantity of combustion gas admitted into the chamber at one time'. At least 10,000 Jews could be killed per day. Treblinka continued in operation until November 1943 but the bulk of the victims had been gassed in 1942.[35]

The sites of the extermination camps had been chosen because they lay near main-line railway routes and could be concealed from prying eyes. For example, the commandant of Auschwitz-Birkenau, Rudolf Höss, noted that the location was chosen: 'first because it was situated at a junction of four lines, and second because the area was sparsely populated and the camp could be completely isolated'.[36] It was also in the area of Upper Silesia that had belonged to Poland before the war, but that had been incorporated into the Reich after Poland's defeat.

Attempts at concealment were not always successful. Professor Stanisław Bohdanowicz, living close to Bełżec, noted that the local inhabitants:

> were complaining about the stench which increased day by day. Everyone understood that in some way the Jews were being killed there. In the end, passengers travelling through Bełżec by train also started to complain that the stench of rotting bodies was unbearable and was even penetrating to the interior of the carriages through tightly shut windows.[37]

Zdzisław Rozbicki lived on a farm by the railway leading to Treblinka and was frightened of the fields near the railway line:

> I was terrified of the transports carrying victims to Treblinka: the faces, on which there still flickered the hope that someone would help them avoid their fate, looking out through the small windows through the barbed wire. This was a daily sight for all of us who worked in the fields. Some tried to escape by tearing through the barbed wire or smashing holes in the floors of the wagons. Most of these, however, were killed by the machine guns mounted on the train. Many nameless graves were dug on both sides of the track – in our fields, as well.[38]

After the Germans discovered the graves of the Polish officers at Katyń, Himmler realised that the graves of the Jews could also be discovered one day and the extent of the German crimes made public. He ordered that the mass graves in the extermination camps should be dug up and the bodies burnt. There were so many corpses that the burning of them was carried out on massive griddles. When the mass graves of the early killings at Auschwitz-Birkenau were dug up and the bodies burned, ashes spread as far as Kraków.[39]

Over 1,300,000 Polish Jews perished in the Operation Reinhard extermination camps of Bełżec, Sobibor and Treblinka; they had a negligible chance of survival once they had been rounded up for deportation. It may seem strange that being sent to Auschwitz-Birkenau represented a chance of life, given that over 1,000,000 Jews were gassed there, but this was because Auschwitz-Birkenau was not an Operation Reinhard extermination camp but was, like Majdanek, a combined labour and extermination camp. On arrival the Jews were subjected to a selection and those deemed unfit for work were slated for extermination.

The remainder would enter the main camp, where they would be forced to undertake hard labour on such low rations that they were destined for a slow death through overwork and starvation. Some could not cope with the conditions:

> The name Musselmann was well known. It referred to those who had given up the will to live. Hunger and despair, the giving up of hope, something about the eyes, something about the way these people walked, dragging their feet with their heads lowered. Once you looked into their eyes, you could see quite clearly that they hadn't got long to live.[40]

Selections were carried out regularly to weed out those deemed no longer capable of work and to ease the overcrowding caused by the arrival of more Jews from the whole of German-occupied Europe. 'The key to survival was instant adjustment, and having a sixth sense of where danger came from, and finding a way of being totally invisible, hiding behind in crowds so that your face would never be known to anyone in charge.' Prisoners had to develop the ability to 'organise', the camp term for bartering for food, for bribing or bartering their way into the work parties with the least sadistic kapos, for obtaining work sheltered from the elements if possible, in the kitchens, hospital or best of all in 'Canada', the giant sorting house for the clothes and luggage of the arrivals, most of whom had already been gassed.[41]

Majdanek, on the outskirts of Lublin, was another vast labour and extermination camp where the Jews were also subjected to selection on arrival. The population of Majdanek was not exclusively Jewish: there were around 2,000 Soviet POWs, who mostly perished from the harsh conditions or from a typhus epidemic in summer 1943, and over 1,000 ethnic Poles, including those seized from their homes during the Zamość clearances. No one segment of the mixed population was specifically targeted for extermination until October 1943. Then, at a meeting between Frank and his police chiefs, it was agreed to carry out Himmler's orders:

> The Jews in the Lublin District have developed into a serious danger. This state of affairs must be cleared up once and for all. I have charged the 'unit Globocnik' with the execution of this matter. The Higher SS and Police Leader East, and the SS and Police Leader Lublin, are requested to assist Globocnik with all resources at their disposal.

Operation *Erntefest* (Harvest Festival) began on 3 November 1943. Over a period of three days, Polish Jews were brought from camps in the Lublin district, Trawniki and Poniatova, and then, along with the Jewish population of Majdanek camp, were taken to previously prepared large pits and shot. At the end of the process 42,000 Polish Jews were dead.[42]

Two ghettos survived for a little longer, though their numbers had been scaled down. Both were engaged in manufacturing goods for the German war economy: the population of Białystok ghetto was about 50,000 and of Łódź ghetto around 80,000. Białystok would be finally liquidated in November 1943, and Łódź in August 1944. Poland was still not *Judenfrei* since a few work camps remained in operation until the Germans began their withdrawal from Poland. For example, the camp at Płaszów where Oscar Schindler ran a factory. As the Soviet armies approached, Schindler drew up a list of Jewish workers and arranged for their evacuation westwards. Furthermore, there were an unknown number of Jews maintaining a tenuous existence in hiding. Recent research has suggested that 28,000 Jews remained hidden in Warsaw after the liquidation of the ghetto. Of these about 40 per cent survived the war, compared to the 99 per cent death rate among those deported to the death camps, meaning that in effect about 5 per cent of the pre-war Jewish population of Warsaw survived.[43] It is thought that between 50,000 to 100,000 Polish Jews survived the war across Poland, hidden by their fellow Poles.[44] In addition about 250,000 escaped Poland during the war, principally into the Soviet Union.

The deportation of the Jews from the Warsaw ghetto is perhaps the best documented by the victims themselves, and serves as an illustration of how the Germans went about their work in clearing the ghettos. On 21 July 1942, the Germans demanded that the *Judenrat* deliver 7,000 Jews for deportation on the following day and 10,000 on the day after that. This request was too much for the chairman of the *Judenrat*, Adam Czerniaków, who committed suicide rather than accede. Chaim Kaplan noted that he 'may not have lived his life with honour but he did die with honour. Some merit paradise by the deeds of an hour but President Adam Czerniaków earned his right to paradise in a single moment.'[45] He was succeeded by Marc Lichtenbaum. The victims would be rounded up by the Jewish police and failure to comply would lead to the death of the families of members of the *Judenrat* and Jewish police. Those chosen were informed that they would be resettled in the east to work and were urged to take items such clothes and money with them. Exemptions were given to members of the *Judenrat*, the police force, those employed by German business, administrators and shopkeepers selling rationed goods.[46] This led to the belief, common in all ghettos and ultimately to prove erroneous, that holding a work permit led to exemption from deportation. Suddenly workshops were flooded by job applicants, and many were accepted even when there was insufficient work for them all. On 29 July the Germans adopted a policy of offering bribes of food to those reporting for deportation, and about 20,000 starving Jews accepted. Despite the lack of news from those taken first, there was still a widespread disbelief that they were destined to be killed: no one could believe that 'a cultured race like the Germans would have a policy of gassing people and burning them'. Even when an escapee from the transport to Treblinka, Dawid Nowodworski, returned to the ghetto with the news of the ultimate destination, few believed him. The first wave of deportations continued until 12 September, by which time around 265,000 Jews had been sent to Treblinka, leaving only 55,000 Jews remaining in the Warsaw ghetto.[47]

Those listed for deportation were taken to the *Umschlagplatz* (collection point) by Ukrainian and German guards to wait for the trains that would take them to their deaths at Treblinka. The lingering image in many witnesses' minds was the deportation of an orphanage run by Janusz Korczak:

> On the day that they left the ghetto they made a strange procession as they walked along Sliska Street led by an elderly, dignified man, and accompanied by only a few policemen. The orphans, dressed in their finery, marched in twos, the younger ones followed by the older. With them were the teachers and all the orphanage staff. Were it not for the expression of stony peace and overbearing sadness on the face of the elderly gentleman, it could have been taken for a children's excursion or a peaceful stroll. But he knew where he was leading his children, this man whose supreme love was for his little homeless wards.[48]

At the *Umschlagplatz* Korczak was offered the opportunity to remain in the ghetto but told the SS: 'Where my children are going, I must go as well.'[49] He died alongside his charges.

The Germans relied on the Jewish police, most of whom had been lawyers before the war, to coerce their brethren into the cattle trucks. There were 2,000 Jewish policemen in the Warsaw ghetto, and their conduct has been uniformly condemned by witnesses to their work. One inmate wrote:

> These policemen became merciless; they had horse-drawn carts, they'd close a house, everyone had to come down, and they'd go from door to door pulling people out . . . They worked because they thought they could save themselves and their families and get some allocation of food. Eventually, when it became more difficult to make up the numbers, they broke doors and dragged people out, pushed them down the stairs and onto the waiting carts.[50]

Abraham Lewin noted in his diary in August 1942: 'The Jewish police have received an order that each one of them must bring five people to be transported. Since there are 2000 police, they will have to find 10,000 victims. If they do not fulfil their quotas they are liable to the death penalty.'[51] The Jewish police were so desperate that they tore up the work papers of their selected victims, but they also accepted bribes to save lives. Emanuel Ringelblum wrote: 'Jewish policemen distinguished themselves with their fearful corruption and immorality. But they reached the height of viciousness during the resettlement. They said not a single word of protest against this revolting assignment to lead their own brothers to the slaughter.'[52] Their conduct was so reprehensible that on 29 October 1942 the commandant of the Jewish police, Jakub Lejkin, was assassinated. Some Jewish police refused to collaborate with the Germans, and 20 to 30 paid for their moral courage with their lives.[53]

The subject of Jewish collaboration with the Germans is naturally an extremely sensitive topic and one which has been little researched. After the war the great Nazi hunter Simon Wiesenthal noted:

> We have done very little to condemn Jewish collaboration with the Nazis. When, after the war, I demanded that those who had abused their office in ghettos or concentration camps be removed from Jewish committees, I was told that 'this would diminish the guilt of the Nazis'.[54]

A survivor of Treblinka, Jankiel Wiernik wrote: 'Another amazing character trait of the Germans is their ability to discover, among the populace of other nations, hundreds of depraved types like themselves, and to use them for their own ends.'[55] It has been estimated that at the end of 1941 the Gestapo controlled 15,000 Jewish agents in the General Government. The Jewish Militia (*Żydowska Gwardia Wolności*), led by Abraham Gancwajch, assisted the Germans in finding Jews who were living in hiding: more will be said on its activities later in this chapter. There was also the Society of Free Jews (*Towarzystwo Wolnych Żydów*), under Captain Lontski, which spied on the Jewish underground, the Jewish Fighting Organisation (*Żydowska Organizacja Bojowa*, ŻOB). In January 1943, the Jews resisted the renewal of the deportations but the locations of their secret bunkers were revealed to the Germans. The ŻOB then issued a warning to the betrayers: 'that if they do not stop their degenerate deeds immediately they will be executed', and this proclamation resulted in the assassination of the Jewish Gestapo informant Professor Alfred Nossig. The Jews ran their own secret court in the Warsaw ghetto and sentenced 59 collaborators to death.[56] Polish archives have an incomplete list of 1,378 Jewish collaborators and betrayers.[57]

Faced with deportation to their deaths the Jews of Poland had two options: resistance or going into hiding. But the first barrier to be overcome was that of disbelief: shared alike by the Jewish victims, by the Polish population as witnesses and by the world at large as unaffected observers. A Pole who was very active in saving Jews, Władysława Chomsowa, noted: 'The greatest difficulty was the passivity of the Jews themselves.'[58] This opinion has been echoed by a major historian, Raul Hilberg: 'In fact, the behaviour of the population during the killing operations was characterised by a tendency towards passivity.'[59] An inmate of the Łódź ghetto, Jakub Poznański, wrote in his diary on 27 September 1943: 'Persistent rumours circulate about the liquidation of the ghettos in various Polish cities. In my opinion, people are exaggerating, as usual. Even if certain excesses have taken place in some cities, that still does not incline one to believe that Jews are being mass-murdered. At least I consider it out of the question.'[60]

The Holocaust was such an unprecedented action that it is perhaps unsurprising that no clear response was possible to the events even as they unfolded. Above all there was the persistent belief that only those incapable of work would be killed, as Emanuel Ringelblum noted:

So strong is the instinct of life of the workers, of the fortunate owners of work permits, that it overcomes the will to fight, the urge to defend the whole community, with no thought of consequences. This is partly due to the complete spiritual breakdown and disintegration, caused by unheard-of terror which has been inflicted upon the Jews for three years and which comes to its climax in times of such evacuations.

The effect of all this taken together is that when a moment for some resistance arrives, we are completely powerless and the enemy does to us whatever he pleases.[61]

The Germans encouraged such beliefs: in the middle of August 1942, they issued 30,000 employment cards to workers in the Warsaw ghetto and made them feel that this excluded them from deportation. The highly controversial leader of the *Judenrat* in the Łódź ghetto, Chaim Rumkowski, was convinced that working for the German war effort exempted the Jews from deportation, and he was therefore willing to sacrifice the aged and sick, and even all the children under 10 years old. On 4 September 1942, Rumkowski told the gathered Jews: 'Give into my hands the victims so that we can avoid having further victims, and a population of a hundred thousand Jews can be preserved. So they promised me: if we deliver our victims ourselves, there will be peace.'[62] A survivor of the Łódź ghetto, Roman Halter, was appalled and believed that Rumkowski should have refused to give up the children. Interviewed after the war, he criticised Rumkowski but later in the same interview excused him on the grounds that 'these times were abnormal, so horrendous, that one cannot rationalise in the circumstances in which we live today, how people behaved and what they did'.[63] Like Rumkowski, the head of the *Judenrat* in the Białystok ghetto, Ephraim Barasz, was also convinced that working for the German war effort would keep the Jews alive. Ultimately both men were proved wrong: the inhabitants of the Białystok ghetto were deported to Treblinka, Majdanek and Auschwitz-Birkenau before the end of 1943. The Łódź ghetto lasted longer, only in June 1944 did the deportations, including Rumkowski, to Chełmno and Auschwitz-Birkenau begin.

The inability to believe that all Jews were destined for extermination, not on the grounds of age, sex or occupation, but simply because they were considered Jewish by the Germans also led the Jews to be taken in by schemes designed by the Germans to ferret out those in hiding. One put into practice in the summer of 1943 was when the Germans let it be known that Jews holding passports from South American countries or for Palestine should report to the Hotel Polski in Warsaw, and then they would be allowed to leave the General Government. The news spread among the hidden Jews and 3,500, one in seven of those in hiding, went to the hotel. For many years it was thought that they were deliberately lured out of hiding on the promise of being sent abroad but instead were either killed soon after or sent to concentration camps. Later research has shown that in the middle of 1943 the Germans did actually genuinely plan to exchange Jews with South American passports, albeit often forged ones, in return for Germans interned in those countries. The Jews were sent to holding centres at Vittel in France and at Bergen-Belsen, but at this point the South American governments withdrew the passports and the scheme collapsed; the 420 Jews still at Hotel Polski were taken to the Pawiak prison and shot. All the others, except for the few hundred with papers for Palestine who were exchanged for Germans interned there, were sent to their deaths at Auschwitz.[64]

By no means all the Jews were passive. Some of their resistance was spontaneous, as a German train superintendent, Jäcklein, discovered when he encountered problems during the transport of 8,200 Jews to Bełżec:

> We had only been travelling a short time when the Jews attempted to break out of the wagons on both sides and even through the roof. Some of them succeeded in doing so . . .

Jäcklein contacted the stationmaster at the next large town, Stanisławów, to have materials ready to repair the train. The train set off again:

> However, all of this was of very little help, for only a few stations later when the train was stationary I established that a number of very large holes had been made and all the barbed wire on the ventilation windows had been ripped out. As the train was departing I even established that in one of the cars someone was using a hammer and pliers. When these Jews were questioned as to why they had these tools in their possession they informed me that they had been told that they might well be of use at their next place of work. I immediately took away the tools. I then had to have the train boarded up at each station at which it stopped, otherwise it would not have been possible to continue the journey at all.[65]

Jews risked their lives by jumping off trains despite the presence of armed guards on the roofs. There was resistance too within the extermination camps. At Treblinka a revolt was carefully prepared for 2 August 1943, by placing all the fittest men on the afternoon shift. When the signal, a gunshot, was given to start the revolt, offers of gold were made to the Ukrainian guards to bribe them down from their watchtowers. Then the Jews ran: 'Our objective was to reach the woods, but the closest patch was five miles away. We ran across swamps, meadows and ditches, with bullets pursuing us fast and furious.'[66] Elsewhere, notably at Sobibor, the *Sonderkommando* revolted and escaped for the forests, where they joined existing partisan groups or formed their own. The German method of dealing with this problem will be covered in Chapter 12.

Revolts also took place in numerous ghettos. During the height of the extermination of the Jews in the summer of 1942, there were mass escapes of several hundred or several thousand at a time from 27 ghettos in Wołyń, with a total of around 47,500 Jews escaping, a quarter of the pre-war Jewish population of Wołyń. Many would later perish in the forests. There was also opposition to German selections in the ghettos elsewhere in eastern Poland, notably at Nieświecż and Słonim.[67] In January 1942, the United Partisans Organisation (*Fareynikte Partizaner Organizatsye*) was established in the Wilno ghetto under the leadership of a communist, Yitzhak Witenberg. His proposal to engage in open battle with the Germans should they attempt to dissolve the ghetto was opposed by the head of the *Judenrat*, Jacob Gens, who also opposed plans for the partisans within the ghetto to leave to join those outside. In July 1943, the Germans discovered Witenberg's identity as a communist leader within the ghetto and Gens demanded that Witenberg surrender himself to the Germans, which he did. A month later the Germans began to deport the Jews from the Wilno ghetto to Stutthof and Majdanek without any opposition. A survivor later wrote: 'We should have mobilised and fought.'[68]

In late July 1942, the ŻOB was established by Mordechai Anielewicz in the Warsaw ghetto. There was a clear left-wing and pro-Soviet bias to ŻOB: Anielewicz belonged to the Zionist-Marxist group Hashomer-Hatzair, and communists were represented on the ŻOB committee. This pro-Soviet bias alienated the Jewish resistance from many within the ghetto and from many of those outside the ghetto who were prepared to help the Jewish resistance.[69] Appeals were made to the AK, using pre-war connections made during service in the Polish Army, for a supply of arms. Rowecki telegraphed London on 4 January 1943 informing the government: 'Jews from a variety of groups, among them communists, have appealed to us at a late date asking for arms, as if our own arsenals were full. As a trial I offered them a few pistols. I have no confidence that they will make use of any of these arms at all.' Rowecki was also desperately worried that a rising within the ghetto might inspire a more widespread uprising in Warsaw, which would result in a pointless slaughter and almost certainly irrevocably weaken the AK.[70] The same month the Germans renewed the deportations from the Warsaw ghetto and, as a result, opinion on the utility of resistance began to change both inside and outside the ghetto: 'Here and there one could hear it voiced that any further German action aimed at the deportation of Jews would now be met with resistance.'[71]

The AK was short of arms: the entire Warsaw region possessed only 135 heavy machine guns, 190 light machine guns, 6,045 rifles, 1,070 pistols, 7,561 hand grenades and 7 anti-tank guns.[72] Out of these meagre stocks the AK supplied ŻOB with 90 pistols, 600 hand grenades, 35 pounds of explosives, a light machine gun and a sub-machine gun.[73] In addition the Jews obtained supplies from other sources, including stealing them from German railway transports.[74] It has been alleged that the AK could have done more to arm the Jewish resistance but recent research has suggested that in the spring of 1943 each ŻOB fighter was in fact far better armed than an average AK soldier would be during the 1944 Warsaw Uprising.[75] The AK also undertook the training of the ŻOB, whose fighters began visiting the AK base on Ulica Marszałkowska for training:

> The men from the ghetto were handed various printed instructions on how to use the arms and explosives, studied the techniques of fighting in town, were acquainted on the spot with various anti-tank weapons effective at close range, and were initiated into the manufacture of typical incendiary materials, mines and grenades. The ŻOB fighters showed tremendous ardour, lively interest, and a great deal of military ability.[76]

The AK also advised on the construction of mines and creation of Molotov cocktails.

On 19 April 1943, the Germans began the final liquidation of the

Warsaw ghetto. One of the ŻOB fighters, Marek Edelman, watched the Germans approach:

> On April 19th around 4 a.m. we saw the German troops coming from Nalewki Street. Tanks, armoured vehicles, small-calibre guns and columns of SS soldiers on motorcycles. 'They are going as if to war,' I remarked to a girl standing next to me. I realised how weak we were, how meagre our resources. Just pistols and grenades. But the fighting spirit did not abandon me. It's time we settled accounts with them.[77]

The first Germans to enter were met by rifle fire and a hail of hand grenades. There were at the most 1,200 ŻOB fighters ranged against 2,100 Germans. The SS attempted to enter the ghetto but were driven off by machine-gun fire. Four armoured cars came and started shelling the houses. Danny Falkner, an inmate in the ghetto, later recalled:

> I felt elated that the Jews had fired the first shots; we could see that the Germans were not immune to violence, that violence could be exerted against them as well. Of course we knew it was an impossibility to conquer or resist them completely. We knew that our fate was sealed. But we wanted to bring down as many Germans as possible.[78]

Zivia Lubetkin later wrote: 'we threw those hand grenades and bombs, and saw German blood pouring over the streets of Warsaw, after we saw so much Jewish blood running in the streets of Warsaw before that, there was rejoicing'. On the first day ŻOB killed 6 SS men and 6 Ukrainian auxiliaries.[79]

The AK assisted the ghetto uprising from the outside and managed to smuggle some rifles into the ghetto. On the first day, 19 April, Captain Józef Pszenny led a company of sappers who tried to blow a hole in the ghetto wall to help civilians caught up in the fighting to escape but was forced to withdraw after 2 AK members were killed and 4 were wounded.[80] On 22 April, an AK detachment attacked a unit of Lithuanian auxiliaries near the ghetto walls, and on the 23rd, an AK unit under Lieutenant Jerzy Skupienski attacked the gate at Ulica Pawia but failed to blow it up and retreated after killing 4 SS and police officers.[81] In his post-action report, the SS commander Major-General Jürgen Stroop complained that his soldiers 'have been repeatedly shot at from outside the Ghetto'.[82] Ringelblum noted that the Germans had taken precautions to reduce outside help: the trams were diverted and the Poles 'were forbidden to move freely in the streets bordering the ghetto'.[83]

Only an estimated 5 per cent of Jews took part in the fighting. For the remaining 95 per cent, the uprising was a time of pure terror, hiding in bunkers, hoping not to be discovered or burned out. Indeed, the German tactics appear to have been directed more against the non-participants than the fighters. The ŻOB leadership had predicted that the Germans would fight house to house, a method that would allow the resistance to inflict casualties on the Germans with the limited weaponry at their disposal. Instead, on 25 April, incendiary bombs were dropped to set the entire ghetto on fire, suffocating those hiding in the cellars and bunkers. The Germans also deployed armoured vehicles. On 29 April, the AK helped about 40 ŻOB fighters to escape through the sewers to the forests near Otwock where they could then join the partisan units.[84] By the end of the first week of May, the remnants of the Jewish resistance were concentrated in a bunker at Ulica Miła 18, which the Germans then attacked:

> The fighting lasted two hours, and when the Germans convinced themselves that they would be unable to take the bunker by storm, they tossed in a gas-grenade. Whoever survived the German bullets, whoever was not gassed, committed suicide ... Jurek Wilner called upon all partisans to commit suicide together. Lutek Rotblat shot his mother, his sister, and then himself. Ruth fired at herself seven times. Thus 80% of the remaining partisans perished, among them ŻOB Commander, Mordechai Anielewicz.[85]

The final act of the ghetto uprising was on 16 May when Stroop pressed the button to blow up the Great Synagogue: he then informed his superiors that the uprising was over and that 'the Jewish quarter is no more'. Around 7,000 Jews lay dead, killed in the fighting, and the remaining 30,000 were transported to their deaths at Treblinka.[86]

The ghetto uprising inspired very differing reactions among the Poles and the Jews living in hiding among the Poles. One Jew living outside the ghetto, Ruth Altbeker, provided perhaps the most eloquent description of the response:

> The scum of society stood by the ghetto walls. Some were tempted by the possibility of looting Jewish property, others lurked for easy prey – a Jew who might try to creep over to the Aryan side through a crevice or chink

in the wall. Among the uniformed policemen, manhunters, conmen and all kinds of rascals around the walls, other Poles waited too, looking out for a convenient moment to supply the fighters with arms and ammunition. A girl hungry for thrills would be waiting to convey the needs of the besieged to the Underground Organisation. All of these were called human beings whom God had created in his image – the Jew-insurgent in his desperate fight against domination and the Polish comrade endangering his life in order to supply him with weapons; the blackguard, the scoundrel and the Polish policeman obligingly serving the Germans, and that soldier in a steel helmet.[87]

Another Jew hiding in Warsaw paid tribute to the fighters, seeing their resistance as somehow atoning for 'previous submissiveness': 'They died in glory for those who yet survive, who are being hunted down like animals, who are hiding and waiting for the war to end or plodding along from day to day pretending to be Aryans.'[88] The *Delegatura* sent a report back to London giving details of the uprising and concluding: 'This war between the Jews and the Germans has awakened feelings of sympathy and admiration on the Aryan side of Warsaw, and shame among the Germans, who feel rightly that the situation that has come about in Warsaw is an uncommon blow to German prestige.'[89] Sikorski broadcast to Poland from London on 4 May 1943, thanking the population of Warsaw for the assistance it had given to the ghetto fighters and asking them 'to offer all succour and protection to the threatened victims'.[90]

Before turning to the issue of Jews who went into hiding, it is necessary to examine the attitude of the Poles towards the Jews during the period of the Holocaust. This has provoked intense and highly emotional debates which show no sign of ending. There is little doubt that anti-semitism was widespread in Poland before the war, which led to economic boycotts of Jewish shops and a cross-party general agreement on the desirability of encouraging Jewish emigration. The German attacks on the Jews in the early period of the occupation – identification, expropriation, hard labour and concentration into ghettos – aroused no strong demonstration of opposition from the Poles. Indeed, despite the Polish Government ordering Poles not to profit from the German expropriation of Jewish property and shops, there is evidence to suggest that they did; an underground newspaper noted in 1942: 'Cases of mass robbery of former Jewish property bear eloquent witness to the ongoing moral decay.'[91] Nor did the attitude change when the Germans began the mass shootings of Jews after the invasion of eastern Poland and of the Soviet Union. It should also be remembered that many of the intellectual elites that might have been able to provide leadership had been killed by the Germans during Aktion AB in 1940 or, in the case of eastern Poland, had been deported to the Soviet Union in 1940–41. Rowecki communicated the feelings in the country to the Polish Government, noting that the pro-Jewish sentiments issued by the government were alienating many Poles from the government because: 'Please accept it as a fact that the overwhelming majority of the country is anti-Semitic. Even socialists are not an exception in this respect. The only differences concern how to deal with the Jews. Almost nobody advocates the adoption of German methods ... Anti-Semitism is widespread now.'[92] Yet there must have been substantial resistance among the Poles to the German mass murders for Frank to feel it necessary to issue a decree on 15 October 1941 stipulating: 'those who knowingly give shelter to such Jews or help them in any way' were punishable by death: a decree that was not issued in any other country.[93] Furthermore, as the deportations began, rumours spread throughout Warsaw 'about collective responsibility – that whole blocks if not the neighbouring blocks would be burnt down if Jews were found in hiding'.[94]

The obstacles against the rescue of the Jews were formidable. One major difficulty was the nature of the majority of Polish Jews themselves: around 80 per cent were unassimilated and therefore did not speak Polish, looked different and dressed differently, and had different dietary requirements. Therefore, they would have had to remain for years totally concealed from sight, unable to leave their hiding places: and as a consequence few were saved. A Polish woman, Maria Ossowska, who was later arrested by the Gestapo and imprisoned in Auschwitz spoke of the problem:

> The tragedy of the children who came out of the ghetto to beg for food was that they could not speak Polish – they were from places deep in eastern Poland and only spoke Yiddish – so it was really difficult to help such people because if you don't explain a few things to them, how can you really give them proper help?[95]

Michael Zylberberg, an assimilated Jew in hiding in Warsaw, echoed this: 'The religious ones inhabited a world of their own, and few had friends among the Poles, who might have saved them.' He noted the cry of the orthodox: *Zu Torah Ve'zu Secharah?*, 'We lived by the Torah; is this the reward?', as they were rounded up for deportation.[96] Even after the war a survivor, Roman Halter, recalled that in London he was asked by some orthodox Jews: 'Tell me, if it came to renouncing Jewishness and becoming a Gentile, or losing your life, you would rather lose your life, wouldn't you?' To which he replied that he would choose life.[97]

The significant number of Jews who were assimilated, spoke Polish fluently and understood Polish customs had a far higher chance of survival and, perhaps most importantly, had the necessary pre-war contacts with Poles to whom they could turn for help. Wanda Grosman-Jedlicka was not only assimilated but her family had converted to Christianity, yet under the Nuremberg Laws they were all considered to be Jews. After the war she paid tribute to those who helped her family:

> And now it must be stated that survival would have been absolutely impossible were it not for the generous disinterested help which often defied all limits of self-sacrifice and bravery on the part of many people, friends and strangers alike. Most often it was given by those who had no moral duty, on a personal level, toward me and my family.[98]

Adam Neuman-Nowicki, an assimilated Jew, had the good fortune to have blond hair, as did his brother, so both fled the ghetto and lived openly in the small town of Staszów using false papers but their parents remained in the ghetto. When news arrived of the impending clearance of the ghetto:

> My brother and I, more than once thought about how we could save our parents from certain death. We reached the conclusion that their Semitic appearance excluded any possibility of arranging Aryan papers for them, and the shortage of money made it impossible to find a Polish family with whom to hide them ... My conscience is clear.[99]

Ruth Altbeker, who did leave the Warsaw ghetto, wrote of the fears of her sister-in-law: 'She feared her Polish was not good enough, that her looks were perhaps not sufficiently Aryan, and argued that she might betray herself by her behaviour.'[100]

It has been estimated that out of the Jews who either did not enter the ghettos or escaped from them, 46 per cent hid, another 10 per cent hid some of the time and lived openly at other times, while the remaining 44 per cent lived openly.[101] Ringelblum described their situation eloquently and accurately because he himself spent time in hiding in Warsaw before being betrayed:

> Life 'on the surface' is not at all easy. A Jew on the surface lives in constant fear, under constant tension. Danger lurks at every step. In the block of flats – the landlord, smelling a Jew in every new subtenant, even if he produces a guarantee of Aryanism from a trustworthy source; the gas and electricity account collectors; next, the manager and the porter of the block, a neighbour, etc., – all these constitute a danger for the Jew 'on the surface', because each of them can recognise him for a Jew. Yet there are far fewer dangers than the Jew imagines. It is these imaginary perils, this supposed observation by the neighbour, porter, manager or passer-by in the street that constitute the main danger; because the Jew, unaccustomed to life 'on the surface', gives himself away by looking round in every direction to see if anyone is watching him, by the nervous expression on his face, by the frightened look of a hunted animal, smelling danger of some kind everywhere.[102]

The Germans had deliberately flooded Poland with virulent anti-semitic materials which played on existing Polish anti-semitism and encouraged the existing belief in the danger of the *żydo-komuna* – the link between being Jewish and communism.[103]

Then there was the attitude of the Catholic Church, which is important, given its centrality to the Poles. Many of the Catholic clergy and religious orders did provide great assistance to the Jews, but equally many priests continued to preach anti-semitic sermons. Irene Gut had witnessed the liquidation of the Radom ghetto and later while working as a housekeeper for a German officer, Major Rügemar, in Tarnopol hid 11 Jews in the cellar of the house. He found out but promised to keep the secret if she would start sleeping with him. Gut went to confession:

> 'Father, there is something else,' I said, and when he nodded I drew a deep breath. 'Father I have become the mistress of a German officer in order to preserve the lives of my Jewish friends.'
>
> 'My child, this is a mortal sin,' he said without hesitation.
>
> I frowned, and leaned closer to the screen. 'But Father, if I don't do this, eleven people will lose their lives.'

'If you do this, it is your immortal soul that you will lose. They are Jews.'[104]

She was refused absolution. In contrast, Michael Zylberberg remembered that when his saviour, Mrs Klima, confessed to hiding Jews, her priest reassured her that 'she was performing a noble service in helping those in danger'.[105]

Almost all Jewish survivors remember the ever-present threat of the *szmalcowniki*, the Polish and Jewish blackmailers, who demanded constant payment for not betraying the Jews in hiding and their Polish protectors. In the case of the Poles, the *szmalcowniki* were usually youths or young men who, deprived of an opportunity for education and under threat of being deported to the Reich for forced labour, resorted to blackmail in order to make a living. The Germans also gave money to those who betrayed Jews, leading to one SS man remarking: 'You Poles are a strange people. Nowhere in the world is there another nation which has so many heroes and so many denouncers.'[106] In the case of the Jewish *szmalcowniki*, these were usually members of the Jewish Militia (*Żydowska Gwardia Wolności*), who would trawl Warsaw looking for Jews in hiding, often driving up behind a person they suspected of being Jewish and calling out in Yiddish or Polish some verses from the Torah in order to gauge the reaction: 'Their eyes were penetrating and the Jews pointed out by them were lost without hope.'[107]

Adolf Berman, a Jew who liaised between the Polish and Jewish undergrounds, wrote that too much had been written about the threats to the Jews in hiding and too little about the Poles who risked their lives to save them: 'The flotsam and jetsam on the surface of a turbulent river is more visible than the pure stream running deep underneath, but that stream existed.'[108] It is extremely difficult to establish with any degree of certainty how many Poles helped Jews. The fact that Yad Vashem in Jerusalem honours over 5,000 Poles as 'righteous' because of their work in saving Jews during the Holocaust is used as evidence to suggest that *only* 5,000 Poles actively worked to save Jews, but this is not a legitimate inference, because Yad Vashem requires the testimony of Jews who were saved. Since any capture of hidden Jews by the Germans resulted in the immediate execution of the Jews *and* their Polish protectors, there was no chance for a later Jewish survivor to bear witness. Furthermore, Yad Vashem also requires that the Gentiles received no financial reward for hiding Jews, so this means that the many people who were too poor to keep a Jew unless he could contribute financially to his upkeep are automatically excluded.[109] The last point is worth comment, because, as has already been noted, Polish rations were so low that most Poles were forced to rely on the black market or on the relief agencies in order to survive. The Jews in hiding could not contribute to their upkeep by working nor did they receive any rations, so that many had to be asked to pay for their board and lodging. Certainly some Poles asked extortionate sums but equally others cared for Jews without charge. Zofia Ryszewska-Brusiliewicz's family hid 13 Jews in a small flat in Warsaw and remembered: 'It was a big problem to buy food for so many people without attracting the attention of the neighbours.' Her father did not earn enough to feed even his own family, so those Jews had to contribute financially. She also noted another problem: she was forbidden to join the AK 'because of the possible danger to the thirteen people', and therefore 'I often had to face the disapproval of my peers because of my passive attitude.'[110]

Icchak Cukierman, a participant in the Warsaw ghetto uprising, claimed: 'One swine could betray a hundred Jews to the Germans. But to save one Jew, you needed the participation of a hundred Poles.'[111] Just as there can be no reliable statistics on how many Poles were involved in hiding Jews (claims range from 1,000,000 to 3,000,000), so we can never know how many Poles were killed trying to save Jews. For example, in 1968 the Jewish Historical Institute in Warsaw confirmed the cases of 343 Poles killed for assisting Jews and were still investigating many others; the Association of Former Political Prisoners raised the estimate to 2,500; the Maximilian Kolbe Foundation identified by name 2,300 executed Poles; some have even claimed as many as 50,000 Poles were killed.[112] A member of the German Reserve Police Battalion 101, Bruno Probst, provided evidence of the German attitude towards Poles helping Jews:

> Even at that time denunciations or comments from envious neighbours sufficed for Poles to be shot along with their entire families on the mere suspicion of possessing weapons or hiding Jews or bandits. As far as I know, Poles were never arrested and turned over to the competent police authorities on these grounds. From my own observations and from the stories of my comrades, I recall that when the above-mentioned grounds for suspicion were at hand, we always shot Poles on the spot.[113]

Even as late as October 1943, when most of the Polish Jews had been exterminated, the SS and Police Leader in the General Government, Krüger, complained to his superiors: 'According to reports reaching us from the Galicia District, the number of cases immediately pending before the special court in Lwów, regarding people providing refuge for Jews, has in the last period increased greatly in number and in scope.'[114]

The attitude of the Underground Government and the AK has led to the strongest criticism of Polish-Jewish relations during the war, which can be summarised:

> The leadership of Polish clandestine organisations was in the position to mould the attitudes of Polish society towards the fugitives and towards those who sought an opportunity to escape from a ghetto or from a camp . . . [but] This inaction and utter callousness concerning Jewish suffering on the part of those who had been entrusted with responsibility for the welfare of Polish citizens under the occupation is beyond comprehension . . . In Poland both the civil and military branches of the underground regarded Jews to be an alien presence on Polish soil for which they felt no responsibility.[115]

The evidence provided comes from examination of underground publications which were widely read. While the *Biuletyn Informacyjny* did reveal the extent of the German crimes against the Jews and did encourage people to assist the Jews, detractors argue that this was not enough. Furthermore, critics point out that the virulent anti-semitism of right-wing groups like the National Radical Camp (*Obóz Narodowno-Radykalny*), or the NSZ, and the small Sword and Plough (*Miecz i Pług*), was perpetuated in their publications, which also had a wide readership.[116]

The Underground Government did, however, establish Żegota, the Council to Aid the Jews, in September 1942, after the main deportations from the Warsaw ghetto. This was the initiative of two Polish women, Zofia Kossak and Wanda Filipowicz. Kossak had previously led the Catholic Front for the Reborn Poland, which advocated a Poland without the Jews, but nonetheless she was appalled by the German extermination policy and was determined to save as many as possible.[117] Her appeal to the Polish population reveals a curious mixture of anti-semitism and humanitarianism:

Our feeling towards the Jews has not changed. We continue to deem them political, economic and ideological enemies of Poland. Moreover, we realise that they hate us more than they hate the Germans, and that they make us responsible for their misfortune . . . We do not want to be Pilates. We have no means actively to counteract the German murders; we cannot help, nor can we rescue anybody. But we protest from the bottom of our hearts, filled with pity, indignation, and horror . . . Who does not support the protest with us, is not a Catholic.[118]

Despite Kossak believing that it was impossible to save the Jews, Żegota set out to do precisely that. Those who condemn the Poles for making insufficient efforts to save the Jews should remember:

In no other country of Europe under the Nazi occupation was a similar council created to attempt to rescue the Jewish population, within which such a wide spectrum of socio-political convictions would be represented, which would be attached to the central underground authorities, whose activities would be financed by the state budget and which would manage to continue for so long.[119]

Żegota began in Warsaw but soon extended its operations to cover most of the General Government. The aim was to provide financial assistance to Jews in hiding: at the beginning Żegota gave each Jew 1,500 złoty per month from its relief funds, but as the number of applicants increased, this dropped to 1,000 złoty and finally to 500 złoty: 'The money was paid in special well-hidden places, sometimes brought directly to the Jew in hiding.'[120] Funds were frequently short and dependent on the unpredictable arrival of couriers carrying money into Poland from Britain.

Żegota was particularly concerned with the rescue of children from the ghettos. Irena Sendler was very active in this respect and organised the placement of more than 2,500 children in orphanages and private homes and with religious orders. The children frequently had to be moved from one place to another because the small children often could not understand what danger they were in and why they had to stay undercover. Sendler recalled being asked by one small boy: 'Madam, how many mothers is it possible to have because I'm going to [my] 32nd?' She kept a card index listing the children's real names and their new names, which she buried in bottles, and after the war passed it to

Dr Adolf Berman, the first president of the Jewish Committee, so that he could try to reunite the children with any surviving relatives. The children were taught Polish and Catholic prayers in the hope that they could survive questioning by the Germans.[121] Sometimes this did not work as Elżbieta Szandorowska recalled: 'A six-year-old girl, Basia Cukier, automatically brought the death sentence upon herself by refusing to say her prayers in the presence of the Gestapo.'[122]

The Catholic Church played an important role working alongside Żegota to save Jews. Władysława Chomsowa, who ran Żegota's operations in Lwów reported:

> The Catholic clergy were of invaluable assistance in enabling us to obtain certificates of baptism, for which they provided blank forms, instructions on what to do, and ready-made certificates. How much effort and nerves went into the making of one document! With time we became more experienced. Żegota from Warsaw began to supply us with blanks of documents and the Home Army legalising cell with beautifully made official stamps. The fury of the Gestapo at our graphic skills was correspondingly great for they realised what was going on.[123]

Although the Jewish children, even those hidden by the religious orders, were taught Catholic prayers to survive questioning, there appears to have been very little attempt made to convert them. Indeed, when Karol Wojtyła, the future Pope John Paul II, was approached by a woman who wanted the Jewish child she was hiding to be baptised, he refused on the grounds that it was against the wishes of the child's parents.[124] The Salesian Brothers in Warsaw hid a number of Jewish boys, and the Germans discovered them:

> They hanged the arrested Salesian Brothers and their young foster-children on the balcony of one of the highest burnt-out buildings, opposite the Courts of Justice. Their tragic bodies were left hanging for several days. In the business area, in a bustling, thriving street, with its trams, cars, cabs and people hurrying in all directions, living their otherwise normal daily lives – there on the balcony, in full view of everybody, still hung the blackened corpses of the heroic priests and boys.[125]

If the Polish, or indeed the European, Jews were to be saved in any large numbers, the international community had to take action. There is no

bt that the allied governments knew of the Holocaust at the time. Prob-
oly the first report to reach the west (via a Swedish businessman) was
written in May 1942 by the Jewish Bund and gave the details of the mass
shootings in the east. Jan Karski's mission to the west in late 1942 was
more important since he had visited the Warsaw ghetto to see the conditions there for himself and had met with a leader of the Jewish Bund and a
leading Zionist. The message he carried from them was uncompromising:

> We are only too well aware that in the free and civilized world outside, it
> is not possible to believe all that is happening to us. Let the Jewish people,
> then, do something that will force the other world to believe us. We are
> all dying here; let them die too. Let them crowd the offices of Churchill,
> of all the important English and American leaders and agencies. Let them
> proclaim a fast before the doors of the mightiest, not retreating until they
> will believe us, until they will undertake some action to rescue those of
> our people who are still alive. Let them die a slow death while the world
> is looking on. This may shake the conscience of the world.[126]

The Jewish leadership also wanted the Allies to threaten the Germans
with reprisals against German POWs and civilians and with collective
action against the German people if the exterminations did not cease.
Neutral countries could help by supplying Jews with blank passports.
Furthermore, the Vatican should threaten the perpetrators with excom-
munication.[127]

On 10 December 1942, the Polish Foreign Ministry issued a statement *The Mass Extermination of Jews in German Occupied Poland*, in
which it announced that the Germans 'aim with systematic deliberation
at the total extermination of the Jewish population of Poland'. The
Poles also provided fully authenticated documentation of the scale of
the Holocaust now overwhelming the Jews in Poland. A week later
eleven allied governments condemned the policy and promised retribution against the perpetrators,[128] but little action was actually undertaken.
On 31 December 1942, Churchill told the chiefs of staff that he hoped
that the RAF would mount several heavy raids on Berlin during January and 'during the course of the raids leaflets should be dropped
warning the Germans that our attacks were reprisals for the persecu-
tions of the Poles and Jews'.[129] These raids were carried out and dropped
over 1,000,000 leaflets. More evidence continued to reach the west
from Poland: in March 1943, information was given that the new

crematorium at Auschwitz-Birkenau was burning 3,000 people per day; in April 1943, Korboński reported on the discrepancy between the numbers arriving at Auschwitz-Birkenau and the size of the camp population along with the conclusion that these 22,000 had been killed shortly after arrival; in April 1943, a Polish courier, probably Jerzy Salski, provided more information on Auschwitz-Birkenau; towards the end of 1943, Jan Nowak reached London and gave details of the Warsaw ghetto uprising.[130]

By then the world was tired of the news of the sufferings of the Poles and the Jews, and often found the news impossible to believe. Karski's report appalled Szmul Zygelbojm, the representative of the Bund in London and a member of the Polish National Council. In May 1943, after hearing of the Warsaw ghetto uprising, he committed suicide, and left a note addressed to Raczkiewicz and Sikorski: 'I cannot continue to live and to be silent while the remnants of Polish Jewry, whose representative I am, are being murdered. My comrades in the Warsaw ghetto fell with arms in their hands in the last heroic battle. I was not permitted to fall like them, together with them, but I belong with them, to their mass grave.'[131] When Karski met Roosevelt in 1943, he found that the president was more interested in the opinions on the Soviet Union held by the Underground Government and the AK and rather dismissive of the plight of the Jews. Karski met with an even more dramatic reaction from the Jewish Supreme Court judge Felix Frankfurter, who told him clearly: 'I am unable to believe you.'[132] When Jan Nowak arrived in Britain from Poland in 1943, he was warned by Ignacy Szwarcbart, a Zionist activist on the Polish National Council in London, not to mention the figure of 3,000,000 Polish Jews because no one, not even the Jews, would believe it.[133] The gross inflation of German atrocities during the First World War, which had been revealed during the interwar years to be largely fabrications, had made governments disbelieving. Nor was the west in any event prepared to do anything to save the Jews. In 1943 the United States Government proposed the evacuation of 60,000–70,000 Bulgarian Jews, who could reach the sanctuary of the Middle East with relative ease, but Eden's response was: 'If we do that, then the Jews of the world will be wanting us to make similar offers in Poland and Germany. Hitler might well take us up on such an offer and there are simply not enough ships and means of transportation in the world to handle them.'[134]

Given the helplessness or indifference of the Christian world to the extermination of the Jews, one is forced to agree with the conclusion drawn by Władysław Bartoszewski, a 'Righteous Among Nations': 'From the moral point of view it must be stated clearly that not enough was done either in Poland or anywhere else in occupied Europe. "Enough" was done only by those who died while giving aid.'[135] But at the same time one must remember that in the case of Poland, the Poles too were in terror of what might happen to them and their families and scarred 'by the crime committed on their soil before their eyes'.[136] The Polish Underground Government and resistance reacted too slowly to the tragedy unfolding in Poland, and resources were put in place to rescue Jews only after the major deportations had taken place, but the underground authorities also did not resist the massive deportations of Poles for forced labour in the Reich. The Holocaust was the defining moment in Polish-Jewish relations but one that was largely confused for many years in Poland by the debates concerning the clashes between different partisan forces in the forests, and especially by the controversy surrounding the high number of Jewish participants in the communist government forcibly foisted on to the country immediately after the war. Because the Holocaust itself and the response to it is not just a matter of numbers but of difficult moral decisions which faced both Polish Christians and Polish Jews alike, the arguments will and probably should continue.

# II

# Sikorski's Diplomacy, 1941–1943

The subject of the diplomatic relations between the members of the Grand Alliance – Britain, the United States and the Soviet Union – and between their leaders – Churchill, Roosevelt and Stalin – is a vast and complex one. The relations of these three countries and their leaders with the Polish Government and its leaders – Sikorski and Mikołajczyk – are barely less complex and daunting. On one level the story appears to be simple: Poland was betrayed by her allies. At the end of July 1941, the prospects for Polish diplomacy appeared to be bright: with the Germans now in occupation of all of Poland, Sikorski had nonetheless signed an agreement with Maisky which had restored full diplomatic relations between Poland and the Soviet Union. The Soviet recognition of the Polish Government in London negated the Molotov–Ribbentrop Pact and created a partnership that made clear there would be an 'independent' Poland after the fighting ended. By the end of 1943, however, it appeared that Polish interests had been sacrificed by Churchill and Roosevelt at the Teheran conference in their efforts to accommodate or appease Stalin. This interpretation views Poland as the helpless victim of Grand Alliance diplomacy, but it is not the whole story.

It is important to look first at the character of the man at the forefront of Polish diplomacy – Sikorski himself. His contemporaries and later biographers have all agreed that he was an extremely able man but also very arrogant. The United States ambassador to the Polish Government, Drexel Biddle, wrote an interesting analysis of Sikorski's character prior to his second visit to Washington:

> While he is a thoroughly honest, sincere and courageous character, he has
> gained, during the past few months, an inordinate ambition, a thirst for

publicity. He pictures himself on the one hand as the leader of post-war Poland, on the other hand, now that France has disappeared as a dominant influence on the continent, the leader of continental Europe.[1]

Sikorski had a vision of the shape of post-war Poland and post-war eastern Europe but faced formidable, if not insuperable, obstacles in achieving his aims. His tendency towards arrogance appears time and time again as he refused to face the facts before him and believed, often without adequate evidence, that the western allies supported his aims.

So what was Sikorski's vision for the future? He carefully analysed Poland's rapid defeat in 1939, looking at both the military reasons (which do not concern us here) and the diplomatic reasons. Sikorski had been a vociferous opponent of the *Sanacja* regime and, in particular, he despised the illusions held by its foreign minister, Józef Beck, that Poland was a 'great' power. For Sikorski the events leading up to the outbreak of the war with Germany, as well as the disastrous military campaign, illustrated the country's fundamental weaknesses. Poland was geographically in a poor position, with the German territory of East Prussia and part of Pomerania providing the ideal launching pad for the German conquest. Poland was far too economically weak to be a great power. Her access to the sea had been limited to a corridor through German territory, which could be and was cut off in a rapid attack. She lacked the industrial resources to ever become a great power, since the post-war plebiscites in Silesia had deprived her of most of the wealth of coal in that region. Furthermore, Poland had antagonised her neighbours, Czechoslovakia and Lithuania, and had therefore become diplomatically isolated.

Sikorski's solution was radical. A member of the Foreign Office, Rex Leeper, wrote in November 1939 that Sikorski appeared to have come to the conclusion that 'the reconstruction of Poland within her pre-war frontiers is very problematic. If it proves impossible to recover from Russia what has been lost, he aims at finding compensation elsewhere which would at the same time increase Poland's security.'[2] In particular, Sikorski believed that Poland's strategic and economic weakness would be eliminated if she occupied East Prussia, German Pomerania and Silesia. To the east she needed to retain the economic resources of East Galicia, especially the oil wells at Drohobycz, and had a strong argument for so doing since the Soviet Union had never controlled that region prior to September 1939. The remainder of the eastern provinces consisted primarily of agricultural land which Poland could afford to bargain away if necessary. No single country in eastern Europe would ever be in a strong enough position to resist the might of Germany and the Soviet Union alone, and so Sikorski formulated a novel solution: confederation. Initially he planned for the confederation of Poland and Czechoslovakia, which could later be expanded to include Lithuania, Hungary and Rumania.

The obstacles lying in the path of achieving these plans were challenging. In the first place, Sikorski's own position within his government was weak and the opposition to him both inside and outside the government had to be taken into consideration. His government had been shaken by the resignation of three ministers – August Zaleski, the foreign minister, Marian Zeyda, the minister for justice, and General Sosnkowski, the minister for military affairs – over the Sikorski–Maisky agreement. The last loss was important not only because Sosnkowski commanded the loyalty of the Polish Army in training in Scotland, many of whose officers still felt that their responsibility belonged not to Sikorski but to the *Sanacja* regime, but also because after his resignation Sosnkowski was then dismissed by Sikorski from his role as minister responsible for the ZWZ, the Polish underground army, the precursor to the AK. The government delegate reported that Polish public opinion supported the Sikorski–Maisky agreement but that there was criticism over the dismissal of Sosnkowski: criticism to which Sikorski reacted angrily.[3] Sikorski also had to face opposition from General Anders, the commander of the Polish Army now forming in the Soviet Union, and to conduct his diplomacy with regards to Poland's eastern frontier in the full knowledge that the men in this army came from the very provinces whose future was disputed by Poland and the Soviet Union.

Sikorski was not, of course, at liberty to pursue his vision independently, because Poland was a member of the alliance, and, indeed, a very junior member. What becomes apparent in 1941–3 is the extent to which the military fortunes of the Soviet Union determined the policies of the members of the Grand Alliance. When the Soviet Union was reeling under the weight of the German attack, Britain and the United States sought to woo Stalin. Mindful of the impact of the peace treaty of 1917 between revolutionary Russia and Germany which had led to a temporary German breakthrough on the Western Front, Churchill and Roosevelt sought to assure Stalin that they understood his demands for future security, among which was the recognition of the 1941 frontiers which gave him eastern Poland. Then, later, when the Soviet Union was stronger and advancing westwards, Churchill and Roosevelt were aware that the military performance of their armies did not match that of the Red Army, and that they were now in no position to resist Stalin's demands.

The frontier issue had nearly ended the Sikorski–Maisky talks in July 1941 before an agreement had been reached, which was unsatisfactory in that the Soviet Union was only prepared to go so far as to state that it 'recognises the Soviet-German Treaties of 1939 as to territorial changes in Poland as having lost their validity'.[4] Sikorski only signed it because Eden convinced him that Britain would not recognise territorial changes made in time of war. In December 1941, Sikorski visited Stalin in Moscow to discuss the outstanding matters arising from the formation of the Polish Army in the Soviet Union and the application of the amnesty freeing the Polish citizens who had been deported from eastern Poland in 1940–41. The question of the frontier arose at the dinner held at the Kremlin on 4 December. According to the official Polish record, Stalin appeared unwilling to discuss the issue of the frontier and it was Sikorski who made the running. Towards the end the following exchange took place:

STALIN: We should settle our common frontiers between ourselves, and before the Peace Conference, as soon as the Polish Army enters into action. We should stop talking on this subject. Don't worry, we will not harm you.
SIKORSKI: The 1939 frontier must not be questioned. You will allow me, Mr President, to return to this problem.
STALIN: Please, you will be welcome.[5]

Those were the final formal words between the two men and the remainder of the evening passed with inconsequential conversation.

On this slender basis Sikorski presented a lengthy and upbeat report to his council of ministers on 12 January 1942. He reassured his ministers that he had remained firm on the question of a revision of Poland's eastern frontier, and gave the misleading impression that Stalin would give the Poles assistance 'in our disputes with the Ukrainians in the matter of the Polish city of Lwów'.[6] Yet in private Sikorski appeared to have doubts that the pre-war eastern frontier could be regained. His intelligence chief, Leon Mitkiewicz, revealed in his diary that Sikorski:

> has accustomed himself to the thought that we will have to cede something to Russia in the east. For example, about Wilno and about the whole Wilno region, the General spoke in a manner which indicated that it would be necessary to cede this area to the Lithuanians [in exchange] for [their] joining a Central European Federation together with the Poles. About Lwów, too, the General said – rather it was possible to surmise and feel – that he is thinking of defending Eastern Galicia with Lwów and the oil basin, at the possible cost of concessions in the rest of our East.[7]

Sikorski was only too well aware that only days after Stalin had seemed to agree to postpone discussion of the frontier, he then had challenged Poland's pre-war territorial integrity during Eden's visit to Moscow. As Eden recalled: 'The conversation, which up to that moment had been smooth in character, suddenly changed and Stalin began to show his claws. He opened by asking for our immediate recognition of Russia's 1941 frontiers as the Soviet frontiers in the peace treaty.'[8] When Eden refused to discuss the issue, citing the Atlantic Charter and the need to consult with the United States, Stalin's angry response was: 'I thought the Atlantic Charter was directed against those people who were trying to establish world domination. It now looks as if the Atlantic Charter was directed against the USSR.'[9]

On 14 August 1941, Churchill and Roosevelt had issued the eight-point Atlantic Charter from on board the ill-fated British ship *Prince of Wales*.* Article 1 stated of the signatories that 'their countries seek no aggrandisement, territorial or other'. This article appeared to provide security for Poland's eastern frontier, and was used as such for Eden's refusal to entertain Stalin's demands for the Baltic States and for eastern Poland. But, on the other hand, it threatened to thwart Sikorski's plan to gain territory from Germany, particularly East Prussia and Western Pomerania. Article 2, 'they desire to see no territorial changes that do not accord with the freely expressed wishes of the people concerned', also threatened Polish interests. Stalin could point to the (blatantly

---

* It was sunk off the coast of Malaya by a Japanese air attack in December 1941.

rigged) elections and plebiscite during the Soviet occupation of eastern Poland as evidence that the population of these provinces had voted for incorporation into the Soviet Union. Biddle wrote to the secretary of state on 12 September 1941, explaining the Polish memorandum submitted to the United States Government on the Atlantic Charter, that the 'mass deportations which had taken place in certain sections of Poland, rendered the principle of self-determination set forth in point 2 of the Declaration, difficult, to say the least'.[10] Notwithstanding its reservations about the Charter, Poland became a signatory on 24 September 1941.

Sikorski was acutely aware of the relationship between Soviet military fortunes and their diplomatic demands. When he visited Moscow in December 1941, Soviet military fortunes were at a nadir, with German forces on the brink of taking Moscow. In hindsight it is apparent that this situation presented Sikorski with the best opportunity he would ever have to settle the frontier question directly with Stalin. During the winter the Soviet counteroffensive relieved the pressure on Moscow and they were able to transport supplies into the besieged city of Leningrad. The British ambassador to the Soviet Union, Sir Stafford Cripps, warned Sikorski at the end of January 1942: 'Russia has acquired a much stronger position. In the matter of State frontiers she has established certain principles which she considered as being beyond discussion.'[11] Sikorski was alert to the threats posed to Polish interests, warning his ministers on 4 February: 'The successes enjoyed by the Soviet army, have electrified public opinion here in Great Britain, and along with British defeats in both the Near and Far East, are doubtless causing a certain state of mind that is disadvantageous for Poland.' He believed that there was a great danger that Britain would take any action it could to keep the Soviet Union in the war, even to the extent of allowing the Soviet Union a free hand in communising Europe.[12] He had already despatched his trusted foreign minister, Raczyński, to the United States to alert the government there of Soviet demands and the British reaction to them. Intelligence reports from Poland reaching London in early 1942 indicated that the Germans were preparing for a massive offensive into the southern region of the Soviet Union in the spring, which the Soviets would temporarily be unable to withstand. The solution, as Sikorski outlined to Eden, was the immediate launch of a Second Front: 'A single armoured division employed on the European continent in 1942 at the moment of the fiercest battles on the eastern front, will represent a greater force if compared to the adversary, than five such divisions employed against the Germans in 1943.' This gamble was necessary 'in order to establish a United Nations, rather than chiefly a Russian peace'. By showing that the western allies were prepared to make sacrifices, they would be in a stronger diplomatic position with regard to the Soviets. In the meantime, no promises regarding post-war frontiers should be made.[13]

The British reaction to the danger of Soviet reverses in the spring of 1942 was rather different: it wanted to conclude a treaty with the Soviet Union which would bind the two countries closely together both during and after the war. The question was: what would Britain offer the Soviet Union? The first step in this accommodation, if not actual appeasement, of the Soviet Union was taken by Churchill in his telegram to Roosevelt on 7 March 1942:

> The increasing gravity of the war has led me to feel that the principles of the Atlantic Charter ought not to be construed so as to deny Russia the frontiers she occupied when Germany attacked her ... I hope therefore that you will be able to give us a free hand to sign the treaty which Stalin desires as soon as possible. Everything portends an immense renewal of the German invasion of Russia in the spring and there is very little we can do to help the only country that is heavily engaged with the German armies.[14]

The phrase 'the frontiers she occupied' subtly sacrificed the whole of the Polish territories occupied by the Soviets after their invasion in September 1939. This also reflected Churchill's own personal opinion, for on 26 April 1942, he wrote to Sikorski: 'The current war is a continuation of the first. Russia demands only the return of that territory with which she entered the war in 1914.'[15] This, of course, was not true, both because East Galicia had never been a portion of the Russian partition, and because in 1914 cities like Łódź had been part of the Russian Empire, but Stalin was not claiming these. The reaction of the American under-secretary of state, Sumner Welles, to Churchill's telegram was shared by Roosevelt: 'The attitude of the British government is not only indefensible from every moral standpoint, but likewise extraordinarily stupid.'[16] When Sikorski was in the United States in March and April 1942, during his meetings with Roosevelt and Welles he emphasised his belief that although the Soviet Union had only demanded the recognition of Soviet incorporation of the three Baltic States (Lithuania, Latvia and Estonia), this should be viewed as just Stalin's opening play. If the British agreed, then the principles of the Atlantic Charter would have already been breached, leaving Stalin free to demand, first, eastern Poland, and then hegemony over the whole of eastern Europe. His opinions fell on receptive ears, particularly since Sikorski outlined his preferred solution: a confederation of eastern European states, beginning with Poland and Czechoslovakia. Sikorski also drew Roosevelt's attention to the strength of the anti-German underground in Poland and its determination to reject German suggestions for Polish participation in an anti-Soviet campaign. He informed both Roosevelt and the Soviet ambassador to the United States, Maxim Litvinov, that Poland had 'a friendly attitude towards the Soviet Union, conditioned, however, by its respecting our rights and our territory'.[17]

Back in Britain the Polish Government mounted a sustained campaign on Eden, virtually begging him not to conclude a treaty with the Soviet Union that included any decisions on post-war frontiers. Sikorski even threatened to release the 'Red Book', the list of Soviet crimes committed during the occupation of Poland in 1939–41.[18] Churchill himself was becoming considerably less keen on an Anglo-Soviet treaty, telling his colleagues: 'We must remember that this is a bad thing. We oughtn't to do it, and I shan't be sorry if we don't.'[19] He wanted some sort of treaty with the Soviet Union but not one that covered post-war frontiers. But it was American opposition that led to the removal of these clauses. The American ambassador to Britain, John Winant, warned Churchill and Eden 'that should a British-Russian treaty be concluded, admitting Soviet territorial demands, the President would be forced to make a public statement disassociating the United States very definitely from any part in such an agreement'.[20] The Anglo-Soviet Treaty, signed on 26 May 1942, did not confirm the Soviet Union's 1941 frontier with Poland and promised that the two powers 'will act in accordance with the two principles of not seeking territorial aggrandizement for themselves and of non-interference in the internal affairs of other peoples'.[21] Eden later gave Sikorski all the credit for the final treaty: 'It is 100% to your merit that this treaty has its present shape and not a different one. The United States have also supported your point of view, and therefore

50% of the merit is theirs.'[22] Sikorski wrote to Roosevelt to thank him for his assistance with the treaty.[23]

This marked the high point of Sikorski's diplomacy and it was all downhill from then on. Negotiations between the exiled Poles and exiled Czechs had begun in London in November 1940, and a Mixed Commission was set up to discuss the prospects for a confederation of the two countries. The future of Teschen, the disputed area of Silesia which the Czechs had seized in 1920 only to lose it to the Poles in 1938, was a stumbling block and one which Beneš, the Czech leader, particularly resented. The real challenges were to establish the purpose of the confederation and then to convince the members of the Grand Alliance that such a confederation would be a positive step. Sikorski was adamant that it should be a bulwark against any future expansionist plans by either Germany or the Soviet Union. In contrast, the Czechs, and in particular Beneš, were strongly in favour of allying the confederation to the Soviet Union in some form. As Raczyński wrote: 'unfortunately, the Czechs, having only the Germans as their enemies and chronically seeking support from Russia, support the Russian claims to our south-eastern territories, counting on assuring for themselves Carpathian Ruthenia in this matter'.[24]

Therefore, the prospects for the confederation were not good. Indeed, Roosevelt warned Sikorski in March 1942 that the Soviets were unlikely to favour it, especially since Sikorski wanted to expand it to include Lithuania, which the Soviets intended for themselves, and ultimately he wanted a southern confederation to include all the countries in the Balkans. Churchill had been in favour of the confederation to begin with but when, during the negotiations for the Anglo-Soviet Treaty, he learned of Soviet opposition he changed his mind. While Molotov was in London negotiating the treaty, he had an important conversation with Beneš, who assured him that 'if your relations with Poland are not friendly there would be no confederation'; Sikorski also met Molotov, but the confederation issue was not raised. Sikorski wrote to Beneš urging him that the matter of Teschen could be settled amicably and that a confederation was really the only guarantor of the future independence of both countries, but in vain. The last meeting of the Mixed Commission was held on 23 July 1942, although talks between the two exiled governments continued for the rest of the year. The Czechs moved even further towards the Soviet camp, and the American embassy in Moscow reported: 'evidence was accumulating to the effect that the Czechoslovak Legation is spending a good deal of its time serving the interests of the Soviet Government'. After the break in relations between Poland and the Soviet Union, Beneš offered to act as an intermediary between them. The Polish Government had no trust in him. It felt that he lacked 'objectivity' and that, indeed, 'in the course of the last year the Czechoslovak Government appears to have become a fervent advocate of USSR aims and, in connection with this attitude, has shown a marked tendency to withdraw from the engagements which it had previously undertaken with regard to Poland'. Beneš achieved his own goal when he signed the Soviet-Czech treaty in Moscow on 12 December 1943.[25]

The question of the future frontiers of Poland continued to dominate Sikorski's diplomacy. Stalin had offered Sikorski a new Polish western frontier on the Oder but Sikorski told Hugh Dalton, the former minister of economic warfare and a friend of the Poles, that he dismissed this idea as a 'provocation'.[26] Certainly, Sikorski envisaged a realignment of the German-Polish frontier with Polish gains in East Prussia, Danzig and Pomerania, because this would give Poland a shorter and therefore a more defendable frontier with Germany. It is also likely that Sikorski also wanted to see the whole of Upper Silesia in Polish hands: part of this rich industrial area had been lost to Poland in the disputed post-war plebiscite. A thesis has been advanced that Sikorski actually had wanted to advance the frontier all the way to the Oder and Neisse, roughly where the border now lies, but the evidence for this is fragmentary.[27] Indeed, when Stalin had made the offer of a new frontier on the Oder, Sikorski had demurred on the grounds that Lower Silesia contained a predominantly German population. The Polish council of ministers warned Sikorski to be cautious on the subject of gains from Germany: 'The advancement of such boundless territorial demands discredits the Poles in the eyes of Anglo-Saxon opinion as a people of unrestrained greed; which does irreparable harm to our real territorial aspirations', which were more limited.[28] The real danger in opening any discussion of the western frontier was that the Big Three might use the prospect of substantial territorial gains from Germany as a bargaining chip to win over Polish support for a revision of the eastern frontier in line with Stalin's demands.

At the end of 1942 it appeared that the tide of the war was beginning to turn in the Allies' favour: Stalingrad was encircled by the Soviets and the western allies had almost cleared North Africa. Sikorski set out for Washington in December 1942 to present his case on the future shape of Poland to Roosevelt, telling the commander of the Polish underground army, Rowecki, that he was seeking recognition of 'our rights in the East with a simultaneous support for our claims in the West'.[29] In addition, Sikorski was also trying to gain an increase in supplies for the underground army in Poland so that it could make its contribution to the defeat of Germany at the opportune moment, and he and his aide Colonel Andrzej Marecki held a series of meetings with senior American generals about this. In a memorandum Sikorski prepared for Sumner Welles, after his first round of conversations with Roosevelt and Welles, he set out the Polish defence of the 1920 eastern frontier. He made the point that the northern and central provinces were primarily agricultural and of no great value, but in contrast East Galicia was of great value to Poland:

> The southern part which contains our only oil-fields is of great importance to Poland, whereas the high cost of production and the comparatively low output [400,000–500,000 tons per annum] would make it insignificant to our neighbour, nor would it bear comparison with his vast capacities or economic facilities of production. In this part of Poland there is also ozocerite, natural gas, potassium chloride, timber and water-power.

He countered the Soviet argument that the river Bug was a strategic barrier by stressing that the Pripet marshes, on the existing frontier, formed a much stronger defensive shield. Sikorski also pointed out that Lwów had never belonged to Russia, and Wilno only when Poland was partitioned.[30]

Sikorski returned to London convinced that his visit had been a great success. He informed his council of ministers that their fears that the Grand Alliance was entertaining the idea of 'depriving Poland of a part of the eastern territories in exchange for acquisitions in the west' had been misguided.[31] He said that Roosevelt supported Polish claims for East Prussia but was concerned about the claims for part of Silesia. A jubilant Sikorski, throwing off all earlier constraint, then reported to the Foreign Office that Roosevelt was in favour of Polish expansion at the expense of Germany and that he would support Poland's claims in the east. Furthermore, he stated that Roosevelt had suggested that Stalin would be content to absorb part of Finland, Estonia and Latvia but not Lithuania, and Bessarabia but not Bukovina. The Foreign Office was bewildered and asked Lord Halifax, the British ambassador in the United States, for clarification. The response was: 'General Sikorski had in fact done all the talking', and that it was he who had hoped that Stalin would be satisfied with more limited gains. Welles had also made the American position on the western frontier clear: no binding statement on the western frontier would be issued and the United States would not guarantee the integrity of any frontier.[32]

Sikorski viewed his visit to Washington as both a personal success and important because he believed that it had demonstrated that the United States was prepared to stand up to Soviet demands detrimental to Polish interests with more determination than Britain. His optimism was entirely unjustified. Shortly after Sikorski's return to London, Welles had asked the Polish ambassador, Jan Ciechanowski, to clarify the Polish position on the eastern frontier: 'Am I to understand that the Polish Government is determined not to sacrifice even an inch of its Eastern Territory', and Ciechanowski was forced to reply in the affirmative.[33] Eden complained that Sikorski was now taking a harder line than before: whereas earlier there seemed a chance that Sikorski might agree to give up the eastern provinces, although certainly not Lwów, now he had returned to demanding the Riga Line and, to make matters worse, was also demanding the Oder Line in the west.[34]

Sikorski appears to have been in danger of falling into the trap of being punctilious about the restoration of Poland's eastern frontier while at the same time being acquisitive in the west. He was unwilling or unable to recognise that Poland was in an extremely weak position diplomatically. The evacuation of the Polish Army from the Soviet Union during 1942 had reinforced the British forces in the Middle East, but the British had neither been approached for, nor had offered, any commitments to the Polish cause in return for this reinforcement. The evacuations were a diplomatic disaster, for, at the dinner at the Kremlin on 4 December 1941, Stalin had explicitly stated that the correct time to discuss the frontiers would be when the Polish Army had begun fighting the Germans. With the evacuation of the Anders army, Stalin lost patience with the Poles, and refused to allow recruitment to the Polish Army to continue because, as he told the new Polish ambassador, Tadeusz

Romer, they would only go to Iran.[35] The evidence of Stalin's absolute determination to secure eastern Poland for the Soviet Union is overwhelming: communiqués on German atrocities in the Soviet Union included references to the cities of Lwów and Wilno, and the Soviet definition of eligibility for recruitment to the Polish Army had sought to exclude Polish citizens of Belorussian, Ukrainian, Lithuanian and Jewish ethnicity. Polish complaints were ignored. In January 1943, Stalin raised the stakes by withdrawing Polish citizenship from the Poles left in the Soviet Union, who were now to be considered simply as Soviet citizens.

It is likely that this withdrawal of Polish citizenship was Stalin's angry reaction to Sikorski's visit to Washington. Indeed, the American ambassador to the Polish Government, Drexel Biddle, reported to the State Department that Stalin's action should be seen as a warning to Sikorski that he should go to Moscow to discuss Poland's eastern frontier directly with Stalin. In the same despatch Biddle noted that Sikorski had told him that he had received 'secret information today that the Russians are hinting that Stalin may be prepared for his part to make concessions'. Sikorski was willing to go to Moscow but, because 'Stalin is riding the wave of military successes', wanted Britain and the United States to prepare the ground for him first.[36] Both Britain and the United States appealed to the Soviets to reverse their ruling on Polish citizenship and to allow the evacuation from the Soviet Union of the families of Polish soldiers who were already in the Middle East, but to no avail. Their lack of success forced the American ambassador in Moscow, Admiral William Standley, to conclude: 'it was precisely because of the fact that Sikorski took his problems to Washington before discussing them with Stalin that Soviet-Polish relations have deteriorated to their present state'.[37]

Sikorski made no plans to go to Moscow for talks with Stalin, as it was politically impossible for him to contemplate making concessions to him at this time. His government was greatly alarmed by reports coming in from the Middle East about the attitude of the officers in the Anders army, 'who, in their hatred towards Russia overstep the mark, and are even considering reaching a compromise with the Germans'.[38] It was, however, equally dangerous for the Polish Government to depend on Britain and the United States to defend its interests. For example, on 10 March 1943 a leading article in *The Times*, written by E. H. Carr, suggested that eastern Europe should be under Soviet hegemony.[39] The Poles were outraged and, although Eden made it clear that this did not reflect government policy, the Soviets were convinced that *The Times* was a government organ and that opinions stated in it were official government policy.[40] Also in March, Eden visited Washington and had interesting talks with Roosevelt, who told Eden that, in his opinion, after the war no country other than Britain, the United States and the Soviet Union should have armaments more powerful than rifles. This proposal was so absurd that it could be safely ignored. Another statement did, however, have far more serious implications for Poland: Roosevelt did not 'intend to bargain with the Poles or other small countries at the peace conference', and 'in any event Britain, the United States and Russia should decide at the appropriate time what was a just solution, and Poland would have to accept'.[41]

On the surface it seemed that there was still a great deal of sympathy for the Poles in government circles. At the end of March, the permanent under secretary at the Foreign Office, Cadogan, ably summed up the situation:

> The indications are that the Russians are trying to force the Poles to agree to accept the Curzon Line frontier under the threat of working against General Sikorski's Government and of making the position of the Poles in Russia impossible. General Sikorski cannot accept such a frontier settlement now and neither we nor the United States Government could advise him to do so. The Russian attitude is, therefore, playing into the hands of German propaganda by stirring up disunity among the United Nations, and by encouraging anti-Soviet feelings in the U.S.A. and among the smaller European nations. It is also undermining the morale of the Polish Fighting Forces here and in the Middle East, which is a matter of very direct interest to us.[42]

Cadogan's mention of German propaganda was prescient given the news the Germans were about to broadcast to the world, which would for ever damage both Polish-Soviet and Polish-British relations.

On 12 April 1943, the German news agency Transocean made public the German discovery of the graves of the Polish officers murdered at Katyń by the NKVD in April and May 1940. The next day the news was broadcast on German radio and repeated by radio stations worldwide.

A giant pit was found, 28 metres long and 16 metres wide, filled with 12 layers of bodies of Polish officers, numbering about 3000. They were clad in full military uniform, and while many of them had their hands tied, all of them had wounds in the back of their necks caused by pistol shots. The identification of the bodies will not cause great difficulties because of the mummifying property of the soil and because the Bolsheviks had left on the bodies the identity documents of the victims.[43]

The Poles had been pressing the Soviets to account for the missing Polish officers ever since the formation of the Anders army had begun, and were appalled now to learn of their fate. Two days later TASS issued a denial and insisted that the Germans themselves had killed the Polish officers in 1941 when they first overran the area. The Poles had no doubt that the Soviets were responsible: for nearly two years they had repeatedly asked the Soviet authorities for details of the whereabouts of these officers without receiving satisfactory responses. General Kukiel, the Polish minister responsible for POW matters, issued a statement, agreed to by Sikorski and other ministers, requesting that the IRC investigate the matter. There were precedents for this appeal: when the Germans murdered some British officers, and when the news of murders of British and American soldiers by the Japanese was made public, the British Government had appealed to the IRC for assistance. An important difference now, of course, was that those murders had been committed by the enemy and not by an ally, the Soviet Union.

The former Polish ambassador to the Soviet Union, Stanisław Kot, now minister of information, drafted a communiqué to be issued by the Polish Government, in which all the steps taken by the Poles to discover the fate of the officers were listed with all the evidence pointing to the Soviets as the guilty party.[44] Later, when the full implications of this communiqué had become evident, the Polish Government tried to explain to Biddle what had happened:

> I am informed by Sikorski's closest associates that after Kot had written the communiqué he succeeded in influencing Sikorski over the telephone, at moment when latter was tired and ill, to permit him to release it; that when on second thought, Sikorski had wanted to withdraw it, it was already in the hands of the press.[45]

On 24 April, Sikorski had a meeting with Eden at the Foreign Office during which Eden subjected him to an intense interrogation concerning the evidence against the Soviets. Finally, Eden was reluctantly forced to accept Sikorski's conclusion but made a passionate appeal: 'Great Britain was in a desperate position. Her two allies were involved in a serious and public dispute, weakening the common front and splitting up the United Nations.' He urged Sikorski to withdraw the invitation to the IRC and to 'make a declaration stating that the Katyń affair was an invention of German propaganda'. Sikorski's response was that he could not do the latter but would withdraw the request for the IRC and control the Polish press if the British and Americans appealed to Stalin to release more Poles from the Soviet Union.[46]

It was too late: on the night of 24–25 April, Molotov summoned the Polish ambassador in Moscow, Romer, and read out a note which began: 'The Soviet Government consider the recent behaviour of the Polish Government with regard to the USSR as entirely abnormal and violating all regulations and standards of relations between two Allied States.' It then accused the Polish Government of being in collusion with the Germans before concluding: 'On the strength of the above, the Soviet Government has decided to suspend relations with the Polish Government.'[47] Romer refused to accept the note, which was then delivered to his hotel. On 28 April, the Polish Government issued a statement affirming that their policy was 'a friendly understanding between Poland and the Soviet Union on the basis of the integrity and full sovereignty of the Polish Republic'.[48] The Soviet use of '*prervat*' meaning 'suspend' rather than '*porvat*' meaning 'break off' meant that many, Sikorski and Romer, among them, hoped that the break would be only temporary.[49] Yet the Polish mention of 'integrity' suggested that they would not relent on the question of the 1941 frontier, so the Soviets were not prepared to alter their stance, and, on 5 May, Romer left the Soviet Union. Goebbels wrote in his diary: 'One can speak of a complete triumph of German propaganda. Throughout this whole war we have seldom been able to register such a success.'[50]

It might be argued that the Polish Government should have approached the matter differently. Quite obviously it could not have condoned the murder of its officer corps as silence would have implied. Still less could it have declared, as Eden suggested, that the Germans were the guilty party. Sikorski's pro-Soviet policy had already proved controversial, and if he had shown any weakness at this point, it would almost certainly have led to mutinies within the Polish Army, whose friends and relatives had been murdered, and to his sacking by the Polish president Raczkiewicz, who had never liked Sikorski's policy towards the Soviet Union. Nor would Sikorski have been supported by the Poles within Poland. The Underground Government and resistance had approved of the plan for a thorough investigation of the Katyń graves by the IRC, and when the official request was withdrawn, the commander of the underground army, Rowecki, notified Sikorski of the country's disappointment and anger and asked him to clarify his position. Rowecki then continued to keep the government informed of how the Germans and the communists were making use of Katyń in their propaganda.[51]

One criticism can be made of Sikorski's leadership at this difficult time. The rising in the Warsaw ghetto and the Germans' brutal suppression of it coincided with the revelations of Katyń. Indeed, it has been suggested that the Germans, who had known about the discovery of the graves since the winter of 1942–3, deliberately delayed releasing the news until the liquidation of the Warsaw ghetto was in progress, in the hope that world opinion would be diverted away from their crimes and focus instead on Soviet crimes.[52] If so, then Sikorski fell into the trap laid by the Germans: he could have easily countered the Soviet accusations of Polish collusion with the Germans by highlighting ongoing German crimes on Polish soil against the Jewish population, but missed the opportunity.

Stark military facts governed the response of the British and American governments to the Katyń revelations and the break in diplomatic relations between the Polish Government and the Soviet Union. The Soviets had inflicted a massive defeat on the Germans when General Friedrich von Paulus was forced to surrender the Sixth Army at Stalingrad, and the Germans were in retreat on the Eastern Front. In contrast the western allies were concentrating their resources on the strategic bombing campaign in Germany and in winning the battle of the Atlantic, for until the latter was won, an invasion of the continent could not be started. Therefore, the choice was clear: the war could be won without the Poles, should they withdraw from the alliance, but not without the Soviets. Churchill informed Stalin that he was opposed to an investigation by the IRC, and Roosevelt went further in his telegram to Stalin: 'It is my view that Sikorski has not acted in any way with Hitler gang, but rather that he made a ~~stupid~~ mistake in taking the matter up with the International Red Cross.' While Roosevelt may have deleted 'stupid' from the final telegram, this is obviously what he thought of the response of the Polish Government.[53]

The British certainly agreed with the Poles that the Soviets were guilty. The British ambassador in Moscow, Archibald Clark Kerr, wrote: 'In a horrible way it seems to fit in with the Poles' story of the disappearance of 8300 officers. The anger and unconvincing terms of Soviet denials suggests a sense of guilt.'[54] Cadogan wrote in the privacy of his diary: 'How can the Poles ever live amicably alongside Russians, and how can we discuss with Russians execution of German "war criminals", when we have condoned this.'[55] On 24 May 1943, the British ambassador to the Polish Government, Owen O'Malley, presented a lengthy and very thorough analysis of the entire Katyń affair to the Foreign Office. He made the case for Soviet guilt but concluded that it was strongly inadvisable for the British Government to allow this belief to become public even if this meant that the government would have to put moral scruples to one side:

> In handling the publicity side of the Katyń affair we have been constrained by the urgent need for cordial relations with the Soviet Government to appear to appraise the evidence with more hesitation and lenience than we should do in forming a common-sense judgment on events occurring in normal times or in the ordinary course of our private lives; we have been obliged to appear to distort the normal and healthy operation of our intellectual and moral judgments; we have been obliged to give undue prominence to the tactlessness or impulsiveness of Poles, to restrain the Poles from putting their case clearly before the public, to discourage any attempt by the public and the press to probe the ugly story to the bottom. In general we have been obliged to deflect attention from possibilities which in the ordinary affairs of life would cry to high heaven for elucidation, and to withhold the full measure of solicitude which, in other circumstances, would be shown to acquaintances situated as a large number of Poles now are. We have in fact perforce used the good name of England like the murderers used the little conifers to cover up a massacre; and, in view of the immense importance of an appearance of Allied unity and of the heroic resistance of Russia to Germany, few will think that any other course would have been wise or right.[56]

Churchill forwarded O'Malley's despatch to Roosevelt, describing it as 'a grim, well-written story'. He also asked Roosevelt to return it to him, 'when you have finished with it as we are not circulating it officially in any way'.[57] Roosevelt's reaction is not known. Churchill's own response was: 'If they are dead nothing you can do will bring them back.'[58] While it was understandable that the British Government should have perceived the necessity of concealing the truth concerning Katyń during the war, the extent and length of the cover-up during and after the Cold War is inexcusable, and this subject will be returned to in Chapter 18.

Churchill promised Stalin that he would muzzle the Polish press, which was publishing strongly anti-Soviet opinions. It had long been a thorn in Sikorski's side, being particularly critical of his policy towards the Soviet Union, and for the anti-Soviet journalists the news of Katyń justified their earlier scepticism. The British censored not only Polish broadcasts on the BBC to Poland and the Polish press in Britain, but also the Polish press in the Middle East. In contrast, the Soviet press continued to make anti-Polish statements virtually without criticism from British quarters. The British authorities in the Middle East, Reader Bullard in Teheran and Richard Casey in Cairo, noted the anger of the Polish troops at being unable to respond to the TASS statements circulating in the region.[59] In London the *Soviet War News* criticised the Polish Government and finally, after a particularly hostile article on 30 April, Churchill summoned Maisky and as Cadogan noted: 'Then we kicked Maisky all round the room, and it went v. well.'[60]

Sikorski, Churchill and Roosevelt all hoped that the breach in Soviet-Polish relations would be temporary, yet evidence quickly mounted up to suggest otherwise. Soon after the break the American ambassador to the Soviet Union, Standley, informed the State Department that while the foreign correspondents in Moscow had at first been ordered by the Soviet censors to use 'suspension of relations', a few days after the announcement they were ordered to use 'break' or 'rupture'. Furthermore, both Standley and Clark Kerr informed their governments that an article in *Izvestiya* by Wanda Wasilewska of the Union of Polish Patriots was sharply critical of the Polish Government. Indeed, Standley reported: 'the consensus here is that the publication of the aforementioned article has now definitely closed the door to any *rapprochement* between the present Polish Government and Moscow'. Biddle drew the same conclusion after a conversation with Bogomolov, the Soviet ambassador to the exiled governments in London.[61] In contrast, Sikorski was optimistic: during a meeting with Eden on 24 May, he let it be known that he was still pressing for the formation of new Polish divisions in the Soviet Union. This meeting occurred after the Soviet announcement of the creation of the Berling army had been made.

Stalin's reaction to the break in relations suggested that he had been preparing for it for a long time, for he quickly threw his support behind the wider activities of the Union of Polish Patriots and despatched more Soviet partisans to Poland.[62] He then upped the stakes by demanding a reorganisation of the Polish Government before he would even consider a restoration of relations. He wrote to Churchill:

> Although you informed me that the Polish Government wanted to work loyally with the Soviet Government, I question its ability to keep its word. The Polish Government is surrounded by such a vast pro-Hitler following, and Sikorski is so helpless and browbeaten that there is no certainty at all of his being able to remain loyal in relations with the Soviet Union even granting that he wants to be loyal.[63]

The Polish politicians in question were Raczkiewicz, Kot and Kukiel. Churchill and Roosevelt were desperate for relations to be restored but warned Stalin that they could not interfere in the internal composition of a foreign government. Nevertheless, both men urged Sikorski to make changes to the council of ministers, and it seems likely that he was planning to do so after his trip to the Middle East.[64]

Sikorski was extremely aware that the news of the murder of their relatives and friends had greatly unsettled the Polish soldiers in the Middle East. On 25 May 1943, he left London for a long overdue visit to the Anders army. He toured the army camps from 1 to 17 June and then held talks with Anders in Cairo to discuss current political and military problems. According to Anders, the visit and the talks were a great success.[65] On 3 July, Sikorski flew from Cairo to Gibraltar. On the evening of 5 July, the plane carrying Sikorski and his daughter, his chief of staff, Klimecki, his British liaison officer, Victor Cazalet, and several other passengers, including a recently arrived courier from Warsaw, Colonel Jan Gralewski, crashed into the sea on takeoff from Gibraltar, killing all the passengers. The Czech pilot, Eduard Prchal, survived but was badly injured.[66] Sikorski's body was found and was transported by ship to

Plymouth, and his funeral was held at Westminster Cathedral on 15 July. The British CIGS, Field Marshal Lord Alanbrooke, wrote in his diary:

> The service was too theatrical and fussy to stir up my feelings till the very end. But when I saw the empty stand where the coffin had been with 6 'sierges' burning round it, and on either flank representative 'colours' of regiments borne by officer parties it struck me as a sad picture of Poland's plight: both its state and its army left without a leader when a change of the tide seems in sight. I was very fond of Sikorski personally and shall miss him badly.[67]

Sikorski's coffin was buried in Newark Cemetery, which already contained the graves of over 200 Polish pilots who had died fighting for the Allies.

The British convened a Court of Inquiry into the crash of Sikorski's Liberator, under the chairmanship of Group Captain J. Elton, and 30 people were questioned. The Polish Government sent Major Stanisław Dudziński as its representative. The inquiry was unable to determine with any certainty why the plane had crashed and concluded:

> It is apparent that the accident was due to jamming of elevator controls shortly after take off with the result that the aircraft became uncontrollable.
>
> After the most careful examination of all available evidence, including that of the pilot, it has not been possible to determine how the jamming occurred but it has been established that there was no sabotage.[68]

The Poles were unhappy about the readiness of the British to rule out sabotage but two separate commissions conducted by the Poles themselves in September and November 1943 were unable to find any evidence of sabotage and concluded that 'the cause had to remain as due to unknown factors'.[69]

The lack of a definite cause led many to believe that the plane must have been deliberately sabotaged and gave rise to a number of surprisingly long-lasting conspiracy theories blaming the British, the spy Kim Philby acting on Soviet orders, the Soviets or the Poles themselves. Perhaps the longest-running was that Churchill wanted Sikorski dead because he was a strong leader and Churchill preferred someone weak whom he could bully into agreeing to Soviet demands.[70] But Frank

Roberts took Churchill the news of Sikorski's death and later said that the prime minister 'was deeply moved and wept over what he felt was a personal loss, that of a great Polish patriot and of a war leader for whom he had real friendship and admiration'.[71] This is corroborated by Retinger's account of Churchill's reaction:

> I was ushered into the big room at 10 Downing Street which had just been vacated by the Cabinet, and which was dense with smoke. I found the Prime Minister alone, wearing his light blue siren suit. As soon as he saw me he got up and started to cry. He told me that he had loved General Sikorski as a younger brother, and had watched his career not only with interest, but with affection. He was profoundly moved and shocked by the news of the crash, and deplored the fact that he would not be able to cooperate with General Sikorski when peace came. He went on to recall with emotion the many critical days they had spent together.[72]

Suspicion also fell on to the British because on two previous occasions Sikorski's life had been in danger when leaving their territory: a bomb was found on a plane carrying him from Canada to the United States in March 1942, and on an earlier occasion the plane taking him south from Scotland was found to have been sabotaged.

The presence on Gibraltar of Kim Philby, ostensibly working for SIS (Secret Intelligence Service), but later discovered to be working for Soviet intelligence, lent credence to the theory that the Soviets had somehow killed Sikorski. This claim centred on the movements of the crew of the plane carrying Maisky from London to Moscow, which was parked on the same airfield, and it was generally acknowledged that security on Gibraltar was lax. Yet why would the Soviets want Sikorski dead? He was the one Polish leader who was a strong enough character to engage in negotiations with them, and even if the Soviets did not want to negotiate with the Polish Government, they would hardly take the risk of throwing suspicion on themselves so soon after the Katyń revelations. The last theory concerns the Poles themselves. There were rumours before Sikorski even arrived in the Middle East that an attempt would be made on his life by Poles.[73] An extraordinary claim was made in 1947 by General Gustaw Paszkiewicz: he stated that he was approached by Anders to join a plot to assassinate Sikorski but refused. This theory has some plausibility since, as has already been explained earlier in this chapter, Sikorski was prepared to consider alterations to Poland's pre-war frontier in the east and this would have made homeless a number of soldiers under Anders's command. It is, however, unlikely that Anders himself was involved in any plot, and much likelier that Paszkiewicz, who had returned to Poland after the war, made this claim as part of the communist Polish Government's campaign against Anders.[74] While Sikorski's death was almost certainly an accident, and there were other such fatal accidental crashes during the war, if sabotage was involved, then the involvement of members of Anders staff cannot be entirely ruled out.

Sikorski's death threw the Polish Government into turmoil. In Poland the underground forces were in a similar state of confusion following the arrest of their leader, Rowecki, by the Gestapo. For all his faults, Sikorski had been a strong and determined man who as Harold Nicolson observed, 'was the only man who could control the fierce resentment of the Poles against Russia, and force them to bury their internecine strife. He is one of those rare people whom one can describe as irreplaceable.'[75] Sikorski had filled two posts, prime minister and commander-in-chief, and it appears that the decision was quickly taken to separate them. The Allies watched with anxiety as the Poles created their new government.

President Raczkiewicz immediately seized the initiative by suggesting that General Sosnkowski, who shared his staunchly anti-Soviet stance, should be appointed commander-in-chief. The only alternative seemed to be Anders. Raczyński kept the Foreign Office informed of Polish plans, and the Foreign Office in turn consulted Clark Kerr in order to discover whom the Soviets might favour. Clark Kerr responded that he knew nothing of Sosnkowski, but was sure that Anders was *persona non grata* with the Soviets. Sosnkowski was extremely popular within the army and had many supporters in Poland in the AK command, but he also had his detractors. Within Poland there was opposition to his appointment from the right-wing NSZ, who felt he was too involved in politics, and from the left wing, who remembered that Sosnkowski had resigned from the government over the Sikorski–Maisky agreement and doubted that his political views had changed. The British hoped that Sosnkowski's appointment, made by Raczkiewicz before the appointment of a prime minister, 'will be offset by the immediate formation of a "democratic" Government under a Prime Minister who will hold the ship of State to the course plotted by Sikorski'.[76]

Retinger and Raczyński were deeply involved in the appointment of the new prime minister. Both favoured Stanisław Mikołajczyk, the leader of the largest political party, the Peasant Party, as someone who had been earmarked by Sikorski for the job. When Retinger saw Eden and Churchill separately on 5 July to suggest Mikołajczyk, Churchill could not remember him but when Retinger described him, replied: 'The man who looks like a fat, slightly bald, old fox.' Mikołajczyk indicated his willingness to accept the job but attached conditions; the most important was a restriction of the wide powers of the president, granted under the 1935 constitution, to appoint his successor and to make political appointments without consultation. Sikorski had forced Raczkiewicz to accept such changes during the formation of the original Polish Government-in-Exile in 1940, and Mikołajczyk wanted the same restrictions to apply now. He also wanted to restrict the powers of the commander-in-chief. He did not want Sosnkowski to be a member of his cabinet, in a position to interfere in political affairs, and also sought to restrict his authority over the underground army, giving some of the responsibilities to the minister of national defence. The two ministers, Kot and Kukiel, whom the Soviets wanted dismissed, both retained their posts. One significant change was that Raczyński was replaced as minister for foreign affairs by Tadeusz Romer, but continued as the Polish ambassador to Britain. The new government was announced on 17 July, after Sikorski's funeral. The names of the new ministers were transmitted to the Polish Army in the Middle East and to Poland, and problems soon arose. The telegrams from Poland from the government delegate and from Bór-Komorowski, the new commander of the AK, indicated that the Poles in Poland were anxious about the new government, while Anders was damning: 'This government is utterly bereft of our trust and our view of it is decidedly negative.'[77]

There was another important diplomatic development in mid-1943. In June Stalin suddenly recalled Maisky, his ambassador in Britain, and Litvinov, his ambassador in the United States, to Moscow. Maisky was replaced by Fedor Gusev, who had been the Soviet ambassador in Canada. Cadogan had met Gusev before and noted: 'If M. Gusev is the man I remember, I should say he was not a good choice. His English was sparse and peculiar.' Clark Kerr described Gusev as 'like a sea calf and apparently no more articulate'. Indeed, when Harold Nicolson met Gusev he recorded: 'The Russian Ambassador cannot speak one word of any known language and is accompanied by an interpreter who grins horribly.'[78] Churchill and the Foreign Office were greatly concerned about the wider implications of Maisky's removal, since it occurred when the Soviet front seemed stalled, prior to the battle of Kursk, whereas the Allies were about to invade Sicily: a move which might lead Stalin to believe that the Allies would then turn their attention to an invasion of the Balkans, a region he wanted to control himself. Sir Orme Sargent came up with another possible reason for the changes:

> May he not have convinced himself that H.M.G. are not going seriously to discuss any political issues arising out of the present war situation; and that since M. Maisky has never been able to get down to any concrete discussions on these matters, he may as well abandon the idea of working through the Soviet Embassy in London.
>
> If this is really the case it has alarming possibilities, for it means that the Soviet Government, when we eventually do decide on negotiating with them and invite their collaboration, will have by that time made up their minds to plough a lonely furrow. It makes it all the more necessary, to my mind, that we should without delay put our cards on the table and show that we are ready to discuss with them questions such as the Polono-Russian frontier, the future of Germany, the handling of the States of Central Europe, the Balkans, etc.

Clark Kerr felt that these fears were exaggerated.[79] Whatever Stalin's motives were, it was now more apparent that there was an urgent need for the leaders of the Allies to have a face to face meeting to discuss the numerous challenges facing them.

With relations severed between Poland and the Soviet Union, Mikołajczyk's government was entirely dependent on the goodwill of Britain and the United States to act as intermediaries. Mikołajczyk himself was inexperienced in international affairs, and Retinger noted that Churchill showed little sympathy and: 'He acted like a kind of steamroller, hating any obstacle in his path and trying by sheer force of personality to crush anything which stood in the way of his own wishes and views on Polish-Russian relations.' Frank Roberts, who had many dealings with Mikołajczyk, believed that he 'had a very practical approach to what could be done and what couldn't'.[80] The question was: what did the Polish Government want, and to what extent were the British and American governments prepared to take on Stalin to achieve Polish wishes?

Mikołajczyk was never in a strong enough position in London to conduct foreign relations with the degree of independence demonstrated by Sikorski. Both Raczkiewicz and Sosnkowski were so strongly anti-Soviet that Mikołajczyk was in no position to make compromises on the issue of the future frontiers of Poland, nor did he have the permission of the main four political parties in Poland. On 15 August 1943, they issued a declaration setting out their aims in war and peace. Among the principles were:

a. The basic principle of the foreign policy should be the collaboration with the Allies, based on equality with a distinct emphasis on self-determination in affairs concerning Poland, her sovereign rights and the integrity of her territory.
b. A constant watchfulness concerning Soviet influence, which is becoming increasingly marked in the Allied countries and a ceaseless recalling to their consciousness of the latent danger in Russian-Communist totalitarian peace aims.
c. The securing to Poland of a Western and Northern frontier, which would guarantee to her a wide access to the sea, together with integrity of her Eastern frontier, as well as suitable indemnities.
d. The formation of a confederation of states of which the Polish-Czechoslovak union might be the nucleus.[81]

The overwhelming impression that is given by this document is that the political parties in Poland had no idea of the true impact of the break in relations between Poland and the Soviet Union. It was in broad agreement with the policy Sikorski had pursued but already, even before his death, this diplomacy had failed.

The Mikołajczyk government was determined to fight for the restoration of Poland's pre-war eastern frontier after the war, but did not realise the extent to which the British and American governments no longer believed that this was possible, and, indeed, were now forming arguments as to why it might not be even desirable. At the Quebec conference in August 1943, Eden sounded out Roosevelt's foreign policy adviser Henry Hopkins on American opinion, and, as he reported to Cadogan, Hopkins had told him that he 'knew that the President's mind about Russia's frontiers was almost exactly the same as my own'.[82] In other words, Roosevelt supported Britain's approval of the Curzon Line. Eden was preparing for the Moscow conference of the three foreign ministers, himself, Molotov and Cordell Hull, which was designed to iron out any difficulties and sound out opinions before Churchill, Roosevelt and Stalin met together for the first time, at Teheran. Eden very much wanted to resolve beforehand the question of Poland's eastern frontier at Moscow. Therefore, on 9 September 1943, he asked Mikołajczyk:

> Supposing that as a result of the war you would get East Prussia, valuable territories in Silesia and in the East, territories up to the Curzon Line extended by the inclusion of Lwów – so far as Wilno is concerned the prospects are much worse – would you consider such a solution acceptable?

Mikołajczyk responded by saying that he could not discuss the question, and the Polish record noted: 'Mr Eden evaded further discussion on that subject.'[83] Alerted now to the line Eden wanted to take at the Moscow conference, the Poles prepared their position. At another meeting with Eden, on 5 October, Mikołajczyk said that he welcomed the forthcoming conference but: 'At the same time the Polish Government was against entering into any conversation relating to Polish-Soviet frontiers, and it considered the resumption of mutual diplomatic relations to be the most important and urgent issue.'[84] Eden was both surprised and disappointed by the response, and wrote to O'Malley on the next day that he would have to go to Moscow 'as a mediator with a very weak hand'.[85]

The question remains: should the Poles have given more leverage to Eden at this point? Certainly, had the Poles been willing to negotiate on their frontiers, the Moscow conference would have provided the best opportunity, as it, as opposed to the subsequent conference at Teheran, had a clear agenda and many important issues were resolved there. Indeed, the assistant under secretary at the Foreign Office who accompanied Eden to Moscow, Sir William Strang, described it as 'perhaps the most fruitful of all the international ministerial conferences held during the war'.[86] It can be argued that if Eden and Hull had been able to demonstrate to Molotov that the Poles were prepared to go some distance towards meeting Soviet demands, then Molotov and Stalin might have been prepared to make the concession of granting Lwów to Poland. This, after all, could still have been represented as conforming to the Curzon Line, which divided into two as it entered East Galicia. It was also possibly the compromise that, had he still been alive and in power, Sikorski would have settled for. But the reasons against making such concessions at this point were, however, equally compelling. In the first place, Mikołajczyk did not have the political support necessary to give away a large portion of Polish territory. Second, he would have faced the opposition of the troops in the Middle East, something also of concern to the Allies. Whereas Mikołajczyk knew that the Poles would oppose concessions, Eden was uncertain about the extent of American support. From private conversations with Hopkins and State Department officials, Eden had been given the impression that the Americans accepted the Curzon Line and were in favour of Poland retaining Lwów, but he was also aware that in public the United States Government 'have always taken a very firm line against the recognition of any territorial changes effected by force and in an election year they will pay great attention to the well-organised Polish vote'.[87] Consequently, Eden was in a weak position regardless of what the Poles said.

The Moscow conference enabled the British and Americans to learn more about the Soviet attitude towards Poland. The reports of the new American ambassador in Moscow, Averell Harriman, who was present at the most important meetings, are revealing: he wrote to Roosevelt that 'the problem of Poland is even tougher than we believed'. Although the frontiers were not discussed, Harriman gained the strong impression that the Soviets were adamant in their demand for the 1941 border. He noted of a conversation with Litvinov, in which Eden participated: 'Litvinov started with a torrent of abuse against the Poles, the gist of it being that they would have to learn to live within their ethnographical boundaries as a small nation and give up the idea that they were a great power.' Both Eden and Harriman noted that the main matter of concern to the Soviets was the composition of the current Polish government: 'They regard the present Polish government in exile as hostile and therefore completely unacceptable to them.' The person who caused most offence was Sosnkowski. Eden had hoped to demonstrate the friendliness of the Polish Government by informing Molotov that the AK was preparing to rise up against the Germans and that the British were arming them, but Molotov was clearly not interested. The AK was loyal to the government in London and Molotov was not convinced that it would not resist the Soviet armies when they advanced into Poland. All three foreign ministers confirmed their desire to see 'the rise of an independent Poland'.[88] This would become a kind of mantra repeated so often by so many people as to become meaningless. When Mikołajczyk later asked him to define what was meant by 'an independent Poland', Eden had a 'fit of pique', and denied that the Soviets were planning to impose a communist-style government on Poland.[89]

The Moscow conference achieved nothing beneficial for the Poles. At their request the frontier issue had not been discussed and instead the spectre of a Soviet-imposed government in Poland had arisen. The Poles felt that the communiqué issued at the end showed that the Allies had split Europe into spheres of influence, with Poland placed firmly within the Soviet sphere. Ciechanowski transmitted a memorandum from the Polish Government to the State Department outlining the Poles' objections and their alarm that:

> The USA is willing to admit the occupation of Polish territory exclusively by Soviet forces, without the participation, in some form at least of American, British and Polish forces ... On the basis of past tragic experiences, as well as our intimate knowledge of Soviet methods, this would be equivalent to delivering Poland to the USSR for immediate and complete sovietisation.[90]

The Poles were now deeply apprehensive about the forthcoming meeting between the Big Three at Teheran.

On 16 November, the Polish Government set out its position in a memorandum for Churchill and Roosevelt. It is worth quoting at length because it represents the standpoint of the Polish Government which would remain largely unchanged over the next year:

> The unwillingness of the Polish Government to enter into discussions on frontier questions is based on the following considerations:
>
> 1) Poland, who entered the war in 1939 in defence of her territory, has never given up the fight and has not produced any Quisling, is fully entitled to expect that she will emerge from this war without reduction of her territory.
>
> 2) The Polish Eastern lands which are the object of Soviet claims extend to half of the territory of the Polish Republic. They contain important

centres of Polish national life. They are closely knitted with Poland by ties of tradition, civilization and culture. The Polish population which has resided there for centuries forms a relative majority of the population of these lands. On the other hand the lower density of their population and their possibilities of economic development furnish Poland with a socially sound means of solving the problem of the over-population of her Western and Southern provinces.

3) The Polish Government could not see their way to enter a discussion on the subject of territorial concessions above all for the reason that such a discussion in the absence of effective guarantees of Poland's independence and security on the part of Great Britain and the United States would be sure to lead further and further to ever new demands.

The attribution to Poland of Eastern Prussia, Danzig, Opole Silesia and the straightening and shortening of the Polish Western frontier are in any case dictated by the need to provide for the stability of future peace, the disarmament of Germany and the security of Poland and other countries of Central Europe. The transfer to Poland of these territories cannot therefore be treated fairly as an object of compensation for the cession to the USSR of Polish Eastern lands which for reasons adduced above do by no means represent to the USSR a value comparable to that which they have for Poland.

The Poles were also disappointed that no progress had been made towards the resumption of relations between Poland and the Soviet Union at the Moscow conference.[91] This was now an urgent matter because the Soviet armies were approaching the pre-war Polish frontier and their attitude towards the Polish underground was unknown. Therefore, Mikołajczyk 'appealed for guarantees and the safeguarding of the right of the Allied Polish Government to assure administration on Polish territory immediately after its liberation from German occupation'. The Poles received no response to their memorandum before Teheran, but were reassured by Eden that the talks there would primarily be on military strategy.[92]

The most striking point about the Teheran conference at the end of November 1943, viewed widely as a turning-point in the war, is the sheer casualness with which the decisions were reached. The American interpreter later wrote:

No one was in charge of organising meetings, setting up schedules, or handling any of the numerous technical preparations for the conference. Moreover, Roosevelt had no position papers on questions that would be discussed. It was my first experience with Roosevelt's informal method of operation. He preferred to act by improvisation rather than by plan.[93]

Churchill had wanted to meet Roosevelt prior to Teheran in order to reconcile their approaches on military strategy, but Roosevelt took steps to avoid such a meeting. The conference at Cairo, immediately preceding Teheran, was devoted to meetings with Chiang Kai-shek, designed to encourage the Chinese leader to take a more active part in the war against the Japanese. Consequently, the two western leaders arrived in Iran with their differences unresolved. As Roosevelt had once told Churchill, he was convinced: 'I can personally handle Stalin better than your Foreign Office or my State Department. Stalin hates the guts of all your top people. He thinks he likes me better and I hope he will continue to do so.'[94] Roosevelt treated the talks with Stalin with the same casualness as his fireside chats to the American people. His method of befriending Stalin was to mock Churchill openly in front of him, which naturally put Churchill on the defensive and forced him to attempt to curry favour with the Soviet leader.[95] The pawn to be sacrificed in this diplomatic game of chess was Poland.

The British position on Poland going into the conference was to accept the Curzon Line as Poland's future eastern frontier, to obtain compensation for Poland in the west and north in the form of territory taken from Germany, and to attempt to gain the guarantees the Polish Government wanted on the future political freedom of their country. Roosevelt's position was more complex: he believed that the frontier between Poland and the Soviet Union should lie east of the Curzon Line, with Lwów going to Poland. He also wanted the Poles to have the freedom to choose the government they wanted.[96] Given the aims of Churchill and Roosevelt prior to the conference, why then did they sacrifice Poland?

The answer lies in the discussions during the first plenary session on 28 November, which was devoted to military strategy. Stalin had been pressing the Allies to launch a Second Front since 1941. Now he became aware that, although both Churchill and Roosevelt were adamant that the Second Front would be launched in late spring or early summer 1944, there were significant differences of opinion between them as to the emphasis that should be placed on the invasion of France as opposed to continuing operations in Italy and launching a new front in the Balkans. Broadly speaking, Roosevelt wanted to concentrate on France, with a major invasion across the Channel into northern France and a subsidiary operation in southern France. While Churchill accepted the importance of the invasion of northern France, he was concerned about the consequences on operations elsewhere necessitated by diverting all available landing craft to the cross-Channel operation. He was also keen to explore the concept of an invasion of the Balkans to be carried out in collaboration with the Yugoslav partisans, a strategy the Poles were also extremely eager on seeing pursued because it would bring the forces of the western allies closer to Poland. But Roosevelt was not interested in what he saw as sideshows, and Stalin was opposed to allied operations in the Balkans because this was an area in which he saw the opportunity to dominate politically.

Therefore Stalin was in agreement with Roosevelt on the primacy of what would become Operation Overlord. As Cadogan noted in his diary: 'President promises everything that Stalin wants in the way of an attack in the West, with the result that Winston, who has to be more honest, is becoming an object of suspicion to Stalin.'[97] Churchill needed to do something to restore his prestige in Stalin's eyes. At dinner that evening Roosevelt was taken ill and retired early, leaving Churchill and Stalin to continue their talks. Totally unprompted, Churchill brought up the subject of Poland:

> Churchill then remarked that it would be very valuable if here in Teheran the representatives of the three governments could work out some agreed understanding on the question of the Polish frontiers which could then be taken up with the Polish Government in London. He said that, as far as he was concerned, he would like to see Poland moved westward in the same manner as soldiers at drill execute the drill 'left close' and illustrated his point with three matches representing the Soviet Union, Poland and Germany.[98]

Stalin did not indicate his opinion then but suggested postponing the discussion on Poland. Before Poland was discussed formally, Stalin learnt of Roosevelt's opinion when they had a private talk on 1 December. Roosevelt told Stalin that he believed that Poland should be moved westwards 'even to the River Oder'. Stalin now knew that, barring the exact definition of Poland's frontiers on the map, he had got what he wanted. Furthermore, and arguably even more importantly, Roosevelt's revelation of his position with the rider that he would not be able to make his position public for the next year because he could not risk alienating 6,000,000 American voters of Polish extraction before the 1944 presidential election was significant.[99] Stalin also now knew that Roosevelt would have to remain on the sidelines while Poland's future was decided. As Field Marshal Sir Alanbrooke expressed it, Stalin now had 'the president in his pocket'.[100]

Poland was discussed at the plenary section on the afternoon of 1 December. It was at this point that Stalin put forward his demand for the port of Königsberg, then in East Prussia, with the remainder of East Prussia going to Poland, and Churchill was taken aback by this but made no objection. Nor did he appear concerned about the implications of extending the Polish frontier as far westwards as the Oder nor of the consequent transfers of populations these frontier changes required. The main question was the Curzon Line. The Soviets were offended by the British reference to a period of the war they would prefer to forget, when asked how the Molotov–Ribbentrop Line differed from the Curzon Line. (The answer was that the province of Białystok remained in Poland according to the Curzon Line.) Roosevelt remained silent during the discussion of the frontiers, and Stalin was free to interpret this as acquiescence. At the Moscow conference, the Soviets had made the claim that the Polish Government and its underground forces in Poland were agents of the Germans, and at Teheran Stalin repeated this claim. Churchill was so determined to settle the frontier matter that he ignored Stalin's provocative statement.[101]

The Teheran conference was a complete victory for Stalin with regards to Poland. Churchill now faced the challenge of obtaining the agreement of the Poles in London, but they were never told formally of the decisions taken at Teheran, and remained ignorant that the fate of eastern Poland had been settled there. The Polish Government did, however, know that Stalin was convinced the Poles would be hostile to the arrival of the Soviet armies on their territory, and it was now up to the government to order the underground forces in Poland to come out into the open. The Soviet reaction to the appearance of these well-armed Poles would shape Poland's ever more desperate diplomacy during the course of 1944.

# 12

# Threats to the Standing of the Polish Government-in-Exile and the Polish Underground Authorities

By the end of 1943, the Polish Government had been comprehensively outmanoeuvred by the Big Three: it had become diplomatically isolated, and eastern Poland had been given to Stalin by Churchill and Roosevelt at the Teheran conference. But for Stalin to be able to absorb eastern Poland into the Soviet Union after it had been liberated from German occupation, and for him to ensure political dominance over the entire population of Poland, the authority of the Polish Government in London had to be undermined. Hence Stalin sponsored communist Poles resident in the Soviet Union, who could be relied upon do his bidding. Stalin and the Polish communists had two powerful tools: the Polish people who remained in the Soviet Union after the evacuations in 1942, and the Polish Army formed from these people, which was for the most part loyal to the Polish communists. It would fight alongside the Red Army and bring many of the exiled Poles back to Poland.

Events in eastern Poland, of which the Polish Government had only a limited knowledge, facilitated the process of destroying its authority there. The Ukrainian insurgency and the ethnic cleansing of the Polish population in Wołyń and East Galicia began the process of depolonising the east. At the same time, there was a state of near anarchy in the forests of eastern Poland, which were an ideal terrain for partisan warfare against the Germans, and a safe haven for fugitives from German oppression. Only one group in the forests, the AK, was loyal to the Polish Government, while others owed allegiance to the Soviet Union, or to the Polish communists. All of these groups spent more time fighting each other than fighting the Germans, and only one thing was certain: that no one group of any political persuasion or loyalty was in total control.

The Ukrainian population of pre-war Poland had felt no great loyalty to the Polish Government, and in September 1939 they had greeted the Soviet invasion hopeful that they would be freed from Polish rule. They were, but far from the independent Ukrainian state the nationalists desired, the new 'Western Ukraine' was incorporated into the Soviet Union and many of their leading agitators were deported to Siberia. Consequently, in June 1941, the Ukrainians greeted the Germans as liberators, and the OUN declared the independence of Ukraine in Lwów on 31 June. The Germans, however, responded by imprisoning OUN leaders, such as Stepan Bandera, in Sachsenhausen concentration camp and killing or imprisoning about 80 per cent of the Ukrainian leadership. Worse still, the lands the Ukrainians laid claim to were split between two Nazi administrations: Wołyń was included in Ostland Ukraine, ruled over by Reichskommissar Erich Koch, while East Galicia was incorporated into the General Government. But the Germans also exploited the disloyalty of the Ukrainians towards the Poles by recruiting large numbers into their auxiliary units and into the Roland and Nachtigel battalions. They became the Germans' most willing assistants and received German uniforms, arms and training before undertaking their main task, the destruction of the Jews: both in the concentration camps, where the Ukrainians acted as guards, and by shooting huge numbers of Jews in the eastern provinces. The Ukrainians also provided the Gestapo with lists of prominent Poles, whom the Germans then shot.

The German defeat at Stalingrad in February 1943 and the prospect of a Soviet advance into eastern Poland led the ethnic Ukrainian Poles to reconsider how they could win their independence. The OUN feared a rerun of the end of the First World War, when German defeat and Russian exhaustion had left a power vacuum in the region which the Poles had filled through armed action. Indeed, this appears to have been exactly what the Poles themselves were thinking: the AK informed the Polish Government that a rapid campaign against the Ukrainians would be necessary as a corollary to the national armed uprising against the Germans, and Wołyń and East Galicia would have to be subjected to an 'armed occupation'. The OUN had split into two parts in 1940, with the older and more moderate members supporting the OUN-M led by Andriy Melnvk, but the younger and more radical members supporting the aims of their mentor Bandera and establishing the OUN-B. At a meeting of the OUN-B in February 1943, they decided to create their own army, the Ukrainian Insurrectionist Army (*Ukrains'ka Povstans'ka Armiia*, UPA), which at its height numbered 40,000 men. The principal aim of the UPA was not to attack the Germans but to cleanse eastern Poland/Western Ukraine of all Poles:

> We should undertake a great action of liquidation of the Polish element. We should take advantage of the occasion, before German forces withdraw, to liquidate the entire Polish population from 16 to 60 ... We cannot lose this battle and, without counting the cost, we should diminish the Polish strength. Forest villages and those near forests should disappear from the face of the earth.[1]

A later order urged the UPA to 'pay attention to the fact that when something remains that is Polish, then the Poles will have pretensions to our land'.[2]

In April 1943, the UPA began their attacks on the defenceless Polish population of Wołyń before extending their operations southwards to encompass East Galicia and westwards into the province of Lublin. Sometimes the UPA repeated the tactics used against the Jews, gathering the Poles together in a large group before marching them to a sheltered spot to murder them: 'They drove us from the clearing into a field of stubble. There, they took a few people at a time, made them lie down, and shot them.' Between 300 and 400 Poles in this group had been killed before the UPA abandoned the remainder when they learned that the Germans were approaching. Elsewhere whole villages were slaughtered:

> In the garden by a linden tree, a pit was dug. In it lay about 70 murdered, half-buried people. The blood, which flowed like a river onto the road from the pit, was now congealed. They threw the children into a potato cellar and covered them with dirt. Those still alive were finished off with clubs that still lay nearby, all bloody. Dead children floated in the well. The buildings were burned to hide all traces.[3]

A feature of the UPA action was its sheer barbarity. They were not content merely to shoot their victims but often tortured them first or desecrated their bodies afterwards. A fifteen-year-old girl, Bronisława Murawska-Żygadło came home to find a dreadful scene:

> I saw my father lying in a pool of blood by the entrance to the house. Not too far away lay the butchered remains of my brother, Adam. Two-year-old Basia lay outside by the window. She was also dead, pierced through either with a bayonet or a knife. I found my mother's lifeless body next door in my uncle's yard; her head was cut to shreds. Not far away lay my Uncle Aleksander, murdered together with his two daughters aged seven and nine.[4]

The Poles were murdered with guns, knives, scythes, burnt alive, buried alive, thrown down wells to drown: it appeared that the UPA left no method of killing untried. Simple methods were used to distinguish between the Poles, who were normally Roman Catholic, and the Ukrainians, who were usually Eastern Orthodox. For example, a UPA member would ask his victim to make the sign of the cross, since each faith did this differently, and if the victim did it the Catholic way then death followed. The UPA also took advantage of the fact that the Poles celebrated Christmas earlier than those Ukrainians who followed the Eastern rite, and murdered hundreds of Poles as they prayed in their highly flammable wooden churches. Not all Ukrainians joined the UPA and many Ukrainians tried to shelter their Polish neighbours and ended up sharing the same appalling fates.

The local AK reported back to its headquarters, which transmitted the news of the slaughters to the government in London. The AK seemed unable to save the Poles from the wrath of the UPA. Orders were received to retaliate against the UPA and those villages which supported them, but not to mount indiscriminate attacks on the Ukrainian population.[5] Tens of thousands of Poles fled the region, but others remained and formed self-defence units to take revenge against the Ukrainians. These avengers faced a difficult choice: the only people able to give them protection and arms were the Germans and the Soviet partisans. In April 1943, the Germans had stood aside and taken no action while the UPA murdered 600 Poles in Janowa Dolina.[6] In July 1943, however, shocked by the scale of the anarchy, the Germans deployed a battalion of Polish policemen, *Schutzmannschaftbataillon* 202, recruited to replace Ukrainian deserters, in Wołyń to attack Ukrainian villages in retaliation for the night of 11–12 July when the UPA coordinated attacks on 167 localities and killed around 10,000 Poles.[7] The AK attempted to reassert the authority of the Polish Government by calling for the self-defence units to place themselves under its command, but it was not in a strong position in Wołyń and took time to build up its forces. In January 1944, the 27th Volhynian Infantry Division was formed by the AK and its 6,558 members fought the UPA and then the Germans.[8]

The campaign of ethnic cleansing was most successful in Wołyń because its Polish population was more scattered and so did not learn of events elsewhere until it was too late to run and hide, and also because the AK was relatively weak there. While Ukrainian nationalism was probably stronger in East Galicia, the UPA had less success there. It mainly recruited from Ukrainians who had previously served the Germans but had now either deserted or had their units disbanded. In East Galicia the Germans offered an alternative to the UPA: the SS *Galizien* Division. This was the brainchild of the German governor, SS Grüppenführer Dr Gustav Wächter, who saw the recruitment of a Ukrainian division as part of the solution to the growing manpower shortage in the Wehrmacht. On 28 April, the formation of SS *Galizien* Division was announced, and within ten days, 32,000 recruits had come forward and 26,000 were accepted for training: by the beginning of July, this number had risen to 28,000.[9] The AK issued a warning that anyone joining this division would be branded as a traitor and face the ultimate penalty, death. The SS *Galizien* recruits were sent for training in Dębrica in southeast Poland, while their officers went to officer training camps scattered throughout German-occupied Europe. SS *Galizien* first saw action in July 1944 when it was sent to reinforce the 13th German Army Corps near Brody in south-east Poland, but only 3,000 of the 11,000 men survived the Soviet attack. Some of the survivors deserted; the remainder were sent to Germany for further training and received reinforcements before seeing action in Slovakia in autumn 1944 and in Slovenia in early 1945.[10]

As the German-Soviet front neared the pre-war Polish frontier at the beginning of 1944, the UPA attacks grew more desperate and daring and extended into East Galicia. Adela Zacharko in the county of Boków in Tarnopol province recalled of February 1944:

At this time, Podhajce was caught in a game of see-saw between Soviet and Germans troops. Once, when the Germans reoccupied it, the Ukrainian Nationalists struck again to finish off the survivors of their previous attacks now convalescing in hospital. During that siege Wiktor Jaźwinski and Sister Janina, the head nurse in the hospital, gathered all their patients (predominantly children) into one room, barricaded the door, and began to pray.

As the Ukrainian Nationalists hacked away at the door, shots rang out in the rear of the hospital and shouts were heard in the Russian language. Under Soviet threat, the UPA abandoned its attack and retreated.[11]

The AK was much stronger in East Galicia and was able to protect the Poles. The Germans also protected the Poles there. For example, the Carmelite monastery in Wiśniowiec became a Polish sanctuary under the protection of the German and Hungarian troops stationed there. The UPA launched an attack as soon as they left and murdered almost all the Poles together with the monks who had been sheltering them. The slaughter was stopped only when the Germans briefly returned.[12] When the Soviets had secured an area, they would help the Poles flee westwards, because it suited their political purposes to denude the provinces of former eastern Poland of the Polish population. After the war the Soviets would turn their attention to the UPA, to destroy it in turn. It has been estimated that 30,000–40,000 Poles died in Wołyń, 10,000–20,000 in eastern Galicia and 10,000–20,000 in Lublin province in this often-overlooked civil war. About 10,000 Ukrainians were killed by Polish self-defence units, Soviet partisans and the German military and police.[13]

Poles fled from the Ukrainians into the forests of eastern Poland, and so did Ukrainians who no longer wanted to serve the Germans, adding another layer to the confusion already existing there. These forests were both dense and extensive and became the safe haven for numerous groups: Soviet deserters from 1941; escaped Soviet POWs; Jews who had fled from the ghettos, some of whom would form family camps and hope to escape the Germans, and others who formed partisan bands to take their revenge on the Germans; and local people of Polish, Belorussian or Ukrainian ethnicity who wanted to escape being rounded up and transported to Germany as forced labour. All had one aim in common: the desire to survive. They had few means at their disposal and consequently preyed on the local population for food: 'At night the partisans would come with their demands; during the day, the Germans.'[14] There were also more organised groups sheltering in the forests: the AK, lying in wait for the opportune moment to launch a national uprising against the Germans, and the Soviet partisans and units of the Polish communist People's Army (*Gwarda Ludowa-Armia Ludowa*, GL-AL). Their strategies were very different. The AK engaged in sabotage and diversionary operations but launched no direct attacks on the Germans so as to save the local population from severe German reprisals. Their units were led by the *Cichociemni*, the 'unseen and silent', Polish paratroopers trained in Britain and despatched to Poland by SOE. The GL-AL had no such scruples and launched small-scale and largely purposeless attacks against German outposts regardless of the consequences. The result could be tragic for the local population: for example, in May 1942, after the GL-AL had assassinated one German officer and two German officials, 1,200 Poles were shot by the Germans in Święciany (Švenčionys).[15]

During 1943 the situation in the forests of eastern Poland became more complicated because both the Poles and the Soviets were determined to stamp their authority over it. In May 1942, a Central Partisan Staff had been established at Soviet headquarters under the command of Marshal Voroshilov, and Soviet parachutists were despatched into pre-war Polish territory to organise the disparate Soviet soldiers into cohesive partisan units; this process really took effect during 1943. The first Polish partisan units loyal to the AK also began operating at this time. The unit commanded by Flying Officer 'Dzwig' started with 44 men but, after a successful raid on a German garrison to steal arms and ammunition, grew rapidly so that soon it was battalion strength with 3 infantry companies and 1 cavalry squadron. A member of the group recalled: 'We had all sorts of difficulties. Equipment, food, liaison, intelligence, training – everything was badly lacking or non-existent ... Thanks to the generosity of the population we were also fed and armed, as, after the defeat of General Popov's Soviet armies, the peasants hid a lot of ammunition and arms.'[16]

The history of the partisans operating in eastern Poland is controversial. From German records it is possible to establish that a great deal of sabotage was conducted against the German rail communications to the front, but not necessarily by whom.[17] Indeed, one historian has claimed:

Among all partisans a discrepancy existed between the value placed on fighting and the actual number of attacks on Germans. It was as if the pressure to oppose the Germans lost its momentum somewhere on the way to the real strikes. This lack of correspondence between ideas and actions was probably responsible for some of the exaggerated claims about extraordinary anti-Nazi escapades.[18]

Historiography has further confused the matter: for post-war political purposes, the communists claimed that only the GL-AL and Soviet partisans undertook armed action against the Germans. Jewish historians tend to agree with this claim, adding that the AK not only failed to attack the Germans but concentrated on killing Jews. In its defence, loyalists to the AK claim that both the Soviet partisan bands and the GL-AL attacked the Polish partisans and that the Jews often helped. It does not help that the loyalty of units such as the Kościuszko unit operating in the Nalibocka forest in the Nowogródek province is claimed by both the AK and the GL-AL.[19] To make matters still more confusing, individuals sometimes moved from one group to another. For example, Florian Mayevski began with the AK and then was persuaded by the Soviets that as a Jew he would be happier working with the Soviet partisans.[20] The position of the Jews who wished to fight was undoubtedly the most complex. Some AK units were anti-semitic but others allowed Jews to join them, while the Soviet partisans claimed to welcome Jews, particularly if they possessed their own weapons, but also accepted Ukrainian recruits who earlier had shot large numbers of Jews at the behest of the Germans. Poles sometimes even joined Jewish partisan groups. For example, a Jewish partisan recalled: '15 Poles joined us. Their homes had been burned and they barely escaped alive. They stayed with us for 4–5 months, and we fought the Banderites four times. Each time Jews and Poles were killed, as were Banderites.'[21]

An American report by the OSS accurately summed up the situation in the forests: 'One thing is certain, the Germans are helped by the lack of unity in the underground and by the fact that each side has other aims than fighting the Germans.'[22] Nevertheless, the Germans were extremely disturbed by the anarchy prevailing in part of the territory they claimed to control – and by the extent of the sabotage. They were clear about classifying the inhabitants of the forests: they were not 'partisans', which would necessitate treating them as POWs, but were 'bandits' who could be executed upon capture. Indeed, they had an entire doctrine devoted to the eradication of what they termed banditry: *Bandenbekämpfung*.[23] In the summer of 1943, the Germans devoted

10 per cent of their forces on the Eastern Front to the destruction of the partisans, and, on 1 August, launched a 'Big Sweep' of the Nalibocka forest, which led to a temporary alliance between the Polish partisans and a local Soviet partisan unit commanded by Comrade Sidoruk. As the Germans entered the forest, with several thousand troops, including an SS division, and with armoured cars and tanks, the Poles managed to ambush and destroy their advance guard. The Germans soon, however, regained the initiative.

> The German round-up resulted in the complete disintegration of the battalion and in the loss of most of the arms. Our losses were about twenty killed and about a hundred missing. Some of them dispersed over the countryside, and some were picked up by the Germans from the villages, as civilians, and sent to concentration camps.[24]

The Soviet partisans attempted to place the blame for the debacle on the Poles, and relations between them worsened. After the 'Big Sweep', which failed to capture or kill many partisans, the Germans burnt all villages within a 10-mile radius and deported 20,000 local peasants for forced labour in Germany.[25]

The German anti-partisan action exacerbated the poor relations already existing between Polish and Soviet partisan units. In late August, the Soviet 'Voroshilov' Brigade attacked an AK unit, disarmed it and executed 8 of its members; the AK retaliated by attacking Belorussian villages in the Nowogródek region where the peasants were suspected of giving aid to the Soviet partisans.[26] At the end of November 1943, as the Soviet forces neared the pre-war Polish-Soviet frontier, General Panteleimon Ponamarenko, the chief of staff of the Soviet partisan command, issued an order calling for the disarming of all Polish partisan units and the shooting of those who resisted.[27] As the Polish partisans knew nothing of this order, their commanders had no fear when invited to meet the Soviet partisan commander, Major Wasiliewicz, on 1 December 1943. The Soviets asked the Poles to assemble their units and then surrounded the Poles with sub-machine guns at the ready and disarmed them.[28] On the one hand, Poles operating with the AK noted that on occasion the Germans and Soviets would collaborate: 'Sometimes the Germans and Russian-led communists were quite close to each other, each in turn attacking the Home Army partisans while leaving the other alone.'[29] On the other, the duplicity of the Soviet partisans led to some

AK units giving a favourable response to the suggestion by the Germans in the Nowogródek and Wilno provinces that the AK should accept arms and supplies from the Germans in return for engaging in anti-partisan warfare. On 9 December 1943, days after the bulk of his unit had been disarmed by the Soviet partisans as described above, Captain Adolf 'Góra' Pilch signed an agreement with the Germans and began to receive supplies from them, as did Lieutenant Józef 'Lech' Świda in Lida and Aleksander 'Wilk' Krzyżanowski in the Wilno area. All these agreements were condemned by AK command and by General Sosnkowski in London.[30]

There have been claims that the AK attacked Jews rather than Germans. Again this is a misunderstanding of what was really happening in the forests. In general, Jews were killed in armed clashes not because they were Jews but rather because their ideological leanings had led them to join the GL-AL rather than the AK. Indeed, the Jews sometimes killed the Poles: in late 1943, the Soviet partisans mounted an attack on the Polish Kościuszko unit in the Nalibocka forest and the Bielski camp was requested to send 50 men to help the Soviets and did so. When in September 1943, a rogue AK unit *Orzeł*, commanded by Lieutenant Leon Szymbierski, wiped out a ŻOB unit in the Koniecpol area, killing 5 Jews, he was put on trial by the AK in Kielce and condemned to death.[31] The principal perpetrators of anti-Jewish violence in the name of anti-communist activity were units owing allegiance to the right-wing NSZ, which remained outside the structure of the AK until March 1944 and even after then some units retained their independence. The NSZ newspaper, *The Rampart*, called for action against the communists:

> It is time to awake and commence with the systematic liquidation of centres under the command of the Communists, and as soon as territory is cleared in this fashion to undertake the planned struggle with the German occupier. The sincere joint work of Polish military and civilian organizations will certainly make it possible for us to pull out the Bolshevik weeds and cleanse the terrain. The PPR, Peoples' Guard, and various 'red' partisans must vanish from the surface of the Polish land.[32]

The NSZ was quick to take up the sword. On 22 July 1943, they destroyed a GL-AL unit *Waryński* at Stefanów near Kielce in retaliation for a GL-AL attack on the NSZ earlier that year. The most notorious clash between the two groups came on 9 August 1943, when a NSZ detachment ambushed and murdered 26 GL-AL partisans and 4 civilians near the village of Borów in Lublin province.[33] The NSZ was openly anti-semitic and would kill Jews in the forests or betray them to the Germans. When Marian Skowerski was released from Gestapo custody in Kielce, he went into the forests in search of the AK. He instead found the NSZ, who asked him to kill some nearby Jews as a test of faith before being allowed to join them. Skowerski refused and travelled on until he found an AK unit, which he joined.[34] The AK condemned the anti-semitic conduct of the NSZ and its part in the murders at Borów.[35]

Stalin wanted to create a Polish government that was 'friendly' towards the Soviet Union and he followed several strategies simultaneously. He cultivated the Polish communists, who were despatched to Poland to seek support for a new communist-dominated government and to create its own underground army, the GL-AL, which would challenge the claim of the AK to be the principal resistance movement. At the same time Stalin encouraged the Polish communists in the Soviet Union to become an organised political force, whose strength was to be underpinned by the creation of a communist Polish army. His policies preceded the break in diplomatic relations with the Polish Government in London and continued apace after it and as the Soviet armies began to approach the pre-war Polish-Soviet frontier.

The pre-war history of the Polish Communist Party, the KPP, had not been a happy one. It had had few members, mostly concentrated in the cities, and many future important personalities, such as Władysław Gomułka, Bolesław Bierut, Stefan Jędrychowski, Edward Ochab and Aleksander Zawadzki, had been imprisoned by the Polish Government. This, ironically, saved their lives because in 1938 Stalin disbanded the KPP for its 'Trotskyist and nationalist tendencies', and during the Great Terror 46 full members and 24 non-voting so-called candidate members of the Central Committee of the KPP who had fled to the Soviet Union were shot. Following the German invasion of Poland, the surviving communists fled to the Soviet zone of occupation, where they were now welcomed, and settled in Lwów, Białystok and Mińsk. There they disseminated Soviet propaganda through their newspaper *Czerwony Sztandar* (*Red Banner*). After the German invasion of the Soviet Union, they were evacuated with Soviet officials, first to Moscow and then to

Kuibyshev where they continued to produce a number of journals and also made Polish-language broadcasts for Poland.[36]

Soon after his meeting with Sikorski at the Kremlin in early December 1941, Stalin began to explore the possibilities of creating a new Communist Party in Poland and designated the head of the Comintern, Georgi Dimitrov, as his spokesman. In late December, a group of Polish communists, led by Marceli Nowotko, Paweł Finder and Bolesław Mołojec, were parachuted into Poland, with the aim, as discussed with Dimitrov, not to re-form the old Communist Party, but to appeal to a broader front of left-wing parties. The Polish Workers' Party (*Polska Partia Robotnicza*, PPR) was formally established in Warsaw on 5 January 1942, and throughout the year Nowotko sent Dimitrov optimistic reports concerning the possibilities of collaboration with the Polish Socialist Party and the Peasant Party. Actually recruitment for the PPR was slow, and by June 1942 it had only between 3,000 and 4,000 members and about the same number in its military wing, the *Gwarda Ludowa* (GL). Indeed, this congruity has led to the suggestion that the PPR was inflating its membership figures by deliberately assuming that every GL member was also a party member.[37] This was likely to be the case since communism had already been unpopular in Poland before the war and had became more so since 1939 with the Soviet occupation of eastern Poland. Communism was perceived by most people as an agency of a foreign power.

On 15 January 1943, the PPR issued an open letter to the Underground Government calling for active armed resistance to the Germans and for a statement from the Polish Government in London condemning the anti-Soviet stance of the pre-war *Sanacja* regime. With Sikorski's permission, the Underground Government held talks with the PPR in February, but they were unsure of the PPR's motivation: it was calling for a new 'democratic' government without defining its interpretation of 'democracy'. The Underground Government leaders were highly suspicious of the PPR's links with the Soviet Union. Before they could reply to the PPR's proposals, the PPR had issued a political programme – 'What are we fighting for?' – and TASS had put out a new statement castigating the Polish Government over its refusal to allow the ethnic minorities in Kresy to be reunited in one country, the Soviet Union. The PPR also suggested that it wanted to forge closer links between its army, the GL, and the AK, and attempts had been made in this direction earlier. However, as Jan Karski reported to the American ambassador to the Polish Government, Drexel Biddle, in March 1943, when contacts were established and the PPR and GL had discovered the identities of those working in the Underground Government and AK, those men had been betrayed and were arrested by the Gestapo. As a result anyone who was contacted by the communists had to be immediately quarantined from his colleagues.[38] The Underground Government consequently broke off all contacts with the PPR and the GL.

Events had intervened to grant the PPR a period of temporary independence from Soviet control during which it could develop its own programme. On 28 November 1942, Nowotko had been killed by an unknown assassin in Warsaw and his position as leader of the PPR had been taken over by Mołojec. Members of the PPR suspected that he might have had something to do with Nowotko's murder and in late December 1942, Mołojec himself was killed in Warsaw, and the party leadership passed to Paweł Finder.[39] Contact with the Soviet Union was then broken in November 1943 when the Gestapo penetrated the PPR, arrested a number of leaders, including Finder, who was later executed by the Germans, and seized a crucial codebook. The leadership was now taken over by Władysław Gomułka. This freed the surviving PPR to abandon the Popular Front approach favoured by the Soviet Union and to launch a radical programme blatantly designed to establish communist rule in post-war Poland. It established a National Council for the Homeland (*Krajowa Rada Narodowa*, KRN) with Bierut as its president. The first manifesto was issued on 31 December 1943. This expressly denied that the Polish Government in London had any right to represent the Polish people, and stated that the future frontiers of Poland were to follow the Curzon Line in the east and reach the Oder and the Baltic in the west and north. This was much the same policy as that adopted by the Union of Polish Patriots (*Związek Patriotów Polskich*, ZPP), sponsored by Stalin, in the Soviet Union. The KRN, however, adopted a far more radical programme: only the PPR was to be viewed as a party, all other parties were relegated to the status of 'groups'. The economic programme was more radical than that promoted by the Polish communists in the Soviet Union: industry was to be nationalised, and large estates and those owned by Germans were to be expropriated by the state without compensation. Furthermore, the PPR/KRN created its own army, which it would later use to impose its will over the country after liberation. The *Gwarda Ludowa* was renamed the *Armia Ludowa* (AL), with General Michał 'Rola' Żymierski as its head. Rola-Żymierski, as he became known, claimed command of all Polish armed forces whether in Poland or abroad in the Soviet Union or in the west.[40]

Stalin cultivated the friendship of prominent Polish communists in the Soviet Union. The most important undoubtedly was Wanda Wasilewska. Her father Leon had been active in left-wing politics in pre-war Poland and a close associate of Piłsudski. Wanda shared his interest from a young age, finally turning towards the communists in the mid-1930s. She married Aleksandr Korniejczuk, a deputy commissar of Soviet foreign affairs, and was admitted to membership of the Soviet Communist Party. Wasilewska had a direct telephone line to Stalin, and this indicated her far greater influence with Stalin than many older and more experienced members of the former KPP. According to one of them, Jakub Berman, they bore no resentment for this state of affairs but rather 'we were rather glad that she was clearing the way with Stalin for reactivating the Polish communist party, since this reactivation had, after all, been the most sacred aim of our efforts'.[41]

In February 1943, despairing of ever achieving what he wanted from the Polish Government, Stalin summoned Wasilewska, Hilary Minc and Wiktor Grosz to a meeting to discuss the future of Polish communism and left-wing activism. He made it clear that he expected a formal break in diplomatic relations between the Soviet Union and the Polish Government in London to be only a matter of time. The result of this meeting was the establishment of the Union of Polish Patriots. Wasilewska claimed that Stalin proposed the name of the party, deliberately choosing one that was vague enough to appeal to Poles of all political persuasions.[42] This broad appeal was confirmed by the articles published in the Union of Polish Patriots' new weekly newspaper, *Wolna Polska* (*Free Poland*), the first issue of which appeared on 1 March 1943. It concentrated on the promotion of patriotism and tried to conceal its political origins, aiming at 'uniting all Polish patriots living in the USSR, regardless of their past, their views and convictions, in the joint task of waging an uncompromising struggle against the German invaders'. A number of articles called for lasting friendship with the Soviet Union and denounced the Polish Government in London.[43]

Stalin did not want the ZPP to be an overtly communist party since that would alienate the Polish population in the Soviet Union, and his sponsorship would risk alarming the Allies, who might then thwart his desire for the Curzon Line. Consequently, the membership of the presidium of the Union of Polish Patriots was deliberately designed to persuade everyone that the Union was a broad-based political movement based on the Popular Front model that had ruled France between 1936 and 1937. To further this end, the chairmanship was given to Andrzej Witos, the brother of Wincenty Witos, who had been a famous and popular leader of the Peasant Party in pre-war Poland. At its first congress in Moscow on 9 and 10 June 1943, the Union of Polish Patriots announced its economic programme, which was designed to appeal to as many people as possible. It included policies such as the confiscation of large landed estates and the free redistribution of land to small farmers and landless agricultural workers. The landowners, except for the Germans, would receive compensation. Industries would be nationalised and cartels broken up, but this nationalisation would end after the post-war reconstruction of industry.[44]

Towards the end of 1943, with the advance of the Soviet armies towards the frontier of pre-war Poland, the ZPP established the Polish National Committee (*Polski Komitet Narodowy*, PKN). Jakub Berman later explained the reasons:

> The rapidly changing international situation demanded that we take some steps. The idea was born of establishing a representative body in the form of the Polish National Committee. The ZPP was concerned with refugees, welfare and education, while we wanted to broaden our base of influence and, in the face of the rapid progression of the war, to prepare the ground for a Polish government.[45]

The PKN hoped to be the precursor of a provisional Polish government that would care for Polish interests in Poland until the liberation of the country when elections would be held. It still planned to appear to be a coalition of all but the *Sanacja* parties, while actually ensuring that the communists controlled all the key ministries.[46]

The Union of Polish Patriots claimed to represent those Poles who were still in the Soviet Union. So who were these Poles and how many of them were there? They fell into several categories. There were many who had been unable to reach the Anders army before the evacuation; some had been in remote labour camps and heard of the amnesty too late or not heard of the amnesty at all. Others had been stopped on their way south and directed to work in kolkhozy and in industry to allevi-ate the acute manpower shortage occasioned by the call-up of every able-bodied male for the Red Army. Then there were those families of servicemen who qualified for evacuation but who lacked the money to travel, or who, fearing an uncertain future, did not make their way inde-pendently to the evacuation port of Krasnovodsk on the Caspian Sea. In addition, the NKVD had informed many Poles that they did not qualify for recruitment to the Anders army and thus for evacuation: most com-monly because they were not considered to be ethnic Poles. Accurate statistical information on their numbers is hard to find. A Polish Gov-ernment estimate in April 1943 gave a number of 271,325 Polish citizens with many thousands still unaccounted for, while a report sub-mitted to Stalin by Beria that January had given a lower total figure and a more detailed breakdown: 92,224 ethnic Poles, 102,153 Jews, 14,202 Ukrainians and 6,502 Belorussians, making a total of 215,081 pre-war Polish citizens.[47]

These Polish citizens were now a tool in Stalin's policy towards Poland. He had issued a challenge to the freedom of operation granted to the Polish Government by the Sikorski–Maisky agreement when, in the summer of 1942, the NKVD began arresting members of the Polish *Delegatura*, the network through which the Polish Government com-municated with the scattered Poles and looked after their welfare. Stanisław Kot resigned his post as Polish ambassador to the Soviet Union in July 1942, on the grounds of ill-health and was replaced by Tadeusz Romer. Prior to his departure he held a final conversation with Andrei Vyshinsky, the deputy commissar for foreign affairs, on 8 July. Kot brought up the question of the arrests of the delegates, but Vishin-sky was adamant that they had been arrested because they had been engaged in espionage rather than welfare activities. Kot denied this charge and referred to specific delegates, such as Arlet and Rola-Janicki, but Vyshinsky was unwilling to discuss the cases of individuals. Kot asked who was now to look after the welfare of the Poles, many of whom were too young, too old or too sick to work, and was not content with the reply that the Soviet authorities would take up the responsibil-ity. Further proof of the Soviet authorities' determination to curb the independence of the delegates came when the Polish chargé d'affaires, Juliusz Sokolnicki, reported to Kot, by then in Teheran, that there had been further arrests. Vyshinsky had issued a statement: 'because all the delegation had engaged in hostile activity and espionage instead of welfare they are to be liquidated and the authorities have been given instructions'.[48] Some of the delegates disappeared into the Gulag, but international intervention on behalf of those who held diplomatic passports ensured the release of 93 in October 1942. Romer suggested that the Poles and Soviets should set up a joint agency to distribute the aid, but this appeal was rejected by the Soviets.[49]

In January 1943, Stalin made an overt challenge to the Polish Government's refusal to recognise the 1941 borders as the new Polish-Soviet frontier, when his government informed the Polish embassy in Moscow that henceforward all Polish deportees in the Soviet Union were to be regarded as Soviet citizens. The reason given was the lack of recognition of the validity of the Curzon Line by the Polish Government. The Polish Government immediately appealed to the British and United States governments: on 2 February, the Polish foreign minister, Raczyński, approached Eden, and on 16 February, the Polish ambassador in Washington, Jan Ciechanowski, met Roosevelt. Churchill and Roosevelt were, however, in a very weak negotiating position because of the disparity between the military fortunes of the Allies. While Stalin was in the process of inflicting a crucial defeat on the Germans at Stalingrad, the western allies were taking a long time to clear North Africa, the Arctic convoys were slow in bringing substantial levels of aid to the Soviet Union, and the launch of the Second Front appeared no closer.

All over the Soviet Union the 25,000 Poles who had received Polish passports were summoned to their local NKVD office and forced to surrender their papers and their amnesty documents which they had received in the second half of 1941. Then they would either be issued with a Soviet passport or have to sign a form applying for such a passport. Their despair over relinquishing their precious documents, the only papers which could secure their release from the living hell of life in the Soviet Union, is not hard to imagine. Whereas in November 1939, traumatised by the complete upheaval in their lives occasioned by the German and Soviet invasions, relatively few Poles in eastern Poland had resisted the issue of Soviet citizenship papers, the situation was very different now. It seemed that all hope of survival and of departure was being extinguished and so the majority resisted: they felt that they had nothing to lose. Tens of thousands of Poles refused to sign and were imprisoned, and one wrote of their treatment:

> We were placed in cells, one Pole in each. Into these cells, almost at once, five or six Soviet prisoners of the criminal class were also introduced. These criminals not only stole our food but also beat us and persecuted us day and night. The NKVD chief or other officials would summon me several times a day and ask me whether I would not now accept a Soviet passport.

Small children, terrified and starving, were brought to see their mothers in prison to persuade them to change their minds.[50] Janka Tuzinkiewicz, in Kazakhstan, was imprisoned until, weak with hunger and deeply concerned about the Kochański children in her care, she accepted a Soviet passport. Those who held out were tried by the Soviet courts and received sentences of from 2 to 5 years in the Gulag.

Concern about the plight of their families in the Soviet Union adversely affected the morale of the Anders army. The British recognised the seriousness of the problem and in February, March and August 1943, both the British and American governments appealed to Stalin to allow the remaining members of military families and orphans to leave the Soviet Union.[51] The number was estimated at 50,000, which caused a degree of concern among the British authorities in the Middle East as to their ability to care for so many.[52] In September Stalin responded:

> The Soviet Government on several occasions has stated and states again that from the side of the Soviet Government no obstacles were placed in the way of the departure from the Soviet Union of Polish citizens in the USSR, the number of which was not large, or of the families of Polish soldiers who have been evacuated to Iran.[53]

This was disingenuous, for the challenges of the previous evacuations had already been considerable: reaching the nearest railway and then travelling to the Caspian Sea before taking a ship across to Pahlevi. At least the Soviets had provided transport then: now the situation was very different, and the amnesty documents and Polish passports had been taken away. Indeed, it can be safely assumed that any Poles who had attempted to leave the Soviet Union would have been arrested and thrown into the Gulag. The Soviets were taken aback by the scale of the protest and the international reaction, and on 1 April 1943, issued a new decree on Polish citizenship which exempted ethnic Poles who in 1939 had been living in the part of Poland occupied by the Germans.[54]

Later that month the Soviet Union broke off diplomatic relations with the Polish Government in London in the wake of the Katyń dispute. The Polish Government approached the British asking them to look after the Poles in the Soviet Union but Cadogan informed Raczyński on 4 May: 'Had to tell him we *can't* take on active charge of Polish interests in Russia. I'm awfully sorry, but I'm *sure* that could only lead to disaster.'[55] The Australian embassy stepped in. The closure of the welfare agencies run by and loyal to the Polish Government provided the Union of Polish Patriots with an opportunity to appeal to as many Poles as possible through action and not just rhetoric. The Union established a social welfare department, *Wydział Opieki Społecznej*, to take over the welfare activities of the former *Delegatura*. The Soviets set up a parallel organisation, *Uprosobtorg*, and the Poles and Soviets worked together to reach the widely dispersed Polish population.[56]

The Soviets wanted the Poles to remain in the Soviet Union because by the summer of 1943, the creation and organisation of a new Polish army, owing its allegiance to the Union of Polish Patriots, was well under way. There had been a proposal to create a Polish rifle division within the Red Army in 1940, when Colonel Zygmunt Berling and his fellow pro-Soviet officers were invited to draw up plans. During discussions with Beria and his deputy, General Vsevolod Merkulov, Berling learnt that most of the officers he planned to work with were 'unavailable'; he was not told explicitly that they had been murdered but some other officers present at the relevant meeting later claimed that Beria told them: 'We made a big mistake.' The plans became irrelevant in the chaos following the German invasion of the Soviet Union.[57] When the creation of the Anders army was announced, Berling made his way to and was employed by the Polish headquarters but deserted when that army left for Iran, and in July 1943 was court-martialled *in absentia*. In September 1942 and during the following winter, Berling and Wasilewska appealed to Stalin for permission to form a Polish division. On 8 April 1943, Berling approached the Soviet authorities with a proposal to establish a new Polish army and permission was granted after the break in diplomatic relations between the Soviet and Polish governments.

On 6 May 1943, the day after the Polish ambassador left the country, the Soviets moved ahead with the creation of a Polish army. On 8 May, an announcement appeared in *Wolna Polska*:

> The Soviet Government has decided to comply with the request of the Union of Polish Patriots in the USSR to create a Polish division named after Tadeusz Kościuszko on the territory of the USSR, which is to fight jointly with the Red Army against the German invader. The formation of the Polish division has already been started.[58]

The division was to be formed in Seltsy, about 110 miles from Moscow.* There would be three infantry regiments and a regiment of light artillery and also a women's regiment, with a strength of 1,095 officers, 3,258 NCOs and 7,093 rank and file. Its name, 'Kościuszko', after the general who led the uprising in 1794 against Russia and Prussia, was a deliberate attempt to stress the patriotic nature of the division, reinforced by the use of Polish uniforms and of the Piast eagle as its symbol.[59] Recruitment was open to all 'people formerly living in the Western Ukraine and Western Belorussia who, though Polish by nationality, were in fact Soviet citizens'.[60] On enlistment the recruits would be offered the opportunity to regain their Polish citizenship and the offer was extended to their family members.[61] The recruits were people who had not heard of the amnesty in time to join the Anders army, those who had been told they were ineligible to join, and those who were too young for military service in 1942, and some were Poles who had been living in the Soviet Union for generations since their ancestors had been deported to Siberia in the nineteenth century, or those who had entered the Soviet Union voluntarily after the outbreak of war. Although the impression was given that recruitment was to be voluntary, there was an element of conscription. At the end of May 1943, Nina Kochańska received a summons to appear before the *Wojenkomaty*, the military commissariat, and after a perfunctory medical inspection, she was ordered to return to her work and lodging until June when she received her call-up papers and left for Seltsy. She was reluctant to leave her mother alone but was given no choice.[62]

So many recruits flooded into Seltsy that by July 1943, there were already 14,380 men at various stages of training, and a second infantry

* Poles will be more familiar with the name Sielce nad Oką.

division, under Colonel Antoni Siwicki, had to be formed. By August it was clear that there were sufficient numbers to justify the creation of the 1st Polish Army Corps. On 10 August, a decree was published sanctioning its formation and Berling, now promoted to the rank of general, was appointed to command it with General Karol Świerczewski as his deputy.[63] Berling was appalled by the state of the recruits: 'There were people in rags which had once been jackets, with bundles, or with some kind of boxes which had once been suitcases, in shoes, moccasins, and felt boots.'[64] The motives of the recruits were varied. For most of them service in the army represented an opportunity for revenge against the German invaders and despoilers of Poland, a chance of a regular supply of food and clothing, and, ultimately, a way to return home to Poland. It was also quickly apparent that political motivation played little part: the recruits had seen too much of communism in action to be open to the political overtures of the Union of Polish Patriots.

The Union of Polish Patriots recognised that the composition and political outlook of the Polish army presented numerous challenges. There was a shortage of officers of Polish descent, and the solution was to send Red Army officers on secondment. The scale of this shortage is revealed by the statistics: between May 1943 and July 1944, 7,206 Soviet officers served with the Poles, making up nearly three-quarters of the officer corps. The Red Army sent the Poles 6 generals, 17 colonels, 54 lieutenant-colonels and 113 majors. Later a cadet school was established to train Polish officers.[65] Few of the Soviet officers spoke Polish well, if at all, which created endless communication difficulties within the army and caused a great deal of resentment among the Poles.[66]

Approximately half the Polish population remaining in the Soviet Union after the departure of the Anders army were Jewish. The majority of the members of the committee of the Union of Polish Patriots and the PKN as well as many of the most prolific journalists on the Polish-language newspapers were Jews. Because the Union wished to emphasise the Polish nature of the Berling army, it took steps to restrict their recruitment and to conceal the Jewish background of those who did join. No clear orders appear to have been given on whether the recruitment of Jews was permitted, so some commissions enlisted all the Jews who wanted to join, others restricted the numbers and some forbade such recruitment. Indeed, the Union of Polish Patriots received over 6,000 letters from Jews pleading to be allowed to join the army. Ultimately the desire to see the Polish army as large as possible dictated the Union's policy: as the available source of non-Jewish Polish manpower began to dry up, more Jews were accepted. Jewish officers, usually serving as political officers, were encouraged to conceal their origins by adopting Polish-sounding names; for example, Garber became Garbowski and Rozental became Rozański.[67]

The vast majority of the Polish recruits were not favourable to the communists and retained their loyalty to the Polish Government-in-Exile. Indeed, the NKVD warned Wanda Wasilewska that her safety was in doubt when she planned to visit the Polish army in the summer of 1943.[68] Since the Union of Polish Patriots had a secret plan to form the new communist government of Poland and to use the army to enforce its position in power, a massive programme of political indoctrination was initiated. Jews were very prominent in the political department: its first two heads, Major Hilary Minc and Captain Roman Zambrowski, were Jewish. All but one of the regimental deputy commanders for political affairs was Jewish, and more Jews filled the lower ranks of the political education structure, including most of the journalists of the divisional newspaper, *Żołnierz Wolności*.[69] Political education took the form of compulsory lectures on Marxist-Leninist doctrine, usually in the evenings, but few Poles took much notice, preferring instead to use the time to mend their kit or surreptitiously to catch up on sleep.[70]

The Polish army received the same three-month basic training as a Red Army Guards infantry division. Men and women alike were trained in the use of the modern weapons of war. Although the women were not expected to take part in front-line fighting, they would undertake patrols in the rear areas. The training was arduous and the marches grew longer as the starved Poles regained their physical strength. The Soviets demonstrated their commitment to the establishment of a Polish army through a generous allocation of weapons. The Soviet liaison officer, General Georgi Zhukov, remarked that the Poles were seven times better armed than a pre-war Polish division: 80 per cent of the equipment was automatic or semi-automatic, every company had some anti-tank rifles, and there were specialist machine-gun and artillery units. The Poles also received about 30 T-34 tanks. Heavy equipment was transported on American-made trucks and jeeps.[71]

On 15 July 1943, the Polish army was shown to the public. War correspondents, including Alexander Werth of the BBC, were invited, along with allied representatives to view a ceremony at which the men and women of the Kościuszko Division would swear their oath of allegiance, and be presented with the divisional banner before a march past. The day was designed to emphasise the Polish character of the division with lavish symbols of Polish statehood. It was also Grunwald Day, celebrated in Poland as the day on which, in 1410, the Polish army had successfully held back any further advance by the Teutonic Knights. The ceremony began with an open-air Mass celebrated by the Polish army chaplain, Father Kupsz. Then the division was presented with its banner, which showed the white Polish eagle on a red and white background and was inscribed with the words 'For Country and Honour' on one side and with a portrait of Kościuszko on the other. The oath of allegiance, however, showed the political nature of the division: the soldiers swore to liberate Poland from the Germans but also swore fidelity to their Soviet allies. At a press conference given by Berling and Wasilewska after the parade, she made some political points of which the most important was that the Union of Polish Patriots 'had no pretension of being an ersatz Polish Government. But it strongly felt that the future Government of Poland must come from the people, not from the émigrés.'[72]

In August 1943, the Kościuszko Division held a large tactical exercise, and at the end of the month a special Soviet army commission with Polish representatives declared the division ready for combat, despite the fact that it was actually only half trained. It seems likely that Wasilewska was the main proponent of this premature despatch, as she was very politically aware. She contacted Stalin directly and asked permission for the division to enter combat. According to Wasilewska:

> Stalin asked me: 'Are you telling me that they will fight properly?' To that question I answered with a one thousand per cent conviction that they would. And I stated it in such a way that the question would not be repeated. The division received permission to move to the front.[73]

There was no military urgency for the Poles to take to the battlefield so soon. Since the battle of Kursk the Red Army had been steadily pushing the German army back: on 25 September, Smolensk was captured and, at the end of the month, the Red Army had reached the Dnieper river and was starting to clear its eastern bank of German forces.[74] There was, however, a political necessity for the Polish army to take the field. The Big Three were soon to meet at Teheran and Stalin wanted to be able to show the western allied leaders that 'his' Poles were already fighting the Germans in contrast to 'their' Poles in the Anders army, who remained in training in the desert after leaving the Soviet Union over a year earlier.

The Red Army autumn campaign, in which the Poles were to take part, aimed at the liberation of Mińsk, the capital of Belorussia, and Kiev, the capital of Ukraine. The Kościuszko Division was transferred to Wiaźma by train and then began to march towards Smolensk. They marched 10 to 20 miles every night because the front line was close and the Luftwaffe still controlled the skies. In Smolensk Nina Kochańska and the women auxiliaries

> were positioned along the roads and had to show the army the direction of the march. My place was near the corner of the square where some gallows still stood. The town was being bombed. Some bombs landed nearby and some further away. In the light of the explosions and through the glow of the fire which followed, these gallows kept appearing before me. It was a bad night and I cannot forget it.[75]

The division went through the Smolensk marshes to where the battle would take place on 12–13 October 1943.

The battle of Lenino was a tactical engagement that has been overlooked by western historians of the Eastern Front but which received enormous publicity in post-war communist Poland.[76] The Kościuszko Division had 3 infantry regiments and was accompanied by tanks from the 1st Polish Tank Regiment and was placed under the Soviet 33rd Army, commanded by General Vasili Gordov. Light artillery regiments from the Soviet 144th and 164th Infantry Divisions would provide support, and the 42nd and 290th Rifle Divisions would cover the Poles' flanks. Berling was not told by Gordov that the attack on Lenino was only a subsidiary operation to tie down German forces while the main action took place elsewhere; in fact part of Gordov's army had been sent to reinforce the right flank of the main advance. The Poles were facing the battle-hardened German 113th and 337th Infantry Divisions. The Germans were well aware that it was the Poles who would attack their positions: careless reconnaissances-in-force prior to the opening of the main assault had alerted the Germans, and they reinforced their positions with men from the 36th Infantry Division on the 11th.

When the battle proper began on 12 October, it was a disaster. Fog delayed the artillery barrage, and when it had eventually started Gordov called it off prematurely. The infantry assault was reminiscent of the trench warfare on the Western Front during the First World War. The Germans had dug narrow trenches and strung barbed wire in front of them, but they had also had time to build more substantial shelters. As the artillery barrage opened, the Germans moved to their reserve trenches to take cover, but because it stopped too early they had ample time to return to the front-line trenches. As the Polish infantry crossed the open ground to the front-line German trenches, they were massacred by German machine guns and, unfortunately, simultaneously shelled by the Soviet artillery. The Polish tanks lost half their complement crossing the Mereya river and the surviving tanks then became bogged down in the marshy terrain and so took little part in the battle. Throughout that first day, the Poles fought hard to retain the ground they had gained, despite being short of ammunition and left unsupported because the adjacent Soviet forces had not reached their objectives, and also fought off numerous German counterattacks. The Poles took their objectives on the 13th but were so weakened that the division had to be replaced by the Soviet 164th Division.[77]

The casualties suffered by the Kościuszko Division were appalling: 510 men killed in action, 1,776 wounded and 765 men missing, or roughly 30 per cent of the troops sent into the battle. The Germans also lost heavily, with 1,500 men killed or wounded. They announced that 600 of the missing Poles had in fact deserted because they did not want to fight alongside the Soviets. Wasilewska was so appalled by the casualty rate, although it was a normal rate for a Red Army division, that she demanded that the division be withdrawn from the front line on the grounds that the casualty rate 'meant that within the next three days we would not have a division left'. It was moved to Bobyry for further training and expansion and would not see action again until the middle of 1944. During the post-mortem on the battle, the Soviet general with overall responsibility, Gordov, strongly criticised the performance of the Poles, stating that it was 'below any standards', but his superiors did not agree and he was removed from his command. It was clear that the Poles had received an insufficient amount of ammunition, because at one point the front-line troops ran out completely. Cooperation with the Soviet forces had been poor, for not only were the Soviets slow to reinforce the Poles but their artillery frequently shelled their ally.

Nevertheless, for propaganda purposes, the battle was seen as a success since the 1st Polish Division had been in battle with the Germans. Highly controversially the Union of Polish Patriots usurped the status of the Polish Government by awarding Polish military medals, including the *Virtuti Militari* and the *Krzyż Walecznych*.[78]

The Polish army remained in training throughout the Soviet 1943 winter campaign, which brought the Soviets to the pre-war frontier on the night of 3–4 January 1944. On the 5th the Polish Government in London issued a statement: 'In their victorious struggle against the German invader, the Soviet forces are reported to have crossed the frontier of Poland' and repeated the assertion that it was 'the only and legal steward and spokesman of the Polish nation'. But even the first part of this statement was open to challenge by the Soviets and the Polish communists, for the Soviets believed that they were liberating Soviet territory. For them the Polish frontier now lay along the river Bug.

# 13

# The Polish Dilemma: The Retreat of the Germans and the Advance of the Red Army

On 4–5 January 1944, the Red Army crossed the pre-war Polish-Soviet frontier at Sarny and advanced into Wołyń towards Łuck and Równe (Rivne). On 5 January, the Polish prime minister, Stanisław Mikołajczyk, made a broadcast to Poland stating: 'We should have preferred to meet the Soviet troops not merely as allies of our allies, fighting against the common enemy, but as our own allies as well.'[1] Therein lay the central dilemma facing both the Polish Government in London and the Underground Government in Poland: were the Soviet armies liberators or conquerors? Without direct diplomatic contact with the Soviet Government, the Poles were forced to adopt a strategy towards the advancing Red Army without any knowledge of the likely Soviet reaction. The omens were not good. The Soviet response to Mikołajczyk's speech appeared in the *Soviet Monitor* on 11 January and reiterated the Soviet claim for a revision of Poland's eastern frontier.[2] To the Soviets, the Polish frontier would not be crossed until the Red Army reached the river Bug. To complicate matters further, within Poland itself there were two diametrically opposed political groupings seeking to form a government in liberated Poland: the Underground Government, representing the Polish Government in London, and the communists.

The Underground Government had long been preparing to govern Poland in the interim before the Poles in London could return and new elections held. On 9 January, it established the Council of National Unity (*Rada Jedności Narodowej*, RJN) as a quasi-parliament under the chairmanship of Kazimierz Pużak. This had a wider membership than its predecessor the Home Political Representation (*Krajowa Reprezentacja Polityczna*, KRP), and included three members of each of the four large parties: the Polish Socialist Party (*Polska Partia Socjalistyczna*, PPS); the Peasant Alliance (*Stronnictwo Ludowe*, SL); the National Alliance (*Stronnictwo Narodowe*, SN); and the Labour Alliance (*Stronnictwo Pracy*, SP). It also included one member from each of the three smaller parties: the Democratic Alliance (*Zjednoczenie Demokratyczne*); the Peasant Freedom Organisation (*Chłopska Organizacja Wolności*); and Motherland (*Ojczyzna*); and one representative of the clergy and one for the cooperatives. In May, a cabinet, the National Council of Ministers (*Krajowa Rada Ministrów*, KRM) was created with four members: Jan Jankowski as the government delegate, Adam Bień, Stanisław Jasiukowicz and Antoni Pajdak.[3]

On 15 March 1944 the Council of National Unity issued its political manifesto, *O co walczy naród polski*, 'What the Polish nation is fighting for'. This demonstrated a certain amount of political wishful thinking, but it also reflected awareness of the attraction of communist plans. The first section was the most idealistic and was the most in tune with the opinions of the Polish Government in London. It called for an international organisation more powerful than the League of Nations to regulate the relations between states and thereby prevent future war. It adopted Sikorski's scheme of a Central European Federation of states to create a strong bulwark between the powerful countries Germany and the Soviet Union. The manifesto was clear on the future shape of Poland: the eastern frontier would remain unchanged but Poland would be increased in size with the absorption of German territories to the north and west. The second section covered the future political structure of Poland: it would not be ruled by a narrow band of men like the pre-war *Sanacja*, but would be a parliamentary democracy with a strong executive. The third and final section reflected the influence of the communist plans: key industries, large financial institutions, public utilities and the forests would all be nationalised; land reform would split up large private estates; social reforms included more power to trade unions and an expansion in education.[4]

The communists were making their own plans. For much of 1943 the German arrests of key Polish communists meant that communications between them and the Polish communists in the Soviet Union had ceased. Now, at the beginning of 1944, communications were restored and it quickly became apparent that the plans of the two communist movements had been developing along differing lines. The situation could only be clarified and resolved by a meeting between the two groups. In March a delegation of four members of the National Council for the Homeland (*Krajowa Rada Narodowa*, KRN), led by Marian Spychalski, left Warsaw and arrived in Moscow on 16 May. Six days later the delegation met Stalin, who pointed out their dilemma: 'The KRN has no army and the Polish army in the Soviet Union has no government.'[5] If the communists wanted to administer Polish territories after the Red Army had liberated them, then the two groups would have to thrash out an agreement now. On 22 July 1944, the complex and extremely fraught negotiations ended with the creation of the Polish Committee of National Liberation (*Polski Komitet Wyzwolenia Narodowgo*, PKWN), known more commonly as the Lublin Committee after the city in Poland in which it first established its base. The Lublin Committee included both communists from Poland and Polish communists from the Soviet Union. Wanda Wasilewska, who had been so instrumental in creating the Polish communist movement in the Soviet Union, did not, however, travel to Poland; she preferred to remain in Moscow with her husband.[6] Stalin did not see the Lublin Committee as a provisional government but only as a body capable of administering liberated Polish territories until the end of the war. He explained his position in a letter to Churchill:

> The Polish Committee of National Liberation intends to set up an administration on Polish territory, and I hope this will be done. We have not found in Poland other forces capable of establishing a Polish administration. The so-called underground organisations, led by the Polish Government in London, have turned out to be ephemeral and lacking influence.[7]

The two communist armies, the underground AL and the 1st Polish Army, were merged under one overall commander, General Michał Rola-Żymierski, although General Zygmunt Berling retained command of the 1st Polish Army.[8]

Poland had a long tradition of uprisings against occupying powers, most notably in 1863 against the Russians. Thus it is not surprising that such a concept, an uprising against the Germans, should form a central plank in the strategy of the Polish Government. The plan, conceived early in the war, stipulated that it should occur at the moment of the German collapse under the military pressure from the western allies. In early 1943, it was clear that this plan would have to be revised since the western allies had no troops at all in Europe and the Soviets had just defeated the Germans at Stalingrad. This meant that it was increasingly likely that the forces that would bring about a German collapse would in fact be Soviet. This in turn led to the crucial question of how the AK and the Underground Government should respond to the entry of Soviet armies into Polish territory. Sikorski was adamant that the Soviets should be greeted as allies but, should the 'Russian attitude to us become clearly hostile', then it would be advisable 'to reveal only the civilian administration and to withdraw the AK units into the interior of the country to save them from destruction'. The AK commander Grot-Rowecki was convinced that the Soviet attitude would be hostile and wanted permission to make preparations to resist their armies. Sikorski's order of March 1943 was issued when Poland and the Soviet Union still had diplomatic relations and had not been revised when they were broken off in April. A historian of these plans has noted: 'To the last, Sikorski refused to revise his instructions ordering the Home Army to treat the Russians as allies and to cooperate with them. Stefan Grot-Rowecki, for his part, remained unconvinced, to the day of his arrest, of the wisdom of these instructions.'[9] The double tragedy of Sikorski's death and Grot-Rowecki's arrest in July 1943 meant that new men, Mikołajczyk as prime minister, General Sosnkowski as commander-in-chief and Bór-Komorowski as commander of the AK, would have the opportunity to revise these plans.

At the beginning of August 1943, Bór-Komorowski sent a despatch to London outlining the situation in Poland and requesting advice. He believed that the AK could not remain passive, awaiting the opportune moment for an uprising, for much longer. The AK was growing impatient and wanted to take reprisals against the increasing German terror, and morale was suffering because of the lack of overt activity. Worse still, the increased activity of the Soviet partisans on Polish soil was proving attractive to those AK soldiers keenest on revenge. Furthermore, there was the danger that the Polish communist party, the PPR, would exploit the situation, which would make its aim of taking over the government of Poland after liberation all the easier to achieve. Above all, Bór-Komorowski wanted advice on how the AK should respond to the arrival of the Red Army, and an update on how the London Poles conceived the purpose of a national uprising.[10]

On 26 October 1943, the Polish Government radioed Bór-Komorowski instructions to prepare plans for a national uprising, which became known as Operation *Burza*. It considered several possible scenarios. The first would be that the Red Army would halt on the border of Poland, satisfied with having cleared its own territory, and that its offensive would only be resumed when the western allies were pressing the Germans in the west. During this interim period the role of the AK would be to wrest control of areas of Poland from the Germans, which the Underground Government would then administer. This scenario was pure fantasy: whereas it was true that no one knew for certain whether the Red Army would advance further west once the territory of the Soviet Union had been liberated, it did not take into account the fact that the only troops of the western allies on European soil were at the foot of Italy and therefore a long way from Poland. Another scenario envisaged that the Soviet armies would cross into Poland and continue to fight the Germans. If this happened, then the Polish Government hoped that diplomatic relations between Poland and the Soviet Union would be restored, and the AK and Underground Government should then reveal themselves to the Soviets. If, however, diplomatic relations were not restored, as the London Poles knew was likely but did not explicitly inform Bór-Komorowski, then the AK and Underground Government should remain hidden.[11]

Bór-Komorowski and Jankowski considered the government's instructions to be fatally flawed, as it appeared to have completely ignored Bór-Komorowski's view of the political situation in Poland. As he later explained, 'the only chance of gaining anything was a constant demonstration of our will to fight Germany to the last, sparing no effort, in the teeth of every adversity'.[12] The political purpose of an uprising could only be fulfilled if the AK came out into the open. Therefore on 26 November 1943, Bór-Komorowski replied to London that he had sent orders to all provinces and districts:

> As can be seen from the order, I have given all commanders and units instructions to emerge into the open after taking part in operations against the retreating Germans. Their task at that moment will be to give evidence of the existence of the Republic of Poland ... In the event of a second Soviet occupation, I am preparing a skeleton network of a new organisation which will be at the General's [Sosnkowski's] disposal.[13]

As Jan Nowak, a Polish courier present in London when Bór-Komorowski's order arrived, put it: 'a storm blew up in Polish circles'.[14]

Sosnkowski in particular was incensed because he believed that an uprising should only occur when three events had happened: the Allies had expressed their support for the Polish position on the eastern frontier, the western allies were on the frontiers of Germany and the German Government was on the point of collapse.[15] He told Mikołajczyk that the AK plan was little more than a 'hopeless gesture of self-immolation', because he believed that the Soviets would not accept the AK or any form of Polish authority in the eastern provinces to which they laid claim, and would at the very least demand that the AK units join the 1st Polish Army.[16] The government, however, was more optimistic, and so in February 1944, Sosnkowski sent Bór-Komorowski an amended order giving the terms on which the AK units were to reveal themselves to the Soviets: 'By order of the Government of the Polish Republic, we present ourselves as the representatives of the Polish administration (as commanders of AK units) with proposals to establish collaboration on these territories with the armed forces of the Soviet Union, for mutual action against the common enemy.'[17]

Bór-Komorowski issued the orders for the launch of Operation *Burza*, and later described how they were put into practice:

> Partisan groups were assembled into larger units and directed to districts which lay across the German lines of retreat. In the eastern provinces, which were the first to start Burza operations, all soldiers of the Home Army were being mobilised. Regiments, battalions and divisions received names and numbers as in 1939. Arms and ammunition, radio and other equipment, stores, warm clothing (short uniform overcoats, caps and boots), hospital equipment, etc. – all these things manufactured at home in secret workshops – were being gradually smuggled to the forests. The Polish partisan groups in the east grew into substantial regular forces long before the Red Army front reached them.[18]

Because chances were high that the Soviets would attempt to disarm the AK units, every unit was issued with a short wave radio transmitter so that Bór-Komorowski would be kept fully informed and could amend orders as required.

Operation *Burza* was begun by the AK 27th Division, commanded by Major Wojciech 'Oliwa' Kiwerski, which was operating near Kowel

(Kovel) in the Wołyń province. It was a well-equipped division with 7,300 men divided into 8 battalions and 2 cavalry squadrons, as well as signals, engineers and military police units. These soldiers were armed with 4,500 rifles, 700 pistols, 140 sub-machine guns, 100 machine guns and 3 anti-tank guns.[19] During January and February 1944, the division engaged the Germans and their Ukrainian auxiliaries in some fierce actions, leading to AK control of small areas of Wołyń, and in March it encountered the leading units of the Red Army and cooperated with them in the capture of Turzysk (Turiysk) and Kowel. The Soviet commanders, General Sergeyev and Colonel Charytonov, praised the action of the AK division and agreed to allow them to fight alongside the Red Army and under its operational command while still maintaining direct contact with AK command. Bór-Komorowski was delighted with this response from the Soviets and radioed back his agreement.[20] The Germans then attacked the 27th Division and the Soviet 56th Cavalry Regiment with four divisions which included SS Panzer Division Viking. 'Oliwa' was killed and his place was taken by Major Tadeusz 'Żegota' Sztumberg-Rychter. After five days of heavy fighting, the Polish and Soviet troops became separated and the Poles were left to fight alone.[21] As their losses mounted the decision was taken to flee for the relative security of the nearby marshes. Most of the supplies and heavy equipment were destroyed and 900 horses let loose, then 'we took light automatic weapons, as much ammunition as we could carry, and we set off towards the Pripet marshes'. The remnants of the division fought the Germans for another two months before AK command ordered them to retreat westwards across the river Bug.[22]

Thus the first major battle of Operation *Burza* was a military failure. It was also a political failure despite the hopeful nature of the first contacts with the Soviets. Unknown to the AK an order had been issued to Soviet commanders in November 1943 for the disarming of AK units and the murder of those soldiers who resisted. During the spring and early summer of 1944, the Soviet armies made no further advances against the Germans. The Soviets now occupied parts of the Polish provinces of Wołyń, Stanisławów and Tarnopol but were too weak to undertake military operations to liberate any major cities. Instead, they were occupied with the disarming of any AK units they found in Wołyń and East Galicia. In April orders were issued for the conscription of all men aged between 17 and 35 into the 1st Polish Army, and those who refused either to be disarmed or to join that army were arrested; many were deported to an unknown location in the Soviet Union. By July over 6,000 AK soldiers had been arrested.[23] The Polish units were also under pressure from the Germans: in June and July, the Luftwaffe regiments mounted large-scale anti-partisan hunts in the forests of Białowieża in Podlesie and near Biłgoraj, 55 miles south of Lublin.[24]

The first battle of Operation *Burza* was also a political failure on the international front because the AK was not being given any credit for its actions: the Soviets publicised the activities of their partisans but failed to mention the AK units who had worked alongside them. In March, Sosnkowski warned Bór-Komorowski:

> The Allies, under influence of unfavourable propaganda, suspect that neither the central H.Q. nor the Home Army Command are really in control of the Underground as a whole. The dates and events of battle and sabotage are taken as accidental and unintentional from our side.[25]

Bór-Komorowski's response was to ask Sosnkowski to approach the British Government to ask it to despatch a military mission to Poland to observe what the AK was doing and 'which could serve as a witness to Soviet moves and oppose them'.[26] In April Churchill gave a final and unequivocal refusal to this.[27] The AK command kept the Polish Government in London fully informed about the progress of Operation *Burza* and the conduct of the Soviet authorities, and the Polish ambassador, Edward Raczyński, in turn, passed the information on to Eden.[28] The British Government, however, was not prepared to make public any news that detracted from the reputation of its ally, the Soviet Union.

An uprising in Poland had no place in allied strategic planning. If it had been given a central role, then more effort would have been made to parachute adequate supplies into Poland. Instead, the Allies wanted the AK to continue its operations aimed at disrupting German communications. On 11 March, Sosnkowski told Bór-Komorowski:

> The Allies have approached us suggesting preparations for action against communications. The political situation may render such action necessary from our point of view, to demonstrate our goodwill in respect of the 'Friends' . . . We are ensuring secrecy at our end to prevent the Soviets from taking propaganda advantage for themselves or placing any obstacles in our way.[29]

The result was Operation *Jula*, which took place at the beginning of April. One of the *Cichociemni*, a Polish paratrooper from Britain, 'Szyb', took part in the operation to blow up a 150-foot span of the railway bridge over the Wisłoka, in the Przeworsk–Rozwadów sector:

> Two trains were coming, one in each direction. They were going to pass each other on the bridge. One locomotive thundered over the bridge and already a long stream of trucks was following. I waited as long as I could; then as the second locomotive was coming over the bridge, we detonated the charges.[30]

Elsewhere, two munitions trains were blown up at Rogoźno and near Nowosielce. German records show that during this period 34 main railway routes were attacked in over 6,000 separate incidents.[31] The Allies gained independent verification of the AK operation through Enigma decrypts, and the head of SOE, Lord Selborne, wrote to Sosnkowski expressing his delight at the success of the operation.[32]

On 22 June, the Soviets launched Operation Bagration, designed to destroy the German Army Group Centre and thrust the 1st Belorussian Front, under General Konstantin Rokossovsky, deep into central-eastern Poland.* Other Soviet armies would drive against Wilno to the north, and advance along the Lwów–Sandomierz axis in the south. The sheer weight of the Soviet attack took the Germans by surprise, and within two weeks the Army Group Centre had been routed, leaving a gap 250 miles wide and almost 100 miles deep in the German front. One by one major cities fell to the Soviet forces: Minsk, the capital of Belorussia on 3 July; Wilno on 13 July; Lublin on 23 July; Brześć on 26 July; and Lwów on 27 July. By the end of July, the 1st Belorussian Front had crossed the Vistula near Dęblin, Puławy and Magnuszów. The 1st Ukrainian Front had reached the Vistula near Baronów, south of Sandomierz. The Soviet armies were now converging on Warsaw.[33] The casualty figures were high: of nearly 2,400,000 Soviet troops, 178,507 were killed, missing or taken prisoner, and a further 578,308 were wounded. The German losses were about 300,000 dead, 250,000 wounded and 120,000 taken prisoner.[34]

---

* Rokossovsky had been born in Warsaw and was of Polish ancestry. He served in the Russian Army in the First World War and then joined the Red Army.

Following Rokossovsky's 1st Belorussian Front was the 1st Polish Army. After its blooding in the battle of Lenino in October 1943, the 1st Polish Army 'Kościuszko' Division had been withdrawn to Bobyry in the Ukraine for reinforcement and further training. While it was there, the political commissars informed the troops about the Katyń massacre, making it clear that the Germans were responsible. The Polish army chaplain, Father Kupsz, held Mass in the Katyń forest. One Polish soldier chanced upon an old man in the woods who whispered to him: 'If these trees could talk, they would tell you much.'[35] By the end of March 1944, the 1st Polish Army consisted of 3 infantry divisions, tank units, artillery, as well as auxiliary units, numbering 43,508 men and women.[36] An article in *Pravda* greeted the creation of the 3rd Division:

> This Division has been trained and prepared for fighting on the Soviet-German front. To a considerable extent the Division is composed of Poles who lived in the western regions of the Ukraine, recently liberated by the Red Army from German occupation. Among the men of the Third Division are a number of former members of the underground organisations created by the London émigré Polish Government. These men, however, could not reconcile themselves to the humiliating position in which they were placed by their leaders. This Division was named 'Romuald Traugutt'.[37]

Other recruits included Poles from Silesia, Pomerania and Warthegau, who had been conscripted into the Wehrmacht and then captured by the Red Army.[38] At the end of March, the 1st Polish Army began to move towards the front in stages via Kiev to the Berdichev–Zhitomir area. The army was commanded by General Berling, with General Świerczewski, his deputy commander responsible for operations, and General Aleksander Zawadzki, deputy commander responsible for political affairs.[39]

On 29 April 1944, the 1st Polish Army joined the 1st Belorussian Front, commanded by Rokossovsky. The first Polish province it entered was Wołyń, and the first Polish towns it passed through were Równe and Łuck. After three years of exile in the Soviet Union, the Poles were delighted to be on home territory at last. The towns looked familiar but it was the countryside that made the most lasting impact on them:

> We came to a large village where not a single house was left standing. Only smoky chimneys were sticking up everywhere. In this cemetery, cherry orchards were ripening, full of red juicy fruit as though in defiance of death

and of this genocide. A sense of something sinister increased the deep silence which hovered over the place.[40]

The Germans were not responsible for this destruction: the Ukrainian UPA had massacred the Polish inhabitants. Soldiers of the AK also remembered their first encounter with the 1st Polish Army, particularly their impression of the officers:

> Making such a parody! You dress up a Russian who doesn't even speak Polish . . . They were unruly. They were not elegant. They had no discipline. They looked more like riff-raff . . . You see, a few months earlier he was a forestry worker and [now] has to pretend he's a captain, a major, a colonel! And they would address themselves as 'comrade', stressing the political character of the army.[41]

While in Wołyń the soldiers of the 1st Polish Army received an increased level of political indoctrination designed to convince them of the legitimacy of the Curzon Line and of the Union of Polish Patriots and the PPR, and efforts were made to discredit the Polish Government in London. On the night of 22–23 July, the army crossed the river Bug, the new Soviet-Polish frontier, and advanced towards Lublin. The crossing of this new frontier 'was given a very solemn character – with flags flying and the band playing'.[42]

The AK had played its part in the Soviet successes. In January 1944, the AK in the Wilno province had launched Operation *Burza*. By the end of April they had fought more than 20 major actions, capturing German arms, ammunition and stores, and taking control of areas of the province. At the end of June, the Red Army was approaching the city of Wilno. The AK wanted to seize it first in the name of the Polish Government, so Lieutenant-Colonel Aleksander 'Wilk' Krzyżanowski ordered over 10,000 AK soldiers to attack the German garrison. On 7 July, the battle began with the AK attacking Wilno from four directions with artillery, air and tank support from the Soviet forces. The city fell to the AK on 13 July, and for two days the Polish 'red and white flag flew for the last time on the Giedymin Tower' before being hauled down by the Soviets. 'Wilk' was invited to talks with General Ivan Tchernyakhowski, commander of the 3rd Belorussian Front, during which it was suggested that the Poles should form an infantry division and a cavalry brigade from their troops. The Poles opposed the offer and, on

17 July, the NKVD arrested 'Wilk' and 70 of his officers and deported them to the Soviet Union.[43]

In Lwów, the AK commander Colonel Władysław 'Janka' Filipkowski and 3,000 poorly armed soldiers fought to wrest control of the city from the Germans as the Red Army advanced into the suburbs. As the Germans retreated, Filipkowski established his headquarters in the city and disclosed his identity to the Soviet forces. He was then invited to talks with General Ivanov, representing General Koniev, the commander of the 1st Ukrainian Front, and with the NKVD General Gruczko. During their meeting a message was read out from Koniev thanking the AK for its 'brotherly cooperation'. On 27 July, Filipkowski reported to AK command that Gruczko had informed him: 'finally Lwów is Soviet and Ukrainian but this does not exclude later modifications between the governments'. The Soviets had also demanded the disbandment of the AK units and their enlistment in the 1st Polish Army. On 31 July, Filipkowski returned to the Soviet headquarters for further talks, whereupon he and 5 of his staff officers were flown to the 1st Polish Army base near Zhitomir in the Ukraine and arrested – and never returned. Back in Lwów, the NKVD surrounded the AK headquarters and arrested everyone there, including the local government delegate, Professor Adam Ostrowski, and sent them all to the prison in Ulica Lacki.[44]

It was clear that Operation *Burza* had failed completely in the disputed eastern provinces, and, at the end of July, Bór-Komorowski acknowledged this and issued an order disbanding AK units east of the Bug, specifically ordering the enlistment of the soldiers into the 1st Polish Army.[45] The operation was not cancelled, however, because now the Soviets had entered 'Poland proper' there was still a chance that the Soviets would acknowledge the legitimacy of the AK and the Underground Government. The Soviet attitude appeared at first to be to deny that the AK was fighting the Germans at all; when General Vasily Chuikov first encountered AK units near Lubartów in Lublin province,

> Its formations numbered about twenty thousand men and were officially organised into companies, battalions, regiments and even divisions. But they simply did not fight the Germans at all, and the latter in turn did not touch them.[46]

Nothing could be further from the truth. Fighting on its own, the AK captured 7 towns, and fighting alongside the Red Army it captured 11 more, including the city of Lublin itself. As Bór-Komorowski wrote: 'It even happened sometimes that during the battle Home Army officers took over command and led Red Army units into action.'[47]

Lublin proved the test case of Soviet goodwill. As soon as the Germans left the city, the local government delegate, Władysław Cholewa, took over the town hall and began organising the administration, and the AK opened a recruitment office for a Lublin battalion. Their authority was challenged by the arrival of a delegation of the communist PKWN, or Lublin Committee, led by Edward Ochab, followed a day later by the first units of the 1st Polish Army, which paraded through the city on 26 July.[48] The delegation approached Cholewa and the local AK commander, Colonel Kazimierz 'Marcin' Tumidajski, but both men denied that the PKWN had any legitimacy: however, they stated that they were willing to hold talks with the Soviets. These talks took place on 27 July, and the AK was faced with the stark choice: either disband and be disarmed, or join the 1st Polish Army. The AK units operating in 'Poland proper', in Zamość, Białystok, Przemyśl and Rzeszów, all strongly resisted being disbanded. Their officers were arrested and despatched to the Soviet Union, and the men sent to recently vacated former German concentration camps. By the beginning of October, over 21,000 AK soldiers had been arrested and many more had fled westwards.[49]

The western allies were embarrassed by the reports from Poland on the conduct of the Soviet authorities and chose to ignore them. They were also not inclined to believe reports on the German terror regime: when the Soviets liberated Majdanek, they invited journalists to view the evidence of German extermination policies – partly demolished gas chambers and piles of clothing taken from the dead. Detailed reports appeared in *Pravda*, and the war correspondent Alexander Werth sent a despatch to the BBC. An item in the *New York Herald Tribune* summed up the reaction in the west:

> Maybe we should wait for further corroboration of the horror story that comes from Lublin. Even on top of all we have been taught of the maniacal Nazi ruthlessness, this example seems inconceivable ... The picture presented by American correspondents requires no comment except that, if authentic the regime capable of such crimes deserves annihilation.[50]

The BBC declined to use Werth's report, dismissing it as Soviet propaganda. It was certainly true that the state of the survivors of Majdanek had immense propaganda value: Soviet and Polish soldiers and new recruits were taken to see the concentration-extermination camp. The Soviets then filled the camp with AK soldiers who had refused to join the 1st Polish Army.

Operation *Burza* had exposed the soldiers of the AK to the full wrath of the Germans, and so the Polish Government asked the western allies to grant combatant rights to the AK, which would give them the protection of the Geneva Convention. The British Government was asked to make a radio broadcast on the following lines:

> Detachments of the Polish Home Army form part of the Polish Armed Forces and remain at war with the Germans since 1 September 1939. Cases have occurred when soldiers of the Polish Home Army, even when fighting openly in close formation, were after their capture shot or handed over by the German military authorities to German civilian authorities to be shot by these.
>
> The German authorities and German soldiers are hereby warned that further disregard of rules of international law regarding combatants will force the Polish Home Army to take reprisals in the shape of shooting captured German soldiers.[51]

The AK command and the government delegate also asked the Polish Government to ensure that combatant rights for the AK would be guaranteed by the Soviet Union: 'We must do all we can to safeguard these people and not let them be liquidated either by the NKVD or by their obedient Polish tools.'[52] Since the Soviet Union was not a signatory to the Geneva Convention, it is unlikely that an allied statement would have had any effect on the conduct of the Soviet authorities and Polish communist bodies in Poland. The AK would only receive combatant rights during the Warsaw Uprising.

Operation *Burza* continued because everywhere there appeared to be signs of an imminent total collapse of the German Army. The *Volksdeutsche* were the first to leave, along with German administrators from eastern Poland. Before leaving they attempted to sell the properties and goods that they had stolen from the Poles back to the Poles for very low prices. Zygmunt Klukowski noted in his diary: 'Our own people are busily buying ... Today's picture of German misery makes us all feel good.'[53] As the Germans left Lwów, Simon Wiesenthal and some Jewish survivors of the concentration camp at Janów were used as cover, taken with them by the fleeing SS:

> Now we understood why Warzok had spared us. As long as the SS had someone to guard, they might get out of front-line duty. We 34 Jews became the life insurance for almost 200 SS men. We were all going to be a happy family. Warzok said we would try to reach the woods of Slovakia, where we would hide until the war was over.[54]

Elsewhere the Germans frantically attempted to erase all traces of their murderous regime, using prisoners from concentration camps to dig up and burn the corpses.[55] By July the retreating German armies had reached Warsaw and the Poles turned out to watch them: 'On the road, an endless column of German soldiers was slogging along wearily, in a state we had never seen them before. They were in rags, dirty, many without arms, and without boots, on foot, on bicycles and carts, in a disorderly retreat, frequently without officers.'[56] Even Jews who had been hiding in the city came to watch the Germans, glorying in the fact:

> These members of the Herrenvolk now looked like the Jewish victims they had hounded out of the cities of Europe to their death. Thousands of people stood all day to watch the beggarly procession of soldiers. The atmosphere was relaxed. No one was afraid any more. The Poles openly made cheap jokes about the former murderers and rulers of Europe.[57]

But the Germans were not totally beaten yet.

Bór-Komorowski had outlined his theory of a national uprising in a lengthy despatch to London in October 1943. His principal maxim was that 'the uprising must not fail'. He considered a range of possible courses of action: from total inaction through to limited operations against the Germans, to a full-scale war against the Soviet armies. The main thrust of his argument was in favour of uprisings in a number of localities of central importance to the Germans. Of these the most essential was, of course, the capital:

> Warsaw, with her airports, communications, railway junction, the river crossings and, what is of supreme importance, her wealth of informed

population, which will not only be a great attacking force in the uprising, but also, immediately after being cleared of the Germans, will be the largest and the most valuable source to replenish our power quickly and in strength. I also believe it is necessary to gain control of Warsaw in a smooth fashion, because here are our main political and military centres, and their speedy liberation is of immense significance. Also I have concrete grounds for believing that Warsaw and her surrounding countryside is a region which could soonest receive reinforcement from our armed forces in exile.

Bór-Komorowski also outlined the assistance required from outside Poland: greater numbers of weapons, 'air forces in various guises' and, as soon as the situation allowed, the relocation of the Polish armed forces in exile into Poland.[58]

Bór-Komorowski's despatch displayed a considerable degree of naïveté concerning the real military and political situation, which was alarming because the Polish Government failed to enlighten him. He was clearly unaware that the importance of the AK in allied military strategy was diminishing, and consequently the level of supplies remained low. Between February 1941 and June 1944, only 305 tons of war materiel had been received.[59] Bór-Komorowski also remained ignorant that the Polish Air Force was not independent but under allied command. This meant that even when the small Polish heavy bomber wing was transferred to Italy in the summer of 1944, it was not free to concentrate on conveying supplies to Poland but also had to make flights to the partisans in Yugoslavia. Bór-Komorowski was on more certain ground when he assumed that the Polish Independent Parachute Brigade would be sent to Poland in the event of an uprising, since this was the very purpose behind its creation, yet the Polish Government failed to inform him that, after heated negotiations between March and May 1944, it too had been put at the disposal of the British. Nor had anyone informed Bór-Komorowski that the shortage of suitable aircraft to lift the men in the brigade and the difficulty of transporting its heavy equipment by glider were such insuperable challenges that no serious planning had even been attempted. The blame for leaving Bór-Komorowski in the dark lies primarily with the Polish commander-in-chief Sosnkowski. In his despatches to the AK commander, Sosnkowski counselled against an uprising largely on political grounds; for example, on 28 July, he telegraphed Bór-Komorowski: 'In present conditions, I am categorically opposed to a general uprising ... Your appraisal of the situation must be sober and realistic. A mistake would be enormously expensive. It is essential to concentrate all forces, political, moral and physical, to prevent Moscow's annexation designs.'[60] But Sosnkowski did not expressly forbid an uprising in Warsaw, nor at the crucial moment was he available to give orders in light of the rapidly changing circumstances: at the end of July, he was visiting the Polish troops in Italy and refusing all calls from his government to return to London.[61]

In the original plans for Operation *Burza*, no role had been assigned to Warsaw, therefore the question has to be asked: why did the Warsaw Uprising take place? In a radio broadcast on 1 September, the government delegate, Jankowski, gave what is probably the best analysis:

> There were several reasons for our uprising. We wanted to repel by force of arms the last blow the Germans were preparing to deal at the moment of their departure to all that was still living in Poland; we wanted to thwart them in their aim of revenge on insurgent Warsaw. We wanted to show the world that although we wanted to have an independent Poland, we were not prepared to accept this gift of freedom from anyone if it meant accepting conditions contrary to the interests, traditions and dignity of our nation. Finally, we wanted to free Poland from the nightmare of the Gestapo punishments, murder and prisons.
>
> We wanted to be free and to owe this freedom to nobody but ourselves.[62]

In interviews and memoirs after the war, decision makers, such as Bór-Komorowski and the head of the AK Information and Propaganda Bureau, Colonel Jan Rzepecki, expressed similar sentiments.[63] They were acutely aware of the threat of the communists. The communist radio station Kościuszko was making broadcasts calling on the population of Warsaw to rise up and liberate themselves, and, on 29 July, leaflets appeared in Warsaw containing a call to battle addressed to the AL, the communist resistance, and issued in the name of Molotov and Edward Osóbka-Morawski. The radio broadcasts were picked up by the radio monitoring stations in Britain.[64]

But this does not explain why the uprising was launched on 1 August. The evidence on the totality of the German collapse was conflicting. While, on 24 July, the German governor of Warsaw, Ludwig Fischer, ordered the evacuation of the German civilian administration to Łódź, two days later he reversed this decision and the Germans returned in strength. Executions of prisoners continued and an increased number of German police and SS patrolled the main thoroughfares through Warsaw in tanks and armoured cars.[65] On 27 July, Fischer ordered the mobilisation of 100,000 Polish men and women to report for work building defences. This placed the AK in a quandary because obedience would deprive it of manpower but disobedience could lead to massive reprisals. In the event the order was generally ignored and the Germans took no reprisals.[66] This led the AK commanders to believe that the German hold on Warsaw was shaky and that the Germans would abandon the city as soon as the Soviets attacked, suggesting that an uprising could succeed. The crucial question still to be answered was: where were the Soviet armies and what were their intentions towards Warsaw?

The Poles knew that the Hermann Goering Brigade had passed through Warsaw on its way to the front, but they did not know of the heavy fighting taking place at the Soviet bridgeheads on the Vistula at Puławy and Magnuszów. The AK commanders gathered in Warsaw knew that they only had sufficient equipment for about a week's fighting so the timing of the uprising was absolutely crucial. They met daily, and sometimes several times a day, to deliberate. On 29 July, there was an important meeting during which Colonel Janusz 'Sek' Bokszczanin reported:

> Soviet artillery fire is so far only intermittent and light. It does not seem to be an artillery preparation for a general forced crossing of the Vistula and an attack on the city. The armoured reserves which the Germans are directing to the front near Warsaw are fully equipped and prove that they intend to fight at the bridgehead. Until the Soviet army shows clear intention of attacking the city, we should not start operations. The appearance of some Soviet detachments on the outskirts of Praga does not signify anything. They may simply be reconnaissance patrols.

Also present at the meeting was Jan Nowak, who had just returned from London. He gave several vital pieces of information to Bór-Komorowski: Sosnkowski was against an uprising; the AK could not count on support from outside Poland because both the Polish Parachute Brigade and the Polish Air Force were now under allied command; and the Polish squadron in Italy was very small.[67]

The importance of knowledge concerning the movements of the Soviet armies is well illustrated by the meetings of the AK command on 31 July. In the morning, it was clear that opinion on calling an uprising on 1 August was split. Crucially the man who was to command the Warsaw Uprising, General Antoni 'Monter' Chruściel, was against launching it, because of the lack of arms in the city for his troops, as was the AK head of intelligence, Colonel Kazimierz 'Heller' Iranek-Osmecki. Opposing him was General Leopold 'Kobra' or 'Niedźwiadek' Okulicki, who had been a prisoner of the NKVD in 1941, had been released under the terms of the Sikorski–Maisky pact and had returned to Poland by parachute. His hatred for the Soviets knew no bounds and he was willing to take any risks in the cause of Polish independence. Bór-Komorowski and his chief of staff General Tadeusz 'Grzegorz' Pełczyński abstained. That afternoon Bór-Komorowski and Jankowski decided that the uprising would start soon but would only last for 3–5 days. In the late afternoon 'Monter' told the meeting of the AK command that he had received information that Soviet tanks were entering Praga, Warsaw's eastern suburb on the banks of the Vistula.[68] This news electrified the meeting and so the die was cast: the uprising would begin at 5 p.m. on 1 August. Bór-Komorowski wrote later that this time was selected because: 'The traffic in the city was at its heaviest, with people returning home from work. It would then be less difficult to conceal units moving to their appointed places in the hurrying crowd of workers coming out of offices and factories.'[69]

The last-minute decision to include Warsaw in Operation *Burza* had far-reaching consequences. Because Warsaw had not been in its original design, far from accumulating supplies in Warsaw from neighbouring areas, the reverse had happened, and, in early July, 900 sub-machine guns with supplies of ammunition had been sent out of Warsaw to units fighting further east.[70] There were an estimated 50,700 members of the AK in Warsaw and, although statistics vary, it can be safely assumed that only between 5,100 and 8,500 could be armed. On 1 August 1944, the AK arsenal consisted of 1,000 rifles, 300 pistols, 60 light machine guns, 7 heavy machine guns, 35 special carbines and bazookas, 1,200 revolvers, and 25,000 hand grenades. The Germans had found two large AK arms caches in the spring, with 70,000 hand grenades and 450 flame-throwers. Ammunition was also in short supply with 190 bullets

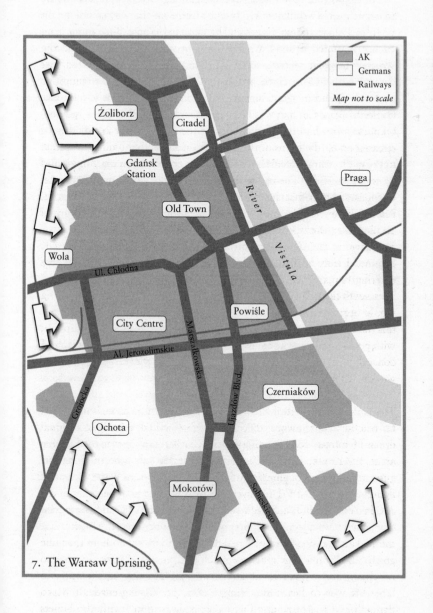

7. The Warsaw Uprising

per rifle, 500 rounds per light machine gun and 2,300 rounds per heavy machine gun. Two major AK arsenals were on the wrong side of the river, in Praga, and so could not be accessed. There were more arms caches scattered around Warsaw but, because these had been constructed in great secrecy, some locations had been lost. Indeed, one arsenal with 678 machine pistols and 60,000 rounds of ammunition was only found in 1947, and another cache so large that it took two weeks to empty in 1957.[71] The members of the AK wore a red-and-white armband but few had more formal uniforms. Most wore a mixture of old Polish uniforms, British uniforms that had been used to cushion the arms in canisters, and about 3,000 German uniforms stolen from a warehouse. The use of the latter caused confusion when the AK encountered the Soviets and led to allegations that the AK were on the German side.[72] Secret food caches had been created in five locations throughout the city, containing 90,000 rations. In the event all five were in areas that the AK never controlled, and so the population of the city suffered greatly from hunger during the uprising.[73] Indeed, food supplies were particularly low as the retreating German armies had taken everything with them.[74]

The AK were strengthened by cooperation with other armed units. The AL, which had about 400 men in the city, put itself operationally under AK command but fought separately; it was woefully underarmed. About 1,000 Jewish survivors also took part: one ŻOB platoon joined the AL while another joined the AK. During the uprising 348 Jews kept imprisoned by the Germans in Warsaw were liberated and about 130 of them joined in the fighting. One Jewish fighter, whose name is unknown, earned the instant award of Poland's highest medal, the *Virtuti Militari*, when he jumped into an immobilised German tank and turned its gun on another tank, successfully destroying it. Various other nationalities present in Warsaw helped: Italians who had deserted the Germans, escaped Soviet POWs, Hungarians, Slovaks and a Frenchman.[75] An escaped British POW, John Ward, had joined the AK and during the uprising would telegraph reports to London. Once the Air Ministry had verified his identity, he was invited to submit daily bulletins on the fighting to *The Times*.[76]

The insurgents had two main aims in the first days of the uprising. The first was to secure the bridges over the Vistula, especially Poniatowski and Kierbedź, and the main east–west thoroughfares to assist the Soviet advance. The second was to seize control of the main municipal districts on the west bank: Stare Miasto (the Old Town) and Śródmieście (the city centre), Żoliborz, Wola, Ochota, Mokotów and Czerniaków; and Praga on the east bank, in order to establish Polish control over the city. But the insurgents lacked the arms and manpower to achieve all these objectives. The German defences were so strong that the AK attacks on the university buildings, the police and Gestapo headquarters, and other major buildings, all failed. The AK's attacks on both of Warsaw's airports met with defeat and heavy losses. They failed to cut or even hinder German communications by telephone and telegraph. None of the bridges or main thoroughfares were wrested from German control, nor was the main railway station. There were some successes: by the end of the first day, the Poles had varying degrees of control over five municipal districts on the west bank, but had been forced to retire from Praga. A propaganda victory was scored when the Poles occupied the tallest building in Warsaw, belonging to the Prudential Insurance Company, and hung a large Polish flag that could be seen across the city.[77] The German garrison was caught by surprise and, according to the report of the German commander of the Warsaw garrison, Luftwaffe Lieutenant-General Reiner Stahel, the Germans suffered 500 casualties on the first day.

The civilian population flocked to assist the AK by tearing up paving stones, overturning trams and other vehicles, and providing furniture to build barricades. They also made other defensive preparations:

> At the very beginning all tenants of a building were entrusted with the task of organising life in their area. Guards were put at the entrances, taking it in turns to check all those who entered, for fear that a German or Volksdeutsche who had run away from another house might try to hide where he was unknown. In case of fire on the roofs or in attics, pails of water and sand were prepared and two voluntary wardens were continuously on duty. Trenches were dug, connecting buildings with one another so that one might walk considerable distances without emerging on the street. Directions, names of streets, and numbers of houses were clearly marked by inscriptions on the cellar walls.[78]

The mood in the city was optimistic and it appeared that the entire population backed the actions of the AK. The Underground Government was caught by surprise, since there had been no time to inform it of the exact time of the start of the uprising, but it quickly moved to establish civilian control in the liberated areas.

Hitler's first reaction when informed of the uprising was to issue an order to 'raze Warsaw completely' from the air, using the Luftwaffe present on the Eastern Front. He was informed that this would cause an enormous number of German casualties because their military units and civilians could not be extracted from the city. Therefore, Himmler and Guderian were ordered: 'upon stifling the uprising with all available means, Warsaw was to wiped from the face of the earth, all the inhabitants were to be killed, there were to be no prisoners'. The Wehrmacht concentrated on wresting control of the main thoroughfares from the AK, and also creating an impenetrable ring around the city to prevent reinforcements reaching the insurgents within it. Himmler ordered SS units to be rushed to the city. A special SS brigade, commanded by SS Obersturmbahnführer Oskar Dirlewanger, was rushed from East Prussia to the Wola suburb of Warsaw with the order to 'kill anyone you want, according to your desire'. The Dirlewanger brigade was mostly composed of recently released criminals. On the same day Himmler ordered the Russian National Liberation Army (*Russaya Osvobodityelnaya Narodnaya Armya*, RONA brigade), commanded by SS General Bronisław Kaminski, to go to Warsaw from Częstochowa.[79] Placed in overall command was the experienced anti-partisan commander General Erich von dem Bach.[80]

German tactics were clear from the outset: no distinction was to be made between AK soldiers wearing identifying armbands and the civilian population. The SS units were responsible for terrible atrocities in the suburb of Wola, where they went from house to house pulling out all inhabitants regardless of age or sex and slaughtering them. On one day alone, 'Black Saturday', 5 August, it is estimated that 40,000 civilians were murdered. The Germans impressed a group of Poles to burn the bodies in improvised crematoria created in the cellars of buildings. Von dem Bach recalled what he witnessed on entering Warsaw:

> Already on the main road leading from Warsaw toward the west near a cemetery I realised that unbelievable confusion was reigning. Wild masses of policemen and soldiers were shooting civilians. I saw the heap of bodies splashed with gasoline and set afire. Toward that fire a woman with a small child in her arms was being led. I turned her about and asked her, 'What

is going on here?' [From her escort] I received the answer that Hitler's order, which did not allow for taking prisoners, but called for the total destruction of Warsaw, was being carried out.

I went alongside the battle-line, and then called all the officers, who authenticated the existence of such an order. On my own responsibility, I nullified it immediately.[81]

Even after Von dem Bach had ordered an end to this massacre, there were occasions when German police murdered unarmed civilians, notably in Mokotów and Żoliborz. The effect of the slaughter in Wola was that survivors fled into AK-held areas, and the knowledge that the Germans drew no distinction between civilians and fighters led to an increased feeling of solidarity between them.[82]

The Germans killed patients in hospitals, making no attempt to distinguish between civilian patients and wounded AK soldiers. They also used Polish civilians to shield their advance. Groups of men and women would be tied to ladders held horizontally and forced to advance on foot ahead of the German infantry, and women were forced to get on to German tanks to prevent Polish attacks. A nurse at an AK nursing station noted: 'The legs of these women were like sieves, full of holes.'[83] The AK began the uprising planning to treat all Germans they took prisoner according to the Geneva Convention, and the evidence suggests that soldiers of the Wehrmacht were treated well. But the SS were tried by the underground courts and shot: 'One SS officer who had murdered Jews in the Ghetto offered a suitcase full of jewellery for his life. It was not accepted.'[84]

AK tactics were to allow the Germans to come close to their positions before showering the Germans with grenades, Molotov cocktails and machine-gun fire. Shortages of weapons was, however, a major problem and led to frustrating encounters, as when Ruth Altbeker witnessed an attack on a German tank:

Near to me two boys were watching. They quickly threw two bottles filled with petrol at the passing tank. Their aim was precise and the tank burst into flames. Two SS men with their hands up jumped from the burning vehicle. It was an exciting moment when the two Germans, trembling with fear, stammered 'Pardon, pardon.' I looked at the boys – neither had any weapon. The SS men stood dazed for a moment, uncertain about their fate.

They looked at the boys, the boys looked at them and eventually the Germans, their hands still raised high, their frightened eyes still staring at the lads, started slowly retreating in the direction of Szucha Street where at last they began running wildly. I gnashed my teeth in powerless anger. One of the boys was on the verge of tears. The tank was still burning on the roadway.[85]

If the uprising was to continue for more than a week, it was essential for the AK to receive supplies through airdrops, but the allied governments were under no obligation to do so: after all, they had repeatedly warned the Polish Government that such operations carried impossibly high risks. Nevertheless, as soon as news of the uprising reached London, Raczyński requested the British Government to do all that it could to assist, and Churchill was in favour of sending support. Requests were sent to the Brindisi air base in Italy to start making airdrops over Warsaw, but Air Marshal Sir Jack Slessor, deputy air commander for the Mediterranean area, later explained the difficulties:

> It was one thing to drop supplies to pre-arranged dropping-zones marked by light signals in open country ... It was quite another to bring a big aircraft down to a thousand feet ... over a great city, itself the scene of a desperate battle and consequently a mass of fires and flashes from guns and bursting shells ... and ringed by light AA [anti-aircraft] weapons.[86]

The round trip from Italy to Warsaw was 1,800 miles. Southern Italy was in the throes of bad weather which prevented all long-distance flights: on 2, 3 and 5–8 August, no flights could be made to Poland. The Poles also made emotional requests for the despatch of the Polish Parachute Brigade, arguing that even the arrival of one battalion would be an enormous morale boost as well as providing military support, but Alanbrooke turned them down.[87]

The Soviet Union was ideally placed to give assistance, since it controlled 6 airfields in Poland, the nearest of which was at Dęblin, a mere twenty minutes' flying time from Warsaw.[88] Churchill cabled Stalin informing him that the British and Poles were making airdrops, and requesting him to do the same. Stalin was in the middle of negotiations between Mikołajczyk, who had just arrived in Moscow, and representatives of the Lublin Committee. The latter had informed him that no uprising was in progress and so Stalin turned down Churchill's request. As evidence mounted that there was indeed an uprising in Warsaw,

Stalin then promised Mikołajczyk that the Soviets would make airdrops over the city, and Mikołajczyk reported this back to his government.[89] Lest it be thought that he was hearing what he wanted to hear, it should be noted that the American ambassador in Moscow, Averell Harriman, reported the same belief to the secretary of state, Cordell Hull, on 10 August. Yet Stalin did nothing, for reasons which will be discussed below. Churchill continued to put pressure on Stalin, and enlisted the support of Roosevelt, which he needed because he wanted the American-Soviet agreement regarding shuttle bombing of Germany, Operation Frantic, to be used to assist Warsaw. On 15 August, Vyshinsky delivered a firm refusal to allow American bombers to land at the base at Poltava in the Ukraine if they had dropped supplies to Warsaw. Churchill and Roosevelt responded by sending a joint appeal to Stalin on 20 August but received another refusal two days later.[90] In Moscow the chief of staff of the British military mission was making almost daily visits to the Soviet Ministry of Defence.[91] The deputy chief of the American military mission in Moscow, George Kennan, thought that the Allies should threaten to cut off aid to the Soviet Union if it did not help the Warsaw Uprising with airdrops or at least help the Allies make their own.[92]

Bór-Komorowski believed that if his government wanted the uprising to continue then it must make greater efforts to send supplies. In a telegram of 6 August, he stated: 'We are not asking for help – we are demanding that it be granted immediately.'[93] Regular airdrops were essential not just to enable the AK to keep fighting but also for the morale of the population of Warsaw, which was being badly affected by the lack of communication from London or airdrops. The government delegate Jankowski told London on 10 August:

> We have neither material nor moral help, because apart from a short speech by the Vice-Premier on 8 August, you have not even shown any acknowledgement of our action. In vain the soldiers and inhabitants of the city gaze into the sky, expecting help from the Allies. Only German planes are to be seen in the smoke. The people are surprised, they are deeply disappointed, and begin to revile you.[94]

One woman recalled her disgust with the Polish Government:

> Hungry, thirsty, often wounded, we would stand in courtyards, frequently under a hail of bullets, to hear at last a voice bringing real help. We listened,

we waited, but in return we received only words. Not only empty, but often painful words. Warsaw was in flames, the soldier-child was dying in the hospital cellar, and the Polish authorities in London were transmitting pathetic songs to give us strength! Sometimes we thought they were mocking us.[95]

John Ward made broadcasts to London which were printed in *The Times*:

Today a battle is going on in Warsaw that I think is very difficult for the British nation to understand. It is a battle that is being carried on as much by the civilian population as by the AK ... It is total warfare. Every street in the city has been a battlefield for the last twenty four days. The enemy mine-throwers, artillery and aircraft are taking a heavy toll of human life. The damage to property is incalculable. Normal life in the city is of course at a complete standstill.[96]

As the uprising continued, Bór-Komorowski and Jankowski sent further warnings to London that the lack of assistance was doing enormous political damage to the entire cause: 'Of course, after the fall of Warsaw, power in the whole country will fall into the hands of the communists.'[97]

The statistics certainly bear out the difficulties faced by the brave aircrews making the hazardous flight to Warsaw. Between 4 August and 21 September, a total of 199 aircraft took off from southern Italy – 94 Polish and 105 British and South African – but Warsaw itself only received 30 airdrops and the nearby Kampinos forest another 28. The difficulties in supplying Warsaw were immense. Flight Lieutenant R. Chmiel described one sortie:

Fires were blazing in every district of Warsaw. The dark spots were places occupied by the Jerries. Everything was smothered in smoke through which flickered ruddy, orange flames. I had never believed a big city could burn so. It was terrible: must have been hell for everybody down there.

The German flak was the hottest I have ever been through, so we got down just as low as we could – 70 or a 100 feet above ground; it was really too low, but we had to get out of the line of fire ... We nearly hit the Poniatowski Bridge as we cracked along the Vistula: the pilot hopped over it by the skin of his teeth ... We dropped the containers and knew we had made a good job of it.

It was time to clear out. The pilot came down a little lower, keeping an eye for steeples and high buildings. The cabin was full of smoke which got into our eyes and made them smart. We could feel the heat from the walls of the burnt-out district.[98]

Jan Nowak and John Ward witnessed a successful airdrop from a Polish plane but then: 'I could not help crying out in anguish at the explosion far away, beyond the city. In the flash when it was hit, for a split second we could see parts of the wings and the fuselage scattering in all directions.'[99] The cost of the allied airdrops was high, and Slessor later estimated that one bomber was lost for every ton of supplies delivered. The 1586th Polish Special Duties Squadron alone lost 16 crews in flights to Warsaw. The British also lost planes, and one landed on a Soviet-controlled airfield where the crew were interned by the Soviets until the British embassy in Moscow intervened on their behalf.[100] The AK command sent orders out to the districts to give details concerning the fate of allied aircrew, which would be radioed back to London so that, ultimately, the British Air Ministry could inform the relatives of the airmen.[101] The airdrops had, however, provided the AK with 1,344 small arms, 3,855 machine pistols, 380 light machine guns, 237 bazookas, 13 mortars, 130 rifles, around 14,000 hand grenades and over 3,000 anti-tank grenades, over 4,500,000 rounds of ammunition, 8½ tons of plastic explosive and 45 tons of food. The AK managed to retrieve about 50 per cent of the canisters in the early airdrops but this percentage fell steadily as the insurgent-held areas shrank.[102]

Within Warsaw the AK insurgents were beginning to lose ground: Wola and Ochota had been lost, and there had been a temporary withdrawal of AK units from Mokotów and Żoliborz. The Germans began to concentrate all their resources on the reduction of individual sectors. The first area to experience the full impact of an all-out German attack was the Old Town, a six-centuries-old warren of narrow streets, overlooking the Kierbedź and railway bridges. Bór-Komorowski described the German tactics:

The Goliaths [remote-controlled miniature tanks filled with explosives] were the first to attack. Their object was to blow up barricades and heavy concrete structures. They were opposed by our forward soldiers, who watched for them on the far side of barricades, hidden in ruins or in the angles of walls. They would try to cut the control wires with precision grenade-throwing. The Goliaths were followed by heavy Tigers which attacked while firing at short range. Only then did the infantry begin – by that time they were usually faced with ruins. The enemy was allowed to advance unchallenged, sometimes to within a grenade's-throw, sometimes into a building. It was often hand-to-hand.[103]

The Germans sent 8,000 troops into the battle and the result was catastrophic for the Poles: 'A sea of fire and bombs had swallowed up a square kilometre of ancient, dry-rotted buildings, packed with tens of thousands of people.'[104] On 13 August, a booby-trapped German tank, captured by the AK, blew up in the middle of a crowd of onlookers, killing over 400. An AK fighter, Jan Dobraczyński, noted that incident 'seemed to presage defeat in the Old Town. From that day there was a considerable increase in the number of victims. More and more graves appeared in the courtyards and on the grass.'[105] By the beginning of September, it was clear that the AK would have to withdraw.

Before the uprising had begun no plans had been made on how the insurgents in different areas of Warsaw were to communicate with each other, and radio traffic between them had to go via London. Therefore, the AK command established an impromptu communications network using the complicated labyrinth of sewers running under Warsaw. Signposts were painted on the sewer walls and a system of guides and messengers issued with special passes was created. Supplies were brought in to the Old Town via the sewers and the severely wounded evacuated. A veteran and historian of the uprising recalled a journey through the sewers:

> We advanced slowly in the slime and after a while the smell did not seem so overwhelming. We crossed several intersections where the sewage fluid moved swiftly and light penetrated from open manholes. Our hands, our shoes, in fact everything was covered in slime. Periodically we rested. The trip seemed to go on forever although it did not last more than three hours.[106]

As it became evident that the AK could no longer hold the Old Town, an evacuation of AK units via the sewers began, but, controversially, many civilians and the wounded were left behind to face the wrath of the Germans. About 5,000 insurgents were killed in the battle for the

Old Town, which ended on 2 September, and the Germans also suffered casualties to over half their force.[107] Shortly afterwards the area of Powiśle by the Vistula fell.

The western allies continued to work on behalf of the beleaguered Poles. On 25 August, Churchill sent Roosevelt the draft of a telegram which he proposed to send to Stalin on the subject of sending American planes from Britain to make an airdrop on Warsaw which asked Stalin bluntly: 'Why should they not land on the refuelling ground which has been assigned to us behind the Russian lines without enquiry as to what they have done on the way?' Roosevelt's reply the following day demonstrated that he was not willing to join Churchill in such a bold statement: 'I do not consider it advantageous to the long range general war prospect for me to join with you in the proposed message.'[108] Churchill did not send the telegram, but continued to apply pressure in other ways. On 4 September, the British Government sent a telegram to Molotov informing him that British public opinion was beginning to question why the Soviets were doing nothing to help the Poles in Warsaw.[109] The Soviet embassy in London also noticed that the normally pro-Soviet British press was becoming embarrassed by Soviet inactivity.[110] Churchill was so enraged by Stalin's refusal to allow allied planes to land on Soviet airfields that he even suggested to Roosevelt that the Allies should ignore the embargo and just go ahead and land on them anyway. Roosevelt was not prepared to risk the alliance, especially since his chief of staff, Admiral William Leahy, had confused the fall of the Old Town with the collapse of the whole Warsaw Uprising.[111]

On 29 August, the governments of Britain and the United States did take a step of immense importance: they issued separate but identically worded declarations granting combatant rights to the AK: 'The Polish Home Army, which is now mobilised, constitutes a combatant force forming an integral part of the Polish Armed Forces.'[112] On 9 September, the British Government went further in another declaration that effectively extended combatant rights to the civilians.[113] These statements were extremely important to Bór-Komorowski and to 'Monter' because, at the beginning of September, they had to decide whether or not to continue the uprising, which had already extended far beyond the week they had originally envisaged. Now they knew that, if the AK surrendered, the western allies would do their utmost to ensure that the AK soldiers would be treated as POWs and not be massacred.

The situation in Warsaw was deteriorating rapidly. Bór-Komorowski telegraphed London on 6 September: 'The civilian population is undergoing a crisis, which could have a fundamental influence on the fighting units.' The withdrawal from the Old Town had taken its toll, and the civilians were now badly demoralised by the incessant bombardment, starvation rations, and the lack of water and electricity. As John Ward reported in *The Times*, conditions were appalling:

> On every conceivable little piece of ground are graves of civilians and soldiers. Worst of all, however, is the smell of rotting bodies, which pervades over the whole centre of the city. Thousands of people are buried under the ruins ... Soldiers defending their battered barricades are an awful sight. Mostly they are dirty, hungry and ragged. There are very few who have not received some sort of wound. And on and on, through a city of ruins, suffering and dead.[114]

The Poles knew that Paris had been liberated on 25 August, but otherwise had little idea of the overall progress of the war; hence Bór-Komorowski's extraordinary question: 'Do you think that action in the west will bring about the end of the war within the next few days?'[115] On 6 September, he and Jankowski sent a joint communiqué outlining the seriousness of the situation in Warsaw and the three options facing the AK: the evacuation of the civilian population of the city with the agreement of the Germans, after which the AK would 'fight to the end'; the unconditional surrender of the entire city; or to continue the battle and surrender each district in turn when overwhelmed by the German forces. The two men appeared to favour the last: 'This solution would gain a little time, but at the same time destroy the whole city.'[116] They hoped that the time gained would enable further supplies to reach them through airdrops and for the Soviet forces to advance to their rescue.

At the same time as this telegram was despatched and before a reply could be received, talks between the Poles and Germans had opened on the possibilities of evacuating civilians from Warsaw. On three days, 8–10 September, there were brief ceasefires to allow this. The underground newspaper *Biuletyn Informacyjny* warned that, although the Polish Red Cross would supervise the evacuation, no one knew how the Germans would behave. On 9 September, the Underground Government distributed leaflets explaining the events of the previous day:

According to news received the Germans confiscate all larger pieces of baggage from those leaving, therefore there is no point in burdening yourselves with large amounts of food, clothing, linen etc.

It has been ascertained that men are separated from their families by the Germans.

Everyone must spend a few days in the camp at Pruszków and from there the men are sent to do fortification work and women and children will be sent west.

The Underground Government advised the sick, the old and mothers with children to leave, but expected all the young men to stay to continue the fight. Estimates on the number who did leave vary, but it can be assumed that it was between 20,000 and 25,000.[117]

On 10 September, General Rohr, commanding the Germans forces in the south part of Warsaw, invited Bór-Komorowski or his representatives to talks to discuss the terms for surrender. Bór-Komorowski was prepared to surrender on three conditions: that combatant rights for the AK soldiers would be respected and no reprisals taken against them for their activities in the period before combatant rights had been granted by the western allies; clarification of the fate of the civilians; and clarification of the German attitude towards the Underground Government. Rohr responded with assurances that there would be no reprisals against either the AK or the Underground Government, that combatant rights would be assured and that the civilian population would be evacuated westwards out of the range of the Soviet advance. Bór-Komorowski responded with a request that the civilian population be allowed to remain in Warsaw, and demanded that the agreement should be endorsed by General Georg-Hans Reinhardt, the commander of the Central Front, and announced on German radio.[118] These conditions, as Bór-Komorowski informed London on 10 September, were designed to delay the surrender because: 'Today there was a marked weakening of artillery fire and bombing of the enemy ... Combat aircraft over Warsaw and the sounds of fighting from the direction of Praga. If we hear more gunfire today we will try to continue fighting. Further airdrops daily will allow us to continue resistance.'[119]

Because it seemed that the Red Army was renewing its advance on Warsaw, the AK command made two important decisions: to continue the uprising, particularly now that the most vulnerable civilians had been evacuated, and to prepare to greet the Soviet Army. The plans prepared by Bór-Komorowski and Jankowski followed similar lines to those that had failed in Operation *Burza*. All the AK units fighting in the city would be incorporated to form an *Armia Krajowa* Warsaw Corps, which would open the thoroughfares through Warsaw to enable the Soviets to clear the city of Germans and advance further west. Then the corps would fight as an independent unit alongside the Red Army. Under no circumstances would it allow itself to be disarmed by the Soviets or incorporated into the 1st Polish Army. Jankowski expanded on these plans:

> In the Centre City Sector there [will] be Polish civilian and military authorities. The Deputy Prime Minister the Delegate, as rightful host of the city and of the country, will welcome the Red Army. The Armia Krajowa will be concentrated in the same region to provide security in the case of unfriendly activities or provocation. The Government Delegate of the city of Warsaw will undertake the civilian administration of the city as temporary mayor. The preconceived attitude toward the Red Army [will] be one of friendship and willingness to cooperate, on condition [that] the Polish authorities are respected.[120]

Throughout the uprising Bór-Komorowski had been receiving further reports from Soviet-occupied Poland, all of which contained the same message: the Soviets disarmed the AK, arrested many of the officers and conscripted the men into the 1st Polish Army. Therefore, there appears to be no good reason why he should have assumed that the Soviet entry into Warsaw would lead to any other result.

There can be no doubt that Stalin did not welcome the outbreak of the Warsaw Uprising. After all, a few days earlier, he had telegraphed Churchill to explain his endorsement of the Lublin Committee as the administrators of liberated Poland, justifying his support on the grounds that there appeared to be no organised underground army or underground government. The uprising had proved him wrong. It is clear from his telegrams to Churchill that Stalin expected the uprising to be crushed soon; he called it a 'reckless and fearful gamble', and told Churchill: 'Soviet headquarters have decided that they must disassociate themselves from the Warsaw adventure since they cannot assume either direct or indirect responsibility for it.'[121] The uprising continued, however, much longer than anyone, including its commanders, had predicted. This put Stalin in a dilemma: to refuse all help brought international criticism, but to provide airdrops, to assist the Allies with their airdrops and to provide artillery and air support to the uprising would necessitate a reversal in the position taken towards the participants in Operation *Burza* and force him to recognise the existence and authority of the AK and Underground Government.

It is indisputable that when the uprising began the Soviet 1st Belorussian Front under Rokossovsky was not in a position to mount an all-out attack to take Warsaw. In the first place, the Soviet armies were too spread out. The 48th and 65th Armies were still over 60 miles away from Warsaw, the right wing had only just reached the Narew river, the 70th Army was engaged in taking control of Brześć and the 47th Army was fighting at Siedlce; only the lead elements of the 2nd Tank Army were approaching Praga. In the second place, the two bridgeheads over the Vistula at Magnuszów and Puławy, to the south of Warsaw, held by the 8th Guards and 69th Armies and the 1st Polish Army, were temporarily subjected to a strong counterattack by the German forces. As Rokossovsky quite correctly claimed later, a rising in Warsaw could assist the Soviet advance but 'the question of timing was of the utmost importance'.[122] It should be remembered that General 'Monter' Chruściel had been opposed to launching the uprising until the whereabouts of Soviet troops were known; it was the faulty intelligence that Soviet tanks were in Praga that had made him change his mind.

Even without an attack on Warsaw, the Soviet forces could still have given air and artillery support during August. Air support would have been particularly valued since the Luftwaffe operated freely over Warsaw: 'Reconnaissance planes flew over the houses with impunity, spotting targets for the artillery and the bombers.'[123] A Soviet captain, Konstanty Kalugin, whose reasons for being in Warsaw are obscure, sent a lengthy message to Stalin on 5 August:

> Having been informed of the general military situation, I have come to the conclusion that, despite the heroic attitude of the army and of the civilian population of Warsaw, there are certain requirements which, when fulfilled, would speed up the victory in the struggle against our common enemy.

He not only went on to list the types of weaponry required but also provided details of where airdrops could be made, and listed some targets for Soviet artillery. Kalugin had no direct contact with Rokossovsky, so his message was sent by the roundabout route of the AK command to Polish headquarters in London, to the British Government, from their Foreign Office to the British embassy in Moscow, and finally to the Soviet authorities.[124]

The 1st Polish Army had taken part in the attempt to force the Vistula at Dęblin and Puławy, but fierce German resistance and the combat inexperience of the Poles meant that the operation failed at the beginning of August. The Polish troops were withdrawn and sent to reinforce the Soviet bridgehead at Magnuszów. After the heavy German counter-attack had stalled, on 8 August Rokossovsky informed Stalin that he would be in a position to attack Warsaw around the 25th, but Stalin did not respond. Instead, the main Soviet effort was turned southwards into the Balkans, and it seemed that the 1st Belorussian Front was to remain on the defensive outside Warsaw.[125] Rokossovsky was permitted to undertake limited operations to secure the bridgeheads, and the momentum of the 1st Belorussian Front and 1st Polish Army carried them into Praga on 11 September. On the 13th, the Germans were forced to blow up all the bridges joining Warsaw to the east bank. General Rola-Żymierski reported to the Lublin Committee:

> On 13 and 14 September the 1st Polish Division was engaged in fighting. Marshal Rokossovsky is full of praise for it. The 1st Division showed such speed in its advance that it had to be restrained so that the rest of the line could catch up. The soldiers are full of enthusiasm. After much heavy fighting their losses are 3,400 dead and wounded. These are serious losses, but then this was street fighting. The size of these losses will have a large political impact.[126]

The Poles in the 1st Polish Army were keen to take the fight into Warsaw to help the uprising, but 'we were made to gaze, powerless, as Warsaw went up in flames. Our Soviet officers, under penalty of death, forbade us to come to the aid of the dying city.'[127] Nina Kochańska was visited by a friend in the Polish artillery, who told her that 'they were sitting in dugouts by the Vistula unable to fire because they had no ammunition'.[128] The Lublin Committee needed to do something to assist the uprising because to do nothing would have been politically suicidal and have forfeited it all the support it had worked so hard to gain. International pressure was also beginning to have an effect on Stalin.

Stalin finally gave in and on the night of 13–14 September, the Soviets made a massive airdrop on Warsaw with 382 planes carrying a total of 64,000 pounds of food, 18,000 rounds of ammunition and 1,200 grenades.[129] These flights continued until 29 September. The AK was squeezed into ever-shrinking sectors, meaning that to achieve pinpoint accuracy the Soviet airdrops had to be made from such a low level that parachutes did not have time to inflate, so many of the canisters split open on hitting the ground, rendering their contents useless. For example, Janusz Zawodny witnessed the descent of a Soviet long-barrelled anti-tank rifle which bent into a pretzel when it hit the ground. Most of the ammunition dropped was of Soviet manufacture and did not fit the Polish weapons and those seized from the Germans. It should have been possible for the Soviets to have sent German war materiel which they had captured, but only 350 German carbines were dropped.[130] The Soviets offered some other assistance with sporadic artillery support and air support, but they did not succeed in knocking out the single most fearsome weapon in the German artillery, the Karl Morser heavy mortar, last used in the siege of Sevastopol in 1942, which sent shells 2 feet wide and nearly 3 feet long and weighing half a ton into Warsaw, causing immense destruction. A single shell could demolish an entire apartment building.[131] The Soviets could have given more efficient assistance had communications been established between AK headquarters and Rokossovsky's headquarters. Rokossovsky later denied that the AK attempted to make contact with him, yet AK sources list the liaison officers sent across the Vistula and the instructions on how to open direct telephone contact.[132]

Stalin also at last permitted the shuttle bombing facilities at Poltava to be used by the Americans for an airdrop on Warsaw. On 18 September, 110 B-17s accompanied by 73 fighters from the Third American Air Division flew to Warsaw from its bases in Britain and dropped almost 1,300 containers over the city. As Stefan Korboński watched, he heard the cries of 'too high, too high' as the American bombers came overhead, followed by groans of frustration as the containers drifted out of reach: only 388 canisters were retrieved by the AK. No planes were lost during the airdrop.[133]

In Warsaw the AK was running out of soldiers and arms. On 14 August, Bór-Komorowski had sent messages to the AK units outside the city to come Warsaw's aid but few got through.[134] Indeed, the AK partisan units outside the city were unwilling to help, because they had not been trained for urban fighting and could see the futility of such a gesture. A gleam of hope remained to the south of the city, where Hungarian units were stationed; they were wavering in their loyalty to Germany and, on 23 August, 'Monter' could report: 'Hungarian units placed south of Mokotów display great cordiality towards the Polish population; they also warn us about the Germans and do not interfere with our actions.' One AK platoon commander was given coffee by the Hungarians on his way to Warsaw. Polish approaches to the Hungarians for further assistance, such as joining the AK or giving them artillery, were turned down. The policy of the Hungarian Government appeared to be not to allow its troops to join the Poles but also not to intervene against them.[135] As the areas under AK control shrank, more airdrops were made into the nearby Kampinos forest, and from there smuggled into Żoliborz, with the Hungarians turning a blind eye to the AK's activities.

With Praga lost to them, the Germans turned their attention to attacking Czerniaków, the area directly across the Vistula from the 1st Polish Army, in order to prevent the Poles from crossing the river. On 15 September, Berling issued orders for such an attempt to be made. The main attack was to be towards Czerniaków by the 4rd Infantry Division, under General Stanisław Galicki, with subsidiary operations towards Żoliborz by the 2nd Infantry Division, under General Antoni Siwicki, and to the area between the Poniatowski and Kierbedź bridges by the 1st Cavalry Brigade, under Colonel Włodziemierz Radwonowicz. The first attempt at crossing the river on the night of 15–16 September ended in disaster: 120 men out of 150 in the leading company were killed or wounded. According to the artillery commander, Colonel Frankowski, many of the Soviet officers were drunk and never took up their commands. Also the crossing started late, just before dawn, and the boats were spotted by the Germans and destroyed.[136] The Poles retreated to Praga, bringing with them two AK officers, one of whom, Major Kmita, had been assigned as a liaison officer to the 1st Polish Army.

A second crossing was made to Żoliborz on the night of 18–19 September with 3,370 soldiers but they were unable to make contact with the AK. A renewed attempt to cross into Czerniaków was more successful and two battalions of the 9th Infantry Regiment established contact with the AK units under the command of Lieutenant-Colonel Jan 'Radoslaw' Mazurkiewicz. The AK noted the appearance of the soldiers of the 1st Polish Army:

> Our new friends wore long khaki coats of the pre-war Polish cut and large Soviet helmets with a 12th century Polish eagle – without a crown – painted on them. Some had the four-cornered Polish field caps. They addressed us as 'brothers' or 'citizens', and spoke of their 'political education officer'. It all made us feel somewhat uneasy. We noticed that while they were armed to the teeth, including the brand-new semi-automatic rifles which even the powerful *Wehrmacht* did not have at that time, their personal equipment consisted of simple sacks hanging on their backs. They were mostly peasants from the eastern plains and marshes conscripted only a few months before. Most had never seen a city before – and were now looking at a ruin.[137]

The Germans sent an armoured column and the SS to crush the Czerniaków bridgehead, and in the fierce eight-day battle the 1st Polish Army suffered the loss of 4,892 men.[138] The casualty rate was so high largely because: 'They had had no battle experience, they did not know how to seek cover on the ground, and they were decimated like flies.'[139] The most experienced Polish division, the 1st, had been withdrawn from Praga after the heavy fighting there, and the men in the 2nd and 3rd Divisions had been recruited only recently. The withdrawal took place on the night of 22–23 September. The 1st Polish Army would not enter Warsaw again until January 1945.

The collapse of the Czerniaków bridgehead left the Germans free to concentrate on the reduction of Mokotów and Żoliborz. On 24 September, Jan Nowak met Okulicki, the AK chief of staff, who warned him that the AK would have to surrender soon because there was no more ammunition or food. Nowak was concerned about the Soviet reaction but Okulicki assured him:

> The Russians will accuse us whatever we do. The accusation about starting the fighting prematurely would have made sense had the Rising collapsed after a few days or a week, but we gave the Russians nearly two months, more than enough advantage for them to renew the attack and liberate the city. But don't be afraid. Before we fly the white flag, Marshal Rokossovsky will be forewarned, and if we get any sort of indication from him

that the Russians are willing to renew their offensive, all talk of surrender will be suspended at once.[140]

On 28 September, a meeting was held between General von dem Bach and Lieutenant-Colonel Zygmunt Dobrowolski, representing Bór-Komorowski. Von dem Bach made four proposals: the recognition of combatant status for all AK male and female fighters; officers would be allowed to keep their personal arms; the International Red Cross would supervise the surrender; and the civilian population would be evacuated from Warsaw. If the AK wished to continue fighting, then the Germans still wanted the evacuation of the civilian population, after which 'the fighting would be carried out with every available means until the town and the army were totally destroyed'.[141] That evening Dobrowolski reported to a meeting of the AK command attended by Bór-Komorowski, Jankowski, the deputy commander of the AK, General Pełczyński, Okulicki, 'Monter' and three other leading members of the underground. After a long discussion, opinions on surrender were divided, and Bór-Komorowski concluded that he was in favour of the evacuation of the civilian population but wanted to delay the surrender of the army. The excuse given, which was accepted by von dem Bach, was that the Poles wanted time to inspect the civilian camp at Pruszków.[142]

On 29 September, Bór-Komorowski contacted Rokossovsky asking him to renew his offensive and Mikołajczyk sent a final appeal to Stalin: 'At this extreme hour of need I appeal to you, Marshal, to issue orders for immediate operations which would relieve the garrison of Warsaw and result in the liberation of the capital.' No response was received.[143] Although the Poles were not satisfied with the conditions at Pruszków, the decision was made to go ahead with the civilian evacuation then. On 1 October, under a ceasefire in the city centre, about 8,000 civilians left, but, on the following day, a mass exodus began:

I looked closely at the faces of the people around me. They all looked extremely exhausted; their faces bore the traces of two months spent mostly in dirty, dark, damp cellars, pervaded by a terrible stench, without light or water and with little food, subjected to shelling, bombing, and bursting mines, all the time expecting the cellar to collapse, burying them alive in a common grave. All this misery and pain had been in vain. It was now to end in a stream of homeless people wandering out into the unknown.[144]

Gradually, Warsaw was emptied of its civilian population, about 280,000, who were then processed in the camp at Pruszków. Around 4,500 Jews had been killed in the uprising: some were civilian casualties, some died fighting with the AK or AL, and a few were killed by anti-semitic Poles. After the surrender the remaining 'hidden' Jews of Warsaw mostly departed for Pruszków and shared the fate of the other Polish civilians, but some, such as Władysław Szpilman, hid in the ruins, and a number crossed the Vistula and were saved by the Soviets.[145]

Over 100,000 civilians were sent as slave labour to the Reich and thousands were sent to the concentration camps at Auschwitz, Ravensbrück and Mauthausen.[146] Those unable to work were abandoned to find somewhere to live and some means by which to survive. The German governor of the General Government, Hans Frank, 'urged the population to be generous to the stricken survivors, to give refuge, accumulate relief funds for them, and on top of that he initiated a public collection of money'. The Poles responded well: 'Along the railway track peasant carts from various neighbouring villages waited, and the peasants simply invited the refugees into their huts.'[147] The Underground Government left with the civilians, hoping to escape detention and to re-form later.

At 9 p.m. on 2 October, Bór-Komorowski signed the capitulation agreement. On the same day, the Polish Government informed him that he had been appointed as commander-in-chief of the Polish Armed Forces in succession to Sosnkowski, who had controversially been sacked. On the 3rd, Bór-Komorowski transmitted the terms of surrender to London, and then he and 'Monter' broadcast a farewell to the AK. On 4 October, Bór-Komorowski informed London that he had appointed Okulicki to succeed him as commander of the AK with orders to continue the underground fight. He also told London that he felt morally obliged to march into captivity with the soldiers he had commanded: 'My escape would have been looked upon by the Germans as a breach of the agreement I had signed with them, and would undoubtedly have had repercussions on the fate of both soldiers and civilians.'[148] He was accompanied by other leading AK commanders, including 'Monter' and the chief of staff, Pełczyński. The AK was ordered by the Germans to supervise the evacuation of the civilians and the surrender of the insurgents and their weapons:

I recall the surprise on the faces of the German soldiers on seeing the equipment we were handing over – old revolvers, rifles that had long seen no use, rusty bayonets. It was nothing strange really, most of our functioning weapons had been carefully wrapped and buried: they just might come in handy later.[149]

In general the Germans treated the AK fighters with respect as is illustrated by a meeting between a Polish patrol and a German patrol:

When the Home Army patrol was only a few yards away from the Germans, the German officer in command raised his hand to his cap, the soldiers slapped the butts of their rifles, and holding themselves stiffly, they stamped the pavement briskly with their boots. The Home Army patrol did a smart 'eyes left'; and in this way the mortal foes, the Poles and the Germans, exchanged honours.[150]

At 9.45 a.m. on 5 October, the AK marched out of Warsaw and a total of 15,378 insurgents and 922 officers, including 3,000 women, became POWs.[151]

The men were despatched to join other Polish POWs in camps run by the Wehrmacht in Germany. The women, however, suffered a very different fate, as the Wehrmacht had no idea of how to treat them since their only experience of women captives were those in various resistance movements without POW status. The women were sent to various camps in Germany, usually adjacent to the men's camps, but lived in tents rather than huts like the men. Pressure was put on them to renounce their POW status and to become civilian workers, and those who refused to do so, 1,721 of the 3,000, were sent to a penal camp at Oberlangen. This had been a POW camp until October 1944 when the International Red Cross was informed that it was now disused, so the IRC did not know of the presence of the women POWs there. The women received no aid and lived in appalling conditions until they were liberated by General Maczek's 1st Polish Armoured Division in April 1945.[152]

The human cost of the Warsaw Uprising was very high, with casualty figures varying from 150,000 to 200,000. Most were civilians, who had been killed in mass executions, died of disease, malnutrition or exhaustion, or, during the fighting, were buried in the cellars, blown to bits by shell-fire or drowned in the sewers trying to escape. About 40,000 AK soldiers took part and the figures give testimony to their determination: 10,200 killed, 7,000 missing presumed killed, 5,000 seriously wounded, making a casualty rate of over 50 per cent. The 1st Polish Army lost 4,892 killed, wounded or missing. Von dem Bach gave the German casualty figures as: 10,000 dead, 7,000 missing and 9,000 wounded.[153]

As Warsaw was emptied the Germans sent in workers to strip the buildings systematically of everything of any value:

> Thousands of wagon-loads of furniture, carpets, pictures and clothing were being despatched into the Reich. All museums, libraries, collections, factory equipment, workshops and laboratories were transported to Germany. The looting assumed gigantic proportions. All efforts to save as much as possible on the part of the Poles who, with the approval of the underground, worked in the German administration of the city under Burgomeister Leist remained ineffective; as were all the attempts at intervention with Governor Fischer, who now resided in Sochaczew.[154]

Then the special German force, the *Verbrennungs und Vernichtungskommando* (Burning and Destruction Detachment), began the well-planned destruction of the city. Out of Warsaw's 24,724 buildings, 10,455 were completely destroyed. All major public buildings, including St John's Cathedral, the Royal Palace, the Opera and Ballet House and the main library, were blown up.[155] The destruction took three months, and a soldier with the 1st Polish Army, Jan Karniewicz, watched helplessly with his fellow Poles as the Germans burned Warsaw: 'there was an aura over Warsaw in the evening – a red aura, a pink aura'.[156] Even the Soviets were moved, for a Soviet bomber pilot Alexandr Markov wrote: 'We knew that Warsaw was once the most beautiful capital in Europe. Now, when we flew over it we saw huge palls of smoke, and even from the air we could smell burned flesh. My spine crawled, to see so much beauty transformed into ruins ... all those golden bell towers gone.'[157]

So what if anything had been achieved by Operation *Burza* and the Warsaw Uprising? By early October 1944, most of the leading AK commanders and their best soldiers had been killed, murdered, arrested or imprisoned in the German prisoner of war camps, in Soviet prisons in Poland or in the Soviet Gulag. The remnants of the AK command and the Underground Government were in a state of total disarray, searching for a new base of operations and a redefined purpose. The Polish

Government in London had lost a considerable amount of credibility because it had manifestly failed to keep its representatives in Poland fully informed about the international situation, and then had proved unable to support the uprisings either politically through publicity or militarily by ensuring adequate supplies through airdrops. General Okulicki wrote in spring 1945:

> If a political error was made, the politicians, who were supposed to have taken care of relations with the Soviet Union, are responsible for it. The leadership and the soldiers of the Home Army only did their duty in service for their nation, when they started the battle for Warsaw and conducted it for sixty-three days. They could not have done otherwise, it would have been fainthearted and cowardly.[158]

Another nail in its coffin was added when Mikołajczyk resigned as prime minister in November, following the failure of his talks with Stalin in Moscow in October. He was succeeded by Tomasz Arciszewski, whose government became known as the 'Government of National Protest'. The decline in the influence of the Polish Government in London did not necessarily lead to support for the Lublin Committee; rather, the Poles felt cast adrift and leaderless.

The Allies had fared no better: the inability of Churchill and Roosevelt to convince Stalin to provide aid to Warsaw during the first critical month of the uprising demonstrated uncomfortably his pre-eminent position in the alliance. Stalin's reputation, too, was damaged: before the uprising the western allies had been unwilling to believe Polish reports of the hostility of the Soviet authorities towards the AK, but his refusal to assist Warsaw awakened suspicion in the western allied camp concerning his future intentions towards Poland and the other countries the Red Army was in the process of 'liberating'.

For the remainder of 1944, the territories of pre-war Poland were effectively split into three zones of occupation. The Germans held the territory to the west of the Vistula. East of the Bug river were Poland's eastern provinces, to which the Soviet Union laid claim, and which were administered directly by their authorities. In the middle, between the Bug and the Vistula, the Lublin Committee sought to establish itself as the only legitimate administrative body in liberated Poland.

The German attitude towards the Poles after the uprising was confused. While they attempted to encourage the natural anti-Soviet stance of the majority, the regime of terror still continued. In an effort to woo the Poles, Hans Frank made a proposal to create a Polish National Committee in Kraków. In addition, the Germans would select prominent Poles, including priests, to serve on local committees in every district. Okulicki quickly saw through the scheme and 'decided in a flash that all the people nominated should be warned so that they could choose between a German and a Polish bullet'.[159] The Germans ran out of time to implement their plan. The regime in Auschwitz I even became more lenient, as one inmate recalled:

> I remember in '44 the paint Kommando had to go about seven kilometres away from the main camp to do some work on houses near the fish-ponds: Auschwitz was very famous before the war for its carp farms. One of the older SS came with us, instead of the young one we'd been expecting, and when we had our meal break, one of us asked him if we could supplement our soup with a carp from the ponds. 'Go ahead', he said, and we took a couple of carp out and baked them on a fire – and he ate with us. We asked him why the young SS man hadn't been put in charge of us, and he said that it was because it wasn't felt that the young SS man had enough experience to deal with us 'old' numbers.[160]

The Germans had been impressed by the performance of the AK and its commander, so they approached Bór-Komorowski several times to ask him to assist in the formation of an anti-Bolshevik Polish legion; he declined.[161] As the prospect of a Soviet invasion and occupation of Germany became likelier, the head of German intelligence in the east, General Reinhard Gehlen, was asked what preparations should be made, and his response was that the Germans should follow the model of the AK.[162]

At the same time the Germans acknowledged that the security situation was deteriorating and consequently issued a draconian order:

> The Reichsführer SS, in agreement with the Governor General, has given the order that in every case of assassination or attempted assassination of Germans, not only the perpetrators shall be shot when caught, but that, in addition, all their male relatives shall also be executed, and their female relatives above the age of sixteen put into a concentration camp.[163]

This was the same sort of order, *Sippenhaft*, that the SS had applied within Germany with regard to the relatives of the 20 July 1944 conspirators; it was now applied to the AK. Extermination of the Jews continued: during the autumn of 1944, the Jews, including a number of Polish citizenship, were deported from Hungary to Auschwitz-Birkenau, and virtually all of them were gassed on arrival. The Polish underground resistance within Auschwitz I attempted to warn the Jews of their impending fate and to encourage them to rush the SS, but to no avail.[164] On 7 October, the SS received a major shock when the *Sonderkommando* staged an uprising, blowing up one crematorium and damaging others. At the end of October, Himmler ordered the demolition of the gas chambers and crematoria, bringing to an end the genocide at Auschwitz-Birkenau.[165]

Polish men and women were conscripted by the Germans to build anti-tank defences along the front line. Teresa Kicińska and other young women were ordered to join a work party digging ditches about 20 miles east of Kielce. They were guarded by equally young Wehrmacht soldiers, who preferred to take them for drives and to flirt with them rather than treat them brutally or see the anti-tank ditches dug, which, since they were in very sandy soil, was a pointless exercise. The situation was, however, potentially flammable as Teresa Kicińska discovered when she slapped one young German officer across the face when he became too frisky. The German overseer threatened to withdraw her papers, and without them she would have no means of getting food. On the advice of her fellow Poles, she fled back home to Kielce and, before the Germans came looking for her, left Poland for Austria at the end of October 1944.[166] The work regime could also, however, be brutal. In East Prussia, Jan Korzybski was ordered to dig trenches near the Masurian Lakes where the work was hard, rations barely above starvation level, accompanied by frequent brutal beatings, and workers were shot if they took unauthorised breaks. In the winter his work party was taken to the Augustowskie Lakes and forced to cut out blocks of ice to make a patchwork of ice pyramids as an anti-tank defence on the lakes.[167]

Okulicki, named by Bór-Komorowski as his successor as commander of the AK, left Warsaw with the civilian population and travelled via Kielce to Częstochowa to rebuild the AK. The Polish Government in London had not been consulted about this appointment and did not confirm it until 21 December 1944.[168] Okulicki reported on the state of the AK on 9 December:

> Many provincial units, and in particular those which were operating in the Kampinos Forest, have been destroyed, while the soldiers of these units have taken shelter in the area on their own or in small groups. In the desperate situation in which these people find themselves, there lies the danger of the transformation of these small groups into common plundering bands or of their defection to the People's Army, which serves Russia. To sum up: as a result of the loss of the Battle of Warsaw, grave signs of demoralization have appeared in the ranks of the Home Army in the provinces. New attitudes have arisen as well in society, as has a new reality, which must be taken into account.[169]

The Kampinos group, operating in the vast forest to the west of Warsaw, had taken little part in the fighting for Warsaw and had been destroyed in an attack launched on 27 September by three battalions of the Hermann Goering Panzer Division and the SS Panzer Divisions *Totenkopf* and *Wiking*.[170] The Radom district still had two untouched infantry divisions of 7,000 soldiers, and the AK was also active near Kielce, engaged mostly in ambushing small German units, with other small units operating near Łódź.[171] Sometimes the AK was approached by German deserters wishing to join it, and all were screened. As Ralph Smorczewski recalled, some were 'members of the notorious Kaminski Brigade so were directed to a shed at the edge of the village and given plenty of alcohol before being killed during the night'. Another member of the AK remembered: 'All over Poland, the forests echoed with the executioners' guns', as the AK took revenge against the SS.[172]

The surviving remnants of the AK and the Underground Government clearly needed to redefine their plans. Both Okulicki and the government delegate, Jankowski, knew that Operation *Burza* had failed. The Underground Government, now in Kraków, informed Mikołajczyk on 19 November that in their opinion: 'It makes no difference to us whatsoever that some locality which will become known because of our further bleeding will thereby be occupied by the Soviets a half day sooner.'[173] Reports reaching the AK command from all over Soviet-occupied Poland indicated that, as the Soviets were making widespread arrests of all members of the Polish civilian and military underground. So the days of the AK in its existing form appeared to be numbered. The Polish Government in London thought, however, that it was still possible for the AK to act as hosts for the Soviet armies.

The ability of the Poles to continue resistance against their occupiers, both German and Soviet, was limited by the lack of support from outside Poland. Allied flights from Italy faced the risk of being shot down by the Soviets if they flew across Rumania or by German air defences between Vienna and Kraków. From Italy, Air Marshal Slessor informed Air Marshal Portal at the Air Ministry on 20 November:

> To continue to ask our crews to run the gauntlet of German night fighter defences in the Vienna-Cracow area where they could reach their targets just as easily while flying in safety behind Russian lines is a grave reflection on the status of the Russians as Allies.[174]

The Air Ministry attempted to obtain Soviet permission for operations to Poland to cross Soviet-occupied territory, but it was refused, and Portal wrote to Churchill: 'If it is politically necessary to continue to supply the Poles by air, I suggest that we ought to try to get this absurd decision reversed.'[175] Churchill refused to intervene personally. Worse news still was to be delivered by the British Government, when, on 22 December, Eden wrote to Raczyński outlining British requirements for the censorship of all communications between the Poles in London and their representatives in Poland. When the two men met on the following day, Raczyński was informed 'that in future all communications by wireless transmission between this country and Russian-occupied Poland must cease'. The British Government was anxious not to offend its ally, the Soviet Union, and determined to take steps to ensure that the Poles did no damage to relations with the Soviet Union by continuing an underground conspiracy.[176]

East of the Bug the Soviet policy was mass arrests of the members of the Underground Government and AK. It is estimated that during 1944 around 100,000 Poles were arrested; some were murdered outright, some were deported to the Soviet Union and some were given the option of joining the 1st Polish Army. Polish civilians were encouraged to move west of the Bug, and this mass movement of the Polish population would continue in the following years.

In liberated 'Poland proper', the Lublin Committee began to recreate the organs of local government and administration and to put its own policies into effect. The new administration was dominated by the communists. The Politburo consisted only of communists: from Poland, Bolesław Bierut and Władysław Gomułka, and Poles from Moscow, Jakub Berman, Hilary Minc and Aleksander Zawadzki. Until October 1944, the cabinet included other political groups: five PPR members, four from the Peasant Party, three Socialists, one Democrat and two unaffiliated members, General Berling and Emil Sommerstein.[177] The Lublin Committee worked quickly to restore some semblance of normal life after five years of occupation, the deaths of many pre-war administrators and the void left by the departure of the Germans. Secondary education had been forbidden under the Germans and the universities had been closed, so the Lublin Committee encouraged schools to reopen and, in October 1944, Lublin University was ready to welcome new students. Local Polish administrators were kept in their jobs, to be purged, based on their politics, at a later date. Industries which had been run by the Germans were kept running by the Poles who had worked in them. The Lublin Committee's policy of land reform began slowly with the break-up of estates which had been owned by the Germans, the land going to the peasantry.[178] These positive activities aimed at winning over the hearts and minds of the Poles.

The policy of encouraging members of the AK to join the Polish Army had been in operation since the Soviet armies had first encountered and disarmed the AK in early 1944. The Lublin Committee wanted to expand the size of the Polish Army to 300,000 men. There were few volunteers from among the AK or local Poles, so, on 15 August, the Lublin Committee issued a decree requiring everyone eligible for military service to register. This covered men born between 1921 and 1924, as well as officers and NCOs from the reserve and the AK up to the age of 40. Rola-Żymierski called up 100,000 men at the beginning of August but, as of October, only 66,000 men had been successfully mobilised, and there was a huge shortfall in the number of officers.[179] This meant that conscription had be forced: 'Late in the evening on Sunday [8 October], Soviet troops encircled the village of Maszów. Going from house to house, they arrested approximately three hundred men, all of draft age, and transported them to the military barracks in Zamość. It seems that this is the new way of forcing enlistment in the so-called Polish army under Russian command. Until now, voluntary recruitment has been a complete fiasco.'[180]

In October the policy of the Lublin Committee towards the AK took another downward turn. The communists realised that large numbers of soldiers forced to join the Polish Army still owed their loyalty to the government in London. Gomułka wrote:

> Recently we have tried to build the Polish Army with AK people. Now we discover that the majority of them are hostile to us. The danger is great in view of the possibility of an understanding with Mikołajczyk. The army which we have built could become an instrument of the reactionaries. We are in control of the top levels, but by no means do we control the whole machine.[181]

Evidence of political unreliability was reinforced by the mass desertion of almost the entire 31st Infantry Regiment of the 1st Polish Army near Krasnystaw in the Lublin province on 13 October.[182] The NKVD started to arrest former AK officers and men, and political education of the troops increased. The original commander of the 1st Polish Army, Berling, became a casualty of the new hardline approach, probably because of his actions in support of the Warsaw Uprising. He was dismissed from his post and sent to the Frunze Military Academy in Moscow, but went on hunger strike, until Jakub Berman placated him by promising a swift return to Poland.[183]

From October 1944 onwards, the Lublin Committee virtually ruled by terror. On 30 October, the decree for the defence of the state created new categories of crimes that could be punished by death: possession of, or knowledge of someone who possessed, a radio receiver; failure to fulfil quotas of foodstuffs; and failure to reveal membership of the AK or of the Underground Government.[184] Bierut summarised the policy:

> The work of the security department must neutralise not only perpetrators, that is, people caught red-handed, but also should ensure safety and carry out preventative action. The public security policy should be directed at the neutralisation of those who oppose the programme of the PKWN.[185]

Stanisław Kujawiński and his radio operator were working for the AK in the Lublin region when they were arrested by the NKVD at the end of November, taken to Lublin and interrogated. After a week Kujawiński was transferred to the care of the Polish Security Service and imprisoned in Lublin Castle, where he found many other AK members. He was first sentenced to death for belonging to the AK and for not reporting to join the Polish Army, but this was commuted to five years' imprisonment.[186] Either Kujawiński or another radio operator in the area had reported to London at the end of October: 'Mass arrests of Home Army soldiers and also of civilians faithful to the London Government have intensified since 10 October, with the simultaneous seizure of landowners, teachers, doctors and educated people.'[187]

The Lublin Committee was able to enforce terror because of the presence of the Red Army. From October to the end of 1944, there were nearly 2,000,000 Red Army soldiers on Polish territory. Working alongside them was the NKVD. An NKVD division was established in Poland in October of 11,000 well-equipped troops, under the command of General Ivan Serov, and, by the end of the year, this division alone had arrested nearly 17,000 people.[188] At the end of July, the Lublin Committee had established a Citizen's Militia to replace the Blue Police, and a Security Service whose members were recruited from the AL and Polish Army. By October the Militia numbered 13,000 men and was taken over by the Security Service, Poland's own version of the NKVD.[189] The AK resisted the Soviets' and the Lublin Committee's reign of terror. Any large-scale action against the Soviets was pointless given the massive presence of Soviet troops, but the AK did implement a policy of assassinating members of the Lublin Committee and Red Army, and, between August and December 1944, over 400 PKWN members and 277 Red Army soldiers were killed.[190] Poland was now dangerously close to civil war before the world war had even ended.

# 14

## Poland: The Inconvenient Ally

During the course of 1944, Poland was reduced to the status of an inconvenient ally in the eyes of Britain and the United States. The Polish ministers were seen as intransigent and viewed with increasingly less sympathy. The Poles themselves felt trapped. As the Soviet armies advanced into Polish territory at the beginning of 1944, it became evident that they viewed the Polish Government's units, the AK, as hostile forces. Throughout the year, the Soviets murdered, or arrested and deported, members of the AK and, at the end of July, went so far as to recognise the communist Poles, the Lublin Committee (PKWN), as the rightful administrators of liberated Polish territory. In vain did the Polish politicians in London try to press upon the western allies their fears that the Soviet Union was determined to dominate Poland or even turn it into its seventeenth republic. The Polish Government was also handicapped by its lack of knowledge of the secret decisions reached at the Teheran conference. When, in February 1944, Churchill made a speech to the House of Commons indicating his support for the Curzon Line, the Poles turned to the United States. But Roosevelt's strategy was one of subterfuge because he was facing a presidential election in early November. Although he wanted to be seen as the honest broker, attempting to reconcile Polish and Soviet differences, at Teheran he too had told Stalin that he was in favour of the Curzon Line. For his part, Stalin now concentrated his attention on the composition of the future Polish Government.

British policy after the Teheran conference was to persuade the Polish Government in London to accept the Curzon Line, including the loss of Lwów, as the new eastern border. It is unnecessary to repeat the contents of the seemingly endless number of memoranda exchanged and the meetings held between Churchill, Eden, Mikołajczyk, Romer and Raczyński, in which British tactics alternated between gentle advice and outright bullying. The British ambassador to the Polish Government, Owen O'Malley, provided the most moderate comments, urging the Poles to accept the Curzon Line on the grounds that the population to the east of it was mixed and 'that the whole trend of modern history has been in the direction of the homogeneity of states'. His argument was that Poland would be strengthened by the loss of her ethnic minorities, especially since he was in favour of an exchange of populations to achieve this, to be carried out 'under the auspices of His Majesty's Government and the United States Government'. Churchill's opinions were frequently more aggressively couched: the Soviet Union 'after two wars which have cost her between twenty and thirty millions of Russian lives has a right to the inexpugnable security of her western frontiers'. Neither Britain nor Poland should 'ignore the fact that only Russian sacrifices and victories hold out any prospects of the restoration of a free Poland'. In any case exchanging the largely agricultural eastern provinces for the rich industrial resources of the territory to be seized from Germany would give 'the Poles a fine place to live in'. Then there was the possibility that worried many observers: if the Poles did not agree to Stalin's demands, 'the advancing Russian armies will set up their own men to run the country from which will certainly result dissension, bloodshed and great evils to Poland'.[1]

The Polish defence was that the Polish Government, safe in London, would lose the support of the Underground Government in Poland and of Poles everywhere if it agreed to give away the eastern provinces. Mikołajczyk did hint that he was prepared to negotiate but was adamant that the Riga Line, Poland's pre-war frontier, must be seen as the basis of discussion and not the Curzon Line. Furthermore, he pointed out that the original Curzon Line had two variants, one of which gave Lwów to Poland. By the middle of February 1944, Mikołajczyk had bowed to British pressure and was ready to at least consider the Curzon Line as a demarcation line, leaving the final settlement of the frontier to the post-war peace settlement. He was alarmed by Stalin's repeated calls for changes in the composition of the Polish Government, informing Churchill: 'Any change in the Polish Government or changes relating to the commander-in-chief of its Armed Forces, cannot be dictated by a foreign power.' He also told Churchill: 'while it might look as if only the frontier line were in question, he was convinced that his Government were in reality defending the independence of Poland itself'. The Poles were making every effort to demonstrate their goodwill towards the Soviet Union. Operation *Burza* had been launched and the AK had come out into the open and was attempting to collaborate with the Soviet armies in the fight against the Germans. The omens from the early stage of the fighting in Wołyń were not auspicious with regards to Soviet intentions towards the armed forces loyal to the Polish Government in London. The Polish Government wanted the British and United States governments to give guarantees that they would uphold Poland's post-war frontiers and that the Soviet occupation of Poland would end as soon as the war did.[2]

Some members of the Foreign Office were also becoming alarmed by Soviet conduct. At the end of January, Orme Sargent wrote of the dangerous situation facing the western allies:

> Stalin no doubt is convinced that however much we may protest, in fact the Russians are going to reach Warsaw one of these days, and when they do so he will be able to set up a Polish Government which will negotiate a settlement giving the Soviet Government full control of Polish territory up to the German frontier. For this, I feel sure, is what Stalin is determined to have. He knows he could never get this from the present Polish Government, and as he does not intend to be rebuffed he prefers to wait until he can ensure full and prompt acceptance of his demands by dictating his terms in Warsaw.[3]

At the end of January, Churchill wrote to Stalin outlining the concerns that the Poles had, and also warning Stalin that there were limits to what Britain and the United States would accept as being fair to the Poles:

> The Poles wish to be assured that Poland would be free and independent in the new home assigned to her; that she would receive the guarantee of the Great Powers against German revenge effectively; that these Great Powers would also assist in expelling the Germans from the new territories to be assigned to Poland; and that in the regions to be incorporated in Soviet Russia such Poles as wished would be assisted to depart for their new abodes. They also inquired about what their position will be if a large part of Poland west of the Curzon Line is to be occupied by the advancing

Soviet armies. Will they be allowed to go back and form a more broad-based government in accordance with the popular wish and allowed to function administratively in the liberated areas in the same way as other governments who have been overrun? In particular they are deeply concerned about the relations between the Polish underground movement and the advancing Soviet forces, it being understood that their prime desire was to assist in driving out the Germans. This underground movement raises matters important to our common war effort.

He warned Stalin against interfering in the composition of the Polish Government in London and added: 'The creation in Warsaw of another Polish Government different from the one we have recognized up to the present, together with disturbances in Poland, would raise an issue in Great Britain and the United States detrimental to that close accord between the three Great Powers upon which the future of the world depends.'[4] Stalin's response was to repeat his demands that the Poles in London recognise the Curzon Line and dismiss President Raczkiewicz, the minister for the interior, Stanisław Kot, and Generals Kukiel and Sosnkowski.[5]

Churchill then attempted a new tack in weaving an intricate path through the conflicting demands of the Poles and Soviets. On 20 February, he informed Stalin: 'The Polish Government are now ready to declare that the Riga Line no longer corresponds to realities', but that they would not make this opinion public until the government had returned to Poland and could consult the Polish politicians there. In the meantime, Churchill wanted to be 'able to assure them that the area to be placed under Polish civil administration will include at least all of Poland west of the Curzon Line'. He added that the Poles would reconstitute their government as soon as diplomatic relations between Poland and the Soviet Union had been resumed.[6] Churchill also sent instructions to the British ambassador in Moscow, Clark Kerr, asking him to convey to Stalin that the Poles had gone as far as they could at this stage, given that they were now moving against the will of the Poles inside Poland, and that 'we should feel alarmed by the effect upon opinion here and in the USA, and therefore upon the United Nations war effort, of a Soviet refusal to give sympathetic consideration to the present proposals'.[7] It was in this context, buoyed up with optimism, that Churchill made clear his support for the Curzon Line in the House of

Commons on 22 February. The reaction of the MPs was mostly positive, with the exception of the MP for Chester, Wirral, Captain Alan Graham, who felt that Poland deserved to be treated better by the Soviet Union.[8]

The Polish Government had taken a massive gamble since all the information it was receiving from Poland indicated no support for any compromise. For example, on 16 February, there was a despatch from the government delegate in Poland setting out the position of the Underground Government:

> We do not agree to a junction, joining the problem of the western boundaries with the eastern. The western territories cannot be considered as an equivalent, since they are restored lands formerly taken away from Poland . . . We categorically oppose the taking up of any discussions with the Soviets as far as our eastern frontiers are concerned . . . Nobody here would understand why Poland should pay for the Soviet war effort by her territories or her freedom.

This statement was supported by communications from the commander of the AK, Bór-Komorowski, and by a declaration from the Council of National Unity (RJN) in Warsaw.[9] Given the strength of this opposition to compromise with the Soviets, it seemed only fair that Stalin should recognise the difficulties faced by the Polish Government and react to their first step towards a solution with magnanimity. Instead, Stalin raised the stakes.

Clark Kerr had already intimated his concern to Eden regarding Poland's future and that of the present Polish Government: 'Soviet Russia genuinely favours the revival of an independent Poland, but at the same time expects so much from the Poles in the way of exemplary behaviour that it would require a miracle for them to live up to the standard demanded of them without complete subservience.'[10] It now seemed that the Soviets were seeking out people whom they believed they could trust to form a Polish government to do their bidding. In January the American ambassador in Moscow, Averill Harriman, reported to the State Department on a recent meeting during which Molotov had suggested that a future Polish government should be composed of 'some of the present members of the Polish Government, prominent Poles in the United States and Poles now in the Soviet Union'.[11] Now, in the middle of February, Clark Kerr, following a 'dreary and exasperating conversation' with Stalin to discuss Churchill's telegram and instructions, was forced to inform Eden of Stalin's latest proposal. After repeating his demands for the Curzon Line and the reconstruction of the Polish cabinet, Stalin added a new proposal: to invite two pro-Soviet Polish-Americans, Professor Oskar Lange and Father Stanislaus Orlemański, to come to Moscow 'to see what was going on here and advise on the choice of appropriate Poles'.[12]

Stalin picked a new quarrel with Churchill, informing him on 16 March that he had heard that his telegrams to Churchill had been getting into the British press 'with serious distortions at that', and this made it difficult 'for me to speak my mind freely'. The British investigated and it became apparent that, although Kot had leaked one message, the Soviet embassy was the source of most of the leaks. Churchill responded to Stalin: 'The information was given both to the American *Herald Tribune* correspondent and to the London *Times* correspondent by the Soviet Embassy in London. In the latter case, it was given personally by Ambassador Gusev.' Caught out, Stalin reacted with anger and indicated his fury at British support for the Poles and the delay in settling the outstanding issues regarding the Polish frontiers. Jock Colville, Churchill's private secretary, noted in his diary: 'During the weekend the PM had a really rude telegram from Stalin and it seems that our efforts to promote a Russo-Polish understanding have failed.' Raczyński was equally despondent, writing in his diary: 'The facts are that British mediation is a fiasco. Moscow is ominously silent, the British are unperturbed, and we now never see either Churchill or Eden.' Yet Churchill had another trick to play: he suggested to Roosevelt that he should invite Mikołajczyk to visit because 'it may at any rate make the Russians more careful if they see that Poland is not entirely without friends'.[13]

Roosevelt's strategy was to try to avoid making any binding statements on Poland until after the presidential election in November 1944. His personal opinion can be ascertained in other ways. For example, in January 1944, he asked the Polish ambassador, Jan Ciechanowski: 'Do you expect us and Great Britain to declare war on Joe Stalin if they cross your previous frontier?' He then caused offence by suggesting that a plebiscite might show that the eastern provinces did not want to return to Poland, before adding further insult by commenting that the

Poles had been foolish about the 'graves question', a tactless reference to the Soviet murder of the Polish officers at Katyń.[14] Further evidence concerning Roosevelt's opinions of the Polish Government is provided by his conduct over the appointment of the United States ambassador to the Polish Government. After Drexel Biddle resigned in early 1944, Roosevelt appeared to be in no hurry to appoint a successor. This alarmed the Polish Government, which

> felt that the absence of a new Ambassador was causing them considerable embarrassment in their present difficult position as this was being interpreted by the Soviet Government, as well as by the German government, to indicate that the United States Government did not consider the Polish Government at the present time worthy of a new Ambassador.[15]

Arthur Bliss Lane was not appointed until September 1944 and never even presented his credentials to the Polish Government in London.[16] Roosevelt also repeatedly postponed Mikołajczyk's planned visit to Washington, fearing that it would incite Polish-American opinion against him. Mikołajczyk felt that the delays were playing into the hands of the Germans, whose propaganda machine was broadcasting the news of a split in the alliance.[17] At the beginning of April, Roosevelt wrote again to Mikołajczyk postponing the visit for at least a month because he was suffering from bronchitis.[18]

The pro-Soviet publicity machine was active in the United States and the Office of War Information (OWI) ensured that newspapers followed that line. In 1942 the influential *Time* magazine made Stalin its 'Man of the Year' and, notoriously, its 29 March 1943 issue was dedicated to the Soviet Union and described the NKVD as 'a national police force similar to the FBI'.[19] In 1943 the film was released of the former American ambassador to the Soviet Union, Joseph Davies's book *Mission to Moscow*. Its producer, Robert Buckner, later described it as an 'expedient lie for political purposes, glossily covering up important facts with full or partial knowledge of their false presentation'.[20] Ships returning to the United States after carrying Lend-Lease supplies to the Soviet Union carried thousands of copies of the pro-communist Polish paper *Free Poland*.[21] To counter this support for the Soviet Union, the Polish Government funded a Polish Information Center in the United States, which published numerous books, articles and journals publicising the news of the Polish armed forces and the conditions in German-occupied

Poland. Polish-Americans also made fifteen-minute broadcasts in English which were transmitted by over 300 radio stations across the United States.[22]

Yet the Polish-Americans were themselves divided. The majority were hostile to the Soviet Union and supported KNAPP, the Committee of Americans of Polish Descent, formed in 1942, which opposed any rapprochement with the Soviet Union and, in particular, any hint of negotiation on Poland's eastern frontier. Yet in early 1944, the activities of *Komitet Narodowy Amerykanów Polskiego Pochodzenia* (KNAPP) were temporarily overshadowed by the activities of the left-wing Kościuszko League, whose membership was centred around the industrial city of Detroit. Out of their ranks emerged the two men Stalin had identified as being in favour of the Curzon Line and friendly towards the Soviets: the Chicago economics professor Oskar Lange and a parish priest from Springfield, Massachusetts, Father Stanislaus Orlemański.[23]

In February 1944, the Soviet ambassador to the United States, Andrei Gromyko, asked Roosevelt to intervene personally to obtain passports for Lange and Orlemański to visit the Soviet Union. The State Department was opposed because as the undersecretary of state, Edward Stettinius explained: 'these two men represent a specific and heavily slanted view of the Polish-Soviet question which is not shared by Americans of Polish descent nor American public opinion as a whole'. The State Department opinion was that the visit must be presented as private, otherwise it could be seen as an abandonment of the Polish Government.[24] The Foreign Office was also against the visit: 'I am afraid that this visit will not be helpful. These men are clearly being sent to assist the overthrow of the Polish government.'[25] Roosevelt allowed the visits to go ahead probably because he wanted to hear what Stalin would tell them.

The choice of Orlemański, a parish priest from Massachusetts, may seem extraordinary, but Stalin wanted to meet him in order to garner the support of American Catholics for his policies. Father Orlemański was greeted in Moscow by Soviet dignitaries and given many photo opportunities which he appeared to relish. He was described by the war correspondent Alexander Werth as 'either a well-meaning simpleton or else a practical joker'. Orlemański was taken to visit the 1st Polish Army, then in the Ukraine, before meeting Stalin on 28 April, who explained his aim to create a new Polish government that would include some prominent Polish-Americans. Orlemański returned to the United States expecting praise for his mission to the Soviet Union. Instead, he was reprimanded by his bishop for meddling in politics and Roosevelt refused to meet him and later told Mikołajczyk that he thought that Orlemański's 'heart was bigger than his brain'.[26] The most damning indictment came from Monsignor Michael Ready of the National Catholic Welfare Conference, who described the visit as 'a political burlesque, staged and directed by capable Soviet agents'.[27]

The visit of Oskar Lange was far more important to Stalin because he had earmarked the Marxist professor of economics as a member of a future Polish government. Lange's report of his meeting at the Kremlin with Stalin and Molotov on 17 May is extremely interesting. According to Lange, he opened the conversation by referring to the concerns he had heard voiced in the United States and by the soldiers he had met in the 1st Polish Army about the welfare of Polish citizens trapped in the Soviet Union. He then turned to another topic which concerned the British and American governments, the question of how much territory the Poles would receive in compensation for the loss of their eastern provinces, and voiced the opinion held by Polish-Americans, by the Polish Government in London and by the Polish soldiers in the Soviet Union that Lwów should be retained by Poland. Stalin was remarkably coy about making Soviet policy explicitly clear: while he did inform Lange about the territorial decisions reached at the Teheran conference, he left open the question of Lwów. Stalin's thinking appeared to be that once Poland's western frontier had been settled finally, it would become easier for all Poles to accept the Curzon Line, with or without Lwów. On the subject of a future Polish government, Stalin stated: 'No Polish government will be formed by the Union of Polish Patriots: the Polish government must emerge out of Poland itself.' Stalin was favourably disposed towards Mikołajczyk and neutral on Romer, the Polish foreign minister. The message Stalin wanted Lange to convey to the United States was that the Soviet Union did not wish to encroach on Poland's sovereignty and independence but did genuinely want to see a Polish government formed from Poles from the Union of Polish Patriots, and suitable Poles from the present Polish Government, as well as Poles from within Poland and from the United States.[28]

Lange's visit to the Soviet Union unleashed a storm of protest in the

United States. The Polish ambassador complained strongly to the State Department that no American private citizen had the right to discuss matters of such importance 'which involved the relationships of governments friendly to the United States'. One historian has concluded: 'No event had unified Polish-American opinion against the Soviet Union more than the Orlemański-Lange visit to the USSR.' The visit led directly to the creation of the Polish-American Congress in May 1944, under the leadership of Charles Rozmarek, which united various separate Polish-American organisations that between them represented every shade of opinion other than that of appeasement of the Soviet Union and stood behind the Polish Government's demand for Polish independence within the pre-war frontiers.[29] Polish-Americans were mostly Democrats and supporters of the New Deal, so this demonstration of opposition to the American policy towards the Soviet Union greatly alarmed Roosevelt. So on 23 May, he agreed to meet Mikołajczyk in Washington in early June.

Mikołajczyk had high hopes for his visit. He aimed to emphasise Poland's contribution to the allied war effort, as Polish soldiers had recently taken Monte Cassino. He was accompanied to Washington by General Tabor,[30] who had left Poland only weeks before and could give up-to-date information on the activities of the AK and on events in Poland as the Soviets advanced. Mikołajczyk felt that this was important because he believed that the Americans were naive about Stalin's true intentions. He also wanted to reverse the progress of what he perceived as Poland's growing isolation, demonstrated by the fact that Poland was not allotted a zone of occupation in Germany and was asked to play only a minor role in the international monetary talks at Bretton Woods and in the creation of the United Nations Relief and Rehabilitation Administration (UNRRA). Of course, Mikołajczyk also wanted to gain Roosevelt's support for the Polish Government's intransigent stance on the frontier issue and his assistance in securing the resumption of diplomatic relations between Poland and the Soviet Union.

Mikołajczyk's visit to Washington was conducted in an atmosphere of optimistic euphoria. The day of his arrival, 5 June, was the day that Rome was liberated, and, on the 6th, troops poured ashore on to the Normandy beaches and the Second Front was finally a reality. Mikołajczyk had several meetings with Roosevelt, as well as with the acting secretary of state, Stettinius, and met Polish-American members of Congress. Stettinius warned Mikołajczyk that now was not the opportune moment to approach the Soviet Union, urging him to wait a few weeks while the Normandy bridgehead was consolidated and then the western allies would be in a stronger position to take on Stalin. Mikołajczyk's response was that the Soviets were bound to launch an advance soon (as they indeed did), which would take them deeper into Poland, making the necessity for the restoration of diplomatic relations all the more urgent. Roosevelt warned Mikołajczyk on several occasions that he could not act as an intermediary in the Polish-Soviet dispute, because of the 'American political year of 1944'. The president suggested that Polish relations with the Soviet Union would be eased if Mikołajczyk would only make the changes in the cabinet that the Soviets wanted, 'after all, it was only four people and it might be the deciding factor'. But Mikołajczyk disagreed, arguing that such a move 'would be misunderstood and that he would be losing face', especially since one of the people whose dismissal Stalin was demanding was the Polish president.[31] Roosevelt also urged Mikołajczyk to go to Moscow for direct talks with Stalin but wavered on whether he would approach Stalin asking him to issue an invitation.[32]

At Roosevelt's request, Mikołajczyk met Lange in Washington to hear about his meeting with Stalin. Mikołajczyk dictated a note of his conversation to Ciechanowski in which Lange had recounted his talk with Stalin and his own conversations with soldiers serving under General Berling. Lange made it clear that the soldiers favoured Poland retaining Lwów and that, while Stalin did not appear to dismiss this, he had nevertheless pointed out that the Ukrainians wanted the city. Lange could not enlighten Mikołajczyk on the attitude of the Soviets towards the AK. Lange also appeared to believe that Stalin did not want to communise Poland, since he realised that the communist PPR had only limited support.[33] Nothing appears to have been achieved by this meeting, other than the opportunity for the two men to meet for the first time.

The political sensitivity of Mikołajczyk's visit meant that steps were taken to ensure that any statements regarding United States foreign policy were accurate. Therefore, it is surprising to find that the following statement in a memorandum by Mikołajczyk summarising the meetings held and the conclusions drawn was approved by the State Department:

The President said that at the Teheran Conference he had made it clear that he held the view that the Polish-Soviet conflict should not be settled on the basis of the so-called Curzon Line and he assured the Prime Minister that at the appropriate time he would help Poland to retain Lwów, Drohobycz and Tarnopol and to obtain East Prussia, including Königsberg, and Silesia.[34]

It is no wonder that Mikołajczyk left Washington feeling confident that the president would support the continued intransigent attitude of the Polish Government on the eastern issue. As he told the Council of Ministers on his return: 'Roosevelt believes that he can get what he wants from Stalin and understands him better than Churchill.' In fact, the secretary of state, Cordell Hull, wrote to Harriman of Mikołajczyk's visit: 'He brought no concrete plan for the solution of the Polish-Soviet question and no detailed plans were discussed with him. No binding commitments made.'[35] Mikołajczyk briefed the government delegate in Poland on the visit, stating again that Roosevelt opposed the Curzon Line and that 'Roosevelt considers his own influence with Stalin and his possibilities of obtaining concessions as greater than Churchill's.'[36] Eden was appalled when he heard of Roosevelt's promises concerning Lwów and the East Galician oilfields and concluded: 'The Poles are sadly deluding themselves if they place any faith in these vague and generous promises.' Roosevelt's opinion is found in his telegram to Stalin:

> You know that his visit was not connected with any attempt on my part to insert myself into the merits of the differences which exist between the Soviet Government and the Polish Government-in-exile. I can assure you that no specific plan or proposal in any way affecting Polish-Soviet relations was drawn up, although we had a frank and beneficial exchange of views on a wide variety of subjects affecting Poland.[37]

Despite his earlier reluctance, Roosevelt urged Stalin to invite Mikołajczyk to Moscow to explore the possibilities of resuming Polish-Soviet diplomatic relations.

Some tentative moves towards direct talks between the Poles and the Soviets had begun in London, for, as early as December 1943, Eden had heard that an official at the Soviet embassy in London, Mr Zinchenko, had proposed this. Eden was intrigued because 'Russians don't speak like that as a rule without instructions, and it is conceivable that Russians would offer Poles better terms direct than through us.' This opening coincided with the conversation Beneš had with Stalin in Moscow that month in which Stalin had asked his advice on various members of the Polish Government. News of the Soviet initiative reached Washington, and, in January 1944, Cordell Hull told Harriman that the United States 'would be glad to extend its good offices in the matter' of promoting Soviet-Polish talks.[38] Yet between January and May nothing happened, possibly because Stalin was waiting to see whether Churchill could bully the Poles into accepting the Soviet demands. In May, with Beneš acting as an intermediary, a meeting took place between the president of the Polish National Council, Stanisław Grabski, and the Soviet ambassador to the Czech Government, Viktor Lebedev, to prepare the ground for a meeting between Mikołajczyk and Lebedev. Grabski felt that the Soviets were attempting to decide which members of the Polish Government in London were well disposed towards the Soviet Union and whether it would be possible to gain their acquiescence to Stalin's demands.[39] An emboldened Mikołajczyk met Lebedev on his return from Washington and made it clear that he wanted the frontier issue left until the end of the war. Lebedev repeated the Soviet demands for the immediate recognition of the Curzon Line and for changes in the composition of the Polish Government, and, failing to achieve these, broke off the talks on 23 June. Eden met Mikołajczyk for dinner six days later and commiserated with him over the failure of the talks but also 'hinted that Poles might have made use of the better atmosphere to make some salutary changes in their own set-up'.[40]

On 22 June 1944, the Soviets launched Operation Bagration, which destroyed the German Army Group Centre and opened the way for the Soviet invasion of Poland. As the Soviets moved into Poland their policy became clearer. While the Polish Government was urging the AK and Underground Government to come out into the open, to fight the Germans alongside the Soviets and then to take over the administration of liberated areas, the Soviets were pursuing the opposite course. Apart from the widespread arrests of soldiers of the AK and their commanders, Stalin was moving closer towards recognising the Polish communist-dominated PKWN as the future Polish government. On 22 July, Stalin formally recognised the PKWN, now on Polish soil in Lublin, as the body best positioned to take over the administration of liberated Polish territories west of the Curzon Line. The Polish Government issued a formal protest and sought the assurance of the British Government that the Polish Government in London would still be recognised by the western allies as the only Polish government.

Churchill pressed Mikołajczyk to go to Moscow for talks with Stalin, and cabled Stalin once Mikołajczyk was on his way that the purpose was: 'the Poles who are friendly to Russia should join with the Poles who are friendly to Britain and the United States in order to establish a strong, free, independent Poland, the good neighbour of Russia, and an important barrier between you and another German outrage.' He concluded: 'It would be a great pity and even a disaster if the Western democracies found themselves recognising one body of Poles and you recognising another.'[41] At the Council of Ministers meeting on 26 July, Mikołajczyk had outlined his position: as a last resort he would agree to the Curzon Line being considered a temporary demarcation line until a final settlement at the peace conference; he would only agree to reorganise his government on its return to Warsaw; and he hoped that the Polish Government and Lublin Committee could sign an agreement on the administration of liberated Polish territory.[42]

It was not clear whether Stalin actually wanted to meet Mikołajczyk; in June he had told Roosevelt that he was uncertain as to the value of such a visit.[43] Even as Mikołajczyk was on his way to Moscow, George Kennan, chargé d'affaires at the American embassy in Moscow, voiced concerns, noting that Stalin had not issued the invitation but had admitted only that he would not refuse to meet Mikołajczyk when he arrived.[44] The talks with Lebedev had broken down when the Soviets had issued a list of demands: changes to the composition of the Polish Government and the inclusion in it of Poles in Poland and Poles from the United States; the acceptance of the Curzon Line, while leaving open the question of Lwów; a statement that the Soviets were not responsible for the Katyń massacre and that the Polish Government accepted the findings of the 1944 Burdenko Commission.[45] This commission had used evidence falsified by the NKVD to prove that the Germans were responsible.[46] Clark Kerr wrote to Romer, the Polish foreign minister, who accompanied Mikołajczyk to Moscow, that the Soviet demands had not changed, and suggested that the Polish Government needed to come to 'some kind of working arrangement with the Polish Committee of National Liberation', and to an agreement regulating relations between the AK and Soviet armies. In return the Poles could expect the restoration of diplomatic relations and Soviet assistance in gaining German territory in the north and west and the expulsion of the German population from those areas.[47] There was no chance that Mikołajczyk could accept these conditions, so why did he go to Moscow? He told the Polish president that he was going 'in order to avoid being burdened with the accusation that in this critical moment he did not exhaust all possibilities to reach agreement'.[48] He was not optimistic regarding the chances for success. Indeed, Kennan's view that Mikołajczyk, Romer and Grabski were 'the doomed representatives of a doomed regime' seems an accurate assessment.[49]

On the morning of 3 August, the three men met Stalin and Molotov. This was the first meeting between Stalin and Mikołajczyk, and gave Stalin an opportunity to assess the character of the Polish prime minister, a leader of the Peasant Party and a very different kind of man from his predecessor, Sikorski. Mikołajczyk opened the proceedings by attempting to find common ground with Stalin based on their similar backgrounds, since both were working men who had risen to positions of political power through their own exertions. He then outlined his reasons for going to Moscow, namely to discuss the future government of Poland now that the Soviet armies were pushing the Germans back across Poland and in the light of the Warsaw Uprising. He hoped to set up a government based on the four main political parties along with the communists. He also wanted to hear Stalin's 'views on the future frontiers of Poland and discuss this problem with you'. Stalin's first point was to note that Mikołajczyk had omitted any reference to the Lublin Committee, which had begun to administer liberated Poland; Mikołajczyk's response was that this administration was the responsibility of the Underground Government, which represented four political parties, and not just of the one party which comprised the PKWN. Stalin made lengthy statements arguing that the Lublin Committee now represented the true reality of politics in Poland, which had moved towards the left during the German occupation, and denigrated the power and influence of the AK, suggesting that it was an insignificant force because it did not possess artillery. Stalin was adamant that unless Mikołajczyk made a settlement with the Lublin Committee, the present unsatisfactory arrangement of two Polish administrations, one recognised by the west, and one by the Soviets, would continue and there would be no peace in Poland, which would hamper the fighting efforts of the Soviets against the Germans.

At this point Mikołajczyk turned the subject to the future frontiers of Poland. Stalin made his position clear: the Curzon Line to the east, Poland's western frontier on the Oder and Neisse, and Königsberg going to the Soviet Union. Mikołajczyk naturally protested about the Curzon Line and Stalin responded:

> But, Mr Prime Minister, it was not we who invented the Curzon Line; neither Russians nor Poles did; Lloyd George, Clemenceau and Curzon were its authors. Russia was not represented when the line was established during the Paris Peace Conference. The Curzon Line was the result of unbiased scholarly research, it was a compromise solution.[50]

Mikołajczyk replied that Galicia had never been part of Russian territory, even during the partitions, but was outdone in his appeal by Grabski, who, according to Clark Kerr, 'made an impassioned appeal for Vilna and Lemberg using all his limbs and even banging his table to drive his arguments home'. Mikołajczyk then asked whether Stalin expected the frontier issue to be settled then or whether it could be postponed, and after reflection Stalin responded: 'We shall be able to come to a final agreement on the question of frontiers with a new, united Polish Government. It is up to you to bring about this unity. This is the most important matter.'[51] The Lublin Committee had already been discussing the frontier issue with Stalin, having set up a border commission which 'proposed that the border should be modified to give Poland the Białowieża forest, Lwów and the oil-bearing areas'. But its initial talks with the Soviets revealed that Stalin was determined to have the whole of eastern Poland, including areas that had no historical links with the Russian Empire.[52]

On 7 and 8 August, Mikołajczyk met Bolesław Bierut and Edward Osóbka-Morawski, the Lublin Committee representatives, and they met Molotov to report on the results. Mikołajczyk seemed most upbeat about the prospect of achieving cooperation with the PKWN. He pointed out that their demand for a reversion to the 1921 constitution was a non-issue since the Polish Government in London agreed with the desirability of this step and had only remained subject to the 1935 constitution because of the necessity of retaining continuity between the government in Poland before the war and the one established in exile.

The main difference between the two constitutions rested on the powers of the president and Mikołajczyk had been able to inform the Lublin Committee that these were already limited by wartime agreements. He was, however, dissatisfied with the offer of only four seats in the new eighteen-member Polish government, with the remainder going to the Lublin Committee. He believed strongly that this proportion did not reflect political opinion in Poland and that the proportion should be reversed. This was totally unacceptable to Bierut, who launched into a lengthy tirade criticising the Polish Government in London, the Underground Government and its army, the AK.[53]

No agreement was reached but, as Stalin wrote to Churchill, the meetings were useful for 'an exchange of views'.[54] Harriman told Cordell Hull that Mikołajczyk was returning to London to consult his colleagues and was optimistic:

> His primary interest is to join all factions at this time in a government which will have a legal basis and which can hold the country together until such time as a truly free general election can be held to establish a new constitution and government. He is satisfied that the Committee of Liberation has not the standing with the Polish people to take control of Poland without the force of the Red Army, but is fearful that if it once gets control, there will not be a free election.[55]

This optimism was reflected in Mikołajczyk's report to the government delegate in Poland on his visit. His impression of the Lublin Committee was that 'these gentlemen cut a sorry figure in the Soviet eyes'. He drew five conclusions:

1. The Soviet Government secured a favourable position for itself by stating that it was ready to discuss all matters and to review the conditions of the establishing of Polish-Soviet relations, providing the Poles could agree between themselves.
2. In this way the Soviet Government has not yet finally sided with the communists, still leaving a margin for compromise.
3. However, it has given a free hand to communists, on the understanding that for the time being it would wait for further developments.
4. The Soviet Government – such is my feeling – has not yet decided whether Poland should be sovietised, reserving for itself a breathing-space for making a final decision on that matter. On the other hand,

Polish communists are determined to exploit the situation for turning Poland into a communist State.

5. In my view, foreign public opinion carries weight with the Soviet Government and the latter is anxious to preserve good relations with England and America. Moreover, it wants peace in the rear of Soviet troops. In the last instance, it tries to keep up the appearance that the Poles will be free to organise the administration of Poland and it seems to me that, at this stage, it will not resort to violence to back Polish communists.[56]

This was written while the Warsaw Uprising was still raging and still had a chance of success. During his final meeting with Stalin, Mikołajczyk had issued a strong appeal for Soviet aid to it.[57] Yet, as was seen in Chapter 13, this aid was slow to appear and then only in insignificant quantities, so the apparent goodwill in Moscow died away in the face of their failure to assist the uprising. Not only did Mikołajczyk begin to requestion Stalin's attitude but, now, so did the British and American governments.

The Polish Council of Ministers discussed the results of Mikołajczyk's visit to Moscow with considerable care. On 29 August, it drew up a memorandum outlining its plans for the future. After the liberation of Warsaw, a new government would be formed with five parties – the Peasant Party, the National Democratic Party, the Socialist Party, the Christian Labour Party, and the communists – all having an equal number of seats; the extreme right-wing parties and the pre-war *Sanacja* ruling group would be excluded. This government would resume diplomatic relations with the Soviet Union and administer liberated Poland. 'Elections will take place as soon as normal conditions are established in the country', whereupon a new constitution would be drawn up and a new president elected. There would be alliances with France, Britain and Czechoslovakia, and close friendship ties with the United States. On the frontier question there was the statement: 'In the East the main centres of Polish cultural life and the sources of raw materials indispensable to the economic life of the country shall remain within Polish boundaries.'[58] This was as far as the Polish Government was prepared to go and, in the light of the existence of the Underground Government, arguably as far as it could go. Yet the plan was controversial. The Polish president had already communicated his anxieties regarding Soviet intentions to the government delegate and to the chairman of the

Council of National Unity a few days earlier.[59] The commander of the AK, Bór-Komorowski, immediately sent a despatch from Warsaw giving his reaction to the memorandum:

> This plan means a complete surrender and provides for several political measures of primary importance, depending on the good will of the Soviets and without previous guarantees from the USSR and the Allies. The plan means an abandonment of the line of policy followed heretofore and the forswearing of the idea of an independent Poland.[60]

The level of distrust of the Soviets felt by the Polish politicians in Warsaw is clear from the Council of National Unity's response, for it was adamant that an agreement must be reached with the Soviet Union before a new government was established: 'The representatives of the Government and the National Council proceeding to Poland should be accompanied by official representatives of Great Britain and the United States.'[61] The Polish politicians in London were greatly alarmed by the conduct of the Soviets, not only over their failure to give any meaningful assistance to the Warsaw Uprising but also because of stories now flooding in of the arrests of AK commanders and soldiers in areas liberated by the Soviets. This is why the Poles continued to press the British to send a military mission to Poland to report on the situation.

On 1 September, Mikołajczyk met Churchill, who was still convalescing from an illness contracted on his recent visit to the front in Italy. This was to be the last meeting between the two men that could be described as being held 'in a particularly cordial spirit'. The main topic was naturally the question of further allied assistance for Warsaw. Churchill informed Mikołajczyk of his meeting with Anders in Italy during which he had urged the Polish soldiers to 'concentrate on what could still be saved rather than mourn over what they had lost'. Churchill recognised that Mikołajczyk was under immense pressure from the warring factions in his cabinet and was threatening to resign, and he wanted to warn the Poles: 'should the Polish Premier resign, he, Churchill, would see no other alternative but to wash his hands of them, in spite of his friendship for Poland'.[62] Churchill actually began to wash his hands of the Polish Government almost immediately, because of the conduct of the Polish commander-in-chief, General Sosnkowski.

Sosnkowski was a somewhat controversial figure whose anti-Soviet stance had led to his resignation from the Polish cabinet in protest at the

Sikorski–Maisky agreement in July 1941. He had been appointed commander-in-chief by Raczkiewicz after Sikorski's death, without consultation with Mikołajczyk, and the prime minister and commander-in-chief rarely met. The Soviets had been demanding the dismissal of Sosnkowski for over a year, and the British and the Americans believed that he had to go if the Polish Government was to have any success in its negotiations with Stalin. Now Sosnkowski went too far with his Order of the Day for 1 September 1944, the fifth anniversary of the outbreak of the war:

> It has been five years since the day when Poland, encouraged by the British government and provided with its guarantee, entered into an isolated battle against the German power ... [Today] the people of Warsaw are left to their own devices, abandoned on the front of the common fight against the Germans – a tragic and horrible riddle that we Poles cannot decipher on the background of the technical possibilities of the Allies at the beginning of the sixth year of the war ... If the population of the capital had to die under the rubble of their houses for lack of help, if they are to be delivered to the slaughter through passivity, indifference, or some other calculation – the conscience of the world will be burdened by a horrible, historically unprecedented sin.[63]

This caused widespread outrage. There could be no doubt: Sosnkowski had to be relieved of his post. Yet the president stubbornly refused to dismiss him, and Mikołajczyk threatened to resign. Churchill, on the way to meet Roosevelt at Quebec, left the task of persuading Mikołajczyk to stay to Eden, who made it very clear that the British Government would not deal with any other Polish prime minister.[64] Finally, on 30 September, Sosnkowski was dismissed.

The Polish Government had a choice of two men who could succeed him: Bór-Komorowski or Anders – although neither would be acceptable to the Soviets. Bór-Komorowski was appointed, but the Warsaw Uprising was on the point of collapse and he was planning to accompany his soldiers into German captivity. This left Anders as acting commander-in-chief. When Churchill had met Anders in Italy in August, he noticed a photographer taking a picture of them talking and told Anders: 'If Stalin sees this photograph of me calling on you and at this particular moment, General, he will be furious', since he knew that Anders was unacceptable to the Soviet Union.[65] Churchill was prepared to allow the photograph to be published because he was angry with Stalin over his attitude towards the Warsaw Uprising. But, at the end of September with the end of the uprising, the appointments, first of Bór-Komorowski and then of Anders, were seen as deliberate snubs to the Soviets, ones which the British felt were unnecessary. The British had been greatly offended by Sosnkowski's Order of the Day and they were no more happy to hear the words of the despatch from Warsaw by the Council of National Unity: 'May the just God estimate the terrible wrong which the Polish nation has suffered, and let Him deal justly with those who have committed that wrong.'[66]

Churchill pressed Mikołajczyk to return to Moscow for further talks with Stalin and with the Lublin Committee. The Polish Government was not optimistic about the prospect of success. Romer sent a letter to the British and United States governments on 7 October commenting on political events in Poland:

> The formation of the National Council of the Homeland, the Polish Committee of National Liberation and the Supreme Command of the Polish Army is tantamount to the Soviet Government taking over the attributes of Polish state sovereignty through the medium of Polish communist elements and of Soviet citizens of Polish descent.[67]

Mikołajczyk informed Churchill that he was prepared to go to Moscow but that his position remained the same as on 29 August, and he wanted to know 'what terms for a settlement will be put forward by the Soviet Government'.[68] Stalin had not budged from his demand for recognition of the Curzon Line and, now that he had the Lublin Committee doing his bidding in Poland, he only needed to be seen to be talking to Mikołajczyk in order to satisfy the British and American governments; he had no intention of making a deal with the Polish Government in London.

The conference on Polish affairs in Moscow opened on 13 October and was attended by Stalin, Molotov and Gusev for the Soviets; Churchill, Eden and Clark Kerr for the British; and Mikołajczyk, Romer and Grabski for the Polish Government. The Americans did not want to be included as the results could alienate the Polish-American voters only weeks before the presidential election; the American ambassador in Moscow, Harriman, was present only as an observer. The talks themselves covered old ground and only served to show that neither side was prepared to give way.[69] What is far more interesting is the differing reactions of the participants to the talks and to the meeting with the Lublin Committee's representatives, Bierut and Osóbka-Morawski.

The impression Churchill left from his speech on Poland in the House of Commons on 28 September and his attitude towards the Poles at the Moscow conference suggested that he was convinced that the issue at stake was the future eastern frontier of Poland, and that he completely failed to take into account the Polish Government's anxieties regarding the conduct of the Lublin Committee in the liberated areas of Poland.[70] Indeed, Churchill actually thought that Stalin would withdraw support from the Lublin Committee if the two Polish bodies came to an agreement. This is probably why he lost his temper with Mikołajczyk on the morning of 14 October:

> I wash my hands off; as far as I am concerned we shall give the business up. Because of quarrels between Poles we are not going to wreck the peace of Europe. In your obstinacy you do not see what is at stake. It is not in friendship that we shall part. We shall tell the world how unreasonable you are. You will start another war in which 25 million lives will be lost. But you don't care ... 25 years ago we have reconstituted Poland although in the last war more Poles fought against us than for us. Now again we are preserving you from disappearance, but you will not play. You are absolutely crazy ... Unless you accept the frontier you are out of business forever. The Russians will sweep through your country and your people will be liquidated. You are on the verge of annihilation.

There was a second meeting between them, during which Churchill was even more intemperate.[71] Eden was far more sympathetic and attempted without success to get at least Lwów for Poland. He described Mikołajczyk as showing 'a calm courage throughout this ordeal' but, in a telegram to the Foreign Office, was forced to concede: 'And so at this time, after endless hours of the stiffest negotiations I have ever known, it looks at though Lwów will wreck all our efforts.'[72]

For all his bullying of Mikołajczyk, Churchill could see why he was deeply worried about the future government of Poland. After all, Mikołajczyk represented the largest political party in Poland, the Peasant Party, yet he was supposed to allow the communists to dominate the new government. Neither Churchill nor Eden had been impressed by the Lublin Committee's representatives; Churchill described them as 'a kind of inverted Quislings', and Eden described Bierut and Osóbka-Morawski as 'the rat and the weasel'.[73] Yet Churchill was equally adamant that the only hope to save Poland from communisation was for the London Poles and Lublin Poles to reach an agreement and, to achieve that, both sides would have to make compromises. As Harriman informed Roosevelt: 'Churchill gave the Committee a sound and useful drubbing along the lines that all the Allies were united to beat Hitler except for the Poles who were fighting among themselves.'[74] Nevertheless, Churchill was a supreme realist and recognised that the Soviet Union was set to dominate politics in eastern Europe. This is why he drew up the secret and notorious percentages agreement* in Moscow with Stalin, his so-called 'naughty document', dividing eastern Europe and the Balkans into spheres of influence.[75]

Mikołajczyk returned to London from Moscow shattered by what he had learned. It was clear to him that both the British and American governments had accepted the Curzon Line. The battle now was to secure a fair representation for the non-communist parties in a new Polish government. The deal offered by the Lublin Committee in Moscow was clearly unacceptable: 75 per cent of the new government would be drawn from the Lublin Committee and 25 per cent from the non-communist parties. The Lublin Committee had tried to appeal to Mikołajczyk's ambition by offering him the post of prime minister but he, knowing that his Peasant Party was the largest party in Poland, thought that a better deal could be secured. At a meeting on 26 October, Churchill urged Mikołajczyk to return to Moscow as soon as possible to resume negotiations and assured him of the British Government's support for his demand for greater political representation for non-Lublin Committee members if the London Poles accepted the Curzon Line.[76] On 27 October, Mikołajczyk made a speech to the Polish National Council outlining the state of affairs, and he also communicated with the government delegate.[77] The Council of Ministers urged Mikołajczyk to ask Roosevelt for a statement of his position, and Mikołajczyk duly wrote to Roosevelt to see what guarantees of Poland's new western

---

* This agreement divided the Balkans: Rumania: Soviet Union, 90%, others, 10%; Greece: Britain, 90%, Soviet Union, 10%; Bulgaria: Soviet Union, 75%, others, 25%; Yugoslavia and Hungary: Soviet Union 50%, others 50%.

frontier and political independence the United States was prepared to offer the Polish Government.[78] Ciechanowski was informed by the State Department that Roosevelt would reply after the election. In a similar vein, Raczyński and Romer approached the Foreign Office seeking guarantees of Poland's new western frontier on the Oder, including the port of Stettin, and asked whether the British Government would defend the independence and integrity of the new Poland. Cadogan gave the assurances the Polish Government needed, although with the rider that the guarantee of the integrity and independence of Poland would be given jointly with the Soviet Government.[79]

On the morning of 2 November, the Council of Ministers held a stormy session during which it was decided to take no decision until after the Polish Government had received a reply from Roosevelt.[80] Churchill was, however, impatient for a decision, and later that day he had a difficult meeting with Mikołajczyk, Romer and Raczyński. The Polish ambassador wrote of Churchill: 'Like a big sheep-dog, watch-dog rather, he barked imperiously at his Polish flock, who were spared neither warning bites nor shafts of sarcasm.'[81] When Mikołajczyk argued that the British Government's guarantees in Cadogan's letter were insufficient, Churchill became very angry and replied: 'Please consider it, therefore, cancelled as of this moment. I withdraw our proposals.'[82] After another meeting of the Council of Ministers on the 3rd, it passed a resolution:

> Despite appreciating the urgent need for a Polish-Soviet agreement, desiring this desperately and not giving up on attempts and efforts to achieve one, it does not find it possible to agree to the conditions proposed at the Moscow conference and therefore asks for a re-examination in the near future of all of these matters by the main Allied Powers with the participation of the Polish Government-in-Exile.[83]

The Polish Government would discuss the matter again when it had received a reply from Roosevelt.

Roosevelt, however, was not to be trusted, as is shown by the duplicity of his treatment of the Polish-American Congress. The Polish-American vote was an important element in securing eleven states, particularly Connecticut, Michigan, New York, Illinois and New Jersey. On 8 October, the Polish-Americans celebrated Pulaski Day to commemorate the Polish cavalry officer Kazimierz Pułaski, who had served under George Washington during the American War of Independence. At the celebration, the Republican presidential candidate and governor of New York, Thomas Dewey, spoke in favour of a free and independent Poland. Three days later the chairman of the Polish-American Congress, Charles Rozmarek, met Roosevelt and voiced their concerns about the future of Poland. At that meeting Roosevelt confined his statements to generalities, but his duplicity comes, not from what he said, but from the fact that the meeting was conducted in front of a map showing Poland with her pre-war frontiers. After a second interview with Roosevelt at the end of October, Rozmarek publicly endorsed Roosevelt as the candidate of choice for Polish-Americans. Over 90 per cent of them voted for him on 7 November, and their vote counted: of the states where the Polish-American vote was the largest, two, Michigan and New Jersey, were won by Roosevelt with only a 1 per cent majority.[84]

On 6 November, Romer transmitted to Ciechanowski the Polish Government's questions to the United States Government: its views on the new western frontier, whether the United States could guarantee Poland's 'real' independence within the new frontiers, and what economic aid for the transfer of populations and for post-war reconstruction would be provided. Ciechanowski reported back the opinion of the State Department's expert on Soviet affairs, Charles Bohlen, that the United States would approve the new frontiers but would not offer any guarantees, but it would provide financial assistance. Stettinius added that, in his opinion, Polish matters should be postponed until the next meeting between the Big Three, scheduled for early 1945, and that Mikołajczyk should attend.[85] Harriman, who was in Washington at the time, had several conversations with Roosevelt. He wrote later of his frustration with Roosevelt's whimsical idea that Lwów could be ruled by an international committee, believing that the concept had been proved impracticable given the history of the League of Nations' tenure of Danzig. Most alarmingly, he noted that Roosevelt was seemingly unaware that the real importance lay in seeing that 'the Soviets do not set up puppet governments under the Soviet system of government of a few picked men supported by the secret police'.[86] Roosevelt's belated reply to Mikołajczyk's appeal was sent on 17 November: 'The United States Government stands unequivocally for a strong, free and independent Polish state with the untrammelled rights of the Polish people to order their internal existence as they see fit.' There would, however, be no guarantees of specific frontiers.[87] On his way back to Moscow from Washington, Harriman stopped off in London and held three conversations with Mikołajczyk, further expanding on Roosevelt's letter: the American position was in line with the British, with the exception that Roosevelt was prepared to intervene personally with Stalin to obtain Lwów for Poland.[88] Eden wrote: 'Harriman has shown us the president's reply to the Polish questions. It does not give much to the Poles and I can't imagine that they were counting on much more although maybe they were nurturing such hopes.'[89]

Mikołajczyk was on the point of resignation. On 15 November, a vote of no confidence in the head of the National Council, Stanisław Grabski, had been proposed by Stanisław Jóźwiak, and Mikołajczyk interpreted this as a vote of no confidence in himself. At the meeting of the Council of Ministers on 16 November, he offered two choices: either the government resign or dissolve the National Council. He was willing to resign his position if the National Democratic Party, his most vociferous opponents, would work with the Socialist Party in a new government. Since the Polish Government had not yet received a reply from Roosevelt, a decision on the future of the government and, indeed, on Mikołajczyk's own position was postponed.[90]

The Council of Ministers met again on 22 November, where Mikołajczyk urged his ministers to accept the deal currently on the table and to rely on Britain and the United States to provide guarantees of Poland's new frontiers and political independence. Three party leaders, Jan Kwapiński, Marian Seyda and Karol Popiel, all opposed the abandonment of Wilno and the eastern provinces of Poland. On the 23rd, Mikołajczyk told Harriman that there was no point in asking Roosevelt to intervene on Lwów. On 24 November, Mikołajczyk submitted his resignation to the Polish president. Jan Kwapiński, the leader of the Socialist Party, was unable to form a government, so Tomasz Arciszewski, the veteran Socialist Party politician who had arrived in Britain from Poland earlier that year, became the prime minister of the last Polish Government-in-Exile of the Second World War. The Peasant Party declined to serve under him.

The British reaction to Mikołajczyk's resignation and to the new Polish Government was anger and disbelief. Eden suggested to Churchill that the ambassador to the Polish Government should be withdrawn and replaced by a chargé d'affaires, but Churchill replied: 'One does not cease to recognise a State every time the Prime Minister changes.'[91] He told Roosevelt that he was convinced that the new government would not survive for long and that Mikołajczyk would soon be back in power, ready to do a deal with the Soviet Union.[92] In the meantime he promised Stalin that the British attitude towards the new government would be 'correct, though it will certainly be cold'. Stalin was not interested: he replied that Mikołajczyk had lost touch with developments within Poland and that he, Stalin, was not interested in negotiating with him again. He hinted that he was turning his full support to the PKWN, and this alarmed both Churchill and Roosevelt, who separately asked Stalin to delay turning the PKWN into a provisional government until after the three leaders had met in the new year.[93] The new Polish government was unpopular in Poland too: the Underground Government demanded the immediate reorganisation of the Polish Government to be fully representative of all the parties. Mikołajczyk was more cautious concerning the chances of a swift return to power, warning Schoenfeld, the American chargé d'affaires: 'there was an active ferment within the Polish political parties with respect to the present Polish Government, but he thought it would be a mistake to overestimate the likelihood of any change of government in the immediate future'.[94]

Churchill gave a speech to the House of Commons on 15 December in which he not only effectively washed his hands of the Poles, but also insulted them for failing to come to an agreement with Stalin. Sir Cuthbert Headlam observed that it 'was rather a sorry performance – he tried to explain away our surrender to Russia and he was not convincing'.[95] Poland had few supporters in Parliament. Indeed, as Hugh Dalton told the Polish courier Jan Nowak:

> I feel sick when I listen to your defenders in the House of Commons. With few exceptions, they are the same people who supported appeasement of Germany and sided with Chamberlain at the time of Munich. Today, for fear of Russia and communism, they want to save not Poland but Germany, as a potential barrier against the Soviets.[96]

Poland did have some well-connected defenders: at court there was the circle around the Duke and Duchess of Kent, and the former permanent under secretary at the Foreign Office, Lord Vansittart, was another powerful voice, but this was patently insufficient.[97]

The lack of public and political support for Poland stemmed from two factors: ignorance about Poland and the power of the pro-Soviet propaganda machinery. Although Poland was Britain's first ally in the war against Germany, relatively little was known about Poland in Britain. Józef Retinger had attempted to correct this with the publication in 1940 of a short book of facts and statistics entitled *All About Poland*.[98] The impression many of the British had was that Poland was a class-ridden society of large landowners who oppressed the masses and whose pre-war government had been a dictatorship. In fact, the number of large landowners and the size of the estates they controlled was comparable with Britain. While the British people took to their hearts the Polish pilots who had contributed to victory in the Battle of Britain, they never understood what the Polish Government was fighting for. Their impression of Polish diplomacy was gathered from the hostile cartoons in the *Evening Standard* by David Low, a friend of the Soviet ambassador, Ivan Maisky. Furthermore, *The Times* published articles by E. H. Carr advocating a division of Europe into spheres of influence, placing Poland firmly within the Soviet sphere.[99] The British ambassador to the Polish Government noted that pro-Soviet and therefore ani-Polish publicity was 'stimulated by all Government departments, nearly all newspapers, the BBC, the Army Bureau of Current Affairs, the Army Education Department, the Political Warfare Executive, and every other organ of publicity susceptible to official influence'.[100] Churchill himself appears to have been deluded into believing that the Soviet Union was now a benevolent power, telling the House of Commons in May 1944:

> Profound changes have taken place in Soviet Russia; the Trotskyite form of Communism has been completely wiped out. The victories of the Russian Armies have been attended by a great rise in the strength of the Russian State, and a remarkable broadening of its views. The religious side of Russian life has had a wonderful rebirth. The discipline and military etiquette of the Russian Armies are unsurpassed.[101]

Efforts by the Polish press to counter pernicious pro-Soviet publicity were met by attempts at censorship and threats to cut off the supply of paper from Polish newspapers. Indeed, an entire issue of *Wiadomości Polskie* (*Polish News*) was suppressed at the end of 1944 because it published a well-documented account of the Soviet arrests of AK soldiers in Poland and the deportation of many to Siberia.[102]

When the Poles did hit the news it was not always for good reasons.

At the beginning of 1944, 68 Jews serving in the Polish Army in Britain deserted and demanded to be allowed to enlist in the British Pioneer Corps, claiming they were the victims of anti-semitism in the Polish Army. The response of the Polish Government was to secure British permission for the soldiers' enlistment in the Pioneer Corps, and to launch its own commission of inquiry into their complaints. Before it could report, another group of 136 Jewish soldiers deserted and demanded the same rights as the first one, which were also granted. In March the Polish Army announced that any future deserters would be punished by court martial, but the desertions continued, accounting for a third of Jewish Polish soldiers, and the ensuing courts martial led to short sentences of two years. Both the British and Polish governments suspected that these desertions were a put-up job by the Soviet embassy, aiming to discredit the Polish Government and the Polish Army. For example, the deserters were all told to report to a particular place in London and were given £5 spending money. There had been anti-semitism in the Polish Army in the early part of the war but the Polish Government had dealt with the matter then by establishing a scheme to educate its soldiers on the nature of Judaism. The publicity was enormously damaging to the Polish cause: questions were asked in Parliament by Tom Driberg, who may actually have been one of the instigators of the desertions in the first place, and windows at the Polish embassy were smashed. President Raczkiewicz was persuaded to grant an amnesty to the deserters.[103]

Public sympathies for the Poles and political disquiet were voiced during the Warsaw Uprising. The spectacle of ill-armed AK soldiers taking on the might of the German Army while the Soviet armies sat idle on the other side of the Vistula deeply moved many in Britain. Vita Sackville-West wrote to her husband, Harold Nicolson, an MP:

> I went to my Biddenden institute [Women's Institute], which I found seething with indignation over Warsaw. They had been listening to the 6 o'clock news. Very shrewd and shrewish they were, and I thought what good sense the English usually display when put to the test. In the course of business the Chairman had to announce that there was going to be a 'day' for Mrs Churchill's Aid to Russia Fund, at which there was just one hoot of derision from the whole audience.[104]

Yet these sympathies were short-lived. To the British public at large, Stalin was 'Uncle Joe' and the Soviet Union was the country that had suffered most in the war and whose armies were taking on most of the German Army. The British public, secure on an island, simply did not understand the arguments over the frontiers between two countries deep in eastern Europe. The poet A. P. Herbert attempted to explain the Polish dilemma in a moving poem:

> 'Unreasonable' Poles, why do you falter?
> Be sensible – be realistic, pray.
> Yours are the only frontiers that must alter:
> You are the one crusader in the way.
>
> Unreasonable Poles, you will be fatter:
> Things of the spirit are not your concern.
> Oxford and Cambridge do not greatly matter:
> And you shall have Lough Swilly in return.
>
> Unreasonable Poles, preserve tradition.
> In just two centuries, you must allow,
> You've thrice enjoyed benevolent partition.
> For Heaven's sake, why start to argue now?[105]

At the end of 1944, Poland was widely seen as the inconvenient ally. This view would soon be tempered, but too late, and only when the agreements reached at the Yalta conference at the beginning of 1945 reached the public domain.

# 15

# Fighting under British Command,
# 1943–1945

During the course of 1943, the Polish Government was forced to acknowledge that its armed forces could never reach the size sufficient for it to operate independently of the British and Americans: there could be no Polish theatre of operations. Size was not the only determinant: allied strategy played a role too. The Poles were forced to follow the strategic planning of the western allies without having a voice in those decisions. They sought the shortest road back to Poland, but the evacuation of the Polish Army from the Soviet Union during 1942 had sealed the most obvious route. In a memorandum for Churchill in November 1942, Sikorski outlined his favoured strategy:

> Operations organised here in the Balkans, and provided with well-developed bases in the Middle East, will bring the Allies to the Rumanian oil fields, which are vital to the German industries, and the capture of which would deprive the Germans of one of their main assets in their arguments concerning their invincibility. Even comparatively small forces used in this route, which would pass through Allied countries such as Greece and Yugoslavia, or through countries quarrelling with each other such as Bulgaria, Rumania or Hungary, might penetrate fairly easily. An attack from the Balkans coinciding with an armed rising in Poland, and subsequently supported by Czechoslovakia, would completely separate the German forces and cut them off from German armies fighting in Russia.[1]

Success in this region would also have the advantage of thwarting Soviet ambitions there. Now that North Africa had been cleared of Axis troops, Churchill was in favour of attacking the 'soft underbelly' of the Axis in the Balkans or in Italy. The Americans, however, were adamant that all strategic planning should be directed towards the opening of the main front in northern France, with a subsidiary but complimentary landing in the south of France. The result was a compromise, reached at the Trident conference in Washington in May 1943, where the Americans were forced to agree that sufficient forces had not been built up in Britain for an invasion of northern Europe to take place that year, and therefore, reluctantly, assented to the British plan for an invasion of Sicily.[2]

On 9 July 1943, Operation Husky, the invasion of Sicily, began. The Allies made slow progress across the island and by the time they reached the capital, Messina, on 17 August, the Germans and Italians had managed to withdraw the bulk of their forces to the mainland of Italy. But the political effect of the allied invasion was enormous: on 25 July, the Fascist Grand Council demanded the resignation of *Il Duce*, Benito Mussolini, as prime minister. He was then arrested and King Victor Emmanuel took direct command of the Italian armed forces. Marshal Pietro Badoglio was appointed as the prime minister. Secretly this new government opened negotiations with the Allies, while assuring Hitler that they were doing nothing of the kind. The harsh armistice terms made the Italians delay signing until 3 September. The Italians had hoped that the Allies would move quickly, making a landing north of Rome and seizing the capital before the Germans had time to react, but the Allies had no such plans. Indeed, while the negotiations with the Italian Government were being conducted, the allied military commanders were finalising plans merely for landings in the south of Italy, at Salerno and Taranto. These landings on 9 September provoked Hitler into launching Operation *Alarich*, the takeover of Italy by German forces. The Italian fleet escaped but German forces were rushed from France and the 1st SS Panzer Division temporarily from the Eastern Front. Rommel's troops crushed the Italian military and civilian resistance in the northern industrial cities of Milan and Turin, while Field Marshal Albert von Kesselring organised the German Tenth Army in the south and began to build strong defensive lines. On 16 September, a daring glider landing, led by SS-Obersturmbannführer Otto Skorzeny, released Mussolini from his imprisonment in the mountain resort of Gran Sasso, and he was taken away to set up a new fascist state in northern Italy.

The allied forces made slow progress northwards from their landing areas at Salerno and Taranto. The mountainous terrain of southern Italy proved ideal for defence but, by early October, the British 8th Army and the American 5th Army had established a continuous line across the peninsula, from a point north of Naples on the Mediterranean to Termoli on the Adriatic. The Allies had given Kesselring ample time to prepare the Gustav Line, a complex set of fortifications crossing the peninsula and centred on the great monastery of Monte Cassino, located on the massif overlooking the Liri valley through which ran Highway 6, the direct road to Rome. Even reaching the Gustav Line led to heavy allied casualties, especially the crossings of the Sangro and Rapido rivers. Frustrated by the slow advance, the allied planners hoped to outflank the German forces by a landing at Anzio, 30 miles south of Rome. Although the Germans were caught by surprise, the American forces, commanded by Major-General John Lucas, proved so dilatory in breaking out of their bridgehead that the Germans forces were able to keep them trapped on the Mediterranean shoreline.[3]

The commander of the allied forces in Italy was General Harold Alexander. He recognised the challenge posed by the Gustav Line and sought to gather as many troops as could be spared from other planned operations for an assault on it. The Polish II Corps, commanded by General Anders and composed of the men who had been evacuated from the Soviet Union in 1942, was an obvious candidate for transfer. Since then they had done nothing but regain their health, receive equipment and training, and be organised into a corps. The lack of any opportunity for these men to see action was politically disastrous for the Polish Government. In 1942 Stalin had derided the Polish Army in the Soviet Union for its refusal to send a division to the Eastern Front. Since then, relations between the Polish Government and the Soviet Union had been broken off after the Katyń crisis, and a new Polish Army formed in the Soviet Union under communist control, which had already seen highly publicised action at Lenino, but the II Corps had been wholly inactive. Furthermore, the Polish Government was under intense pressure from the British Government to agree to the annexation of eastern Poland into the Soviet Union, so it was politically imperative to put the II Corps into action as soon as possible. Churchill recognised this and, as early as July 1943 when the invasion of Italy was being planned, suggested: 'The Polish troops in Persia should be brought to Egypt for this task. These Poles wished to fight ... and once engaged will worry less about their own affairs, which are tragic.'[4]

Forward elements of the II Corps began arriving in Italy in December

1943. Men from the 3rd Carpathian Division were sent to relieve British troops on the allied defence line on the Sangro river, where they endured the bitter cold of the Italian winter and lost 17 officers and 182 other ranks in minor raids on German positions and on patrols.[5] During the early part of 1944, the rest of the II Corps was transported from its training areas in Palestine and Egypt to Italy. Some of the troops disembarked in Naples and took the opportunity to climb up Mount Vesuvius, four days before the volcano erupted on 18 March with 'great flames shooting out, and hot lava running in two red-hot streams down the mountain side'.[6] By April there were 50,000 Polish military in Italy, organised into the 3rd Carpathian Division, commanded by Major-General Duch; the 5th Kresy Division, commanded by Major-General Nikodem Sulik; the 2nd Armoured Brigade, commanded by Major-General Bronisław Rakowski; and a considerable artillery force, commanded by Major-General Roman Odzierzyński. The II Corps might have looked strong on paper and had its full complement of equipment, but it was hampered by a shortage of manpower: the divisions had two rather than three brigades and there was a very limited reserve.[7]

General Anders arrived in Italy on 6 February, and five days later at the allied headquarters at Caserta he met the commander of the British 8th Army under whom he would work, Lieutenant-General Oliver Leese. The two men were obliged to converse in French, a language in which Anders was fluent but Leese spoke badly: the Poles later claimed that Leese ruined their commander's knowledge of French. Leese immediately formed a favourable impression of Anders, and became sympathetic to the Polish situation after hearing that Anders's wife was in German-occupied Poland and Anders had heard nothing of or from her since 1939 and that Anders's ADC, Prince Eugene Lubomirski, and Anders himself had both spent time imprisoned by the Soviets. Leese wrote to his wife: 'They hate the Russians even more than the Germans.'[8]

The Monte Cassino massif totally dominates the Rapido and Liri valleys and is a natural defensive position. The great Benedictine monastery of Monte Cassino on Monastery Hill can be viewed from almost everywhere in the area, and from this hill and the surrounding high ground, the German defenders could see every movement by the Allies in the valleys below, bringing their artillery to bear at will on allied operations.

There were two hills defending the approaches to the monastery, Castle Hill and Hangman's Hill, while behind Monastery Hill ran Snakeshead Ridge and below that a Gorge (also known as Cavendish Road) along which it might be possible to bring armoured formations, a possibility recognised by the German defenders. The rear of Monastery Hill was, however, in full view of the Germans stationed on the dominant heights of Monte Caira.

The first attack on Monte Cassino was mounted by the 135th Regiment of the US 34th Division on 1 February. The troops advanced along the line of Snakeshead Ridge towards Monte Calvario, best known as Point 593, which was a hill with steep sides about 2,000 yards from the monastery. Units of the 135th also advanced along the parallel Phantom Ridge towards Colle Sant' Angelo. The Germans counterattacked in force and the Americans quickly discovered the strength of the German defences. By 11 February, it was clear that they could advance no further and the first battle of Monte Cassino ended in failure, amid the snow and freezing rain. The presence of the monastery exerted a strong psychological effect on the allied troops, for although the Germans had promised not to fortify the monastery itself, the hill on which it rested was pockmarked with dugouts, mortars and artillery. On 15 February, the monastery was bombed by the US 15th Strategic Air Force, causing almost total destruction. The abbot left for Rome to complain about the bombing; the Germans were meanwhile free to fortify the resulting ruins.

General Alexander gathered a multinational force for a renewed assault on the Monte Cassino massif: the 4th Indian Division and the 2nd New Zealand Division. The plan was for the Indian Division to follow the same path as the Americans to reach the monastery, while the New Zealand Division was to cross the Rapido north of Sant' Angelo, capture the town of Cassino and open up Highway 6 for the advance of the US 1st Armoured Division. The attack was timed to take advantage of the confusion caused by the bombing of the monastery, but little progress was made and, on 18 February, the attacks on Monastery Hill were called off.

The third battle opened on 15 March and the attacks were made again by the New Zealanders and the Indian Division. Castle Hill and Hangman's Hill were captured but a determined defence of Monastery Hill by the German 1st Parachute Division precluded any assault being made towards the monastery. Higher on the massif, tanks from the 20th Armoured Brigade had been creeping along the Gorge when they were spotted by the Germans, who destroyed them. On 23 March, the attack was called off.[9]

General Alexander now set about planning Operation Diadem – the fourth attempt to break the Gustav Line. This was on a much larger scale than the previous attacks, comprising an advance along a 20-mile front by the British 8th Army on the right, the French expeditionary force, under General Alphonse Juin, in the middle, and the US 5th Army, commanded by General Mark Clark, on the left. On 24 March, Leese met Anders to outline the contribution the II Corps could make to the coming battle: an attack on the Monte Cassino massif, the capture of the monastery, followed by an advance on the German reserves in the village of Piedimonte on the Senger, or Hitler, Line. He gave Anders ten minutes to consider the proposal, designed to give Anders an honourable way to refuse to commit his limited forces to an attack on the position that had already defeated men from several nations. A precedent had been set for such a refusal during discussions with Lieutenant-General Sir Bernard Freyberg, who commanded the also limited numbers of New Zealanders. But Anders had an acute sense of political awareness and could see the beneficial publicity which could be gained should the Poles succeed in taking Monte Cassino. His thinking was:

> Monte Cassino is a fortress for which many nations have battled; it is a fortress which is known the world over. If I refuse, then the Corps will be deployed in the Liri River Valley, where the assault will also cause heavy losses but scattered over a longer period of time . . . If we do capture Monte Cassino, and capture it we must, then we will bring Poland's cause – currently so hard-pressed – to the fore of world opinion.[10]

Anders agreed to take on the task and was prepared to accept losses of around 3,500 men. His superior, General Sosnkowski, was less enthusiastic, telling Anders, on 12 April, that in his opinion the II Corps was too weak to carry it out, and that either Anders should operate within the British 13th Corps in the Liri valley or at the very least should request reinforcement by an infantry brigade and more artillery. Leese did give the Poles more artillery but could spare no infantry.[11]

Anders set about visiting the generals who had commanded divisions in the previous attacks and found General Bernard Freyberg and

General Charles Keightley, of the British V Corps, particularly helpful. He also took a plane on 7 April and flew over the Monte Cassino massif, and he and his staff studied air reconnaissance photographs and topographical maps. Ground reconnaissance was virtually impossible since the Germans overlooked the whole area, so the detailed layout of their defences was unknown. A staff officer, Colonel Piatkowski, noted: 'There were no orthodox defence works on the position, such as old-type trenches or barbed wire – nothing, in fact, which could give any clue to the system of fortifications.'[12] They were helped a little by a German who deserted on 5 May and helpfully described the defences on the Cassino massif and of Piedimonte and the Liri valley. Anders decided that these basically consisted of two rings joined together to form a figure of eight: the first ran from Massa Albaneta, Phantom Ridge, Colle Sant' Angelo to Albaneta Farm; the second ran from Massa Albaneta to Colle d'Onofrio and included Monastery Hill itself. The II Corps report written after the battle explained: 'The system of such ... defences may be compared to a Roman amphitheatre where every single spectator can see the result of the ... [spectacle] and vice versa. Each single weapon sited on the circumference of such a ring, could, therefore, take part in the battle for any point on the periphery.'[13] Anders concluded that at least half a ring needed to be captured in a single attack. He identified the two main bastions as Point 593 and Colle Sant' Angelo, and allocated each of his divisions to attack one apiece before the monastery itself would be approached. The 5th Division would take the ridge and advance on Colle Sant' Angelo as well as capturing the nearby hills. This would put them in a position to cover the operations of the 3rd Division, which would capture Point 593 and the Massa Albaneta before assaulting the monastery.[14]

The II Corps moved into its positions during the night of 23–24 April: 'We filled the Rapido valley with smoke-screens to obscure the moonlight, and we employed every possible trick of camouflage to hide from the enemy our artillery positions, our traffic and our dumps.'[15] The British soldiers explained the positions to the incoming Poles:

> At night we took them round the battle positions. We got along very well together, though they could never wholly conceal their slight impatience with our attitude. They hated the Germans, and their military outlook was dominated by their hate. Their one idea was to find out where the nearest

Germans were and go after them . . . They thought we were far too casual because we didn't breathe blind hate all the time.[16]

Conditions at the front were appalling: there was a shortage of rations and water, the Poles lay in shallow foxholes surrounded by decomposing corpses from the earlier battles, and the Germans shelled the area unremittingly. Wiesław Wolwowicz, an officer in the 16th Lwów Rifle Battalion, remembered: 'When the German army started shelling us there was no green grass, there were no bushes, there were just rocks and rubble . . . It wasn't easy . . . When the guns were shelling the rocks, the rocks used to break up.'[17] Stanisław Kochański, in the heavy anti-aircraft artillery down in the Rapido valley, wrote in his diary that the men were terrified by the shelling: when he ordered one of his gun crew out of the trench, he received the reply, 'If you order me, then of course I'll come out, Sir, but I'm sure to shit myself.'[18]

The Polish troops were champing at the bit and keen to get their revenge on the Germans. A British officer, Brigadier T. P. D. Scott, remembered that when Anders explained his plan to his commanders an argument broke out:

> There was some question about which Brigade was to lead the ball. One Brigadier rose to his feet and asserted with much vigour that his men had fought at Tobruk, were seasoned warriors and would therefore do the attack. The other Brigadier at once rose to his feet and said, No, he was the senior, therefore his Brigade would do the attack . . . Such a display of keenness to attack in our Army might be misinterpreted.[19]

Lieutenant Władek Rubnikowicz of the 12th Polish Lancers stated: 'We all wanted to be able to fight for our country. All of us, 100 per cent and 100 per cent more, felt a sense of honour at going into battle for Poland.'[20] This sentiment was shared by those Poles who had already been wounded. Stanisław Kochański, who had been evacuated to the Casualty Clearing Station located in a palace at Venafro after receiving severe facial burns from an exploding shell, recalled the efforts he and other men made not to be sent further to the rear. A week before the battle began, he was discharged from hospital with his wounds not yet healed, thanks to the connivance of a friendly nurse who used her make-up to conceal them. Later, out searching for a break in the telephone cable from his battery to the headquarters, Kochański startled a jittery tank commander who spotted his heavily bandaged face in the dark and thought that he had seen a phantom of death.[21]

The bombardment before the infantry assault on Monte Cassino was intense. One British participant, John Tweedsmuir, wrote:

> There was a silence before the barrage started at 11.00, and then we heard the most lovely nightingale song imaginable. Then the barrage started with heaven knows how many guns, then, over the noise of the guns, the nightingales sang even louder . . . so that you could hear their song above the barrage of the guns.[22]

The artillery was firing virtually blind: the mountains were so steep that the German positions could not be identified. Even the anti-aircraft artillery was used in the bombardment because their guns had the required elevation. Kazimierz Bortkewicz noted that there was a problem with the shells only bursting if they hit something really hard, so they adjusted the fuses to burst the shells in the air hoping to pepper the German trenches with shell splinters.[23] After the first day of the battle, German POWs said that the sheer intensity of the artillery bombardment had come as a great surprise to them.

At 1 a.m. on 12 May, the assault on Monte Cassino by the Polish infantry began, followed closely by tanks attacking the Gorge, which were soon stalled:

> One tank from the support troop came to a stop amongst some rocks, the second one struck a mine and went up in flames, the third one received a direct hit by a heavy shell and had its track damaged. The leading tank of the tank troop following also struck a mine. Sappers engaged in clearing a path for tanks found that the . . . Gorge was unusually heavily mined and . . . they suffered such casualties that they were unable to continue their work.[24]

The infantry failed to occupy the whole of Phantom Ridge and were thwarted in their attempts to advance towards Colle Sant' Angelo and Point 575. The Polish infantry briefly held Point 593 on Monte Calvario and Point 569, but were driven back by German counterattacks. One Polish infantry officer recalled that German artillery fire made progress almost impossible:

> The German guns blasted us so effectively that we were obliged to throw ourselves flat and crawl around looking for cover . . . It seemed impossible

that men could live in such a holocaust. Breathing a prayer, I groped blindly towards a shell hole. It was filled with bodies, sprawling on top of each other. Most of them were lifeless, but . . . I clawed frantically at those on top in an effort to burrow deeper . . . We were fast approaching the end of our tether. We no longer knew where to shoot or whom to aim at. We were mentally blank, stupefied, exhausted.[25]

The slow progress of the 13th Army Corps in the Liri valley, the news of German reinforcements and the high Polish casualty rate forced Anders to issue orders to return to the starting line.[26]

The high number of casualties shocked the Poles: 'The day of the first Polish attack the line of jeeps with wounded was endless, just going and going.' Tomasz Piesakowski visited the temporary cemetery 'to find out where the graves of my friends were' and was appalled by the sheer number of graves.[27] Leese visited Anders, who was visibly distressed by the lack of success. Leese responded with great sympathy and informed Anders that the Polish lack of reinforcements meant that they could only fight one more battle, so they should take a few days to recover before attacking again.

Five days later, on 17 May, the Poles renewed the assault. The plan was essentially unchanged from the first attack except that its timing would coincide with that of the 13th Corps in order to force the German artillery to split its defensive firepower. Initial progress was slow because the troops were still exhausted from their efforts of a few days earlier. Lance Corporal Dobrowski described the battle:

We lie there waiting . . . and then at last comes the order to move. Always the same old cry. We must take ammo, ammo, ammo. Apart from our normal ammunition each of us must take between thirty and forty pounds of grenades. It is a hot day and the going is difficult. When we begin to ascend Hill 593, the weakest soldiers can no longer keep pace. We are in no particular formation. No sections; no platoons. The situation is such that we must use our own initiative. Later we can reorganize – those of us who are left. Now we engage the enemy. All is confusion and the Germans' positions are mixed with ours. With munificent impartiality we hurl our hand-grenades. From the neighbouring heights Spandaus, Schmeissers and heavy machine guns catch us in a murderous cross-fire.[28]

By the end of the first day, the Poles had broken the northern defence ring, and captured Colle Sant' Angelo and Point 593. Their situation was precarious, as Colonel Klemens Rudnicki, second-in-command of the 5th Division, recalled: 'Casualties had been enormous. Most of the ammunition was used up and there was nothing left to fight with. The platoons and battalions were hopelessly intermixed ... It was impossible to say what dawn would bring.'[29]

During the night of 17–18 May, the commander of the German Tenth Army, General Heinrich Vietinghoff-Scheel, had a conversation with Field Marshal von Kesselring, and they agreed that the Monte Cassino monastery position was now untenable.[30] Its German troops were withdrawn but continued to resist the Polish attack elsewhere. At 8 a.m. on 18 May, a patrol of thirteen men under Lieutenant Gurbiel moved towards the ruins of the monastery, and he described the scene:

> A thick haze, mixed with the morning mist, rolled up the valley. The sun appearing over the mountains, was like a tarnished golden ball. The stink of decay hung over the hill, and the light breeze made it even more unbearable. Only the shimmering, blood-red poppy fields, defying the shells and bombs, waved softly in the wind.[31]

Seven men climbed into the monastery and, after having checked that the ruins were deserted, at 10.20 a.m. hoisted an improvised Polish flag over the remains of the monastery at Monte Cassino. Then one of the lancers played the *Kraków Hejnał** on his bugle. One soldier remembered:

> There was a lump in my throat as, through the echo of the cannon's roar, the notes of the *Hejnał* rang out from the Abbey ... These soldiers, hardened by numerous battles, only too well acquainted with the shocking wastefulness of death on the slopes of Monte Cassino, cried like children, as, after years of wandering, they heard not from the radio, but from the previously invincible German fortress, the voice of Poland, the melody of the *Hejnał*.[32]

The British attack had made considerable progress in the Liri valley and the Gustav Line had finally been broken.

---

* This military signal dates from the fourteenth century when Poland was attacked by the Tartars. It breaks off with a broken note, allegedly when an arrow had pierced the bugler's throat. It has since become a powerful symbol of Poland's identity and independence, and for centuries has been played hourly from the tower of the Mariacki church in Kraków.

Leese visited Anders and they drank sweet champagne in celebration, and Leese wrote to his wife: 'The success has made up for all the casualties.'[33] The BBC broadcast that evening: 'Cassino and the monastery have been captured. The final assault was carried out by British troops, while Polish troops occupied the monastery.' Anders was jubilant that, after all that his men had gone through in the Soviet Union, they had now proved their mettle in battle. He wrote to Sosnkowski: 'All who took part in the battle have abundantly deserved decorations, and I think that at least one-third of them ought to receive the Cross for Valour. I will make separate recommendations for the award of the *Virtuti Militari* Cross [Poland's highest medal].'[34]

The Poles had faced the most formidable German opposition, the German 1st and 3rd Parachute Regiments. One German paratrooper, Josef Klein, paid tribute to them:

> They were brave soldiers. They were the bravest of them all, in fact. But it was more like an inner drive that went almost to the level of fanaticism . . . They looked at death but marched ahead nevertheless, which nobody else did . . . This was a devastating thing – the order and sense of duty the Poles had. The thinking that 'We have to get through. We have to show the Allied forces that we are worthy of belonging to them. We must make the breakthrough' . . . We often couldn't believe it.[35]

Polish casualties were high: 72 officers and 788 other ranks killed, and 204 officers and 2,618 other ranks wounded, much as Anders had predicted when he took on the task. These numbers were so high, however, that after taking Piedimonte the II Corps was withdrawn from action and sent to the rear for a rest. The shortage of reinforcements was a serious problem and plans were made to transfer some men from the artillery, especially the underemployed anti-aircraft artillery, to the infantry. Stanisław Kochański viewed the prospect with misgivings: 'I don't have the vocation to be a hare even though I have great admiration for the infantry, their courage and sacrifice.' German POWs were sifted and those of Polish origin were given the opportunity to join the Polish Army they had just been fighting.[36]

On 5 June, troops from the US 5th Army entered Rome, and to some it seemed that the greatest objective of the Italian campaign had been achieved. In his memoirs General Alexander mourns what happened next: he wanted to retain the number of troops he had under his command, clear the Po valley and advance to the north-east towards the Ljubljana Gap and on to Vienna. Churchill agreed with this strategy but the Americans were committed to the launching of Operation Dragoon, the invasion of southern France in August 1944, so a substantial proportion of the United States army and the French expeditionary force was removed from the front line in readiness.[37] Therefore, Alexander's options were limited, and the operations on the Adriatic front were temporarily halted while the main effort was made on the northward advance from Rome.

Then supply problems started to slow the allied advance and it became essential to capture a northern port on the Adriatic. Anders was ordered to 'pursue the enemy at the highest possible speed and capture Ancona harbour', since opening it would considerably ease the Allies' supply concerns. The II Corps was lent a number of British units, including the 7th Queen's Hussars, and an Italian corps, *Corpo Italiano di Liberazione*, commanded by General Umberto Utili, consisting of 13 poorly equipped infantry battalions. The Germans ferociously defended the many river crossings and their artillery exacted a high toll in casualties. Finally, at 2 p.m. on 18 July, the Polish troops entered Ancona. Within days the minefields had been swept and the port was restored to full working order, bringing fuel to the 8th Army. The Polish casualties in the advance on Ancona and the battles to capture the port were high: 150 officers and 2,000 other ranks. Afterwards the Poles were given a short period of rest and a chance to absorb 4,111 reinforcements, 856 of whom had previously fought in the Wehrmacht.[38] Leese visited the troops after the battle and wrote to his wife that they were 'much younger and in many ways of finer physique than they were before the Cassino battle. So many [of] them bore the marks of their sufferings in prison in Russia. The new ones are deserters and prisoners from the Germany [*sic*] Army.'[39]

The Poles pursued the Germans northwards, clearing the way for the launching of the next major allied operation, the breaking of the Gothic Line to gain entry into the plain of Lombardy. This line ran from Pesaro on the Adriatic, along the river Foglia to Pistoia, north of Pisa, and consisted of a defensive belt about 4 miles in depth with well-prepared infantry and artillery defensive positions, anti-tank obstacles and minefields. Because of the departure of troops for the invasion of southern France, Kesselring's divisions outnumbered those of the Allies, even though the German divisions were under strength.[40] Before the attack on the Gothic Line, the Polish troops received a morale boost created by two important visitors, King George VI and their commander-in-chief, General Sosnkowski. On 23 July, Anders and Sosnkowski were presented to the king and together they watched a march past of some Polish units. On 27 July, they had dinner with the king, and Leese reported to his wife: 'We also made Anders sing his folk-song of Lwów – and the King and I sang the chorus in what we called Polish!' The chorus had been written down phonetically for them.[41]

The attack on the Gothic Line was launched on 19 August, with the Poles operating next to the Adriatic, the Canadians in the middle and the British on the left flank. The II Corps took Pesaro and then, on 2 September, was ordered out of the line for a rest in the Ancona area and took no further part in the fighting on the Gothic Line. In October the Poles returned to the fray and their most notable achievement was the ten-day battle for Forlì, which 'took place on mountainous ground in extremely adverse conditions, cold, lack of accommodation and trans-port difficulties'. These battles in the Apennines took a heavy toll: 226 officers and 3,257 other ranks killed or wounded. The new commander of the 8th Army, Lieutenant-General Richard McCreery, sent congratu-lations to Anders.[42] The Allies were now so exhausted and the weather so bad with torrential rain that the front stalled on the Senio river throughout the winter of 1944–5.

Before the offensive could be renewed in the spring, the II Polish Corps faced its worst crisis – morale. Throughout its operations in Italy the Germans had attempted to undermine Polish morale. The German radio station *Wanda* had broadcast from Rome in Polish twice daily informing the Poles of the progress of the talks between the western allies and the Soviet Union over the fate of eastern Poland and encour-aging them to desert. As the Germans retreated, they left leaflets in every trench, full of photographs and copies of documents from the Inter-national Red Cross, which made a great impression on the Polish soldiers: 'Today I looked through a leaflet the Germans published in Polish about the murders at Katyń. When will they [the Soviets] be paid back for that?'[43]

Worse news was to hit the Poles when the agreement at Yalta was made public in February 1945. Virtually all the men in the II Corps came from eastern Poland, which was now to be part of the Soviet Union. Tadeusz Żukowski, in the 3rd Division, recorded his reaction:

From that moment on, we knew that there was no way back for us, no hope. We knew that now we were fighting solely for our honour and dignity, nothing else. The despair amongst our ranks was overwhelming. We lost faith in the allies, our own officers weren't able to tell us what went wrong and what would happen to us in the future. They themselves, were deeply affected by the sudden unfavourable news. Still, we fought on, wherever they sent us, only this time, we did not feel like Polish soldiers fighting for a good cause, but merely mercenaries.[44]

Anders's first reaction was that the Poles should cease fighting and dying for the Allies who had betrayed them. On 13 February, he formally asked McCreery for permission to take the Poles out of the line and repeated this in a report to the chief liaison officer at allied headquarters, Major-General Frederick Beaumont-Nesbitt. Anders then had meetings with Alexander, McCreery and Clark between 15 and 21 February, during which Alexander told Anders that his troops were essential, particularly now that the Canadian corps had been sent to north-west Europe.[45] Anders then flew to London to talk to his government and to meet Churchill and the CIGS, Field Marshal Alanbrooke. In his memoirs Anders alleged that Churchill cruelly told him that he could take his troops out of the line because they were simply no longer needed.[46] There is no evidence to substantiate Anders's assertion. For example, Sir Alexander Cadogan, who was present at the meeting, makes no mention of it, nor does Alanbrooke, who certainly knew that the Poles were still very much needed. Anders, now acting commander-in-chief of the Polish army since Sosnkowski's controversial dismissal, returned to Italy, where, on 13 March, he issued an Order of the Day stating that, although the Polish Government would not recognise the decisions made at Yalta, he expected the 'maintenance of dignity and discipline worthy of the highest morale, which is the attitude of every soldier of II Corps'.[47]

Harold Macmillan, British minister resident in the Mediterranean, still worried about the morale of the Polish troops: 'At the worst, they will disintegrate into a rabble of refugees. At the best, they will be kept enough together to hold a sector of line, without attacks or counter-attacks. I do not think they could now be used offensively.' He was proved wrong during the battles of the spring when the Poles 'fought with distinction in the front of the attack ... they had lost their country, but they kept their honour'.[48] Indeed, the Poles themselves felt that they were fighting for honour alone: 'It was like a crusade ... I honestly believed that I was fighting for a better world based on Roosevelt's Four Freedoms and the Atlantic Charter.'[49] Others like Stanisław Kochański wanted to hold themselves in readiness for future battles:

> Really it would be a shame to die here on the Italian front, or be crippled. I have to keep my strength for something else. Here is one more believer who wants to pay them back for 17 September, 10 February, 13 April, and so many other dates, for the Urals, Kazakhstan and Katyń. There I won't be sitting in the anti-aircraft artillery, I'll be pushing myself forward. There it would be worth dying, as long as it's not too soon.

The men of the II Polish Corps held on to the belief that after Germany was defeated they could go into action against the Soviet Union, regain the lost territories and have a freely elected democratic government.[50]

In April 1945, phase I of the allied spring offensive in Italy opened, aimed at launching the 5th and 8th Armies through the Argenta Gap into the Po valley and capturing or isolating Bologna. The Poles suffered an early setback when, on 9 April, a wave of American heavy bombers erroneously dropped their payloads on top of the forward troops of the 3rd Division, killing 38 and wounding 188. The loss of these men was sorely felt not least because they were the specialists at river crossings. After very hard-fought battles the Poles entered Bologna at 6 a.m. on 21 April, two hours ahead of the Americans. They hoisted the Polish flag from the highest tower they could find and received a letter of thanks from the mayor of Bologna, Joseph Dozza.[51] Macmillan was quick to praise the Poles in his diary:

> The Poles have fought splendidly and were in crashing form. Not a word about politics or the future of Poland; nothing but triumphant exposition of their operations. I hardly recognised General Anders, whom I had last seen in very gloomy mood at Caserta. '*Une très jolie petite bataille; nous avons tué plus que deux mille Boches; on les sent partout*'.[52]

The Germans knew that their forces were defeated in Italy and, on 2 May, they surrendered. The Poles, though facing an uncertain future, celebrated the end of their war: Stanisław Kochański had to knock out one of his soldiers who was drunkenly waving his machine gun around and firing it.[53]

The Poles, however, received very little public recognition for their contribution to the final defeat of German forces in Italy. Ever since Monte Cassino they had been seen as a political embarrassment. For example, an article, 'The Carpathian Lancers', written by the American war correspondent Martha Gellhorn, who had joined the Poles during their advance on Ancona, was not published by *Collier's Magazine*, because it mentioned how the Poles worried about the Soviet advance in their country:

> All the Poles talk about Russia all the time. The soldiers gather several times a day around the car which houses the radio and listen to the news; they listen to all the news in Polish wherever it comes from. They follow the Russian advance across Poland with agonized interest. It seemed to me that up here, on the Polish sector of the Italian front, people knew either what was happening ten kilometres away or what was happening in Poland, and nothing else. We never found out what the Eighth Army was doing in front of Florence or how the French were getting on above Siena or whether the Americans had raced ahead to take Pisa. And Normandy was another world. But what went on in Poland could be seen in every man's face, in every man's eyes.[54]

The Polish war cemetery at Monte Cassino, however, has a prominent position near the monastery, and there are two memorials, one to each division on Points 575 and 593. The reconstruction of the abbey at Monte Cassino took over a decade and was funded exclusively by the Italian Government: donations from the nations who had contributed to its destruction were refused.

On 6 June 1944, Operation Overlord – D-Day – the Second Front – was launched when the armies of Britain, Canada and the United States landed on the beaches of Normandy. All Polish surface ships, bar *Garland*, took part in Operation Neptune, the naval part of D-Day, covering Canadian and British landings. The town of Caen was an objective of the British forces that day but lay beyond their reach then. Several small and two major attacks – Operations Epsom and Goodwood – in June and July failed to dislodge the Germans. To the west the Americans found the going easier and cleared the Cotentin peninsula and began to push the Germans back into the Cherbourg peninsula: Cherbourg surrendered on 26 June. Both Allies then encountered problems caused by the terrain, the bocage, which favoured the defender: 'narrow, steep, deep, wriggling, overgrown, hedged, banked and densely watercoursed', where no one could predict what was around the corner, or on the other side of the banks, with the lanes so narrow that the destruction of a single vehicle could hold up a whole column. The battle was relentless and casualties high on both sides, but finally, at the end of July, the British captured Caen and the Americans were able to break out and begin the drive eastwards. The Allies and the Germans were all converging on one point: Falaise.[55]

In accordance with the 1943 directive of the Combined Chiefs of Staff, the 1st Polish Armoured Division was not used in Operation Overlord but held in reserve. The division had struggled to reach its full establishment, and in 1943 Sosnokowski had stripped the infantry regiments in Scotland to fill it. On 1 August, the strength of the 1st Armoured Division was 13,000 officers and men, equipped with 381 tanks, 473 artillery pieces and 3,050 vehicles.[56] Its commander was General Maczek, who had led an armoured unit in Poland in September 1939 and in France in 1940. The insignia of the division was the helmet and Husaria eagle wings, which had been worn on the shoulders of the Polish soldiers who, under King Jan Sobieski, had stopped the Turks at the gates of Vienna in 1683 and saved Christendom in Europe. The division was nicknamed 'The Black Devils'. On 1 August, the day on which the Warsaw Uprising was launched, the 1st Armoured Division crossed the Channel. It was placed under the 1st Canadian Army, commanded by Lieutenant-General Henry Crerar, and its objective was to assist in trapping the bulk of the German armies at Falaise.

Operation Totalise was the name given to the drive by the II Canadian Armoured Division, commanded by Lieutenant-General Guy Simonds, and the 1st Polish Armoured Division towards Falaise to cut off the German retreat to the Seine. It was launched on 7 August and began disastrously when the American bombers dropped their bombs on the Polish and Canadian front lines, killing 315 men. Attempts on the ground to alert the bombers to their error by throwing yellow smoke grenades came to nothing because the Americans were using yellow flares to mark their target.

A Canadian Spitfire pilot, after vainly trying to divert the first two waves of Fortresses that were bombing the gun lines, deliberately shot down the leader of the third wave to the accompaniment of tumultuous applause from the scattered, frightened soldiery below. The crew baled out.[57]

Operation Totalise failed in the face of fierce resistance by the SS *Hitlerjugend* Panzer Division.

On 13 August, Operation Tractable opened with an attack by the Canadians towards Falaise and a drive by the Poles on the left flank towards Thun. Again American bombers bombed the allied positions, this time in the rear, causing 391 casualties. The Poles succeeded in breaking through the German defences and, on 15 August, the Polish reconnaissance regiment, the 10th Mounted Rifles, reached and secured a crossing over the river Dives near Jort. Further south the American army had reached Argentan. A Polish participant, Ryszard Zolski, recalled the tempo of the battles:

> Falaise will be remembered as the most murderous battlefield of the invasion, where the might of the German Army clashed with the armies of America, England, Canada and Poland – where the Germans were determined to fight – not counting the cost, even to the last man. My God, how they fought – bravely and with determination, until at the end, hardly recognisable as human at all, only tattered remnants of clothing, flesh of men and horses, jumbled up with smashed armour, tanks and the like. Attack from the air, bombing, rockets, machine guns, together with our artillery, grenades and armour of every sort, finally annihilated their mighty army, and halted their retreat. Falaise – one of the most costly battles of the war, both in men and armament.[58]

Maczek now split his limited forces: on 17 August he ordered the 24th Lancers, 10th Mounted Rifles and 2nd Armoured Regiment to advance towards Chambois, while the remainder of the division occupied a vital piece of high ground, Mont Ormel, also known as Hill 262 and 'The Mace'.[59]

The Poles had mixed fortunes on the road to Chambois, when the 2nd Armoured Regiment ended up in Les Chameaux, a few miles from Chambois, because their French guide had become disorientated in the dark. It was fortuitous because at Les Chameaux the Poles found and destroyed the rearguard of the 2nd Panzer Division before turning towards their target. On the way when they encountered a German motorised column in the dark:

The Germans halt their units and allow our column to pass. They even post a German soldier to regulate the traffic. He should be able to discern the American Shermans and those large white stars on the tanks and on my carriers. But it is still totally black. We just ride in front of the German column.[60]

The 2nd Tactical Air Force flew sortie after sortie as Chambois 'was delivered to the flames ... The roads leading to it and the side streets were jammed with German armour already alight or smouldering, enemy corpses and a host of wounded soldiers.'[61] The Poles took so many prisoners that they struggled to spare enough men to guard them. On 19 August, the Poles linked up with the 90th United States Infantry Division. Lieutenant George Godrey noted of the Poles: 'They were excellent fighters and very cold-blooded.'[62]

The main body of the Poles was on 'The Mace', so nicknamed by Maczek because of its shape. This high, wooded escarpment overlooked the Chambois–Vimoutiers road along which the German forces were trying to escape eastwards under allied artillery fire. The Polish force expected an early reinforcement by the Canadian 4th Armoured Division under Major-General George Kitching, as they were rapidly running out of food and ammunition, despite receiving a limited resupply by a parachute drop, and they asked the Canadians to speed up their relief. Kitching, however, refused to do so and was sacked by Simonds. Then on 20 August, elements of *Der Führer* Regiment of the 2nd SS Panzer Division and of the 9th SS Panzer Division *Der Hohenstaufen* mounted an assault directly on the Mace: 'Every combination of tactics was used: conventional infantry assaults, combined panzer and grenadier, unsupported Panther attacks, savage bombardments or no barrage at all.'[63] Second Lieutenant Tadeusz Krzyżaniak commented on the fighting:

> Where are we? Where are they? In fact I know very well. THEY are in front of us, WE behind. At the same time, THEY are behind us, WE in front. Then it's the opposite. Everywhere explosions, and everywhere blood: the blood of horses, the blood of others, and my blood.[64]

All day the battle raged, with high casualties among both the attacking SS formations and the Polish defenders. Finally, on 21 August, the Canadians reached the beleaguered Poles and Ed Borowicz noted their reaction:

On the top of Hill 262 stands Lieut. Col Nowaczyński, the battalion commander, with the commander of the Canadian tanks, staring in silence at the battlefield. Over the khaki uniforms, at the emerald-blue lance pennons of the dead soldiers of the 8th Battalion, the disfigured faces, jutting jaws and teeth in deathly smiles, human parts – torsos, legs, blood-ied stretchers, pieces of an anti-tank gun, and nearby a barrel of a broken mortar in the convulsive grip of a dead gunner. In the middle of a few blackened, smoking Shermans, on their turrets hangs a leaning torso, half scorched hands lying listlessly.[65]

Tomasz Potworowski and a friend visited the scene a few days later and observed: 'Already by then the Canadian sappers charged with clearing the mess had erected a sign on the "Mace" which read: "A Polish Battle-field."[66] Polish losses up to 22 August were 325 killed and 1,116 wounded or missing: this was 10 per cent of the division's strength. Sosnkowski telegraphed his troops from London: 'Your sacrifices will enable the rights of Poland to be established on an indestructible foun-dation.' The Germans left behind 50,000 dead and 200,000 taken prisoner in the Falaise Pocket.[67]

Field Marshal Walter Model, who had replaced Field Marshal Günther-Hans Kluge in the middle of August, realised that the Germans had no option but to retreat to the Seine and try to mount a defence there. The allied breakout from Normandy and the drive eastwards was, however, now in full swing, and, after a brief rest, the Poles joined in the chase, moving quickly, 'sometimes as fast as the tanks could drive'.[68] The Poles advanced through Rouen, Abbeville and St Omer before crossing the Belgian frontier. There was fierce fighting on the approach to Ypres, 'after which we were hampered in our advance, as orders from General Maczek decreed that there was to be no bombardment on the town, as Ypres and its unfortunate population had suffered terrible destruction during the Great War'.[69] Ypres was eventually taken by hand-to-hand fighting with minimal damage to the town. On 9 September, the Polish division reached Ghent, the capital of Flanders. There, after a ceremony at the town hall, Maczek signed the visitors' book, putting his name next to that of General Foch, who had signed in 1918.[70]

The Poles now chased the Germans across the Dutch border, where the Polish division was transferred to the command of the I British Corps, under Lieutenant-General John Crocker. In October there was a fierce eight-day battle for the Turnhout Canal, and the Polish victory there removed the German threat to Antwerp. The Poles now advanced on the major Dutch city of Breda and on 28 October, after a six-day battle, took it just before the Canadian and American troops arrived. The road along which the 8th Battalion fought was renamed Poolsche Weg in honour of Maczek's troops. The Poles rested in the region of Breda over the winter, and received and trained reinforcements sent from the small reserve in Britain and absorbed those Poles who, having been conscripted into the Wehrmacht, had been combed out of allied POW camps.[71]

In April the Poles rejoined the allied offensive with further operations in the Netherlands. The armoured division was expected to fight in the country around the Friesian islands, an area so criss-crossed with canals and channels that a member of Maczek's staff pointed out 'that boats would be more useful to us than tanks'. The objective was the German port of Emden and, as the division crossed the Dutch-German border, Maczek noted the contrast 'between the houses decorated with flags and masses of flowers and relatively untouched houses in Holland with the white flags in Germany and the deserted streets and shuttered houses'.[72] The Germans resisted the Allies strongly on their own territory but slowly and surely the Allies advanced, and the Polish objective was altered to the important German naval base at Wilhelmshaven. From 19 to 29 April, the Poles fought hard to advance, as the terrain proved ideal for defence since it was extremely marshy with a thin layer of peat covering the tracks along which the tanks and armoured vehicles had to pass. The obvious routes that the Poles had to advance along meant that the Germans knew precisely where to place their defences.[73]

The Germans were collapsing on all fronts and Hitler committed suicide in his bunker in Berlin on 30 April. On 6 May, Maczek attended a meeting between General Simonds and a German delegation led by General Erich von Straube. Simonds made it clear that only unconditional surrender was on offer. The 1st Polish Armoured Division was given the honour of occupying Wilhemshaven, and Colonel Antoni Grudziński, second in command of the Polish 10th Armoured Brigade, noted the reaction of the Germans to this news:

An officer on my staff, a former student at Gdańsk Polytechnic, translated every sentence into German. When the words 'Polish Division' were uttered by the translator, and as if by inattentiveness repeated, it seemed the Germans whitened and unease flashed in their eyes. I enquired if they understood – 'Jawohl' – they replied. I gave a sign that they might leave. But, a thought passed through my mind, 'This is for September 1939'.[74]

The Poles took control of Wilhelmshaven and accepted the surrender of 19,000 German officers, including a general and an admiral. Three cruisers, 18 submarines, 205 lesser ships and support vessels plus a vast array of artillery and infantry weaponry were taken into Polish custodianship. The division had lost 304 officers and 5,000 other ranks since August 1944.[75] Despite all that Poland had suffered at the hands of the Germans, Maczek maintained strict discipline to ensure that the Poles did not take reprisals. This, despite the fact that the division had liberated a concentration camp at Oberlangen full of emaciated women POWs, members of the AK who had surrendered after the collapse of the Warsaw Uprising and had been held there without the protection of the Geneva Convention.[76] On 19 May, General Anders visited Wilhelmshaven and Maczek had prepared for the visit by ordering the German population to sew Polish flags using white sheets and the red portion of the Nazi flags. The result was an impressive array of Polish flags on 25-feet-high posts shimmering along the avenue where the division marched past Anders. Maczek was then replaced as commander of the 1st Polish Armoured Division by General Rudnicki, and the armoured division joined the Polish Parachute Brigade to take part in the occupation of Germany.[77]

The Polish Parachute Brigade had been a unit looking for a purpose. The rationale behind its creation was that it should be used only for operations in Poland, in support of a national uprising. Neither the Poles nor the British gave serious consideration to exactly how a parachute brigade could be transported there, and the reality was that the only aircraft with the adequate range were Dakotas, and they were in strictly limited supply. Gliders would be needed to carry the brigade's heavy equipment, but these were extremely vulnerable to anti-aircraft artillery and would in all likelihood suffer high losses on its way. Questions about its validity had arisen during the planning conference Sikorski convened in London in April 1942, and the commander of the 3rd Infantry Brigade Group, Major-General Gustaw Paszkiewicz, had suggested then that if the parachute brigade, then only a cadre unit, was brought up to full strength the British would demand its use for their own purposes. The brigade's commander, General Stanisław Sosabowski, argued that if the men could be found, the British would equip the brigade and that would be the time to debate its ultimate purpose.[78]

In August 1942, the British accepted the 1st Parachute Brigade as an allied unit under Polish command and placed it under the commander of the British Airborne Corps, Lieutenant-General Frederick Browning. In March 1944 the CIGS, Field Marshal Alanbrooke, wrote to Sosabowski setting out conditions under which the Polish Parachute Brigade could be used for operations in Europe, not necessarily in Poland. The Polish cabinet replied with its own list of conditions, which the British found unacceptable. In May 1944, it was clear that General Bernard Montgomery would not accept any conditions attached to its use, and, on 6 June, Sosnkowski reluctantly agreed to place the Polish Parachute Brigade, now at a strength of 3,100 men, at the disposal of the British planning staff.[79] On 1 August the Warsaw Uprising was launched. This was the moment for which the men of the parachute brigade had been waiting, the time when they would return to Poland to fight for their country's liberation. On 12 August 1944 Sosabowski wrote to Alanbrooke:

> The question of employing part of the Polish Paratroop Brigade in the Battle of Warsaw has not been decided upon. The date of the participation of this brigade in the fighting in France is approaching. Therefore, I would be very much obliged to you if you would give instructions for one battalion to be diverted from operational duties in France and designated for use in Poland.

Alanbrooke replied that this was impossible because of lack of transport. Sosnkowski responded by warning: 'a crisis of morale may occur in the ranks of the brigade which could deprive the unit of its fighting value'. On 13 August, the soldiers in the brigade went on a twenty-four-hour hunger strike to protest at the failure to aid Warsaw.[80]

The Polish Parachute Brigade played no role in the airborne landings on D-Day but was earmarked for later airborne operations, for example, near Paris or across the Belgium border, but these were cancelled because the allied front moved so rapidly after the breakout from Normandy. The Polish Parachute Brigade's establishment was then 2,000 officers and men divided into 3 battalions. The Poles felt frustrated at the inaction:

> It was obvious to all that the brigade would see combat in a short time. We all considered and argued amongst ourselves as to where and when that drop would take place. The wish of us all was that we would go to Warsaw. The heart and minds of all us soldiers, particularly those of the Parachute Brigade, were consumed by Warsaw's tragedy; everybody wanted to help. The privilege of fighting in the ranks of its defenders was our most heartfelt desire.[81]

The Allies were advancing fast and, by 14 September, the whole of Belgium and Luxembourg as well as a small portion of Holland had been liberated. The pace of the allied advance was now being dictated by the speed with which supplies could be brought to the front from Normandy, and the allied planners viewed the port of Antwerp as being in the ideal position for supplies for the advance into Germany. The Channel ports of Boulogne, Le Havre, Calais and Dunkirk were still in German hands. But they appear to have failed to recognise that the port of Antwerp could not be opened until the Scheldt estuary had been cleared. Instead, Montgomery, still in command of allied ground forces until 10 September, when General Dwight Eisenhower took over, planned an audacious leap over the Meuse river and the Lower Rhine by airborne troops to open the way into the Ruhr and the north German plain. This was the genesis of Operation Market Garden, the attempt by airborne and ground forces to seize the bridge over the Rhine at Arnhem. Called by many 'a bridge too far', the operation could also be described in the words of the commander of the Polish Parachute Brigade, General Sosabowski: 'But the Germans, General . . . the Germans!'[82] Operation Market Garden has been the subject of much study and the reasons for its failure carefully analysed. It is impossible here to give more than a basic overview of the flaws in the planning stage, the operation itself, Poland's role in it and the assignment of the blame for the failure of the operation.

Before Operation Market Garden came Operation Comet, the first plan to seize the bridges at Arnhem, Grave and Nijmegen and hold them until the ground forces arrived. Sosabowski was briefed on Polish participation by Major-General Robert Urquhart, commander of the British 1st Airborne Division. Sosabowski raised so many questions that

Urquhart invited him to put them to Browning, who appeared to agree with Sosabowski's points: the distance of the drop zones from the target meant that surprise would be lost, and if the bridges were destroyed or could not be taken and held then there was no other way to cross the rivers; but told Sosabowski: 'The Red Devils and the gallant Poles can do anything.'[83] Operation Comet was cancelled on 10 September, but Browning had become aware of Sosabowski's readiness to question orders, and this would tell against him in the future. Indeed, Browning was later to criticise the performance of the Poles at Arnhem and the performance of Sosabowski personally. Urquhart, who had more contact with Sosabowski during the actual operation, did not share his superior's opinion: he dedicated his book on Arnhem: 'To all ranks who served in the 1st Airborne Division in September 1944 and their Comrades in Arms of the 1st Polish Parachute Brigade Group'.

Operation Market Garden was even more ambitious: the US 82nd and 101st Airborne Divisions were added to the British 1st Airborne and the Polish Parachute Brigade. The plan was for the American divisions to seize the bridges at Eindhoven, Grave and Nijmegen, and the British the bridge over the Rhine at Arnhem. The German parachute landing at Maleme in Crete had proved so costly that thereafter the Germans had abandoned airborne landings, but the British believed that the lesson of Crete was that the landings should be made further away from the objective and the troops concentrated before the advance on the target: for example, the closest drop zone to Arnhem was 6 miles away. The obvious disadvantage was that surprise would be lost. No matter, thought the allied military planners, there were insufficient German troops in the vicinity to affect the landings, the concentration of the troops and the advance. Because the Dutch resistance had been heavily penetrated by the Gestapo earlier in the war, the allied planners now discounted a report from Holland of the presence of the remnants of the 9th and 10th SS Panzer divisions refitting near Arnhem. Worse still, the RAF seemed either unable or unwilling to spare the aircraft and crews to make more than one airdrop per day, which meant that the troops would be landed in stages and thus the build-up of their strength would be slow.

The role allocated to the Poles was split over two days. On the second day of the operation, the glider force of 45 Horsa gliders carrying the entire anti-tank weaponry of the brigade as well as the Polish liaison and signals officers would be landed north of the Rhine within the perimeter held by the British division that would have landed on the first day. The rest of the Polish Parachute Brigade would land on the south bank of the Rhine near the bridge at Arnhem. Sosabowski suspected from the outset that the Poles would find themselves being expected to clear up the mess created by flawed planning. He believed that the British 1st Airborne would have insufficient troops for the tasks allotted to it: taking and holding the bridge at Arnhem and holding open the bridges for the Poles to cross the river to join the British, or, indeed, controlling the drop zone for the Polish paratroopers. Urquhart informed Sosabowski: 'If by any chance the 1st Brigade has not taken the Arnhem bridges, you will have to capture them on the way through.'[84] No one seemed to question the overly ambitious ground part of Market Garden: an 80-mile advance by Lieutenant-General Brian Horrocks's XXX Corps up a virtually single-lane road to relieve the airborne forces.

Operation Market Garden opened on 17 September. The US airborne divisions were dropped on their objectives, the three bridges, which they took successfully. The British force had mixed fortunes. Only half the airborne division could arrive on the first lift, which meant that this force had to be split: the 1st Parachute Brigade advanced on the bridge at Arnhem but the remainder had to remain behind to guard the landing ground for the second lift in the vicinity of Oosterbeek. The Germans quickly recovered from their surprise and, though short of tanks, they still had the full complement of artillery and anti-aircraft artillery and the determination to thwart the British attempt to leap the Rhine and open the road to the Ruhr. Communications between the British units broke down and there were none at all between the force at Arnhem and the military commanders back in Britain. This meant that the second British drop and the Polish glider force landing on 18 September would be made with limited knowledge of the events on the ground. The British airdrop and first Polish glider landing encountered little opposition, but the second Polish glider landing, on 19 September, encountered far more. Germans fighters intercepted the defenceless gliders with the result that five anti-tank artillery guns were lost, and also harassed the glider troops on the ground, causing high casualties. Further losses ensued when the British thought that the Poles, who had different kit and grey berets, were the Germans and opened fire on them.[85]

Poor weather precluded air reconnaissance flights, limited the supply drops to the beleaguered British troops and delayed the departure of the main portion of the Polish Parachute Brigade. Eventually, on 21 September, an air armada of 114 planes carried the Polish airborne troops into battle. While the planes were in the air the British called off the airdrop, but only 61 planes received the message and turned back; the remainder continued to their destination and dropped 1,067 paratroopers, including Sosabowski. Only the day before had Sosabowski been informed that his brigade would no longer be dropped south of Arnhem bridge but instead was to be dropped near Driel and then moved across the Lower Rhine using the ferry at Heveadrop to join Urquhart's forces which were trapped in Oosterbeek. The British assured them that the ferry was under allied control but in fact they had only seen it from the Westerbouwing Heights. When the British troops checked on 21 September, the ferry was missing and the cable cut.[86] Unknown to the Poles, their landing ground was under German control, and they shot at the Polish paratroopers as they floated down and then pinned the survivors on the ground with heavy firepower. One Pole, who had served in the Wehrmacht, saved his group by calling out in perfect colloquial Wehrmacht German: 'Stop shooting at us, you horse's arse!' The machine gun ceased firing and the Poles made their escape.[87]

Sosabowski found that not only was he missing most of his 1st and part of his 3rd Battalion, whose planes had turned back, but also that he had no communications with Urquhart and so knew nothing of events on the north bank. Searching for the promised ferry at Heveadrop, the Poles met Cora Baltussen, linked to the Dutch underground, who informed the Poles that it was out of commission. Sosabowski finally heard about the situation confronting the British when:

> an incredible figure staggered in. Dripping with water and spattered with mud stood a near-naked man, clad only in underpants and a camouflage net round his face. Suddenly I recognised Captain Zwolański, whom I had sent as Liaison Officer to Urquhart. 'Oh!' I uttered rather pointlessly. 'What are you doing here?' 'I have just swum the Rhine to bring you the latest news, sir.' 'Yes,' I said. 'It looks as if you have. Well, tell me about it.' One of my staff threw a blanket over Zwolański's shoulders, who had begun to shiver. He gratefully accepted a chair and started to talk.[88]

Zwolański said the British would send rafts to transfer the Poles across the river, and while waiting the Poles set up a defensive perimeter and the Dutch people, grateful for their liberation, helped them. Sosabowski used a ladies' bicycle to ride round the perimeter checking on his troops. A Polish chaplain, Father Bednorz, knocked on the door of the rectory in Driel and the pastor, Father Poelman, greeted him enthusiastically and gave him an antique crucifix as a remembrance of the Dutch liberation from the Germans.[89]

Urquhart's chief of staff, Colonel Charles Mackenzie and the chief engineer, Lieutenant-Colonel Eddie Myers, arrived at Sosabowski's headquarters. Together the three men hatched a plan to ferry the Poles across the river that night using a total of 4 dinghies, salvaged from downed planes, allowing 6 men to cross at a time, and some hastily constructed rudimentary rafts. On the night of 22–23 September only 52 Polish troops succeeded in crossing the Rhine to the British perimeter; the Germans fired on them, puncturing the dinghies and exacting a heavy toll on the Poles: 'Many were drowned in the fast-flowing waters, and some were swept down into the hands of the enemy.'[90] The Driel perimeter was now strengthened by the arrival of the small advance party of Horrocks's ground troops, the 43rd Wessex Division. The Poles then faced a Panzer attack and Sosabowski persuaded a reluctant British tank officer to go on the offensive. Sosabowski wrote:

> I pedalled towards the tank and, waving my arms, which made the cycle wobble dangerously, I indicated that they should follow me. The tank roared and off I went, pedalling like hell in front of the clattering monster to avoid being run over. My aide chugged along behind, the map-board swinging madly from his shoulders. Amazed paratroopers looked at us from their trenches: it must have been quite a sight.

The Germans backed down at the sight of the British tank. The 43rd Division was able to provide more boats, so on the night of 23–24 September 200 Poles made the hazardous journey to join the beleaguered British.[91]

On 24 September, there was a conference at the headquarters of the 43rd Division at Valburg between Horrocks, Browning, Thomas and Sosabowski, in which Horrocks laid out the plans for reinforcing the Oosterbeek bridgehead using the Wessex Division and the Poles in two crossings.[92] No information was given on the number or type of boats available. Sosabowski was unimpressed, especially as he had been ordered to release the 1st Battalion for this crossing, and he argued for a larger crossing at a different location. Horrocks was outraged at Sosabowski's impertinence and told him: 'And if you, General, do not want to carry out your orders, we will find another commander for the Polish Para Brigade who will carry out orders.' At a private meeting with Browning later, Sosabowski also learnt that apparently there were no boats at all – they were trapped far back in the road column. Sosabowski did not hold back on his opinions and wrote later: 'I fear that my forthrightness hurt Browning's feelings, for he quickly indicated the end of our conversation.'[93] That night Sosabowski was asked to relinquish the limited number of boats he had to aid the crossing by the Dorset Regiment, and then he watched in horror as the Germans massacred the British.[94]

By this time it was clear that Operation Market Garden was a total failure, and the troops who had made it to the north bank of the Rhine had to be withdrawn back to the south. The evacuation took place on the night of 25–26 September, but only 2,163 men from the 1st Airborne Division were rescued and 140 Poles. During the entire operation the Poles lost 49 dead, 159 wounded and 173 missing: these figures represented 23 per cent of the officers and 22 per cent of the other ranks.[95] Sosabowski now asked Browning to release the Polish brigade in accordance with prior agreements on the level of casualties the Poles could sustain before withdrawal from active operations. Browning refused, stating that he needed the Poles to defend the airstrips in the area of Neerloon and the bridges at Heumen and Nijmegen. The Polish brigade was reinforced between 27 and 29 September by the arrival of the part of the brigade, including its pack artillery, which had travelled to Holland by sea and land transport.[96] On 7 October, the Polish Parachute Brigade returned to Britain by ship from Ostend, and at Tilbury docks the customs officer asked the Poles if they had anything to declare. Sosabowski replied that they did: 'We have a large quantity of Eau de Cologne – or Rhine Water.'[97]

Sosabowski suspected that his poor relations with Browning might have an impact on how the Polish side of the failed operation was portrayed. He attempted to pre-empt criticism by despatching back to London the Polish war correspondent Marek Swiecicki, who broadcast his report on the Polish Parachute Brigade at Arnhem on the BBC. The broadcast was also transmitted to Poland and translated into other languages and went out on the BBC World Service. None of this helped Sosabowski. On 7 October, having heard complaints from Browning, Montgomery wrote to Alanbrooke suggesting that the Poles had fought badly and should be sent to Italy because he no longer wanted them under his command.[98] Sosabowski knew nothing of this and arranged for Browning to be awarded the Star of Order *Polonia Restituta*, a high Polish order, but Browning responded by saying that the award was 'unfortunate' and that the relationship between the two men 'has not been one of the happiest'. Browning also wrote to the deputy CIGS, Lieutenant-General Sir Ronald Weeks, in November suggesting that Sosabowski should be removed from his command because he was too difficult to work with and had acted with insufficient urgency during Market Garden. Sosabowski was deeply hurt and puzzled by the criticism, feeling that he and his men had done their best under the difficult circumstances of a flawed plan. Furthermore, because Browning was about to depart for a new post in South East Asia, he saw no reason why he should be dismissed.* The Polish Government sacked him: he was replaced by Lieutenant-Colonel Stanisław Jachnik and appointed inspector of disposal units. Two of his parachute units were so outraged that they went on hunger strike in protest, until Sosabowski visited and calmed them.[99]

Until Urquhart and Sosabowski published their memoirs, in 1958 and 1960 respectively, the blame for the ultimate failure of the Arnhem operation was placed on the Poles. Urquhart summarised his operations with the Poles: 'I could not fault them for cooperation. I never had any worries about that. Everything I asked was done, unless there was a very good reason.'[100] More recently a reassessment of the Arnhem operation has quite rightly questioned whether there was any point in sending the Poles there at all since by the time they landed the operation was well on its way to being a complete failure. The forward ground forces reached Driel at the same time as the Poles were being summoned across the river, but there was too little bridging equipment and too few boats to get more than a limited number of men across to the north bank. A recent historian of the campaign concluded:

> The scapegoating of Sosabowski and his men was a spiteful, unwarranted and unforgivable slur on a competent and conscientious commander whose

* The inept Browning was incredibly now appointed chief of staff to Mountbatten.

only crime was to refuse to play the Whitehall game to Browning's satisfaction, and upon a courageous body of men whose only failing was an
inability to walk on water.[101]

With the benefit of hindsight, it is possible to say that the Polish airborne participation in the Arnhem operation was futile since all it did
was damage the reputation of the Polish armed forces. The brave Poles
at Arnhem fought under impossible circumstances and their sacrifices
were in vain.

Poland continued to provide important intelligence to the western allies
in the last years of the war. Polish forced labourers in the Third Reich
were in an ideal position to report on the state of the German war economy. Indeed, the AK intelligence section even trained some men who
would then go to work in German factories as forced labour. The Poles
reported on seventeen ports in Germany and Poland, following a
detailed questionnaire provided by the British, on subjects ranging from
the types of ships at berth and their armaments, the names, tonnage,
cargo and route of merchant ships, to coastal defences and the location
of minefields. The Poles also supplied intelligence on the construction of
the new 'snorkel' U-boat. The Allies were also interested in the state of
the German war economy: output as well as the effect of the strategic
bombing campaign. The Poles provided vital intelligence, particularly
after the allied bombing of Germany forced the relocation of various
aircraft factories to Poland. Reports were generated by agents working
in the German factories in Mielec, Rzeszów, Poznań, Bydgoszcz and
Grudziądz, all of which produced German bombers and fighters.[102]

Undoubtedly the most vital contribution of the Poles towards allied
intelligence was on Hitler's secret weapons, the V-1 – the pilotless flying
bomb – and the V2 – the rocket. The Germans had begun the construction of a top-secret rocket research station at Peenemünde on the Baltic
island of Usedom in 1936. During the winter of 1942–3, the Baltic
cell of the AK, led by Bernard 'Wrzos', 'Jur' Kaczmarek and later by
Lieutenant Stefan 'Nordryk' Ignaszak, was able to penetrate the island
because the Germans were making heavy use of forced labour to extend
the facilities. The AK sent reports back to London on the new rockets
which the Poles passed to the British. The chief of the Polish intelligence
in London, Lieutenant-Colonel Michał Protasewicz, recalled:

The area of Peenemünde was of much interest to the British. What they asked for was the plan of the area (or camp). A bit of a tall order ... Amazingly, a few weeks later, the plan of the camp arrived, via Vienna or possibly Sweden ... with the buildings where the alleged research was conducted marked with pencilled dots. The plan was accompanied by a brief description of the camp. I do not remember whether it contained any mention of the trials.

Further reports followed and reconnaissance flights confirmed the presence of the V-1 and V-2 weapons. On the night of 17–18 August 1943, the British bombed Peenemünde with 597 planes, and Polish intelligence reported on the results: 735 people, including two of the most important subordinates of Wernher von Braun, Germany's leading rocket scientist, had been killed. The raid did not affect the actual production of the V-1, which was located in Germany, but the production of V-2 weapons was now moved to the underground Dora works in the Harz mountains near Nordhausen. The testing site for the V-2 rockets was moved out of allied bomber range to the Polish village of Blizna near Mielec, at the junction of the Vistula and San rivers. From the end of November 1943 onwards, the AK kept a register of every test launch, the time and direction of flight, and attempted to reach the landing site ahead of the Germans. Fragments were recovered, including a sample of fuel used (80 per cent hydrogen peroxide) and reports sent to London.

On 10 May 1944, the AK had a stroke of luck when one of the rockets landed in a marsh on the left bank of the Bug near the village of Mężenin. It did not explode and the local AK managed to hide the rocket in a barn 5 miles away and called upon experts from Warsaw, Antoni Kocjan and Stefan Waciórski, to come and dismantle it. They made a thorough report, which included 80 photographs, 12 diagrams and a sketch of the range at Blizna. Eight parts of the rocket were retained. Abridged reports were transmitted to London on 12 June and 3 July 1944. On 8 July, Bór-Komorowski was informed of the reaction in London, which had been under bombardment by V-1s since 12 June:

> Your projectiles may be an improved type of a flying bomb, currently used against London. We are very keen to reconstruct the weapon you have, and our friends are organising the pick-up of all the documents, data and parts, most importantly the radio and fuel samples, by a two-way flight. The friends consider this to be of the highest priority.[103]

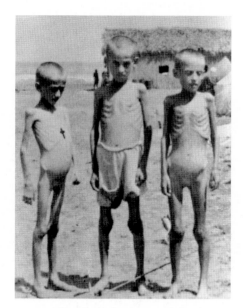

17. Starving Poles on arrival in Iran

18. Orphaned Polish boys on PE parade in Palestine, August 1942

19. The site of the Katyń massacre, a Nazi photograph from 1943

20. The Warsaw Ghetto uprising, April 1943

21. The Warsaw Ghetto uprising, May 1943

22. Tanks of the 1st Polish Armoured Division assembling for
Operation *Totalize*, Normandy, 8 August 1944

23. Troops of the 3rd Carpathian Rifles Division taking up ammunition supplies during the last battle of Monte Cassino

24. Scene at Majdanek after Soviet liberation, July 1944

25. General Berling and members of the Polish Committee of National Liberation, Lublin, July 1944

26. Troops of the *Armia Krajowa* with captured Germans, 20 August 1944

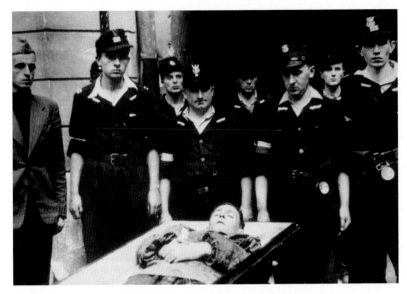

27. Funeral of an AK soldier, September 1944

28. General Tadeusz 'Bór' Komorowski after surrendering
to the Germans, 1 October 1944

29. Soldiers of the 1st Polish Armoured Division after liberating Breda, the Netherlands, 30 November 1944

30. Polish and Soviet women slave-workers in Germany after their liberation by the US 9th Army, Jülich, 31 December 1944

31. Polish male prisoners at Dachau after liberation, 1 May 1945

32. Thousands of Polish troops aboard SS *Banfora* at
Tilbury Docks being repatriated, December 1945

It was not easy to organise flights to Poland from Italy and the only plane capable of the long flight was a Dakota. On 25 July, the weather in Italy cleared and Operation Wildhorn III was launched. It had, however, been raining in Poland and when the Dakota landed on the airfield at Wał Ruda near Tarnów, it became stuck in the mud. The rocket parts were loaded on to the aircraft along with a lengthy report and accompanied by an AK intelligence officer, Captain Jerzy Chmielewski. The plane also collected two important passengers, Józef Retinger, who had been investigating conditions in Poland on behalf of the Polish Government, and Tomasz Arciszewski, the veteran socialist politician who would soon become the last prime minister of the wartime Polish Government-in-Exile. Haste was needed because earlier that day two German Storch planes had landed on the airstrip, and there was every chance that they might return.[104] The plane engines roared in the night and the aircraft lights lit up the area: 'A crowd of helpers scraped the mud away with spades and bare hands, while local farmers brought up cartloads of planks, ripped from the fences around their houses. These they forced under the wheels and then laid a track.'[105] The parts and the report, still accompanied by Chmielewski, arrived in London on 28 July.

Intelligence was not the only contribution the Poles made to the fight against the V-weapons. A Polish fighter wing, 133, was sent back to Britain to defend London against the V-1s. The Polish pilots learnt to fly close enough to the V-1 in flight and then nudge the wing, tipping it so that it fell to earth short of London. Polish fighter pilots accounted for 10 per cent of all V-1s destroyed.[106] The Polish 300 Squadron took part in the strategic bombing campaign of Germany, and 278 Polish aircrew were shot down and taken POW by the Germans. Some were sent to Stalag Luft III at Sagan (Żagań), the location of what was later called the Great Escape. This was a plan for 200 allied aircrew to escape through a tunnel: the Poles not only assisted in the construction of the tunnel but were particularly active in the tailoring department, making civilian clothing for the escapees. Only 78 men did escape on the night of 24–25 March 1944, including 6 Poles. Most were quickly recaptured, and on Hitler's orders 50 were killed including all the Poles – Squadron Leader Antoni Kiewnarski, Flight Lieutenant Włodzimierz Kolanowski, Flight Lieutenant Jerzy Mondszajn, Flight Lieutenant Stanisław 'Danny' Król, Flight Lieutenant Kazimierz Pawluk and Flight Lieutenant Paweł Tobolski.[107]

In February 1945, the Polish Air Force was informed about the Yalta agreements. The news came as a terrible shock, especially since 300 Squadron was about to take off to bomb Dresden to aid the Soviet advance. Pilot Officer Magierowski wrote to a friend:

> The sorties have been ordered, so we're going to fly – it's the proper thing to do, they say – although anger and despair are in our hearts. It's a funny feeling, but sometimes I wonder if all this has any sense. If the Germans get me now, I won't even know what I'm dying for. For Poland, for Britain, or for Russia?[108]

The men threatened to mutiny and the British officers removed the Poles' side arms, but the Polish Government ordered them to continue the fight to 'keep peace, dignity and solidarity, as well as to maintain brotherhood in arms with the soldiers of Great Britain, Canada, the United States, and France'.[109] They did not mention the Soviet Union in this list of allies. During the entire war, 1,903 Polish airmen were killed in action.[110]

# 16

# The End of the War

Polish fortunes were at a nadir at the end of 1944. The battle for the restoration of the pre-war eastern frontier had been lost, and Mikołajczyk was unable to convince his government to accept this and resigned as prime minister in November. His replacement, Tomasz Arciszewski, was largely ignored by the British and American governments, and the Polish Government-in-Exile was not recognised by the Soviets. Since the middle of 1944, Poland had been effectively split into three zones of occupation: east of the Bug river, the Curzon Line, the Soviets remained in control; west of the Bug river and in territory liberated from the German occupation, the communist-dominated Lublin Committee, sponsored by Stalin, held sway; all of western Poland and much of the central region were still under German occupation. The failure of Operation *Burza* and the Warsaw Uprising had left the Underground Government and the AK in a state of considerable disarray and with their reputations badly damaged. The battle was now for the restoration of Poland's independence, and the omens were not good.

The opening shot was fired by Stalin when, on 3 January 1945, he informed Churchill that on 31 December 1944 the Supreme Soviet had recognised the Lublin Committee as the Provisional Government of Poland. He justified this decision on the grounds:

> The decision to make it the Provisional Government seems to us quite timely, especially now that Mikołajczyk has withdrawn from the émigré Government and that the latter has thereby lost all semblance of a government. I think that Poland cannot be left without a government.[1]

Churchill immediately replied deprecating Stalin's action, and making it clear that neither the British nor the American governments would follow suit. He wanted the discussion of the make-up of the future Polish government left to the next meeting of the Big Three, scheduled to take place in Yalta in early February. The Polish Government also issued its own statement criticising Stalin's action.[2]

On the eve of the Yalta conference, both the British and American governments considered how to approach the question of the future governance and with it the independence of Poland. Neither believed that the new Provisional Government nor the Arciszewski government was representative of the Polish people. In an important memorandum of 8 January, Sir Orme Sargent argued against trying to reform the Polish Government in London and urged that attention should now be focused on broadening the support base of the Provisional Government by persuading Mikołajczyk and some of his colleagues to join it. Eden's opinion was that 'there are no good candidates from the Government in London', but that Mikołajczyk and perhaps others like Romer and Grabski could be persuaded to join the Provisional Government to make it 'far more representative' of Poland. Although the Arciszewski government was still officially recognised by the British Government, it was held at arm's length and not approached for its views. Instead, the British preferred to deal with Mikołajczyk, who was seen as being more of a realist. In a series of meetings at the Foreign Office, he was questioned on his willingness to return to Poland and collaborate in 'a government which would include, and no doubt, be based largely on, the Lublin party as well as Poles from liberated Poland'. Mikołajczyk tentatively agreed but put forward his own ideas: efforts should be made to secure equal representation for each of the five major political parties in Poland, and that, in the interim period before elections could be held, Poland should be run by a presidential council, to be formed 'of the most widely known leaders and representatives of political life, the churches and science'.[3]

The Arciszewski government reacted sharply to the rumours of Mikołajczyk's negotiations with the Foreign Office and saw the dangers implicit in the forthcoming meeting at Yalta. On 22 January, it sent a memorandum to Roosevelt and Churchill demanding that all discussion of Poland's frontiers should be postponed until the peace conference and that, in the interim and until elections could be held, an inter-allied commission should be formed to administer the country.[4] Cadogan told the Polish ambassador, Raczyński, that this was 'not very realistic', to which 'he, with a wry smile, agreed'. Cadogan then saw the Polish foreign minister, Adam Tarnowski, and said much the same thing. Tarnowski was, however, very defensive, and, in the privacy of his diary, Cadogan voiced his indignation, especially regarding the Polish Government's claim 'that it was up to us to save Poland'.[5]

Churchill, Roosevelt and Stalin all approached the Yalta conference with different aims. Churchill was in a position of considerable weakness since Britain was financially bankrupt, her fighting efforts dwarfed by the manpower of the United States and the Soviet Union, and her imperial prestige gravely damaged by her early defeats in the war. The advance of the Soviets into the Balkans in the latter half of 1944 and the ensuing Soviet political dominance of the region greatly alarmed Churchill, who felt honour-bound to obtain a satisfactory settlement for Poland. The Foreign Office briefing paper for Yalta stipulated that Churchill and Eden should work towards a completely new Polish government, based on neither the existing Polish Government in London nor the Provisional Government.[6]

Roosevelt had lost interest in European affairs, and either did not realise or did not care about the danger of Soviet domination in Europe. He was concerned with two issues: to obtain a promise from the Soviet Union to enter the war against Japan as soon as the war in Europe had ended; and to win Soviet support for and participation in the United Nations Organisation. With regards to Poland, the State Department briefing paper suggested that the Provisional Government should not be recognised 'until more conclusive evidence is received that it does in fact represent the basic wishes of the Polish people'. Roosevelt personally liked Mikołajczyk's idea of a presidential council, but was willing to settle for an enlargement of the Provisional Government by the incorporation of 'democratic' Poles from inside and outside Poland.[7] Stalin's position was the simplest: he wanted the western allies to agree to what can only be termed a 'Russian peace', achieved by the force of Soviet arms, which would give him domination over eastern Europe.

Several factors affected the relative negotiating powers of the Big Three at Yalta. The armed forces of the western allies were still engaged in undoing the damage wrought by Hitler's desperate thrust through the Ardennes in mid-December 1944 – better known as the Battle of the Bulge – and the Soviet January offensive in Poland had been brought forward to relieve the pressure on the western allies. Indeed, Churchill opened proceedings at Yalta by acknowledging the western allies' debt to the Soviet forces. The British and American negotiating positions were weakened because each did not know what the other hoped to achieve or what tactics it would be employing. The blame for this lies firmly with Roosevelt, who, as with the run-up to the Teheran conference, had taken deliberate steps to avoid holding meetings with Churchill prior to Yalta lest Stalin feel that they were ganging up on him. This ignorance would prove to be damaging because Stalin in fact 'knew what questions the British considered important, what they were planning to raise themselves, and what would be raised by the Americans. The Soviets were also aware of points of agreement and discord between the western allies and of their intended line of approach to Stalin on all these issues.' Stalin's British spies, Guy Burgess in London and Donald Maclean in Washington, had provided him with this priceless information.[8]

The Yalta conference opened on 4 February and, although the future of Poland was only one of the many issues to be discussed, it dominated the proceedings. The two points to be settled were the future frontiers of Poland and its future government. The agreement made at Teheran that the Curzon Line should be Poland's eastern frontier was confirmed without challenge at Yalta, but there was considerable discussion over the extent of the geographical compensation Poland should receive to the north and west. No challenge was made to Poland's absorption of East Prussia, with the exception of Königsberg, which Stalin claimed for the Soviet Union. The discussion centred on Silesia. Upper Silesia had been claimed by both Germany and Poland after the First World War and had been split between them. There was general agreement that the Polish frontier should certainly advance as far as the river Oder, but considerable disagreement over who should control the territory lying south of where the Oder turned eastwards. There were two tributaries running southwards from the Oder: the Eastern Neisse and the Western Neisse. Stalin stated that he had promised the Lublin Committee the Western Neisse and thereby the whole of Lower Silesia, centred on the city of Breslau (Wrocław). Churchill was alarmed, remarking that 'it would be a pity to stuff the Polish goose so full of German food that it got indigestion', since he knew that Lower Silesia had a predominantly German population. Stalin dismissed the concerns of the two western leaders that millions more Germans than anticipated would have to be relocated from the territory to be given to Poland by assuring them that the Germans had already run away.[9] Poland's western frontier was not settled at Yalta and required lengthy discussion at the post-war Potsdam conference.

At the third plenary session on 6 February, Churchill raised the question of the composition of the future government of Poland. He insisted on a new provisional government representative of all shades of Polish political opinion and wanted guarantees of free elections in Poland. Stalin launched into a lengthy tirade arguing that the Lublin Committee was truly representative of the Polish people, the agents and supporters of what he now termed the 'émigré' government in Poland were little more than terrorists, and if the Provisional Government wished to invite Polish politicians from outside Poland to join it, it was free to make that decision.[10] That evening Roosevelt intervened by writing to Stalin with the ingenious suggestion that the leaders of various Polish political parties should be brought to Yalta and made to agree on a new government.[11] This took Stalin by surprise and he initially prevaricated. At the fourth plenary session, Stalin informed the western leaders that neither Bierut nor Osóbka-Morawski could be contacted since they were not in Warsaw, and no one knew where the two men Roosevelt wanted brought to Yalta, Wincenty Witos, leader of the Peasant Party in Poland, and Archbishop Sapieha, were. Stalin also argued there was no time to bring these men there. Molotov then made a proposal to break the deadlock: a commission of himself, Clark Kerr and Harriman should be formed in Moscow to confer with Polish political leaders in the hope of augmenting the existing Provisional Government with the inclusion of other Polish politicians until elections were held.[12] The fifth plenary session made no progress, and that evening Eden recorded in his diary: 'Stuck again over Poland'.[13]

At the sixth plenary session on 9 February, Roosevelt introduced a new proposal which had been discussed by the foreign ministers earlier that day. This called for 'the present Polish Provisional Government [to] be reorganised into a fully representative government based on all democratic forces in Poland and including democratic leaders from Poland abroad, to be termed "The Provisional Government of National Unity"'. Its composition would be settled by Molotov, Clark Kerr and Harriman. Molotov requested that 'non-fascist and anti-fascist' be added in reference to the democratic parties. This spelled great danger to Churchill since he already had ample evidence from Poland of the Soviet and Polish communist habit of labelling all their opponents 'fascist', but Roosevelt appeared oblivious to this danger. He was, however, determined to ensure that the elections in Poland should be 'free and unfettered', as was Churchill. Indeed, Eden had already informed the meeting of the foreign ministers that he thought it essential that the western ambassadors should act as observers for the elections, but this proved a sticking-point. Stalin was clearly insulted that the western allies should suspect that his puppets would not hold free elections.[14]

The accords signed at Yalta by the Big Three reflected their satisfaction at the end of the conference. In many ways it is true to say that 'Yalta was basically a summary of every discussion that had taken place between the Big Three up to 1944. There was little new, little that had not already been conceded to the Soviet Union by force of arms.'[15] Agreement had been reached on how to bring about the final defeat of Germany, the subsequent occupation and control of Germany, German reparations, the United Nations, Yugoslavia, the intention to try major war criminals, the repatriation of each other's national POWs after their liberation, and the entry of the Soviet Union into the war with Japan within three months of the conclusion of the war in Europe. A Declaration on Liberated Europe was issued, and among its points were two with a bearing on Poland:

> To foster the conditions in which the liberated people may exercise their rights [sovereign rights and self-government], the three governments will jointly assist the people ... to form interim governmental authorities broadly representative of all democratic elements in the population and pledged to the earliest possible establishment through free elections of governments responsive to the will of the people; and ... to facilitate where necessary the holding of such elections.[16]

The declaration showed signs of being written in haste, with no definitions given to 'democratic', nor to 'broadly representative', terms which Stalin was highly likely to interpret in a different light from Churchill and Roosevelt.

There were also signs of haste in the drafting of the accord on Poland, which would have serious consequences for the negotiations of the commission soon to start proceedings in Moscow:

A new situation has been created in Poland as a result of her complete liberation by the Red Army. This calls for the establishment of a Polish Provisional Government which can be more broadly based than was possible before the recent liberation of Western Poland. The Provisional Government which is now functioning in Poland should be reorganized on a broader democratic basis with the inclusion of democratic leaders from Poland itself and from Poles abroad. This new government should then be called the Polish Provisional Government of National Unity.

Mr Molotov, Mr Harriman and Sir Archibald Clark Kerr are authorized to consult in the first instance in Moscow with members of the present Provisional Government and with other Polish democratic leaders from within Poland and from abroad with a view to the reorganization of the present government along the above lines. This Polish Provisional Government of National Unity shall be pledged to the holding of free and unfettered elections as soon as possible on the basis of universal suffrage and secret ballot. In these elections all democratic and anti-Nazi Parties shall have the right to take part and put forward candidates.

After the formation of the Provisional Government of National Unity, the governments of the three Great Powers would recognise it and exchange ambassadors with Poland. On the subject of frontiers, the Curzon Line was confirmed but, as to the western frontier, the resolution was restricted to the generality that Poland would receive substantial territories to the north and west: but that the final delineation of the western frontier would be left until the peace conference.[17] Charles Bohlen, a member of the American delegation, later highlighted a fundamental weakness: no stipulation was made regarding the ratio of communist to democratic politicians from inside and outside Poland.[18] The gravest weakness was in the phrase 'to consult in the first instance in Moscow'. As will be seen, Molotov interpreted this phrase in a very different way from Clark Kerr and Harriman.

The importance of the Yalta conference lies far less in what was agreed there and far more in the fact that, unlike those of the Teheran conference, the Yalta agreements were made public, on 13 February. At last the world learnt what its armed forces had been fighting for. It was only to be expected that the Poles in the west would be hostile. On 17 February, Anders met Alexander at Caserta in Italy and asked him: 'By a conference at which Poland was not represented, not invited to state her views, the Government is displaced, the Constitution annulled and hence all treaties abrogated, what therefore is the position of the loyal Poles?'[19] A few days later a deeply distressed Anders was in London and had a meeting with Churchill during which Anders threatened to take the II Corps out of the line, and Churchill challenged him to do so.[20] Indeed, Churchill was so furious with Anders and offended by his appointment as acting commander-in-chief that the two men only ever had that one meeting, a stormy one, Churchill cancelling a second.[21] Only an announcement by the Polish Government persuaded Anders and the other Polish commanders to keep the Polish troops in the war against Germany.[22] The Polish Government made a series of protests, arguing that the Yalta agreements were 'a fifth partition of Poland, now accomplished by her Allies'.[23] A more measured response was sent to London by the Underground Government, now operating in hiding near Warsaw:

> The Council of National Unity expresses the conviction that the decisions of the Crimean Conference taken without the participation or consent of the Polish State ... impose new, arduous and unjust sacrifices on Poland. The Council of National Unity, whilst strongly protesting against the unilateral decisions of the Conference, is nevertheless, obliged to adapt itself to them, seeing in them a chance of saving the independence of Poland, to prevent the further destruction of the Polish nation and to lay the foundation for the organisation of her own forces which would enable Poland to carry out an independent policy in the future ...
>
> By adopting this line of policy – a painful one for the Polish nation – the Council of National Unity wishes to show its willingness to come to an agreement with its eastern neighbour and establish with it durable, friendly and peaceful relations ...

The council expected that the Allies would ensure that the Provisional Government of National Unity would be truly representative of all parties, and its pragmatic reaction also signalled a split from the intransigence of the Arciszewski government and reflected what it knew of the prevailing realities in Poland.[24]

On 27 February, the debate on Yalta began in the House of Commons. Churchill covered all the main points of the agreements reached, but the issue of Poland held centre stage. Churchill began by confirming and approving of the Curzon Line, and repeated the assertion, first made public in the Commons in December 1944, that Poland would gain East Prussia and an undefined amount of territory in the west as compensation. He then turned to the vexed matter of its future government, and, after explaining that the composition of a new provisional government would be decided in Moscow by a commission of the two western ambassadors and Molotov, Churchill placed the blame for the delay in the formation of a new government squarely on the shoulders of the Polish Government in London:

> Let me remind them that there would have been no Lublin Committee or Lublin Provisional Government in Poland if the Polish Government in London had accepted our faithful counsel given to them a year ago. They would have entered into Poland as its active Government, with the liberating Armies of Russia. Even in October, when the Foreign Secretary and I toiled night and day in Moscow, M. Mikolajczyk could have gone from Moscow to Lublin, with every assurance of Marshal Stalin's friendship, and become the Prime Minister of a more broadly constructed Government, which would now be seated at Warsaw, or wherever, in view of the ruin of Warsaw, the centre of government is placed.

He went on: 'The impression I brought back from the Crimea, and from all my other contacts, is that Marshal Stalin and the Soviet leaders wish to live in honourable friendship and equality with the Western democracies. I feel also that their word is their bond.' Yet almost immediately he added that he recognised that the Polish forces fighting under British command were deeply unhappy about the Yalta agreements and so made the extraordinary offer: 'I earnestly hope it may be possible to offer the citizenship and freedom of the British Empire' to those members of the Polish forces who did not wish to return to Poland. It seemed then that Anders's impassioned reaction to the news of the Yalta agreements had made some impact on Churchill.[25]

Churchill's speech was subject to frequent interruptions, reflecting the growing disquiet among the Members of Parliament. Harold Nicolson reflected the mood of the House with his summary of Churchill's performance:

> He makes an extremely good case for arguing that Poland in her new frontiers will enjoy an independent and prosperous existence. But in his

closing words before luncheon he rather destroys all this by saying that we will offer British citizenship to those Polish soldiers who are too frightened to return.[26]

Jock Colville, Churchill's private secretary, noted in his diary that the under secretary at the Foreign Office, Orme Sargent, 'tells me that the Polish Government's propaganda against the Crimea Agreement has been both extensive and effective'.[27] On the second day of the debate, the effectiveness of their campaign was shown by the proposal of an amendment by the Conservative MP Maurice Petherick that the House

> regrets the decision to transfer to another power the territory of an ally contrary to treaty and to Article 2 of the Atlantic Charter and furthermore regrets the failure to ensure to those nations which have been liberated from German oppression the full right to choose their own government free from the influence of any other power.[28]

The supporters, mainly Conservative MPs, objected to the imposition of the Curzon Line by 'an act of force', and voiced deep concern that elections in Poland would not be free. A junior minister, H. G. Strauss, resigned his office. The amendment was defeated by 396 votes to 25.[29] Across the Atlantic, Roosevelt addressed Congress on the Yalta agreements on 1 March. His speech was very well received, and Roosevelt suffered no criticism of the Polish clauses. A Gallup poll showed that the majority of those Americans surveyed thought that the Yalta agreements were the best possible solution to the Polish question, but a larger majority also believed that they were not 'fair' to the Poles.[30]

Ultimately the success of the Yalta conference would rest on whether or not Churchill and Roosevelt had been correct in assuming that the Soviets could be trusted not to impose communist-dominated governments on the countries of eastern Europe. The omens were not good from the outset. The Soviets rapidly made a mockery of the Declaration on Liberated Europe in six countries: in Austria the Soviets allowed Dr Karl Renner to form a provisional government without agreement with the other occupying powers; in Bulgaria the Soviets backed the communists' plans for elections to be held on a single electoral list, which would give them a disproportionate number of seats; in Hungary the Soviets pushed for immediate land reform; in Rumania Soviet pressure forced King Mihai to dismiss the Rădescu government and install the

Soviet stooge Petru Groza; in Yugoslavia an agreement was made between Josip Tito and Ivan Šubašić without reference to the western powers; and in Czechoslovakia Beneš faced communist demands out of all proportion to their electoral strength. On 8 March, Churchill confessed to Roosevelt that, although he wanted to publicise his displeasure at these events, he was unwilling to do so lest Stalin turn round and remind him that he, Stalin, had stood aside while the British had crushed the pro-communist rising in Greece at the end of 1944.[31]

The tripartite commission of Clark Kerr, Harriman and Molotov began work in Moscow on 23 February. Harriman's first report to Stettinius was optimistic: Molotov appeared to have agreed that the Provisional Government would be invited to send representatives to Moscow, and that invitations would be issued to five other Poles from Poland. This, however, turned out to be an erroneous impression. The British and American position was:

> the Commission should at once invite representatives of 'Lublin' and an unspecified number of representative Poles from inside and outside Poland to Moscow to discuss among themselves under the Commission's auspices how representative government can be formed, allocation of key posts and how presidential functions should be performed pending elections.[32]

But Molotov was adamant that the agreement at Yalta stipulated that the Provisional Government should be called to Moscow first and be given the right of veto over the list of names from outside its ranks who might be invited to join the government. The dispute rested on the different interpretations of the words 'to consult in the first instance in Moscow'. Dean Acheson, the acting secretary of state, advised Harriman that Bohlen, who had drafted that section of the agreement, had been consulted:

> In the English text the words 'In the first instance' come before the words 'in Moscow' and could therefore only relate to the fact that consultations of the Commission were to begin in Moscow but could later be transferred elsewhere. The consultations were however clearly stated to be with three specified categories of Poles, one of which was 'Members of present Provisional Government'. There is nothing in [the] English text to suggest that they should take place with the present Provisional Government before 'other Polish Democratic leaders from within Poland and abroad'.[33]

Molotov's response to the receipt of this information was that the phrase meant 'that the Commission should consult in the first instance with the Polish Provisional Government'.[34] Bohlen later wrote that he did not think that the Soviets had agreed to the words 'in the first instance' at Yalta with the intention to misinterpret them later, but that they then 'saw in this phrase a loophole allowing them to promote their own cause'.[35] The determination of the Provisional Government to assume the dominant position in the new Provisional Government of National Unity is amply demonstrated by its reaction to the names of eight Poles the British and Americans wished to invite to Moscow. Of the eight names from outside the Provisional Government – the list included Mikołajczyk, Romer and Grabski from London – the communists rejected Mikołajczyk and Romer – and from those Poles inside Poland accepted only Professor Stanisław Kutzreba, a historian from Kraków.[36] Molotov also refused to allow allied observers into Poland, arguing that their despatch would 'sting the national pride of the Poles to the quick'.[37]

The Moscow Commission was making no progress. The Soviet position was the simplest: as Stalin had told Zhukov after Yalta, 'Churchill wants the Soviet Union to share a border with a bourgeois Poland, alien to us, but we cannot allow this to happen.'[38] Churchill was alarmed by the stalemate in Moscow. He had been badly bruised by the criticism in the House of Commons, and, for him, the creation of a broad-based new Provisional Government of National Unity was essential for the British Government to be able to convince Parliament and the public that Britain had discharged its debt of honour and loyalty to its longest-serving wartime ally. Furthermore, as Clark Kerr stated in a letter to Eden: 'for us the Polish question is, and must remain, one of the utmost consequence, for upon its satisfactory solution rests a great part of our hope and belief in the possibility of a real and cordial understanding between the Soviet people and our own'.[39]

Roosevelt was also worried about the lack of progress in Moscow but had a different concern: the future of the United Nations. He was only interested in the negotiations on the new Polish provisional government insofar as they impacted on it. The League of Nations had been established after the First World War as a body designed to prevent quarrels between nations escalating into armed conflict. It was weak from the start because Russia, then in the throes of a civil war, was not invited to join, and the United States' membership was not ratified by the Senate. Roosevelt's ambition to create a more powerful organisation than the League had forced him to face similar challenges to those that had confronted Woodrow Wilson. In order to convince the Senate that the United Nations would be a body capable of preserving peace in the world, Roosevelt needed to ensure the participation of all allied and neutral countries, and the Soviet Union was the most important. To gain its support Roosevelt and Churchill had agreed at Yalta to allow the Soviet Union three votes in the assembly while all other countries would have one apiece. Poland, a signatory to the document launching the United Nations, introduced an unwelcome complicating factor into the negotiations leading up to the opening of the founding conference of the United Nations in San Francisco on 25 April. Molotov threatened to boycott the proceedings if the Soviet Union did not get its own way in the Moscow Commission, which caused Eden to question whether there was even any point in the conference: 'How can we lay the foundations of any new World Order when Anglo-American relations with Russia are so completely lacking in confidence?'[40]

Churchill took the lead in communicating to Roosevelt his alarm at the stalemate in the Moscow Commission and repeatedly urged Roosevelt to join him in making a joint approach to Stalin. On 8 March, he wrote to Roosevelt voicing his fears: 'if we do not get things right now, it will soon be seen by the world that you and I by putting our signatures to the Crimea settlement have underwritten a fraudulent prospectus'.[41] A week later he asked Roosevelt: 'Poland has lost her frontier. Is she now to lose her freedom?' and warned: 'the moment that Molotov sees that he has beaten us away from the whole process of consultations among Poles to form a new government, he will know that we will put up with anything'. Roosevelt agreed that something needed to be done to break the deadlock in Moscow but disagreed about the tactics.[42] After Molotov's rejection of the Anglo-American interpretation of the Yalta agreements, Churchill sent another barrage of communications to Roosevelt urging action. On 27 March, he asked Roosevelt whether he felt that Molotov's threat not to attend the San Francisco conference could be interpreted either as a Soviet withdrawal from the entire concept of the United Nations or as an attempt at blackmail. He concluded: 'if the success of San Francisco is not to be gravely imperilled, we must both of us make the strongest possible appeal to Stalin about Poland'.[43]

This threat to his beloved United Nations spurred Roosevelt into action. On 31 March, both he and Churchill wrote to Stalin independently, demanding that the commission be free to invite a representative set of Poles. Stalin's response to them both, on 7 April, indicated that no progress had been made: he still demanded that the new Polish government be built around the Provisional Government and that its representatives would be consulted on which other Poles should be invited to Moscow. He also stipulated: 'only those leaders should be summoned for consultation from Poland and from London who recognise the decisions of the Crimea Conference on Poland and who in practice want friendly relations between Poland and the Soviet Union'.[44]

Mikołajczyk had been approached by representatives of the Provisional Government who urged him to come to an agreement with them independently of the commission in Moscow. Mikołajczyk, however, rejected this attempt to separate him from the western powers and stated firmly that he would only meet the members of the Provisional Government when invited to do so by the Moscow Commission.[45] He was prepared to do all he could to move the Moscow proceedings forward and therefore, when he was asked to make a public statement signalling his acceptance of the Yalta agreements, he did so and the statement was published in *The Times* on 15 April.[46] This should have opened the way for Mikołajczyk to take part in the negotiations in Moscow, but Stalin was not satisfied, and stalled by insisting on a statement from Mikołajczyk explicitly accepting the Curzon Line.

Roosevelt died on 12 April and there was a brief hiatus before the new president, Harry Truman, took up the sword in the battle for Poland. In a joint letter to Stalin, Churchill and Truman attempted to make some progress by suggesting:

(1) That we instruct our representatives on the Commission to extend invitations immediately to the following Polish leaders to come to Moscow for consultation: Bierut, Osóbka-Morawski, Rola-Żymierski, Bishop Sapieha, one representative Polish political party leader not connected with the present Warsaw Government (if any of the following were agreeable to you he would be agreeable to us – Witos, Zuławski, Chachiński, Jasiukowicz), and from London: Mikołajczyk, Grabski and Stańczyk.

(2) That once invitations to come for consultation have been issued by the Commission, the representatives of the Warsaw Provisional Government would arrive first if desired.

(3) That it be agreed that these Polish leaders called for consultation could suggest to the Commission the names of a certain number of other Polish leaders from within Poland or abroad who might be brought in for consultation in order that all the major Polish groups be represented in the discussions.

(4) We do not feel that we could commit ourselves to any formula for determining the composition of the new Government of National Unity in advance of consultation with the Polish leaders . . .

Stalin was having none of it. His reply to this letter and to subsequent communications during April indicated that he would not change his mind on anything concerning the government of Poland. The only apparent good news was that Molotov would be attending the San Francisco conference after all.[47]

The negotiations in Moscow remained deadlocked and were now moved to the San Francisco conference, where the three foreign ministers were present. But before this conference opened, one outstanding issue had to be resolved: which Polish government would represent the Poles? The Soviet embassy in Washington sent several memoranda to the State Department demanding that an invitation should be issued to the Provisional Government, while the Polish Government in London sent appeals to the governments of Britain, the United States and China demanding an invitation on the grounds that it had signed the original charter launching the United Nations on 1 January 1942.[48] Questions were asked in Parliament in support of the right of the Polish Government in London to send representatives to San Francisco, but Eden could only reply that invitations were issued by the four Great Powers and that, since the Soviet Union did not recognise the Polish Government in London, and Britain, the United States and China did not recognise the Provisional Government: 'Poland can only be invited to the Conference if a Polish Provisional Government of National Unity, which will be recognised by all four Powers, can be formed in Poland in accordance with the recommendation of the Crimea Conference.'[49]

On 25 April, the San Francisco conference on the United Nations opened without the participation of Poland. The Polish ambassador to the United States, Jan Ciechanowski wrote:

> The empty chair of Poland at the San Francisco conference weighed heavily on that assembly. There was something uncanny in the fact that, at the end of a victorious world war ... Poland, an Allied nation ... was prevented from taking her part in a gathering of nations allegedly held to apply the terms of justice and democracy to a future system of world security.[50]

Goebbels was unimpressed by the conference, terming it the 'San Fiasco' conference.[51] The unofficial delegation led by Stanisław Kot sent to San Francisco by the Polish Government in London received mixed messages from the delegates: there was an apparent reluctance even to be seen talking to the Poles lest they be accused of anti-Soviet sentiments, while Kot gained the impression: 'The idea of war with Russia is said to be growing in influential US circles, particularly Army and Navy whose influence is strongly growing.'[52] A few days after the conference opened there was a concert by the great pianist Arthur Rubinstein at the San Francisco Opera House. After playing the United States national anthem, he stood up and announced to the audience that although the flag of his native country, Poland, was not displayed, he would like to play its national anthem, *Jeszcze Polska nie zginęła* ('Poland is not yet lost'). This was followed by long and loud applause.[53] On 26 June, the United Nations Charter was signed by 153 delegates, with a space left for the signature of Poland.

At San Francisco the three foreign ministers, Eden, Stettinius and Molotov, held numerous meetings to discuss Poland,[54] but made no progress. On 21 April, the Soviet Union had demonstrated its firm commitment to the Provisional Government by concluding a treaty of friendship, mutual assistance and post-war cooperation with it. The Polish Government in London issued an immediate protest: 'From the point of view of international law none of the treaties concluded by the Lublin Administration is valid, considering that this body is not the government of the Polish Republic and does not represent the will of the Polish nation.'[55] Stettinius and Eden were equally appalled by the treaty. The Soviet Union also effectively made the talks pointless with the arrest of sixteen underground leaders in Poland by the NKVD. Among them were Józef Chachiński and Stanisław Jasiukowicz, whom Harriman and Clark Kerr had wanted to invite to consultations in Moscow. No one knew of the whereabouts and fate of the arrested men until, on 3 May, Molotov revealed that the men had indeed been arrested by the NKVD, transported to Moscow and would shortly be put on trial. The Polish Government in London immediately issued an appeal to Stettinius, as chairman of the San Francisco conference, asking him to intervene to secure their release.[56] The arrests made it quite clear to the British and American governments that the Soviet Union had no intention of allowing the Polish people to choose their own government. The joy felt in San Francisco at the announcement of the end of the war in Europe on 8 May was tempered by fear for the Poles.

The London Poles had been sidelined, above all, by the brutal military facts of the eastern front at the beginning of 1945. The Soviet plan for the liberation of Poland, the clearance of East Prussia and the drive to the Oder was daring and dramatic in its execution. Witold Sągajłło was awakened in the early hours of the morning of 11 January:

> The whole house was shaking. I got up and went to the window. From it I could see well beyond Ostrowiec across the Plain of Sandomierz. From the foot of the Holy Cross Mountains to my right and stretching to the east, there was across the whole horizon a continuous band of fire – thousands of Russian guns delivering a heavy barrage. The Russian breakout from the Baranów bridgehead had started.[57]

The 1st Ukrainian Front under Marshal Ivan Koniev launched its attack from the Sandomierz bridgehead west of the Vistula and, by the night of the 15th, had advanced 60 miles on a broad front. Polish cities fell one after the other: on 16 January Radom, Częstochowa and Kielce were liberated, and a Polish girl recalled the advent of Soviet troops in Kielce:

> Then a door opened with a great noise and the soldiers barraged [sic] in, strange, I thought, they were wearing extremely worn out uniforms, they were unshaven with a rifle hanging on a string, they were shouting and kept running everywhere, knocking anything on the way, there were lots of them.[58]

The soldiers then searched the house, looking not for German soldiers but for watches and vodka. She was lucky that these Soviet soldiers were only interested in loot, because the fate of other Polish women was far worse. The escaped British POW John Ward heard that 'within a few days the Russians had raped every female in the district over fourteen years of age'.[59] It is commonly assumed that the Soviet soldiers only raped German women but in fact the rapes began as soon as the Soviet frontier had been crossed. The subject is, naturally, an extremely sensitive one.

The 1st Ukrainian Front then advanced on Kraków, from which Hans Frank and the German administration had fled on 17 January, and the city fell to the Soviets two days later. On 27 January, the Soviets advanced into Upper Silesia and liberated Auschwitz. There they found 7,600 survivors: 1,000 at Auschwitz I; 6,000 at the extermination camp, Auschwitz-Birkenau; and 600 at Auschwitz III, the Buna works.[60] The Germans had begun the reduction of the camp population during the last half of 1944, despatching around 65,000 westwards to the concentration camps at Buchenwald, Dachau and Ravensbrück. On 17 January 1945, most of the remaining 56,000 prisoners, mostly Jews from all over Europe, were marched westwards out of the camp, and many died on the road, too weak from starvation or too poorly clad to withstand the harsh winter conditions. The SS attempted to hide the evidence of the exterminations by blowing up the crematoria and gas chambers but much remained to reveal to the world the extent of the crimes of the SS.[61]

The Soviet armies continued to drive towards the Oder, which Koniev's troops reached in early February and created bridgeheads across the river to the north and south of Breslau. Adjacent to the 1st Ukrainian Front, the armies of the 1st Belorussian Front, commanded by Marshal Zhukov, operated on the Poznań–Łódź axis and went on to the Oder. Further to the north, the 2nd Belorussian Front, commanded by Rokossovsky, attacked north-west from Warsaw towards the Baltic, aiming to cut off the German forces in East Prussia which were under attack from the 3rd Belorussian Front, commanded by Ivan Chernyakhovsky. The 1st Polish Army, operating under Rokossovsky, was given the honour of liberating Warsaw, which it achieved on 17 January, four days after the offensive had opened. The Germans had withdrawn most of their troops before the Poles attacked. Warsaw was a deserted and destroyed city where only a few intrepid survivors such as Władysław Szpilman had eked out a tenuous existence between the evacuation of the city at the beginning of October and its liberation three months later. It was during this period that Szpilman met Captain Wilm Hosenfeld, who supplied him with food in return for Szpilman playing the piano for him.[62]

The Germans put up a strong defence at certain points, and one strongpoint was the ancient fortress of Poznań, which was left to Chuikov's 8th Guards Army while the forces of Zhukov and Rokossovsky were directed northwards to relieve pressure on the 3rd Belorussian Front, which was facing a fierce and lengthy battle for Königsberg in East Prussia. The battle for Poznań took nine days, and Chuikov described the battle for the fortress to the Soviet war correspondent Vasily Grossman: 'Our men were walking around on top of it, and Germans were shooting up at them [from inside]. Then sappers poured in one and a half barrels of kerosene, set it on fire, and the Germans sprang out like rats.' Finally, after a total of 28,000 of the 40,000 German defenders had been killed, its commander, Major-General Ernst Gomell, shot himself and the fortress surrendered.[63]

The 1st Polish Army was tasked with guarding Zhukov's flank by mounting a direct assault on the Pomeranian Wall. This complex defensive position had been constructed by the Germans using the advantages presented by the 'post-glacial landscape, with rolling hills cut across with sequences of deep lakes and densely wooded areas'. The rapidity of the Soviet advance had led to complacency and to a strong belief that the Germans were finished as a fighting force, but the Poles were to discover that this was not true. The Polish offensive in western Pomerania opened at the end of January in appalling weather conditions, and a lack of reconnaissance meant that the advance of German units, including the SS division *Lettland*, had gone unnoticed. Command mistakes made the situation worse: on 31 January, the 1st Polish Infantry Division was ordered to cross the Gwda river near Grudna and advance in the direction of Jastrow (Jastrowie), but its commander, Colonel Aleksander Archipowicz, became disorientated and advanced instead towards Flederborn (Podgaje), which lay outside the operational area. The German resistance was so strong that the Poles only breached the Pomeranian Wall on 5 February.[64]

The 2nd Belorussian Front aimed at the East Pomeranian coast between Kolberg (Kołobrzeg) and Köslin (Koszalin). The Poles were given a leading role in the assault on Kolberg. This Prussian port was famous for having resisted five sieges, including one by the French in 1807, and for that reason had been the subject of Goebbels's last, lavish propaganda film. In 1945, however, it was defended by a motley group of Wehrmacht units, two Volkssturm battalions and assorted personnel of the Luftwaffe and Kriegsmarine. The port was home to 68,000 civilian refugees fleeing the Soviet advance through East Prussia and awaiting evacuation to the Reich.* Kolberg was a natural defensive position, surrounded by the sea or by marshes, which limited the use of tanks and heavy artillery. The battle opened at the beginning of March and again the Poles suffered from the excessive optimism of their commanders. The ferocity of the German defence forced the Polish commander, General Stanisław Popławski, to feed more and more troops into the battle. The Germans held out until all the civilians and wounded had been evacuated before withdrawing on the night of 17 March, which went unnoticed by the Poles. The battle cost the Poles 4,004 casualties, of which 1,266 were dead. In contrast the German casualties were only 2,300 men.[65]

The 2nd Belorussian Front then attacked eastwards towards Gdynia and Danzig and reached the Baltic at Sopot, thereby splitting the German defences and leaving each city to be destroyed in turn. The Soviets were assisted in the attack on Gdynia when a Polish girl reached the commander of the VIII Guards Mechanised Corps, I. F. Dremov, and handed him a map of the entire German defensive positions: 'Mixing Polish words with Russian, the girl drew attention to the most vulnerable locations of the fortresses and the sectors where it could be attacked to the best advantage.'[66] Gdynia was liberated on 28 March, and on 30 March Danzig fell to the Soviet armies.

Poland was now liberated from the Germans, and the Polish armies had played their part. A report from the 1st Belorussian Front to Beria testified to the anger the Polish soldiers felt towards the German soldiers who had occupied their country:

Soldiers of the 1st Polish Army are known to be particularly ruthless towards Germans. There are many places where they do not take captured German officers and soldiers to assembly points, but simply shoot them on the road. For instance, [in one place] 80 German officers and men were

---

* The Germans successfully evacuated thousands of civilians from East Prussia by sea, but on 30 January 1945, the *Wilhelm Gustloff* carrying over 9,000 refugees was torpedoed off Gdynia.

captured, but only two were brought to the POW assembly point. The rest were shot. The regimental commander interrogated the two, then released them to the Deputy Chief of Reconnaissance, who shot these men too. The deputy political officer of 4th Infantry Division, Lieutenant Colonel Urbanovich, shot nine prisoners who had voluntarily deserted to our side, in the presence of the divisional intelligence officer.[67]

Not all the soldiers in the 1st and 2nd Polish Armies wanted to fight under Soviet command. Most had been forcibly conscripted and some took any opportunity to desert. Zygmunt Klukowski noted in his diary:

> Desertions from the Polish army are increasing. Lately many soldiers have left the garrison in Zamość. The underground is trying to take care of the deserters by giving them lodging and food. Even the nuns in Michalów are hiding six deserters. Mass desertions are expected in the spring, probably into the forest.[68]

His diary entries for the following month record the difficulties encountered in feeding the growing number of deserters. Other examples include: in March the commanding officer of the Polish 9th Infantry Division, who persuaded 380 soldiers to desert on their way to the front; and a junior officer at the Polish army tank school, who was also a member of the AK, who called on 70 cadets to desert and take their weapons with them. The NKVD hunted down deserters ruthlessly and killed many of those they recaptured.[69]

All the Polish armies took part in the final battles of the Second World War. The Polish armies in the west continued fighting to the end, with Maczek's armoured division crossing into Germany and occupying Wilhelmshaven, and the II Corps in Italy ending the war having taken Bologna. The Polish armies on the Eastern Front had also played their part in the final defeat of the Third Reich. The 1st Polish Army was tasked with forcing the Oder river at Siekierki and then advancing with the 2nd Belorussian Front to approach Berlin from the north. Operations commenced on 16 April, but crossing the Oder was no easy task, as General Jurij Bordziłowski, the 1st Army's chief engineer, recalled:

> I have forced many rivers, I saw many more, sometimes I crossed them, sometimes I defended them, but the Oder in early spring 1945 looked the worst and made a depressing impression. I did see rivers that were larger

and wider, but they were just rivers, and here we saw an infinite expanse of water, where it was hard to tell the river bed from the shallow back-waters, often a kilometre or more in width. I knew very well what we could be in for – there was no way to swim and no way to walk.

The 1st Polish Army then broke the German defensive line at Stara Odra, advanced on the Hohenzollern Canal and pursued the Germans back to the Laba river, which they reached on 6 May. Further south, elements of the 1st Polish Army, including the 1st Division, took part in the final battles for Berlin, reaching the centre as the city capitulated.[70]

The 2nd Polish Army, under General Karol Świerczewski, operated under the command of the 1st Ukrainian Front. These troops had been conscripted in the second half of 1944 and they were undertrained and underequipped, and many even lacked uniforms and were forced to go into battle wearing their civilian clothing. The 2nd Polish Army contained many former AK soldiers who were politically unreliable and took any opportunity for desertion. Nonetheless, the Soviets threw these men into the battles to cross the Neisse river and then advance towards Dresden. The operation opened on 16 April, and poor reconnaissance meant that the Poles were ignorant of the strength of the Germans. Worse was to unfold when the Germans managed to gather together sufficient forces to mount a counterattack which decimated the rear of the 2nd Polish Army near Bautzen and led to the successful recapture of Bautzen. The seriousness of the situation necessitated the withdrawal of Polish and Soviet troops from the Dresden area and the evacuation of Bautzen. Towards the end of April, the officer carrying the order of retreat was killed and his papers captured by the Germans who now knew exactly how and when to attack the Polish troops. The result was a slaughter and, by the time the situation had been restored, the 2nd Polish Army had suffered 4,902 dead and 13,000 wounded or missing, and had lost over half its tanks and over 20 per cent of its artillery. Despite these losses the 2nd Polish Army took part in the final operations for the capture of Dresden before turning south, crossing into Czechoslovakia and taking part in the final battles of the war for Prague, which it entered on 11 May.[71]

The reaction of the Poles to the liberation of Poland by the Soviet armies was mixed. For most it appears that there was a feeling of quiet relief that the Germans had gone, but little joy and a great deal of suspicion directed towards the Soviets. Michał Zylberberg, a Jew who had survived hidden in Warsaw and then moved to the country when Warsaw was evacuated after the uprising, wrote of the Soviet liberation of the village where he was sheltering:

> It was silent and shuttered, without a soul in the street. The local population were awaiting a different sort of liberation. They hoped that the Polish government in exile would set them free. The market square was filled with thousands of Russian soldiers, playing on mouth organs and performing Cossack dances.[72]

The Soviet soldiers were equally unimpressed by their reception by the Poles: 'When you look at them, you feel such anger, such hatred. They're having fun, loving and living. And you are fighting to liberate them! They just laugh at us Russians. Bastards!'[73] The Jews who had survived, whether in camps, in hiding or as partisans in the forests, were naturally overjoyed to see their Soviet liberators.

The Poles faced several choices after the liberation of Poland and its occupation by the Soviet armies and administration by the communist-dominated Provisional Government: leave Poland, wait and see what would happen, or resist the new occupation. The winter of 1944–5 provided the last opportunity for those in the south of Poland to flee the Soviet advance by crossing into Austria, a move for which the Germans would grant permission. Among those who took the opportunity were Teresa Kicińska, her half-brother Jurek Strążewski and the Smorczewski family. The decision at the Moscow conference of the foreign ministers in 1943 to treat Austria as the first victim of Hitler's aggression meant that as Germany moved inexorably towards defeat the Austrians tended to adopt a more friendly approach towards the recent Polish arrivals. For example, in Vienna Ralph Smorczewski's father approached a police officer for residential permits:

> 'What do you need them for?'
> 'Well, if somebody enquires as to the reason why we are here, we will be in trouble.'
> 'Nobody will enquire.'
> 'We need these permits to obtain some food.'
> 'You can get it on the black market.'[74]

Also in Vienna, Teresa Kicińska and her half-brother, although they were technically members of a subject race, were offered a suite in a hotel in Vienna in exchange for cigarettes on the grounds that: 'soon the war will be over and you will be coming here as visitors'. Finally, however, the Austrians were desperately short of food and wanted to get rid of the refugees. Just as the war was ending the Smorczewski family crossed into Bavaria, and the Austrians all but threw Teresa Kicińska and her half-brother across the border into Switzerland.[75]

Away from the south, no escape was possible and the situation was far worse. The Germans forced the Poles into labour gangs to dig defences against the Soviet attack, and as the Germans withdrew westwards, so the Poles were forced to follow:

> In the course of two weeks we covered on foot tens of miles, both during the day and night. Without any supplies. We were starving, begging, and stealing whatever we could eat, sleeping along the way in whatever farm buildings we came across. Along the way we met terrified people from Prussia escaping with their things. The look of them reminded us of our own September 1939, except then the direction of the exodus was different.[76]

Indeed, all over Poland various marches were taking place westwards under the German jackboot: Jews who had survived the concentration camps and labour camps and allied POWs – and, of course, the German administrators and their families were fleeing westwards along with the Germans who had been settled in Poland as part of Himmler's great resettlement programme. A German prison governor ordered to move his prisoners westwards described the problems:

> The weather conditions were disastrous. The progress of the trek was hindered by the heavy snowfall, the cold, the mass of refugees and army vehicles as well as the flooding back of masses of troops, prisoners of war, etc. Every road was jammed, so that the treks sometimes had to wait for hours in one spot, just to move a few hundred metres forward.[77]

Also going westwards were the Poles from east of the Curzon Line under the repatriation agreements signed between the PKWN and the Soviet Union in the autumn of 1944, of which more in Chapter 17.

As the Soviet armies liberated the country, the Provisional Government extended its rule over the whole of Poland. It aimed to consolidate its position as the sole ruling body in Poland before any agreement on a new Provisional Government of National Unity, including non-communist elements, was decided by the Moscow Commission. To this end the Provisional Government began by reforming the economy. It caused total chaos through a sudden abolition of the złoty issued by the Germans in Kraków and its replacement by a new złoty printed in Lublin. The Provisional Government took the first steps towards the nationalisation of industry by seizing the cash stocks of businesses and granting short-term credits in their place, with failure to repay these leading to the seizure of the businesses. The 2,000,000 troops in the Soviet armies attempted to live off the land; for the peasants this meant an immediate replacement of German agricultural quotas by those imposed by the Soviets and the Provisional Government. The quotas were enforced with draconian efficiency, leading to great shortages of food for the Poles in the countryside and near starvation in the towns and cities.[78] The Provisional Government attempted to woo the peasants away from its greatest political rival, the Peasant Party, by quickly introducing agrarian reform, a subject about which all parties were in fact in agreement. A Soviet soldier, Vsevolod Olimpiev, noted the impact of agrarian reform on the village where he was billeted:

> Our host had abandoned his work and was spending his time at meetings of some sort. When asked by me he answered that land redistribution was underway in the village then. After one of those meetings he came back home upset and gloomy because he had been given a bad allotment. He declared that he would write a letter of complaint not to Lublin but to Comrade Stalin in Moscow and asked me for a piece of paper for it. I gave him a double sheet torn away from a notepad. Next day the host came back in a good mood for he had received a better allotment. To achieve this it was enough to show a piece of paper obtained from 'Mister Russian Sergeant' and announce the address he was intending to write to![79]

The agrarian reform was put into practice so incompetently that many peasants received under 4 hectares, too little even to provide a living for their families.

The tool used by the Provisional Government in alliance with the NKVD to impose its rule on liberated Poland was the application of terror against all those it viewed as its opponents. These opponents were all members of the AK and the Underground Government. Okulicki assumed command of the AK after Bór-Komorowski had gone into German captivity, and the reports he sent to London during the last months of 1944 reflect the extreme demoralisation within the ranks of the AK and the belief that there was no point in harassing the German retreat solely to replace the German occupation with a Soviet one.[80] The Polish Government in London agreed with his assessment and on 19 January 1945 Okulicki issued his final order disbanding the AK:

> Conduct your future work and activity in the spirit of the recovery of the full independence of the state and defence of the Polish population from annihilation. Try to be the nation's guides and creators of an independent Polish state. In this activity each of us must be his own commander. In the conviction that you will obey this order, that you will remain loyal only to Poland, as well as to make your future work easier, on the authorisation of the President of the Polish Republic, I release you from your oath and dissolve the ranks of the AK.[81]

The Underground Government remained in existence in secret, hoping that some of its members would be invited to take positions in the future government of Poland.

Although continued resistance to occupation might have seemed futile, nonetheless the Poles were not going to see their country occupied by the Soviets without a fight. In the aftermath of the Warsaw Uprising, General Emil 'Nil' Fieldorf was ordered to set up a new conspiratorial underground organisation from the ranks of the AK, which became known as Independence (*Niepodległość*, NIE).* It aimed at infiltrating and undermining the organs of the Provisional Government where possible and the boycotting of government decrees. Okulicki took over command after disbanding the AK, but NIE had little chance of success given the widespread terror perpetrated by the NKVD and the Provisional Government, and it withered away when Okulicki was arrested in March.[82] In its place, as the war in Europe ended, Colonel Jan Rzepecki established the Delegation of the Armed Forces (*Delegatura Sił Zbrojnych*), which aimed to bring some organisation to the resistance, necessary because many AK units were refusing to give up the fight. This *Delegatura* was in turn replaced by Freedom and

---

* NIE is also 'No' in Polish, which is effectively what the resistance was saying to Soviet occupation.

Independence (*Wolnośc i Niezawisłość*, WiN), aimed at organising the resistance for political ends rather than military activities and to give some sense of purpose to those former AK soldiers who refused to accept that Poland had been abandoned to the communists.[83]

The National Armed Units (*Narodowe Siły Zbrojne*, NSZ) had operated in loose cooperation with the AK during 1944 but completely separated itself in November 1944. The NSZ was loyal to the aims of the National Party, representing the right wing of Polish politics, and was highly anti-semitic. The NSZ had been the main culprit in attacks on Jewish partisan bands during the German occupation. It was equally anti-Soviet, and so continued to fight the Soviet forces even after the disbandment of the AK. The most famous brigade in the NSZ was the Świętokrzyska Brigade of 700 men, commanded by Colonel Antoni Dąbrowski, which managed to cross into Czechoslovakia in February 1945 and establish contact with the US 3rd Army as the war came to an end.* NSZ units unable to leave Poland continued hit-and-run attacks on the Soviet forces and on the Polish security forces.[84]

The Polish resistance might have been fragmented after the dissolution of the AK, but it was active and widespread. It has been estimated that before the end of the war there were 80,000 anti-government guerrillas operating across Poland, particularly in the Lublin, Białystok and Rzeszów provinces. Their death count rose during the first five months of 1945: 800 PPR members were murdered and 2,000 militiamen. The Red Army was also attacked, with 317 soldiers killed and a further 125 wounded. The response of the Provisional Government was to depend largely on the NKVD for assistance. As early as October 1944, Beria had already established a special NKVD division, Division 64, to arrest not only members of the AK but also Polish professionals, such as lawyers and professors, who had somehow survived the German occupation. The Provisional Government set up its own Internal Security Corps, but with mixed results: one unit was sent out before its training was complete and as Gomułka wryly noted: 'the 3rd Battalion of the Internal Army went out into the terrain and 2,000 people deserted'.[85]

---

* The Świętokrzyska Brigade caused controversy immediately after the war: the British refused to accept the brigade as reinforcements to the Polish Army in the west. The Polish communist authorities demanded its return to Poland so that its members could be tried as German collaborators. In August 1945, the US Army disarmed the brigade and the soldiers were sent to a DP camp.

The situation was worst in the area of Poland that now lay beyond the Curzon Line, where the NKVD had launched Operation *Sejm*, designed to stamp out the AK and any sign of Polish nationalism. The transcripts of NKVD interrogations of the Poles reveal the chief pre-occupation of the Soviet authorities: to cut off all communication between eastern Poland and the Polish territories west of the Curzon Line, and indeed also with London. The Soviets knew that the AK and some members of the Underground Government had radio contact with the west and the tenor of many interrogations was to identify who had access to these now forbidden communications. Those arrested were either transported to Siberia or, if they were fortunate, despatched across the river Bug into Poland.[86] The NKVD could change their minds very quickly as to who was a threat. For example, Leon Kochański had been tried by the Soviet authorities in May 1940 because of his former position as a senior Polish civil servant in Stanisławów, but had been acquitted, and during the German occupation he had worked in the Underground Government. At the beginning of 1945, he was re-arrested by the NKVD because they were convinced that he had the means of communicating with the west. In fact, the records of the interrogation of another underground operative, Adam Ostrowski, suggest that a radio was supposed to reach Kochański but had never done so. Because the NKVD were uncertain, they released Kochański and ordered him to cross into Poland where he hoped to join his family. On 29 March, he embarked on the train to Poland but was then taken off it and re-arrested by the NKVD. He contracted spotted typhoid in prison and died a broken man, twelve days later on 10 April 1945.[87]

In Poland itself, NKVD tactics were to surround a village and seize all the men in it for interrogation. A report to London stated:

> The NKVD are keeping those arrested in cellars, air raid shelters and in every possible place. Those arrested sit in darkness, without any bedding or warm clothes. In the course of interrogations, the NKVD beat prisoners, torture them morally, keep them in the cold without clothes. They accuse those arrested of espionage on behalf of the British and of the Polish Government in London, and of collaboration with the Germans. There is a high rate of mortality among the prisoners.[88]

It has been estimated that at least 50,000 Poles were sent to labour camps in Siberia between November 1944 and May 1945, and at least twice as many were interned in camps in Poland. In May 1945, there were 8,000 prisoners in the Royal Castle in Lublin, and large camps were established in Rebertów, Piotrków and Skrobów and other places.[89] It was small wonder that many people took to the woods to escape the Soviet round-ups and joined together to form resistance units.

As early as February 1944, Mikołajczyk had become sufficiently disturbed by the reports of the hostile attitude of the Soviet authorities to the AK in the Wołyń province to appeal to Churchill to despatch a mission of British observers to provide independent reports. Churchill and SOE were keen but the Foreign Office objected on the grounds that it could be viewed as a hostile act by the Soviets. Therefore, in April, Churchill replied to Mikołajczyk that there would be no mission. This reluctance to send a mission may in part be blamed on the fact that the initial Soviet advance and its hostile reaction to the appearance of the AK took place in the provinces the Soviet Union laid claim to, which might have been interpreted as some sort of excuse. By July this was no longer the case, as the Soviet armies had crossed the Curzon Line and showed no signs of altering their attitude towards the AK. The Soviet failure to support the Warsaw Uprising greatly disturbed the British Government, and as a result the continued Polish appeals for a mission began to bear fruit. In October the members were nominated and their purpose decided, and they were despatched to Italy to await an opportune moment for insertion into Poland. On 2 November 1944, Clark Kerr informed Molotov that the British were sending liaison officers to Poland to obtain 'direct trustworthy information about events in Poland'. This was to be Operation Freston.[90]

The Freston mission was led by Colonel Bill Hudson, and the members were Major Peter Kemp, Sergeant-Major Donald Galbraith, Major Peter Solly-Flood and Major Alun Morgan. The interpreter was a Polish lieutenant, Antoni Pospieszalski, using the *nom de guerre* Captain Tony Currie. Adverse weather conditions and British vacillations on the desirability of the mission after Mikołajczyk's resignation caused further delays. Finally, on the night of 26–27 December 1944, the mission parachuted into Poland, landing near Włoszczowa Końskie in the district of Radom. They kept on the move, escorted by the AK, but lost their radio equipment after a brief skirmish with the Germans. At the beginning of January 1945, the mission met Okulicki and was briefed on the state of the resistance in Poland and the attitude of the Red Army. On the night of 13 January, the sound of Soviet artillery was heard and the mission managed to send a message back to London asking for confirmation, which they received, of their orders to hand themselves over to the Soviets. Peter Kemp recalled that London reassured them that 'our names and location and the nature of our mission had been communicated to the Russian political and military authorities'. This appeared not to be the case. On 15 January, the British mission presented themselves to the nearest Soviet unit and were taken to the Soviet Army corps headquarters at Zytn and interrogated by an NKVD general who asked them: 'Why have you been spying on the Red Army? Allied soldiers would not be found living with bandits, collaborators, war criminals and enemies of the Red Army.' They were all arrested and, in the middle of February, arrived in Moscow before being repatriated via Cairo. The mission had accomplished nothing other than prove the hostility of the Soviets towards the AK, which had in any case been officially disbanded while the mission was still on Polish soil.[91]

In January 1945, Churchill and Eden, alarmed at the scale of arrests in Poland, approached the Polish Government with a new proposal: if they supplied the British with a list of the names of the main underground leaders, the British would pass this on to Stalin at Yalta in order for these men to receive protection against arrest. It was a wildly optimistic assumption by the British that Stalin would offer Soviet protection to the Polish Underground Government given that he had recognised the Lublin Committee as the Provisional Government and that it was the NKVD who was making most of the arrests in Poland. The Polish Government was extremely wary. In a memorandum submitted to the Foreign Office, the Poles raised two important points: the Polish Government would release the names of the most prominent members of the underground 'if they could rest fully assured that such a disclosure would not bring about fatal consequences for those concerned', and 'The Polish Government would be grateful to learn what steps designed to assure the safety of the Polish citizens are visualised by the British Government.' This was much further than the British were prepared to go.[92] Nevertheless, on 8 March, the Polish Government decided to furnish Eden with the names of the four party leaders – Jan Stanisław Jankowski, Antoni Pajdak, Stanisław Jasiukowicz, and the pseudonym 'Walkowicz', whose name was undisclosed but was in fact Adam

Bień – in the hope that these men would be invited for consultation with the Polish Commission in Moscow.[93]

On 1 March, NKVD General Ivan Serov was appointed head of the Polish Ministry of Public Security and wasted little time in attempting to crush the Polish Underground Army and Underground Government. Okulicki and the government delegate, Jankowski, received invitations from Soviet Colonel Pimienov to attend a meeting with General Ivanov, a representative of Marshal Zhukov, to discuss cooperation.[94] In fact Ivanov was the pseudonym of Serov. The first meeting between Jankowski and Serov took place on 17 March at Pruszków, and in his report to the Polish Government in London Jankowski was optimistic about the possibilities of cooperating with the Soviets and received permission from the government to continue the talks.[95] Okulicki had already been a 'guest' of the NKVD in the Lubyanka prison in 1941, after having been arrested in Lwów in January 1941, and this made him wary of accepting the invitation to the talks. Indeed, the Polish Government forbade him to reveal himself, but, under pressure from the politicians in Poland, he decided to do so. On 27 March, Jankowski and Okulicki, accompanied by Jankowski's three deputies – Bień, Pajdak and Jasiukowicz – the chairman of the Council of National Unity, Kazimierz Pużak, and members of the Council – Kazimierz Bagiński Eugeniusz Czarnowski, Stanisław Mierzwa, Franciszek Urbański, Józef Chachiński, Kazimierz Kobylański, Stanisław Michałowski and Zbigniew Stypułkowski – and their translator Józef Stemler Dąbski, met Serov. On 28 March, they were all arrested, and on, 1 April, Stefan Korboński, the most senior surviving member of the Underground Government, informed London of this and of the suspicion that they had been taken by plane to Moscow to await trial. A sixteenth Polish politician, Aleksander Zwierzyński, was already in prison there.[96]

Raczyński immediately informed Eden of the arrests and appealed for British assistance. The Soviet authorities did not disclose that they had arrested the sixteen Polish leaders; even the Provisional Government was not informed and, according to Korboński's sources, considered the arrests a great mistake. With the San Francisco conference about to open, the Polish foreign minister, Tarnowski, sent an impassioned appeal to Eden and Stettinius at the end of April to find out from Molotov the fate of the arrested men. Finally, on 3 May, Molotov did admit that the Soviets had arrested and imprisoned them, and

Eden and Stettinius angrily confronted him and demanded their immediate release. As both Eden and Cadogan noted: 'I have never seen Mr
Molotov look so uncomfortable.' On 5 May, Eden and Stettinius issued
identical statements at the San Francisco conference deprecating the
conduct of the Soviets and demanding a full explanation. This came in
a statement by TASS on 5 May: Okulicki was accused of 'preparing
diversionary activities in the rear of the Red Army', and the others were
accused of 'the installation and maintenance in the rear of Soviet troops
of illegal radio transmitters'. The British and American governments
responded by breaking off the talks on the future composition of the
Polish Government and continued to appeal for the release of the sixteen men.[97]

The arrest of the Polish leaders cast a dark shadow over the celebrations accompanying the end of the war in Europe on 8 May.* Polish
armies had contributed to the final success of the Allies but found little
satisfaction in the advent of peace. The soldiers of Anders's II Corps in
Italy in particular had mixed feelings about the end of the war. For
them, the decisions taken at Yalta had deprived them of their home, and
apparently had left Poland at the mercy of the communists. One officer
at Bologna described the mood of his soldiers:

> Our soldiers look down from their vehicles on the enthusiastic crowd,
> return smiles and greetings, but they do not share the general joy; they are
> rather serious and sad ... In a few days the life in town will return to
> normal, while we will go further north. We will continue to liberate towns
> and villages, to carry on bloody battles, because all roads lead to Poland.
> And this Poland is closer and closer but so desperately distant.[98]

In Germany, the soldiers of General Maczek's division were caring for a
large number of Polish displaced persons (DPs) who had been brought
to Germany as forced labour and now faced an uncertain future. Maczek took over the town of Harn, evacuated the German population, and
for the next two years Harn became Maczków, a Polish town in Germany. Polish POWs, most of whom had been in camps since 1939, were
also liberated, and one of them, Piotr Tareczyński, noted:

> We were unofficially told that anyone who had any personal grievance to
> settle with any German could do so within a fortnight of the announcement,

* 9 May in the Soviet Union.

and would be immune from prosecution, regardless of what form his revenge took. Personally, I had no personal accounts to settle with anyone, and just wanted to be left alone.[99]

Many Polish DPs and POWs began to travel south to enlist in the II Corps in Italy. Polish Jews, who formed a large proportion of the DPs, now faced the challenge of coming to terms with the scale of the slaughter of their people and the search for any family members who might have survived. One Polish Jew, George Topas, summed up his feelings: 'I began to feel a sense of anxiety that displaced the mood of hopeful expectation. I was not yet fully aware that the world I had once known existed no more.'[100]

Within Poland the mood was despondent. Zygmunt Klukowski noted in his diary: 'The war with Germany is over; the people are free in many countries, but we still live in difficult conditions, exposed to violence, terror, and barbarian attacks from our so-called friends who are in fact no better than the occupying Germans.'[101] Other Poles were even more forthright. Stefan Baluk, whose war had taken him to France and Britain before being parachuted back to Poland as one of the unseen and silent, wrote:

> As the smoke cleared from the battlefield it began to emerge that we had suffered a huge national defeat, yet we did not want to, or were simply unable to, believe this. We clutched at the last illusory straws of hope. We had yet to adapt to the new situation, and now faced an enemy within.[102]

Of the 24,000,000 Poles who had survived the war, over 5,000,000 were abroad: in the Polish armed forces in the west, in DP camps scattered across the world, in other countries as refugees and in what had been eastern Poland, waiting to be repatriated to the new Polish state.[103] The shape and government of the new Poland were as yet undecided. There were many battles still to be fought.

# 17

# The Aftermath of the War

The Second World War left Poland devastated. Around 6,000,000 Poles had died during the conflict, 20 per cent of the pre-war population; only around a tenth as a result of military action. The deaths of the remainder bore testament to the brutality of the German occupation from 1939 to 1945 and to the Soviet occupations from 1939 to 1941 and from 1944 to 1945. Of the dead, half were Polish Jews, representing approximately 90 per cent of the pre-war Jewish population of Poland. Of the 24,000,000 Poles who survived the war, at least 5,000,000 were outside Poland's borders.[1]

Poland was an economic wreck: 60 per cent of industrial capacity had been lost, and her agricultural output had been devastated by the loss of 72 per cent of all sheep and 60 per cent of all cattle. Her cities lay in ruins: almost 85 per cent of Warsaw had been destroyed in the fighting or deliberately demolished. The new United States ambassador, Arthur Bliss Lane, noted: 'the scene was depressingly lacking in the normal bustle and movement of a city'. There was hardly any electric lighting or running water in the city. The bridges across the Vistula had all been destroyed and 'only a temporary wooden bridge and a small pontoon bridge for the use of troops joined Warsaw and Praga'.[2] In September 1945, General Eisenhower arrived in Poland from Germany for a day, toured Warsaw and 'continually exclaimed at the extent of the destruction, the equal of which he had never seen'.[3] Poland's cultural and intellectual elite had also been targeted and massacred: a third of all those who had received higher education and a third of those who had received a secondary education during the interwar years had been killed. A third of all academics, scientists and doctors had been killed, and over half of all lawyers.[4]

Poland would clearly require a great deal of outside assistance in order to rebuild the country. First, however, she needed a government that was recognised by Britain, the United States and the Soviet Union. The negotiations of the Moscow Commission and the three foreign ministers who had met during the San Francisco conference had failed to break the deadlock. In May 1945, Truman despatched Roosevelt's trusted foreign policy adviser Harry Hopkins to Moscow for talks with Stalin in the hope that moves towards the creation of a new Polish Provisional Government of National Unity could be made through a bi-partisan agreement. Truman sidelined Churchill, believing him to be too personally involved in the issue. Hopkins himself felt the omission of a British representative weakened his position in Stalin's eyes, signalling an apparent breach in the unity of the western allies; Hopkins was, however, a personal friend of the British ambassador, Clark Kerr, and told Truman that this would enable him to gauge the degree of British support for his mission. While Hopkins was in Moscow, Churchill signalled his alarm at Soviet breaches in the agreements made at the Yalta conference by asking his chiefs of staff to consider Operation Unthinkable, war with the Soviet Union.[5]

Hopkins had six meetings with Stalin, conducted in a relaxed and friendly atmosphere with Harriman as an observer; both sides saw the outcome as a success. It was settled that the representatives of the Provisional Government, politicians from inside Poland and from Britain would all be invited to Moscow at the same time to hammer out a deal with the assistance of the Moscow Commission. It was also agreed that only those Poles who accepted the Yalta agreements, particularly the reference to the Curzon Line, would be invited. Hopkins made an appeal for Stalin to release the sixteen imprisoned Poles but he refused. Only George Kennan, chargé d'affaires at the American embassy in Moscow, saw danger: he urged Harriman not to renew talks in the Moscow Commission, on the grounds that there was no chance of Poland regaining her freedom from NKVD control, and that any American attempt to take part in establishing a new government would only be viewed as bowing to and acknowledging Soviet control over Poland.[6]

On 15 June 1945, the Moscow Commission extended invitations to Władysław Gomułka, Bolesław Bierut, Edward Osóbka-Morawski and Władysław Kowalski as representatives of the Provisional Government; Wincenty Witos, Zygmunt Żuławski, Adam Krzyżanowski,

Stanisław Kutrzeba and Henryk Kołodziejski as politicians in Poland; and Stanisław Mikołajczyk, Jan Stańczyk and Józef Żakowski from London. Mikołajczyk later gave his reasons for taking part:

> I felt it was my duty, as one who had sent Polish soldiers into battle, to share the fate of my own people in those most difficult days ... There was the danger, too, that if independent Polish leaders did not participate in the work of the three Ambassadors, the Polish people and not the Big Three would later be blamed for the failure of Yalta.[7]

When the Provisional Government representatives arrived in Moscow, they were greeted at the airport by Molotov and Vyshinsky and their photographs appeared on the front page of the newspapers; no public mention was made of the arrivals of the other Poles.

Mikołajczyk brought with him a long list of demands which he presented to Bierut, Osóbka-Morawski and Gomułka on 17 June. Among them was his plan for a presidential council composed of Bierut, Witos and Sapieha with the post of prime minister going to a member of the Peasant Party, as the largest political party in Poland, and the majority of seats in the cabinet going to non-communist parties. Gomułka attempted to put Mikołajczyk in his place:

> We will never give up power ... If no understanding is reached here, then we will return to Poland without you ... You should know for certain that in two or three months the Western powers will recognise our government ... And even if we have to wait longer for this recognition – then we will wait – but we will never give up power.[8]

The reality was that the Soviet Union and its lackeys in the Provisional Government were in such a dominant position that Mikołajczyk had to give way and hope that free and unfettered elections, to be held at some unknown date in the future, would bring the non-communist parties to power.

The composition of the Polish Provisional Government of National Unity was thrashed out on 21 June. Agreement was reached that the communists and their political allies would have 17 of the 21 cabinet posts, including the key portfolios for security, national defence, foreign policy, information and justice. Osóbka-Morawski would remain as prime minister. Mikołajczyk had to be content with scraps: the non-communist Poles received the portfolios for agriculture and land reform (Mikołajczyk), education (Czesław Wycech), public administration (Władysław Kiernik) and labour and social welfare (Stańczyk). Mikołajczyk and Gomułka became deputy prime ministers.[9] Harriman summed up why he believed that Mikołajczyk had settled for such a poor deal: 'In frankness I must report that this settlement has been reached because all the non-Lublin Poles are so concerned over the present situation in Poland that they are ready to accept any compromise which gives some hope for Polish independence and individual freedom.'[10]

Two outstanding issues dampened any elation that might have been expected with the announcement of the formation of the Provisional Government of National Unity. One was the lack of any firm agreement on the timing and freedom of elections. Harriman had reminded the commission of the desirability of guarantees for freedom of assembly and speech before the elections but Molotov had brushed this aside, saying that it should be left to the new Polish Government to determine. The statement first agreed at Yalta for 'free and unfettered elections' was repeated but again no definition was provided, nor was a time frame discussed. This would prove to be an enormous miscalculation on the part of the British and Americans.

The other issue was the trial of the fifteen underground leaders, which opened in Moscow on 19 June.* The charges were 'transmitting information about Soviet armed forces collected by espionage to the Polish government in London and to the command of the AK, openly provocative distortions about the behaviour of Soviet soldiers on Polish territory liberated from the invaders', maintaining armed resistance groups and committing sabotage. Leopold Okulicki explained that his organisation NIE had vowed to oppose the deportations from the eastern provinces of Poland and the repatriations from those areas to Poland, and while he admitted that lives had been lost in the attacks on NKVD and repatriation offices, he argued that this had not been intentional. He was also accused of provoking war against the Soviet Union and was shown a communication to a subordinate in which he predicted war between the western powers and the Soviet Union: 'We shall then come to the front in the defence line, and we shall probably even see

---

* Antoni Pajdak was ill in June; his trial took place in November. He was sentenced to 5 years in prison.

some Germans there who will be under Anglo-Saxon command.'[11] The trials were widely reported and Harriman even attended the first day:

> Fifteen of sixteen accused (one was reported to be ill) were marched in between NKVD guard and seated in crudely built wooden dock where they were attended by two NKVD guards with fixed bayonets. They were well dressed, apparently well nourished, seemingly composed and gave no indication of mistreatment . . . It is difficult to see how conduct of the trial during the present conversations in Moscow can fail to have a most unfortunate effect on the non-Warsaw Poles and greatly diminish prospects for a satisfactory understanding.[12]

Appeals by the Polish Government in London, then still recognised by the British and American governments, fell on deaf ears. The threat that the trials could damage the prospect of the negotiations for a new Polish government probably contributed to the sentences being lenient by Soviet standards. On 21 June, the court sentenced Okulicki to ten years in prison; Jankowski to eight, Bień and Jasiukowicz to five. Three men, Michałowski, Kobylański and Stemler, were acquitted; the remaining men were sentenced to serve between four months and a year. Okulicki and Jankowski died in prison; Pużak was arrested by the Polish Security Office (*Urząd Bezpieczeństwa*, UB) on his return to Poland and died in prison in 1950; after their release Bagiński and Stypułkowski returned to Poland, and then left for the United States and Britain respectively.[13]

The creation of the new Provisional Government opened the way for British and American recognition on 5 July 1945. This meant that recognition was withdrawn from the Polish Government in London. Raczyński sent a note of protest to the British Government:

> Now the territory of the Polish Republic is under foreign military occupation and the arbitrary power of foreign military and political forces. The events which have transpired in Poland since the outbreak of the war, are not the result of the intent of the Polish nation expressed constitutionally or by revolution. A war begun in the defence of the inviolability and independence of Poland has ended with the deprivation of Polish independence and the placing of the country under the rule of a foreign power. Under these conditions, neither I nor my government can acknowledge *faits accomplis* in Poland imposed unilaterally.[14]

The British Government made great efforts to secure a smooth transition from one set of Poles to the other. On 4 July, Raczyński signed an agreement at the Foreign Office whereby ownership of all the buildings and property of the Polish Government was passed to the newly established Interim Treasury Committee for Polish Questions. This was to be an entirely British affair staffed by Treasury officials, but in practice Raczyński was invited to take part in all discussions and signed official correspondence as the 'Chief Polish Representative'. The committee assumed responsibility for the welfare of the 65,000 family members of the Polish soldiers scattered in camps across India, Africa and the Middle East, and for the pay and supply of the Polish forces.[15] This gentle approach rankled with Stalin, who at the Potsdam conference voiced his displeasure at the leisurely liquidation of the Polish Government in London. Stalin of course had a history of ruthless eradication of political opponents. He saw the continued existence of the Arciszewski government, even in exile and unrecognised by the British and American governments, as a threat. On 26 July 1945, Raczyński handed over the keys to the Polish embassy in Portland Place, whereupon the Foreign Office sealed the premises to await the incoming Polish ambassador from the government in Warsaw, Henryk Strasburger, an ally of Mikołajczyk.[16]

On 2 September, the Arciszewski government agreed to continue in existence in exile to influence foreign policy issues, to maintain contacts with the anti-communist resistance movements in Poland and elsewhere, and to care for Poles in exile. Its continued diplomatic dealings with countries that did not recognise the Polish Provisional Government* led to complaints from Poland's deputy foreign minister, Zygmunt Modzelewski, during his visit to Britain at the end of 1945. Bevin assured him that Britain had a long history of offering asylum to prominent politicians, such as Trotsky and Chicherin, and had no plans to impose restrictions on the Poles.[17] The Polish Government-in-Exile continued in existence until 1991.

The war had ended before the western frontier of Poland had been settled. The British and American position was that the broad concept of

---

* States which did not immediately recognise the Polish Provisional Government included Spain, Portugal and the Vatican.

advancing Poland's frontier to the Oder was not in dispute, but neither wanted the whole of Lower Silesia incorporated into Poland, rather they wanted the new frontier to run along the Oder and the Eastern Neisse. Stalin, on the other hand, signalled his support for the demands of the Provisional Government for a border running from Stettin (Szczecin) on the Baltic south along the Oder, and then along the Western Neisse to the Czech border when he allowed the publication of an article on the subject in *Pravda* by Dr Stefan Jędrychowski, the propaganda chief of the PKWN.[18] As soon as the Soviet armies reached the Oder in February 1945, the Provisional Government was allowed to administer the region. The British and Americans objected. Kennan was requested to gain clarification of what was going on in Silesia since, according to the State Department, the situation would be acceptable if the local Polish administration was responsible not to the Provisional Government but was acting 'as administrative officials for the Soviet Union as occupying power'. Kennan pointed out that all the evidence pointed towards the incorporation of Silesia into Poland, with Polish press reports celebrating the return of Piast Poland to Polish rule after seven centuries of German rule and Polish politicians taking part in ceremonies of incorporation into Poland. Vyshinsky was approached by both the British and United States governments for comment but gave evasive replies and, indeed, appeared 'disconcerted' and 'confused' by the question being raised at all.[19]

The western border of Poland was an economic issue too. The European Advisory Commission had settled the frontiers of the zones of occupation in Germany and its recommendations had been adopted at Yalta. Furthermore, all plans for German reparations were based on Germany being treated as a single economic unit within its pre-1937 frontiers. At a preliminary meeting in Berlin just before the Potsdam conference opened, Marshal Zhukov, commander of the Soviet zone, dropped a bombshell when he stated that Silesian coal could not be taken into consideration because 'territory east of the Oder–Neisse line was not within his jurisdiction'.[20]

When the conference opened on 16 July, the Polish western frontier was immediately controversial. Truman wanted the matter postponed until the peace conference, but Churchill pointed out that this was undesirable because 'the Poles, who had assigned themselves, or had been assigned this area, would be digging themselves in and making themselves masters'.[21] He was also appalled by the prospect of the uprooting of 8,000,000–9,000,000 Germans rather than the 4,000,000 predicted earlier. The Polish delegation, which included Mikołajczyk, Bierut and Modzelewski, sent several memoranda to the British and American delegations stating the Polish case for the absorption of the western territories. Their arguments were: Poland needed to emerge from the war strengthened economically given that she had lost her eastern provinces; the western territories were needed to absorb the Poles repatriated from those eastern provinces and those returning from the west, to relieve overcrowding in central Poland; the issue needed to be settled now or there would be no chance of free elections in the area; and, finally, with some extraordinary massaging of statistics, they suggested that the German character of the claimed regions had been in decline before the war.[22]

The British position was one of total hostility to the Oder–Western Neisse line but the departure of Churchill to learn the results of the general election and the gap before Clement Attlee and Ernest Bevin, the new Labour prime minister and foreign secretary, arrived in Potsdam gave the Americans an opportunity to embark on some horse-trading with the Soviets. On 31 July, the American secretary of state, Joseph Byrnes, offered Molotov a deal whereby the United States would accept the Soviet position on the Polish frontier in return for their acceptance of the American position on reparations and on the admission of Italy to the United Nations. The matter was discussed at the plenary session that day.[23] The protocols issued at the end of the conference stated: 'The three Heads of Government reaffirm their opinion that the final delimitation of the western frontier of Poland should await the peace settlement.' In the meantime, the area up to the Oder and Western Neisse 'shall be under the administration of the Polish State and for such purposes should not be considered as part of the Soviet zone of occupation in Germany'.[24]

Two weeks after the Potsdam conference ended, the Soviet Union signed an agreement with the Polish Provisional Government of National Unity fixing the Polish frontier along the Oder–Western Neisse, but the matter did not end there. On 6 September 1946, Byrnes gave a speech in Stuttgart in which he raised the possibility that Poland's western frontier was still open to revision. The Poles reacted with great hostility to Byrnes's speech: there was a large demonstration in front of

N

LITHUANIA

Kaliningrad (Königsberg)

Gdańsk (Danzig)

Wilno (to Lithuania)

Szczecin (Stettin)

Białystok

Baranowicze

Poznań

■ Warsaw

Brześć

Łódź

P O L A N D

Lublin

Wrocław (Breslau)

Kraków

Lwów

Stanisławów

C Z E C H O S L O V A K I A

Subcarpathian Ruthenia

Bukovina

Annexed by Poland in 1945
Polish territory annexed by Soviet Union in 1945
Other annexed territory

0      100 miles
0      150 km

8. Poland in 1945 with Territorial Losses and Gains

the American embassy in Warsaw and the American ambassador, Bliss Lane, reported that the speech had united the Polish population in defence of the western territories and weakened Mikołajczyk's position because the Warsaw Government called him a lackey of the west who would deprive Poland of her new western frontier.[25] The British position was that the western frontier was intimately linked with the assurance of free elections in Poland,[26] but the elections would not be free, and the Polish-German frontier would remain unchanged. Only in 1990 did a free Poland and a now reunited Germany sign a treaty ratifying the Oder–Western Neisse border.

The Big Three had agreed that the Germans should be expelled from the territories ceded to Poland but had not foreseen the drama and human misery that would accompany this removal. The departure of the Germans from territories east of the Oder and Western Neisse took place in three phases from early 1945 to the end of 1947. The first phase was a voluntary flight ahead of the Soviet advance, often impeded by the conduct of the local Nazi officials. The second phase began in May and June 1945, the so-called 'wild' phase: the disorganised and brutal rounding up of Germans in the border regions and their precipitate expulsion across the Oder with little more than they could carry. This mirrored the treatment of the Poles in the areas annexed to the Reich in 1939 and 1940 and was designed explicitly as revenge for the suffering of the Poles at the hands of the Germans during the war. The commander of the 2nd Polish Army, General Świerczewski, expressed the policy in an order of 24 June 1945:

> We are behaving with the Germans as they behaved with us. Many have already forgotten how they treated our children, women and old people ... One must perform one's tasks in such a harsh and decisive manner that the Germanic vermin do not hide in their houses but rather will flee from us of their own volition ... We do not forget that Germans always will be Germans.[27]

Around 274,000 Germans were expelled during the 'wild' phase, 40,000–45,000 in a few days at the end of June alone, and they were often systematically robbed by the Polish militia carrying out the expulsions. The mass of destitute German refugees spreading across Germany caused great alarm in allied quarters because the commanders of its zones of occupation were already struggling to feed the population there. The issue was discussed at the Potsdam conference, where it was agreed that 'any transfers that take place should be effected in an orderly and humane manner'.[28] The Poles (and indeed the Czechs and Hungarians, who were also expelling Germans) ignored allied appeals to suspend the deportations until the Allied Control Council had prepared plans for their reception. The third phase, beginning in August 1945, was more orderly but the numbers overwhelmed the Allied Control Commission. Only in November 1945 did the Allied Control Commission agree plans to accept 2,000,000 Germans into the Soviet zone and a further 1,500,000 into the British zone. Thereafter the transport of Germans from the east was better regulated and the casualty rate fell.

Nonetheless, the sight of traumatised and starving German refugees in the western zones of Germany provoked the British and American governments to ask their ambassadors to approach the Polish Provisional Government to mitigate the harshness of the expulsions. Neither Bliss Lane nor Victor Cavendish-Bentinck were responsive since both were on the ground in Poland and could see for themselves how the Poles had been treated by the Germans. Bliss Lane reported that he had toured the western regions and felt that the Germans were not being badly treated and concluded: 'Many of the reports regarding ill-treatment come from the Germans themselves who, in keeping with their characteristic of whining after losing war, make the picture as black as possible.' Cavendish-Bentinck was ordered by Bevin to make an official complaint but Bliss Lane informed the secretary of state: 'As Bentinck was authorised and not instructed to make representations he proposes like Nelson at bombardment of Copenhagen to hold his telescope to his blind eye.'[29] In the 1950s, the West German Ministry for Expellees, Refugees and War Disabled argued that the allied principle of German collective responsibility for the war had been inhumane, pointing to the suffering of the German people during the expulsions. One historian has commented:

Focused on German suffering and its comparability to that of the victims of German crimes, this type of rhetoric enabled West Germans to address the Nazi past while evading questions of collective responsibility and to suggest that the German people, too, had ultimately been victims of Hitler and his psychopathic henchmen.[30]

The West Germans claimed that 1,000,000 had died during this period, but more recent estimates have cut that number by half, still a substantial figure. In 1947, when the deportations had largely ceased, there were around 250,000 Germans in Poland, and there is still a German presence in Poland today.

The Polish authorities had to define who was German and who was Polish, and this was not always easy. In East Prussia the so-called autochthons – the Mazurs, Kashubs and Warmiaks – could fall into either category: most had been German citizens before the war but had claims to be considered Polish now. For example, the Mazurs were Germanised Protestants of Polish ethnicity, whereas the Warmiaks and Kashubs were partly Germanised Catholic Poles. These autochthons had been able to sign the *Volksliste* during the war but were now able to revert to being considered Poles.

Silesia proved even more problematic since the region had been split between Poland and Germany before the war, but now the whole region was in Poland. The Polish authorities forced the Silesians through a process of 'verification and rehabilitation' designed to prove whether they were Polish or German. Those who wished to stay had to prove that they had lived in Poland or Silesia before the war and had demonstrated a 'positive attitude' towards the Poles before and during the war. The 300,000 people who failed the test were expelled into Germany. This was a better fate than befell many other Silesians, who were interned by the Soviet military authorities. It has been estimated that around 25,000–30,000 Silesians were deported to the Soviet Union in 1945, mostly miners to work in the Soviet mines in the Donbas region. Many more were interned in camps in Poland, including Auschwitz, alongside AK members and anyone else who had incurred the displeasure of the Soviet and Polish authorities. The conditions in Camp Lamsdorf (Łambinowic) were particularly bad and a German doctor recorded the deaths of 6,488 of the 8,064 inmates through starvation, disease and hard labour. Its Polish director, Czesław Geborski, was later tried by the Poles for his brutality towards the German inmates. Some of these Silesians the Poles claimed as their own, and appealed to the Soviets for their release. By 1947 the Polish Provisional Government had managed to secure the release of most of the Polish Silesians from labour camps in Poland run by the NKVD but could do little for those who had been deported to the Soviet Union.[31]

Revenge against the Germans was not the only motive for the Polish Provisional Government in the western territories, or the 'recovered territories' as they became known. The expulsion of the Germans enabled the government to build a society according to their communist principles without having to impose their will on a recalcitrant local population. Gomułka was able to state at a meeting of the central committee of the PPR in May 1945: 'The western territories are one of the reasons the government has the support of the people. This neutralises various elements and brings people together. Westward expansion and agricultural reform will bind the nation with the state.' The Polish Provisional Government confiscated the property of the Germans and allocated it to its supporters or to people, such as the peasants, whom it wanted to win over. Of the 6,000,000 hectares distributed in the land reform, nearly 5,000,000 had been owned by the Germans.[32] Given that the western territories formed around a third of post-war Poland, this was an enormously significant political tool for the communists.

The settlement of Poles in the western territories was slow. In August 1945, Wrocław had a population of 189,000 Germans and only 16,000–17,000 Poles.[33] Six months later Stefan Korboński visited the city and noted that from the air one could see 'charred yellowish spots indicating burned settlements', and that between 75 and 90 per cent of the city had been destroyed in the fighting.[34] Early settlers had ample opportunity to enrich themselves. Wiesław Lauter noted of Świebodzin (formerly Schweibus): 'Our walk through the town was strange. It was entirely quiet, our steps echoes on the pavement of the empty streets as in a well ... The town was entirely depopulated.'[35] Another Polish settler on reaching Lignica (formerly Liegnitz) said: 'One could take possession of a flat, a villa, a block of flats left behind by a doctor, a banker, a general.'[36]

It had been agreed at Potsdam that Poland would receive reparations from the Soviet share. The Polish portion was estimated at $350,000,000 but as Mikołajczyk was informed, the Soviet authorities 'stated that since they had arranged to have large sections of eastern Germany annexed to Poland and that since these areas contained factories and equipment valued at $950,000,000, Poland had already been paid three times the reparations which were due to her'. The reconstruction of industry in the region was hampered by the conduct of the Soviets who, according to

Jakob Berman, treated the area 'as their personal spoils of war and considered the wealth there to be not ours but German, and thus their claim to it incontestable'. Appeals to Molotov by Berman and Hilary Minc eventually put an end to Soviet seizures of factories and plant.[37]

At Yalta it had been agreed that the Polish population from the former Polish provinces now behind the Curzon Line would be allowed to be transferred to Poland. In fact this was just confirming a process that had already begun. On 9 September 1944, Osóbka-Morawski, for the Lublin Committee, and Nikita Khrushchev, for the Soviet Union, had signed an agreement for the population exchanges: the Poles east of the Curzon Line would go westwards and the Ukrainians, Belorussians and Lithuanians in Poland eastwards. The Polish Government in London complained to the British Government that this agreement was illegal since the Lublin Committee was not a government, and pointed out that it left in limbo those Polish citizens who had been deported to the Soviet Union in 1940–41 and forced to accept Soviet citizenship in 1943. This situation was rectified on 6 July 1945, with a new agreement signed in Moscow between the Polish Provisional Government of National Unity and the Soviet Union, which granted: 'Poles and Polish Jews living in the USSR the right to renounce their Soviet citizenship in favour of Polish and the choice of returning to Poland if they so wished'. The agreement excluded those Belorussians, Ukrainians and Lithuanians who had been Polish citizens before the war. The transfers were organised by the National Repatriation Bureau (*Państwowy Urząd Repatriacyjny*), replaced in the spring of 1945 by the General Government Plenipotentiary for Repatriation.

The transfer process began in the autumn of 1944 when 117,212 Poles left the Ukraine, before being temporarily halted because of overcrowding in central Poland. After the end of the war, the process restarted and accelerated: in 1945 511,877 Poles 'returned' from the Ukraine, 135,654 from Belorussia, 73,042 from Lithuania, and 22,058 from Siberia and Kazakhstan. In 1946 a total of 640,014 Poles were 'repatriated', but thereafter the process slowed down and over the next two years only 18,000 Poles returned. The total number of 'repatriates' from the east was 1,517,983.

There was resistance to the 'repatriation' process. The Polish

Government in London opposed it and in March 1945 sent an order to the government delegate on the policy to be adopted. This was basically to urge the Poles not to leave, but not to resist to the extent that repressive measures against them would increase. The attacks on repatriation offices by the former AK were one of the charges brought against Okulicki during his trial in Moscow. Even at the end of the war the Foreign Office received reports from Lwów that the Poles were refusing to leave because they hoped that the United Nations, then meeting in San Francisco, would reassign the city to Poland.

Ultimately it was fear that forced the Poles to accept the 'repatriation' process. There appears to have been unofficial cooperation between the NKVD and the UPA in ethnically cleansing the east of the Polish communities. It has been suggested not only that did UPA units attack Poles who had not registered for 'repatriation', but that the NKVD even formed false UPA units to attack the Poles. The Poles were led to believe that 'whoever doesn't go to Poland goes to Siberia', and had great suspicion of the entire registration process: 'the Commission registers Poles to send them behind the Bug, and the administrators hand out cards to send people to the Donbas'. Above all, the Poles felt an enormous wrench on being forced to leave Kresy, their homeland. One 'repatriate' wrote: 'Each Pole felt torn by his conscience: Poles truly love Poland, but they also love their villages where they were born, where they had their forests and ponds, where their fathers', grandfathers', and great grandfathers' farms were, and where ashes rested in ancestral graves.'

Considerable incentives were offered for the Poles to be 'repatriated'. They were released from all outstanding taxes and insurance contributions and would be offered a loan of 5,000 złoty to replace farm machinery left behind. Those who had the title deeds of their property in the east were eligible to receive a farm in the west, but those who had lost these precious documents were not. Farming families were allowed to take up to two tons of farming equipment and household articles with them as well as livestock; urban families were allowed one ton. The export of valuables such as precious metals or stones and objects of artistic value was forbidden. The 'repatriation' process was often chaotic. Stanisław Grabski submitted a report in September 1945:

> The Plenipotentiary was notified that a train departed on a given day and that he was supposed to get one thousand registered persons to the station.

The repatriates assembled for that purpose on open-air platforms. As a rule, they waited for the train for 10 to 15 days, unable to cook food, unable to find shelter from rain or wind, and exposed to robbery at night. They could not go back to their homes because they had sold their flats and furniture.[38]

Others were uncertain about the 'repatriation' process and fell through the official net. In October 1944, Józefa and Krzysia Kochańska were relocated from their exile in Kazakhstan to the Ukraine, but appeals for their relocation home to eastern Poland fell on deaf ears. They took matters into their own hands and, with the connivance of a Ukrainian family that was being relocated to the Ukraine legally, the Kochańskas bribed the conductor to allow them on to a train to Lwów, and they travelled on to join Józefa's brother Czesław, a parish priest in Białohorszcze. The village was being prepared for 'repatriation' to Poland but the Kochańskas were not registered: indeed, they were in the area illegally. The solution was an odd and fortuitous one: the Soviet village leader had accidentally shot dead a recently married man and, traumatised by his action, had turned to Father Czesław for forgiveness and help; in return for the comfort he received, he registered the Kochańskas for 'repatriation'.

The authorities attempted to resettle the Polish 'repatriates' in the western territories by moving entire communities together, but the chaos of the process often made this impossible, and so entirely new communities had to be forged from people of very different backgrounds. The people from cities in the east did congregate in cities in the western territories: Wrocław, Szczecin and Olsztyn (formerly Allenstein) attempted to replace the lost cities of Lwów, Wilno, Stanisławów and Grodno. Despite the official prohibition on the export of works of art, in practice transfers were possible. For example, the Lwów Catholic bishop appealed for the transfer of parish registers and 10,000 works of theology and philology. The transfer of the icon from the Armenian cathedral in Stanisławów was explicitly forbidden, but the bishop convinced the local NKVD officer that the large replica of the icon on the front of the church was actually the real thing, and so managed to smuggle the true icon to Gdańsk. Other transfers included the statue of Jan Sobieski from Lwów to Gdańsk, the Ossoliński library from Lwów to Wrocław and the icon of the Blessed Virgin Mary from the Dominican Cathedral in Lwów to the Dominican church of St Nicholas in Gdańsk.[39]

The 'repatriation' agreements between Poland and the Soviet Union called for the 'repatriation' of the estimated 700,000 Ukrainians living within the borders of post-war Poland, who were mostly concentrated in the eastern and south-eastern regions. Like the Poles in the east, many of these Ukrainians, particularly their blood-brothers the Lemkos in the south-east, had been settled in Poland for generations and did not want to be transferred to the Ukraine. Nor did the UPA want them to leave Poland since the UPA laid claim to areas of Poland mostly around Przemyśl and Chełm. The AK attacked the Ukrainians to encourage them to leave, just as the UPA attacked the Poles east of the Curzon Line, killing certainly hundreds but probably thousands. The Polish Provisional Government also wanted the Ukrainians out, and between 1944 and 1947 482,000 Ukrainians were forcibly deported to the Ukraine. In April 1946, Operation Group Rzeszów was formed in the Polish Army to speed up the expulsion, and about 4,000 Lemkos and Ukrainian civilians were killed. At the end of August 1946, the Soviet Union closed its borders and refused to accept the remaining 200,000 Ukrainians, as it concentrated on 'pacifying' the regions of the Ukraine, Belorussia and Lithuania now within its borders, brutally suppressing all separatist nationalist movements. In Poland, after the assassination of the deputy Polish minister for defence, General Świerczewski, in April 1947, Operation Vistula was launched under the command of General Stefan Mosser, and this forcibly deported the remaining Ukrainians and Lemkos to western Poland, killing those who resisted; it was undertaken with the approval of the Soviet Union and with the military assistance of 13,000 Czechs. The Polish determination to expel Ukrainians and to crush Ukrainian nationalism was in part revenge for the brutal wartime murders of Polish communities in Wołyń. Other minorities, the Belorussians, Lithuanians and Czechs, were allowed to stay within the new Poland.[40]

The Polish Provisional Government was determined to make the new Poland a mono-ethnic country. It remained to see whether it wanted it to be a mono-racial one too. The end of the war meant that the full scale of the destruction of Poland's pre-war population of over 3,000,000 Jews slowly began to emerge. The Central Committee for Polish Jews estimated that only about 50,000 Jews had survived in Poland, either in hiding or liberated from concentration camps. During 1945 another 30,000 Polish Jews who had survived through either voluntary or forced exile in the Soviet Union returned to Poland under the same repatriation agreements which had brought back the Poles who had lived behind the Curzon Line; a further 200,000 would return before the end of the decade. The total number of Polish Jews who had survived the war, either in Poland or abroad, was estimated at 380,000.[41] At the end of the war it was by no means clear that the Jews would want to resettle in Poland or would want to emigrate – or, indeed, whether they would be welcome in the new Poland.

The Jews felt a natural inclination to return to their homes in the search for surviving members of their families. The movements of Jews across Poland in the immediate post-war period make it difficult to gauge accurate numbers: a census by the Provisional Government in June 1946 gave a figure of around 240,000. The Jews faced an enormous emotional trauma on their return to their former homes: their communities had been devastated by the Holocaust and few found their relatives. For many it seemed that Poland was little more than a vast Jewish cemetery. Some had become influenced by Zionist ideas and sought to leave for a new life in Palestine, while others travelled west in search of a more prosperous existence.[42]

The Jews were also uncertain of their welcome in Poland. There were numerous instances of anti-semitism among the Polish population directed towards the survivors, which stemmed from a number of factors. There was a severe shortage of housing because of the damage caused by the war, and some of the reluctance of the Gentile Poles to vacate Jewish homes had its roots not in anti-semitism but in a simple fear of homelessness. Indeed, the state passed a series of decrees during 1945 which placed 'abandoned and formerly German properties' under state administration, but many of these 'abandoned' properties had been owned by Jews, who faced the prospect of court action against the state to reclaim them. Then there was also an ideological clash: most of the returning Jews had passed the war in the Soviet Union, and this, coupled with the fact that a number of the political leaders in the communist-dominated Polish Provisional Government, such as Minc, Berman, and Roman Zambrowski, were Jews, renewed the old spectre of the *żydo-komuna* ('communist Jew'). In 1947 the Jewish section of the PPR had 7,000 members. Even Israel Gutman, a historian normally extremely critical of Poles, was forced to comment: 'It was certainly undeniable that Jews were to be found amongst the upper echelons of the regime and within the government bureaucracy', but he also noted: 'In reality, the Polish public entertained a greatly exaggerated notion of the numbers and influence of Jews in the administration of the government and the Communist Party.'[43]

According to some estimates, 500–600 or 1,500 Jews were murdered in Poland between November 1944 and the middle of 1947. This was a period of near civil war in Poland, and it is by no means always clear whether they were murdered because they were Jews or because they were communists. Bliss Lane met two prominent Jewish leaders in January 1946, and they agreed with his assessment that reports of anti-semitism were greatly exaggerated and that the main reason that Jews were leaving Poland was a psychological reaction to the war years.[44] On 4 July 1946, however, there was a pogrom in Kielce which killed 40 Jews. Some facts surrounding the pogrom are indisputable: on 1 July, a small Polish boy disappeared, and when he reappeared two days later he told his father that he had been held in the cellar of a Jewish house and had seen the bodies of other Polish children there, and his father reported this to the police. On 4 July, the police and militia surrounded the house, where 250 Jews recently repatriated from the Soviet Union lived and a mob of around 4,000 people soon gathered. According to a report written by Bliss Lane, who sent representatives to investigate shortly after the events, it was not clear whether the militia opened fire on the house or whether the frightened Jews inside fired the first shots, 'but almost all the sources agreed that the militia had been responsible to a great extent for the massacre, not only in failing to keep order, but in the actual killing of the victims, for many had been shot or bayoneted to death'.[45] Later studies have failed to clarify who fired the first shots but generally agree that the uniformed representatives of the state, whether policemen, militia or soldiers, attacked the Jews exclusively. Twelve Poles were charged with the pogrom and nine immediately sentenced to death. The deputy governor, the chief of the UB and the chief of the militia in Kielce were all arrested, but no member of the militia was ever put on trial. The communists indeed took steps to ensure that they were not seen to be siding with Jews against the Catholic Poles.[46] The Kielce pogrom led to an acceleration in the rate of Jews leaving Poland and would also be exploited by the government seeking to discredit its political opponents.

The Polish Provisional Government of National Unity pursued two parallel courses with regard to the Jews. A memorandum issued on 5 June 1945 stated: 'all loyal citizens of the Polish Republic, irrespective of nationality and religious domination, should be treated the same'.[47] As has been shown above, this did not seem to apply to the Germans or Ukrainians within Polish borders, so what then would be the attitude towards the Jews? The government was keen for the Jews to settle in the western territories. This would solve the problem of what to do about their houses and businesses which had been taken over, often innocently, by Poles during the war, for in the western territories they could take over properties and businesses vacated by the Germans. Furthermore, the Jews could move away from areas, such as the regions of Warsaw, Lublin and Białystok, where the pre-war Jewish population had been largely exterminated, and could build new and perhaps more hopeful communities in the west, particularly around Wrocław and Szczecin. Before the war all the main political parties had been in favour of Jewish emigration and the post-war government proved no exception. It would be an exaggeration to say that the government actively encouraged emigration, but it certainly facilitated it. The government allowed the Jewish Agency in Poland to establish an emigration bureau, passports were easily obtainable and no attempt was made to curb the activity of Zionist organisations. Indeed, on 30 July 1945, a secret agreement was signed between the government and the Jewish Agency, under which the former promised not to interfere with the emigration of Jews. This was in line with the policy of the Soviet Union to support the exodus of Jews, anticipating that the influx of a large number of Jews into Palestine would damage British and American influence in the Middle East.[48]

Jewish emigration from Poland had begun as soon as concentration camps were liberated. The initial wave was by *Brichah* (Flight), an organisation formed by Jewish survivors in Poland. At the end of the war contact was made with the Jewish Brigade stationed in Italy and an escape route was organised over the Alps into Italy. In August 1945 the Jewish Brigade was transferred to occupation duties in Germany because the British became aware of its smuggling of Jewish survivors into Italy and then onto ships travelling illegally to Palestine. The route was now taken over by the Polish II Corps, with an unofficial agreement between

Anders and Zionist organisations, by which the II Corps would provide transport for Jews from the Austrian-Italian frontier to Italian ports and in return the Jews would also smuggle out family members of soldiers in the II Corps. For example, the daughter of General Nikodem Sulik and her two siblings were smuggled out of Poland to join their father, commanding the 5th Division; they travelled on a train with 800 Jews and were taught some Yiddish phrases to act as cover. At the Italian border she observed the collection of the Jews by soldiers in Polish army uniforms, and her story is backed up by other witnesses. Most Jews, however, travelled to Czechoslovakia and then to the American zone in Austria before ending their exodus in the American zone in Germany, where they joined the mass of Polish DPs already there. Prior to the Kielce pogrom about 70 Jews per week left Poland but after the pogrom the numbers rose sharply to 700 per day. The UNRRA representative on the spot noted the connivance of the Polish and Czech border guards in the exodus. The American political adviser in Austria, John Erhardt, raised the alarm, stating that the US forces there could not cope. Dean Acheson, acting secretary of state, contacted Bliss Lane requesting him to intervene with the Polish and Czech governments. He responded that it was his belief that the Polish Provisional Government was encouraging the emigration of the Jews and noted that Jews could obtain passports with ease, whereas Polish citizens who were not Jews could not.[49]

At the end of the war there were millions of Poles outside the borders of Poland. These fell into several categories: members of the Polish armed forces who had fought alongside the western allies during the war; Polish prisoners of war now liberated from German captivity; Poles who had been deported to Germany as forced labour and were now massed in DP camps in western Europe; the families of Polish soldiers in Anders's II Corps scattered across the world; and an unknown number of Polish refugees who had fled Poland either in 1939-40 or towards the end of the war. The challenge facing the western allies, especially Britain, and the Polish Provisional Government was how to encourage them to return to Poland. In his speech to the House of Commons, in February 1945, explaining the Yalta agreements, Churchill had offered 'the citizenship and freedom of the British Empire' to those Poles who felt that they could not return home. This statement had been made without considering the possible consequences, as Herbert Morrison, the Home Secretary, commented at the cabinet meeting on 28 March 1945:

> It is to be much hoped that a situation in which we are obliged to offer British nationality to large numbers of Poles will not arise. If and when it should arise, it will be necessary to consider carefully how to present the case for differentiating in favour of the Poles with a view to avoiding any permanent policy of accepting as British subjects, with a right of permanent residence in the UK, all those many aliens who desire to stay here and claim they have rendered assistance to the war effort of the United Nations.[50]

The cabinet concluded that the Polish armed forces could be considered a special case. Britain felt bound to offer a home to those Poles who had fought under their command and whose homes lay behind the Curzon Line. This pledge was honoured by the incoming Labour Government after the 1945 general election. At the same time, British policy was to encourage as many Poles as possible to return to Poland and to take whatever steps necessary to facilitate their repatriation.

At the end of the war there were a total of 194,275 officers and other ranks in the Polish military establishment: 54,234 in Britain; 55,780 in Italy; 16,000 in Germany; and 36,506 in the Middle East, as well as 6,700 members of the Polish Women's Service Corps, 19,400 in the Polish Air Force and 4,000 in the Polish Navy.[51] In addition there were about 1,500 German POWs of Polish nationality who had been accepted into the Polish Army, and a further 155 who were joining the Polish Army from German POW camps in the United States.[52] The Polish armed forces were under British operational command but owed allegiance to the Polish president and to the Polish Government in London. Anders had been acting commander-in-chief while Bór-Komorowski was a POW, but in May 1945 Bór-Komorowski assumed his post.*

---

* Bór-Komorowski was imprisoned in Colditz as a 'Prominente' to be used as a hostage by the Germans as the war ended. In the middle of April 1945, the 'Prominente' were moved first to Königstein in Germany and then to Laufen in Austria where, as US forces approached, they were put under Swiss protection. Shortly after the end of the war, Bór-Komorowski was flown from Innsbruck to London. He resigned as commander-in-chief in September 1945 and the day-to-day running of the staff was entrusted to Kopański.

The future of the Polish armed forces had been under consideration by the War Office and Foreign Office and by Anders himself before the war ended. The Foreign Office was aware that the Polish armed forces had the potential to become a political minefield should the Moscow negotiations on the formation of a provisional government acceptable to the three allies fail. Indeed, Anders, on 9 March 1945, in a lengthy memorandum, 'The Future of the Polish Armed Forces at the Side of Great Britain', warned: 'If the new government be unconstitutional and should it not obtain recognition from the President of the Republic, Polish soldiers, sailors and airmen, would be unable to recognise it.' The Foreign Office noted that if the British Government recognised a Polish government which the Polish armed forces viewed as unacceptable, then the relationship between Britain and the Polish armed forces would have to be altered. At the same time, the British wanted to maintain the operational value of the Poles.[53] This is why, during late 1944 and early 1945, the Poles were given permission to increase their establishment by enlisting ex-Wehrmacht Poles and liberated Polish POWs and DPs,[54] and by July 1945 it had risen to 228,000. The role of the Poles after the war was also under discussion: Anders wanted the Polish Army to take part in the occupation of Germany, an idea that was welcomed by some of the British. For example, Churchill believed that using the Poles for occupation duties would enable the demobilisation of his troops to progress at a faster pace.[55] Yet the presence of a large number of Polish troops in Germany would almost certainly be totally unacceptable to the Soviets, given the strongly anti-Soviet stance of Anders and his troops in the II Corps, the majority of whom had endured exile in the Soviet Union. Indeed, it was Anders himself who caused most alarm for the British; the British ambassador in Italy, Sir Noel Charles, said that he 'enjoys the position of a Commander of an independent army, fighting alongside but not subordinate to the British'.[56] The British CIGS, Field Marshal Sir Alanbrooke, at a meeting on 2 May 1945, discovered that Anders wanted his troops to take part in the occupation of Germany: 'and then has wild hopes of fighting his way home to Poland through the Russians!'[57]

The British Government was aware of the potential hostile reaction to Britain's imminent recognition of the Polish Provisional Government of National Unity at the beginning of July 1945 and at a meeting at the War Office before recognition appealed to the Polish high command to send a directive to their field commanders calling for calm while the future of the Polish armed forces was decided. In return, the British promised to continue responsibility for the pay and maintenance of the Polish armed forces through the Interim Treasury Committee.[58] The statements issued by the two most senior and respected Polish commanders, Bór-Komorowski and Anders, disappointed the British. While Bór-Komorowski, as commander-in-chief, did call for calm in his directive issued on 29 June 1945, he added that the Polish armed forces should not submit to another authority, meaning the Warsaw Government, until free elections had been held. Then, when Poland had regained her freedom, the Polish armed forces in exile would return home as a whole.[59] Anders, predictably, was rather more belligerent and issued an Order of the Day in which he criticised the British Government, and made clear his hostile opinion of the Polish Government in Warsaw and of the Soviet Union, and ordered his men to 'wait in closed and disciplined ranks for a favourable change of conditions'.[60]

Anders was ordered to cease recruitment to the II Corps in July 1945. The corps had, however, become a magnet for the Poles who had left or been forced to leave Poland during the war. Maja Puchalik had been in various German camps since the Warsaw Uprising and after liberation made her way to Italy with her fiancé, and they both joined the II Corps: 'It was an extraordinarily difficult passing, because it took place at night, through the Alps, across ravines. I remember that we encountered a rainstorm.'[61] Teresa Kicińska was a refugee in Switzerland and made the illegal crossing of the Swiss-Italian border near Lugano. The Italians turned a blind eye to the Poles appearing in their midst and even provided transport to the nearest Polish army camp.[62] The II Corps was much more than a military organisation, for it provided for the welfare of Polish refugees and DPs in Italy, and operated Polish schools and vocational schools, and persuaded Italian universities to admit Polish soldiers as students.[63] Consequently, within a very short space of time Anders had added a further 20,000 to his establishment. This led to a showdown with General Alexander in September 1945, and Anders was ordered to reduce his strength to 85,000, but he resorted to subterfuge, reducing pay and rations so that the British supplies and funds went further, and by January 1946 the establishment of the II Corps was 110,000.[64]

British policy was to encourage as many Poles as possible to return to Poland voluntarily to rebuild their country. The Potsdam declaration on the issue stated:

> The Three Powers are anxious to assist the Polish Provisional Government in facilitating the return to Poland as soon as practicable of all Poles abroad who wish to go, including members of the Polish Armed Forces and Merchant Navy. They expect that the Poles who return home will be accorded personal and property rights on the same basis as Polish citizens.[65]

The Polish commander-in-chief in Warsaw, General Michał Rola-Żymierski, initially stated in August 1945 that he wanted the return of all Polish troops as a military unit. The Polish Provisional Government issued a decree that officers and soldiers returning to Poland would receive the same entitlements to pay, decorations and pensions as the Polish Army that had fought under Soviet command. Polish citizenship would be granted to those Poles whose homes now lay east of the Curzon Line.[66] Ideally, the Poles wanted the military to return with its equipment, but the British objected since they had supplied it in the first place. British policy was to demobilise those Poles opting for repatriation and to treat them as civilians, but the Polish Provisional Government pressed for a reversal of this policy: they wanted the troops refusing repatriation to be demobilised. The British Government also demanded written assurances that the returning troops would receive guarantees against persecution.[67] The Polish Provisional Government reacted with indignation, and during December 1945 and January 1946 the British negotiated terms in London with Modzelewski. No sooner had the agreement been drawn up and signed by the Polish ambassador in London, Strasburger, than the Polish Provisional Government changed its tune. In February 1946, it declared that the Polish forces would no longer be considered as units but those soldiers seeking repatriation would have to apply individually to Polish consulates. This threw open the whole question of the future of the Polish armed forces again.[68]

The Polish Provisional Government's change of heart stemmed from several factors. First, there was the growing realisation that the highly politicised Polish Army was hostile towards communism and its soldiers would be likely to vote against the communists in any future elections. This had become apparent during the vicious propaganda war that had accompanied the Polish military missions in western Europe. The Polish Provisional Government made the initial error of designating General Świerczewski as 'Commander of the Polish Forces in the West'. His background as the commander of the Polish troops in the International Brigade during the Spanish Civil War, a Soviet general and the commander of the 2nd Polish Army, was hardly likely to endear him to the strongly conservative and anti-Soviet Polish forces. He was replaced by the less controversial General Izydor Modelski, whose military mission arrived in London in October 1945 to encourage Polish soldiers to seek repatriation. Bevin was so keen to see the Poles go that he made scarce shipping available. In Italy matters were complicated by the activities of the Polish embassy, where the new Polish ambassador in Rome was Stanisław Kot, Anders's *bête noire* from the time when Kot had been Polish ambassador to the Soviet Union in 1941 and Anders had been building up the Polish Army there. The two men clashed again on a personal and political level. Matters were made worse by the activities of the military attaché, Colonel Kazimierz Sidor, who engaged in a such a poisonous campaign against Anders that the British recommended Sidor's recall to Poland and refused to acknowledge his position as head of the Polish military mission in Italy. The communists alleged that Anders imprisoned those soldiers opting for repatriation; a Polish Army newspaper retaliated by printing pictures of the execution of soldiers who had returned to Poland.[69]

The Soviets demanded the return of Polish soldiers born east of the Curzon Line, an issue of extreme political sensitivity. It took place against the background of the forced repatriation of Soviet citizens by the British and the rumours, later confirmed, that these soldiers were executed on their arrival in the Soviet Union. The British position was clear: all soldiers in the Polish armed forces who had been Polish citizens at the outbreak of the war were entitled to be considered as Poles now, which covered most of the soldiers serving under Anders. The British remained firm, despite frequent Soviet demands for a reversal of the policy. For example, there was a heated exchange between Alexander and Major-General Iakov Basilov, the Soviet Special Delegate on Repatriation Matters, during which Basilov demanded the return of 30,000 'Soviet' citizens in the II Corps and Alexander responded: 'It must be understood that the Poles were Allies.'[70] The consequences of the British policy of considering all Polish citizens before the war as eligible for

British citizenship would have unforeseen consequences. It would include those Ukrainians born in Poland who had volunteered for the SS *Galizien* and were now in allied captivity. The British and Polish military authorities agreed that these men should be released from captivity and not be sent back to the Soviet Union, and in 1947 they were allowed to emigrate to Canada and Britain. The 1999 British War Crimes Commission concluded that some war criminals might well have slipped through the net and become British citizens, having originally either served in SS *Galizien* or been late recruits to the II Corps.[71]

The future of the Poles who had been conscripted to serve in the Wehrmacht was a more serious problem. The Polish Provisional Government did not want ex-Wehrmacht Poles to be repatriated, and there was a rumour that they would be screened on arrival to see who was to be executed, imprisoned or allowed to return home.[72] The western embassies in Warsaw confirmed to their governments that the ex-Wehrmacht Poles were receiving appalling treatment on repatriation.[73] During the war the Poles had instituted a thorough screening process for those Poles who had served in the Wehrmacht. Those who had been conscripted, the majority of whom had not served in the front line, were welcomed into the Polish Army, but those who had been officers or had joined the SS were excluded from joining the Polish Army, on the grounds that they had effectively renounced Polish citizenship through their service. Of a total of 54,500 German POWs who passed through the Polish Selection and Interrogation Pool, 1,151 were not admitted into the Polish Army, and of these 371 were not admitted for various security reasons.[74] These men continued to be treated as German POWs and not as Poles.

On 21 September 1945, a plebiscite on repatriation was conducted in all units of the II Corps at the request of the British authorities. One soldier wrote:

> I was given the choice whether I wished to go back to Poland from the II Corps. I didn't want to go back. Nobody in the Polish army said straight out that it was better for us not to go back – no officers, for instance. But the Polish paper was against it. Also there were army shows with actors, and though this was not pressure exactly, an atmosphere was built up that we should stay.[75]

In an effort to persuade the Poles to return to Poland, in March 1946

Bevin issued a leaflet with words of encouragement, but it met with a distinctly muted response, as Zbigniew Wysecki related:

> I can tell you what happened in my company. There was a British officer, I believe it was a major, and he was the person who handed this letter to every soldier personally. It wasn't just distributed, no, the company was attended, you know, stood and every soldier individually walked up to that major, he sat behind a table, and the major handed him that letter and if I'm not mistaken only about, maybe, fourteen or fifteen soldiers accepted the letter, all the rest just saluted and turned around and did not take the letter from him. So he just stood there holding a pile of letters.[76]

The leaflet was in poorly translated Polish which increased the soldiers' suspicions. There was also hostility to Bevin personally because back in 1920 the arms shipments for Poland needed for the war with the Soviet Union were prevented from leaving Liverpool dockyard because of a strike organised by Bevin.

Those soldiers who opted for repatriation were sent to a separate camp in Italy at Cervinara. By the middle of January 1946, it had 14,500 soldiers and another 12,000 had already been repatriated. Those opting for repatriation were recent recruits and soldiers of the Independent Carpathian Brigade, none of whom had been through exile in the Soviet Union. A total of 105,000 Polish servicemen returned to Poland: 86,000 from Britain, 5,000 from Germany, 2,000 from the Middle East and 12,000 from Italy. Of the 85,000 men who had accompanied Anders out of Soviet captivity, only 310 opted to return to Poland, and of those, only 60 had fought at Cassino. The rest of Anders's corps remained in the west to await the outcome of the elections in Poland.[77]

The British then had to decide what to do with the Poles who would not return to Poland. The troops were in Italy, British-occupied Germany, Palestine, Egypt and Britain. There was pressure to solve the matter quickly. The Italians wanted the Poles to leave because they were beginning to face hostility from the local Italian population who not only resented their success with the Italian women but also hated their politics. The deeply conservative Poles were in camps in the heavily socialist region of Bologna and elections in Italy were imminent. Furthermore, the frontier between Yugoslavia and Italy was in dispute and the Yugoslav Government also wanted the Poles out. The Soviet Union, through Zhukov at the Control Commission, made many complaints about the continued existence of a Polish army in the west and felt particularly threatened by its occupation duties in the British zone in Germany. Molotov was also belligerent: the Soviet Union would not tolerate 'maintaining at allied cost tens of thousands of soldiers in the Polish fascist army of General Anders'. The British themselves were finding the Polish Army to be a financial burden they could no longer bear, given that the army cost £2,500,000 a month to maintain, and that Britain was effectively bankrupt. On 4 April 1946, a ministerial Polish Forces Committee met for the first time, under the presidency of Hugh Dalton, the chancellor of the exchequer, who had had close contact with the Poles during the war. The Polish commanders had already been briefed that the British Government planned to demobilise the Polish Army and that the only questions to be answered were how and where.[78]

On 12 May 1946, Anders was summoned for a meeting with General William Morgan and the British ambassador in Italy, Noel Charles, to be informed that the II Corps was to be transferred to Britain for disbandment. Three days later Anders was in London for a meeting with Attlee and Bevin to learn more details. He informed Bevin that the II Corps was more than a military unit – it had become a large family – and asked that its welfare facilities, including the schools, should be transported to Britain too.[79] Bevin agreed, and outlined the plans for the formation of the Polish Resettlement Corps (*Polski Korpus Przysposobienia i Rozmieszczenia*, PRC). He announced his plans to Parliament on 26 May 1946.[80] The PRC was designed as a transitional arrangement to keep the Poles in disciplined units, accommodated in army camps and receiving army pay while at the same time facilitating their transfer to civilian life through training and instruction in the English language. Soldiers would be loaned to employers, but still receive their pay from the PRC, or could find a job through the Labour Exchange and be released from the PRC. Soldiers who wished to continue in military service received the unattractive offer of being allowed to enlist in the British Army as privates, with promotion only allowed after naturalisation. Enrolment was voluntary, but encouraged by the Polish commanders, including Anders, and would last for a period of two years. It was estimated that around 160,000 were eligible to join and a separate corps was established for the Polish Air Force. The commander of the PRC was General Kopański. Anders was considered too dangerous to be given command, especially since he believed that the PRC was a good idea if only because it kept the Poles in units that, should relations between the western powers and the Soviet Union break down, could be quickly mobilised as an army. Anders did not join the PRC but received a pension from the British Government.

The creation of the PRC was controversial. The trade unions feared that the Poles would take jobs from British ex-servicemen and took steps to prevent their employment in many industries, even those critically short of manpower. The Polish Provisional Government raised objections to the PRC, seeing it as a military unit and a continued political threat, and warned that enlistment in a foreign army, which is how it viewed the PRC, would lead to the loss of Polish nationality. In September 1946, the Polish Provisional Government relented and restricted its withdrawal of citizenship to Anders and 75 other high-ranking officers for 'conducting abroad activities detrimental to the Polish State'. About 5 per cent of the Poles would not accept repatriation or enlistment into the PRC: they became known as 'recalcitrants'.[81]

The demobilisation of the Polish Army started with the II Corps, which began to leave Italy for Britain on 10 June 1946. Most of the soldiers travelled by ship and their dependants followed overland. On 31 October 1946, the last transport left Italy: it included Anders. Some Poles remained in Italy because they had married Italian women and the British would not allow their wives to come to Britain. Anders had faced much resentment at his acquiescence in the formation of the PRC from his commanders, especially those in the 5th Division who wanted to fight its way back to Poland, but he pointed out that there was no other course and that in any case the II Corps only had enough fuel to reach the Austrian Alps. The 21,000 Polish troops from Germany arrived in Britain in April and May 1947, and those from the Middle East between July 1947 and April 1948.

The PRC was successful in placing the Poles in employment and eventually even the trade unions relented and reluctantly began to accept the Poles. After the fraudulent elections in Poland in January 1947, it was apparent to the British Government that no more Poles would want to be repatriated, and accordingly on 27 March 1947 the Polish Resettlement Act was passed offering the right to remain in Britain to the exiled Poles. The PRC was finally wound up in July 1948.[82] Settlement in Britain was facilitated from 1947 onwards by the Committee for Education of Poles in Great Britain run by the Department of Education, which oversaw Polish education in schools and places of higher education in Britain and ensured that the students would receive British qualifications. There was a Polish University College in London, which operated between 1947 and 1954 and offered degrees in engineering, architecture and economics, validated by the University of London; a Polish Architectural School in Liverpool and a Polish agricultural college in Glasgow. The 1951 census recorded an increase of 117,700 people born in Poland from the number recorded in the 1931 census.[83]

The Poles found it hard to adapt to life in Britain and many felt unwelcome. Edward Wierzbicki explained why he later emigrated to Australia:

> I knew I did not want to settle in England because I felt pretty bitter towards the country for its two-faced political attitude towards Poles and Poland. It was far from pleasant trying to explain to the indigenous population why I'd no intention of returning to my own country. The pro-Communist angling of the news did its bit as well. By a certain class of people we were hated and held in deep disregard. It seemed to me that at that time England was governed by pro-Communist sympathisers and workers' unions. Poles were accused of all manner of things probably because of their real contribution to the common victory. In such an atmosphere there was no chance for co-existence and therefore, in my search for a better future, it was necessary to find a more peaceful corner of the world.[84]

Poles were hurt by questions such as 'Just how long will you Poles want to continue eating British bread? Haven't you heard the war is over?', or having their experiences as exiles in the Soviet Union dismissed as shellshock because every Briton knew that Stalin was a good guy. The Poles quickly learnt that the British did not believe that Stalin was responsible for the Katyń massacre. Stefan Knapp, who had fought in the Battle of Britain, said: 'I was choking with the bitterness of it. Not so long ago I had enjoyed the exaggerated prestige of a fighter pilot and the hysterical adulation that surrounded him. Suddenly I was turned into the slag everybody wanted to be rid of, a thing useless, burdensome, even noxious. It was very hard to bear.'[85]

Polish resentment at their treatment by the British after the war was exacerbated by their exclusion from the 1946 Victory Parade. This politically sensitive matter was handled carelessly by the Labour Government when invitations were issued to all allied nations to send military delegations to take part. The Polish Army in Poland was loyal to the Provisional Government, but had not fought alongside the British, while the Polish troops who had fought in the west under Anders, Maczek and Sosabowski remained loyal to the government-in-exile, but this government was no longer recognised by the British Government and so could not receive an invitation. The British Government did extend invitations to the Provisional Government and to 25 Polish pilots who had fought in the Battle of Britain, but this apparent injustice towards the Poles led to an outcry. Harold Macmillan, minister in Italy, apologised personally to Anders; questions were asked in the Commons and Churchill voiced his displeasure at the conduct of the government, whose response was that it regretted that it did not see any way for the Poles to be represented in the march. Ten MPs sent a letter of protest to the *Daily Telegraph* pointing out:

> Ethiopians will be there, Mexicans will be there, the Fiji Medical Corps, the Labuan Police and the Seychelles Pioneer Corps will be there – and rightly too.
>
> But the Poles will not be there.
>
> Have we lost not only our sense of perspective but our sense of gratitude as well? We fear so.

Taken aback by the response – the refusal of the pilots to take part and the failure of the Polish Provisional Government to send a delegation – the British Government hastily sent out invitations to General Kopański, other senior Polish generals and the heads of the Polish Air Force and Polish Navy. These were respectfully declined, and the march took place on 8 June without any Polish representatives.[86]

The war had caused an immense dislocation of people in Europe, and in 1943 the United Nations Relief and Rehabilitation Administration (UNRRA) had been established to provide relief to nearly 7,000,000 DPs in Europe until their repatriation was possible.[87] The scale of the problem emerged as the Allies liberated Europe: by the winter of 1944–5, there were 39,300 Polish DPs in France and 22,700 in Belgium, but by the end of September 1945 there were 910,000 Poles in the British and

American zones of Germany and Austria requiring care.[88] The DPs were herded into camps, where the conditions varied tremendously.[89]

In the summer of 1945, the majority of the DPs in Europe were Soviets. Repatriation was effected swiftly for them and for the west Europeans. It was initially estimated that 378,000 of the 500,000 Polish DPs in the British zone wished to return to Poland. The new Polish Provisional Government of National Unity launched a campaign accusing the western allies of deliberately hindering their repatriation, but the fault lay not with the British and Americans, who were keen to see them leave before the winter, but with the Soviets, who insisted that their own DPs be repatriated first. In addition, the Soviets put all sorts of obstacles in the way of the repatriation of the Poles; for example, by refusing to allocate petrol for trucks to convey them across the Soviet zone, or by insisting that the western allies supply the rolling stock for those travelling by train. Some Poles were desperate to return to Poland. They had been seized for forced labour during the war and often had left home without having a chance to bid farewell to their families. For example, Barbara Makuch was liberated from Ravensbrück concentration camp:

> My dream was to return to Poland to find my mother and sisters if they were still alive. I joined a group of twenty other women and we started our march. For more than a month, we wandered through defeated Germany in its ruins, with groups of German soldiers hiding in the woods and criminals at large. Mostly we walked, but occasionally we received lifts in cars or trains. The most comfortable part of the journey was on a coal car. Food was scarce, but sometimes people gave us soup of a few potatoes.[90]

She spent a few years in Poland before emigrating to Canada at the invitation of the family of a Jew she had hidden during the war. The large-scale repatriation of the Poles only began in October 1945, through Czechoslovakia. Even then things did not move smoothly: two American officers reported back from the repatriation centre at Dziedzice that some DPs were being forced to sign statements agreeing to work as informers for the UB, the Polish Security Office, under assumed names. Bliss Lane realised that assurances guaranteeing the freedom of repatriated Poles needed to be obtained from the Polish Provisional Government.[91]

During the winter of 1945–6, there were still nearly 2,000,000 DPs awaiting repatriation. Most were located in the western occupation zone of Austria and Germany and three-quarters were Poles. The delay in repatriation proved disastrous for the project: it gave the DPs time to feel at home in the camps, to open schools, to resume cultural activities and, worst of all, to become prey to every rumour surrounding conditions in Poland. In late 1945, a secret UNRRA report told of a repatriated Pole who had returned to the DP camp at Eller, near Düsseldorf: 'This man claims that the conditions there [in Poland] were absolutely horrible and no Pole should be influenced to return to Poland. There is no food, accommodation, coal and, what is worse, no work.' The man travelled round the Polish DP camps telling everyone who would listen what it was really like in Poland. Polish officers loyal to the Polish Government-in-Exile were operating as welfare officers in the camps and advised the Poles not to return until free elections had been held. The Provisional Government sent its own liaison officers into the camps to arrange repatriation, but a report noted that their conduct was 'most inept' and that following their visits the numbers wishing to be repatriated actually dropped. A thousand Poles rioted in Wildflecken Camp when seven liaison officers loyal to the Warsaw Government appeared. Only at the end of August 1946, was the influence of the Polish Government-in-Exile eliminated from the camps, but by then it was too late: the majority of Poles in the DP camps did not wish to return to Poland.[92]

The Poles were unpopular with the military occupation authorities and with the UNRRA, particularly with General Frederick Morgan, its chief of operations.[93] Margaret McNeill was working in a DP camp at Frankenburg and noted:

> The more we got to know the Poles, the more they baffled us ... They respected their Church and counted honour something to be defended to the death, yet they earned for themselves a reputation for drunkenness, dishonesty and cruelty. They were often hopelessly lazy and unreliable as far as steady routine work went, but in a crisis they would, at the eleventh hour, rally and work with unparalleled speed and determination.[94]

McNeill displayed considerable sympathy for the Poles who agreed to repatriation: 'Where was the joy and triumph of their homecoming? In cattle-trucks they had arrived, defenceless and despised, to meet cruelty and degradation; and in cattle-trucks they returned, bruised, embittered and distrustful, to meet an unknown future in their devastated country.'[95] The Poles in Germany gained a largely unfair reputation for criminality although most of the crimes they were accused of, especially those against property, had in fact been committed by Germans.[96] Admittedly the Poles did engage in some crime and, if the crime was serious enough, could face the death penalty: in September 1945, 4 Poles were sentenced to death and another 27 to terms of imprisonment by a court in Paderborn. Michael Howard, a young intelligence officer in the British Army, recounted that when a British officer was shot by Polish DPs who were ransacking a German farm, the Poles were caught, tried and condemned to death by firing squad.[97]

During summer 1946, when the UNRRA found it more difficult to get the Poles to volunteer for repatriation, Operation Carrot was instituted by its director-general, Fiorello La Guardia: offering sixty days' rations to any Pole volunteering, with these goods put on display at the camps. Kathryn Hulme was well aware of the conditions facing those Poles in Wildflecken should they return, and wrote of Operation Carrot: 'Gradually we forgot the secret shame we had felt when we had first stood beside the free food displays and had watched our DPs stare at the terrible fascination of the bait, thrashing, twisting and turning before they took the hook.'[98] The UNRRA screened a film, *Return to Homeland*, and the Polish Provisional Government initiated a letter-writing campaign among Poles in Poland to their relatives in the west, encouraging them to return.[99] The numbers coming forward were still unsatisfactory so the UNRRA hardened its stance and issued an order: 'Effective October 1st 1946, all educational, recreational and other cultural activities are to be discontinued in all camps caring for one hundred or more Polish Displaced People.' The president and vice president of the Polish-American Congress, Charles Rozmarek and Ignacy Nurkiewicz, visited Polish DP camps that autumn and Rozmarek's comment was an indictment of the UNRRA: 'UNRRA has embarked on a course to make life so miserable for Displaced Persons that they will accept repatriation as the lesser of two evils.'[100] But the UNRRA actions were not entirely successful, for by June 1947, when its remit expired and it was replaced by the International Refugee Organisation, there were still 166,181 Polish DPs in the western zones of Germany. In 1947 Poles were included in the European Voluntary Workers scheme, which brought workers to Britain to undertake poorly paid menial jobs.[101] Many of those who remained behind were not repatriated but later took the opportunity to find new homes abroad when countries, such as Canada and Australia, opened their frontiers to immigrants.[102]

The Jewish DPs were originally classified according to their country of origin and were only segregated at the end of 1945. Jews leaving Poland generally gathered in Łódź and then travelled in groups to the Czech border before making their way to DP camps in Germany and Austria. The numbers leaving were manageable to begin with but after the Kielce pogrom about 700 Jews a day left Poland. Major Jewish DP camps were established in the British zone at Höhne near the former camp at Belsen, and there were twelve DP camps in the American zone, three of the largest being at Landsberg, Wolfratshausen and Felafing. The Jewish DPs were unpopular with the UNRRA and allied military personnel. General Morgan was convinced that the flood of Jews into Germany after the Kielce pogrom was 'nothing short of a skilful campaign of anti-British aggression on the part of Zion aided and abetted by Russia', and this and other even more anti-semitic remarks led to his eventual sacking. Certainly the scale of Jewish DPs posed a major dilemma for the UNRRA, and Bliss Lane was ordered by the State Department to approach the Polish Provisional Government to ask it to curb Jewish emigration because there was nowhere for them to settle permanently. When a questionnaire was distributed to 19,000 Jewish DPs, 18,700 listed Palestine as their destination of choice. Until the British could be prevailed upon to allow significant numbers of Jews into Palestine or other countries proved willing to accept large numbers of Jewish immigrants, the problem appeared insoluble.[103]

Not all the Polish DPs were in Europe: the families of the soldiers evacuated from the Soviet Union in 1942 were scattered in Africa, India and the Middle East. The UNRRA's task was not easy because these DPs had experienced Soviet life and consequently few wished to be repatriated, and even registering them was difficult. The UNRRA representative in India, R. Durant, visited the Valivade camp in India and met with an unexpected reaction:

> No one is certain who this newcomer is. Some say he is a communist! A group of hostile women surrounded him yesterday to have a closer look and one poked him with the tip of her umbrella. The pros and cons of registration were discussed in school, but it was difficult to make one's mind up as different teachers expressed conflicting opinions.[104]

The camp members voted to ask their husbands and relatives, soldiers in the II Corps, for advice before registration. This was a wise move because, under the terms of their settlement in Britain, the Polish soldiers were allowed to bring their relatives with them. The actions of the UNRRA were not helped by tactlessness. A report to the Colonial Office in February 1945, concerning the Poles in Africa, noted that trouble was caused when 'the refugees were asked to state to which place in pre-war Poland they wished to return, irrespective of whether that place was in the part of Poland claimed by Russia or whether or not Poland would be controlled by a Government developing out of the Lublin Committee after the war'.[105] The Poles feared compulsory repatriation to Poland but in fact British policy was encapsulated in an instruction to all British commanders in July 1945: 'Latvians, Estonians, and Lithuanians and Poles whose homes are east of the 1939 demarcation of the Curzon Line will not be repatriated to the Soviet Union unless they affirmatively claim Soviet citizenship.'[106]

The British faced the additional problem that the Polish DPs in India and in the Middle East were located in politically sensitive areas. The Congress Party was agitating for Indian independence and the presence of Poles there was awkward. The situation in Palestine was even worse, because the Jews were conducting a brutal underground war against the British forces, and there was a real danger that the Poles, mostly Polish cadets, could be caught in the crossfire:

> But the Jewish community, and in particular its insurgent element, well remembered the indulgent attitude of General Anders towards his Jewish deserters. The terrorists did not wish to quarrel with us, and said so through intermediaries. Naturally, the Polish commanders consulted their British colleagues and superiors, and an informal tri-partite deal was struck: the Poles would stay neutral, and in return they would not be targeted by the Jews, provided they did not carry arms, and remained clearly identifiable.[107]

The arrangement worked. Nevertheless the British authorities hastened to facilitate the departure of the Poles from all these regions. Those Poles in India who opted for repatriation were despatched overland to Egypt and then by sea to Gdynia or by train from Trieste. The remaining Poles left India and the Middle East for Britain in the course of late 1946 and early 1947, where they joined their family members who had served in the Polish armed forces. The Polish settlements in British East Africa were closed at the beginning of 1947, and many of those who did not have family members in Britain travelled to Australia to begin a new life.

One of the most poignant tragedies in the post-war years were the desperate and heartbreaking attempts by the parents of Polish children who had been kidnapped under the *Lebensborn* programme to find their children and bring them back. The Polish Red Cross found German records indicating that 3,000 children had been kidnapped from Silesia, 5,000 from Łódź and 30,000 from the Zamość region. The UNRRA established child-tracing agencies in January 1946 to search for Polish and other eastern European nationals in the three western zones of Germany. By the middle of 1946, 10,000 lost Polish children had been located and a year later this rose to 15,000. The Austrians voluntarily gave up 8,000 Polish children but in general there was greater resistance in Germany. The agencies discovered that many children who had failed the tests designed to check their suitability for Germanisation had been murdered during the war. A few stories ended more happily: Gita Sereny traced two Polish children to a farmhouse in Bavaria, and the UNRRA was able to reunite them with their parents, whom they had not seen since they were kidnapped in 1942 in Lwów. But not all the children wanted to return: some had been so young when they were taken that they were convinced they were German and rejected their Polish parents. Other children were orphans since their parents had been killed by the Germans, and their future was less certain and questions were asked at the time and later whether it was in these children's best interests to remain with their adopted German families or to return to Poland and be placed in orphanages. Ultimately only about 15 per cent of the children kidnapped from Poland were reunited with their Polish parents.[108]

The Poles who found themselves outside Poland's borders at the end of the war anxiously observed events at home before deciding whether or not to return. Mikołajczyk returned in July 1945. Stanisław Grabski, who had accompanied him from London via Moscow, wrote to his nephew in London that the public received him so enthusiastically that 'in Kraków his car was lifted up and they wanted to carry it'. Stefan Korboński explained the reaction of the crowds:

Tens of thousands of people welcomed him in the streets of Kraków, Warsaw, Poznań and Katowice. I am not a bit surprised: all these people believe that Mikołajczyk has come with the approval of the British and American governments, bringing a recipe for relieving Poland of its eastern guests. Moreover, he is the first arrival from the legendary West, and as a result he garnered the applause destined for our exiled army, navy, and air force, and their leaders, Sikorski, Anders and others.

All hopes for a free Poland appeared to rest with Mikołajczyk despite the communist domination of the Provisional Government of National Unity. Korboński himself was optimistic, believing that Mikołajczyk must have a plan, devised with the approval of the British and American governments: 'Surely Mikolajczyk wouldn't be so stupid as to come on his own with nothing at all.'[109] Mikołajczyk believed that he, as the leader of the largest political party, the Peasant Party, would win the elections. He thought that, so long as he pledged friendly relations with the Soviet Union, Poland would be allowed to act, like Czechoslovakia, as a bridge between the east and the west. The communists, however, feared not only losing power to Mikołajczyk, but that this would trigger a total occupation of Poland by Soviet forces. Many other Poles believed that there would soon be a war between the Soviet Union and the west.

The challenges facing the Provisional Government of National Unity were immense. The country needed to be settled and restored to economic life, and free elections held and the result of the elections accepted by the Soviet Union, Britain and the United States. Mikołajczyk had made a successful appeal to Roosevelt during his visit to Washington in June 1944 for American financial aid for the restoration of Poland. Aid flooded in from the American Red Cross, which cooperated with the Polish Red Cross until the latter was taken over by the communists, and spent around $7,000,000 in 1945–6; and from other American aid agencies including American Relief for Poland, the National Catholic Welfare Conference and the Committee for American Relief in Europe. The first shipments of UNRRA relief began arriving in Poland in September 1945, and it was quickly apparent that distribution was subject to political manipulation. Ration cards were given out according to political reliability rather than need, so that much aid ended up in the hands of government employees who then sold it on the black market. Bliss Lane wrote numerous memoranda to the State Department recommending linking political freedom with the granting of credits for the rebuilding of industry:

> We would be making a great mistake to grant half a billion dollars to the Polish Government: the Polish people would interpret our action as acquiescence in non-democratic and brutal practices. On the other hand, our refusal to give financial aid to an imposed government having the support of less than ten per cent of the population would be appreciated as a mark of sympathy for the people's plight.

The State Department ignored his advice and, in April 1946, was prepared to give two credits worth $50,000,000 and $40,000,000. Aid also came from Britain: Józef Retinger approached its government requesting that surplus war supplies be sent to Poland without payment. The British Government agreed and about £4,000,000 worth was despatched, including materials to build bridges, uniforms, 150 tons of field kitchens and domestic utensils, and machine tools. Retinger asked the Polish Provisional Government to thank the British for their gift but received a flat refusal to do so.[110]

The restoration of Poland's economic life could not be achieved until the country was more settled. Nor could the communists risk elections while the opposition was so demonstrably strong. The Underground Government, the Council of National Unity, dissolved itself on 1 July 1945, recognising that the imminent transfer of diplomatic recognition to the Provisional Government of National Unity made its continued existence pointless. Yet underground armed resistance against the communist security forces, the Polish Army and occupying Soviet forces continued. The government issued an amnesty in August 1945 calling on former members of the AK to turn their weapons in, whereupon they would not be punished for their opposition to the government; the deadline was extended to the end of September, then the middle of October and various amnesty periods were offered until the end of April 1947. According to communist records, 42,000 people revealed themselves during the first period, and by April 1947 a further 55,277 members of underground organisations had come into the open, including members of the NSZ and WiN. It was also revealed that a large quantity of weapons had been surrendered, ranging from small artillery pieces to pistols. In early 1947, the communists began to release some political prisoners, with over 25,000 being allowed to return home.[111]

These numbers reveal the scale of the opposition to the government. The situation in Poland from 1945 to 1947 was close to a civil war. Two prominent communists of the time later explained how they had viewed the situation. Roman Werfel described it as 'the law of the Wild West . . . Whoever shoots first will be the one to survive.' Jakub Berman commented: 'They shot us and we, out of necessity, shot at them; the shooting was fierce and people were often ruthlessly liquidated. Hundreds of party people, security people, and soldiers from the Internal Security Corps were killed; everyone who was suspect was stopped on the road.'[112] The western diplomats witnessed the scale of the internal strife for themselves. Robin Hankey, British chargé d'affaires in Warsaw, recalled that the resistance controlled the forests:

> Once we had to send a car down to Katowice with various diplomatic things and our driver gave a lift to another Pole in the car. The car was stopped by the underground army – in the forests on the way to Katowice. The passenger who was there unfortunately had the same name as a communist the Home Army wanted, and they took him out and shot him and left him in the ditch. And so our car went on without him.[113]

The Polish forces launched a major campaign in 1947 to crush the resistance for good, during which 1,486 were killed for the loss of only 136 members of the security forces.[114] The Polish forces were commanded by General Gustaw Paszkiewicz, who had returned from Britain. He caught one resistance commander in the Białystok region who, as a former AK parachutist, recognised his former commander from Britain and spat in his face. He was executed on the spot.[115]

The communists had no interest in setting an early election date, despite the Yalta undertakings, since they hoped that their consolidation of power would be strengthened by delay. The failure to fix a date was an oversight by the western allies and one which they soon regretted. The responses of the Polish Provisional Government to enquiries as to the date of the elections revealed a great deal. Cavendish-Bentinck reported: 'When I discuss the elections with these Communists, I can see that they regard this as an obstacle which will be quietly surmounted, and that it is a boring topic that I am compelled to discuss with them as a result of the out-moded ideas prevalent in London.' Hilary Minc, on a mission to Washington to obtain economic aid for Poland, told Acheson quite openly: 'Elections were ephemeral things which raised strong passions which however soon subsided.'[116]

The communists resorted to numerous tactics to weaken Mikołajczyk's position. They tried to split his Peasant Party by establishing a new Peasant Party loyal to the communist position, and, above all, the government embarked on a campaign to link him and his supporters to the resistance. Arms would be planted in the houses of Peasant Party members and then uncovered during searches by the UB; the size of the Citizens' Militia was greatly increased; and tens of thousands of non-communists were arrested and imprisoned. The communists also proposed a new electoral law and elections on a single electoral list. The British and American governments were firmly opposed to the concept of a single electoral list, while Mikołajczyk weakened his position within his own party and with the western governments by demanding his Peasant Party have 75 per cent of the names on the list, which was, of course, rejected by the communists. Instead of holding elections in 1946, the government called a referendum on three issues of importance. The text was agreed by the government on 27 April 1946, the electorate was to be asked:

1. Are you in favour of abolishing the Senate?
2. Do you want consolidation, in the future constitution of the economic system founded on agricultural reform and the nationalisation of basic national industries, including the statutory rights of private enterprise?
3. Do you want the consolidation of the western border of the Polish State on the Baltic, Oder River and Lusatian Neisse?

This was a challenge to Mikołajczyk because as one of his deputies expressed it: 'There have probably never been such minor programme differences among parties in Poland as now.' In fact the Peasant Party was in favour of an affirmative reply to all three questions, but Mikołajczyk believed that, with no sign of imminent elections, the referendum needed to be used as an expression of opposition to the government. Therefore, he decided that the Peasant Party must recommend voting against the first question, or as Korboński put it: 'The mysterious recipe for the liberation of Poland, prepared by world-famous physicians and communicated only to Mikołajczyk, required a negative answer to the first question.'[117]

The communists launched a huge propaganda campaign, *Trzy razy tak* ('Three Times Yes'), and also increased the terror campaign against the Peasant Party, as described by its chairman:

> There are no more killings, such as occurred during the winter, instead there are harassments, arrests, oppression, and actions forcing people to collaborate with the UB. Our people are being dismissed from administrative and economic posts. In Lower Silesia only one of our county administrators remains out of eighteen. They were dismissed in the course of two weeks. In one county administration eighteen people were dismissed. In the province of Lower Silesia our hamlet heads and village heads are being replaced by PPR members ... In Białystok province our party's provincial board is summoned to the UB often for questioning ... A strong tendency exists toward eliminating our people in the national councils ... Currently our opponents have undertaken action to connect us to the NSZ.[118]

Both Bliss Lane and Cavendish-Bentinck sent reports back to Washington and London citing examples of the violence being directed against the Peasant Party, and Byrnes and Bevin responded by making public their concerns over the scale of arrests and political malpractice in Poland.

The referendum took place on 30 June 1946, and the results were announced on 12 July. According to the official figures, 68.2 per cent voted in favour of the first question; 77.3 per cent in favour of the second; and 91.4 per cent in favour of the third. Yet the Peasant Party rightly disputed the results, citing those from Kraków where the 'weak nerves' of the communist chairman of the election board had enabled the results to be correctly tallied. According to the Kraków representative of the Peasant Party:

> When they began to count the ballots in the presence of our representatives, and found that an overwhelming majority of the cards bore negative answers to the first question, the chairman suddenly felt ill and left, bestowing the task to his deputy. A few minutes later, he too felt ill, and the same thing happened to all the Communist members of the board. Those who remained quickly completed the count and announced the results so that it could no longer be falsified.[119]

The results in Kraków showed that 84 per cent had voted no to the first question. This show of strength by the opposition terrified the

communists and provoked them to take action to damage the reputation of the opposition. After the Kielce pogrom, Osóbka-Morawski and
Berman both told Bliss Lane that the opposition was behind it. The fraud
surrounding the referendum was widely reported in the west by British
and American correspondents, and the government hoped that by blaming the pogrom on the opposition: 'the West, hearing of such a horrible
atrocity as a racial pogrom, would turn against the Poles and forget
about the referendum'.[120] The tactic worked to some extent as the west
began to lose interest in Polish affairs, but this was probably more a
general disengagement from east European affairs than a reaction to
perceived acts of Polish anti-semitism.

By the end of 1946, it was clear that neither the British nor the American government expected that the elections in Poland, now scheduled
for January 1947, would be 'free and unfettered'. All the signs were
pointing to an increase in terror, and Mikołajczyk estimated that around
50,000–60,000 of his supporters had been arrested, at least 110 murdered, and 142 party candidates had been arrested; and in 10 of the 52
electoral districts the Peasant Party's candidates had been disqualified
from standing. The new electoral law was published in October 1946
and presented the western governments with a dilemma. In a memorandum to the State Department, the British Government, through its
embassy in Washington, concluded: 'while the law contains such loop-
holes that it will enable the elections to be falsified, its actual provisions
do not seem to provide very solid ground for objection', except on
minor points. Mikołajczyk considered boycotting the elections but both
the western ambassadors in Poland advised him against this. He concluded
that the only chance for free elections was to make an appeal directly to the
three governments, British, American and Soviet, who had been party to
the agreements at Yalta and Potsdam on free elections. Accordingly on
18 December 1946, he sent a letter to all three governments listing pre-
electoral abuses. Bliss Lane urged the State Department to frame a
suitable protest quickly which he would give to the Polish Provisional
Government: speed was necessary to ensure that the American response
at least reached the press prior to the elections, or else there was the
risk that if the protest arrived after the elections then the Polish Government would claim that it had had no knowledge of electoral abuses
before the elections and so could not have been expected to act.
Cavendish-Bentinck made a similar appeal to the Foreign Office. The

American ambassador in Moscow, Walter Bedell Smith, also added his voice of protest in a note to Molotov. The western protests were delivered on 9 January and stated that neither the British nor the American government believed that elections on a single electoral list fulfilled the pledges made at Yalta and Potsdam. On 14 January, Bliss Lane informed the secretary of state of the Polish Provisional Government's response that the allegations were 'based on distorted facts and unfounded reproaches raised by anti-democratic elements' in Poland, and Molotov similarly responded to Bedell Smith that the Polish Provisional Government had not done anything wrong.[121]

The elections were held on 19 January 1947 and fraud was widespread. Candidates for opposition parties were disqualified, their representatives forbidden access to the polls and the secret ballot was widely disregarded. The falsification of the results was predictable: according to the official figures, 80 per cent of the electorate had voted in favour of the communist bloc and only 10 per cent for the Peasant Party. There was no repetition of the brave actions at Kraków during the referendum, so the true figure cannot be obtained. The western governments had decided not to send observers to the elections, partly because there were too few linguistically qualified impartial people available and partly because of a fear that they by their very presence could be interpreted as partaking in the electoral fraud. Although the communists maintained the façade of a coalition by making the general secretary of the Socialist Party, Józef Cyrankiewicz, prime minister, in fact communist domination was assured. The reins of power were held by the communists: Gomułka was vice premier and controlled nearly half the country through his role as minister for the recovered territories, Radkiewicz was minister of security, Minc was minister for industry and Modzelewski was foreign minister. A new 'little' constitution on the Soviet model was adopted, and in December 1948 the Socialist Party merged with the PPR to form a single Polish United Workers' Party (*Polska Zjednoczona Partia Robotnicza*) which fulfilled much the same purpose as the Communist Party in the Soviet Union. Both the British and American governments protested that the 1947 elections had not been 'free and unfettered', but they were ignored by the Polish Government. Indeed, the British seemed to signal their approval by signing a trade agreement with the new government on 27 April 1947. Bliss Lane reacted more strongly when, on 23 January, he asked to be recalled because he believed that remaining in Poland would be 'considered a tacit acceptance in the recent fraud'. Cavendish-Bentinck also left Poland in 1947 and was replaced as British ambassador by Donald St Clair Gainer.[122]

After the election, Mikołajczyk and his allies realised that they had no political future in Poland. The western diplomats agreed that Mikołajczyk's life might be in danger, and Bliss Lane urged the State Department to take action: 'As we took such an important role in urging Mikołajczyk to join the Provisional Govt I feel that we have far more than a humanitarian responsibility to endeavour to protect him from the fate of Mikhailovitch [the Yugoslav partisan commander]'. The British actually prepared plans to extract Mikołajczyk from Poland.[123] Mikołajczyk's life was indeed in danger. On 18 October 1947, he heard that he, Korboński and Wincenty Bryja, the treasurer of the Peasant Party, were to be stripped of their parliamentary immunity at a session of parliament due to start within the week, and he also learnt that a military court in Warsaw had already been ordered to try them and sentence them to death. Korboński felt that Mikołajczyk was exaggerating: 'Surely his arrest would cause an international scandal, and the British and American governments would intervene.' But in Bulgaria the opposition leader Nikola Petkov had just been executed, and in Rumania the opposition leader, Iuliu Maniu, was on trial for his life. Korboński and Mikołajczyk conferred and made separate plans for escape. On 26 October, the press announced that Mikołajczyk had crossed into the west, smuggled through the Soviet and British zones of Germany; on 5 November, Korboński followed via Sweden. Bryja remained in Poland and was arrested and imprisoned until 1954.[124]

The lack of international reaction from the west depressed the Polish people: 'foreign observers noted that an atmosphere of despondency, apathy, and fatalism prevailed over society'.[125] The Poles asked themselves, what had the war been all about? Britain had ostensibly gone to war to preserve the Polish state yet was now willing to sit back and see an alien political culture thrust on the country. Far from being a call to arms, as a number of Poles had interpreted it, Churchill's speech at Fulton on 5 March 1946 was a recognition that Europe had been split into two spheres of influence for the foreseeable future:

From Stettin in the Baltic to Trieste in the Adriatic an iron curtain has descended across the Continent. Behind that line lie all the capitals of the ancient states of Central and Eastern Europe. Warsaw, Berlin, Prague, Vienna, Budapest, Belgrade, Bucharest and Sofia, all these famous cities and the populations around them lie in what I must call the Soviet sphere, and all are subject in one form or another, not only to Soviet influence but to a very high and, in some cases, increasing measure of control from Moscow.[126]

The Polish novelist and dramatist Witold Gombrowicz, who had spent the war in exile in Argentina, described the effect of the end of the war:

The end of the war did not bring liberation to the Poles. In the battle-grounds of Central Europe, it simply meant swapping one form of evil for another, Hitler's henchmen for Stalin's. While sycophants cheered and rejoiced at the 'emancipation of the Polish people from the feudal yoke', the same lit cigarette was simply passed from hand to hand in Poland and continued to burn the skin of people.[127]

Poland now became a forgotten backwater, trapped behind the 'Iron Curtain', and largely ignored by the world until the rise of Solidarity (*Solidarność*) in the late 1970s and early 1980s.

# 18

# The Final Chapter

The memoirs of General Anders, published in 1949, carried the title *Bez ostatniego rozdziału* (*Without the Final Chapter*). The Second World War might have finished, but the battle for the history of the war had begun. He and other leading diplomats and politicians believed that the war had ended before Poland had regained her freedom. Other titles also reflected this. Jan Ciechanowski, the wartime Polish ambassador in Washington, called his memoirs *Defeat in Victory*. Stanisław Mikołajczyk went even further, entitling his *The Rape of Poland*. The belief that the western allies had betrayed Polish interests to the Soviet Union was shared by non-Polish politicians. Arthur Bliss Lane, the first post-war American ambassador to Poland, wrote of his two years in Poland under the title *I Saw Freedom Betrayed*. All these memoirs have one thing in common: a belief that there was unfinished business at the end of the Second World War.

The battle for the history of the Second World War was fought throughout the Cold War and followed its fortunes. What was said about the Second World War often depended on where it was said and the stage that the Cold War had reached. Already in 1949, the English translation of Anders's memoirs carried the less controversial title of *An Army in Exile*, although the contents, including much about wartime politics and diplomacy as well as the military matters that directly concerned him, were unchanged.

The Cold War formed the backdrop to the reappraisal of an issue that caused continued offence to the Polish community: the correct attribution of responsibility for the murder of the Polish officers whose graves had been found by the Germans at Katyń in 1943. The Polish-American community had been greatly angered by what they considered to be the pro-Soviet policies of the Roosevelt administration and the wartime State Department. The Truman administration after the war had a very different approach as demonstrated by the proclamation of the Truman Doctrine in 1947, American support for the Berlin Airlift in 1948 and the formation of NATO in 1949. As the Cold War was getting under way, it was now possible to enquire into the actions of the Soviet Union without being seen to denigrate a wartime ally. Consequently, in April 1949, the president of the Polish-American Congress (PAC), Charles Rozmarek, asked the American ambassador to the United Nations, Warren Austin, to 'demand an immediate and impartial investigation of one of the world's most heinous crimes'. Austin refused, but the PAC continued to press for an inquiry. In July 1949 a journalist, Julius Epstein, had a series of articles on Katyń published by the *New York Herald Tribune* which included a request for the establishment of an American Committee of Investigation of the Katyń Murders. His articles aroused the interest and support of a Democrat congressman from Indiana, Ray Madden, whose proposal for an investigation by the International Red Cross won no congressional support. Epstein then approached Bliss Lane with the suggestion of forming a private committee to press for an investigation, to which he responded warmly, and a committee was established under his presidency. Committee members included the former director of the Office of Strategic Services, William Donovan, and Allan Dulles. The committee had no impact until the revelation that American POWs in Korea had been shot in the base of the back of the skull, which eerily resembled the Katyń murders. Thus, when Madden introduced a motion on 18 September 1951 for an investigation to be carried out into Katyń by a committee of seven members of the House of Representatives, it was passed unanimously.[1]

The Madden Committee began its hearings on 4 February 1952. Its aim was to 'record evidence, data and facts that will eventually and officially establish the guilt of the nation that perpetrated the greatest crime of genocide in all recorded history', and also to investigate whether the massacre had been reported fairly in the free world since April 1943.[2] The Madden Committee sent letters of invitation to the governments of the Soviet Union, Poland and the Federal Republic of Germany and to the Polish Government-in-Exile in London. The London Poles and the Germans responded favourably. The Soviet embassy in Washington responded on 29 February 1952 that it was insulted by the request and reminded the committee that the Soviet Union had thoroughly investigated the matter in 1944 and that the Burdenko Commission had reported that the Germans were undeniably responsible. The Soviets also launched a publicity campaign designed to restate its arguments on German responsibility.[3] The reaction to the Madden Committee in the corridors of Whitehall was distinctly muted, for, although few believed that the Germans were responsible, the Foreign Office had no desire to see its wartime attempts to suppress the evidence of Soviet culpability laid bare. Some British politicians, however, viewed the matter differently. One hundred MPs of all political persuasions signed a motion by Sir Douglas Savory, Ulster Unionist MP for South Antrim, calling for the government to support the Madden Committee's plan to submit its report to the United Nations and for the United Nations to bring it before the International Court of Justice.[4]

The Madden Committee presented its interim report on 2 July 1952, which concluded unanimously that the NKVD had carried out the massacre, not later than the spring of 1940. The committee's final report, on 22 December 1952, concluded that the American Government had deliberately concealed and withheld evidence that pointed to Soviet guilt, and it was submitted to the United Nations on 10 February 1953. No further action was taken, however, because the United States was then engaged in delicate peace negotiations with North Korea and Soviet support was needed for them. Furthermore, the Madden Committee had become unpopular for besmirching the reputation of the Roosevelt government as a war-winning administration, over what many Americans saw as a minor issue of no interest to the American people.[5]

In 1962 Janusz Zawodny published *Death in the Forest*, a survey of the Katyń murders, which produced little reaction in Britain and the United States. But a reprint in 1971 and the publication of *Katyn: A Crime Without Parallel* by Louis FitzGibbon led to considerable interest in Britain. There was a lengthy correspondence on the issue in *The Times* and the *Daily Telegraph*, and on 19 April 1971 the BBC showed a film about Katyń, *The Issue to Be Avoided*. The Conservative MP for Abingdon, Airey Neave, put down a motion in the House of Commons calling for a United Nations investigation into Katyń which was signed by 60 MPs.

In January 1972, a Katyń Memorial Fund was established in London and 165 MPs signed a motion welcoming it. Its organisers published Owen O'Malley's 1943 memorandum to Eden, quoted in Chapter 11, which indicated Soviet guilt. Airey Neave wrote to the foreign secretary, Sir Alec Douglas-Home, on 28 February 1972, asking if a Katyń Memorial could be constructed in one of London's Royal Parks, but the Foreign Office objected vociferously to the idea of any monument anywhere at all, as it was convinced that such a monument would poison relations with the Soviet Union. Certainly, the Soviets were greatly angered by the proposal, mounting a huge publicity campaign and making an official protest to the British Government. Permission was refused to site the monument in Thurloe Place on land controlled jointly by the Victoria and Albert Museum and by the Department of Education. The next proposal, to place it in the disused churchyard of St Luke's Church in Chelsea, was initially accepted by Kensington and Chelsea Council, but government pressure on the Church authorities and opposition from local residents led to a court case in 1974 which ended the project at St Luke's. Kensington and Chelsea Council then offered a site in the Kensington Church Cemetery in Gunnersbury Park on the outskirts of London, and although the Soviet embassy sent bullying letters to the council, on 18 September 1974 the Katyń memorial, a 21-foot high obelisk with a carved inscription '1940', was unveiled by Maria Chełmecka, a widow of one of the murdered officers. The unveiling was attended by representatives of the British Legion and by 20 MPs. The War Office forbade officers to attend in uniform but a few retired officers did so. Margaret Thatcher, leader of the Conservative Party, then in opposition, sent a representative, and a Labour peer, Emmanuel Shinwell, also broke the official government line by attending. The Foreign Office did not sent a representative on the grounds that 'it has never been proved to Her Majesty's Government's satisfaction who was responsible'.[6] In 1980, however, after a change of government, Barney Hayhoe, under secretary of state at the Ministry of Defence, attended the memorial service on the fortieth anniversary of the Katyń massacre.[7]

Within Poland a veil was drawn over the issue of Katyń. The Polish Government toed the Soviet line on German culpability and joined the Soviets in protesting against the Madden Committee and the construction of the Katyń memorial in London. There is also considerable evidence to suggest that widows and children of the officers murdered at Katyń

suffered from discrimination regarding their jobs, promotions and housing. But as the child of one victim, Stanisława Dec, noted:

> The worst was the silence, the prohibition against speaking openly of their
> death, of a dignified burial, for half a century. It was forbidden even to
> visit the places of execution. My youngest sister, Zosia, always envied those
> friends of hers whose parents had died in Auschwitz. They at least could
> go to the grave sites, and didn't have to hide the truth.[8]

The rise of *Solidarność* led a number of Poles to question the official
version of events publicly. On the 1981 anniversary of the discovery of
the graves, over 2,000 people gathered in the Powązki cemetery in Warsaw for an unofficial ceremony, and their brave action led to a protest
in *Pravda*.[9] The loosening of the communist bloc under the Soviet presidency of Mikhail Gorbachev led to revelations on Katyń, and at an
official ceremony at the Kremlin on 13 April 1990 he presented the last
communist president of Poland, Wojciech Jaruzelski, with two thick
files of NKVD documents on the massacre along with lists of the victims. The Poles reacted strongly to this evidence, demanding an official
Soviet apology, a trial of those who committed the murders and of those
responsible for the cover-up, and compensation for the families of the
victims. The Soviets responded with hostility and the Katyń issue continued to poison Polish-Soviet relations.[10]

The official Soviet line was that the massacre had been carried out by
the NKVD on Beria's orders, but this was breached by the Russian
president, Boris Yeltsin, when he handed the first post-war non-
communist Polish president, Lech Wałęsa, two documents: Beria's order
of 5 March 1940 and an extract from minutes of the Politburo meeting
of that day when Beria's proposal was discussed and approved, bearing
the clear signature of Stalin.[11] In 2002 a chapel was dedicated in the
Military Cathedral in Warsaw that bears the names of the known victims
of Katyń and other massacres in the Soviet Union carried out at the same
time. In 2007 the film *Katyń* was produced by Andrzej Wajda to critical
acclaim: in 2010 it was shown in Russia for the first time. In 2010 the
Russian prime minister, Vladimir Putin, invited Donald Tusk, the Polish
prime minister, to join him at Katyń to commemorate the seventieth
anniversary of the massacre as a gesture of reconciliation between Russia and Poland; both men attended, Putin being the first Russian leader
to do so. Three days later, on 10 April 2010, the Polish president, Lech

Kaczyński, and his entourage were killed in a plane crash on their way to a Polish ceremony at Katyń.

In the years immediately after the war as the communist government of Poland sought to establish its rule over the country, AK members were hunted down and, when caught, were tried, imprisoned and, in some cases, executed. Others were apprehended by the NKVD, which was still active in Poland, and despatched to the Gulag. Most of the leaders of the AK, including Bór-Komorowski, had been liberated from German captivity by the forces of the western allies and few of them returned to Poland, preferring exile in the west.

The fate of the AK affected the commemoration of the cataclysmic event – the Warsaw Uprising. While Stalinisation was in full swing, tending the graves of AK soldiers could lead to arrest. No scholar in Poland could write an account of the uprising, and when Adam Borkiewicz attempted to do so, he had all his documents seized by the Security Police and his wife was imprisoned for collating his material. The communist line was that the AK was to be disparaged. Indeed, on the second anniversary of the Warsaw ghetto uprising, of which the communists approved, Colonel Mieczysław Dąbrowski of the Polish Army stated: 'The [Nazi] air force, the SS, German tanks, Polish hooligans, Polish reactionaries, and, in fact, the Home Army: they all fought against the [Jewish] insurgents.' During this period the only wartime resistance forces acknowledged by and lauded by the authorities were the AL and the Jewish resistance.

After 1956 Poland underwent a period of rapid and thorough de-Stalinisation, and the government's attitude towards the Warsaw Uprising began to change. The primacy of resistance was still given to the AL, despite the fact that only 400 members took part in the uprising. Following an amnesty in 1956, about 25,000 AK members were released from prison, and the Soviet Union was approached to release its AK prisoners from the Gulag. The government also assured AK fighters in exile that they would have full rights of citizenship should they choose to return to Poland. Polish historiography of the uprising now focused on the AK rank and file, while the officers were still portrayed as reactionaries, if not as the fascists they were once called. Borkiewicz's study of the Warsaw Uprising was finally published in 1957. In 1956 *Kanal*, a film by Andrzej Wajda about a group of AK soldiers struggling through the sewers during the uprising, was released. The twentieth anniversary of the Warsaw Uprising was celebrated in Warsaw: speeches at the commemoration spoke of the 'lunacy and political diversion' of the AK leadership, while at the same time praising the efforts of the common AK soldier and the people of Warsaw. In the United States, the twentieth anniversary was marked by President Lyndon Johnson hosting a reception at the White House at which Bór-Komorowski was the guest of honour.

The rise of *Solidarność* influenced attitudes towards the uprising. It drew its own lessons and remained firmly against any attempt to overthrow the communist government by force of arms, determinedly adhering to the principle of passive resistance. *Solidarność* also established its historical links with the wartime Underground Government by publishing a news-sheet with the same title, *Biuletyn Informacyjny*, as that published under the German occupation. The Polish Government attempted to reassert its position as the guardian of the memory of the Warsaw Uprising by agreeing, at the fortieth anniversary celebrations in 1984, to erect a large memorial to the Warsaw insurgents, which was officially unveiled in 1989 by President Jaruzelski, who in 1944 had been a young officer in Berling's army watching Warsaw going up in flames from the other side of the Vistula. The 1980s also saw the construction of the Little Insurgent Monument in Warsaw, depicting a boy soldier weighed down by an adult-sized helmet and clutching a Sten gun.

When the fiftieth anniversary of the Warsaw Uprising was celebrated in 1994, Poland was once again free. Invitations were extended to all the western allies whose pilots had flown support missions during the uprising, and to the presidents of Germany and Russia. The Russian president, Boris Yeltsin, declined, but the German president, Roman Herzog, attended and asked 'forgiveness for what has been done to you by Germans'. In 2004 the Warsaw Uprising Museum was opened in Warsaw on 31 July, and the commemoration reception the following day, the sixtieth anniversary of the start of the uprising, was attended by the German chancellor, Gerhard Schröder; the American secretary of state, Colin Powell; and the British deputy prime minister, John Prescott. Russia again failed to send a representative.[12]

At the end of the war Warsaw lay in ruins. The 840-acre area that had formed the ghetto had been totally destroyed by the Germans after the ghetto uprising. The 1944 Warsaw Uprising had reduced most of the Old Town (Stare Miasto) to rubble, and everywhere else there were damaged buildings from the 1939 campaign and the uprising, as well as the debris from the deliberate dynamiting of important buildings by the Germans after the collapse of the uprising. In January 1945, the Lublin Committee decided that Warsaw would be restored as the capital of Poland and so a vast rebuilding programme was begun, overseen by the Warsaw Restoration Bureau (*Biuro Odbudowy Stolicy*, BOS), under the leadership of the architect and engineer Roman Piotrowski.

BOS had two priorities: to restore historical Warsaw and to provide urgently needed housing for Warsaw's population. Photographs and drawings were collected to recreate the Old Town as a facsimile of the pre-war district, work which was overseen by the Historic Architecture Department, led by Professor Jan Zachwatowicz. By September 1950, the Old Town had been rebuilt, and the department was wound up. The success of its endeavours was reflected in 1980 when the Old Town was added to UNESCO's World Heritage List. The mansions and palaces along the Royal Route, running along Krakowskie Przedmieście, Nowy Świat and Aleje Ujazdowskie, were restored to their pre-war glory and are now mainly the offices of government ministries and public bodies. Reconstruction of the New Town was begun, but then the money ran out.

The architectural development of Warsaw from 1949 to 1956 has been termed 'social realism'. Apart from the restoration of old Warsaw, three major projects were undertaken to rebuild housing and to restore industry and to create a new socialist city: the East-West route (Trasa W-Z), the enormous Marzałkowska Housing project and the rebuilding of the industrial areas. Most of the remaining damaged buildings in Warsaw were gradually demolished and cheap, quickly constructed buildings put in their place. Housing for the workers of Warsaw was built on top of the rubble of the Warsaw ghetto. Despite the shortage of money, finance was found to build the ugly Palace of Culture, which dominates the city centre. Historical reconstruction ended with the assumption of power by Gomułka in 1956. He came from peasant stock, disliked Warsaw and despised its intelligentsia. While he was in power the reconstruction of the Łazienki Royal Palace, begun earlier, was completed but a halt was called to the reconstruction of streets in the New Town such as Ul. Długa. Instead, a massive programme of cheap housing and office buildings was begun – termed 'pauper-modernism'. Gomułka opposed the rebuilding of the Royal Castle, burnt during the 1939 campaign and blown up by the Germans in 1944, on the grounds that it was a symbol of feudalism and of the rule of the nobility. In 1970 Gomułka was replaced by Edward Gierek, an educated man, who in 1971 demonstrated his commitment to the history of Warsaw by supporting the restoration of the Royal Castle.[13]

The historiography of Polish-Jewish relations during the Second World War was subjected to political manipulation in communist Poland. The role of organisations such as Żegota was underplayed because of their loyalty to the Polish Government-in-Exile. Instead, there was an emphasis on Jewish resistance, especially the Warsaw ghetto uprising, a monument to which was constructed shortly after the war using Swedish stone ordered by Hitler for his victory arch in Berlin. The publication of Emanuel Ringelblum's *Notes from the Warsaw Ghetto* in 1958 was heavily edited to omit many favourable references to the Christian Poles who tried to help the Jews, and this distorted version was sold and translated abroad. In April 1967, a stark grey monument was unveiled at Auschwitz in front of an audience of 200,000, many of whom were former inmates, and the government made political capital out of the ceremony, calling it a grand anti-fascist meeting. In 1968 the communist attitude towards Jews changed: the Soviet Union was hostile to the state of Israel, and its victory over the Soviet-supported Arab countries in the 1967 Six Day War led to an anti-semitic campaign in the Soviet Union and in the Soviet satellite countries, including Poland. Under the new historiography, the Jews were seen as ingrates who not only refused to acknowledge the widespread assistance they had received from the Poles but also, after collaborating with the Germans, had perpetrated crimes against the Poles in the last year of the war and during the early post-war years.[14]

In 1987 the debate on wartime Polish-Jewish relations was reignited by the publication of an article by Jan Błoński, 'Biedni Polacy patrzą na getto' ('Poor Poles Look at the Ghetto'), in the weekly Catholic magazine *Tygodnik Powszechny*. He argued that Polish anti-semitism before the war had been widespread, and the result had been that the majority of the Poles had stood by while the Jews were exterminated, neither betraying them nor assisting them. This spurred a furious debate in

*Tygodnik Powszechny.* During an international conference on the history and culture of Polish Jewry held in Jerusalem in February 1988, a special session was devoted to the ethical problems of the Holocaust in Poland and covered many of the issues raised by Błoński and his supporters and detractors. These have been gathered in a volume, edited by Antony Polonsky, *'My Brother's Keeper?'*

A new debate was sparked off in 2001 with the publication of *Neighbors: The Destruction of the Jewish Community in Jedwabne* by Jan Gross. The revelation that Poles had collaborated with the Germans in the murder of the Jews drew an angry reaction since it challenged 'the slogan "Poland brought forth no Quisling", born under German occupation, developed with celerity into an axiom of Polish national life'.[15] Gross's book has been criticised for his failure to use German material, which allegedly led him to underplay the German encouragement of the massacre, and furthermore for entirely ignoring the question of Jewish collaboration both with the Soviets and with the Germans. It was, nonetheless, a milestone in the discussion of this terrible subject.[16]

Poland was the graveyard of Polish and European Jewry. The Germans destroyed the extermination camps before retreating, leaving little to be seen. At Treblinka there are symbolic railway lines leading to the execution area, which is covered in hundreds of jagged memorial stones, each dedicated to a lost Jewish community. There is also a monument inscribed *Nigdy Więcej* (Never Again). There was even less left at Bełżec, but now there is a memorial, erected in 2004, and a museum. Sobibor is marked only by a memorial mound and a small museum. Majdanek was overrun before the Germans had finished their demolitions so there is more left: rows of wooden huts and a mausoleum above reconstructed gas chambers containing the ashes of Jews and Poles murdered there; a memorial was unveiled in 1969, the twenty-fifth anniversary of its liberation.

The commemoration of Auschwitz has been a source of controversy. Auschwitz I, the concentration camp in which Christian Poles and Soviet POWs were the most numerous inmates throughout the war, was built around the former Polish artillery barracks and a tobacco factory. This is why so many of the original buildings have survived and why the main museum facilities, with an area devoted to each nationality of the victims of the whole Auschwitz complex, are located there, with the entrance marked by the wrought-iron sign *Arbeit Macht Frei*. Auschwitz-Birkenau or Auschwitz II, the extermination camp, is approached along the railway lines, and contains the remains of the huts in which the inmates lived and of the gas chambers. The ashes of the victims are scattered between the huts and the entire area is regarded as a graveyard and is on UNESCO's World Heritage List. In 1979 Pope John Paul II said Mass in front of 500,000 people in the grounds of Auschwitz-Birkenau, for which an 85-foot-high cross was erected (and then removed). In 1984 the Carmelite nuns opened a convent near Auschwitz I and erected the 'Pope's cross', which was visible from the camp. The convent was closed in 1993 after Jewish protests, but the cross remained and Jewish protests continued, arguing that the whole of Auschwitz should be regarded as a Jewish memorial. This in turn angered Polish Catholics who argued that the cross honoured Catholic martyrs such as Saint Maximilian Kolbe, the Polish Franciscan friar who volunteered to die in the place of a stranger. The debate over the primacy of remembrance continues to this day at Auschwitz.

Many of the debates on Polish-Jewish relations stem from the ignorance of the importance Poland had for the Jews in the centuries when they were persecuted elsewhere in Europe and of the value of this Jewish presence among the Poles. It can only be hoped that the much-delayed opening of the Museum of the History of Polish Jews in Warsaw, now due in the spring of 2013, will enhance greater understanding.

During the Second World War, members of the Polish armed forces and Polish civilians died all over the world. Many of the Poles who died during captivity or exile in the Soviet Union have no known graves, but restoration of Polish cemeteries in Kazakhstan and Uzbekistan has begun, and in 2002 a memorial to the Poles who died in Uzbekistan was erected in Tashkent. For those who died after leaving the Soviet Union, their graves are tended in cemeteries from Pahlevi and Teheran in Iran, to Iraq, Palestine, India and countries in Africa. Polish servicemen lie buried in cemeteries such as Auberive and Langannerie in France, Newark in Britain, Arnhem-Oosterbeek in the Netherlands and Monte Cassino in Italy.[17] There are also graves of members of the air forces of the western allies who died in Poland: Poznań Old Garrison cemetery contains the graves of British airmen shot down on supply flights to Poland and those shot after the Great Escape; Kraków Rakowiecki cemetery contains the graves of those allied fighters killed while supplying the Warsaw Uprising.

Commemoration has often been difficult. In the summer of 1946, a fund appeal was launched in Britain for a memorial to the Polish Air Force, which received the support of Air Marshals Portal and Trenchard. The Polish Air Force Memorial was erected on Western Avenue on the edge of Northolt Aerodrome, from which many Polish Battle of Britain fighter pilots had flown, on 2 November 1948.[18] In 1993, a memorial in honour of the Battle of Britain unveiled on the cliffs of Dover showed the insignia of all squadrons who had taken part in the battle – except for the two Polish ones, but after a public outcry the insignia of the Kościuszko and Poznań squadrons were added.[19] On 19 September 2009, in front of an invited audience of veterans and guests, including the author, the Polish War Memorial was unveiled at the National Memorial Arboretum in Staffordshire.

In Poland, since the end of communism, Warsaw has seen an explosion in the number of memorials commemorating events in the Second World War. During the communist period, the Tomb of the Unknown Soldier in the Saxon Gardens, badly damaged during the war, was restored, but references to the Polish-Soviet War were omitted, and little mention was made of the battles fought by the Poles under the command of the western allies during the Second World War. In 1990 new plaques were erected reflecting Polish sacrifices from 1918 to 1945. The importance of the Warsaw Uprising in the city's history is reflected by the sheer number of memorials and plaques to individual AK platoons scattered across the city. In 1995 a monument to those deported and murdered in the east was erected on a busy road junction, which lists all the main towns of Kresy from which the victims were taken and which are now outside Poland's borders. After a campaign throughout the 1990s, in November 2008, stones were placed in the streets of Warsaw marking the outline of the Warsaw ghetto. Veterans too have received recognition: in 1992 those from the Polish Air Force were received with full military ceremony in Plac Piłsudskiego by Lech Wałęsa. In September 1993, the body of Sikorski was exhumed from Newark Cemetery and transferred to Poland, and reburied in the royal crypt at Wawel Castle in Kraków. Post-war events have not been forgotten either: in September 2003, the British prime minister, Tony Blair, issued a formal apology for the failure of the British Government to invite the Poles to the 1946 Victory Parade, and amends were made when the Poles led the sixtieth anniversary parade in London on 9 July 2005. Also in 2005, in a speech in Riga marking the sixtieth anniversary of the end of the Second World War, President George W. Bush issued an apology for the consequences of the 1945 Yalta conference: 'The captivities of millions in Central and Eastern Europe will be remembered as one of the greatest wrongs of history.'

Poland has always considered herself to be at the heart of Europe, the last bulwark of civilisation before the alien east began. The communist period was the only time when Poland was cut off from her heritage, forced to become a satellite of her powerful eastern neighbour, the Soviet Union. The end of communism in Poland has meant that the Poles can now look westwards again: hence, Polish pride at Poland's membership of NATO since 1999 and of the European Union since 2004. This return home has taken time, but now that Poland is once again free, the final chapter of the Second World War has at last been written.

# *Appendix 1*

1. Polish Order of Battle – 1 September 1939, 4 a.m.

## COMMANDER-IN-CHIEF: Marshal Edward Rydz-Śmigły

## HIGH COMMAND

Chief of Staff: Brigadier-General Wacław Stachiewicz

Air Force and Anti-Aircraft High Command: Brigadier-General Józef Zając

Chief of Artillery: Brigadier-General Stanisław Miller

Chief of Engineers and Fortifications: Brigadier-General Mieczysław Dąbkowski

Chief of Armoured Troops: Colonel Józef Kapciuk

## ARMY KARPATY   Commander: General Kazimierz Fabrycy

Operational Group 'Jasło'
  2nd Mountain Brigade
  3rd Mountain Brigade
Detachment 'Hungary'
  2nd ('Podole') KOP Regiment
  Karpaty National Guard Brigade
Group No. 2 'Kaw'
  Warsaw Mechanised Brigade
  46th Light Artillery Detachment
  47th Light Artillery Detachment

Group Tarnów
  22nd Infantry Division
  38th Infantry Division
*Army Support Units*: 1st Motorised Artillery Regt; 9th Heavy
  Artillery Detachment; 12 Anti-Aircraft sections.
*Air Command*: 31st Attack Squadron; 56th Reconnaissance Squadron.

## ARMY KRAKÓW   Commander: Brigadier-General Antoni Szylling

Group Śląsk: Commander: Brigadier-General Jan Jagmin-Sadowski
  23rd Infantry Division
  55th Infantry Division
  Katowice Fortress Brigade Group
  95th Heavy Artillery Detachment
  1 Anti-Aircraft section
Group Bielsko: Commander: Brigadier-General Mieczysław Boruta-
Spiechowicz
  1st Mountain Brigade
  21st Mountain Infantry Division
  Group Colonel Misianga
  6th Infantry Division
  7th Infantry Division
  10th Mechanised Brigade
  Kraków Cavalry Brigade
  11th Infantry Division
  45th Infantry Division
  5th Heavy Artillery Regiment
*Army Support Units*: 64th Light Artillery Detachment; 65th Motorised Engineer Battalion; Armoured Trains 51, 52, 54; 1st Motorised
  Anti-Aircraft Battalion; Kraków Local Defence Regiment; 12 Anti-
  Aircraft sections.
*Air Command*: 121st Fighter Squadron; 122nd Fighter Squadron;
  24th Attack Squadron; 23rd Reconnaissance Squadron; 26th
  Reconnaissance Squadron.

## ARMY ŁÓDŹ   Commander: General Juliusz Rómmel

Group Piotrków: Commander: Brigadier-General Wiktor Thommée
  30th Infantry Division

Wołyń Cavalry Brigade
2nd Battalion 4th Heavy Artillery Regiment
7th Heavy Machine Gun Battalion
2nd Infantry Division
10th Infantry Division
(22nd Mountain Division)
28th Infantry Division
Kresy Cavalry Brigade

*Army Support Units*: 6th Heavy Artillery Regiment; 4th Heavy Artillery Regiment; 2nd Tank Battalion, Headquarters; 50th Motorised Engineer Battalion; 3rd Heavy Machine Gun Battalion; Armoured Train 53; 4 Anti-Aircraft sections.

*Air Command*: 161st Fighter Squadron; 162nd Fighter Squadron; 32nd Attack Squadron; 63rd Reconnaissance Squadron; 66th Reconnaissance Squadron.

## ARMY MODLIN    Commander: Brigadier-General Emil Krukowicz-Przedrzymirski

8th Infantry Division
20th Infantry Division
Nowogródzka Cavalry Brigade
Mazowsze Cavalry Brigade

*Army Support Units*: Modlin Regiment (improvised); Kazan Regiment (improvised); Plock Local Defence Unit; Pułtusk Local Defence Unit; Zegrze Local Defence Unit; 98th Heavy Artillery Detachment; 60th Motorised Engineer Battalion; Armoured Trains 13, 14, 15; 1st Heavy Artillery Regiment.

*Air Command*: 152nd Fighter Squadron; 41st Attack Squadron; 53rd Reconnaissance Squadron.

## ARMY POMORZE    Commander: General Władysław Bortnowski

Group East: Commander: Brigadier-General Mikołaj Bołtuć
    4th Infantry Division
    16th Infantry Division
Jabłonowo Local Defence Regiment

Group Czersk: Commander: Brigadier-General Stanisław Grzmot-Skotnicki

Pomorze Cavalry Brigade
Chojnice Local Defence Regiment
Kościerzyna Local Defence Battalion

9th Infantry Division
15th Infantry Division
27th Infantry Division

*Army Support Units*: 46th Motorised Engineer Battalion; Vistula Local Defence Regiment; Toruń Local Defence Regiment; Chełmno National Guard Regiment; River Flotilla (7 vessels).

*Air Command*: 141st Fighter Squadron; 142nd Fighter Squadron; 42nd Attack Squadron; 43rd Reconnaissance Squadron; 46th Reconnaissance Squadron.

## ARMY POZNAŃ   Commander: General Tadeusz Kutrzeba

14th Infantry Division
17th Infantry Division
25th Infantry Division
26th Infantry Division
Wielkopolska Cavalry Brigade
Podole Cavalry Brigade
Pomorze National Guard Battalion

*Army Support Units*: 7th Heavy Artillery Regiment; 5th Heavy Machine Gun Battalion; 47th Motorised Engineer Battalion; Armoured Trains 11, 12.

*Air Command*: 131st Fighter Squadron; 132nd Fighter Squadron; 33rd Reconnaissance Squadron; 34th Attack Squadron.

## ARMY PRUSY   Commander: General Stefan Dąb-Biernacki

Group Brigadier-General J. Kruszewski
Cavalry Group No. 1: Commander: Brigadier-General Rudolf Dreszer
19th Infantry Division
Wilno Cavalry Brigade
Group Brigadier-General Stanisław Skwarczyński
3rd Infantry Division

12th Infantry Division
36th Infantry Division
Northern Group – General Stefan Dąb-Biernacki
13th Infantry Division
29th Infantry Division
39th Infantry Division
44th Infantry Division

*Army Support Units*: 1st Heavy Artillery Regiment; 3rd Heavy Artillery Regiment; 50th Heavy Artillery Detachment; 1st Light Tank Battalion; 81st Motorised Engineer Battalion; 1st Co., 2nd Engineer Battalion; Armoured Train 55; 9 Anti-Aircraft sections.

## GROUP GRODNO   Commander: Brigadier-General Józef Olsyna-Wilczyński

Grodno Local Defence Regiment
Wilno Local Defence Regiment Headquarters
Baranowicze KOP Regiment
Kleck Light Artillery Battalion
9 Anti-Aircraft sections

## GROUP KUTNO   (Never mobilised as a group)

5th Infantry Division
24th Infantry Division
9th Heavy Artillery Regiment
71st Light Artillery Detachment

## GROUP NAREW   Commander: Brigadier-General Czesław Młot-Fijałkowski

18th Infantry Division
33rd Infantry Division
Podlasie Cavalry Brigade
Suwałki Cavalry Brigade

*Army Support Units*: Osowiec Local Defence Unit; Wizna Local Defence Unit; 53rd Motorised Engineer Battalion; 34th Fortress Group; 81st Light Artillery Detachment.

*Air Command*: 13th Reconnaissance Squadron; 5th Attack Squadron; 151st Fighter Squadron.

## GROUP WYSZKÓW    Commander: Brigadier-General Wincenty Kowalski

1st Infantry Division
41st Infantry Division
Armoured Train 55
35th Infantry Division
2nd Heavy Artillery Regiment

### National Guard – *Obrona Narodowa*

82 battalions, of which 11 would be absorbed or combined with active units.
1,600 officers and 50,000 men.

### Frontier Defence Corps – KOP

34 infantry battalions
12 cavalry squadrons
2 light artillery battalions
4 engineer companies

Source: Zaloga & Madeja, *The Polish Campaign*, 41–4

## 2. Norway 1940

### Polish Independent Highland Brigade    Commander: General Zygmunt Szyszko-Bohusz

1st Demi-Brigade
  1st Battalion
  2nd Battalion
2nd Demi-Brigade
  3rd Battalion
  4th Battalion

## 3. France 1940

**1st Grenadier Division    Commander: General Bronisław Duch**

  1st Warsaw Grenadier Regiment
  2nd Wielkopolska Grenadier Regiment
  3rd Silesian Grenadier Regiment
  8th Uhlan Regiment
  1st Wilno Light Artillery Regiment
  1st Pomeranian Heavy Artillery Regiment
  1st Modlin Engineer Battalion
  1st Gdańsk Signals Battalion

**2nd Infantry Fusiliers Division    Commander: General Bronisław Prugar-Ketling**

  4th Infantry Regiment
  5th Infantry Regiment
  6th Infantry Regiment
  2nd Infantry Divisional Reconnaissance Group
  2nd Artillery Regiment
  202nd Heavy Artillery Regiment
  10th Divisional Anti-Tank Battery

**3rd Infantry Division    Commander: Colonel Tadeusz Zieleniewski**

  Under formation

**4th Infantry Division    Commander: General Rudolf Dreszer**

  Under formation

**10th Brigade of Armoured Cavalry    Commander: General Stanisław Maczek**

**Polish Independent Highland Brigade    Commander: General Zygmunt Szyszko-Bohusz**

## 4. Western Desert 1941–1942

**Polish Independent Carpathian Brigade   Commander: General Stanisław Kopański**

  1st Battalion Carpathian Rifles
  2nd Battalion Carpathian Rifles
  3rd Battalion Carpathian Rifles
  Carpathian Artillery Regiment
  Carpathian Anti-Tank Artillery Battalion
  Carpathian Uhlan Regiment

## 5. First Polish Army Corps

**1st Armoured Division   Commander: General Stanisław Maczek**

  10th Armoured Cavalry Brigade
    1st Armoured Regiment
    2nd Armoured Regiment
    24th Lancers Regiment
    10th Dragoons Regiment
  3rd Infantry Brigade
    1st Highland Battalion
    8th Rifle Battalion
    9th Rifle Battalion
    1st Independent Heavy Mortar Gun Squadron
  Divisional Artillery
  10th Mounted Rifle Regiment

**1st Independent Parachute Brigade   Commander: General Stanisław Sosabowski**

  1st Parachute Battalion
  2nd Parachute Battalion
  3rd Parachute Battalion
  Airborne Anti-Tank Battery
  Airborne Engineering Company
  Airborne Signals

Airborne Medical Unit
Airborne Light Artillery Battery

Sources: various used.

# 6. Polish II Corps

**Commander: General Władysław Anders; Deputy Commander: General Zygmunt Szyszko-Bohusz**

**3rd Carpathian Rifle Division    Commander: General Bronisław Duch**

1st Carpathian Rifle Brigade
  1st Carpathian Rifle Battalion
  2nd Carpathian Rifle Battalion
  3rd Carpathian Rifle Battalion
2nd Carpathian Rifle Brigade
  4th Carpathian Rifle Battalion
  5th Carpathian Rifle Battalion
  6th Carpathian Rifle Battalion
3rd Carpathian Rifle Brigade
  7th Carpathian Rifle Battalion
  8th Carpathian Rifle Battalion
  9th Carpathian Rifle Battalion
7th Lubelski Uhlan Regiment
1st Carpathian Light Artillery Regiment
2nd Carpathian Light Artillery Regiment
3rd Carpathian Light Artillery Regiment
3rd Carpathian Anti-Tank Regiment
3rd Light Anti-Aircraft Regiment
3rd Heavy Machine Gun Battalion

**5th Kresy Infantry Division    Commander: General Nikodem Sulik**

4th Wołyń Infantry Brigade
  10th Wołyń Rifle Battalion
  11th Wołyń Rifle Battalion
  12th Wołyń Rifle Battalion

5th Wilno Infantry Brigade
  13th Wilno Rifle Battalion
  14th Wilno Rifle Battalion
  15th Wilno Rifle Battalion
6th Lwów Infantry Brigade
  16th Lwów Rifle Battalion
  17th Lwów Rifle Battalion
  18th Lwów Rifle Battalion
25th Wielkopolski Uhlan Regiment
4th Kresy Light Artillery Regiment
5th Wilno Light Artillery Regiment
6th Lwów Light Artillery Regiment
5th Kresy Anti-Tank Regiment
5th Kresy Light Anti-Aircraft Regiment
5th Kresy Heavy Machine Gun Battalion
5th Kresy Sapper (Engineer) Battalion

## Corps Artillery   Commander: General Roman Odzierzyński

9th Heavy Artillery Regiment
10th Medium Artillery Regiment
11th Medium Artillery Regiment
12th Medium Artillery Regiment
13th Medium Artillery Regiment
7th Anti-Tank Regiment
7th Light Anti-Aircraft Artillery Regiment
8th Heavy Anti-Aircraft Artillery Regiment

## 2nd Warsaw Armoured Division   Commander: General Bronisław Rakowski

2nd Warsaw Armoured Brigade
  1st Lancers Regiment
  4th Armoured Regiment
  6th Armoured Regiment
  2nd Motorised Commando Battalion
16th Pomeranian Infantry Brigade
  64th Infantry Battalion

65th Infantry Battalion
66th Infantry Battalion
Carpathian Lancers Regiment

Source: Madeja, *The Polish 2nd Corps*


## 7. Polish Army on the Eastern Front

**1st Polish Army** **Commander: General Zygmunt Berling (till October 1944); then General Stanisław Popławski**

1st Tadeusz Kościuszko Infantry Division
2nd Infantry Division
3rd Infantry Division
4th Infantry Division
6th Infantry Division
1st Armoured Brigade
1st Warsaw Cavalry Brigade
5 Artillery Brigades

**2nd Polish Army** **Commander: General Karol Świerczewski**

5th Infantry Division
7th Infantry Division
8th Infantry Division
9th Infantry Division
10th Infantry Division
16th Armoured Brigade
2nd Artillery Division

**1st Armoured Corps** **Commander: Colonel Jan Rupasow (till August 1944); General Józef Kimbar**

1st Motorised Infantry Brigade
2nd Armoured Brigade
3rd Armoured Brigade
4th Armoured Brigade

Source: Grzelak, Stańczyk & Zwoliński, *Bez Możliwości Wyboru*

# *Appendix 2*

**Anders, Władysław** (1892–1970) – General; served in the Russian Army in the First World War; various interwar cavalry commands; commander of the Nowogródzka Cavalry Brigade and an independent operational unit, Group Anders, September 1939; taken POW by the Soviets; released after the Sikorski–Maisky agreement and appointed to command the Polish Army in the Soviet Union, 1941–2; commander of II Corps, 1942–5; acting commander-in-chief, 1944–5; active in post-war émigré politics.

**Arciszewski, Tomasz** (1877–1955) – Politician; leading figure in the PPS before the war; led the PPS along with Kazimierz Pużak in the Underground Government; evacuated from Poland, July 1944; prime minister, Polish Government-in-Exile, 1944–7.

**Beck, Józef** (1894–1944) – Politician; served in the Polish Legions during the First World War; minister of foreign affairs, 1932–9; one of the triumvirate with Rydz-Śmigły and Mościcki ruling Poland, 1935–9; escaped to Rumania, September 1939, and died in internment.

**Berling, Zygmunt** (1896–1980) – General; served in the Polish Legions during the First World War; fought in the Polish-Soviet War, notably in the battle of Lwów; held various interwar infantry and staff appointments; held no post during the German invasion; arrested by NKVD, 1939, and imprisoned in Starobel'sk; agreed to cooperate with the Soviets and was moved to Moscow; released under the Sikorski–Maisky agreement and joined the Polish Army being formed in the Soviet Union;

chief of staff of 5th Division, 1941–2; deserted that army, 1942, on its evacuation from the Soviet Union, and sentenced to death in absentia, 1943; commander of 1st Kościuszko Division, 1943; deputy commander, 1st Polish Army on the Eastern Front, 1944; dismissed after despatching units to assist the Warsaw Uprising; worked in Frunze Military Academy, Moscow, 1944–7; returned to Poland, 1947, and commander of the Polish General Staff Academy.

**Berman, Jakub** (1901–84) – Politician; early member of the KPP; fled to Soviet-occupied Poland, September 1939, and then to Moscow, June 1941; trained the future communist leaders of Poland and served on the politburo of the Union of Polish Patriots, (ZPP), 1941–4; head of the UB, 1944–56, and responsible for communist ideology and propaganda; dismissed during the anti-Stalinist purges, 1956.

**Bierut, Bolesław** (1892–1956) – Politician; trained by the Comintern in Moscow and served as a communist agent in Austria, Czechoslovakia and Bulgaria in the 1920s; arrested and imprisoned in Poland, 1933, and released in 1938; fled to Soviet-occupied Poland, September 1939; leader of the Union of Polish Patriots; returned to Poland, 1944, as head of the Lublin Committee and Provisional Government, a position he held until 1947; president of Poland, 1947–56.

**Bór-Komorowski, Tadeusz** (1895–1966) – General; served in the Austrian Army during the First World War; joined the Polish Army, 1918; fought in the Polish-Soviet War; held various interwar cavalry commands; deputy commander of cavalry brigade, September 1939; commanded the resistance in Kraków area, 1940–43; commanded the AK, July 1943–October 1944; taken POW by the Germans; appointed commander-in-chief of the Polish Army, September 1944 but could only take up duties after liberation in May 1945; active in post-war émigré politics.

**Bortnowski, Władysław** (1891–1966) – General; served in the Polish Legions during the First World War; joined the Polish Army, 1918; fought in the Polish-Soviet War; held various interwar infantry commands and staff appointments; commanded Army Pomorze, September

1939; taken POW by the Germans; after liberation went into exile first in Britain and then in the United States.

**Boruta-Spiechowicz, Mieczysław** (1894–1987) – General; served in the Polish Legions and commanded two regiments of Haller's Army in France during the First World War; fought in the Polish-Soviet War; held various interwar infantry commands; commanded an operational group attached to Army Kraków, September 1939; taken POW by the Soviets, 1939–41; indicated an interest in fighting the Germans together with the Soviets when interviewed by Beria and Merulov on the possibility of forming a Polish Division in Red Army, October 1940; released autumn 1941 and briefly commanded 5th Infantry Division of the Polish Army in the Soviet Union; commander of 1st Armoured Corps, 1943–5; returned to Poland and served for a year in the Polish People's Army; active member of the anti-communist opposition.

**Chruściel, Antoni 'Monter'** (1895–1960) – General; served in the Austrian Army during the First World War; joined the Polish Army, 1918, fought in the Polish-Soviet War; held various interwar infantry commands and teaching appointments; commanded the 82nd Siberian Infantry Regiment (part of the 30th Division), most notably in the defence of Modlin, September 1939; joined the resistance and, when this became the AK, was its chief of staff, 1939–44; commanded the AK troops during the Warsaw Uprising, 1944; taken POW by the Germans; after liberation joined the II Corps, 1945–7; after demobilisation remained in Britain and then emigrated to the United States.

**Ciechanowski, Jan** (1887–1973) – Economist and diplomat; served in the Polish embassy in London, 1919–25; Polish ambassador to the United States, 1941–July 1945; settled in the United States.

**Czuma, Walerian** (1890–1962) – General; served in the Polish Legions during the First World War; taken POW by the Russians; after the 1917 Russian Revolution organised Polish units in Siberia and was imprisoned by the Bolsheviks; released after the Treaty of Riga, 1921, and joined the Polish Army; held various interwar infantry commands; commanded the forces defending Warsaw, September 1939; taken POW by the

Germans; after liberation joined the Polish Army in the West, 1945–7; settled in Britain.

**Dąb-Biernacki, Stefan** (1890–1959) – General; served in the Polish Legions during the First World War; commanded a regiment in the Polish-Soviet War; commander of Army Prusy and then Northern Front, September 1939; abandoned his troops after the battle of Tomaszów Lubelski; crossed into Hungary and then to France; not given another command; remained in Britain after the war.

**Dąbrowski, Franciszek** (1904–62) – Lieutenant-Commander in the Polish Navy; one of the principal defenders of Westerplatte, September 1939; taken POW by the Germans; after liberation returned to Poland and rejoined the Polish Navy and became a member of the Communist Party; expelled from the Party, 1950; rehabilitated, 1956.

**Dmowski, Roman** (1864–1939) – Politician; ideologue and leader of the National Democratic movement; worked for Russo-Polish co-operation 1906–16; leader of Polish National Committee, 1914–18; co-leader of the Polish delegation to Versailles and co-signatory with Paderewski of the Treaty of Versailles, 1919; minister of foreign affairs, October–December 1923; opponent of Piłsudski.

**Dreszer, Rudolf** (1891–1958) – General; served in the Russian Army during the First World War; joined the Polish Army, 1918; held various interwar staff appointments; commanded first Army Prusy and then Army Małopolska, September 1939; crossed into Rumania and then to France; commanded the 4th Infantry Division, France, 1940; escaped to Britain after the fall of France; politically opposed to Sikorski and sent to officer internment camp at Rothesay on the island of Bute, Scotland before being placed on the inactive list; emigrated to Canada after demobilisation in 1946.

**Duch, Bronisław** (1885–1980) – General; served in the Polish Legions during the First World War; joined the Polish Army, 1918; commanded 73rd Infantry Regiment, 1936–8; commanded 39th Reserve Infantry Division, September 1939; escaped to France; commanded 1st

Grenadier Division, France, 1940; commanded 1st Rifle Brigade, First Polish Corps, 1942–3; commanded 3rd Carpathian Infantry Division, II Corps, 1943–6; remained in Britain after demobilisation.

**Fabrycy, Kazimierz** (1888–1958) – General; served in the Polish Legions during the First World War; fought in the Polish-Soviet War; deputy minister of military affairs, 1926–34; held various interwar infantry commands; commanded Army Karpaty and the Rumanian bridgehead, September 1939; escaped from Poland and given various minor appointments in the Polish Army in the Middle East; remained in exile in Britain after the war.

**Fieldorf, Emil 'Nil'** (1895–1953) – General; served in the Polish Legions and Austrian Army during the First World War; joined the Polish Army, 1918; fought in the Polish-Soviet War, notably in the campaign to seize Wilno; held various interwar infantry posts; commanded 51st Giuseppe Garibaldi Regiment, 12th Infantry Division, September 1939; escaped to France; returned to Poland, September 1940 and joined the resistance; commanded Kedyw special operation group which carried out the assassination of SS and Police Leader Franz Kutschera in February 1944; deputy commander of the AK under Okulicki, October 1944–January 1945; leader of NIE; arrested by NKVD in March 1945 and sent to a forced labour camp in the Urals; released in 1947 and returned to Poland; arrested by the Polish communist authorities and sentenced to death.

**Gomułka, Władysław** (1905–83) – Politician; district activist of Polish Communist Party, 1926–38 and served two prison terms; head of PPR 1943–8; deputy prime minister in Polish Provisional Government and active in crushing anti-communist agitation; fell from grace in 1948 and kept under house arrest 1948–55; general secretary of communist United Polish Workers' Party 1956–70 and presided over relaxation of communist system in Poland until resignation after crushing revolt of shipyard workers with military force in December 1970.

**Grabski, Stanisław** (1871–1949) – Politician and economist; co-founder of Socialist Party but then joined the National Democrat Party; served in the *Sejm*, 1919–25; negotiator for the Treaty of Riga; minister of religious beliefs and public education, 1923 and 1925–6, and tried to eliminate the Ukrainian language in Polish schools; opposed to Piłsudski and worked as an economist in several universities; arrested by the Soviets in 1939 and released in 1941; travelled to London and served in the Polish Government-in-Exile; returned to Poland in 1945 and served in the provisional parliament before the 1947 elections.

**Grot-Rowecki, Stefan** (1895–1944) – General; served in the Polish Legions during the First World War; fought in the Polish-Soviet War; commanded 55th Infantry Regiment, 1930–35; brigade commander, September 1939; active in the Polish resistance and persuaded several groups to unite into the AK under his leadership in 1942; arrested by the Gestapo in Warsaw, 30 June 1943, and sent to Sachsenhausen concentration camp; rejected German proposals to organise a Polish battalion to fight Soviets; shot after the outbreak of the Warsaw Uprising.

**Grzybowski, Wacław** (1887–1959) – Diplomat; ambassador to Czechoslovakia, 1927–35; ambassador to the Soviet Union, 1936–9; ambassador of the Polish Government-in-Exile to western Europe, 1939–59.

**Haller, Józef** (1873–1960) – General; served in the Austrian Army during the First World War, and then as commander of Second Brigade of Polish Legions on Eastern Front; escaped internment after the Treaty of Brest-Litovsk in 1918 and reached France via Russia, July 1918; appointed to command the Polish Army in France on the Western Front; returned to Poland, 1919, with his army and seized Pomerania for Poland; fought in the Polish-Soviet War; deputy to the *Sejm*, 1920–27; forced to retire after Piłsudski's coup in 1926 and organised the opposition abroad; minister of education in the Polish Government-in-Exile, 1939–45; settled in Britain after the war.

**Iranek-Osmecki, Kazimierz** (1897–1984) – Soldier; served in the Polish Legions on Italian front during the First World War; after the oath crisis returned to Poland and worked in the Polish underground; joined the Polish Army, 1918; held various interwar staff appointments; quartermaster-general, September 1939; escaped to Rumania, where he served as deputy head of Polish intelligence; travelled to France and then Britain, June 1940, where he continued work in intelligence; emissary to Rowecki,

December 1940 and returned to Britain, April 1941; parachuted into Poland, March 1943, and appointed chief of intelligence of the AK; one of the decision makers on the launch of the Warsaw Uprising; negotiated the end of the uprising and became a POW in Colditz; settled in Britain after liberation.

**Jankowski, Jan Stanisław** (1882–1953) – Politician; co-founder of the National Workers' Party, 1920; member of the *Sejm*, 1928–35; one of the leaders of the Labour Party; government delegate, February 1943–March 1945, and approved the decision to launch the Warsaw Uprising; after the uprising continued his duties in hiding until arrested by the NKVD, March 1945; taken to Moscow and was a participant in the Trial of the Sixteen; sentenced to eight years in prison and died or was murdered two weeks before his release.

**Jasiukowicz, Stanisław** (1882–1946) – Politician; prominent National Democrat; member of the *Sejm*, 1920–35; deputy government delegate, 1940–43; minister in the Underground Government until his arrest by the NKVD in March 1945; taken to Moscow and was a participant in the Trial of the Sixteen; sentenced to five years in prison, where he died.

**Karaszewicz-Tokarzewski, Michał** (1893–1964) – General; served in the Polish Legions during the First World War; joined the Polish Army, 1918; fought in defence of Lwów during the Polish-Ukrainian War, 1918; fought against the Lithuanians in Wilno, 1919; held various interwar infantry commands; commander of an operational group attached to Army Pomorze, participated in the battle of Bzura, second-in-command of Army Warsaw during the defence of Warsaw, September 1939; went underground after Poland's defeat and founded ZWZ in September 1939 and commanded it until December 1939; appointed to command the resistance in Soviet-occupied Poland and arrested by the NKVD crossing the border, March 1940, and imprisoned; released, 1941, and appointed commander of 6th Division in the Polish Army in the Soviet Union; second-in-command of the Polish Army in the east, 1943–4; commander of 3rd Polish Corps in Egypt, 1944; settled in Britain after the war.

**Karski, Jan,** born **Jan Kozielewski** (1914–2000) – Courier; graduate of the Jan Kazimierz University in Lwów and joined the diplomatic service; served in Germany, Switzerland and Britain, 1936–8; artillery officer, September 1939, and taken POW by the Soviets; pretended to be a common soldier and returned to Poland during the POW exchanges between the Germans and the Soviets; escaped from German custody and joined the ZWZ; undertook several courier trips from Poland to Polish Government in France; appointed by the government delegate Cyryl Ratajski to travel to London with messages about conditions in German-occupied Poland and about the Holocaust; before his trip he visited the Warsaw ghetto for talks with Jewish leaders and also Izbica labour camp; reached London, 1942, and revealed details of the Holocaust to the Polish and British governments; travelled to the United States, 1943, and met Roosevelt; his news was widely disbelieved; after the war he studied at Georgetown University in the United States and later taught there.

**Klimecki, Tadeusz** (1895–1943) – General; served in the Austrian Army on Italian front during the First World War; joined the Polish Army, November 1919; fought in the Polish-Soviet War; held various interwar commands; served on the general staff, September 1939; escaped to France and joined the general staff there; evacuated to Britain and appointed chief of the general staff, July 1940; accompanied Sikorski on his final trip and was killed with him in the plane crash off Gibraltar, July 1943.

**Klukowski, Zygmunt** (1885–1959) – Physician and diarist; lived and worked for most of his life in Szczebrzeszyn, near Zamość; kept detailed diaries of the German occupation, 1939–44, and of the Soviet occupation, 1944–56.

**Kopański, Stanisław** (1895–1975) – General; served in the Russian Army during the First World War until February 1917 when joined 1st Polish Corps; joined the Polish Army, 1919; fought in the Polish-Ukrainian War and the Polish-Soviet War; held various interwar artillery commands; member of the general staff, September 1939; reached France via Rumania; commander of the Polish Carpathian Brigade, April 1940, then in Syria but moved to Palestine, June 1940; commander of the Polish Carpathian Brigade, Tobruk, August–December 1941; commander of 3rd Carpathian Infantry Division of II Corps, 1942–3; chief of staff, July 1943–5; settled in Britain after the war.

**Korboński, Stefan** (1901–89) – Politician; fought in the Polish-Ukrainian War, 1918; fought in the Polish-Soviet War; took part in the Third Silesian Uprising, 1921; member of the People's Party; lieutenant in the 57th Infantry Regiment, September 1939; taken POW by the Soviets but escaped; co-founder of the Underground Government, 1939; head of the Directorate of Civilian Resistance, 1941–5; last government delegate of Polish Government-in-Exile, March–June 1945; arrested by the NKVD but soon released; served in the People's Party in opposition to the communists, 1945–7; fled Poland after the fraudulent elections, 1947; settled in the United States.

**Kot, Stanisław** (1885–1975) – Politician and historian; professor at the Jagiellonian University in Kraków, 1920–35; dismissed for opposition to the university policies dictated by the *Sanacja* Government; fled to France and assisted in the formation of the Polish Government-in-Exile, 1939; minister for internal affairs, 1939–41; ambassador to the Soviet Union, 1941–2; minister in the Middle East, 1942–3; minister of information, 1943–5; returned to Poland and cooperated with the Provisional Government of National Unity, 1945–7, ambassador to Italy, 1945–7; remained in exile in Britain.

**Kukiel, Marian** (1885–1973) – General; served in the Polish Legions during the First World War; joined the Polish Army, 1918; fought in the Polish-Soviet War; held various interwar command and staff posts; opposed Piłsudski and left the army, 1926; took part in the defence of Lwów, September 1939; deputy minister of war, 1939–40; commander of First Polish Corps in Scotland, 1940–42; minister of war, 1943–5; remained in exile in Britain.

**Lanckorońska, Countess Karolina** (1898–2002) – Resistance fighter; taught history and art history at Lwów University, 1918–41; active in the resistance; arrested, tried and sentenced to death by the Germans in Stanisławów, 1941; family connections secured a stay of execution and instead she was sent to Ravensbrück concentration camp until liberation, 1945; lived in Fribourg, Switzerland and Rome after the war.

**Lange, Oskar** (1904–65) – Polish/American economist and diplomat; born and educated in Poland; emigrated to the United States, 1937, and appointed economics professor at Chicago University; naturalised American citizen, 1943; visited Stalin, 1944; renounced American citizenship and returned to Poland, 1945; served as the first communist Polish ambassador to the United States, 1945–7; Polish delegate to the United Nations Security Council, 1946; returned to Poland, 1947.

**Langner, Władysław** (1897–1972) – General; served in the Polish Legions during the First World War; held various interwar infantry commands; commander of the Lwów garrison, September 1939, defended the city against the Germans and surrendered it to the Soviets; travelled to France via Rumania; commanded 3rd Carpathian Rifle Brigade in Scotland, 1940–41; inspector of military training, 1941–5; settled in Britain after the war.

**Maczek, Stanisław** (1892–1994) – General; served in the Austrian Army during the First World War; joined the Polish Army, 1918; fought in the Polish-Ukrainian War and the Polish-Soviet War; held various interwar infantry commands; commander of the newly formed 10th Motorised Cavalry Brigade, October 1938, and commanded it, September 1939; crossed with his brigade into Hungary, briefly interned before reaching France; commanded 10th Armoured Cavalry Brigade, France, 1940; evacuated to Britain and appointed to command 1st Polish Armoured Division; commanded the division in the fighting in Normandy, particularly the Falaise Gap, Belgium, the Netherlands and Germany, 1944–5; commanded First Polish Corps, 1945–7; retired from the army in 1948 and remained in exile in Britain.

**Mikołajczyk, Stanisław** (1885–1966) – Politician; fought in the Polish-Soviet War, wounded and discharged, 1920; active in the People's Party (PSL) in the 1920s and elected to the *Sejm*, 1929; opposed the *Sanacja* regime; served as a private in the Polish Army in defence of Warsaw, September 1939; escaped to Hungary and then to France; deputy chairman of the National Council in the Polish Government-in-Exile, 1939–41; minister of the interior and deputy prime minister, 1941–July 1943; prime minister, July 1943–November 1944; returned to Poland, July 1945 and deputy prime minister and agriculture minister in the Polish Provisional Government of National Unity 1945–7; leader of the opposition to the communists; resigned from the government after the fraudulent 1947 elections; fled Poland when facing arrest, October 1947; emigrated to the United States; remains returned for burial in Poland, 2000.

**Młot-Fijałkowski, Czesław** (1892–1944) – General; served in the Polish Legions during the First World War; interned after the oath crisis in 1917 but released in May 1918 and worked with the Polish Military Organisation; joined the Polish Army, 1918; and served in defence of Teschen, the Polish-Ukrainian War and the Polish-Soviet War, 1918–21; held various interwar infantry commands; commanded Narew Special Operational Group, September 1939; taken POW by the Germans and died in Oflag Murnau.

**Mościcki, Ignacy** (1867–1946) – Politician; president of Poland 1926–39; interned in Rumania, September 1939; released December 1939 because of his dual Polish-Swiss citizenship and travelled to Switzerland, where he lived for the rest of his life.

**Nowak, Jan,** born **Zdzisław Jeziorański** (1914–2005) – Resistance fighter; NCO in artillery, September 1939; joined the resistance; active in Action N, the black propaganda campaign against the Germans; envoy between the AK commanders and the Polish Government-in-Exile; produced the first report of Warsaw ghetto uprising; fought in the Warsaw Uprising and ordered to leave Warsaw by the AK command before the capitulation and reached London; worked in the Polish division of BBC radio, 1948–76; head of the Polish section of Radio Free Europe, 1952–76; emigrated to the United States and led the Polish American Congress, 1979–96; adviser to the National Security Agency and to presidents Jimmy Carter and Ronald Reagan; visited Poland frequently in 1990s and returned to Poland for final time in 2002 where he died.

**Odzierzyński, Roman** (1892–1975) – General; served in the Austrian Army during the First World War; joined the Polish Army, 1918; fought in the Polish-Soviet War, notably in defence of Lwów; held various interwar artillery commands; commander of the training centre in Trauguttowie on the outbreak of war, September 1939, and evacuated the troops to Rumania; escaped to France and appointed artillery commander of 4th Division, 1940; evacuated to Britain and commander of artillery in 4th Brigade; commander of Polish Army in the east, 1942–3;

commander of artillery, II Corps, 1943–5; active in the post-war émigré politics.

**Okulicki, Leopold** (1898–1946) – General; served in the Polish Legions during the First World War; joined the Polish Army, 1918, fought in the Polish-Soviet War; held various interwar staff commands; served in the defence of Warsaw, September 1939; joined the early resistance movement and arrested in Lwów by NKVD, January 1941; released under the terms of the Sikorski–Maisky agreement and joined the Polish Army in the Soviet Union as chief of staff, 1941–2; sent to Britain for *Cichociemni* training; dropped into Poland and served in Operation Bzura; appointed deputy and successor to Bór-Komorowski and served in Warsaw Uprising; reformed the AK and appointed its commander, October 1944; disbanded the AK, January 1945; arrested by the NKVD, March 1945; sentenced to ten years' imprisonment at the Trial of the Sixteen in Moscow, 1946, and died or was murdered in prison, December 1946.

**Osóbka-Morawski, Edward** (1909–97) – Politician; active in the PPS before the war; leader of the PKWN, 1944–5; prime minister, Polish Provisional Government of National Unity, June 1945–February 1947; dismissed from his posts with advent of Stalinism, 1949; readmitted to the Communist Party, 1956.

**Paderewski, Ignacy** (1860–1941) – Pianist and statesman; worked for Polish independence in the United States during the First World War and active member of the Polish National Committee in Paris; returned to Poland in late 1918 and served as prime minister and foreign minister, January–December 1919; chief Polish delegate to the Paris Peace Conference and signatory to the Treaty of Versailles; Polish ambassador to the League of Nations, 1920–22; active member of the opposition to Piłsudski while living in Switzerland, 1926–36; head of the Polish National Council in the Polish Government-in-Exile, 1940; died in the United States while on a visit; buried at Arlington National Cemetery but remains returned to Poland in 1992 and reburied in St John's Cathedral, Warsaw.

**Pajdak, Antoni** (1894–1988) – Politician, lawyer and activist; served in the Polish Legions during the First World War; lawyer and active in socialist politics in interwar years; deputy government delegate, 1943–5; arrested by the NKVD, March 1945, and sentenced to five years' imprisonment in the Trial of Sixteen; released in 1950 but sent into exile in Siberia; returned to Poland, 1955; opposition activist particularly 1968–81.

**Paszkiewicz, Gustaw** (1893–1955) – General; served in the Russian Army during the First World War; joined the Polish Army, 1918; fought in the Polish-Soviet War; held various interwar staff and infantry commands; led the pacification campaign against the Ukrainians, 1937–8; commander of 12th Infantry Division and deputy commander of Army Karpaty, September 1939; escaped to Rumania and thence to France and Britain; brigade commander, 1940–42; commander 4th Rifle Division, 1942; commander 2nd Armoured Brigade, 1942–3; deputy commander, First Polish Corps, 1943–5; returned to Poland, August 1945; appointed commander of 18th Infantry Division and then commander of Warsaw military district, 1946–8, and hunted down members of the AK; accused Anders of conspiring to kill Sikorski, 1947.

**Pełczyński, Tadeusz** (1892–1985) – General; served in the Polish Legions during the First World War and was interned after the oath crisis; joined the Polish Army, 1918; held various interwar staff appointments; commanded 19th Infantry Division, September 1939; joined the resistance; commander of Lublin District, ZWZ, July 1940–April 1941; chief of staff, ZWZ, July 1941–3; deputy commander, AK, July 1943–October 1944; took part in the decision to launch the Warsaw Uprising; seriously wounded during the uprising and taken POW by the Germans; lived in Britain after liberation.

**Piłsudski, Józef** (1867–1935) – Politician and soldier; active in anti-Russian politics and member of the Socialist Party before the First World War; founder of the Polish Legions which fought with Austrian armies during the First World War; interned after the oath crisis, 1917; released in November 1918, returned to Poland and declared independent Poland on 11 November 1918; provisional chief of state and commander-in-chief, 1918–19; chief of state, 1919–22; commander-in-chief during the Polish-Soviet War; launched a *coup d'état* and founded the *Sanacja* regime, May 1926; prime minister, 1926–8, 1930; general inspector of armed forces, 1926–35; minister of military affairs, 1926–35.

**Piskor, Tadeusz** (1889–1951) – General; served in the Polish Legions during the First World War; joined the Polish Army, 1918; fought in the Polish-Soviet War; held various interwar staff appointments, including chief of the general staff; commanded Army Lublin, September 1939; taken POW by the Germans; settled in Britain after liberation.

**Prugar-Ketling, Bronisław** (1891–1948) – General; member of the Polish Military Organisation and then the Polish Army in France during the First World War; fought in the Polish-Soviet War; held various interwar infantry commands and staff appointments; commander of 11th Infantry Division, September 1939; escaped to France and commander of 2nd Division, 1940; interned in Switzerland after the fall of France, 1940–45; returned to Poland, 1945, and joined the People's Army; held various staff appointments.

**Pużak, Kazimierz** (1883–1950) – Politician; important in the pre-war PPS; founding member of the underground socialist party, 1939; PPS representative in the Underground Government, 1940–44; escaped Warsaw after the uprising; arrested by the NKVD, March 1945, and sentenced to eighteen months' imprisonment in the Trial of the Sixteen; released November 1945 and returned to Poland; active in anti-communist socialist politics; arrested by the Polish security police, 1947 and 1948; sentenced to ten years' imprisonment and died in prison.

**Raczkiewicz, Władysław** (1885–1947) – Politician; served in the Russian Army during the First World War until the Russian Revolution; joined the Polish Army; fought in the Polish-Soviet War; head of Nowogródek province, 1921–4; government delegate to Wilno province, 1924–31; senate marshal, 1930–35; head of Kraków province, 1935; head of Pomorze province, 1936–9; escaped to France, 1939; appointed president of the Polish Government-in-Exile, 1939–45; remained as president when the government was no longer recognised until his death.

**Raczyński, Edward** (1891–1993) – Diplomat; served in the Polish embassies and missions to Berne, Copenhagen and London, 1919–25;

head of the department of international agreements, ministry of foreign affairs, 1925–32; Polish ambassador to the League of Nations, 1932–4; Polish ambassador to Britain, 1934–45; minister of foreign affairs, 1941–3; active in post-war émigré politics.

**Rakowski, Bronisław** (1895–1950) – General; served in the Polish Legions during the First World War; fought in the Polish-Soviet War; commanded 12th Uhlan Regiment, 1931–6; head of the Army Historical Bureau, 1936–9; chief of staff of the Southern Front and defence of Lwów, September 1939; captured by the NKVD and imprisoned in Moscow, released under the Sikorski–Maisky agreement; commander of 8th and then 5th divisions, Polish Army in the Soviet Union; chief of staff of the Polish Army in the east, 1942–3; commander of 2nd Armoured Brigade, 1943–5; commander of 2nd Armoured Division, 1945–7; emigrated to Argentina after demobilisation.

**Ratajski, Cyryl** (1875–1942) – Politician; mayor of Poznań, 1922–4, 1925–35, 1939; minister of the interior, 1924–5; government delegate to the Polish Government-in-Exile, 1940–42; resigned due to ill health.

**Retinger, Józef** (1888–1960) – Political adviser; educated at the Sorbonne, Paris; lived in Britain, 1911–17; unofficial adviser to the president of Mexico from 1917; adviser to Sikorski, 1939–43; parachuted into Poland, 1944, for consultations with the Underground Government; returned to London, 1944; post-war advocate of European unification and helped found the European Movement and the Council of Europe.

**Rola-Żymierski, Michał** (1890–1989) – General; served in the Polish Legions during the First World War; joined the Polish Army, 1918; fought in the Polish-Soviet War; graduated from the École Spéciale Militaire de Saint-Cyr; returned to Poland and served as deputy chief of administration of the Polish Army; court-martialled and found guilty of bribery and embezzlement, demoted to private first class, expelled from the army, and sentenced to five years' imprisonment, 1927; released, 1931, and approached by the NKVD and became a secret member of the KPP; after Stalin disbanded the KPP, 1937, emigrated to France; returned to Poland, 1939; deputy commander of the communist *Gwardia Ludowa*,

1943; commander of the AL, 1944; commander-in-chief, communist Polish Army, 1944–5; minister of defence in the Provisional Polish Government, 1945; appointed head of the Commission of State Security, 1946, and undertook the rounding up of AK members and the expulsion of the Ukrainian minority from Poland; minister of defence, 1946–9; arrested, 1952, during Stalinist purges; released in 1955 and rehabilitated by Polish Government, 1956.

**Romer, Tadeusz** (1894–1978) – Diplomat; secretary to the Polish National Committee in Paris, 1917–19; Polish ambassador to Portugal, 1933–7; to Japan, 1937–41; to the Soviet Union, 1942–3; minister of foreign affairs, 1943–4; emigrated to Canada after the war.

**Rómmel, Juliusz** (1881–1967) – General; served in the Russian Army in the First World War and formed the Polish II Corps in Russia, 1917; commanded the Polish Light Brigade during the Russian Civil War, joined the Polish Army, 1918, commanded the 1st Cavalry Division during the Polish-Soviet War; held various interwar command posts; commanded Army Łódź and then Army Warsaw, September 1939; taken POW by the Germans; on liberation attempted to join the Polish II Corps but was made unwelcome so he returned to Poland; retired from the army, 1947.

**Rowecki, S.,** *see* **Grot-Rowecki, Stefan**

**Rudnicki, Klemens** (1897–1992) – General; served in the Austrian Army during the First World War; joined the Polish Army, 1918; appointed commander of 9th Małopolska Cavalry Regiment, 1938, and commanded it, September 1939; worked for the resistance in Lwów, arrested by the NKVD and imprisoned in Moscow; released under the Sikorski–Maisky agreement, 1941; joined the Polish Army in the Soviet Union as temporary commander of the 6th infantry division, 1941–2; deputy commander of 5th Infantry Division, 1941–5; commanded 1st Armoured Division, May 1945–1947; settled in Britain after demobilisation.

**Rydz-Śmigły, Edward** (1886–1941) – General; served in the Polish Legions during the First World War; commanded the Central Front during the Polish-Soviet War; supported Piłsudski's *coup d'état*, 1926;

inspector-general of the army, 1931–5; marshal, 1936; army inspector general and one of the ruling triumvirate along with Beck and Mościcki, 1935–9; commander-in-chief, September 1939; fled to Rumania on 18 September 1939; interned in Rumania but escaped to Hungary; returned secretly to Warsaw to join the resistance as a private under an alias, 1941, but died from a heart attack a few months after his return.

**Rzepecki, Jan** (1899–1983) – Soldier; served in the Polish Legions during the First World War; joined the Polish Army, 1918; taught at the Infantry Officers School during the interwar years; opposed Piłsudski's *coup d'état*; on the staff of Army Kraków, September 1939; worked with the resistance throughout the German occupation, 1939–44; taken POW by the Germans after the Warsaw Uprising, 1944; returned to Poland, 1945, and deputy commander of NIE and successor clandestine organisations, arrested November 1945 and sentenced to eight years' imprisonment, released under the 1947 amnesty; lecturer at the General Staff Academy, 1947–9; arrested in 1949 and released in 1954.

**Sikorski, Władysław** (1881–1943) – General and statesman; served in the Polish Legions during the First World War; joined the Polish Army; fought in the Polish-Soviet War, notably on the Warsaw front; commander-in-chief, 1921; prime minister and minister of the interior, December 1922–May 1923; chief inspector of infantry, 1923–4; minister of military affairs, 1924–5; commanded the Lwów military district, 1925–8; neutral during Piłsudski's *coup d'état* but then joined the opposition, leading to his dismissal, 1928; spent much of remaining interwar years in Paris; refused a military command, September 1939; escaped to Rumania and then to France; prime minister and commander-in-chief, Polish Government-in-Exile, 1939–43; killed in a plane crash off Gibraltar, July 1943; remains moved from Newark Cemetery to Wawel Castle, Kraków, 1993.

**Sosabowski, Stanisław** (1892–1967) – General; served in the Austrian Army during First World War; joined the Polish Army, 1918; held various interwar staff and infantry commands; commander of 21st Infantry Regiment, September 1939; taken POW by the Germans but escaped and joined the resistance in Warsaw; the resistance ordered him to leave for France with reports on the German occupation; deputy commander, 4th Infantry Division, 1940; commander, 4th Rifle Brigade and then 1st Independent Parachute Brigade, 1940–44; took part in Operation Market Garden, September 1944; unfairly blamed for the failure of the Arnhem operation and dismissed, December 1944; commander of guard troops, 1945–7; remained in exile in Britain.

**Sosnkowski, Kazimierz** (1885–1969) – General; close co-operator with Piłsudski, 1905–18; served in the Polish Legions during the First World War; appointed commander of the Warsaw military district, 1918; commanded the reserve army during the Polish-Soviet War, notably in defence of Warsaw; minister of defence, 1920–24; commander of the Poznań military district, 1935–37; inspector-general of Army Polesie, 1928–39; commander of the Southern Front, September 1939; escaped to France and appointed deputy president of the Polish Government-in-Exile and in charge of the Polish resistance; resigned over the Sikorski–Maisky agreement, July 1941; commander-in-chief, July 1943–September 1944, when dismissed from office; emigrated to Canada after the war.

**Stachiewicz, Wacław** (1894–1973) – General; served in the Polish Legions during the First World War; deputy chief of staff to General Sosnkowski during the battle of Warsaw, 1920; graduated from École Supérieure de Guerre, Paris, 1923; taught at the Polish War Academy and held various staff positions; chief of staff, 1935–9 and responsible for war plans; fled to Rumania, 18 September 1939 and was interned; escaped in January 1940, reached Algiers and was interned by the French; reached London, 1943, but was offered no appointment; emigrated to Canada, 1948.

**Stańczyk, Jan** (1886–1953) – Politician and trade union activist; engaged in socialist politics and trade unionism during the interwar years; left Poland at the request of Sikorski, September 1939; minister of labour and social welfare and the Polish representative to the International Labour Organisation, 1939–44; participated in the Moscow talks on the formation of the Provisional Government of National Unity, June 1945; minister of labour and social welfare, June 1945–July 1946;

director-general for social affairs at the United Nations and Polish representative to International Labour Organisation, 1946–8; instrumental in the merger of the PPS and PPR, December 1948.

**Starzyński, Stefan** (1893–1943) – Politician; served in the Polish Legions during the First World War; joined the Polish Army, 1918 and appointed chief of staff of 9th Infantry Division; served in II Department (Intelligence) of the General Staff during the Polish-Soviet War; deputy minister of the treasury, 1929–30, 1931–2; member of the *Sejm*, 1930–33; mayor of Warsaw, 1934–9; organised the civilian population and the defence of Warsaw, September 1939; refused all offers to help him escape the city; arrested by the Gestapo, October 1939; exact fate unknown but probably executed in Dachau, 1943.

**Sulik, Nikodem** (1893–1954) – General; served in the Russian Army during the First World War; joined the Polish Army and fought in the Polish-Soviet War; held various infantry posts before being appointed to command KOP, and still in command in September 1939; arrested by the NKVD, April 1941, but soon released under the terms of the Sikorski–Maisky agreement; commanded 7th Division of the Polish Army in the Soviet Union, commander of 5th Division, II Corps, 1943–5; settled in Britain after the war.

**Świerczewski, Karol** (1897–1947) – General; evacuated from Warsaw to Moscow during the First World War and joined the Bolshevik party in 1918; served in the Red Army during the Russian Civil War and the Polish-Soviet War; graduated from Frunze Military Academy, Moscow, 1927, and served on the Red Army General Staff; commanded 14th International Brigade and then 35th International Division during the Spanish Civil War; served as a general in the Red Army, 1941–3, but given little responsibility due to alcoholism; one of the founders of the 1st Polish Army in the east, 1943; commanded 2nd Polish Army on the Eastern Front, 1944–5; deputy defence minister, 1946–7 and persecuted the AK and Ukrainians; assassinated by the UPA, 1947.

**Świrski, Jerzy** (1882–1959) – Vice-Admiral; served in the Russian Navy during the First World War; joined the Ukrainian Navy, 1918; joined the Polish Navy, 1919; director of the Polish Navy, 1925–39; escaped to

Britain; director of the Polish Navy in the Polish Government-in-Exile, 1939–47; settled in Britain after the war.

**Szylling, Antoni** (1884–1971) – General; served in the Russian Army during the First World War and then joined the Polish 2nd Corps in Russia, 1917; joined the Polish Army, 1919; held various interwar infantry commands; commander of Army Kraków, September 1939; taken POW by the Germans; after liberation lived in France, Britain and Canada.

**Szyszko-Bohusz, Zygmunt** (1893–1962) – General; served in the Russian Army during the First World War, captured by Austrians, escaped and joined the Polish Legions; fought in the Polish-Soviet War and seriously wounded; held various interwar infantry and staff posts; commander of 16th Infantry Division, September 1939; escaped to France via Hungary; commander of Podole Rifle Brigade, Norway and France, 1940; evacuated to Britain and in charge of training; led the Polish military mission to the Soviet Union, 1941; chief of staff, Polish Army in the Soviet Union, 1942; commander of 5th Infantry Division, 1942–3; deputy commander of II Corps, 1944–5; settled in Britain after the war.

**Unrug, Józef** (1884–1973) – Vice-Admiral; served in the German Navy during the First World War; joined the Polish Navy, 1918; commander of the Polish Navy, 1925–39; taken POW by the Germans; was offered but declined the opportunity to join the German Navy; settled in Britain and then France after liberation.

**Wasilewska, Wanda** (1905–64) – Communist publicist and journalist; left-wing journalist during the interwar years; fled to Soviet-occupied Poland, September 1939, and worked as a journalist on Soviet-sponsored Polish newspapers; fled to Moscow, June 1941, and war correspondent with the Red Army; creator of the ZPP and supporter of the 1st Polish Army, 1943; deputy chief of the PKWN, 1944; remained in the Soviet Union after the war.

**Zając, Józef** (1891–1963) – General; served in the Polish Legions and the Polish Army in France during the First World War; fought in the late stages of the Polish-Soviet War; held various interwar staff appointments; commander of Kraków military district and inspector of the Polish Air Force, 1936; commander of air defence, 1938; commander of the Polish Air Force, 1939; commander of the Polish Air Force in France, 1940; deputy commander of I Corps, 1940–41; commander of the Polish Air Force in the Middle East, 1941–2; deputy commander of the Polish Army in the Middle East, 1942–3; inspector general of training, 1943–6; settled in Britain after the war.

**Zaleski, August** (1883–1972) – Diplomat; member of the Polish National Committee during the First World War; served in the Polish embassies in Switzerland, Greece, Italy and League of Nations, 1920s; minister of foreign affairs, 1926–32; minister of foreign affairs, 1939–41 until his resignation in protest at the Sikorski–Maisky agreement; active in post-war émigré politics.

# Notes

## ABBREVIATIONS

| | |
|---|---|
| *AK Documents* | H. Czarnocka *et al.*, *Armia Krajowa w dokumentach 1939–1945* |
| *APHC* | T. Stirling, D. Nalęcz & T. Dubicki (eds), *The Report of the Anglo-Polish Historical Commission on Intelligence Co-operation Between Poland and Great Britain During World War II* |
| *DBPO* | M. Pelly, H. Yasamee & K. Hamilton (eds), *Documents on British Policy Overseas* |
| *Destiny Can Wait* | Committee of the Polish Air Force Memorial, *Destiny Can Wait* |
| *Documents on the Holocaust* | Y. Arad, I. Gutman & A. Margaliot (eds), *Documents on the Holocaust: Selected Sources on the Destruction of the Jews of Germany and Austria, Poland, and the Soviet Union* |
| *DPSR* | Sikorski Institute, *Documents on Polish-Soviet Relations* |
| *FRUS* | *Foreign Relations of the United States* |
| *German Crimes in Poland* | Central Commission for Investigation of German Crimes in Poland, *German Crimes in Poland* |
| IOR | India Office Records, British Library, London |
| IWM | Imperial War Museum, London |
| PISM | Polish Institute and Sikorski Museum, London |
| *Poles in India* | Association of the Poles in India, *Poles in India 1942–1948* |
| *Protokoły* | W. Rojek & A. Suchciłz (eds), *Protokoły z posiedzeń Rady Ministrów Rzeczypospolitej Polskiej* |
| SSEES | School of Slavonic and East European Studies, University College London |

| | |
|---|---|
| *Stalin Correspondence* | *Correspondence Between the Chairman of the Council of Ministers of the U.S.S.R. and the Presidents of the U.S.A. and the Prime Ministers of Great Britain during the Great Patriotic War of 1941–1945* |
| *Stalin's Ethnic Cleansing* | Association of the Families of the Borderland Settlers, *Stalin's Ethnic Cleansing in Eastern Poland* |
| TNA | The National Archives, Kew |

## PREFACE

1. I. Serraillier, *The Silver Sword* (1956); G. Morgan & W. Lasocki, *Soldier Bear* (1970). A new biography of Wojtek has recently been published: A. Orr, *Wojtek the Bear: Polish War Hero* (2010).
2. Churchill, *The Second World War: The Gathering Storm* (1946), 290.
3. O'Malley, *Phantom Caravan*, 230.
4. Various entries, Danchev & Todman, *War Diaries*, *passim*.
5. Gilbert, *Winston S. Churchill*, vol. VII, 185.
6. Ibid., 260.
7. Quoted in Bartoszewski, 'Poles and Jews as the "Other"'.
8. R. Lukas, 'The Polish Experience of the Holocaust', in Berenbaum, *Mosaic of Victims*, 88–95.
9. Deák, *Essays on Hitler's Europe*, 74.
10. Plokhy, *Yalta*, vi.
11. Cienciala, 'Detective Work'.

## CHAPTER 1: THE REBIRTH OF POLAND

1. Zamoyski, *Polish Way*, *passim*; Davies, *God's Playground*, *passim*.
2. P. Wandycz, 'The Polish Question', in Boemeke, Feldman & Glaser, *Treaty of Versailles*, 313–35.
3. Zamoyski, *Polish Way*, 7.
4. Gerson, *Woodrow Wilson*, 19–25; Stachura, *Poland 1918–1945*, 24.
5. Reddaway, *et al.*, *Cambridge History of Poland*, 463; J. Hapak, 'The Polish Army in France', in Stefancic, *Armies in Exile*, 117–35; Gerson, *Woodrow Wilson*, 71, 79–82; Wandycz, *United States and Poland*, 117–20.
6. Gerson, *Woodrow Wilson*, 101–10.
7. Prusin, *Lands Between*, 80; Snyder, *Reconstruction*, 58–9; Wandycz, *Soviet-Polish Relations*, 95–9; Wandycz, 'Poland's Place in Europe in the Concepts of Piłsudski and Dmowski'.
8. D. Stevenson, 'French War Aims and Peace Planning', in Boemeke, Feldman & Glaser, *Treaty of Versailles*, 91–2; Wandycz, *France and her Eastern Allies*, 35–48.

9. Gerson, *Woodrow Wilson*, 136.

10. Komarnicki, *Rebirth*, 376; Latawski, 'The Dmowski–Namier Feud'.

11. First Report of the Commission on Polish Affairs, 12 March 1919, TNA, FO 608/69.

12. M. Macmillan, *Peacemakers*, 217–39; Lundgreen-Nielsen, *Polish Problem*, *passim*.

13. Gajda, *Postscript to Victory*, *passim*; P. Leśniewski, 'Three Insurrections: Upper Silesia 1919–21', in Stachura, *Poland Between the Wars*, 13–42.

14. Fink, 'The Minorities Question at the Paris Peace Conference: The Polish Minority Treaty, 28 June 1919', in Boemeke, Feldman & Glaser, *Treaty of Versailles*, 249–74; Karski, *Great Powers*, 40, 255.

15. Elcock, 'Britain and the Russo-Polish Frontier'; Karski, *Great Powers*, 48–52.

16. Komarnicki, *Rebirth*, 382.

17. Carton de Wiart, *Happy Odyssey*, 112.

18. Quoted in Elcock, 'Britain and the Russo-Polish Frontier'.

19. Davies, *White Eagle*, *passim*; Zamoyski, *Warsaw 1920*, *passim*; Matuszewski, *Great Britain's Obligations*, *passim*; G. Craig, 'The British Foreign Office from Grey to Austen Chamberlain', in Craig & Gilbert, *The Diplomats*, 31; Debicki, *Foreign Policy*, 13–15; Davies, 'Lloyd George and Poland'; Elcock, 'Britain and the Russo-Polish Frontier'; Kuśnierz, *Stalin and the Poles*, 22–3; Karski, *Great Powers*, 52–70; Rozek, *Allied Wartime Diplomacy*, 12–16; Snyder, *Reconstruction*, 63–4; Wandycz, *Soviet-Polish Relations*, 285–6; *Destiny Can Wait*, 263; Belcarz & Pęczkowski, *White Eagles*, 66–7.

20. Borzęcki, *Soviet-Polish Peace*, 280; Mastny, *Russia's Road*, 16.

21. P. Stachura, 'The Battle of Warsaw, 1920', in Stachura, *Poland Between the Wars*, 43–59.

22. Zamoyski, *Polish Way*, 340.

23. Komarnicki, *Rebirth*, 304; Zamoyski, *Polish Way*, 333; Prażmowska, *Poland*, 64–7; Jasienica, 'The Polish Experience'.

24. Polonsky, *Politics in Independent Poland*, 5–9; Reddaway *et al.*, *Cambridge History of Poland*, 497; Z. Landau, 'The Economic Integration of Poland 1918–23', in Latawski, *Reconstruction*, 145–52.

25. W. Roszkowski, 'The Reconstruction of the Government and State Apparatus in the Second Polish Republic', in Latawski, *Reconstruction*, 159–60; Stachura, *Poland 1918–1945*, 104–5.

26. Polonsky, *Politics in Independent Poland*, 12–15, 278–83; P. Stachura, 'The Second Republic in Historiographical Outline', in Stachura, *Poland Between the Wars*, 1–12; Housden, *Hans Frank*, 79; Zamoyski, *Polish Way*, 348; Davies, *God's Playground*, 411–18.

27. Polonsky, *Politics in Independent Poland*, 317–39.

28. Retinger, *Memoirs*, 77; Zamoyski, *Polish Way*, 343; Holzer, 'The Political Right in Poland'; Seidner, 'The Camp of National Unity'.

29. Davies & Polonsky, *Jews in Eastern Poland*, 4; Gutman & Krakowski, *Unequal Victims*, 8; Stachura, *Poland 1918–1945*, 46.

30. T. Piotrowski, *Poland's Holocaust*, 146.

31. Prusin, *Lands Between*, 106; T. Piotrowski, *Poland's Holocaust*, 179–98.

32. P. Stachura, 'National Identity and the Ethnic Minorities in Early Inter-War Poland', in Latawski, *Reconstruction*, 60–86; Snyder, *Reconstruction*, 143, 150–51; Polonsky, *Politics in Independent Poland*, 374; Prusin, *Lands Between*, 108–16.

33. Stachura, 'National Identity and the Ethnic Minorities', in Latawski, *Reconstruction*; Polonsky, *Politics in Independent Poland*, 463; Mazower, *Hitler's Empire*, 40; Blanke, 'The German Minority in Inter-War Poland and German Foreign Policy'.

34. Lukas, *Forgotten Survivors*, 3.

35. J. Lichten, 'Notes on the Assimilation and Acculturation of Jews in Poland, 1863–1943', in Abramsky, Jachimczyk & Polonsky, *Jews in Poland*, 106–29.

36. S. Korboński, *Jews and the Poles*, 8.

37. Lukas, *Out of the Inferno*, 9.

38. J. Turowicz, 'Polish Reasons and Jewish Reasons', in Polonsky, *'My Brother's Keeper?'*, 134–43; Beck, *Dernier Rapport*, 140; Prusin, *Lands Between*, 93–5; E. Mendelsohn, 'Interwar Poland: Good for the Jews or Bad for the Jews?', in Abramsky, Jachimczyk & Polonsky, *Jews in Poland*, 130–39; Bartoszewski, 'Poles and Jews as the "Other"'; Wynot, '"A Necessary Cruelty"'; Longerich, *Holocaust*, 110; Ringelblum, *Polish-Jewish Relations*, x.

39. Davies, *God's Playground*, 425–9.

## CHAPTER 2: POLISH FOREIGN POLICY, 1920–1939

1. Karski, *Great Powers*, 84.

2. Jędrzejewicz, *Lipski*, 24.

3. Jędrzejewicz, *Łukasiewicz*, 187; Wandycz, *Twilight*, passim.

4. Cienciala, *Poland and the Western Powers*, 21.

5. The principal treaty signed at Locarno was between Germany, France, Belgium, Britain and Italy.

6. Mastny, *Russia's Road*, 16; Snyder, *Bloodlands*, 30, 37.

7. Snyder, *Bloodlands*, 38, 56–7.

8. Beck, *Dernier Rapport*, 37–8.

9. Beneš, *Memoirs*, 10.

10. Gasiorowski, 'Did Piłsudski Attempt'.

11. Steiner, *Triumph of the Dark*, 31.

12. Jędrzejewicz, *Lipski*, 142, 288.

13. Steiner, *Triumph of the Dark*, 365–6.

14. Cienciala, *Poland and the Western Powers*, 17–18, 26; Steiner, *Triumph of the Dark*, 71, 94–5; Wandycz, *Twilight, passim*.
15. Jędrzejewicz, *Lipski*, 402.
16. Debicki, *Foreign Policy*, 117–20; Prażmowska, *Britain, Poland and the Eastern Front*, 16.
17. Karski, *Great Powers*, 237; Haslam, 'The Soviet Union'.
18. Eden, *Eden Memoirs*, 35.
19. Raczyński, *In Allied London*, 9.
20. Polish Ministry for Foreign Affairs, *Official Documents*, 47–8. On 19 November 1938, the Czech Government agreed to allow Germany extraterritorial rights for the section of the planned road from Breslau to Vienna which would cross Czech territory. Newman, *March 1939*, 89; Prażmowska, *Britain, Poland and the Eastern Front*, 18.
21. Jędrzejewicz, *Lipski*, 353; Debicki, *Foreign Policy*, 125–9; Karski, *Great Powers*, 218–19; Prażmowska, *Britain, Poland and the Eastern Front*, 15.
22. Newman, *March 1939*, 163.
23. Prażmowska, *Britain, Poland and the Eastern Front*, 12–14, 39.
24. Minute by Vansittart, 17 March 1939, TNA, FO 371/2306; Chiefs of Staff minutes, 18 March 1939, TNA, CAB 53/10.
25. Newman, *March 1939*, 134–5; Karski, *Great Powers*, 265.
26. Prażmowska, 'Poland's Foreign Policy'.
27. Ibid.; Strang, *At Home and Abroad*, 161; Bruce Strang, 'Once More unto the Breach'.
28. 31 March 1939, *Hansard*, vol. 345, 2415.
29. Prażmowska, 'Poland's Foreign Policy'.
30. Steiner, *Triumph of the Dark*, 738–9.
31. Dilks, *Diaries*, 166.
32. Beck, *Dernier Rapport*, 176.
33. Prażmowska, *Britain, Poland and the Eastern Front*, 19.
34. Cienciala, *Poland and the Western Powers*, 239.
35. Cannistraro, Wynot & Kovaleff, *Poland and the Coming of the Second World War*, 70–71.
36. Debicki, *Foreign Policy*, 130–31.
37. More details on these talks can be found in Prażmowska, 'Poland's Foreign Policy'.
38. 3 April 1939, *Hansard*, vol. 345, 2500, 2509.
39. Debicki, *Foreign Policy*, 149; TNA, FO 371/23073; Craig & Gilbert, *Diplomats*, 610.
40. Karski, *Great Powers*, 355.
41. Prażmowska, *Britain, Poland and the Eastern Front*, 147–9.
42. Debicki, *Foreign Policy*, 145–6; Karski, *Great Powers*, 329–30; A. Suchcitz, 'Poland's Defence Preparations in 1939', in Stachura, *Poland Between the Wars*, 109–36; Jędrzejewicz, *Łukasiewicz*, 211–17.

43. Steiner, *Triumph of the Dark*, 786.

44. Karski, *Great Powers*, 333; Prażmowska, *Britain, Poland and the Eastern Front*, 103–5.

45. Suchcitz, 'Poland's Defence Preparations', in Stachura, *Poland Between the Wars*; Report to the Chiefs of Staff Committee, 15 June 1939, TNA, CAB 53/50; TNA, CAB 23/100; diary entry 10 July 1939, Macleod & Kelly, *Ironside Diaries*, 78; Committee of Imperial Defence report, 28 March 1939, TNA, CAB 53/47; Kennard to Sargent, 30 May 1939, TNA, FO 371/23129; Karski, *Great Powers*, 332; Prażmowska, *Britain, Poland and the Eastern Front*, 93–6; Turnbull & Suchcitz, *Sword*, 33.

46. 31 July 1939, *Hansard*, vol. 350, 1921–2.

47. Debicki, *Foreign Policy*, 144; Karski, *Great Powers*, 334–5; Prażmowska, 'Poland's Foreign Policy'; Turnbull & Suchcitz, *Sword*, 26–7.

48. Kennedy, *German Campaign*, 48–50.

49. Polonsky, *Politics in Independent Poland*, 397.

50. Speech at Sandhurst, January 1939, in Turnbull & Suchcitz, *Sword*, 77–8.

51. Suchcitz, 'Poland's Defence Preparations', in Stachura, *Poland Between the Wars*; Drzewieniecki, 'The Polish Army on the Eve'; Polonsky, *Politics in Independent Poland*, 484–5; author's interview with Teresa Kicińska.

52. Hargreaves, *Blitzkrieg Unleashed*, 85; Garliński, *Poland in the Second World War*, 12; Kennedy, *German Campaign*, 51–4.

53. P. Fleming (born Piotr Tarczyński), IWM 2289 86/17/1; interview with J. Garliński, IWM 10592; A. Suchcitz, 'From Tsarist Subject to Soviet Prisoner: General Anders' Road to Command 1892–1929', in Pyłat, Ciechanowski & Suchcitz, *General Władysław Anders*, 1–17.

54. Zaloga & Madeja, *Polish Campaign*, 26; Turnbull & Suchcitz, *Sword*, 77–8.

55. Garliński, *Poland in the Second World War*, 12; Polonsky, *Politics in Independent Poland*, 490–91; Zamoyski, *Forgotten Few*, 16–19.

56. Suchcitz, 'Poland's Defence Preparations', in Stachura, *Poland Between the Wars*; Prażmowska, *Britain, Poland and the Eastern Front*, 89–92; Plan Zachód can be found in Sikorski Institute, *Polskie Siły Zbrojne*, vol. 1, 257–420.

57. Reports to the State Department, Biddle, 29 March & 6 May 1939, in Cannistraro, Wynot & Kovaleff, *Poland and the Coming of the Second World War*, 48–9, 64.

58. Suchcitz, 'Poland's Defence Preparations', in Stachura, *Poland Between the Wars*; report to the Chiefs of Staff Committee, 15 June 1939, TNA, CAB 53/50; TNA, CAB 23/100; diary entry 10 July 1939, Macleod & Kelly, *Ironside Diaries*, 78.

59. The British Mission to Poland, TNA, FO 371/22925; Suchcitz, 'Poland's Defence Preparations', in Stachura, *Poland Between the Wars*; Harrison, 'Carton de Wiart's Second Military Mission'.

60. Cannistraro, Wynot & Kovaleff, *Poland and the Coming of the Second World War*, 80–81.

61. Karski, *Great Powers*, 366–9.

62. Raczyński, *In Allied London*, 20.

63. Steiner, *Triumph of the Dark*, 839–44; I. Kershaw, *Hitler*, 201–15.

64. Suchcitz, 'Poland's Defence Preparations', in Stachura, *Poland Between the Wars*; Karski, *Secret State*, 9; Hargreaves, *Blitzkrieg Unleashed*, 76–7; Debicki, *Foreign Policy*, 159; Henderson, *Failure of a Mission*, 261–71.

## CHAPTER 3: THE SEPTEMBER 1939 CAMPAIGN

1. Gluza, *Rok 1939*, 85.

2. Hollingworth, *Three Weeks War*, 16.

3. Diary entry 1 September 1939, Macleod & Kelly, *Ironside Diaries*, 9. When Britain declared war on Germany, Ironside was appointed CIGS and Gort commander-in-chief of the British Expeditionary Force.

4. R. Smorczewski, IWM 128787 03/41/1.

5. Krystyna Kuczyńska-Dudli, in Lukas, *Forgotten Survivors*, 67.

6. Zaloga & Madeja, *Polish Campaign*, 108–10, 113–14; Garliński, *Poland in the Second World War*, 14–15; Prażmowska, *Britain and Poland, 1939–1943*, 3.

7. Zaloga & Madeja, *Polish Campaign*, 92–3.

8. Carton de Wiart, *Happy Odyssey*, 156.

9. Lukas, *Did the Children Cry*, 14.

10. R. Zolski, IWM 4211 83/24/1.

11. Author's interview with Anna Kochańska.

12. Hargreaves, *Blitzkrieg Unleashed*, 99–100.

13. Karski, *Secret State*, 12.

14. Hargreaves, *Blitzkrieg Unleashed*, 12–13; Zaloga & Madeja, *Polish Campaign*, 110; Piekałkiewicz, *Cavalry*, 8.

15. Major Stanisław Wojtaszewski, quoted in Gluza, *Rok 1939*, 102.

16. Hargreaves, *Blitzkrieg Unleashed*, 129; Karski, *Secret State*, 13; Zaloga & Madeja, *Polish Campaign*, 117–21.

17. 3 September 1939, *Hansard*, vol. 351, 293.

18. Jędrzejewicz, *Łukasiewicz*, 290–91.

19. Klukowski, *Diary from the Years of Occupation*, 6.

20. Shirer, *Rise and Fall*, 742.

21. Zaloga & Madeja, *Polish Campaign*, 123–6.

22. Carton De Wiart, *Happy Odyssey*, 155.

23. Czarnomski, *They Fight for Poland*, 35.

24. Karski, *Great Powers*, 376–8; Shirer, *Rise and Fall*, 763.

25. Jędrzejewicz, *Łukasiewicz*, 295.

26. Diary entry 18 October 1939, Taylor, *Goebbels Diaries*, 24.

27. Karski, *Great Powers*, 376–8; Prażmowska, *Britain, Poland and the Eastern*

*Front*, 182–4; Dilks, *Diaries*, 215–6; diary entry 29 September 1939, Macleod & Kelly, *Ironside Diaries*, 114.

28. Raczyński, *In Allied London*, 31.

29. TNA, AIR 8/260.

30. Jędrzejewicz, *Łukasiewicz*, 297.

31. TNA, FO 371/23147; Prażmowska, *Britain, Poland and the Eastern Front*, 186–8; TNA, FO 371/23147; CAB 65/1, War Council, 6 September. Norwid-Neugebauer resigned as head of the Polish military mission in January 1940; from November 1942 to 1947 he headed the Administration of the Polish Armed Forces (Norwid-Neugebauer, *Defence of Poland, passim*).

32. Gluza, *Rok 1939*, 105.

33. Klukowski, *Diary from the Years of Occupation*, 16.

34. Gluza, *Rok 1939*, 123.

35. Hollingworth, *Three Weeks' War*, 24.

36. Polish Ministry of Information, *The German Invasion of Poland*, 50.

37. Robbins Landon, *Prüller*, 29.

38. Hargreaves, *Blitzkrieg Unleashed*, 231–8; Rossino, *Hitler Strikes Poland*, 15, 62–72, 79, 90; Gluza, *Rok 1939*, 100–101.

39. Hargreaves, *Blitzkrieg Unleashed*, 130, 142–3; Zaloga & Madeja, *Polish Campaign*, 142. Sucharski's breakdown was concealed by his subordinates and he became a hero in post-war Poland.

40. Corporal Bronisław Grudziński and Bernard Rygielski, quoted in Gluza, *Rok 1939*, 111.

41. Zaloga & Madeja, *Polish Campaign*, 127–30.

42. Sosabowski, *Freely I Served*, 22–30; Prażmowska, *Britain and Poland, 1939–1943*, 3; Zaloga & Madeja, *Polish Campaign*, 126–7; Cannistraro, Wynot & Kovaleff, *Poland and the Coming of the Second World War*, 146.

43. Garliński, *Poland in the Second World War*, 19; Zaloga & Madeja, *Polish Campaign*, 131–3; Williamson, *Poland Betrayed*, 104.

44. Hargreaves, *Blitzkrieg Unleashed*, 151–6; Zaloga & Madeja, *Polish Campaign*, 132–5.

45. Hargreaves, *Blitzkrieg Unleashed*, 163–7.

46. Piekałkiewicz, *Cavalry*, 12–14.

47. Rudnicki, *Last of the Warhorses*, 32–8.

48. Hargreaves, *Blitzkrieg Unleashed*, 145–6; Zaloga & Madeja, *Polish Campaign*, 139.

49. Hargreaves, *Blitzkrieg Unleashed*, 198–9.

50. Czarnomski, *They Fight for Poland*, 53.

51. Gross, *Revolution from Abroad*, 22–3. Langner escaped to Rumania, and then to France where he joined the reborn Polish Army. After the fall of France he went to Britain and was appointed commander of the Polish 3rd Carpathian Rifle Brigade stationed in Scotland. In 1941 he gave up his post and from 1943 served as an inspector of military training of Polish units in Britain.

52. *DPSR*, vol. I, 46.
53. Sword, *Soviet Takeover*, xvi.
54. *DPSR*, vol. I, 42.
55. Hollingworth, *Front Line*, 84.
56. Diary entry 17 September 1939, in Colville, *Fringes of Power*, 23.
57. TNA, FO 371/23103.
58. Chamberlain statement to Commons, 20 September 1939, *Hansard*, vol. 351, 976–8.
59. Raczyński, *In Allied London*, 37–8; Sword, 'British Reactions to the Soviet Occupation'.
60. Halifax to House of Lords, 26 October 1939, *Hansard*, vol. 114, 1565.
61. Gluza, *Rok 1939*, 136.
62. Carton de Wiart, *Happy Odyssey*, 159.
63. Gluza, *Rok 1939*, 139.
64. Szawłowski, *Wojna Polsko-Sowiecka*, vol. 1, 39–46.
65. Apolinary in Grudzińska-Gross & Gross, *War through Children's Eyes*, 205.
66. Zaloga & Madeja, *Polish Campaign*, 151–2.
67. Grudzińska-Gross & Gross, *War through Children's Eyes*, 6.
68. Gluza, *Rok 1939*, 135, 141, 151.
69. Williamson, *Poland Betrayed*, 122–4; Szawłowski, *Wojna Polsko-Sowiecka*, *passim*; Cygan, *Kresy w ogniu*, *passim*.
70. Gluza, *Rok 1939*, 156–7, 161.
71. Zaloga & Madeja, *Polish Campaign*, 140–41; Hargreaves, *Blitzkrieg Unleashed*, 243–4.
72. Szpilman, *Pianist*, 36.
73. Hargreaves, *Blitzkrieg Unleashed*, 247–8; Zaloga & Madeja, *Polish Campaign*, 141; Gluza, *Rok 1939*, 159, 162.
74. Sosabowski, *Freely I Served*, 42, 46.
75. Rudnicki, *Last of the Warhorses*, 53.
76. Gluza, *Rok 1939*, 169.
77. Hargreaves, *Blitzkrieg Unleashed*, 262–3.
78. Ibid., 261.
79. Zaloga & Madeja, *Polish Campaign*, 156.
80. Datner, *Crimes against POWs*, xxx, 20–31.
81. Rossino, *Hitler Strikes Poland*, 180–84; Hargreaves, *Blitzkrieg Unleashed*, 231–8; Garliński, *Poland in the Second World War*, 25; Zaloga & Madeja, *Polish Campaign*, 156.
82. Zamoyski, *Forgotten Few*, 21–32.
83. Czarnomski, *They Fight for Poland*, 233.
84. Zaloga & Madeja, *Polish Campaign*, 145–6.
85. Williamson, *Poland Betrayed*, 73–4.
86. Zaloga & Madeja, *Polish Campaign*, 143–4.
87. Ibid., 156.

88. A. Harvey, 'The French Armée de l'Air'.

89. Carton de Wiart's report, TNA, WO 106/1747; The Biddle Report in Cannistraro, Wynot & Kovaleff, *Poland and the Coming of the Second World War*, 166–73; Harrison, 'Carton de Wiart's Second Military Mission'.

90. Keith Sword interview with Peter Wilkinson, SSEES archives, SWO 1/3.

91. Franciszek Kornicki, IWM 01/1/1; Baluk, *Silent and Unseen*, 74.

92. Hargreaves, *Blitzkrieg Unleashed*, 210.

93. Kesselring, *Memoirs*, 46.

94. *Destiny Can Wait*, 12–13.

95. Tooze, *Wages of Destruction*, 328–9.

96. Diary entry 5 October 1939, Macleod & Kelly, *Ironside Diaries*, 117.

97. Hargreaves, *Blitzkrieg Unleashed*, 264–5.

98. Rudnicki, *Last of the Warhorses*, 62–6; Zaloga & Madeja, *Polish Campaign*, 113.

99. M. Rymaszewski, IWM 11621 02/28/1.

100. Piekałkiewicz, *Cavalry*, 16; Anonymous, 'German Cavalry in World War II'.

101. Hollingworth, *Three Weeks' War*, 72; statement by Halifax, 13 September 1939, *Hansard*, vol. 114, 1051; Sir E. Grigg, House of Commons, 20 September 1939, *Hansard*, vol. 351, 956.

102. Kwiatkowski, quoted in Gluza, *Rok 1939*, 139.

103. Biddle to Secretary of State, 19 September 1939, and Bullitt, ambassador in France, to Secretary of State, 18 October 1939, *FRUS 1939*, vol. II, 689, 697.

104. Cannistraro, Wynot & Kovaleff, *Poland and the Coming of the Second World War*, 163.

105. Jędrzejewicz, *Łukasiewicz*, 351–73.

106. Diary entry 26 September 1939, Dilks, *Diaries*, 219.

107. Raczyński, *In Allied London*, 40–44.

108. Baluk, *Unseen and Silent*, 74.

109. Wood & Jankowski, *Karski*, 60.

110. TNA, FO 371/23153.

111. 'Preliminary guidelines on the opinions and aims of the government, 8 November 1939; report on the visit to England, 23 November 1939', in *Protokoły*, vol. I, 81–4, 94–101.

112. Guidelines for the underground, 23 November 1939, *AK Documents*, vol. VI, no. 1589, 1–4.

113. Karski, *Great Powers*, 355.

## CHAPTER 4: THE GERMAN AND SOVIET OCCUPATION OF POLAND TO JUNE 1941

1. Karski, *Secret State*, 46.

2. Korboński, *Fighting Warsaw*, 8.

3. Łuczak, *Polska i Polacy*, 91–7; I. Kershaw, *Hitler*, 238–9.

4. Chodakiewicz, *Between Nazis and Soviets*, 86; Mazower, *Hitler's Empire*, 74; Lukas, *Forgotten Holocaust*, 111.

5. A. Prażmowska, 'The Experience of Occupation: Poland', in Bourne, Liddle & Whitehead, *Great World War*, 551–65; diary entry 9 February 1940, in Taylor, *Goebbels Diaries*, 118; Kunicki, 'Unwanted Collaborators'.

6. Lukas, *Forgotten Holocaust*, 8; speech by Frank to the army, 3 October 1939, quoted in Shirer, *Rise and Fall*, 1124; diary entry 5 November 1940, Taylor, *Goebbels Diaries*, 165.

7. S. Piotrowski, *Hans Frank's Diary*, 110.

8. Chodakiewicz, *Between Nazis and Soviets*, 78; Karski, *Secret State*, 15; Polish Ministry of Information, *German New Order in Poland*, 129.

9. S. Piotrowski, *Hans Frank's Diary*, 226.

10. Gluza, *Rok 1939*, 181.

11. Housden, *Hans Frank*, 117.

12. S. Milton, 'Non-Jewish Children in the Camps', in Berenbaum, *Mosaic of Victims*, 150–60.

13. J. Garliński, 'The Polish Underground State 1939–45'; Łuczak, *Polska i Polacy*, 475–8.

14. Polish Ministry of Information, *German New Order in Poland, passim.*

15. Housden, *Hans Frank*, 82, 85; Lukas, *Forgotten Holocaust*, 11; S. Piotrowski, *Hans Frank's Diary*, 194.

16. Lukas, *Forgotten Holocaust*, 27–8; J. Gross, *Polish Society under German Occupation*, 96; Chodakiewicz, *Between Nazis and Soviets*, 68; Housden, *Hans Frank*, 96–9.

17. Łuczak, *Polska i Polacy*, 197–200; Lukas, *Forgotten Holocaust*, 29; Tooze, *Wages of Destruction*, 365; Klukowski, *Diary from the Years of Occupation*, various entries.

18. Klukowski, *Diary from the Years of Occupation*, 87.

19. Gilbert, *Second World War*, 40; Tooze, *Wages of Destruction*, 362.

20. Gross, *Polish Society*, 76–80; Łuczak, *Polska i Polacy*, 277–94; Lukas, *Forgotten Holocaust*, 33; U. Herbert, *Hitler's Foreign Workers*, 71.

21. Datner, *Crimes against POWs*, xvii–xviii; U. Herbert, *Hitler's Foreign Workers*, 66; Tooze, *Wages of Destruction*, 363; Peter Fleming (Piotr Tarczyński), IWM 2289 86/17/1.

22. Polish Ministry of Information, *German New Order in Poland*, 117–22.

23. Lanckorońska, *Those Who Trespass Against Us*, 59.

24. Datner, *Crimes against POWs*, 99–105.

25. Bergen, 'The Nazi Concept of "Volksdeutsche"'; I. Kershaw, 'War and "Ethnic Cleansing": The Case of the "Warthegau"', in Robertson, *War, Resistance and Intelligence*, 83–96; Lane, *Victims of Stalin and Hitler*, 40; Stoltman, *Trust Me You Will Survive*, 37.

26. Rutherford, *Prelude to the Final Solution*, 11.

27. Polish Ministry of Information, *German New Order in Poland*, 181.
28. Łuczak, *Polska i Polacy*, 141–5.
29. S. Piotrowski, *Hans Frank's Diary*, 79.
30. Garliński, *Poland in the Second World War*, 27–9; Bór-Komorowski, *Secret Army*, 19; Lukas, *Did the Children Cry*, 19; Tooze, *Wages of Destruction*, 464; Polish Ministry of Information, *German Invasion of Poland*; Karski, *Secret State*, 68; Mazower, *Hitler's Empire*, 84–88.
31. Interview with Z. Szkopiak, IWM 16816.
32. S. Piotrowski, *Hans Frank's Diary*, 217.
33. Chodakiewicz, *Between Nazis and Soviets*, 139–43.
34. Under the Nuremberg Laws there were several definitions of a non-Aryan: '1. A Jew is a person descended from at least two fully Jewish grandparents by race or married to a Jewish person on 15 September 1935, or descended from three or four Jewish grandparents; 2. *Mischlinge* of the first degree – person descended from two Jewish grandparents but not belonging to the Jewish religion and not married to a Jewish person on 15 September 1935; *Mischlinge* of the second degree – Person descended from one Jewish grandparent' (Hilberg, *Destruction of the European Jews*, vol. I, 80).
35. Longerich, *Holocaust*, 160; Gutman & Krakowski, *Unequal Victims*, 32.
36. Diary entry 27 October 1940, Katsch, *Scroll of Agony*, 215–16.
37. Neuman-Mowicki, *Struggle for Life*, 19–20.
38. Marrus, *Unwanted*, 230.
39. Wood & Jankowski, *Karski*, 53.
40. Hilberg, *Destruction of European Jews*, vol. I, 234.
41. Ringelblum, *Notes from the Warsaw Ghetto*, 73.
42. Hilberg, *Destruction of European Jews*, vol. I, 210, 222–3, 226.
43. Edelman, *Ghetto Fights*, 6.
44. Ringelblum, *Notes from the Warsaw Ghetto*, 89, 130.
45. Ringelblum, *Polish-Jewish Relations*, 87.
46. Iwaszkiewicz, *Notaki 1939–1945*, 48.
47. Hilberg, *Destruction of European Jews*, vol. I, 218.
48. Korboński, *Fighting Warsaw*, 15.
49. S. Piotrowski, *Hans Frank's Diary*, 49.
50. Korboński, *Fighting Warsaw*, 56.
51. Diary entry 10 March 1941, Klukowski, *Diary from the Years of Occupation*, 141.
52. Korboński, *Fighting Warsaw*, 50–51.
53. Gumkowski & Leszczyński, *Poland Under Nazi Occupation*, 112–14.
54. Lukas, *Forgotten Survivors*, 53–5.
55. Lukas, *Forgotten Holocaust*, 8–9.
56. Polish Ministry of Information, *German Invasion of Poland*, 22–3.
57. Housden, *Hans Frank*, 120–21.
58. Polish Ministry of Information, *German Invasion of Poland*, 23; Snyder,

*Bloodlands*, 147–8; T. Piotrowski, *Poland's Holocaust*, 28; S. Piotrowski, *Hans Frank's Diary*, 138.

59. Testimony of Hans Frank at Nuremberg, 18 April 1946, Yale University Avalon Project.
60. S. Piotrowski, *Hans Frank's Diary*, 136.
61. *AK Documents*, vol. I, 2.
62. Alexander Maisner, IWM 91/1/1.
63. Garliński, 'The Polish Underground State'.
64. Ibid.; Bór-Komorowski, *Secret Army*, 24.
65. Instruction No. 1, 4 December 1939, Instruction No. 3, 8 April 1940, Instruction No. 6, 3 November 1940, *AK Documents*, vol. I, 10–21, 187–92, 305–24.
66. Harrison, 'The British Special Operations Executive and Poland'.
67. Diary entry 9 November 1940, Klukowski, *Diary from the Years of Occupation*, 124.
68. Sagajllo, *Man in the Middle*, 21.
69. Wood & Jankowski, *Karski*, 63–4; Prażmowska, *Civil War in Poland*, 25–6.
70. Garliński, 'The Polish Underground State'.
71. Bór-Komorowski, *Secret Army*, 33, 47.
72. Karski, *Secret State*, 88.
73. Gross, *Revolution from Abroad*, 13.
74. Despatch of unnamed journalist, 25 September 1939, quoted in Sukiennicki, 'The Establishment of the Soviet Regime'.
75. Gross, *Revolution from Abroad*, 35–40, 50–53.
76. M. Szuba-Tomaszewska, quoted in *Stalin's Ethnic Cleansing* 33.
77. Henryk N., quoted in Grudzińska-Gross & Gross, *War Through Children's Eyes*, 148.
78. E. Piekarski, IWM 16697.
79. Author's interview with Nina Kochańska.
80. Grudzińska-Gross & Gross, *War Through Children's Eyes*, 9.
81. Davies & Polonsky, *Jews in Eastern Poland*, 10–16; Gross, *Revolution from Abroad*, 32–3; Korzec & Szurek, 'Jews and Poles under Soviet Occupation'; Prusin, *Lands Between*, 130–31; J. Gross, 'A Tangled Web: Confronting Stereotypes concerning Relations between the Poles, Germans, Jews, and Communists', in Deák, Gross & Judt, *Politics of Retribution*, 74–129.
82. Julian M. in Grudzińska-Gross & Gross, *War Through Children's Eyes*, 101.
83. Quoted in *Stalin's Ethnic Cleansing*, 156.
84. Interview with S. Kujawiński, IWM 12018.
85. Author's interview with Nina Kochańska.
86. Quoted in *Stalin's Ethnic Cleansing*, 426.
87. Quoted in T. Piotrowski, *Polish Deportees*, 26.
88. Gross, *Revolution from Abroad*, 71–113.
89. Sobieski, 'Reminiscences from Lwów'.

90. Gluza, *Rok 1939*, 186.
91. Henryk N., in Grudzińska-Gross & Gross, *War Through Children's Eyes*, 150.
92. Zajdlerowa, *Dark Side of the Moon*, 47.
93. Kuśnierz, *Stalin and the Poles*, 55; Gross, *Revolution from Abroad*, 188–9.
94. Quoted in Zbikowski, 'The Jewish Reaction to the Soviet Arrival in the Kresy'.
95. Gross, 'A Tangled Web', in Deák, Gross & Judt, *Politics of Retribution*.
96. Sword, *Deportation and Exile*, 10.
97. Witold T., in Grudzińska-Gross & Gross, *War Through Children's Eyes*, 194.
98. Sukiennicki, 'The Establishment of the Soviet Regime'; Prusin, *Lands Between*, 131–2.
99. Gross, *Revolution from Abroad*, 126–38.
100. Witold T., in Grudzińska-Gross & Gross, *War Through Children's Eyes*, 195.
101. B. M. Trybuchowski, in *Stalin's Ethnic Cleansing*, 667.
102. Lanckorońska, *Those Who Trespass Against Us*, 8; author's correspondence with Anna Kochańska.
103. Lukas, *Forgotten Holocaust*, 14–15.
104. Author's interview with Nina Kochańska.
105. Zbigniew & Zeev, in Grudzińska-Gross & Gross, *War Through Children's Eyes*, 217, 230.
106. Rees, *World War Two*, 25.
107. Apolinary H., in Grudzińska-Gross & Gross, *War Through Children's Eyes*, 205.
108. Interview with K. Dobrowolski, IWM 17438.
109. Zajdlerowa, *Dark Side of the Moon*, 47; Strzembosz, *Studia z dziejów okupacji sowieckiej, passim*.
110. Grudzińska-Gross & Gross, *War Through Children's Eyes*, 12–14; Kuśnierz, *Stalin and the Poles*, 59.
111. W. Bonusiak, 'Przemiany ekonomiczne w Małopolsce Wschodniej w latach 1939–1941', in Chmielowiec, *Okupacja sowiecka ziem polskich*, 113–30; Prusin, *Lands Between*, 134.
112. Rees, *World War Two*, 27–8.
113. Author's interviews with Nina and Renia Kochańska.
114. Wiesław R., in Grudzińska-Gross & Gross, *War Through Children's Eyes*, 64.
115. Snyder, *Bloodlands*, 93–104; Gross, *Revolution from Abroad*, 144–86.
116. Author's interview with Nina Kochańska.
117. Maisner, IWM 91/1/1.
118. Piesakowski, *Fate of Poles*, 41.
119. Gross, *Revolution from Abroad*, 144–86.
120. *Stalin's Ethnic Cleansing*, 108.
121. Z. Berling, *Wspomnienia*, vol. I, 37–53.
122. Piesakowski, *Fate of Poles*, 47; N. Lebedeva, 'The Deportation of the Polish Population to the USSR, 1939–41', in Rieber, *Communist Studies*, 28–45;

Cienciala, Lebedeva & Materski, *Katyń*, 26; Sanford, 'The Katyń Massacre and Polish-Soviet Relations'.

123. Rees, *World War Two*, 54-8.

124. Paul, *Katyń*, 81-4.

125. Cienciala, Lebedeva & Materski, *Katyń*, 137-44.

126. Swianiewicz *et al.*, *Crime of Katyń*.

127. Kuśnierz, *Stalin and the Poles*, 69; Z. Siemaszko, 'The Mass Deportation of the Polish Population to the USSR, 1940-1941', in Sword, *Soviet Takeover*, 217-35.

128. T. Piotrowski, *Polish Deportees*, 31.

129. Ibid., 21.

130. Interviews with D. Sobolewska, W. Chmura, K. Dobrowolski, all IWM 13043, 16635, 17438; J. Kucięba & O. Nowicka, in *Stalin's Ethnic Cleansing*, 336, 614.

131. Julian M. & Janusz K., in Grudzińska-Gross & Gross, *War Through Children's Eyes*, 102, 115.

132. T. Piotrowski, *Polish Deportees*, 25.

133. Author's interviews with Nina and Anna Kochańska.

134. T. Piotrowski, *Polish Deportees*, 18.

135. Interview with K. Bortkiewicz, IWM 21562; Nikodem U., in Grudzińska-Gross & Gross, *War Through Children's Eyes*, 154.

## CHAPTER 5: EXILE IN THE SOVIET UNION

1. Z. Siemaszko, 'The Mass Deportation of the Polish Population to the USSR, 1940-1941', in Sword, *Soviet Takeover*, 217-35.

2. Kuśnierz, *Stalin and the Poles*, 68-9; Sikorski Institute, *Polskie Siły Zbrojne*, vol. III, 34.

3. Siemaszko, 'Mass Deportation', in Sword, *Soviet Takeover*; Piesakowski, *Fate of Poles*, 50-51; Gross, *Revolution from Abroad*, used these numbers in the first edition but has acknowledged later research in the 2002 edition.

4. Lebedeva, 'Deportation of the Polish Population', in Rieber, *Communist Studies*; Ciesielski, Materski & Paczkowski, *Represje Sowieckie Wobec Polaków i Obywateli Polskich*, 11-16.

5. Jolluck, *Exile and Identity*, 9-13; Sword, *Deportation and Exile*, 25-7; Cienciala, Lebedeva & Materski, *Katyń*, 153-4.

6. Jolluck, *Exile and Identity*, 14-16; Siemaszko, 'Mass Deportation', in Sword, *Soviet Takeover*.

7. Lane, *Victims of Stalin and Hitler*, 101.

8. Królikowski, *Stolen Childhood*, 19.

9. Zajdlerowa, *Dark Side of the Moon*, 142-3.

10. Author's interview with Nina Kochańska.

11. Diary of the Milewski family, quoted in T. Piotrowski, *Polish Deportees*, 35; interview with Danuta Andresz, IWM 16758; Jolluck, *Exile and Identity*, 38–9.

12. Author's interview with Nina Kochańska.

13. Zajdlerowa, *Dark Side of the Moon*, 147, 151.

14. Ibid., 141; interview with Stanisław Kujawiński, IWM 12018; interview with Zdzisława Kawencka, IWM 16847; Jolluck, *Exile and Identity*, 38.

15. Author's interviews with Nina and Krzysia Kochańska; Zajdlerowa, *Dark Side of the Moon*, 141.

16. Julian M., in Grudzińska-Gross & Gross, *War Through Children's Eyes*, 104; Tadeusz Pieczko, in T. Piotrowski, *Polish Deportees*, 58.

17. For example Danuta G., in Grudzińska-Gross & Gross, *War Through Children's Eyes*, 74–5; interview with K. Dobrowolski, IWM 17438; author's interview with Nina Kochańska.

18. Much of this timber was sent to Germany in accordance with the Molotov–Ribbentrop Treaty. Jolluck, *Exile and Identity*, 57–8.

19. Królikowski, *Stolen Childhood*, 21.

20. Stanisław K., in Grudzińska-Gross & Gross, *War Through Children's Eyes*, 121–4.

21. Lane, *Victims of Stalin and Hitler*, 110.

22. Jolluck, *Exile and Identity*, 59.

23. Dobrowolski, IWM 17438; author's interview with Stanisław Kochański.

24. Author's interview with Nina Kochańska; Huntingdon, *Unsettled Account*, 133.

25. Jolluck, *Exile and Identity*, 63; Dobrowolski, IWM 17438; author's interview with Nina Kochańska; Kawencka, IWM 16847.

26. Author's interview with Nina Kochańska; Zajdlerowa, *Dark Side of the Moon*, 150.

27. Author's interview with Nina Kochańska.

28. Zajdlerowa, *Dark Side of the Moon*, 148.

29. Huntingdon, *Unsettled Account*, 109.

30. Zajdlerowa, *Dark Side of the Moon*, 143.

31. Interview with Elizabeth Piekarski, IWM 16697; Jolluck, *Exile and Identity*, 63.

32. Helena F., in Grudzińska-Gross & Gross, *War Through Children's Eyes*, 216–17.

33. Author's interview with Nina Kochańska.

34. Zajdlerowa, *Dark Side of the Moon*; author's interview with Stanisław Kochański; Kujawiński, IWM 12018.

35. Jolluck, *Exile and Identity*, 74; Huntingdon, *Unsettled Account*, 125.

36. Author's interview with Stanisław Kochański.

37. Ibid.; Dobrowolski, IWM 17438; Pieczko, in T. Piotrowski, *Polish Deportees*, 59.

38. Zajdlerowa, *Dark Side of the Moon*, 145; Grudzińska-Gross & Gross, *War Through Children's Eyes*, 56–8, 110–11, 216–17; Sabina Lukasiewicz, Józefa Pucia-Zawada and Władysław Jarnicki, in T. Piotrowski, *Polish Deportees*, 60, 63, 65.

39. Arnold Rymaszewski, IWM 11621 02/28/1; author's interview with Nina Kochańska; T. Piotrowski, *Polish Deportees*, 72.

40. Pierkarski, IWM 16697; Stanisław J. & Stanisław B, in Grudzińska-Gross & Gross, *War Through Children's Eyes*, 84–7, 143–5.

41. Dobrowolski, IWM 17438; Huntingdon, *Unsettled Account*, 143; author's interview with Nina Kochańska.

42. Królikowski, *Stolen Childhood*, 24.

43. Milewski, in T. Piotrowski, *Polish Deportees*, 35.

44. Eva Sowińska, in ibid., 68–9.

45. Kawencka, IWM 16847; Zajdlerowa, *Dark Side of the Moon*, 144; author's interview with Stanisław Kochański; Adam R., in Grudzińska-Gross & Gross, *War Through Children's Eyes*, 62–3; Huntingdon, *Unsettled Account*, 109; Kelly, *Finding Poland*, 125, 127.

46. Milewski, in T. Piotrowski, *Polish Deportees*; Kuśnierz, *Stalin and the Poles*, 84; Huntingdon, *Unsettled Account*, 166–7; author's interview with Nina Kochańska.

47. Author's interview with Nina Kochańska; Dobrowolski, IWM 17438; Zajdlerowa, *Dark Side of the Moon*, 144; Huntingdon, *Unsettled Account*, 128–31; Danuta G. & Alfred P., in Grudzińska-Gross & Gross, *War Through Children's Eyes*, 74–5, 118.

48. Grudzińska-Gross & Gross, *War Through Children's Eyes*, xxiii, 183–90; Zajdlerowa, *Dark Side of the Moon*, 150–51; Dobrowolski, IWM 17438; author's interview with Nina Kochańska.

49. Zajdlerowa, *Dark Side of the Moon*, 148.

50. Piekarski, IWM 16697; author's interview Kryszia Kochańska; Huntingdon, *Unsettled Account*, 114.

51. Anna Mineyko, in T. Piotrowski, *Polish Deportees*, 72.

52. Stanisław K. and Zeev F., in Grudzińska-Gross & Gross, *War Through Children's Eyes*, 121–4, 230–34; Pieczko, in T. Piotrowski, *Polish Deportees*, 56.

53. Milewski, in T. Piotrowski, *Polish Deportees*, 46; Dobrowolski, IWM 17438; Apolinary H., in Grudzińska-Gross & Gross, *War Through Children's Eyes*, 205–10.

54. Milewski, in T. Piotrowski, *Polish Deportees*, 36–7.

55. Author's interview with Renia Kochańska.

56. F. Lachman, IWM 1191 91/6/1.

57. Vala Miron and Stefania Buczak-Zarzycka, in T. Piotrowski, *Polish Deportees*, 53–5; Dobrowolski, IWM 17438.

58. Kujawiński, IWM 12018; Zajdlerowa, *Dark Side of the Moon*, 144; author's interview with Nina Kochańska.

59. Maria Borkowska-Witkowska, in T. Piotrowski, *Polish Deportees*, 60–61; Huntingdon, *Unsettled Account*, 184–91.

60. Kennard to Halifax, 18 May 1940, TNA, FO 371/5744/116/55; Teresa Lipkowska, quoted in Rozek, *Allied Wartime Diplomacy*, 76–7.


CHAPTER 6: ESCAPE FROM THE SOVIET UNION

1. World Broadcast on the German Invasion of Russia, 22 June 1941, in Churchill, *Great War Speeches*, 122.

2. Sikorski's broadcast to the Polish nation, 23 June 1941, DPSR, vol. I, 108–12.

3. Ciechanowski, *Defeat in Victory*, 39–41.

4. TNA, FO 371/24472.

5. See Gorodetsky, *Stafford Cripps in Moscow*.

6. Protest of the Polish Government to the Allied and Neutral Governments against the conscription of Polish citizens by the Red Army, 3 February 1940, in *DPSR*, vol. I, 93.

7. Retinger, *Memoirs*, 110; Cienciala, 'The Question of the Polish-Soviet Frontier in 1939–1940'; Cienciala, 'General Sikorski and the Conclusion of the Polish-Soviet Agreement'; Prażmowska, *Britain and Poland, 1939–1943*, 64; J. Coutouvidis, 'Sikorski's Thirty Day Crisis, 19 June–19 July 1940', in Sword, *Sikorski*, 116–20.

8. Note made by General Sikorski on his conversation with Sir Stafford Cripps on the imminent outbreak of war between Germany and the USSR, 18 June 1941, *DPSR*, no. 85, 103–8.

9. Diary entry 5 July 1941, Dilks, *Diaries*, 360.

10. Record of a conversation between General Sikorski and Ambassador Maisky on the conditions of resumption of Polish-Soviet relations, 5 July 1941, *DPSR*, vol. I, 117–19.

11. Eden to Zaleski, 18 July 1941, *DPSR*, vol. I, 138–9.

12. Record of a conversation between Sikorski and Maisky, in the presence of Eden, 11 July 1941, *DPSR*, vol. I, 128–32.

13. Quoted in Terry, *Poland's Place in Europe*, 184–5.

14. Cienciala, 'General Sikorski and the Conclusion of the Polish-Soviet Agreement'.

15. Raczyński, *In Allied London*, 95; Retinger, *Memoirs*, 119.

16. Diary entry 27 July 1941, in Gorodetsky, *Stafford Cripps in Moscow*, 132.

17. Diary entry 30 July 1941, in Colville, *Fringes of Power*, 422.

18. Polish-Soviet Agreement, 30 July 1941, *DPSR*, vol. I, 141; Retinger, *Memoirs*, 119.

19. Eden, *Eden Memoirs*, 273.

20. Maisky, *Memoirs of a Soviet Ambassador*, 174.

21. Raczyński, *In Allied London*, 102.
22. Prażmowska, *Britain and Poland, 1939–1943*, 26–7.
23. Rowecki to headquarters, 28 August 1941, *AK Documents*, vol. II, no. 220, 51.
24. Decree by the Presidium of the Supreme Council of the USSR, 12 August 1941, *DPSR*, vol. I, 145.
25. Polish-Soviet Military Agreement, 14 August 1941, *DPSR*, vol. I, 147–8.
26. Garliński, *Poland in the Second World War*, 113.
27. Kot, *Conversations with the Kremlin*, xviii–xix.
28. Sarner, *General Anders*, 36.
29. Sword, *Deportation and Exile*, 35. General A. Wasilewski was also a member of the Soviet military mission.
30. Kot, *Conversations with the Kremlin*, 19.
31. Peszke, *Battle for Warsaw*, 93.
32. Sword, *Deportation and Exile*, 37, 56.
33. General instructions for the Polish ambassador in the Soviet Union, 28 August 1941; Sikorski's instructions to Anders concerning the political conditions under which the Polish forces in the USSR should be used, 1 September 1941, *DPSR*, vol. I, 158–65; Anders, *Army in Exile*, 61–2.
34. Rozek, *Allied Wartime Diplomacy*, 70–71; Kot, *Conversations with the Kremlin*, 10–11; Sword, *Deportation and Exile*, 88.
35. Sword, *Deportation and Exile*, 38.
36. Hulls, 'Russian Polish Relations', 29 October 1942, IWM 4043 84/48/1.
37. Sword, *Deportation and Exile*, 41.
38. K. Colonna-Czosnowski, IWM 5532 96/28/1.
39. A. Maisner, IWM 916 91/1/1.
40. Królikowski, *Stolen Childhood*, 42.
41. A. Gołębiowski, IWM 319 95/6/1.
42. R. Rzepcyński, in T. Piotrowski, *Polish Deportees*, 88.
43. A. Bielińska, in *Stalin's Ethnic Cleansing*, 53.
44. R. Reich, in ibid., 445.
45. W. Godawa, in ibid., 75.
46. A. Belińska, in ibid., 53.
47. E. Hubert, in ibid., 161.
48. Kot to Raczyński, 8 November 1941, Kot, *Conversations with the Kremlin*, 96–7; author's interview with Stanisław Kochański.
49. Sword, *Deportation and Exile*, 43, 46, 48.
50. W. Derfel, in *Stalin's Ethnic Cleansing*, 115.
51. F. Szalasny, in ibid., 456–7.
52. Milewski family, in T. Piotrowski, *Polish Deportees*, 79–80.
53. Huntingdon, *Unsettled Account*, 198.
54. Sword, *Deportation and Exile*, 56.
55. Kot, *Conversations with the Kremlin*, passim.

56. *Destiny Can Wait*, 29.

57. Lane, *Victims of Stalin and Hitler*, 125.

58. Kot, *Conversations with the Kremlin*, 175; Rozek, *Allied Wartime Diplomacy*, 75–7.

59. General instructions for the Ambassador of Poland in the USSR, 28 August 1941, *DPSR*, vol. I, 158–61.

60. Sword, *Deportation and Exile*, 48.

61. Rudnicki, *Last of the Warhorses*, 180, 195–6, 200, 228, 240.

62. Ibid., 203; Czapski, *Inhuman Land, passim*.

63. Sword, *Deportation and Exile*, 3, 37; Z. Siemaszko, 'General Anders in the Soviet Union: September 1939–August 1942', in Pyłat, Ciechanowski & Suchcitz, *General Władysław Anders*, 19–30.

64. Minute of the conversation at the Kremlin between Sikorski and Stalin, 3 December 1941, *DPSR*, vol. I, 231–43.

65. L. Kliszewicz, IWM 7147 97/38/1.

66. Merridale, *Ivan's War*, 66, 92.

67. Summary of despatches received from the Polish Ambassador in Russia, 21 October 1941, in Jędrzejewicz, *Poland in the British Parliament*, vol. II, 14–15.

68. Note from Beria to Stalin, 30 November 1941, in Materski, *Armia Polska*, 19.

69. Kot conversation with Stalin, 14 November 1941, Kot, *Conversations with the Kremlin*, 106–16.

70. British Military Mission, Moscow to Hulls, 8 October 1941; L. Hulls, IWM 4043 84/48/1.

71. Kot to Sikorski, 3 and 8 October 1941, Kot, *Conversations with the Kremlin*, 43–4, 54.

72. A. Gołębiowski, IWM 319 95/6/1.

73. Interview with Z. Kawencka, IWM 16847; D. Maczka, in *Stalin's Ethnic Cleansing*, 212; Sikorski's instructions to Anders, 10 December 1941, *DPSR*, vol. I, 251–3.

74. Memo by the Polish Government-in-Exile to Eden, 28 October 1941, in Jędrzejewicz, *Poland in the British Parliament*, 11–14.

75. Kot conversation with Stalin, 14 November 1941, Kot, *Conversations with the Kremlin*, 106–16.

76. Ciechanowski, *Defeat in Victory*, 76–7.

77. Minute of the conversation at the Kremlin between Sikorski and Stalin, 3 December 1941; note of a conversation between Sikorski and Stalin during dinner at the Kremlin, 4 December 1941; declaration of friendship and mutual assistance, 4 December 1941, *DPSR*, vol. I, 231–46.

78. Materski, *Armia Polska*, 40–44.

79. Cazalet, *With Sikorski to Moscow*, 52–5.

80. Huntingdon, *Unsettled Account*, 216.

81. Sword, *Deportation and Exile*, 57; Grudzińska-Gross & Gross, *War Through Children's Eyes*, xxiv; Rudnicki, *Last of the Warhorses*, 221.

82. Milewski family, in T. Piotrowski, *Polish Deportees*, 80.

83. L. Hulls, 26 July 1942, IWM 4043 84/48/1.

84. Grudzińska-Gross & Gross, *War Through Children's Eyes*, xxiv; Sword, *Deportation and Exile*, 57-8; Siemaszko, 'General Anders', in Pyłat, Ciechanowski & Suchcitz, *General Władysław Anders*.

85. Lane, *Victims of Hitler and Stalin*, 126.

86. Sword, *Deportation and Exile*, 90, 94.

87. Rozek, *Allied Wartime Diplomacy*, 104.

88. Sword, *Deportation and Exile*, 45.

89. K. Barut, in *Stalin's Ethnic Cleansing*, 87.

90. B. Stępniewski, in ibid., 330.

91. J. Kucięba, in ibid., 341.

92. L. Hulls, 'The Polish Army in Russia', 18 June 1942, IWM 4043 84/48/1.

93. Sword, *Deportation and Exile*, 98.

94. Fels, '"Whatever Your Heart Dictates and Your Pocket Permits"'.

95. K. Sword, 'The Welfare of Polish-Jewish Refugees in the USSR, 1941-43: Relief Supplies and Their Distribution', in Davies & Polonsky, *Jews in Eastern Poland*, 145-58.

96. Kot, *Conversations with the Kremlin*, 159-60, 227; D. Engel, 'The Polish Government-in-Exile and the Erlich-Alter Affair', in Davies & Polonsky, *Jews in Eastern Poland*, 172-82.

97. H. Swiderska, in Grudzińska-Gross & Gross, *War Through Children's Eyes*, 46-8; Królikowski, *Stolen Childhood*, 59.

98. Zajdlerowa, *Dark Side of the Moon*, 203.

99. Meeting between Anders and Stalin, 18 March 1942, *DPSR*, vol. I, 301-10; Anders, *Army in Exile*, 96-100.

100. Gilbert, *Second World War*, 226.

101. Sword, *Deportation and Exile*, 64.

102. Hodgkin, *Letters from Teheran*, 128.

103. Sword, *Deportation and Exile*, 65-6; M. Polak, 'An Alternative View: The Controversy Surrounding the Military Decisions Taken by General Anders', in Pyłat, Ciechanowski & Suchcitz, *General Władysław Anders*, 91-111.

104. Sword, *Deportation and Exile*, 66-7.

105. Rudnicki, *Last of the Warhorses*, 229; Berling, *Wspomnienia*, vol. I, 254-68.

106. Interview with Kazimierz Dobrowolski, IWM 17438; author's interview with Stanisław Kochański.

107. A. Gołębiowski, IWM 319 95/6/1.

108. Ryszard Zolski, IWM 4211 83/24/1.

109. Arnold Rymaszewski, IWM 11621 02/28/1.

110. I. Szunejko, in T. Piotrowski, *Polish Deportees*, 90.

111. Sword, *Deportation and Exile*, 67.

112. Kot to Anders, 26 March 1942 and Klimecki to Anders, 27 March 1942, in Anders, *Army in Exile*, 101–2.

113. Note from Beria to Stalin, 4 April 1942, in Materski, *Armia Polska*, 91–3.

114. Woodward, *British Foreign Policy*, vol. II, 617–18; Zajdlerowa, *Dark Side of the Moon*, 204; Sword, *Deportation and Exile*, 100.

115. A. Rymaszewski, IWM 11621 02/28/1.

116. Rudnicki, *Last of the Warhorses*, 242.

117. Churchill to Stalin, received 18 July 1942, in *Stalin Correspondence*, no. 56, 58–61; Terry, *Poland's Place in Europe*, 235–42.

118. Garliński, *Poland in the Second World War*, 155.

119. Rudnicki, *Last of the Warhorses*, 246.

120. Berling, *Wspomnienia*, vol. I, 280–301.

121. Sword, *Deportation and Exile*, 77.

122. Kot conversation with Vyshinsky, 2 June 1942, Kot, *Conversations with the Kremlin*, 239–42.

123. Telegram from Kot to Raczyński, 9 July 1942, *DPSR*, vol. 1, no. 241, 388–9; Siemaszko, 'General Anders', in Pyłat, Ciechanowski & Suchcitz, *General Władysław Anders*.

124. Author's interview with Nina Kochańska and Stanisław Kochański.

125. Teresa Glazer, in *Poles in India*, 23.

126. Sword, *Deportation and Exile*, 78–9; Garliński, *Poland in the Second World War*, 155; Anders, *Army in Exile*, 112; memorandum of the Polish Embassy in the USSR on the restrictions of the rights of Polish Jews imposed by the Soviet Government, 11 August 1942, *DPSR*, vol. I, Supplement no. 9, 679–87.

127. S. Buczak-Zarzycka, in T. Piotrowski, *Polish Deportees*, 85.

128. Sword, *Deportation and Exile*, 81.

129. Z. Stepek, in *Stalin's Ethnic Cleansing*, 251; author's interview with Renia Kochańska.

130. Sword, *Deportation and Exile*, 74.

131. Anders, *Army in Exile*, 127.

132. Ryszard Zolski, IWM 4211 83/24/1.

133. Wójcik, *Polish Spirit*, 153–4.

134. TNA, FO 371/36691.

135. Żaroń, *Armia Andersa*, 242–3; Giedroyć, *Crater's Edge*, 142–53.

136. Ryszard Zolski, IWM 4211 83/24/1.

137. Wójcik, *Polish Spirit*, 157–8.

138. Author's interview with Stanisław Kochański; Tadeusz Walczak, IWM 6441 97/38/1; Alexander Maisner, IWM 916 91/1/1.

139. R. Terlecki, 'The Jewish Issue in the Polish Army in the USSR and the Near East, 1941–1944', and A. Polonsky, 'The Proposal to Establish a "Jewish Legion" within the Polish Army in the USSR', in Davies & Polonsky, *Jews in Eastern Poland*, 161–70, 361–5; TNA, FO 371/31099.

140. Terlecki, 'The Jewish Issue', Davies & Polonsky, *Jews in Eastern Poland*.

141. Sarner, *General Anders*, 118–20, 134–44.

142. TNA, FO 371/39484; TNA, CO 733/445/11.

143. Edward Wierzbicki, quoted in *Stalin's Ethnic Cleansing*, 644.

144. Author's interview with Nina Kochańska.

145. Materski, *Armia Polska*, 98; Sarner, *General Anders*, 73.

146. Sarner, *General Anders*, 126–7. Rozen-Zawadzki had been one of the offi-cers identified by the NKVD as pro-communist and sent to the 'Bungalow of Bliss' rather than the Lubyanka prison or executed at Katyń.

147. T. Żukowski, IWM 8115 99/3/1.

148. A. Gołębiowski, IWM 319 95/6/1.

149. Papers of Colonel Leslie Hulls, IWM 4043 84/48/1; E. Maresch, 'The Polish 2 Corps in Preparation for Action and its Disbandment 1943–1946', in Pyłat, Ciechanowski & Suchcitz, *General Władysław Anders*, 33–54.

150. Żaroń, *Armia Andersa*, 170–85.

151. Anders, *Army in Exile*, 151.

152. Maresch, 'The Polish 2 Corps', in Pyłat, Ciechanowski & Suchcitz, *General Władysław Anders*; Żaroń, *Armia Andersa*, 227–35; Anders, *Army in Exile*, 150, 153.

## CHAPTER 7: POLAND'S CONTRIBUTION TO THE ALLIED WAR EFFORT, 1940–1943

1. Peszke, *Battle for Warsaw*, 41; Peszke, 'The Polish Armed Forces in Exile' (1987), 33–69; Prażmowska, *Britain and Poland, 1939–1943*, 24.

2. F. Kornicki, IWM 8131; Baluk, *Silent and Unseen*, 47.

3. Sword interview with Robin Hankey, SSEES, SWO 1/3.

4. Fai-Podlipnik, 'Hungary's Relationship with Poland and Its Refugees'; T. Frank, 'Treaty Revision and Doublespeak: Hungarian Neutrality, 1939–1941', in Wylie, *European Neutrals and Non-Belligerents*, 150–73.

5. Piekałkiewicz, *Cavalry*, 14.

6. Maczek, *Od Podwody*, 99.

7. *Destiny Can Wait*, 21–2; McGilvray, *Black Devil's March*, 7–8.

8. Only in 1974 was it revealed that the British had read Enigma throughout the war with the publication of F. W. Winterbottom, *The Ultra Secret*. The most complete story of the Polish contribution to the breaking of Enigma can be found in Kozaczuk, *Enigma*, and Budiansky, *Battle of Wits*.

9. The key for each message was the initial position of the rotor wheels and was chosen randomly by the sender. The chosen key was transmitted just before the message itself, encrypted with a prearranged key known to both sender and receiver, and distributed on monthly sheets, with one key for each day through most of the war, several a day at the end. Other pre-

arranged key information was the choice of which rotors to put into the machine and in which order.

10. Sebag-Montefiore, *Enigma*, 15–41; *APHC*, vol. I, 443–4.

11. Kozaczuk, *Enigma*, 64.

12. Modelski, *Polish Contribution*, 92–5; Sebag-Montefiore, *Enigma*, 51–4.

13. Sebag-Montefiore, *Enigma*, 225–43; Modelski, *Polish Contribution*, 97.

14. Sebag-Montefiore, *Enigma*, 271–4.

15. Kleczkowski, *Poland's First 100,000*, 9–10, 19–20; Peszke, 'The Polish Armed Forces in Exile' (1981), 67–113 .

16. Jędrzejewicz, *Łukasiewicz*, 339–40.

17. Waszak, *Agreement in Principle*, 18.

18. Peszke, 'The Polish Armed Forces in Exile' (1981); Zamoyski, *Forgotten Few*, 50–51.

19. Koskodan, *No Greater Ally*, 45.

20. Kornicki, IWM 8131.

21. Baluk, *Silent and Unseen*, 69; Sosabowski, *Freely I Served*, 81.

22. Pruszyński, *Poland Fights Back*, 54.

23. Czarnomski, *They Fight for Poland*, 164.

24. Stella-Sawicki, Garliński & Mucha, *First to Fight*, 58.

25. Pruszyński, *Poland Fights Back*, 62–3; Stella-Sawicki, Garliński & Mucha, *First to Fight*, 69; Kleczkowski, *Poland's First 100,000*, 23–4; Peszke, *Battle for Warsaw*, 52–5; Polish Ministry of Information, *Polish Troops in Norway*.

26. Waszak, *Agreement in Principle*, 18.

27. Czarnomski, *They Fight for Poland*, 125–6.

28. Baluk, *Silent and Unseen*, 84–5; Maczek, *Od Podwody*, 111–13; Peszke, 'The Polish Armed Forces in Exile' (1981); Kleczkowski, *Poland's First 100,000*, 23–8; Potomski, *Maczek*, 182–98.

29. Slizewski, *Stracone Złudzenia*, 74–5, 86–7, 167.

30. Frieser, *Blitzkrieg Legend*, *passim*; M. Alexander, 'After Dunkirk'.

31. Koskodan, *No Greater Ally*, 56.

32. Peszke, *Battle for Warsaw*, 58–9.

33. Diary entry 25 June 1940, Colville, *Fringes of Power*, 170–71.

34. Prażmowska, *Britain and Poland, 1939–1943*, 26; author's interview with Teresa Kicińska; Peszke, *Battle for Warsaw*, 60–61; Kleczkowski, *Poland's First 100,000*, 35–6.

35. Maczek, *Od Podwody*, 115–23.

36. F. Kornicki, IWM 01/1/1; Baluk, *Silent and Unseen*, 87.

37. Report by General Sosnkowski, *Protokoły*, vol. II, 18–24.

38. Maczek, *Od Podwody*, 121.

39. 18 June 1940, *Hansard*, vol. 362, 61.

40. Keegan, *Second World War*, 94.

41. Koskodan, *No Greater Ally*, 93.

42. Stella-Sawicki, Garliński & Mucha, *First to Fight*, 99.

43. *Bloody Foreigners: The Untold Battle of Britain*, Channel 4 documentary screened on 29 June 2010.

44. Olson & Cloud, *For Your Freedom and Ours*, 92–167.

45. Zamoyski, *Forgotten Few*, 92.

46. Sir Alexander Hardinge to Lord Hamilton of Dalzell, August 1940, quoted in Raczyński, *In Allied London*, 70.

47. Diary entry 21 September 1940, in Colville, *Fringes of Power*, 245–6.

48. Olson & Cloud, *For Your Freedom and Ours*, 177, 181.

49. Stella-Sawicki, Garliński & Mucha, *First to Fight*, 196. The names in Fiedler's book were all fictitious to protect the families of the men in Poland, but after the war a new edition used the real names.

50. Kleczkowski, *Poland's First 100,000*, 58–9; Peszke, 'The Polish Armed Forces in Exile' (1981).

51. TNA, FO 371/26751.

52. Stella-Sawicki, Garliński & Mucha, *First to Fight*, 75.

53. Ibid.

54. Cazalet, *With Sikorski to Moscow*, 16–17.

55. Modelski, *Polish Contribution*, 132; Kitchen, *Rommel's Desert War*, 148.

56. Koskodan, *No Greater Ally*, 103.

57. Cazalet, *With Sikorski to Moscow*, 20.

58. Koskodan, *No Greater Ally*, 104.

59. Modelski, *Polish Contribution*, 132.

60. Stella-Sawicki, Garliński & Mucha, *First to Fight*, 76, 166.

61. Gilbert, *Winston S. Churchill*, vol. VI, 678.

62. Baluk, *Silent and Unseen*, 90.

63. Sosabowski, *Freely I Served*, 91, 94.

64. Peszke, 'The Polish Armed Forces in Exile' (1981); Prażmowska, *Britain and Poland, 1939–1943*, 66, 72.

65. Commons, 8 November 1939, *Hansard*, vol. 353, 229–30.

66. Kukiel, *Generał Sikorski*, 147.

67. TNA, PREM 3/351/1; Sztniewski, 'Teofil Starzyński's Activities'.

68. Stella-Sawicki, Garliński & Mucha, *First to Fight*, 70.

69. Cholewczyński, *Poles Apart*, 46–7, 56; Sosabowski, *Freely I Served*, 101, 105–8. The Poles trained a total of 238 Frenchmen, 172 Norwegians, 2 Czechs, 4 Belgians and 4 Dutchmen.

70. Sosabowski, *Freely I Served*, 113–16.

71. Prażmowska, *Britain and Poland, 1939–1943* is particularly strong on this.

72. Ibid., 24; PISM, A.XII.1/129.

73. Sosabowski, *Freely I Served*, 108.

74. 16 June 1942, *Hansard*, vol. 380, 1368.

75. PISM, A.XII.4/102.

76. 13 October 1943, *Hansard*, vol. 392, 90; 26 October 1943, ibid., vol. 393, 23.

77. Schwonek, 'Kazimierz Sosnkowski as Commander in Chief'.

78. TNA, WO 193/41/80751.
79. Peszke, *Poland's Navy*, 30, 36.
80. TNA, ADM 171/9971.
81. Stella-Sawicki, Garliński & Mucha, *First to Fight*, 90.
82. Peszke, *Poland's Navy*, *passim*.
83. Ibid.
84. Padfield, *War Beneath the Sea*, 76; Peszke, *Poland's Navy*, *passim*.
85. Stella-Sawicki, Garliński & Mucha, *First to Fight*, 96.
86. Peszke, *Poland's Navy*, 36, 167, 171; Stella-Sawicki, Garliński & Mucha, *First to Fight*, 97.
87. *Destiny Can Wait*, 113.
88. Ibid., 214.
89. Ibid., 142.
90. Olson & Cloud, *For Your Freedom and Ours*, 227.
91. Garliński, *Poland in the Second World War*, 145; Stella-Sawicki, Garliński & Mucha, *First to Fight*, 180–84.
92. Koskodan, *No Greater Ally*, 98; Peszke, *Battle for Warsaw*, 122; Stella-Sawicki, Garliński & Mucha, *First to Fight*, 105–11
93. *APHC*, vol. II, 837–46; vol. I, 86.
94. Wood & Jankowski, *Karski*, 137–8.
95. *APHC*, vol. I, 194, 223, 232.
96. Report by Słowikowski, 8 January 1942, *APHC*, vol. II, no. 54, 589–92.
97. Winter, 'Penetrating Hitler's High Command'.
98. Special Operations Executive (SOE) general appreciation regarding Polish intelligence reports on German preparations for an attack on the Soviet Union, 22 April 1941, *APHC*, vol. II, no. 89, 742–5; note by MI14 regarding a possible attack on the USSR, which takes into account Polish intelligence reports, 25 April 1941, *APHC*, vol. II, no. 17, 463–5; vol. I, 284, 532.

## CHAPTER 8: POLISH NON-COMBATANTS OUTSIDE POLAND, 1939–1945

1. Łuczak, *Polska i Polacy*, 568–9.
2. R. Ellis, O'Donovan & Wilson, 'Report on the Condition of Polish Refugees'; Łuczak, *Polska i Polacy*, 568.
3. Kapronczay, *Refugees in Hungary*, 23–169; Stasierski, *Szkolnictwo Polskie na Węgrzech*, *passim*; Fai-Podlipnik, 'Hungary's Relationship with Poland and Its Refugees'; Colonel Korkozowicz to London, 2 November 1943, Colonel Matuszczak to London, 3 November 1943, A. Sapieha to London, 6 November 1943, Sapieha to London, 17 November 1943, all in *AK Documents*, vol. III, 193–7, 201–8.
4. Engel, *Facing a Holocaust*, 29; Łuczak, *Polska i Polacy*, 572.

5. P. Stachura, 'The Poles in Scotland, 1940–50', in Stachura, *Poles in Britain* 48–58; Kernberg, 'The Polish Community in Scotland'.

6. Garliński, *Poland in the Second World War*, 241; author's interview with Teresa Kicińska, who arrived in Switzerland in 1945 and was placed in the guardianship of her half-brother by the Swiss authorities.

7. Łuczak, *Polska i Polacy*, 570–71; Sword, *Formation*, 70; Fels, '"Whatever Your Heart Dictates and Your Pocket Permits"'.

8. *Poles in India*, 15.

9. Hodgkin, *Letters from Teheran*, 129.

10. Tadeusz Zukowski, IWM 8115 99/3/1; Alexander Maisner, IWM 916 91/1/1; Wacława Chmura, IWM 16663; author's interview with Renia Kochańska.

11. *Poles in India*, 14.

12. Janina Żebrowski-Bulmahn, quoted in T. Piotrowski, *Polish Deportees*, 103.

13. Sword, *Deportation and Exile*, 81.

14. Stanisław Milewski, in T. Piotrowski, *Polish Deportees*, 105; *Poles in India*, 13.

15. Aniela Molek-Piotrowska, Stefania Buczak-Zarzycka, Andrzej Czcibor-Piotrowski, all quoted in T. Piotrowski, *Polish Deportees*, 107, 118; author's interview with Renia Kochańska.

16. T. Piotrowski, *Polish Deportees*, 98.

17. *The Times*, 20 June 1942.

18. Letter from Bader to Raczyński, 17 July 1942, in Raczyński, *In Allied London*, 118.

19. For example, Anna Giedroyć and her two daughters. See Giedroyć, *Crater's Edge, passim*.

20. Hodgkin, *Letters from Teheran*, 130.

21. Raczyński, *In Allied London*, 117.

22. Kelly, *Finding Poland*, 155.

23. *Poles in India*, 70.

24. Sikorski to Churchill, 5 June 1942, TNA, FO 371/32629.

25. Cairo to Foreign Office, 22 June 1942, IOR, L/PJ/8/412/316.

26. *Poles in India*, 16.

27. Sword, *Deportation and Exile*, 85–6; *Poles in India*, 83.

28. Królikowski, *Stolen Childhood*, 72.

29. T. Piotrowski, *Polish Deportees*, 131.

30. IOR, L/PJ/8/412; L/PJ/8/413; *Poles in India, passim*.

31. Królikowski, *Stolen Childhood*, 85.

32. T. Piotrowski, *Polish Deportees*, 137–81.

33. Królikowski, *Stolen Childhood*, 98.

34. Sarner, *General Anders*, 113.

35. Królikowski, *Stolen Childhood*, 273–4, 294; T. Piotrowski, *Polish Deportees*, 120–25.

36. T. Piotrowski, *Polish Deportees*, 187.

37. Ibid., 194–5.

## CHAPTER 9: THE DARK YEARS: OCCUPIED POLAND, 1941–1943

1. Quoted in R. Kershaw, *War Without Garlands*, 3.
2. Diary entry 31 May 1941, Klukowski, *Diary from the Years of Occupation*, 152.
3. Lanckorońska, *Those Who Trespass Against Us*, 74–5.
4. R. Smorczewski, IWM 128787 03/41/1.
5. For example, both Erickson and Bellamy refer to this first period as the 'Battle of the Frontiers' but do not mention the Poles at all.
6. Erickson, *Road to Stalingrad*, 118–21; A. Chor'kov, 'The Red Army during the Initial Phase of the Great Patriotic War', in Wegner, *From Peace to War*, 415–29; G. Kumanev, 'The Soviet Economy and the 1941 Evacuation', in Wieczyński, *Operation Barbarossa*, 163–93.
7. Lanckorońska, *Those Who Trespass Against Us*, 66.
8. Rowecki to London, 5 August 1941, *AK Documents*, vol. II, 29.
9. Brigadier General Edel Lingenthal, quoted in Glantz, *Initial Period of War*, 337.
10. Diary entry 5 July 1941, Felix Landau, in Klee, Dressen & Riess, *'The Good Old Days'*, 90–91.
11. Lanckorońska, *Those Who Trespass Against Us*, 88.
12. Halina Ostrowska, in Lukas, *Out of the Inferno*, 130.
13. Kosyk, *Third Reich*, 46–7.
14. Kamenetsky, *Hitler's Occupation of Ukraine*, 43.
15. T. Piotrowski, *Poland's Holocaust*, 87, 166–7.
16. Author's interview with Yarema Bogaychuk.
17. Kamenetsky, *Hitler's Occupation of Ukraine*, 49.
18. Lanckorońska, *Those Who Trespass Against Us*, 88–9. Krüger later arrested and interrogated Countess Lanckorońska in Stanisławów, during which he revealed that he had ordered the murder of the Lwów professors. He was later reprimanded by the SS, not for the murders, but for having revealed his part in them.
19. Olszański, *Kresy Kresów Stanisławów*, 115.
20. Ibid., 120–23.
21. Mazower, *Hitler's Empire*, 281.
22. Lukas, *Out of the Inferno*, 4.
23. Korboński, *Fighting Warsaw*, 219.
24. Tooze, *Wages of Destruction*, 545.
25. Gross, *Polish Society*, 107.
26. Ciechanowski, *Defeat in Victory*, 192.
27. Housden, *Hans Frank*, 181.
28. Korboński, *Fighting Warsaw*, 219–20.

29. Quoted in Lukas, *Out of the Inferno*, 26.
30. S. Piotrowski, *Hans Frank's Diary*, 106.
31. Friedrich, 'Collaboration in a "Land without a Quisling"'.
32. Korboński, *Fighting Warsaw*, 222.
33. Łuczak, *Polska i Polacy*, 315–19.
34. Lanckorońska, *Those Who Trespass Against Us*, 108–9.
35. Klukowski, *Diary from the Years of Occupation*, 173.
36. C. Streit, 'Partisans – Resistance – Prisoners of War', in Wieczyński, *Operation Barbarossa*, 260–75; Snyder, *Bloodlands*, 180.
37. Quoted in Lukas, *Out of the Inferno*, 59.
38. Mazower, *Hitler's Empire*, 299.
39. Homze, *Foreign Labour*, 165.
40. Housden, *Hans Frank*, 196.
41. Herbert, *Hitler's Foreign Workers*, 391.
42. Quoted in Lukas, *Forgotten Survivors*, 35.
43. Tooze, *Wages of Destruction*, 536.
44. L. Collingham, *Taste of War*, 371.
45. Tooze, *Wages of Destruction*, 531–2.
46. T. Piotrowski, *Poland's Holocaust*, 28.
47. Bór-Komorowski, *Secret Army*, 60.
48. Gebhardt was later hanged for his crimes. Deák, *Essays on Hitler's Europe*, 76; Lanckorońska, *Those Who Trespass Against Us*, 203–40; Wanda Półtawska wrote of her experience in *And I Am Afraid of My Dreams*.
49. Housden, *Hans Frank*, 185–7.
50. Quoted in Engel, *Facing a Holocaust*, 33.
51. R. Smorczewski, IWM 128787 03/41/1.
52. Tooze, *Wages of Destruction*, 466–7; Mazower, *Hitler's Empire*, 214; Lukas, *Forgotten Holocaust*, 22.
53. S. Piotrowski, *Hans Frank's Diary*, 276.
54. Diary entry 10 August 1943, Klukowski, *Diary from the Years of Occupation*, 276. Globocnik was sent to govern a part of German-occupied Italy in September 1943.
55. Housden, *Hans Frank*, 187–90, 209–10.
56. Lukas, *Forgotten Holocaust*, 21–2; Tooze, *Wages of Destruction*, 468.
57. S. Milton, 'Non-Jewish Children in the Camps', in Berenbaum, *Mosaic of Victims*, 150–60.
58. Hrabar, Tokarz & Wilczur, *Fate of Polish Children*, 206 and *passim*; Lukas, *Did the Children Cry*, 112–31.
59. Nowak, *Courier from Warsaw*, 337–8.
60. Garliński, 'The Polish Underground State 1939–45'.
61. Stanley Sagan, quoted in Lukas, *Forgotten Survivors*, 162.
62. See Korboński, *Fighting Warsaw*, for a detailed description of its activities.
63. Ibid., 166–99.

64. Nowak, *Courier from Warsaw*, 169.

65. Garliński, 'The Polish Underground State 1939–45'; Davies, *Rising '44*, 200.

66. Garliński, 'The Polish Underground State 1939–45'.

67. Bór-Komorowski, *Secret Army*, 79.

68. Lukas, *Forgotten Holocaust*, 67–8; Korboński, *Fighting Warsaw*, 200–14.

69. Stoltman, *Trust Me You Will Survive*, 114, 121.

70. Zbigniew Bokiewicz, quoted in Lukas, *Out of the Inferno*, 28.

71. Davies-Scourfield, *In Presence of My Foes*, 94–120; London to Rowecki, 6 December 1941, *AK Documents*, vol. II, 162.

72. Bór-Komorowski, *Secret Army*, 83–4. Jan Kiliński was one of the leaders of the Kościuszko uprising against the Russians in 1794.

73. Lukas, *Forgotten Holocaust*, 102.

74. Mazower, *Hitler's Empire*, 477.

75. Gross, *Polish Society*, 117–19; Korboński, *Fighting Warsaw*, 141.

76. Kunicki, 'Unwanted Collaborators'.

77. Cienciala, Lebedeva & Materski, *Katyń*, 221–2.

78. Altbeker Cyprys, *Jump for Life*, 137–8.

79. Friedrich, 'Collaboration in a "Land without a Quisling"'.

80. Altbeker Cyprys, *Jump for Life*, 137–8.

81. Connelly, 'Why the Poles Collaborated so Little'.

82. Chodakiewicz, *Between Nazis and Soviets*, 84.

83. Mayevski, *Fire Without Smoke*, 93–4.

84. Korboński, *Fighting Warsaw*, 142–3; Sagajllo, *Man in the Middle*, 40.

85. *German Crimes in Poland*, 28.

86. Ibid., 184; Snyder, *Bloodlands*, 294–5.

87. Quoted in Lukas, *Out of the Inferno*, 44.

88. Author's interview with Anna Skowerski.

89. Author's interview with Nina Kochańska. He had never actually laid eyes on this parishioner who was suspected of being a communist but had been asked to support him by the man's girlfriend; the man survived the war.

90. Jędrzejewicz, *Poland in the British Parliament*, 124–8.

91. Altbeker Cyprys, *Jump for Life*, 171.

92. Klukowski, *Diary from the Years of Occupation*, passim.

93. T. Piotrowski, *Poland's Holocaust*, 28.

94. Friedrich, 'Collaboration in a "Land without a Quisling"'; Connelly, 'Why the Poles Collaborated so Little'.

95. J. Węgierski, 'Kim Byli "Hilary" i "Hugo"'.

96. Nowak, *Courier from Warsaw*, 95.

97. Lukas, *Forgotten Holocaust*, 93. Świerczewski, Kalkstein and Kaczorowska were all sentenced to death for high treason by an underground court. Świerczewski was hanged in the basement of his house in Warsaw by the AK. Kalkstein was protected by the Gestapo and went on to fight with an SS unit during the Warsaw Uprising and survived the war. Kaczorow-

ska's sentence was commuted because she was pregnant; she also survived the war.

98. War Cabinet meeting, 19 July 1943, TNA, CAB 65/35; Mikołajczyk to Churchill, 20 July 1943 and Churchill to Mikołajczyk, 1 August 1943, *AK Documents*, vol. III, 42–5, 52.

99. Sagajllo, *Man in the Middle*, 96–8

100. Garliński, 'The Polish Underground State 1939–1945'; Bór-Komorowski, Situation Report no. 5, 20 April 1944, *AK Documents*, vol. III, 413–17.

101. I. Gutman, 'The Victimisation of the Poles', in Berenbaum, *Mosaic of Victims*, 96–100.

102. Harrison, 'The British Special Operations Executive and Poland'.

103. Bór-Komorowski, *The Secret Army*, 125.

104. Ibid., 75–7.

105. K. Piekarski, *Escaping Hell*, 126–7.

106. Ibid., 145.

107. Garliński, *Fighting Auschwitz*, passim.

108. Blood, *Hitler's Bandit Hunters*, 215–16; author's interview with Teresa Kicińska; A. Huberman, IWM 18050.

109. Frank Blaichman, IWM 02/23/1. He had escaped from the ghetto in Lubartów.

110. Lowell Armstrong, 'The Polish Underground and the Jews'.

111. Author's interview with Nina Kochańska.

112. Quoted in Lowell Armstrong, 'The Polish Underground and the Jews'.

113. Ainsztein and Karkowski have taken selective quotations from Organization Report 220 of 31 August 1943, which mentioned Jews only in passing and was sent to the Polish Government in London but not to AK commanders in Poland: Ainsztein, *Jewish Resistance*; Krakowski, *War of the Doomed*.

114. *AK Documents*, vol. III, no. 482, 62.

115. Lowell Armstrong, 'The Polish Underground and the Jews'.

116. Quoted in ibid.

117. Sagajllo, *Man in the Middle*, 75.

118. Quoted in Lukas, *Out of the Inferno*, 26.

119. R. Smorczewski, IWM 128787 03/41/1.

120. Garliński, 'The Polish Underground State 1939–45'.

121. Quoted in Lukas, *Out of the Inferno*, 126–7.

122. Baluk, *Silent and Unseen*, 123–5; Peszke, *Battle for Warsaw*, 115–16; Sagajllo, *Man in the Middle*, 79; G. Iranek-Osmecki, *Unseen and Silent*, passim.

123. *Destiny Can Wait*, 214–15.

124. Harrison, 'The British Special Operations Executive and Poland'.

125. *Destiny Can Wait*, 217; Stafford, *Britain and European Resistance*, 184.

126. Ciechanowski, *Defeat in Victory*, 193.

127. Alanbrooke to Sikorski, 14 May 1942, *AK Documents*, vol. II, no. 304, 230–31; Stafford, *Britain and European Resistance*, 133–6; Wilkinson &

Astley, *Gubbins and SOE*, 110–12; 130–31; Peszke, *Battle for Warsaw*, 119–21, 141–3, 145–9.

128. Nowak, *Courier from Warsaw*, 105.
129. Housden, *Hans Frank*, 196–7, 209; Sagajllo, *Man in the Middle*, 85–7.
130. Bór-Komorowski, *Secret Army*, 113.
131. Mayevski, *Fire Without Smoke*, 114.
132. Prażmowska, *Civil War in Poland*, 31.
133. R. Lukas, 'The Polish Experience of the Holocaust', in Berenbaum, *Mosaic of Victims*, 88–95.

## CHAPTER 10: THE HOLOCAUST, 1941–1943

1. Gilbert, *Righteous*, 31.
2. Diary entry 5 July 1941, Felix Landau, in Klee, Dressen & Riess, *'The Good Old Days'*, 90–91.
3. Interview with Alicia Melamed Adams, IWM 18670.
4. Gross, *Neighbors*; Dean, 'Where Did All the Collaborators Go?'; Dean, 'Poles in the German Local Police in Eastern Poland'; Connelly, 'Poles and Jews in the Second World War'.
5. Quoted in P. Longerich, 'From Mass Murder to the "Final Solution"', in Wegner, *From Peace to War*, 253–75.
6. Situation report of Gebeitskommissar Gerhard Erren, 25 January 1942, quoted in Klee, Dressen & Riess, *'The Good Old Days'*, 178–9.
7. Pohl, 'Hans Krüger and the Murder of the Jews'.
8. Quoted in Kaczorowska, *Children of the Katyń Massacre*, 140–41.
9. Hilberg, *Destruction of the European Jews*, 316.
10. Olszański, *Kresy Kresów Stanisławów*, 115.
11. Snyder, *Bloodlands*, 199–200.
12. Tec, *When Light Pierced*, 21. The author survived the occupation as a Jew by passing as a Pole.
13. Łuczak, *Polska i Polacy*, 315–19.
14. Diary entry 4 December 1941, Hilberg, Staron & Kernisz, *Warsaw Diary*, 305.
15. Quoted in Smith, *Forgotten Voices*, 108.
16. Lewin, *Cup of Tears*, 116.
17. Altbeker Cyprys, *Jump for Life*, 36, 74.
18. Zylberberg, *Warsaw Diary*, 23.
19. Gutman & Krakowski, *Unequal Victims*, 185.
20. Lukas, *Out of the Inferno*, 57.
21. Altbeker Cyprys, *Jump for Life*, 31–2.
22. Zylberberg, *Warsaw Diary*, 49.
23. R. Smorczewski, IWM 128787 03/41/1.

24. Author's interview with Teresa Kicińska.
25. Author's interview with Nina Kochańska.
26. *German Crimes in Poland*, 158.
27. Gilbert, *The Holocaust*, 283.
28. I. Kershaw, 'Improvised Genocide?'
29. *German Crimes in Poland*, 109–10; Mazower, *Hitler's Empire*, 380–81.
30. Decree by Himmler, 19 July 1942, *Documents on the Holocaust*, 275–6.
31. Hilberg, *Destruction of the European Jews*, vol. III, 1219. The *Sonderkommando* disposed of the corpses of the exterminated Jews.
32. Gilbert, *The Holocaust*, 287.
33. Beevor & Vinogradova, *Writer at War*, 280–306.
34. *German Crimes in Poland*, 95–104.
35. J. Wiernik, 'One Year in Treblinka', in Langer, *Art from the Ashes*, 18–51.
36. Statement by Höss, quoted in Klee, Dressen & Riess, *'The Good Old Days'*, 269.
37. Gilbert, *The Holocaust*, 409.
38. Zdzisław Rozbicki, quoted in Turski, *Polish Witnesses*, 106.
39. Wiernik, 'One Year in Treblinka', in Langer, *Art from the Ashes*.
40. Interview with Michael Etkind, IWM 10486.
41. Interview with Kitty Hart-Moxon, IWM 16632.
42. Blood, *Hitler's Bandit Hunters*, 223–4.
43. Paulsson, *Secret City*; Gutman, *Jews of Warsaw*, 265.
44. Deák, *Essays on Hitler's Europe*, 71.
45. Katsch, *Scroll of Agony*, 385.
46. Announcement of the evacuation of the Jews from the Warsaw ghetto, 22 July 1942, *Documents on the Holocaust*, 281–2.
47. Interview with Stanley Faull, IWM 18272.
48. Altbeker Cyprys, *Jump for Life*, 50–51.
49. Quoted in Smith, *Forgotten Voices*, 122.
50. Quoted in ibid., 121.
51. Lewin, *Cup of Tears*, 179.
52. Ringelblum, *Notes from the Warsaw Ghetto*, 330.
53. Gutman, *Jews of Warsaw*, 447.
54. Wiesenthal, *Justice Not Vengeance*, 231.
55. Wiernik, 'One Year in Treblinka', in Langer, *Art from the Ashes*, 29.
56. T. Piotrowski, *Poland's Holocaust*, 66; Grynberg, *Words to Outlive Us*, 162, 175; Lukas, *Forgotten Holocaust*, 118.
57. T. Piotrowski, *Poland's Holocaust*, 74.
58. Lukas, *Out of the Inferno*, 15.
59. Hilberg, *Destruction of the European Jews*, 307.
60. Gilbert, *The Holocaust*, 608.
61. Ibid., 368.
62. Adelson & Lapides, *Łódź Ghetto*, 330.
63. Interview with Roman Halter, IWM 17183.

64. Grynberg, *Words to Outlive Us*, 444; Yad Vashem Resource Centre, Jerusalem.

65. Report by Jäcklein, 14 September 1942, quoted in Klee, Dressen & Riess, '*The Good Old Days*', 233–4.

66. Wiernik, 'One Year in Treblinka', in Langer, *Art from the Ashes*.

67. Longerich, *Holocaust*, 353.

68. Hilberg, *Destruction of the European Jews*, 385–6.

69. Lukas, *Forgotten Holocaust*, 172; Tzvetan Todorov quoted in Deák, *Essays on Hitler's Europe*, 163.

70. Rowecki to London, 4 January 1943, *AK Documents*, vol. II, 282.

71. Altbeker Cyprys, *Jump for Life*, 86.

72. Sikorski Institute, *Polskie Siły Zbrojne*, vol. III, 234.

73. Lukas, *Holocaust*, 175.

74. Bór-Komorowski, *Secret Army*, 105.

75. Gutman & Krakowski, *Unequal Victims*, 162; research by Teresa Prekerowa, quoted in T. Piotrowski, *Poland's Holocaust*, 108.

76. Quoted in Lukas, *Forgotten Holocaust*, 174.

77. Edelman, *Ghetto Fights*, 35.

78. Interview with D. Falkner, IWM 19783.

79. Gilbert, *The Holocaust*, 558–9.

80. Nowak, *Courier from Warsaw*, 133.

81. Korboński, *Jews and the Poles*, 58.

82. Deák, *Essays on Hitler's Europe*, 73.

83. Ringelblum, *Polish-Jewish Relations*, 178–9.

84. Bór-Komorowski, *Secret Army*, 108.

85. Edelman, *Ghetto Fights*, 41.

86. Gilbert, *The Holocaust*, 563–5.

87. Altbeker Cyprys, *Jump for Life*, 133.

88. Stefan Ernest, quoted in Grynberg, *Words to Outlive Us*, 290. Ernest escaped from the ghetto in January 1943 and died that May.

89. Report on the Warsaw ghetto revolt, 4 May 1943, *AK Documents*, vol. III, 4–6.

90. Engel, *Facing a Holocaust*, 70–71.

91. Mazower, *Hitler's Empire*, 452.

92. Gross, 'Tangled Web', in Deák, Gross & Judt, *Politics of Retribution*.

93. Frank decree, 15 October 1941, *AK Documents*, vol. VI, 208.

94. Ringelblum, *Polish-Jewish Relations*, 152–3; F. Tych, 'Witnessing the Holocaust: Polish Diaries, Memoirs and Reminiscences', in Bankier & Gutman, *Nazi Europe*, 175–98.

95. Interview with M. Ossowski, IWM 19794.

96. Zylberberg, *Warsaw Diary*, 61.

97. Interview with R. Halter, IWM 17183.

98. Quoted in W. Bartoszewski, 'Polish-Jewish Relations in Occupied Poland,

1939–1945', in Abramsky, Jachimczyk & Polonsky, *Jews in Poland*, 147–60.

99. Neuman-Nowicki, *Struggle for Life*, 52–3.
100. Altbeker Cyprys, *Jump for Life*, 121.
101. Tec, *When Light Pierced*, 75.
102. Ringelblum, *Polish-Jewish Relations*, 100–101.
103. Chodakiewicz, *Between Nazis and Soviets*, 148–9.
104. Gut Opdyke, *In My Hands*, 217.
105. Zylberberg, *Warsaw Diary*, 88.
106. Tec, *When Light Pierced*, 51.
107. For example, Altbeker Cyprys, *Jump for Life*, 165.
108. Quoted in Lukas, *Out of the Inferno*, 12.
109. Tec, *When Light Pierced*, 4.
110. Quoted in Lukas, *Out of the Inferno*, 32–5. Twelve of the Jews survived: one was killed in a camp after the Warsaw Uprising when he was identified as a Jew by the Germans.
111. K. Kakol, 'The Eighty-First Blow', in Polonsky, *'My Brother's Keeper?'*, 144–9.
112. Korboński, *Jews and the Poles*, viii, 67; Lukas, *Out of the Inferno*, 13.
113. Browning, *Ordinary Men*, 149.
114. Quoted in Gilbert, *Righteous*, 43.
115. Gutman & Krakowski, *Unequal Victims*, 69, 144, 147.
116. Bartoszewski, 'Polish-Jewish Relations in Occupied Poland', in Abramsky, Jachimczyk & Polonsky, *Jews in Poland*; D. Engel, 'Possibilities of Rescuing Polish Jewry under German Occupation and the Influence of the Polish Government-in-Exile', and S. Krakowski, 'The Polish Underground and the Jews in the Years of the Second World War', both in Bankier & Gutman, *Nazi Europe*, 136–48, 215–30.
117. Gilbert, *Righteous*, 120.
118. Reproduced in Tec, *When Light Pierced*, 111–12.
119. T. Prekerowa, 'The "Just" and the "Passive"', in Polonsky, *'My Brother's Keeper?'*, 72–80.
120. Altbeker Cyprys, *Jump for Life*, 149–50.
121. Gilbert, *Righteous*, 120–22; Lukas, *Forgotten Survivors*, 166–70.
122. Quoted in Lukas, *Out of the Inferno*, 163.
123. K. Iranek-Osmecki, *He Who Saves One Life*, 50.
124. Gilbert, *Holocaust Journey*, 142–3.
125. Altbeker Cyprys, *Jump for Life*, 170.
126. Karski, *Secret State*, 261–77.
127. Engel, *Facing a Holocaust*, 21–2.
128. Gilbert, *Auschwitz and the Allies*, 103.
129. Gilbert, *Winston S. Churchill*, vol. VII, 287.
130. Breitman, *Official Secrets*, 116–20.

131. Wood & Jankowski, *Karski*, 152.

132. Ibid., 188.

133. Nowak, *Courier from Warsaw*, 274–5. There is far more on this subject in Gilbert, *Auschwitz and the Allies*.

134. Dallas, *Poisoned Peace*, 429.

135. Bartoszewski, 'Polish-Jewish Relations in Occupied Poland', in Abramsky, Jachimczyk & Polonsky, *Jews in Poland*.

136. Polonsky, Introduction, '*My Brother's Keeper?*', 1–33.


## CHAPTER 11: SIKORSKI'S DIPLOMACY, 1941–1943

1. Biddle to Hull, 2 February 1942, *FRUS 1942*, vol. III, 102; see, for example, Raczyński, *In Allied London*, 161–3, and biographers, most notably Terlecki, *Generał Sikorski*.

2. Rex Leeper, Head of Political Intelligence Department to Strang, Foreign Office, 25 November 1939, quoted in Polonsky, *Great Powers*, 75–6.

3. Government Delegate to London, 15 August 1941, no. 211; Rowecki to Sikorski, 15 September 1941, no. 236, Sikorski to Rowecki, 10 October 1941, no. 251, all in *AK Documents*, vol. II, 42, 70, 126–8.

4. Polish-Soviet Agreement, 30 July 1941, *DPSR*, vol. I, no. 106, 141.

5. Conversation between Sikorski and Stalin, 4 December 1941, *DPSR*, vol. I, no. 160, 245.

6. Report on Sikorski's journey to the Middle East and Russia, presented by him to the Council of Ministers, 12 January 1942, *DPSR*, vol. I, no. 171, 264–6.

7. Diary entry 9 January 1942, quoted in Terry, *Poland's Place in Europe*, 128.

8. Eden, *Eden Memoirs*, 295.

9. Gardner, *Spheres of Influence*, 91.

10. For the text of the Atlantic Charter, see *FRUS 1941*, vol. I, 367–9; Biddle to Hull, 12 September 1941; and Polish Government memorandum to the State Department, 12 September 1941, both in ibid., vol. I, 373–8.

11. Conversation between Sikorski and Cripps, 26 January 1942, *DPSR*, vol. I, no. 176, 269–71.

12. Meeting of the Council of Ministers, 4 February 1942, *Protokoły*, vol. IV, 136–45. Hong Kong fell on Christmas Day 1941 and Singapore on 15 February 1942. Supplies earmarked for the Polish forces in the Soviet Union were rushed to the Pacific. The British were in retreat in the Western Desert.

13. Sikorski to Eden, 9 March 1942, *DPSR*, vol. I, no. 189, 289–4; Stoler, 'The "Second Front"'.

14. Churchill to Roosevelt, 7 March 1942, Loewenheim, Langley & Jonas, *Roosevelt and Churchill*, 186.

15. Borodziej, *Warsaw Uprising*, 154.

16. Quoted in Rees, *World War Two*, 128.
17. Conversation between Sikorski and Roosevelt, 24 March 1942, *DPSR*, vol. I, no. 194, 310–11; report on visit to United States presented to Council of Ministers, 14 April 1942; and report on meeting with Litvinov, both in *Protokoły*, vol. IV, 207–16, 242–4.
18. Memo from Polish Government to the Foreign Office, 27 March 1942; Raczyński to Eden, 13 April 1942; Sikorski to Eden, 16 April 1942; Raczyński to Eden, 21 April 1942; conversation between Sikorski, Churchill and Cripps, 26 April 1942, all in *DPSR*, vol. I, nos. 196, 202, 204, 209, 211; 312–17, 321–2, 324–5, 332–5, 336–40.
19. Diary entry 7 May 1942, Dilks, *Diaries*, 450–51.
20. Ciechanowski, *Defeat in Victory*, 117.
21. Text of Anglo-Soviet Treaty, 26 May 1942, TNA, FO 371/33017.
22. Conversation between Sikorski and Eden, 8 June 1942, *DPSR*, vol. I, no. 225, 364–6.
23. Sikorski to Roosevelt, 17 June 1942, *FRUS 1942*, vol. III, 155–7.
24. Quoted in the introduction to *Protokoły*, vol. IV.
25. Beneš, *Memoirs*, 149; record of talks between Sikorski and Molotov, 10 June 1942, in Rzheshevsky, *War and Diplomacy*, document 117, 291–4; Sikorski to Beneš, 23 July 1942, *Protokoły*, vol. IV, 377–84; Mastny, *Russia's Road*, 56–9; memorandum from the Polish Foreign Ministry to the State Department, 17 May 1943, *DPSR*, vol. II, no. 16, 19.
26. Diary entry 21 May 1942, Pimlott, *Second World War Diary*, 441–2.
27. See Terry, *Poland's Place in Europe*, *passim*.
28. Resolution of the Council of Ministers on approach to the frontier with Germany, 7 October 1942, *Protokoły*, vol. V, 29–31.
29. Instruction from Sikorski to Rowecki, 28 November 1942, *AK Documents*, Vol. II, no. 357, 369–72.
30. Memorandum by Sikorski presented to Sumner Welles, 23 December 1942, *DPSR*, vol. I, no. 283, 469–73.
31. Resolution of the Council of Ministers on approach to the frontier with Germany, 7 October 1942, *Protokoły*, vol. V, 29–31.
32. Report by Sikorski on his visit to the United States, 21 January 1943, *Protokoły*, vol. V, 158–75; memorandum for Welles, 4 December 1942, PISM, A.XII.23/42; meeting between Sikorski and Welles, 4 December 1942, *FRUS 1942*, vol. III, 199–202.
33. Minute by G. D. Allen, Central Department, Foreign Office, 20 January 1943, in Polonsky, *Great Powers*, 113–14; Courtovidis & Reynolds, *Poland*, 85–6.
34. Eden to Dormer, 22 January 1943, Polonsky, *Great Powers*, 115–16.
35. Conversations between Romer and Stalin, 26–27 February 1943, *DPSR*, vol. I, no. 295, 489–501.
36. Biddle to Hull, 28 January 1943, *FRUS 1943*, vol. III, 324–5.

37. Standley to Hull, 9 March 1943, *FRUS 1943*, vol. III, 346–7.

38. Minutes of the meeting of the Council of Ministers, 11 February 1943, *Protokoły*, vol. V, 265–75.

39. *The Times*, 10 March 1943.

40. Raczyński, *In Allied London*, 136.

41. Eden, *Eden Memoirs*, 372–3; Feis, *Churchill, Roosevelt, Stalin*, 122–3.

42. Cadogan to Churchill, 31 March 1943, in Polonsky, *Great Powers*, 119–20.

43. *DPSR*, vol. I, 523–4.

44. Broadcast by Berlin radio station, 15 April 1943, no. 305; TASS communiqué, 15 April 1943, no. 306; communiqué by Kukiel, 16 April 1943, no. 307; statement by the Polish Government, 17 April 1943, no. 308, all in *DPSR*, vol. I, 523–8; Mikołajczyk, *Rape of Poland*, 61.

45. Biddle to Hull, 2 May 1943, *FRUS 1943*, vol. III, 404–5.

46. Conversation between Sikorski and Eden, 24 April 1943, *DPSR*, vol. II, supplement 15, 696–702.

47. Molotov to Romer, 25 April 1943, Polonsky, *Great Powers*, 126–8.

48. Quoted in Garliński, *Poland in the Second World War*, 189.

49. Werth, *Russia at War*, 648.

50. Quoted in Paul, *Katyń*, 230.

51. Government Delegate and AK commander to London, 29 April 1943, *AK Documents*, vol. VI, no. 1761, 313; Rowecki to Sikorski, 5 May 1943, no. 438; Sikorski to Rowecki, 10 May 1943, no. 440; Rowecki to London, 13 May 1943, no. 441; Rowecki, Special Report no. 198, May 1943, no. 445, all in *AK Documents*, vol. III, 6–7, 10–13.

52. E. Thompson, 'The Katyn Massacre and the Warsaw Ghetto Uprising in the Soviet-Nazi Propaganda War', in Garrard and Garrard, *World War 2*, 215–30.

53. Churchill to Stalin, 24 April 1943, *Stalin Correspondence*, vol. I, no. 151, 126–7; Roosevelt to Stalin, 26 April 1943, ibid., vol. II, no. 81, 56.

54. Clark Kerr to Eden, 21 April 1943, TNA, PREM 3/354/8.

55. Diary entry 18 June 1943, Dilks, *Diaries*, 537.

56. TNA, FO 371/34577.

57. Churchill to Roosevelt, 13 August 1943, Kimball, *Churchill & Roosevelt*, vol. II, 389.

58. Paul, *Katyń*, 220.

59. Bell, *John Bull*, 117–18.

60. Diary entry 30 April 1943, Dilks, *Diaries*, 525.

61. Standley to Hull, 28 April 1943; Biddle to Hull, 2 May 1943, both in *FRUS 1943*, vol. III, 400–402, 404–5.

62. Certainly Wanda Wasilewska and her Polish communist allies believed that Stalin had been waiting for an opportunity to break with the Polish Government in London. Grzelak, Stańczyk & Zwoliński, *Bez Możliwości Wyboru*, 12.

63. Stalin to Churchill, 4 May 1943; Churchill to Stalin, 12 May 1943, *Stalin Correspondence*, vol. I, nos. 156, 159, 131–2, 134.

64. Churchill to Stalin, 12 May 1943, in *Stalin Correspondence* vol. I, no. 159, 134; Roosevelt to Sikorski, 7 June 1943, *Protokoły*, vol. VI, 20–25; Biddle to Welles, 2 June 1943, *FRUS 1943*, vol. III, 424–6.

65. Anders, *Bez ostatniego rozdzialu*, 148–9. This belief is corroborated by the report of General Beaumont-Nesbitt in his report to the Foreign Office (TNA, FO371/34594).

66. Garliński, *Poland in the Second World War*, 215.

67. Danchev & Todman, *War Diaries*, 429–30.

68. Peszke, *Battle for Warsaw*, 134.

69. For more details, see Terlecki, *Generał Sikorski*, vol. II, 270–73 and 289–91.

70. R. Hochhuth, *The Soldiers*, a play produced in 1967.

71. Frank Roberts interviewed by Keith Sword, SSEES archives, SWO 1/3.

72. Retinger, *Memoirs*, 144.

73. Anders, *Bez ostatniego rozdzialu*, 144–5.

74. Sarner, *General Anders*, 155–6.

75. Nicolson, *Harold Nicolson*, 303.

76. Diary entry 6 July 1943, Dilks, *Diaries*, 541–2; diary entry 8 July 1943, J. Harvey, *War Diaries*, 272–3; Raczyński, *In Allied London*, 150–51; Prażmowska, *Civil War in Poland*, 144.

77. Retinger, *Memoirs*, 144; Raczyński, *In Allied London*, 151, 156; Government Delegate to Mikołajczyk and Kot, 15 August 1943; Bór-Komorowski to Sosnkowski, 19 August 1943, both in *AK Documents*, vol. III, 55–8, 60–62; Schwonek, 'Kazimierz Sosnkowski as Commander in Chief'.

78. Litvinov was replaced by Andrei Gromyko. Churchill to Roosevelt, 28 June 1943, Kimball, *Churchill & Roosevelt*, 285; Clark Kerr, quoted in Kitchen, *British Policy*, 160; diary entry 28 March 1944, Nicolson, *Harold Nicolson*, 357.

79. Memoranda by Warner, Sargent and Cadogan, 28 July 1943; Clark Kerr to Foreign Office, 3 August 1943, all in TNA, FO 371/36925.

80. Retinger, *Memoirs*, 144; Frank Roberts interviewed by Keith Sword, SSEES archives, SWO 1/3.

81. Government Delegate to Mikołajczyk and Minister of the Interior, 15 August 1943, *AK Documents*, vol. III, no. 477, 55–8.

82. Memorandum by Eden, 5 October 1943, Polonsky, *Great Powers*, 151–4.

83. Meeting between Mikołajczyk, Retinger, Raczyński, Eden and Strang, 9 September 1943, *DPSR*, vol. II, 49–50.

84. Conversation between Mikołajczyk, Romer, Raczyński, Eden and Cadogan, 5 October 1943; memorandum by Polish Government to Eden, 5 October 1943, both in *DPSR*, vol. II, 61–4, 65–8.

85. Eden to O'Malley, 6 October 1943, Polonsky, *Great Powers*, 155–7.

86. Strang, *At Home and Abroad*, 74.

87. Memorandum by Eden, 5 October 1943, Polonsky, *Great Powers*, 151–5. In fact there were around 6,000,000 Polish-American voters.

88. Harriman to Roosevelt, 4 November 1943, *FRUS Teheran*, 152–5; Eden to Foreign Office, 6 November 1943, Polonsky, *Great Powers*, 157–8; *FRUS 1943*, vol. I, 667–8.

89. Conversation between Mikołajczyk, Romer, Raczyński, Eden, Sargent and Strang, 12 November 1943, *DPSR*, vol. II, 74–8.

90. Ciechanowski to State Department, 17 November 1943, *FRUS 1943*, vol. III, 478–81.

91. Memorandum by the Polish Government for Churchill and Roosevelt, 16 November 1943, *DPSR*, vol. II, no. 51, 53–6.

92. Conversation between Mikołajczyk, Raczyński, Romer and Eden, 22 November 1943, *DPSR*, vol. II, no. 55, 90–93.

93. Bohlen, *Witness to History*, 136.

94. Roosevelt to Churchill, 18 March 1942, Kimball, *Churchill & Roosevelt*, vol. I, 421.

95. Feis, *Churchill, Roosevelt, Stalin*, 276; Mastny, *Russia's Road*, 122; Eubank, *Summit at Teheran*, *passim*; for more on the Anglo-American differences in strategy, see A. Roberts, *Masters and Commanders*, *passim*.

96. Memorandum, 22 November 1943, CAB 66/43/04911; Mastny, *Russia's Road*, 131.

97. Diary entry 29 November 1943, Dilks, *Diaries*, 580.

98. Conversation between Churchill and Stalin, 28 November 1943, *FRUS Teheran*, 511–12.

99. Conversation between Roosevelt and Stalin, 1 December 1943, *FRUS Teheran*, 594–5.

100. Kersten, *Establishment of Communist Rule*, 29.

101. Plenary session, 1 December 1943, *FRUS Teheran*, 597–604.

## CHAPTER 12: THREATS TO THE STANDING OF THE POLISH GOVERNMENT-IN-EXILE AND THE POLISH UNDERGROUND AUTHORITIES

1. T. Piotrowski, *Poland's Holocaust*, 247.

2. Mazower, *Hitler's Empire*, 507.

3. T. Piotrowski, *Genocide and Rescue*, 65, 85.

4. Ibid., 52.

5. For example, Rowecki to London, 4 May 1943; Situation Report, 23 March 1944, both in *AK Documents*, vol. III, nos. 437, 582, 4–5; 380–84. The situation regarding the Ukrainians featured in numerous Situation Reports transmitted by Komorowski to London.

6. Kosyk, *Third Reich*, 160; T. Piotrowski, *Genocide and Rescue*, 24.

7. Snyder, 'The Causes of Ukrainian-Polish Ethnic Cleansing 1943'.

8. Snyder, *Reconstruction*, 174.

9. Dmytryshn, 'The Nazis and the SS Volunteer Division "Galicia"'.

10. M. Yukkevich, 'Galician Ukrainians in German Military Formations and in the German Administration', in Boshyk, *Ukraine During World War II*, 67–87; Snyder, *Reconstruction*, 165–6.

11. T. Piotrowski, *Genocide and Rescue*, 173.

12. Ibid., 80.

13. Ibid., 21.

14. Tec, *Defiance*, 143.

15. T. Piotrowski, *Poland's Holocaust*, 101.

16. G. Iranek-Osmecki, *Unseen and Silent*, 144, 149.

17. Blood, *Hitler's Bandit Hunters*, 101.

18. Tec, *Defiance*, 113.

19. Ibid., 158; Ainsztein, *Jewish Resistance*, 390.

20. Mayevski, *Fire Without Smoke*, 5.

21. Snyder, *Reconstruction*, 164–5.

22. Mazower, *Hitler's Empire*, 506.

23. Blood, *Hitler's Bandit Hunters*, 115–17.

24. G. Iranek-Osmecki, *Unseen and Silent*, 148.

25. Prusin, *Lands Between*, 188.

26. Ibid., 189.

27. Sword, *Deportation and Exile*, 146–7.

28. G. Iranek-Osmecki, *Unseen and Silent*, 152–7.

29. Sagajllo, *Man in the Middle*, 113.

30. T. Piotrowski, *Poland's Holocaust*, 88.

31. Lowell Armstrong, 'The Polish Underground and the Jews'; T. Piotrowski, *Poland's Holocaust*, 91.

32. Quoted in Kersten, *Establishment of Communist Rule*, 21.

33. T. Piotrowski, *Poland's Holocaust*, 95; Kersten, *Establishment of Communist Rule*, 22.

34. Author's interview with Iwona Skowerski.

35. Komorowski to Sosnkowski, 8 December 1943, *AK Documents*, vol. III, no. 511, 215.

36. Sword, *Deportation and Exile*, 114; A. Paczkowski, 'Poland, the "Enemy Nation"', in Courtois, *et al.*, *Black Book of Communism*, 363–93.

37. T. Piotrowski, *Poland's Holocaust*, 103; Prażmowska, *Civil War in Poland*, 41–2.

38. Cienciala, 'The Activities of Polish Communists'; Biddle to Secretary of State, 3 March 1943, *FRUS 1943*, vol. III, 338–42.

39. Prażmowska, *Civil War in Poland*, 42. The case of who murdered Nowotko and why has never been satisfactorily resolved.

40. Polonsky & Drukier, *Beginnings of Communist Rule*, 10–11; Kersten, *Establishment of Communist Rule*, 19.

41. Wanda Wasilewska had been active in the Polish socialist movement since

her early youth and in the mid-1930s drew closer to communism. Jakub Berman had joined the KPP in 1928. Interview with J. Berman, in Torańska, '*Them*', 217.

42. Kersten, *Establishment of Communist Rule*, 10; Cienciala, 'The Activities of Polish Communists'.

43. K. Nussbaum, 'Jews in the Kościuszko Division and First Polish Army', in Davies & Polonsky, *Jews in Eastern Poland*, 183–208; Werth, *Russia at War*, 642–3.

44. Sword, *Deportation and Exile*, 131; Polonsky & Drukier, *Beginnings of Communist Rule*, 11–14.

45. Torańska, '*Them*', 231.

46. Kersten, *Establishment of Communist Rule*, 36.

47. Cienciala, Lebedeva & Materski, *Katyń*, 214.

48. Quoted in Kot, *Conversations with the Kremlin*, 271.

49. Sword, *Deportation and Exile*, 111–12.

50. Zajdlerowa, *Dark Side of the Moon*, 205–11.

51. Ciechanowski, *Defeat in Victory*, 150–60; documents handed to Stalin by Clark Kerr and Admiral Standley, 11 August 1943, Polonsky, *Great Powers*, 139–42.

52. Woodward, *British Foreign Policy*, vol. II, 623–4.

53. Ibid., vol. II, 637.

54. T. Piesakowski, *Fate of Poles*, 134–5.

55. Diary entry 5 May 1943, Dilks, *Diaries*, 527.

56. Sword, *Deportation and Exile*, 136–7.

57. Cienciala, Lebedeva & Materski, *Katyń*, 208.

58. Nussbaum, 'Jews in the Kościuszko Division and First Polish Army', in Davies & Polonsky, *Jews in Eastern Poland*.

59. Garliński, *Poland in the Second World War*, 194–5; Sword, *Deportation and Exile*, 122–3.

60. TNA, FO 371 34576.

61. Biddle to Secretary of State, 6 July 1944, *FRUS 1943*, vol. III, 1291–2.

62. Author's interview with Nina Kochańska.

63. Garliński, *Poland in the Second World War*, 195–6.

64. Berling, *Wspomnienia*, vol. II, 113.

65. Nussbaum, 'Jews in the Kościuszko Division and First Polish Army', in Davies & Polonsky, *Jews in Eastern Poland*.

66. Polonsky & Drukier, *Beginnings of Communist Rule*, 12.

67. Nussbaum, 'Jews in the Kościuszko Division and First Polish Army', in Davies & Polonsky, *Jews in Eastern Poland*.

68. Sword, *Deportation and Exile*, 127–8.

69. Nussbaum, 'Jews in the Kościuszko Division and First Polish Army', in Davies & Polonsky, *Jews in Eastern Poland*.

70. Author's interview with Nina Kochańska.

71. Werth, *Russia at War*, 656.

72. Ibid., 657–61.

73. Wasilewska, *Wspomnienia*, 388.

74. Erickson, *Road to Berlin*, 131–2.

75. Author's interview with Nina Kochańska.

76. For example, neither John Erickson nor Chris Bellamy mentions the battle.

77. Grzelak, Stańczyk & Zwoliński, *Bez Możliwości Wyboru*, 156–61; Berling, *Wspomnienia*, vol. II, 335–424.

78. Wasilewska, *Wspomnienia*, 391; Sword, *Deportation and Exile*, 130.

## CHAPTER 13: THE POLISH DILEMMA: THE RETREAT OF THE GERMANS AND THE ADVANCE OF THE RED ARMY

1. Mikołajczyk, *Rape of Poland*, 305.

2. *DPSR*, vol. II, no. 74, 132–4.

3. Hanson, *Civilian Population*, 60; Garliński, 'The Polish Underground State 1939–1945'.

4. Declaration by the RJN, 15 March 1944, *AK Documents*, vol. III, no. 573, 361–70.

5. Polonsky & Drukier, *Beginnings of Communist Rule in Poland*, 19.

6. Prażmowska, *Civil War in Poland*, 74–8; Polonsky & Drukier, *Beginnings of Communist Rule in Poland*, 15; Kersten, *Establishment of Communist Rule*, 60–64.

7. Stalin to Churchill, 28 July 1944, *Stalin Correspondence*, vol. I, no. 301, 245–6.

8. Prażmowska, *Civil War in Poland*, 78.

9. Ciechanowski, *Warsaw Rising*, 132–47.

10. Bór-Komorowski to Sosnkowski, 2 August 1943, *AK Documents*, vol. III, no. 474, 52.

11. Polish Government to Bór-Komorowski, 26 October 1943, *AK Documents*, vol. III, no. 496, 182–5.

12. Bór-Komorowski, *Secret Army*, 180.

13. Bór-Komorowski to Sosnkowski, 26 November 1943, *AK Documents*, vol. III, no. 509, 209–13.

14. Nowak, *Courier from Warsaw*, 231.

15. Borodziej, *Warsaw Uprising*, 45.

16. Sosnkowski to Bór-Komorowski, 11 January 1944; Sosnkowski to Mikołajczyk, 5 January 1944, *AK Documents*, vol. III, no. 527, 239–42, no. 520, 227.

17. Sosnkowski to Bór-Komorowski, 17 February 1944, *AK Documents*, vol. III, no. 552, 282–4.

18. Bór-Komorowski, *Secret Army*, 183–4.

19. Borowiec, *Destroy Warsaw*, 73.

20. Bór-Komorowski, *Secret Army*, 186–7.

21. Borowiec, *Destroy Warsaw*, 74.

22. G. Iranek-Osmecki, *Unseen and Silent*, 180.

23. Paczkowski, 'Poland, the "Enemy Nation"', in Courtois *et al.*, *Black Book of Communism*.

24. Blood, 'Securing Hitler's *Lebensraum*'. The forest of Białowieża is now split between Poland and Belarus.

25. Bór-Komorowski, *Secret Army*, 188–9.

26. Bór-Komorowski to Sosnkowski, 30 March 1944, *AK Documents*, vol. III, no. 586, 386.

27. Mikołajczyk to Churchill, 21 February 1944; Churchill to Mikołajczyk, 7 April 1944, *AK Documents*, vol. VI, no. 1807, 373, no. 1817, 386.

28. For example, Raczyński to Eden, 24 August 1944, *DPSR*, vol. II, no. 207, 357–62.

29. Sosnkowski to Bór-Komorowski, 11 March 1944, *AK Documents*, vol. III, no. 568, 355.

30. G. Iranek-Osmecki, *Unseen and Silent*, 90.

31. Blood, *Hitler's Bandit Hunters*, 228.

32. Selborne to Sosnkowski, 3 May 1944, *AK Documents*, vol. III, no. 610, 431.

33. Adair, *Hitler's Greatest Defeat*, passim; Erickson, *Road to Berlin*, passim; Overy, *Russia's War*, 243–4.

34. Bellamy, *Absolute War*, 616

35. Author's interview with Nina Kochańska.

36. Garliński, *Poland in the Second World War*, 198.

37. *Pravda*, 27 March 1944, quoted in Rozek, *Allied Wartime Diplomacy*, 203–4. Romuald Traugutt was the commander of the 1863 uprising against the Russians.

38. Garliński, *Poland in the Second World War*, 250–51.

39. Sword, *Deportation and Exile*, 141.

40. Author's interview with Nina Kochańska.

41. Zbigniew Wolak, quoted in Rees, *World War Two*, 296.

42. Grzelak, Stańczyk & Zwoliński, *Bez Możliwości Wyboru*, 50–52.

43. Borowiec, *Destroy Warsaw*, 75; Halina Kalwajt, quoted in Kaczorowska, *Children of the Katyń Massacre*, 130; G. Iranek-Osmecki, *Unseen and Silent*, 182–5. Aleksander Krzyżanowski was released in 1947 and returned to Poland. He was rearrested by the Polish Security Police in 1948 and died in prison in 1951.

44. Filipkowski remained in prison in the Soviet Union until 1947, when he was handed over to the Polish authorities, interrogated and released. Ostrowski was soon released and held public office in the post-war Polish Government and served as Poland's ambassador to Sweden.

45. Bór-Komorowski, *Secret Army*, 197–8; Borowiec, *Destroy Warsaw*, 76.

46. Chuikov, *End of the Third Reich*, 43; Rokossovsky also made similar comments in his memoirs.

47. Bór-Komorowski, *Secret Army*, 198.

48. Reynolds, '"Lublin" versus "London"'; Bór-Komorowski, *Secret Army*, 198.

49. Sword, *Deportation and Exile*, 154.

50. Werth, *Russia at War*, 898–9.

51. AK Command to London, 21 July 1944, *AK Documents*, vol. III, no. 676, 571. This information was passed by Raczyński to Eden on 27 July, ibid., vol. III, no. 685, 580–85.

52. AK Command and Government Delegate to London, 30 July 1944, *AK Documents*, vol. III, no. 693, 590.

53. Diary entry 19 March 1944, Klukowski, *Diary from the Years of Occupation*, 311.

54. Wiesenthal, *Murderers Among Us*, 41.

55. T. Piotrowski, *Poland's Holocaust*, 27.

56. Klukowski, *Red Shadow*, 345–6.

57. Zylberberg, *Warsaw Diary*, 154.

58. Bór-Komorowski to London, 14 October 1943, *AK Documents*, vol. III, no. 492, 157–79.

59. Harrison, 'The British Special Operations Executive and Poland'; Walker, *Poland Alone*, 189. During the same period, over 3,400 tons of supplies were dropped in Yugoslavia.

60. Sosnkowski to Bór-Komorowski, 28 July 1944, *AK Documents*, vol. IV, no. 724, 17.

61. Ciechanowski, *Warsaw Uprising*, 296.

62. Zawodny, *Nothing But Honour*, 15.

63. Bór-Komorowski, *Secret Army*, *passim*; interview in 1969 with Rzepecki, in Kersten, *Establishment of Communist Rule*, 71.

64. Bór-Komorowski, *Secret Army*, 212–13; Nowak, *Courier from Warsaw*, 440.

65. Hanson, *Civilian Population*, 69.

66. Davies, *Rising '44*, 117.

67. Nowak, *Courier from Warsaw*, 333–4; for details of the deliberations, see Ciechanowski, *Warsaw Uprising*, 215–40.

68. Ciechanowski, *Warsaw Uprising*, 237–40.

69. Bór-Komorowski, *Secret Army*, 215.

70. Ciechanowski, *Warsaw Uprising*, 212.

71. Zawodny, *Nothing But Honour*, 25, 30.

72. Ibid., 33.

73. Borodziej, *Warsaw Uprising*, 75.

74. Hanson, *Civilian Population*, 67.

75. Zawodny, *Nothing But Honour*, 29, 24–5; Gilbert, *Holocaust Journey*, 314–15.

76. Walker, *Poland Alone*, 218.

77. Borodziej, *Warsaw Uprising*, 75.

78. Altbeker Cyprys, *Jump for Life*, 190.

79. Borowiec, *Destroy Warsaw*, 99–101. Kaminski was born in Russia and had a Polish father. In 1941 his offer to form a locally recruited force to fight against the Soviet partisans was accepted by the Germans, and Kaminski's brigade became notorious for its brutality against the partisans in Belorussia. His brigade was withdrawn from Warsaw on von dem Bach's orders at the end of August 1944. Kaminski himself was court-martialled by the Germans, sentenced to death and shot on 4 October 1944. Zawodny, *Nothing But Honour*, 56.

80. Von dem Bach-Zelewski had the Zelewski part of his surname removed in 1941 because of its Polish-sounding origin.

81. Zawodny, *Nothing But Honour*, 63.

82. Borodziej, *Warsaw Uprising*, 111.

83. Irene Barbarska, quoted in Lukas, *Out of the Inferno*, 19.

84. Nowak, *Courier from Warsaw*, 348–9; Zawodny, *Nothing But Honour*, 64.

85. Altbeker Cyprys, *Jump for Life*, 194.

86. Harrison, 'The British Special Operations Executive and Poland'.

87. Peszke, *Battle for Warsaw*, 191–4.

88. Bór-Komorowski, *Secret Army*, 211.

89. Conversation between Mikołajczyk and Stalin, 9 August 1944, *DPSR*, vol. II, no. 189, 336.

90. Churchill to Stalin, 4 August 1944; Stalin to Churchill, 5 August 1944, both in *Stalin Correspondence*, vol. I, nos. 311 and 313, 251–3; Mikołajczyk to Polish Government, 9 August 1944, *DPSR*, vol. II, no. 89, 336; Harriman to Cordell Hull, 10 August 1944, *FRUS 1944*, vol. III, 1308–10; Vyshinsky to Harriman, 15 August 1944, TNA, FO 371 1075/8/55; Churchill and Roosevelt to Stalin, 20 August 1944, Loewenheim, *Roosevelt and Churchill*, 565; Stalin to Churchill and Roosevelt, 22 August 1944, *Stalin Correspondence*, vol I, no. 323, 258. Shuttle bombing began on 2 June 1944 with US bombers flying from bases in Britain, bombing targets such as the marshalling yards at Debrecen in Hungary or the oil installations in Rumania before landing at the Soviet airfield at Poltava in the Ukraine for refuelling.

91. Hugh Lunghi, quoted in Rees, *World War Two*, 289. Lunghi was the interpreter with the mission.

92. Bohlen, *Witness to History*, 161.

93. Bór-Komorowski to Sosnkowski, 6 August 1944, *AK Documents*, vol. IV, no. 776, 61.

94. Jankowski to Raczkiewicz, 10 August 1944, *AK Documents*, vol. IV, no. 801, 85.

95. Altbeker Cyprys, *Jump for Life*, 200.

96. John Ward to *The Times*, 24 August 1944, quoted in Hanson, *Civilian Population*, 1.

97. 6 September 1944, *AK Documents*, vol. IV, no. 1006, 282–3.

98. *Destiny Can Wait*, 222–3.

99. Nowak, *Courier from Warsaw*, 358.

100. P. Siudak to Korboński, 30 August 1944, *AK Documents*, vol. IV, no. 959, 237.

101. Bór-Komorowski to AK commanders, 31 August 1944, *AK Documents*, vol. IV, no. 968, 245.

102. Chmielarz, 'Warsaw Fought Alone'.

103. Bór-Komorowski, *Secret Army*, 287–8.

104. Korboński, *Fighting Warsaw*, 367.

105. Hanson, *Civilian Population*, 107.

106. Note written by Borowiec in Stalag XIA in January 1945 and incorporated into his book *Destroy Warsaw*, 129.

107. Zawodny, *Nothing But Honour*, 149.

108. Churchill to Roosevelt, 25 August 1944; Roosevelt to Churchill, 26 August 1944, both in Kimball, *Churchill & Roosevelt*, 295–6.

109. British Government to Molotov, 4 September 1944, in Polonsky, *Great Powers*, 218–19. Molotov replied on 9 September with another refusal.

110. The reaction of the press and public opinion in Britain is covered in detail in Bell, *John Bull*, 161–8.

111. Churchill to Roosevelt, 4 September 1944; Roosevelt to Churchill, 5 September 1944, both in Loewenheim, *Roosevelt and Churchill*, 571–2.

112. Declaration by the British Government, 29 August 1944; declaration by the United States Government, 29 August 1944, *AK Documents*, vol. IV, nos. 952 and 953, 225–8. Eisenhower had issued a similar declaration regarding the French Resistance.

113. Declaration by the British Government, 9 September 1944, *AK Documents*, vol. IV, no. 1030, 303.

114. *The Times*, 10 September 1944.

115. Bór-Komorowski to London, *AK Documents*, vol. IV, no. 1007, 284.

116. Jankowski and Bór-Komorowski to London, 6 September 1944, *AK Documents*, vol. IV, no. 1006, 282–4.

117. Bartoszewski, *Powstanie Warszawskie*, 213–20; Hanson, *Civilian Population*, 156–8.

118. Hanson, *Civilian Population*, 158–9.

119. Bór-Komorowski to London, 10 September 1944, *AK Documents*, vol. IV, no. 1034, 306.

120. Zawodny, *Nothing But Honour*, 186–8.

121. Stalin to Churchill, 16 August 1944, *Stalin Correspondence*, vol. I, no. 321, 257.

122. Rokossovsky, *Soldier's Duty*, 255.

123. *Destiny Can Wait*, 225.

124. Davies, *Rising '44*, 270–71; Borowiec, *Destroy Warsaw*, 109. Kalugin remained in Warsaw until the end of September, when he crossed the Vistula to join the Soviet Army.

125. Grzelak, Stańczyk & Zwoliński, *Bez Możliwości Wyboru*, 166–75; Zawodny, *Nothing But Honour*, 72–4; Zawodny goes into great detail, examining the case of whether the capture of Warsaw was part of the Soviet plans and whether the Soviet armies could have attacked the city; Davies, *Rising '44*, 271.

126. Quoted in Polonsky and Drukier, *Beginnings of Communist Rule*, 286.

127. Wanda Bitner, quoted in *Stalin's Ethnic Cleansing*, 306.

128. Author's interview with Nina Kochańska.

129. Minutes of a meeting of the PKWN, 15 September 1944, quoted in Polonsky and Drukier, *Beginnings of Communist Rule*, 281–3.

130. Zawodny, *Nothing But Honour*, 184–5.

131. Bór-Komorowski, *Secret Army*, 274.

132. Zawodny, *Nothing But Honour*, 202. The author lists the attempts to establish communications during September 1944.

133. Korboński, *Fighting Warsaw*, 379; Chmielarz, 'Warsaw Fought Alone'.

134. Bór-Komorowski to AK units, 14 August 1944, *AK Documents*, vol. IV, no. 829, 107.

135. Zawodny, *Nothing But Honour*, 67–8.

136. Grzelak, Stańczyk & Zwoliński, *Bez Możliwości Wyboru*, 177–8.

137. Borowiec, *Destroy Warsaw*, 151.

138. Zawodny, *Nothing But Honour*, 182; Davies, *Rising '44*, 396.

139. Korboński, *Fighting Warsaw*, 388; Davies, *Rising '44*, 396.

140. Nowak, *Courier from Warsaw*, 384–5.

141. Hanson, *Civilian Population*, 194.

142. Ibid., 194–6.

143. Mikołajczyk to Stalin, 29 September 1944, *AK Documents*, vol. IV, no. 1180, 409. At this time Bór-Komorowski was sending daily information reports to Rokossovsky.

144. Nowak, *Courier from Warsaw*, 386.

145. Paulsson, *Secret City*, 235–6.

146. Davies, *Rising '44*, 437.

147. Altbeker Cyprys, *Jump for Life*, 217, 226.

148. Bór-Komorowski to London, 1 and 4 October 1944, *AK Documents*, vol. IV, nos. 1201, 1217, 423, 441; Bór-Komorowski, *Secret Army*, 372. Bór-Komorowski and his fellow commanders were imprisoned in various camps (Oflag 73 in Langwasser near Nuremberg; Colditz; a civilian camp at Laufen in Czechoslovakia) before being handed over to the Swiss on 4 May 1945.

149. Baluk, *Silent and Unseen*, 249.
150. Korboński, *Fighting Warsaw*, 401.
151. Zawodny, *Nothing But Honour*, 194.
152. Skrzynska, 'A Brief Outline of the History of Women POWs'.
153. Borowiec, *Destroy Warsaw*, 179; Zawodny, *Nothing But Honour*, 210–11.
154. Korboński, *Fighting Warsaw*, 407.
155. Borowiec, *Destroy Warsaw*, 179; Duffy, *Red Storm on the Reich*, 109.
156. Quoted in Rees, *World War Two*, 297.
157. Hastings, *Armageddon*, 123–4.
158. Quoted in Borodziej, *Warsaw Uprising*, 72.
159. Nowak, *Courier from Warsaw*, 398.
160. Zenon Frank, quoted in Gill, *Journey Back*, 341.
161. Bór-Komorowski, *Secret Army*, 380–83.
162. Waskiewicz, 'The Polish Home Army'.
163. Affidavit by Hans Frank in evidence to the Nuremberg Trial, Yale Avalon Project.
164. Pierkarski, *Escaping Hell*, passim.
165. Walker, *Poland Alone*, 264–5.
166. Author's interviews with Teresa and Anna Kicińska.
167. Kaczorowska, *Children of the Katyń Massacre*, 113–14.
168. Kopański to Okulicki, 17 October 1944, *AKDocuments*, vol. V, no. 1257, 75. Okulicki was given fewer powers than his predecessor. Mikołajczyk asked Jankowski to obtain the opinion of surviving AK commanders regarding Okulicki, Mikołajczyk to Jankowski, 25 October 1944, ibid., vol. V, no. 1279, 97.
169. Okulicki to Raczkiewicz, 9 December 1944, *AK Documents*, vol. V, no. 1344, 170–84.
170. Staff Group Kampinos to AK Command, 19 September 1944, *AK Documents*, vol. IV, no. 1110, 356–8; Davies, *Rising '44*, 397.
171. Garliński, *Poland in the Second World War*, 307.
172. R. Smorczewski, IWM 128787 03/41/1; Gut Opdyke, *In My Hands*, 214.
173. Quoted in Kersten, *Establishment of Communist Rule*, 115.
174. Gilbert, *Churchill*, vol. VII, 1068.
175. TNA, PREM 3/352/11.
176. Eden to Raczyński, 22 December 1944, *AK Documents*, vol. V, no. 1361, 202–4.
177. Polonsky & Drukier, *Beginnings of Communist Rule*, 25.
178. A. Paczkowski, *Spring Will Be Ours*, 132.
179. Polonsky & Drukier, *Beginnings of Communist Rule*, 33.
180. Diary entry 10 October 1944, Klukowski, *Red Shadow*, 24.
181. Quoted in Polonsky & Drukier, *Beginnings of Communist Rule*, 56.
182. Sword, *Deportation and Exile*, 159.
183. Torańska, *'Them'*, 228–9.

184. Sword, *Deportation and Exile*, 159–60.
185. Quoted in Kersten, *Establishment of Communist Rule*, 101.
186. S. Kujawiński, IWM 12018.
187. Quoted in Davies, *Rising '44*, 487.
188. Paczkowski, *Spring Will Be Ours*, 130.
189. Polonsky & Drukier, *Beginnings of Communist Rule*, 32.
190. Ibid., 66.

## CHAPTER 14: POLAND: THE INCONVENIENT ALLY

1. Meeting between Eden and Mikołajczyk, 22 December 1943, Eden, *Eden Memoirs*, 434; O'Malley to Mikołajczyk, 3 January 1944, *DPSR*, vol. II, no. 69, 122; Churchill to Eden, 6 January 1944, TNA, PREM 3/399/6; Churchill to Roosevelt, 6 January 1944, Kimball, *Churchill & Roosevelt*, 651; Churchill to Eden, 7 January 1944, TNA, PREM 3/355/7, FO 371/39386; conversation between Mikołajczyk, Romer, Raczyński, Churchill, Eden and Cadogan, 20 January 1944, *DPSR*, vol. II, no. 83, 144–9 ; War Cabinet, 25 January 1944, TNA, CAB 65/45/11/1.
2. Memo by Polish Government, 16 January 1944; Mikołajczyk to Eden, 23 January 1944; Mikołajczyk to Churchill, 15 February 1944, all in Mikołajczyk, *Rape of Poland*, 309–16; meeting between Mikołajczyk and Churchill, 6 February 1944, *DPSR*, vol. II, no. 96, 165–71; meeting between Mikołajczyk and Churchill, 16 February 1944, *DPSR*, vol. II, no. 103, 180–88.
3. Memo by Sargent, 24 January 1944, TNA, FO 371/39386.
4. Churchill to Stalin, 28 January 1944, *Stalin Correspondence*, vol. I, no. 235, 196–9.
5. Stalin to Churchill, 4 February 1944, ibid., vol. I, no. 236, 199–201.
6. Churchill to Stalin, 20 February 1944, ibid., vol. I, no. 243, 205–8.
7. Copied in Churchill to Roosevelt, 21 February 1944, Kimball, *Churchill & Roosevelt*, 740–41.
8. House of Commons, 22 February 1944, *Hansard*, vol. 397, 698–9, 733–6.
9. Resolution of the Council of National Unity, 15 February 1944, *DPSR*, vol. II, no. 102, 179–80.
10. Clark Kerr to Eden, 20 February 1944, TNA, FO 371/43312.
11. Harriman report on a meeting with Molotov, 18 January 1944, *FRUS 1944*, vol. III, 1230–31.
12. Clark Kerr to Eden, 28 February 1944, TNA, FO 371/43312.
13. Stalin to Churchill, 16 March 1944, *Stalin Correspondence*, vol. I, no. 254, 214; diary entry 18 March 1944, Colville, *Fringes of Power*, 479; diary entry 20 March 1944, J. Harvey, *War Diaries*, 336; Churchill to Stalin, 21 March 1944, *Stalin Correspondence*, vol. I, no. 256, 215; Stalin to

Churchill, 25 March 1944, *Stalin Correspondence*, vol. I, no. 258, 218; diary entry 26 March 1944, Colville, *Fringes of Power*, 480; Raczyński, *In Allied London*, 198; Churchill to Roosevelt, 4 March 1944, Kimball, *Churchill & Roosevelt*, 20–21.

14. Gardner, *Spheres of Influence*, 208–9.

15. Memorandum by James Dunn, Director of Office of European Affairs, 10 February 1944, *FRUS 1944*, vol. III, 1247.

16. Bliss Lane spent months in Washington meeting various State Department officials and the Polish ambassador. His departure for London was first delayed by the Yalta conference and then by the hope that the negotiations in Moscow would result in a new Polish government which could be recognised by all three members of the Grand Alliance.

17. Mikołajczyk report of his conversations with Schoenfeld, 15 February 1944, *DPSR*, vol. II, no. 101, 177–9.

18. Roosevelt to Mikołajczyk, 3 April 1944, *DPSR*, vol. II, no. 121, 215–16.

19. Karski, *Great Powers*, 458. *Time* magazine had made Hitler its Man of the Year in 1938.

20. T. Bennett, 'Culture, Power, and *Mission to Moscow*'.

21. Ciechanowski, *Defeat in Victory*, 180.

22. Drag Korga, 'The Information Policy of the Polish Government-in-Exile'.

23. Ibid.

24. Stettinius to Roosevelt, 8 March 1944, *FRUS 1944*, vol. III, 1402.

25. TNA, PREM 3/355/15.

26. Mikołajczyk's report to the Council of Ministers on his visit to Washington, 19 June 1944, *Protokoły*, vol. VII, 170–92.

27. Mastny, *Russia's Road*, 173–4; Szymczak, 'Oskar Lange, American Polonia'; *Time*, 8 May 1944.

28. Lange report, 17 May 1944, *DPSR*, vol. II, no. 132, 235–40; Szymczak, 'Oskar Lange, American Polonia'.

29. Lukas, *Strange Allies*, 55.

30. General Tabor was actually Major-General Stanisław Tatar.

31. Stettinius to Roosevelt, 12 June 1944, *FRUS 1944*, vol. III, 1274–6.

32. Mikołajczyk's report to the Council of Ministers on his visit to Washington, 19 June 1944, *Protokoły*, vol. VII, 170–92.

33. Note of meeting between Mikołajczyk and Lange, 13 June 1944, *DPSR*, vol. II, no. 143, 258–63; Mikołajczyk, *Rape of Poland*, 68–70.

34. Diary entries 7–14 June 1944, Campbell & Herring, *Diaries*, 77–87; memo by Mikołajczyk to the State Department, 12 June 1944, *DPSR*, vol. II, no. 141, 250–56.

35. Mikołajczyk's report (see note 32); Hull to Harriman, 17 June 1944, *FRUS 1944*, vol. III, 1295–9.

36. Mikołajczyk to Government Delegate, 21 June 1944, *DPSR*, vol. II, no. 147, 269–70.

37. Roosevelt to Stalin, 17 June 1944, *FRUS 1944*, vol. III, 1284.

38. Eden, *Eden Memoirs*, 440; Hull to Harriman, 15 January 1944, *FRUS 1944*, vol. III, 1228–9.

39. Kersten, *Establishment of Communist Rule*, 56.

40. Schoenfeld, US Chargé d'affaires to Polish Government, to Hull, 9 July 1944, *FRUS 1944*, vol. III, 1292–6; Eden to Clark Kerr, 8 July 1944, Polonsky, *Great Powers*, 204–6.

41. Churchill to Stalin, 27 July 1944, *Stalin Correspondence*, vol. I, no. 305, 249.

42. Mikołajczyk's report (see note 32).

43. Stalin to Roosevelt, 24 June 1944, *Stalin Correspondence*, vol. II, no. 206, 139.

44. Kennan to Harriman, 27 July 1944, Kennan, *Memoirs*, 206.

45. Schoenfeld to Hull, 9 July 1944, *FRUS 1944*, vol. III, 1292–6.

46. For details of the Burdenko report, see Maresh, *Katyń 1940*, 153–60.

47. Clark Kerr to Romer, 2 August 1944, quoted in Zawodny, *Nothing But Honour*, 233–4.

48. Cienciala, 'The Diplomatic Background of the Warsaw Rising'.

49. Kennan, *Memoirs*, 208.

50. Conversation between Mikołajczyk and Stalin, 3 August 1944, *DPSR*, vol. II, no. 180, 309–22.

51. Clark Kerr to Eden, 4 August 1944, Polonsky, *Great Powers*, 209–11.

52. Minutes of the PKWN, 25 July 1944, quoted in Polonsky & Drukier, *Beginnings of Communist Rule*, 252.

53. Conversation between Mikołajczyk, Bierut and Osóbka-Morawski in the presence of Molotov, 8 August 1944, *DPSR*, vol. II, no. 186, 325–33.

54. Stalin to Churchill, 8 August 1944, *Stalin Correspondence*, vol. I, no. 315, 254.

55. Harriman to Hull, 10 August 1944, *FRUS 1944*, vol. III, 1308–10.

56. Mikołajczyk to Government Delegate, 18 August 1944, *AK Documents*, vol. IV, no. 868, 139–44.

57. Conversation between Mikołajczyk and Stalin, 9 August 1944, *DPSR*, vol. II, no. 189, 334–9.

58. Memorandum on the organisation and programme of the Polish Government following the liberation of Poland, 29 August 1944, *DPSR*, vol. II, no. 214, 372–4.

59. Raczkiewicz to Government Delegate and chairman of Council of National Unity, 24 August 1944, *DPSR*, vol. II, no. 210, 366–8.

60. Bór-Komorowski to Mikołajczyk and Sosnkowski, 29 August 1944, *AK Documents*, vol. IV, no. 939, 213.

61. Council of National Unity to Mikołajczyk, 30 August 1944, *DPSR*, vol. II, no. 217, 376–7.

62. Conversation between Mikołajczyk and Churchill, 1 September 1944, *DPSR*, vol. II, no. 220, 380–82.

63. Order of the Day, 1 September 1944, *AK Documents*, vol. IV, no. 975, 251–4.

64. Conversation between Mikołajczyk and Eden, 5 September 1944, *DPSR*, vol. II, no. 223, 385–7.

65. Anders, *Army in Exile*, 213.

66. Manifesto by Council of National Unity, 3 October 1944, *AK Documents*, vol. IV, no. 233, 398–9.

67. Romer to British Government and to United States Government, 7 October 1944, *DPSR*, vol. II, no. 235, 400–404.

68. Mikołajczyk to Churchill, 9 October 1944, *DPSR*, vol. II, no. 236, 405.

69. For details of these talks see *DPSR*, vol. II, no. 237, 405–15 and TNA, PREM 3/355/13.

70. Churchill to the Commons, 28 September 1944, *Hansard*, vol. 403, 489–90.

71. Conversations between Mikołajczyk and Churchill, 14 October 1944, *DPSR*, vol. II, nos. 239 and 241, 416–22, 423–4.

72. Report on the talks in Moscow, Eden, TNA, PREM 3/355/13.

73. Eden, *Eden Memoirs*, 486–7; Churchill to Attlee, 17 October 1944, TNA, PREM 3/355/13.

74. Harriman to Roosevelt, 14 October 1944, *FRUS 1944*, vol. III, 1324.

75. A. Roberts, *Masters and Commanders*, 526; Churchill, *Second World War*, vol. VI, 198.

76. Conversation between Mikołajczyk and Churchill, 26 October 1944, *DPSR*, vol. II, no. 250, 439–41.

77. Mikołajczyk's speech to National Council, 27 October 1944, *Protokoły*, vol. VII, 578–80; Mikołajczyk to Government Delegate, 27 October 1944, *DPSR*, vol. II, no. 251, 442–3.

78. Mikołajczyk to Roosevelt, 26 October 1944, *FRUS Yalta*, 207–9.

79. Cadogan to Romer, 2 November 1944, *DPSR*, vol. II, no. 256, 449–50.

80. Meeting of the Council of Ministers, 2 November 1944, *Protokoły*, vol. VII, 588–90.

81. Raczyński, *In Allied London*, 240.

82. Conversation between Mikołajczyk, Romer, Raczyński and Churchill, 2 November 1944, *DPSR*, vol. II, no. 257, 450–57.

83. Resolution passed by the Council of Ministers, 3 November 1944, *Protokoły*, vol. VII, 595–6.

84. Lukas, *Strange Allies*, 126–7; Bliss Lane, *I Saw Freedom Betrayed*, 37–9; Drag Korga, 'The Information Policy of the Polish Government-in-Exile'.

85. Romer to Ciechanowski, 6 November 1944; Ciechanowski to Romer, 10 November 1944; Ciechanowski to Romer, 13 November 1944; Ciechanowski to Mikołajczyk and Romer, 16 November 1944, all in *DPSR*, vol. II, nos. 262–5, 461–5.

86. Harriman, *Special Envoy*, 369–70.

87. Roosevelt to Mikołajczyk, 17 November 1944, *FRUS 1944*, vol. III, 1334–5.

88. Conversations between Mikołajczyk, Romer and Harriman, 22–24 November 1944, *DPSR*, vol. II, no. 269, 469–70.

89. Eden, *Eden Memoirs*, 496–7.

90. M. Zgórniak, Introduction to *Protokoły*, vol. VII, xl–xlvix.

91. Eden to Churchill, 26 November 1944, TNA, FO 371/39418.

92. Churchill to Roosevelt, 16 December 1944, Loewenheim, *Roosevelt and Churchill*, 632–3.

93. Churchill to Stalin, 3 December 1944; Stalin to Churchill, 8 December 1944; Roosevelt to Stalin, 16 December 1944, all in *Stalin Correspondence*, vol. I, nos 362, 367, 281–2, 284–5; vol. II, no. 248, 165.

94. Schoenfeld to Secretary of State, 21 December 1944, *FRUS 1944*, vol. III, 1350–53.

95. Churchill to Commons, 15 December 1944, *Hansard*, vol. 406, 1478–1578; Ball, *Parliament and Politics*, 436.

96. Nowak, *Courier from Warsaw*, 239.

97. Davies, *Rising '44*, 55–6.

98. Retinger, *All About Poland*.

99. See Bell, *John Bull, passim*.

100. O'Malley, *Phantom Caravan*, 231. O'Malley had been in line for a Grade 1 post after his stint with the Polish Government. Instead he became ambassador to Portugal, a Grade 2 post.

101. Churchill to House of Commons, 24 May 1944, *Hansard*, vol. 400, 782.

102. Karski, *Great Powers*, 489–90.

103. Sarner, *General Anders*, 422–5; Engel, *Facing a Holocaust*, 108–37.

104. Diary entry 4 October 1944, Nicolson, *Harold Nicolson*, 404.

105. A. P. Herbert, *Light the Lights*, 43.

## CHAPTER 15: FIGHTING UNDER BRITISH COMMAND, 1943–1945

1. Memorandum and letter to Churchill, 17 November 1942, TNA, PREM 3 35/11.

2. A. Roberts, *Masters and Commanders, passim*.

3. Keegan, *Second World War*, 347–58.

4. Prażmowska, *Britain and Poland, 1939–1943*, 190.

5. W. Madeja, *Polish Corps*, 43.

6. H. Macmillan, *The Blast of War*, 485.

7. J. Piekałkiewicz, *Cassino*, 159.

8. Leese letter to his wife, 11 February 1944, quoted in Ryder, *Oliver Leese*, 158.

9. Parker, *Monte Cassino*, 171, 285–6; J. Ellis, *Cassino*, 267–8.

10. Z. Wawer, 'General Anders and the Battle for Monte Cassino', in Pyłat, Ciechanowski & Suchcitz, *General Władysław Anders*, 55–76.

11. M. Polak, 'An Alternative View – The Controversy surrounding the Military Decisions Taken by General Władysław Anders', in ibid., 91–111.

12. Piatkowski, 'The Second Polish Corps'.

13. II Polish Corps, 'The Operations of II Polish Corps Against Monte Cassino', TNA, WO 204/8221.

14. Piekałkiewicz, *Cassino*, 163; Holland, 'The Approach to Battle'; Madeja, *Polish Corps*, 47–9; Anders, *Army in Exile*, 169–72; Linklater, *The Campaign in Italy*, 224–5; H. Stańczyk, 'Dowodzenie gen. Dyw. Władysława Andersa 2. Korpusem Polskim w bitwie o Monte Cassino', in Szczepaniak, *Generał Władysław Anders*, 81–104.

15. Anders, *Army in Exile*, 170.

16. Majdalany, *Cassino*, 68.

17. Rees, *World War Two*, 261.

18. Stanisław Kochański, diary entry 20 April 1944, in author's possession.

19. J. Ellis, *Cassino*, 321.

20. Holland, *Italy's Sorrow*, 9.

21. Stanisław Kochański diary entries May 1944.

22. Ryder, *Oliver Leese*, 165.

23. Interview with K. Bortkiewicz, IWM 21562.

24. II Polish Corps, 'The Operations of II Polish Corps' (see note 13).

25. J. Ellis, *Cassino*, 327.

26. Wawer, 'General Anders', in Pyłat, Ciechanowski & Suchcitz, *General Władysław Anders*.

27. Rees, *World War Two*, 261.

28. J. Ellis, *Cassino*, 334.

29. Ibid., 335.

30. Ibid., 311.

31. Quoted in Piekałkiewicz, *Cassino*, 181.

32. J. Ellis, *Cassino*, 337.

33. Leese to his wife, 19 May 1944, Ryder, *Oliver Leese*, 169.

34. Anders to Sosnkowski, 22 May 1944, in Raczyński, *In Allied London*, 221–2.

35. Rees, *World War Two*, 261–2.

36. Stanisław Kochański, diary entry 24 May 1944. His health prevented him from being transferred to the infantry, but volunteers did transfer from the artillery to the infantry.

37. H. Alexander, *Alexander Memoirs*, 138–9.

38. Anders, *Army in Exile*, 186; Linklater, *Campaign in Italy*, 345–6; R. Orsetti, 'The 2nd Polish Corps Commander in the Adriatic Campaign 1944–46 in Retrospect', in Pyłat, Ciechanowski & Suchcitz, *General Władysław Anders*, 113–28; Madeja, *Polish Corps*, 91.

39. Leese to his wife, 23 July 1944, Ryder, *Oliver Leese*, 179.

40. Anders, *Army in Exile*, 205, 190–91.

41. Leese to his wife, 27 July 1944, Ryder, *Oliver Leese*, 181–2.

42. Madeja, *Polish Corps*, 113; Anders, *Army in Exile*, 235. Leese had been appointed commander-in-chief of allied land forces in South East Asia.

43. Piekałkiewicz, *Cassino*, 165; Stanisław Kochański, diary entry 19 July 1944. Only five Poles deserted to the Germans during the whole Italian campaign.

44. T. Żukowski, IWM 8115 99/3/1.

45. Madeja, *Polish Corps*, 149.

46. Anders, *Army in Exile*, 256.

47. Madeja, *Polish Corps*, 149.

48. H. Macmillan, *Blast of War*, 696–7.

49. Bortkiewicz, IWM 21562.

50. Stanisław Kochański, diary entry 23 July 1944.

51. Madeja, *Polish Corps*, 173–4; Anders, *Army in Exile*, 266–8; Orsetti, 'The 2nd Polish Corps Commander', in Pyłat, Ciechanowski & Suchcitz, *General Anders*.

52. Diary entry 22 April 1945, H. Macmillan, *War Diaries*, 741.

53. Author's interview with Stanisław Kochański.

54. This article was published in Gellhorn, *Face of War*.

55. Peszke, *Poland's Navy*, 152; Keegan, *Six Armies*, 271.

56. McGilvray, *Black Devil's March*, 12.

57. Pickering, 'Tales of Friendly Fire'.

58. R. Zolski, IWM 4211 83/24/1.

59. McGilvray, *Black Devil's March*, 17–40; Potomski, *Maczek*, 232–8.

60. Koskodan, *No Greater Ally*, 144.

61. Keegan, *Six Armies*, 271, 275.

62. Beevor, *D-Day*, 468.

63. Keegan, *Six Armies*, 279–82.

64. Florentin, *Stalingrad en Normandie*, 426.

65. Koskodan, *No Greater Ally*, 147.

66. T. Potworowski, IWM 8288 06/38/1.

67. McGilvray, *Black Devil's March*, 41–54; Potomski, *Maczek*, 259–75.

68. Zolski, IWM 4211 83/24/1.

69. Modelski, *Polish Contribution*, 154.

70. McGilvray, *Black Devil's March*, 58–80.

71. Stella-Sawicki, Garliński & Mucha, *First to Fight*, 120; Modelski, *Polish Contribution*, 155–6.

72. Maczek, *Od Powodny*, 225–7.

73. McGilvray, *Black Devil's March*, 81–99.

74. Koskodan, *No Greater Ally*, 151.

75. McGilvray, *Black Devil's March*, 103–13.

76. Stella-Sawicki, Garliński & Mucha, *First to Fight*, 121.

77. Maczek, *Od Powodny*, 232–7.
78. PISM, A.XII.1/129.
79. Peszke, *Battle for Warsaw*, 112, 191–4.
80. Sosabowski, *Freely I Served*, 129–33.
81. Peszke, *Battle for Warsaw*, 201.
82. Browning's comment to Montgomery at the final planning conference for Operation Market Garden. Ryan, *A Bridge Too Far*, 7; Urquhart, *Arnhem*, 17. The comment by Sosabowski (played by Gene Hackman) was immortalised in the film *A Bridge Too Far* (1977).
83. Cholewczyński, *Poles Apart*, 78–9.
84. Peszke, *Battle for Warsaw*, 202; Sosabowski, *Freely I Served*, 145; Cholewczyński, *Poles Apart*, 80.
85. Urquhart, *Arnhem*, 90–91.
86. Buckingham, *Arnhem*, 178.
87. Cholewczyński, *Poles Apart*, 7.
88. Sosabowski, *Freely I Served*, 164–5.
89. Cholewczyński, *Poles Apart*, 145.
90. Urquhart, *Arnhem*, 143.
91. Sosabowski, *Freely I Served*, 171; Buckingham, *Arnhem*, 188–9.
92. Buckingham, *Arnhem*, 191.
93. Sosabowski, *Freely I Served*, 182–4.
94. Cholewczyński, *Poles Apart*, 221–4.
95. Stella-Sawicki, Garliński & Mucha, *First to Fight*, 126. The 1st Airborne Division lost 1,485 dead and 6,500 captured. Buckingham, *Arnhem*, 197.
96. Cholewczyński, *Poles Apart*, 277, 281.
97. Sosabowski, *Freely I Served*, 191.
98. Cholewczyński, *Poles Apart*, 281, 292, 312.
99. Sosabowski, *Freely I Served*, 199, 202–3. In his memoirs Montgomery makes no criticism of the Polish Parachute Brigade; Montgomery, *Memoirs*.
100. Cholewczyński, *Poles Apart*, 292.
101. Buckingham, *Arnhem*, 199.
102. *APHC*, vol. I, 493–5, 502.
103. R. Wnuk, 'Polish Intelligence and the German "Secret Weapons": V-1 and V-2', *APHC*, vol. I, 473–83. Some of the actual reports radioed back to London can be found in vol. II, 850–902.
104. Garliński, *Hitler's Last Weapons*, *passim*.
105. Jones, *Most Secret War*, 559–60.
106. Stella-Sawicki, Garliński & Mucha, *First to Fight*, 110.
107. *Destiny Can Wait*, 251.
108. Olson & Cloud, *For Your Freedom and Ours*, 373.
109. *Destiny Can Wait*, 169.
110. Stella-Sawicki, Garliński & Mucha, *First to Fight*, 111.

## CHAPTER 16 THE END OF THE WAR

1. Stalin to Churchill, 3 January 1945, *Stalin Correspondence*, vol. I, no. 381, 291–2. Edward Osóbka-Morawski was prime minister and Władysław Gomułka and Stanisław Janusz were deputy prime ministers.

2. Churchill to Stalin, 5 January 1945, *Stalin Correspondence*, vol. I, no. 382, 295; press release of the Polish Government, 6 January 1945, *DPSR*, vol. II, no. 294, 505.

3. Schoenfeld to Secretary of State, 27 January 1945, *FRUS 1945*, vol. V, 115–21; memo by Sargent, 8 January 1945, memo on conversation with Mikołajczyk, 24 January 1945, memo by Mikołajczyk, 26 January 1945, all in TNA, FO 371/47575/2896; Hanson, 'Stanisław Mikołajczyk'.

4. Memo from the Polish Government to the governments of the United States and Britain, 22 January 1945, *DPSR*, vol. II, no. 300, 511–12.

5. Raczyński's note of his conversation with Cadogan, 23 January 1945, *DPSR*, vol. II, no. 301, 512–13; record of conversation between Cadogan and Tarnowski, 26 January 1945, TNA, FO 371/47575/2896; diary entries 23 and 26 January 1945, Dilks, *Diaries*, 698.

6. Foreign Office Briefing Paper, TNA, PREM 3/356/3; Cienciala, 'Great Britain and Poland Before and After Yalta'.

7. State Department Briefing Paper, *FRUS Yalta*, 230–34.

8. Plokhy, *Yalta*, 78.

9. Fourth plenary session, 7 February 1945, *FRUS Yalta*, 717.

10. Third plenary session, 6 February 1945, *FRUS Yalta*, 667–71.

11. Roosevelt to Stalin, 6 February 1945, *Stalin Correspondence*, vol. II, no. 266, 177–9.

12. Fourth plenary session, 7 February 1945, *FRUS Yalta*, 711–17.

13. Eden, *Eden Memoirs*, 517.

14. Fifth plenary session, 8 February 1945, and sixth plenary session, 9 February 1945, *FRUS Yalta*, 776–81, 847–8; Plokhy, *Yalta*, 243–6.

15. Dallas, *Poisoned Peace*, 399.

16. Declaration on Liberated Europe, *FRUS Yalta*, 972.

17. Communiqué issued at the end of the conference, 12 February 1945, *FRUS Yalta*, 973–4.

18. Bohlen, *Witness to History*, 190.

19. Meeting between Alexander and Anders, 17 February 1945, TNA, FO 371/47578/2896.

20. Anders, *Army in Exile*, 256.

21. Gilbert, *Churchill*, vol. VII, 1237.

22. Government resolution on the army, 13 February 1945, *Protokoły*, vol. VIII, 240.

23. Protest by the Polish Government, 13 February 1945, *Protokoły*, vol. VIII,

238–40; Tarnowski to O'Malley, 18 February 1945, *DPSR*, vol. II, no. 312, 523–7; conversation between Raczyński and Eden, 20 February 1945, *DPSR*, vol. II, no. 314, 528–32.

24. Resolution of the RJN, 22 February 1945, *AK Documents*, vol. VI, no. 1916, 460–61.

25. 27 February 1945, *Hansard*, vol. 408, 1276–85.

26. Diary entry 27 February 1945, in Nicolson, *Harold Nicolson*, 436.

27. Diary entry 28 February 1945, in Colville, *Fringes of Power*, 565–6.

28. 28 February 1945, *Hansard*, vol. 408, 1422.

29. Bell, *John Bull*, 176–81.

30. Kersten, *Establishment of Communist Rule*, 123–4.

31. Churchill to Roosevelt, 8 March 1945, Loewenheim, *Roosevelt and Churchill*, 660–65.

32. Eden to Clark Kerr, 18 February 1945, TNA, FO 371/47578/2896.

33. Acheson to Harriman, 18 March 1945, *FRUS 1945*, vol. V, 172–6.

34. Harriman to Secretary of State, 23 March 1945, *FRUS 1945*, vol. V, 176–8.

35. Bohlen, *Witness to History*, 192.

36. The full list was Mikołajczyk, Romer and Grabski from London; Archbishop Sapieha, Wincenty Witos (leader of the Peasant Party), Zygmunt Żuławski (Socialist trade union leader), Professor Franciszek Bujak (chemistry professor in Lwów), and Professor Stanisław Kutzreba (historian from Kraków and president of the Polish Academy of Sciences).

37. Harriman to Secretary of State, 23 March 1945, *FRUS 1945*, vol. V, 176–8; the British correspondence on the Moscow conference is in TNA, FO 371/47582.

38. Gardner, *Spheres of Influence*, 245.

39. Memo by Clark Kerr, 27 March 1945, TNA, FO 371/47941.

40. Eden to Churchill, 24 March 1945, Eden, *Eden Memoirs*, 525–6.

41. Churchill to Roosevelt, 8 March 1945, Loewenheim, *Roosevelt and Churchill*, 660–65.

42. Churchill to Roosevelt, 13, 16, 27, 30 and 31 March 1945; Roosevelt to Churchill, 15, 29 and 31 March 1945, all in Loewenheim, *Roosevelt and Churchill*, 670–96.

43. Churchill to Roosevelt, 27 March 1945, Loewenheim, *Roosevelt and Churchill*, 684–7.

44. Roosevelt to Stalin, 31 March 1945, Stalin to Roosevelt, 7 April 1945, both in *Stalin Correspondence*, vol. II, nos. 284, 288, 191–3, 197–9; Churchill to Stalin, 31 March 1945, Stalin to Churchill, 7 April 1945, both in ibid., vol. I, nos. 416, 418, 310–11, 314.

45. Hanson, 'Stanislaw Mikolajczyk'.

46. *The Times*, 15 April 1945.

47. Churchill and Truman to Stalin, 18 April 1945, *Stalin Correspondence*, vol. I, no. 430, 325–6; Truman to Stalin, 23 April 1945, ibid., vol. II,

no. 297, 207–8; Stalin to Churchill, 18 and 24 April 1945 and 4 May 1945, Churchill to Stalin, 28 April 1945, all in ibid., vol. I, nos. 428, 439, 456, 450, 324, 331–2, 346–8, 339–44; Stettinius to Harriman, 14 April 1945, *FRUS 1945*, vol. V, 213.

48. Soviet Embassy to State Department, 9 and 22 March 1945; meeting between Grew and Gromyko, 23 March 1945; State Department to Soviet Embassy, 29 March 1945; Soviet Embassy to State Department, 17 April 1945, all in *FRUS 1945*, vol. I, 113–14, 147–8, 164, 330; Polish Government to the governments of Britain, United States and China, 12 March 1945, and memo by Polish Government, 21 April 1945, both in *DPSR*, vol. II, nos. 324, 341, 544–5, 569–70; meeting between Ciechanowski and Bliss Lane, 15 March 1945, *FRUS 1945*, vol. V, 165–7.

49. 21 March 1945, *Hansard*, vol. 409, 835.

50. Ciechanowski, *Defeat in Victory*, 387.

51. Diary entry 8 April 1945, in Trevor-Roper, *Goebbels Diaries*, 322.

52. Telegrams from San Francisco, *Protokoły*, vol. VIII, 500–502; Plokhy, *Yalta*, 382.

53. Jędrzejewicz, *Poland in the British Parliament*, 602.

54. The Polish issue was discussed at five meetings between the foreign ministers, *FRUS 1945*, vol. V, 237–51, 259–62, 272–6, 281–4.

55. Protest of the Polish Government, 28 April 1945, *DPSR*, vol. II, no. 346, 574–5.

56. Appeal by the Polish Government to Stettinius, 6 May 1945, *DPSR*, vol. II, no. 354, 589–90.

57. Sagajllo, *Man in the Middle*, 151.

58. U. Dudzic-Ranke, IWM 13318 05/14/1.

59. Quoted in Walker, *Poland Alone*, 277.

60. Rees, *Auschwitz*, 264.

61. Hitchcock, *Liberation*, 288–9.

62. Szpilman, *Pianist*, 177–87.

63. Beevor & Vinogradova, *Writer at War*, 324.

64. Grzelak, Stańczyk & Zwoliński, *Bez Możliwości Wyboru*, 185–8.

65. Erickson, *Road to Berlin*, 447–76, 517–26; Grzelak, Stańczyk & Zwoliński, *Bez Możliwości Wyboru*, 188–90.

66. Duffy, *Red Storm*, 225–7.

67. Hastings, *Armageddon*, 287.

68. Klukowski, *Diary of the Occupation*, 562; Klukowski, *Red Shadow*, 57.

69. Hastings, *Armageddon*, 297.

70. Grzelak, Stańczyk & Zwoliński, *Bez Możliwości Wyboru*, 194–7.

71. Ibid., 198–208.

72. Zylberberg, *Warsaw Diary*, 210.

73. Hastings, *Armageddon*, 123–4.

74. R. Smorczewski, IWM 128787 03/41/1.

75. Author's interview with Teresa Kicińska.

76. Jan Korzybska, quoted in Kaczorowska, *Children of the Katyń Massacre*, 114.

77. Bessel, *Germany 1945*, 53.

78. Arciszewski to Churchill, 8 March 1945, *DPSR*, vol. II, no. 319, 536–41. Churchill included this information in a telegram to Roosevelt on 10 March 1945.

79. Quoted in Rogers & Williams, *On the Bloody Road*, 114.

80. For example, Okulicki to Raczkiewicz, 9 December 1944 and Okulicki to Kopański, 21 December 1944, both in *AK Documents*, vol. V, nos. 1344, 1367, 170–84, 211.

81. Okulicki Order, 19 January 1945, *AK Documents*, vol. V, no. 1391, 239.

82. Okulicki, 22 January 1945, *AK Documents*, vol. VI, no. 1909, 455.

83. Prażmowska, *Civil War in Poland*, 150–51.

84. Kersten, *Establishment of Communist Rule*, 126.

85. Polonsky & Drukier, *Beginnings of Communist Rule*, 106–7; Reynolds, '"Lublin" versus "London"'; Paczkowski, 'Poland, the "Enemy Nation"', in Courtois *et al.*, *Black Book of Communism*.

86. Introduction and interrogation of Adam Ostrowski, in Instytut Pamięci Narodowej, *Operacja 'Sejm'*, 243–77. Ostrowski had been the regional government delegate for Lwów. After the war he joined the government and became the Polish ambassador first to Sweden and then to Italy.

87. Author's interview with Nina Kochańska.

88. Arciszewski to Churchill, 8 March 1945, *DPSR*, vol. II, no. 319, 536–41.

89. Kersten, *Establishment of Communist Rule*, 95; Paczkowski, 'Poland, the "Enemy Nation"', in Courtois *et al.*, *Black Book of Communism*; Polonsky & Drukier, *Beginnings of Communist Rule*, 108–9.

90. Mikołajczyk to Churchill, 21 February 1944; Churchill to Mikołajczyk, 7 April 1944; Clark Kerr to Molotov, 2 November 1944, all in *AK Documents*, vol. VI, nos. 1807, 1817, 1888, 373, 386, 437; Walker, *Poland Alone*, 266, 274.

91. Bines, *Operation Freston*, *passim*; Kemp, *Thorns of Memory*, 233–65.

92. Raczyński to Eden, 28 January 1945, *DPSR*, vol. II, 515–16.

93. Raczyński to Eden, 9 March 1945, *AK Documents*, vol. V, no. 1451, 321.

94. Pimienov to Okulicki, Pimienov to Jankowski, 6 March 1945, *AK Documents*, vol. V, nos. 1445, 1446, 315–16.

95. Jankowski to London, 20 March 1945, *AK Documents*, vol. V, no. 1471, 346–7.

96. Garliński, 'The Polish Underground State 1939–1945'; Okulicki to Kopański, 25 March 1945; Korboński to London, 1 April 1945, both in *AK Documents*, vol. V, nos. 1477, 1483, 352, 359; Kersten, *Establishment of Communist Rule*, 133–4.

97. Raczyński to Eden, 1 April 1945, *DPSR*, vol. II, no. 331, 553–4; Reynolds,

'"Lublin" versus "London"'; Cienciala, 'The Diplomatic Background of the Warsaw Rising'; Tarnowski to Eden and Stettinius, 27 April 1945, *DPSR*, vol. II, 573; diary entry 5 May 1945, Dilks, *Diaries*, 744; Eden, *Eden Memoirs*, 536; Stalin to Churchill, 4 May 1945, *Stalin Correspondence*, vol. I, no. 456, 346-8; statements by British delegation and by Stettinius on arrest of the sixteen, 5 May 1945, and communiqué by TASS, 5 May 1945, all in *AK Documents*, vol. V, 399-403.

98. Sarner, *General Anders*, 201.
99. Quoted in Hastings, *Armageddon*, 570.
100. Gilbert, *Day the War Ended*, 269-70.
101. Diary entry 15 May 1945, Klukowski, *Red Shadow*, 72.
102. Baluk, *Silent and Unseen*, 262.
103. Kersten, *Establishment of Communist Rule*, 164.

## CHAPTER 17: THE AFTERMATH OF THE WAR

1. Gumkowski & Leszczyński, *Poland Under Nazi Occupation*, 215-17.
2. Bliss Lane, *I Saw Freedom Betrayed*, 17.
3. Korboński, *Warsaw in Chains*, 30.
4. Kersten, *Establishment of Communist Rule*, 165-6; Lukas, *Bitter Legacy*, 32-3; Bliss Lane, *I Saw Freedom Betrayed*, 87, 113.
5. Hopkins to Truman, 14 June 1945, *FRUS 1945*, vol. V, 337-8. The British chiefs of staff concluded that war against the Soviet Union was virtually impossible since the rearming of German forces would cause an international outcry and US support was far from guaranteed. Mazower, *Hitler's Empire*, 566.
6. Hopkins Mission, 26 May-6 June 1945, *FRUS Potsdam*, vol. I, 24-62; Kennan to Secretary of State for Harriman, 14 May 1945, *FRUS 1945*, vol. V, 195-6.
7. Mikołajczyk, *Rape of Poland*, 134.
8. Quoted in W. Larsh, 'Yalta and the American Approach'.
9. Kersten, *Establishment of Communist Rule*, 152-6.
10. Harriman to Secretary of State, 21 June 1945, *FRUS 1945*, vol. V, 352-4.
11. Stypułkowski, *Invitation to Moscow*, 317; Kersten, *Establishment of Communist Rule*, 153-5.
12. Harriman to Secretary of State, 18 June 1945, *FRUS 1945*, vol. V, 349-50.
13. The entire transcript of the trial can be found in *Trial of the Organisers, Leaders and Members*. The quotation is from pp. 236-8.
14. Raczyński to Eden, 6 July 1945, *DPSR*, vol. II, no. 378, 626-8.
15. Hope, *Abandoned Legion*, 80.
16. Raczyński, *In Allied London*, 297-8; Sword, *Formation of the Polish*

*Community*, 185–93. Strasburger was recalled in 1949 but decided to remain in London.

17. Introduction to *Protokoły*, vol. VIII; Bevin to Cavendish-Bentinck, 14 December 1945, *DBPO*, series I, vol. 6, 269–73.
18. De Zayas, *Nemesis at Potsdam*, 50–51; Raack, 'Stalin Fixes the Oder-Neisse Line'.
19. Harriman to Secretary of State, 9 April 1945; Stettinius to Kennan, 17 April 1945; Kennan to Secretary of State, 18 April 1945; Kennan to Secretary of State, 11 May 1945, all in *FRUS 1945*, vol. V, 205–7, 227–31, 293–5. Silesia was ruled by the Polish Piast dynasty from the tenth to the fourteenth century.
20. Quoted in Dallas, *Poisoned Peace*, 557.
21. Sixth plenary session, 22 July 1945, *FRUS Potsdam*, vol. II, 247–52.
22. For example, Modzelewski to Harriman, 10 July 1945, *FRUS Potsdam*, vol. I, 757–77; summary of statements made by the Polish delegation to the meeting of the foreign ministers, 24 July 1945, ibid., vol. II, 332–5, memo by Mikołajczyk, 24 July 1945, ibid., vol. I, 1128–9.
23. Meeting between Byrnes and Molotov, 31 July 1945; Eleventh plenary session, 31 July 1945, *FRUS Potsdam*, vol. II, 510, 627–8.
24. Protocols on the Berlin Conference, 1 August 1945, *FRUS Potsdam*, vol. II, 1490–92.
25. Bliss Lane to Secretary of State, 17 September and 3 October 1946, *FRUS 1946*, vol. VI, 494–5, 498–500; Kersten, *Establishment of Communist Rule*, 304.
26. Lukas, *Bitter Legacy*, 18.
27. Bessel, *Germany 1945*, 214–15.
28. *FRUS Potsdam*, vol. II, 1495 (see note 24).
29. Bliss Lane to Secretary of State, 4 and 12 December 1945, *FRUS 1945*, vol. II, 1318–19, 1323.
30. Ahonen, *After the Expulsion*, 272.
31. There is a large literature on the expulsion of the Germans from the east. Notable contributions include: P. Ther, 'A Century of Forced Migration: The Origins and Consequences of "Ethnic Cleansing"'; K. Kersten, 'Forced Migration and the Transformation of Polish Society in the Post-War Period'; S. Jankowiak, '"Cleansing" Poland of Germans: The Province of Pomerania, 1945–1949', all in Ther & Siljak, *Redrawing Nations*, 43–72, 75–86, 87–105; E. Ochman, 'Population Displacement and Regional Reconstruction in Postwar Poland: The Case of Upper Silesia', in Gatrell & Baron, *Warlands*, 210–28; Rieber, *Communist Studies*, 16; De Zayas, *Nemesis at Potsdam*, 81; Prażmowska, *Civil War in Poland*, 177–82; Dallas, *Poisoned Peace*, 211–36; Naimark, *Fires of Hatred*, 124–32.
32. Kersten, 'Forced Migration', in Ther & Siljak, *Redrawing Nations*.
33. Mazower, *Hitler's Empire*, 544.

34. Korboński, *Warsaw in Chains*, 92.

35. Quoted in Curp, *A Clean Sweep*, 42.

36. Dallas, *Poisoned Peace*, 156–7.

37. Torańska, '*Them*', 250–51; conversation between Elbridge Durbrow, Chief of Eastern European Affairs at the State Department, and Mikołajczyk, 8 November 1945, *FRUS 1945*, vol. V, 402–3. Mikołajczyk was in Washington on the Polish Economic Mission to secure funds for the reconstruction of Poland.

38. J. Kochanowski, 'Gathering Poles into Poland: Forced Migration from Poland's Former Eastern Territories', in Ther & Siljak, *Redrawing Nations*, 135–54.

39. K. Stadnik, 'Ukrainian-Polish Population Transfers, 1944–46: Moving in Opposite Directions', in Gatrell & Baron, *Warlands*, 165–87; Czerniakiewicz, *Repatriacja ludności polskiej z ZSRR 1944–1948*; Plokhy, *Yalta*, 174; Snyder, *Reconstruction*, 187–8; Sword, *Deportation and Exile*, 176–95; Romer to British Government, 7 October 1944, *DPSR*, vol. II, no. 235, 400–404; Polish Government to Government Delegate, 14 March 1945, *AK Documents*, vol. V, no. 1462, 331; author's interviews with Nina Kochańska and Igor Korczagin.

40. K. Zieliński, 'To Pacify, Populate and Polonise: Territorial Transformations and the Displacement of Ethnic Minorities in Communist Poland, 1944–49', in Gatrell & Baron, *Warlands*, 188–209; O. Subtelny, 'Expulsion, Resettlement, Civil Strife: The Fate of Poland's Ukrainians, 1944–1947', in Ther & Siljak, *Redrawing Nations*, 155–72; Snyder, *Reconstruction*, 188–94; Statiev, *Soviet Counterinsurgency*, *passim*.

41. Gutman & Krakowski, *Unequal Victims*, 351–2, 363; Y. Litvak, 'Polish-Jewish Refugees Repatriated from the Soviet Union to Poland at the End of the Second World War and Afterwards'; H. Shlomi, 'The "Jewish Organising Committee" in Moscow and "The Jewish Central Committee" in Warsaw, June 1945–February 1946: Tackling Repatriation', both in Davies & Polonsky, *Jews in Eastern Poland*, 227–39, 240–54.

42. Banas, *Scapegoats*, 23.

43. Gutman & Krakowski, *Unequal Victims*, 367.

44. Bliss Lane met Szuldenfrei, a Bundist, and Adolf Berman, brother of Jakub and a communist. Bliss Lane to Secretary of State, 11 January 1946, *FRUS 1946*, vol. V, 132–3.

45. Bliss Lane to Secretary of State, 15 July 1946, *FRUS 1946*, vol. VI, 478–80; Bliss Lane, *I Saw Freedom Betrayed*, 157–9.

46. Gross, *Fear*, 81–99.

47. Gross, 'A Tangled Web', in Deák, Gross & Judt, *Politics of Retribution*, 370–72.

48. Kersten, *Establishment of Communist Rule*, 215; Prażmowska, *Civil War in Poland*, 171–2.

49. Bliss Lane to Secretary of State, 16 December 1945, *FRUS 1945*, vol. II, 1214; Erhardt to Secretary of State, 3 August 1946; Acheson to Bliss Lane, 8 August 1946; Bliss Lane to Secretary of State, 6 September 1946, all in *FRUS 1946*, vol. V, 175–6, 178, 186–7; Shephard, *Long Road Home*, 186; Sarner, *General Anders*, 226–9; Hitchcock, *Liberation*, 333–5.

50. TNA, CAB 66/62.

51. Biegański *et al.*, *Polski Czyn Zbrojny w II Wojnie Światowej*, 716–17.

52. Col. B. Regulski to Lieut.-Col. J. Carlisle, War Office, 13 June 1945; Carlisle to Regulski, 20 August 1945, *PISM*, A.XII.42/19.

53. Memo on 'The Future of the Polish Armed Forces at the Side of Great Britain', Anders, 9 March 1945; Miss Gatehouse's report, 6 April 1945, TNA, FO 371/47662.

54. PISM, A.XII.4/106; A.XII.42/19; TNA, FO 371/47660; WO 32/11090.

55. TNA, FO 371/47661; FO 371/47662; Sarner, *General Anders*, 231–3.

56. E. Maresch, 'The Polish 2 Corps in Preparation for Action and its Disbandment 1943–1946', in Pyłat, Ciechanowski & Suchcitz, *General Władysław Anders*, 33–54.

57. Diary entry 2 May 1945, Danchev & Todman, *War Diaries*, 686.

58. TNA, FO 371/47667; FO 371/56468; WO 204/10454.

59. Bór-Komorowski to field commanders, 29 June 1945, PISM, A.XII.3/10.

60. Sword, *Formation*, 200–203; Hope, *Abandoned Legion*, 77.

61. Quoted in Kaczorowska, *Children of the Katyń Massacre*, 168.

62. Author's interview with Teresa Kicińska.

63. Orsetti, 'The 2nd Polish Corps Commander', in Pyłat, Ciechanowski & Suchcitz, *General Władysław Anders*; Thornton, 'The Second Polish Corps'.

64. TNA, FO 371/56366. In effect the Polish soldiers agreed to receive pay for a rank below their actual rank and the surplus went towards the welfare of the soldiers not officially on the establishment and of the civilians. Author's interview with Stanisław Kochański.

65. *FRUS Potsdam*, vol. II, 1491 (see note 24).

66. TNA, FO 371/47676; FO 371/47691.

67. Hope, *Abandoned Legion*, 140–43.

68. Bevin to Cavendish-Bentinck, 9 September 1945; Cavendish-Bentinck to Bevin, 26 September 1945; Bevin to Cavendish-Bentinck, 11 November 1945; Bevin to Cavendish-Bentinck, 14 December 1945, all in *DBPO*, 75–6, 104–6, 201–4, 269–73.

69. Sarner, *General Anders*, 231; Hope, *Abandoned Legion*, 116–20; Maresch, 'The Polish 2 Corps Commander', in Pyłat, Ciechanowski & Suchcitz, *General Władysław Anders*. Modelski had been deputy minister of national defence in the wartime Polish Government. Kot would later remain in Italy after his term as ambassador expired and then move to London.

70. See, for example, Bevin to Halifax, 11 February 1946, *DBPO*, 290; Tolstoy, *Victims of Yalta*, 340; Hope, *Abandoned Legion*, 138–9.

71. Hetherington & Chalmers, *War Crimes*; Wiesenthal, *Justice Not Vengeance*, 204–5.

72. Sarner, *General Anders*, 209–11.

73. Memo by L. D. Halliday, 13 November 1945, *DBPO*, 211–16.

74. Lieut.-Col. Kamiński to War Office, 28 August 1945, PISM, A.XII.42/19.

75. Quoted in Lane, *Victims of Stalin and Hitler*, 154.

76. Z. Wysecki interviewed by Keith Sword, SSEES archives, SWO 1/7.

77. Peszke, *Poland's Navy*, 167; Proudfoot, *European Refugees*, 283; Anders, *Army in Exile*, 287; Sarner, *General Anders*, 242–3; Lane, *Victims of Stalin and Hitler*, 188; Hope, *Abandoned Legion*, 147–8. Some of the soldiers who returned to their pre-war homes in what had been eastern Poland and was now western Belorussia suffered a later deportation to northern parts of the Soviet Union in response to their perceived political unreliability and opposition to the establishment of kolkhozy. J. Szumski, 'Collectivization of Western Belarus, 1947–1952', in Malicki & Zasztowt, *East and West*, 169–78.

78. Sword, *Formation*, 200–203; TNA, FO 371/46776.

79. Anders, *Army in Exile*, 293–4; Thornton, 'The Second Polish Corps'.

80. Bevin to Commons, 22 May 1946, *Hansard*, vol. 429, 299–306.

81. Sword, *Formation*, 229–45; Lane, *Victims of Stalin and Hitler*, 186–8; Hope, *Abandoned Legion*, 181–8; Sword, '"Their Prospects Will Not Be Bright"'.

82. Sword, *Formation*, 245–67; Sarner, *General Anders*, 245–64; Polak, 'An Alternative View', in Pyłat, Ciechanowski & Suchcitz, *General Władysław Anders*.

83. Lane, *Victims of Stalin and Hitler*, 198. School reports were issued in Polish and English. The author's parents first met when they both were studying at the Polish University College.

84. Quoted in *Stalin's Ethnic Cleansing*, 644–5.

85. Z. Wolak, quoted in Rees, *World War Two*, 392; Z. Kawencka, IWM 16847; S. Knapp, in Zamoyski, *Forgotten Few*, 207; Hope, *Abandoned Legion*, 196.

86. Davies, *Rising '44*, 505; Commons, 4 June 1946, *Hansard*, vol. 423, 308; *Daily Telegraph*, 5 June 1946.

87. The definitions used by Supreme Headquarters Allied Expeditionary Force were: 'Refugees are civilians not outside the national boundaries of their country, who desire to return to their homes, but require assistance to do so, who are: (1) temporarily homeless because of military operations; (2) at some distance from their homes for reasons related to the war.'

Displaced Persons (DPs) are 'civilians outside the national boundaries of their country by reason of the war, who are: (1) desirous but unable to return to their home or find homes without assistance; (2) to be returned to enemy or ex-enemy territory'. DPs sub-classified as evacuees; war or political fugitives; political prisoners; forced or involuntary workers; Todt workers;

former members of forces under German command; deportees; intruded persons; extruded persons; civilian internees; ex-POWs; or stateless persons'. Proudfoot, *European Refugees*, 115.

88. Proudfoot, *European Refugees*, 130, 159.

89. Shephard, *Long Road Home*, 162–74; Wyman, *DPs*.

90. Quoted in Lukas, *Out of the Inferno*, 115.

91. Bliss Lane to Secretary of State, 28 November 1945, *FRUS 1945*, vol. V, 420–12.

92. Proudfoot, *European Refugees*, 237, 281; Wyman, *DPs*, 83; Gallman, American Chargé d'affaires in London to Secretary of State, 28 February 1946, *FRUS 1946*, vol. V, 143–7.

93. Shephard, *Long Road Home*, 158.

94. McNeill, *By the Rivers of Babylon*, 37.

95. Ibid., 92.

96. Bessel, *Germany 1945*, 263.

97. Howard, *Otherwise Occupied*, 119–20; Cavendish-Bentinck to Bevin, 26 September 1945, *DBPO*, 104–6.

98. Wyman, *DPs*, 71; Hulme, *Wild Place*, 151–2; Shephard, *Long Road Home*, 91–4.

99. Proudfoot, *European Refugees*, 284. The letter-writing campaign could be manipulated. Józefa Kochańska wrote to her son Stanisław, now in Britain with the II Corps, describing all the good meals they were eating and contrasting them with rationing in Britain. Unknown to the Polish authorities, she was listing foods that she knew her son detested. Just in case his tastes had changed, she added the postscript, 'Tell Inky not to return. We don't want his kind here.' Inky being Stanisław's family nickname. Author's interview with Stanisław Kochański.

100. Lukas, *Bitter Legacy*, 111–13.

101. Lane, *Victims of Stalin and Hitler*, 190–96.

102. Kelly, *Finding Poland*, 220.

103. Wyman, *DPs*, 136, 139, 145; Dallas, *Poisoned Peace*, 269.

104. *Poles in India*, 484.

105. Kelly, *Finding Poland*, 226.

106. TNA, WO 219/2427.

107. Giedroyć, *Crater's Edge*, 177–8.

108. Hrabar, Tokarz & Wilczur, *Fate of Polish Children*, 147–50; Wyman, *DPs*, 91–3; Shephard, *Long Road Home*, 313–22.

109. Quoted in Kersten, *Establishment of Communist Rule*, 187; Korboński, *Warsaw in Chains*, 19–20, 43.

110. Bliss Lane to Secretary of State, 13 October 1945, *FRUS 1945*, vol. V, 388–90; Bliss Lane to Secretary of State, 21 April 1946, *FRUS 1946*, vol. VI, 432; Bliss Lane, *I Saw Freedom Betrayed*, 136–8; Retinger, *Memoirs*, 197–201.

111. Kersten, *Establishment of Communist Rule*, 228; Korboński, *Warsaw in Chains*, 233.

112. Torańska, *'Them'*, 272.

113. R. Hankey interviewed by Keith Sword, SSEES archives, SWO 1/3.

114. Courtois *et al.*, *Black Book of Communism*, 376.

115. Korboński, *Warsaw in Chains*, 244; Kersten, *Establishment of Communist Rule*, 222–79; Prażmowska, *Civil War in Poland*, 129–59; Paszkiewicz had held various commands in Britain, ending as the deputy commander of the 1st Corps before he returned to Poland.

116. Cavendish-Bentinck to Bevin, 10 October 1945, *DBPO*, 138–43; meeting between Acheson and Minc, 18 December 1946, *FRUS 1946*, vol. VI, 543–4.

117. Korboński, *Warsaw in Chains*, 117.

118. Kersten, *Establishment of Communist Rule*, 257.

119. Quoted in Korboński, *Warsaw in Chains*, 121. There was even a rumour that Kraków's population would be resettled in retaliation for its opposition.

120. Korboński, *Warsaw in Chains*, 122.

121. Kersten, *Establishment of Communist Rule*, 305–39; memo by the British Embassy to the State Department, 17 October 1946, *FRUS 1946*, vol. VI, 510–11. The text of Mikołajczyk's protest is in Bliss Lane to Secretary of State, 29 December 1946, *FRUS 1946*, vol. VI, 552–3; Bliss Lane to Secretary of State, 31 December 1946, *FRUS 1946*, vol. VI, 554; Bedell Smith to Molotov, 5 January 1947, Bliss Lane to Rzymowski, 9 January 1947, Bliss Lane to Secretary of State, 14 January 1947, Bedell Smith to Secretary of State, 15 January 1947, all in *FRUS 1947*, vol. IV, 402–8.

122. Bliss Lane, *I Saw Freedom Betrayed*, 176; Kersten, *Establishment of Communist Rule*, 339; Bullock, *Hitler and Stalin*, 1022; Bliss Lane to Secretary of State, 21 and 23 January 1947, *FRUS 1947*, vol. IV, 410–14.

123. Bliss Lane to Secretary of State, 18 January 1947, *FRUS 1947*, vol. IV, 408–10; Foot, *SOE*, 307.

124. Mikołajczyk, *Rape of Poland*, 267; Korboński, *Warsaw in Chains*, 263.

125. Kersten, *Establishment of Communist Rule*, 340.

126. Gilbert, *Winston S. Churchill*, vol. VIII, 200.

127. Quoted in Courtois *et al.*, *Black Book of Communism*, 22.

## CHAPTER 18: THE FINAL CHAPTER

1. Cienciala, Lebedeva & Materski, *Katyń*, 235–7.

2. Maresch, *Katyń 1940*, 222.

3. Cienciala, Lebedeva & Materski, *Katyń*, 236–7.

4. *The Times*, 18 July 1952.

5. Cienciala, Lebedeva & Materski, *Katyń*, 239.

6. Maresch, *Katyń 1940*, 245–7; Cienciala, Lebedeva & Materski, *Katyń*, 242–5; *The Times*, 23 April 1971, 27 June 1972, 19 March 1976, 17 September 1976.

7. *The Times*, 20 September 1980.

8. Kaczorowska, *Children of the Katyń Massacre*, 150.

9. *The Times*, 16 April 1981.

10. Paul, *Katyń*, 348–9.

11. Maresch, *Katyń 1940*, 261–2.

12. Borodziej, *Warsaw Uprising*, 11–12, 142–9; *The Times*, 17 April 1956; J. Chodakiewicz, 'The Warsaw Rising 1944: Perception and Reality', downloaded from www.warsawuprising.com, Project InPosterum; Bartoszewski, *Powstanie Warszawskie*, 387–445.

13. During the summer of 2011 there was an excellent exhibition on the rebuilding of Warsaw at the Dom Spotkań z Historią in Warsaw.

14. J. Tomaszewski, 'Polish Historiography on the Holocaust', in Bankier & Gutman, *Nazi Europe*, 111–35.

15. Finder & Prusin, 'Jewish Collaborators on Trial'.

16. The debates surrounding the issues raised by Gross's book can be found in Polonsky & Michlic, *Neighbors Respond*.

17. A list of members of the Polish armed forces who fell in action or died from other causes outside Poland during the Second World War was published in 1952: Sikorski Institute, *Wykaz poległych i zmarłych żołnierzy Polskich Sił Zbrojnych na obczyźnie w latach 1939–1946*.

18. *Destiny Can Wait*, 352–3.

19. Olson & Cloud, *For Your Freedom and Ours*, 427.

# Bibliography

All publications are in London unless otherwise stated.

C. Abramsky, M. Jachimczyk & A. Polonsky (eds), *The Jews in Poland* (Oxford, 1986)

P. Adair, *Hitler's Greatest Defeat: The Collapse of Army Group Centre, June 1944* (1994)

A. Adelson & R. Lapides (eds), *Łódź Ghetto: Inside a Community Under Siege* (New York, 1989)

P. Ahonen, *After the Expulsion: West Germany and Eastern Europe, 1945–1990* (Oxford, 2003)

R. Ainsztein, *Jewish Resistance in Nazi-occupied Eastern Europe* (1974)

Earl H. Alexander, *The Alexander Memoirs 1940–45* (1962)

M. Alexander, 'After Dunkirk: The French Army's Performance Against "Case Red", 25 May to 25 June 1940', *War in History*, 14 (2007), 219–64

R. Altbeker Cyprys, *A Jump for Life* (1997)

W. Anders, *An Army in Exile* (1949)

—, *Bez ostatniego rozdziału* (Newtown, 1949)

Anonymous, 'German Cavalry in World War II', *Intelligence Bulletin* (March 1946)

A. Applebaum, *Gulag: A History* (2003)

Y. Arad, I. Gutman & A. Margaliot (eds), *Documents on the Holocaust: Selected Sources on the Destruction of the Jews of Germany and Austria, Poland, and the Soviet Union* (1999)

Association of the Families of the Borderland Settlers, *Stalin's Ethnic Cleansing in Eastern Poland: Tales of the Deported 1940–1946* (Hove, 2000)

Association of the Poles in India, *Poles in India 1942–1948* (2009)

S. Ball (ed.), *Parliament and Politics in the Age of Churchill and Attlee: The Headlam Diaries 1935–1951* (Cambridge, 1999)

S. Baluk, *Silent and Unseen: I Was a Polish WWII Special Ops Commando* (Warsaw, 2009)

J. Banas, *The Scapegoats: The Exodus of Jews from Poland* (1979)

D. Bankier and I. Gutman (eds), *Nazi Europe and the Final Solution* (New York, 2009)

T. Barker, 'The Ljubljana Gap Strategy: Alternative to Anvil/Dragoon or Fantasy?', *Journal of Military History*, 56 (1992), 57–85

W. Bartoszewski, 'Poles and Jews as the "Other"', *Polin*, 4 (1989), 6–17

—, *Powstanie Warszawskie* (Warsaw, 2009)

J. Beck, *Dernier Rapport* (Neuchâtel, 1951)

A. Beevor, *D-Day: The Battle for Normandy* (2009)

— & L. Vinogradova (eds), *A Writer at War: Vasily Grossman with the Red Army 1941–1945* (2007)

B. Belcarz & R. Pęczkowski, *White Eagles* (Ottringham, 2001)

P. Bell, *John Bull and the Bear: British Public Opinion, Foreign Policy and the Soviet Union, 1941–1945* (1990)

C. Bellamy, *Absolute War: Soviet Russia in the Second World War* (2007)

E. Beneš, *Memoirs of Dr Eduard Beneš* (1954)

T. Bennett, 'Culture, Power, and *Mission to Moscow*: Film and Soviet-American Relations during World War II', *Journal of American History*, 88 (2001), 489–518

M. Berenbaum (ed.), *A Mosaic of Victims: Non-Jews Persecuted and Murdered by the Nazis* (New York, 1990)

D. Bergen, 'The Nazi Concept of "Volksdeutsche" and the Exacerbation of Anti-Semitism in Eastern Europe, 1939–45', *Journal of Contemporary History*, 29 (1994), 569–82

Z. Berling, *Wspomnienia*, 2 vols. (Warsaw, 1990)

R. Bessel, *Germany 1945: From War to Peace* (2009)

W. Biegański *et al.*, *Polski czyn zbrojny w II wojnie światowej. Walki formacji Polskich na Zachodzie, 1939–45* (Warsaw, 1981)

J. Bines, *Operation Freston* (1999)

P. Black, 'Rehearsal for "Reinhard"?: Odilo Globocnik and the Lublin Selbstschutz', *Central European History*, 25 (1992), 204–26

R. Blanke, 'The German Minority in Inter-War Poland and German Foreign Policy – Some Reconsiderations', *Journal of Contemporary History*, 25 (1990), 87–102

D. Blatman, 'The Encounter between Jews and Poles in Lublin District after Liberation, 1944–45', *East European Politics and Societies*, 20 (2006), 598–621

A. Bliss Lane, *I Saw Freedom Betrayed* (1949)

P. Blood, *Hitler's Bandit Hunters: The SS and the Nazi Occupation of Europe* (Washington DC, 2006)

—, 'Securing Hitler's Lebensraum: The Luftwaffe and the Forest of Białowieża 1942–4', *Holocaust and Genocide Studies Journal*, 24 (2010), 247–72

M. Boemeke, G. Feldman & E. Glaser (eds), *The Treaty of Versailles: A Reassessment after 75 Years* (Cambridge, 1998)

C. Bohlen, *Witness to History* (New York, 1973)

T. Bór-Komorowski, *The Secret Army* (1951)

A. Borkiewicz, *Powstanie Warszawskie 1944* (Warsaw, 1957)

W. Borodziej, *The Warsaw Uprising of 1944* (Madison, WI, 2006)

A. Borowiec, *Destroy Warsaw! Hitler's Punishment, Stalin's Revenge* (Westport, CT, 2001)

J. Borzęcki, *The Soviet-Polish Peace of 1921 and the Creation of Interwar Europe* (New Haven, CT, 2008)

Y. Boshyk (ed.), *Ukraine During World War II: History and its Aftermath* (Edmonton, 1986)

J. Bourne, P. Liddle & I. Whitehead (eds), *The Great World War 1914–45, Vol. I Lightning Strikes Twice* (2000)

A. Bramwell (ed.), *Refugees in the Age of Total War* (1988)

R. Breitman, *Official Secrets: What the Nazis Planned, What the British and Americans Knew* (1999)

C. Browning, *Ordinary Men* (New York, 1992)

G. Bruce Strang, 'Once More unto the Breach: Britain's Guarantee to Poland, March 1939', *Journal of Contemporary History*, 31 (1996), 721–52

W. Buckingham, *Arnhem 1944* (2002)

S. Budiansky, *Battle of Wits: The Complete Story of Codebreaking in World War II* (2000)

A. Bullock, *Ernest Bevin, Foreign Secretary, 1945–51* (1983)

—, *Hitler and Stalin: Parallel Lives* (1991)

S. Butler (ed.), *My Dear Mr. Stalin: The Complete Correspondence between Franklin D. Roosevelt and Joseph V. Stalin* (2005)

T. Campbell and G. Herring (eds), *The Diaries of Edward R. Stettinius, Jr., 1943–1946* (New York, 1975)

P. Cannistraro, E. Wynot & T. Kovaleff (eds), *Poland and the Coming of the Second World War: The Diplomatic Papers of A. J. Drexel Biddle, Jr., United States Ambassador to Poland, 1937–1939* (Columbus, OH, 1976)

M. Carley, '"A Situation of Delicacy and Danger": Anglo-Soviet Relations, August 1939–March 1940', *Contemporary European History*, 8 (1999), 175–208

A. Carton de Wiart, *Happy Odyssey* (1950)

V. Cazalet, *With Sikorski to Moscow* (1942)

Central Commission for Investigation of German Crimes in Poland, *German Crimes in Poland* (Warsaw, 1946–7)

H. Chandler, 'The Transition to Cold Warrior: The Evolution of W. Averell Harriman's Assessment of the USSR's Polish Policy, October 1943–Warsaw Uprising', *East European Quarterly*, 10 (1976), 101–32

A. Chmielarz, 'Warsaw Fought Alone: Reflections on Aid to and the Fall of the 1944 Uprising', *Polish Review*, 39 (1994), 415–33

P. Chmielowiec (ed.), *Okupacja sowiecka ziem polskich 1939–1941* (Warsaw, 2005)

M. Chodakiewicz, *Between Nazis and Soviets: A Case Study of Occupation Politics in Poland 1939–47* (Lanham, MD, 2004)

G. Cholewczyński, *Poles Apart: The Polish Airborne at the Battle of Arnhem* (New York, 1993)

V. Chuikov, *The End of the Third Reich* (Moscow, 1978)

W. Churchill, *Great War Speeches* (1978)

—, *The Second World War*, 6 vols (1946–54)

J. Ciechanowski, *Defeat in Victory* (New York, 1947)

—, *The Warsaw Rising of 1944* (Cambridge, 1974)

J. Ciechanowski & A. Suchcitz (eds), *General Władysław Sikorski: Poland's Wartime Leader* (2007)

A. Cienciala, 'The Activities of Polish Communists as a Source for Stalin's Policy Towards Poland in the Second World War', *International History Review*, 7 (1985), 129–45

—, 'Detective Work: Researching Soviet World War II Policy on Poland in Russian Archives (Moscow, 1994)', *Cahiers du Monde russe*, 40 (1999), 251–69

—, 'The Diplomatic Background of the Warsaw Rising of 1944: The Players and the Stakes', *Polish Review*, 39 (1994), 393–413

—, 'General Sikorski and the Conclusion of the Polish-Soviet Agreement of 30 July 1941: A Reassessment', *Polish Review*, 41 (1996), 401–34

—, 'Great Britain and Poland Before and After Yalta: A Reassessment', *Polish Review*, 40 (1995), 281–313

—, 'The Katyń Syndrome', *Russian Review*, 65 (2006), 117–21

—, *Poland and the Western Powers 1938–1939: A Study in the Interdependence of East and West Europe* (1968)

—, 'The Question of the Polish-Soviet Frontier in 1939–1940: The Litauer Memorandum and Sikorski's Proposals for Re-establishing Polish-Soviet Relations', *Polish Review*, 33 (1988), 295–323

—, N. Lebedeva & W. Materski (eds), *Katyń: Crime Without Punishment* (2007)

S. Ciesielski, W. Materski & A. Paczkowski, *Represje Sowieckie wobec Polaków i obywateli Polskich* (Warsaw, 2000)

L. Collingham, *The Taste of War: World War Two and the Battle for Food* (2011)

J. Colville, *The Fringes of Power* (1985)

Committee of the Polish Air Force Memorial, *Destiny Can Wait* (1949)

J. Connelly, 'Poles and Jews in the Second World War: The Revisions of Jan T. Gross', *Contemporary European History*, 11 (2002), 641–58

—, 'Why the Poles Collaborated so Little: And Why That Is No Reason for Nationalist Hubris', *Slavic Review*, 64 (2005), 771–81.

*Correspondence Between the Chairman of the Council of Ministers of the U.S.S.R. and the Presidents of the U.S.A. and the Prime Ministers of Great Britain during the Great Patriotic War of 1941–1945* (Moscow, 1957)

S. Courtois *et al.* (eds), *The Black Book of Communism: Crimes, Terror, Repression* (Cambridge, MA, 1999)

J. Coutouvidis, 'Lewis Namier and the Polish Government in Exile 1939–40', *Slavonic and East European Review*, 62 (1984) 421–8

— & J. Reynolds, *Poland 1939–45* (New York, 1986)

G. Craig & F. Gilbert (eds), *The Diplomats 1919–1939* (Princeton, 1953)

D. Curp, *A Clean Sweep? The Politics of Ethnic Cleansing in Western Poland 1945–1960* (New York, 2006)

J. Cwikliński, *The Captain Leaves His Ship: The Story of the SS Batory* (1955)

W. Cygan, *Kresy w ogniu: wojna polsko-sowiecka 1939* (Warsaw, 1990)

J. Czapski, *The Inhuman Land* (1987)

H. Czarnocka *et al.*, *Armia Krajowa w dokumentach 1939–1945*, 6 vols. (1970–89)

F. Czarnomski, *They Fight for Poland* (1941)

J. Czerniakiewicz, *Repatriacja ludności polskiej z ZSRR 1944–1948* (Warsaw, 1987)

G. Dallas, *Poisoned Peace: 1945 – The War That Never Ended* (2005)

A. Danchev & D. Todman (eds), *War Diaries 1939–1945: Field Marshal Lord Alanbrooke* (2001)

S. Datner, *Crimes against POWs: Responsibility of the Wehrmacht* (Warsaw, 1964)

N. Davies, *Europe at War* (2006)

—, 'The Genesis of the Polish-Soviet War, 1919–20', *European History Quarterly*, 5 (1975), 47–67

—, *God's Playground*, vol. 2 (Oxford, 1981)

—, 'Lloyd George and Poland, 1919–20', *Journal of Contemporary History*, 6 (1971), 132–54

—, *Rising '44* (2003)

—, *White Eagle, Red Star: The Polish-Soviet War 1919–20* (1983)

— & A. Polonsky (eds), *Jews in Eastern Poland and the USSR 1929–46* (1991)

G. Davies-Scourfield, *In Presence of my Foes* (Barnsley, 2004)

I. Deák, *Essays on Hitler's Europe* (2001)

—, J. Gross & T. Judt (eds), *The Politics of Retribution in Europe: World War II and its Aftermath* (Princeton, 2006)

M. Dean, 'Poles in the German Local Police in Eastern Poland and their Role in the Holocaust', *Polin*, 18 (2005), 353–66

—, 'Where Did All the Collaborators Go?', *Slavic Review*, 64 (2005), 791–8

A. De Zayas, *Nemesis at Potsdam* (1979)

R. Debicki, *Foreign Policy of Poland 1919–1939* (1963)

D. Dilks (ed.), *The Diaries of Sir Alexander Cadogan* (1971)

—, *Epic and Tragedy: Britain and Poland* (Hull, 1996)

B. Dmytryshyn, 'The Nazis and the SS Volunteer Division "Galicia"', *American Slavic and East European Review*, 15 (1956), 1–10

I. Drag Korga, 'The Information Policy of the Polish Government-in-Exile toward the American Public during World War II', *Polish American Studies*, 64 (2007), 27–45

W. Drzewieniecki, 'The Polish Army on the Eve of World War II', *Polish Review*, 26 (1981), 54–64

C. Duffy, *Red Storm on the Reich: The Soviet March on Germany, 1945* (1991)

M. Edelman, *The Ghetto Fights* (1990)

A. Eden, *The Eden Memoirs: The Reckoning* (1965)

R. Edmonds, *The Big Three: Churchill, Roosevelt and Stalin in Peace and War* (1991)

S. Eizenstat, *Imperfect Justice: Looted Assets, Slave Labor, and the Unfinished Business of World War II* (New York, 2003)

H. Elcock, 'Britain and the Russo-Polish Frontier, 1919–1921', *Historical Journal*, 12 (1969), 137–54

J. Ellis, *Cassino: The Hollow Victory* (1984)

R. Ellis, D. O'Donovan & F. Wilson, 'Report on the Condition of Polish Refugees in Rumania and Hungary', *British Medical Journal* (18 November 1939), 1013–15

D. Engel, *Facing a Holocaust: The Polish Government-in-Exile and the Jews, 1943–1945* (1993)

—, *In the Shadow of Auschwitz: The Polish Government-in-Exile and the Jews, 1939–1942* (Chapel Hill, NC, 1987)

C. Epstein, *Model Nazi: Arthur Greiser and the Occupation of Western Poland* (Oxford, 2010)

J. Erickson, *The Road to Berlin* (1983)

—, *The Road to Stalingrad* (1975)

— & D. Dilks (eds), *Barbarossa: The Axis and the Allies* (Edinburgh, 1994)

K. Eubank, *Summit at Teheran: The Untold Story* (New York, 1985)

J. Fai-Podlipnik, 'Hungary's Relationship with Poland and Its Refugees during World War II', *East European Quarterly*, 36 (2002) 63–77

B. Farrell, 'Yes, Prime Minister: Barbarossa, Whipcord, and the Basis of British Grand Strategy, Autumn 1941', *Journal of Military History*, 57 (1993), 599–625

H. Feis, *Between War and Peace: The Potsdam Conference* (Princeton, 1960)

—, *Churchill, Roosevelt, Stalin: The War They Waged and the Peace They Sought* (Princeton, 1957)

B. Fels, '"Whatever Your Heart Dictates and Your Pocket Permits": Polish-American Aid to Polish Refugees during World War II', *Journal of American Ethnic History*, 22 (2003), 3–30

J. Fenby, *Alliance: The Inside Story of How Roosevelt, Stalin and Churchill Won One War and Began Another* (2006)

G. Finder & A. Prusin, 'Jewish Collaborators on Trial in Poland 1944–1956', *Polin*, 20 (2007), 122–48

L. FitzGibbon, *Katyń: A Crime Without Parallel* (1971)

E. Florentin, *Stalingrad en Normandie* (Paris, 1994)

M. R. D. Foot, *SOE* (1984)

A. Foster, 'An Unequivocal Guarantee? Fleet Street and the British Guarantee to Poland, 31 March 1939', *Journal of Contemporary History*, 26 (1991), 33–47

K.-P. Friedrich, 'Collaboration in a "Land without a Quisling": Patterns of

Cooperation with the Nazi German Occupation Regime in Poland during World War II', *Slavic Review*, 64 (2005), 711–46

K.-H. Frieser, *Blitzkrieg Legend: The Campaign in the West, 1940* (Annapolis, MD, 2005)

P. Gajda, *Postscript to Victory: British Policy and the German-Polish Borderlands, 1919–1925* (Washington DC, 1982)

L. Gardner, *Spheres of Influence: The Partition of Europe from Munich to Yalta* (1993)

J. Garliński, *Fighting Auschwitz: The Resistance Movement in the Concentration Camp* (1975)

—, *Hitler's Last Weapons: The Underground War Against the V1 and V2* (1979)

—, *Poland in the Second World War* (New York, 1985)

—, *Poland, SOE and the Allies* (1969)

—, 'The Polish Underground State 1939–45', *Journal of Contemporary History*, 10 (1975), 219–59

J. Garrard and C. Garrard (ed.), *World War 2 and the Soviet People* (New York, 1992)

Z. Gasiorowski, 'Did Piłsudski Attempt to Initiate a Preventive War in 1933?', *Journal of Modern History*, 27 (1955), 135–51

P. Gatrell & N. Baron (eds), *Warlands: Population Resettlement and State Reconstruction in the Soviet–East European Borderlands, 1945–50* (Basingstoke, 2009)

M. Gellhorn, *The Face of War* (1959)

L. Gerson, *Woodrow Wilson and the Rebirth of Poland 1914–20* (Hamden, CT, 1972)

M. Giedroyć, *Crater's Edge: A Family's Epic Journey Through Wartime Russia* (2010)

M. Gilbert, *Auschwitz and the Allies* (1981)

—, *The Day the War Ended* (1995)

—, *The Holocaust* (1986)

—, *Holocaust Journey* (1997)

—, *The Righteous: The Unsung Heroes of the Holocaust* (2002)

—, *The Second World War* (1989)

—, *Winston S. Churchill: Finest Hour, 1939–1941* (1983), vol. VI

—, *Winston S. Churchill: Road to Victory, 1941–1945* (1986), vol. VII

—, *Winston S. Churchill: 'Never Despair', 1945–1965* (1988), vol. VIII

A. Gill, *The Journey Back from Hell* (1989)

D. Gillies, *Radical Diplomat: The Life of Archibald Clark Kerr* (1999)

D. Glantz (ed.), *The Initial Period of War on the Eastern Front: 22 June–August 1941* (1993)

Z. Gluza (ed.), *Rok 1939 Rozbiór Polski* (Warsaw, 2009)

D. Goldhagen, *Hitler's Willing Executioners* (1997)

G. Gorodetsky, 'The Origins of the Cold War: Stalin, Churchill and the Formation of the Grand Alliance', *Russian Review*, 47 (1988), 145–70

—, (ed.) *Stafford Cripps in Moscow, 1940–1942: Diaries and Papers* (2007)

V. Gromada (ed.), *Essays on Poland's Foreign Policy 1918–1939* (New York, 1975)

J. Gross, *Fear. Anti-Semitism in Poland after Auschwitz: An Essay in Historical Interpretation* (Princeton, 2006)

—, *Neighbors: The Destruction of the Jewish Community in Jedwabne* (Princeton, 2001)

—, *Polish Society under German Occupation: The Generalgouvernement, 1939–44* (Princeton, 1979)

—, *Revolution from Abroad: The Soviet Conquest of Poland's Western Ukraine and Western Byelorussia* (Princeton, 1988, 2002)

I. Grudzińska-Gross & J. Gross (eds), *War Through Children's Eyes: The Soviet Occupation of Poland and the Deportations 1939–41* (Stanford, 1981)

M. Grynberg (ed.), *Words to Outlive Us: Eyewitness Accounts from the Warsaw Ghetto* (2003)

C. Grzelak, H. Stańczyk & S. Zwoliński, *Bez Możliwości Wyboru: Wojsko Polskie Na Froncie Wschodnim 1943–1945* (Warsaw, 1993)

J. Gumkowski & K. Leszcyński, *Poland Under Nazi Occupation* (Warsaw, 1961)

I. Gut Opdyke, *In My Hands: Memories of a Holocaust Rescuer* (New York, 1999)

Y. Gutman, *The Jews of Warsaw, 1939–1943: Ghetto, Underground, Revolt* (Bloomington, IN, 1982)

— & S. Krakowski, *Unequal Victims: Poles and Jews during World War II* (New York, 1986)

J. Hammersmith, 'The US Office of War Information (OWI) and the Polish Question 1943–45', *Polish Review*, 19 (1974), 154–63

H. Hanak, 'Sir Stafford Cripps as Ambassador in Moscow, June 1941–January 1942', *English Historical Review*, 97 (1982), 332–44

—, 'Sir Stafford Cripps as British Ambassador in Moscow May 1940–June 1941', *English Historical Review*, 94 (1979), 48–70

J. Hanson, *The Civilian Population and the Warsaw Uprising* (Cambridge, 1982)

—, 'Stanisław Mikołajczyk: November 1944–June 1945', *European History Quarterly*, 21 (1991), 39–73

R. Hargreaves, *Blitzkrieg Unleashed: The German Invasion of Poland 1939* (Barnsley, 2008)

W. A. Harriman, *Special Envoy to Churchill and Stalin* (New York, 1976)

E. Harrison, 'The British Special Operations Executive and Poland', *Historical Journal*, 43 (2000), 1071–91

—, 'Carton de Wiart's Second Military Mission to Poland and the German Invasion of 1939', *European History Quarterly*, 41 (2011), 609–33

A. Harvey, 'The French Armée de l'Air in May–June 1940: A Failure of Conception', *Journal of Contemporary History*, 25 (1990), 447–65

J. Harvey (ed.), *The War Diaries of Oliver Harvey* (1978)

J. Haslem, 'The Soviet Union and the Czechoslovakian Crisis of 1938', *Journal of Contemporary History*, 14 (1979), 441–61

M. Hastings, *Armageddon* (2004)

A. Henderson, *Failure of a Mission* (1940)

A. P. Herbert, *Light the Lights* (1945)

U. Herbert, *Hitler's Foreign Workers* (Cambridge, 1996)

T. Hetherington and W. Chalmers, *War Crimes: Report of the War Crimes Inquiry (London, 1989)* (1989)

R. Hilberg, *The Destruction of the European Jews*, 3 vols. (New York, 1985)

—, *Perpetrators, Victims, Bystanders: The Jewish Catastrophe, 1933–1945* (New York, 1992)

—, S. Staron & J. Kernisz (eds), *The Warsaw Diary of Adam Czerniaków* (Chicago, 1999)

L. Hill, 'Three Crises, 1938–39', *Journal of Contemporary History*, 3 (1968), 113–44

W. Hitchcock, *Liberation: The Bitter Road to Freedom, Europe 1944–1945* (2008)

E. Hodgkin (ed.), *Letters from Teheran: Reader Ballard* (1991)

J. Holland, 'The Approach to Battle', *Everyone's War*, no. 18 (2008), 9–16

—, *Italy's Sorrow* (2008)

C. Hollingworth, *Front Line* (1989)

—, *The Three Weeks' War in Poland* (1940)

J. Holzer, 'The Political Right in Poland, 1918–39', *Journal of Contemporary History*, 12 (1977), 395–412

E. Homze, *Foreign Labour in Nazi Germany* (Princeton, 1967)

M. Hope, *The Abandoned Legion: A Study of the Background and Process of the Post-war Dissolution of Polish Forces in the West* (2005)

—, *Polish Deportees in the Soviet Union* (1998)

S. Horak, *Poland and Her National Minorities, 1919–1939* (New York, 1961)

M. Housden, *Hans Frank: Lebensraum and Holocaust* (Basingstoke, 2003)

M. Howard, *Otherwise Occupied* (Tiverton, 2010)

R. Hrabar, Z. Tokarz & J. Wilczur, *The Fate of Polish Children During the Last War* (Warsaw, 1981)

K. Hulme, *The Wild Place* (Boston, 1953)

E. Huntingdon, *The Unsettled Account* (1986)

Instytut Pamięci Narodowej, *Operacja 'Sejm'* (Warsaw, 2007)

G. Iranek-Osmecki (trans.), *The Unseen and Silent: Adventures from the Underground Movement* (1954)

K. Iranek-Osmecki, *He Who Saves One Life* (New York, 1971)

A. Iwańska, *Polish Intelligentsia in Nazi Concentration Camps and American Exile* (Lewiston, NY, 1998)

J. Iwaszkiewicz, *Notaki 1939–1945* (Wrocław, 1991)

A. Jaroszynska-Kirchmann, 'The Mobilization of American Polonia for the Cause of the Displaced Persons', *Polish American Studies*, 58 (2001), 29–62

P. Jasienica, 'The Polish Experience', *Journal of Contemporary History*, 3 (1968), 73–88

W. Jędrzejewicz (ed.), *Diplomat in Berlin, 1933–1939: Papers and Memoirs of Józef Lipski, Ambassador of Poland* (New York, 1968)

— (ed.), *Diplomat in Paris, 1936–1939: Papers and Memoirs of Juliusz Łukasiewicz, Ambassador of Poland* (New York, 1970)

— (ed.), *Poland in the British Parliament 1939–45*, 3 vols. (New York, 1946)

—, 'The Polish Plan for a "Preventative War" against Germany in 1933', *Polish Review*, 11 (1966), 62–91

T. Jersak, 'Blitzkrieg Revisited: A New Look at Nazi War and Extermination Planning', *Historical Journal*, 43 (2000), 565–82

K. Jolluck, *Exile and Identity: Polish Women in the Soviet Union During World War II* (Pittsburgh, 2002)

R. Jones, *Most Secret War* (1978)

G. Kacewicz, *Great Britain, the Soviet Union and the Polish Government-in-Exile* (The Hague, 1979)

T. Kaczorowska, *Children of the Katyń Massacre: Accounts of Life after the 1940 Soviet Murder of Polish POWs* (Jefferson, NC, 2006)

W. Kaiser, 'Co-Operation of European Catholic Politicians in Exile in Britain and the USA during the Second World War', *Journal of Contemporary History*, 35 (2000), 439–65

I. Kamenetsky, *Hitler's Occupation of Ukraine, 1941–1944: A Study of Totalitarian Imperialism* (New York, 1956)

K. Kapronczay, *Refugees in Hungary: Shelter from Storm During World War II* (Toronto, 1999)

J. Karski, *The Great Powers and Poland, 1919–45* (1985)

—, *Story of a Secret State* (1945)

A. Katsch (ed.), *Scroll of Agony: The Warsaw Diary of Chaim A. Kaplan* (1966)

J. Keegan, *The Second World War* (1989)

—, *Six Armies in Normandy* (New York, 1982)

M. Kelly, *Finding Poland: From Tavistock to Hruzdowa and Back Again* (2010)

P. Kemp, *The Thorns of Memory* (1990)

A. Kemp-Welch (ed.), *Stalinism in Poland* (1999)

G. Kennan, *Memoirs* (Boston, 1967)

R. Kennedy, *The German Campaign in Poland, 1939* (Uckfield, 1990)

T. Kernberg, 'The Polish Community in Scotland', Ph.D. thesis, University of Glasgow (1990)

I. Kershaw, *Hitler 1939–1945: Nemesis* (2000)

—, 'Improvised Genocide? The Emergence of the "Final Solution" in the "Warthegau"', *Transactions of the Royal Historical Society*, 6th series, 2 (1992), 51–78

R. Kershaw, *War Without Garlands* (2008)

K. Kersten, *The Establishment of Communist Rule in Poland, 1943–1948* (Berkeley, 1991)

A. Kesselring, *Memoirs* (1953)

L. Kettenacker, 'The Anglo-Soviet Alliance and the Problem of Germany, 1941–1945', *Journal of Contemporary History*, 17 (1982), 435–58

W. Kimball (ed.), *Churchill & Roosevelt: The Complete Correspondence*, 3 vols. (Princeton, 1984)

M. Kitchen, *British Policy Towards the Soviet Union During the Second World War* (1986)

—, *Rommel's Desert War* (Cambridge, 2009)

S. Kleczkowski, *Poland's First 100,000* (1944)

E. Klee, W. Dressen & V. Riess (eds), *'The Good Old Days': The Holocaust as Seen by Its Perpetrators and Bystanders* (1991)

Z. Klukowski, *Diary from the Years of Occupation, 1939–44* (Urbana, IL, 1993)

—, *Red Shadow: A Physician's Memoir of the Soviet Occupation of Eastern Poland, 1944–1956* (Jefferson, NC, 1993)

H. Koch, 'The Spectre of a Separate Peace in the East: Russo-German "Peace Feelers", 1942–44', *Journal of Contemporary History*, 10 (1975), 531–49

T. Komarnicki, *Rebirth of the Polish Republic, 1914–20* (1957)

A. Korbonski, 'Civil-Military Relations in Poland Between the Wars: 1918–1939', *Armed Forces & Society*, 14 (1988), 169–89

S. Korboński, *Fighting Warsaw: The Story of the Polish Underground State 1939–45* (New York, 1956)

—, *The Jews and the Poles in World War II* (New York, 1989)

—, *Warsaw in Chains* (1959)

A. Korczyński & S. Swietochowski (eds), *Poland Between Germany and Russia 1926–1939* (New York, 1975)

P. Korzec & J.-C. Szurek, 'Jews and Poles under Soviet Occupation 1939–1941', *Polin*, 4 (1989), 204–25

K. Koskodan, *No Greater Ally: The Untold Story of Poland's Forces in World War II* (Oxford, 2009)

W. Kosyk (ed.), *The Third Reich and the Ukrainian Question: Documents 1934–1944* (1991)

S. Kot, *Conversations with the Kremlin and Dispatches from Russia* (Urbana, IL, 1963)

W. Kozaczuk, *Enigma: How the German Machine Code Was Broken, and How It Was Read by the Allies in World War Two* (Frederick, MD, 1984)

S. Krakowski, *The War of the Doomed: Jewish Armed Resistance in Poland, 1942–1944* (New York, 1984)

L. Królikowski, *Stolen Childhood: A Saga of Polish War Children* (Buffalo, NY, 1983)

M. Kukiel, *Generał Sikorski: Żoinierz i mąż stanu Polski walczącej* (1981)

—, *Six Years Struggle for Independence: A Report on the Polish Fighting Forces in World War Two* (1947)

W. Kulski, 'The Lost Opportunity for Russian-Polish Friendship', *Foreign Affairs*, 25 (1946–7), 667–84

M. Kunicki, 'Unwanted Collaborators: Leon Kozłowski, Władysław Studnicki and the Problem of Collaboration among Polish Conservative Politicians in World War II', *European Review of History*, 8 (2001), 203–20

B. Kuśnierz, *Stalin and the Poles* (1949)

K. Lanckorońska, *Those Who Trespass Against Us: One Woman's War Against the Nazis* (2005)

A. Lane, *Victims of Stalin and Hitler: The Exodus of Poles and Balts to Britain* (Basingstoke, 2004)

— & H. Temperley (eds), *The Rise and Fall of the Grand Alliance, 1941–45* (1995)

J. Langer, 'The Harriman-Beaverbrook Mission and the Debate over Unconditional Aid for the Soviet Union, 1941', *Journal of Contemporary History*, 14 (1979), 463–82

L. Langer (ed.), *Art from the Ashes: A Holocaust Anthology* (Oxford, 1995)

C. Lanzmann, *Shoah: An Oral History of the Holocaust* (New York, 1985)

W. Laqueur, *The Second World War: Essays in Military and Political History* (1982)

W. Larsh, 'Yalta and the American Approach to Free Elections in Poland', *Polish Review*, 40 (1995) 267–80

P. Latawski, 'The Dmowski–Namier Feud', *Polin*, 2 (1987), 37–49

— (ed.), *The Reconstruction of Poland, 1914–23* (Basingstoke, 1992)

A. Lewin, *A Cup of Tears: A Diary of the Warsaw Ghetto* (Oxford, 1988)

E. Linklater, *The Campaign in Italy* (1951)

F. Loewenheim, H. Langley & M. Jonas (eds), *Roosevelt and Churchill: Their Secret Wartime Correspondence* (1975)

P. Longerich, *Holocaust* (Oxford, 2010)

J. Lowell Armstrong, 'Policy Toward the Polish Minority in the Soviet Union, 1923–89', *Polish Review*, 35 (1990) 51–65

—, 'The Polish Underground and the Jews: A Reassessment of Home Army Commander Tadeusz Bór-Komorowski's Order 116 Against Banditry', *Slavonic and East European Review*, 72 (1994), 259–76

J. Lucas, *Last Days of the Reich: The Collapse of Nazi Germany, May 1945* (1986)

C. Łuczak, *Polska i Polacy w drugiej wojnie światowej* (Poznań, 1993)

R. Lukas, 'The Big Three and The Warsaw Uprising', *Military Affairs*, 39 (1975), 129–35

—, *Bitter Legacy: Polish-American Relations in the Wake of World War II* (Lexington, KY, 1982)

—, *Did the Children Cry? Hitler's War against Jewish and Polish Children, 1939–45* (New York, 2001)

—, *The Forgotten Holocaust: The Poles under German Occupation, 1939–1944* (New York, 1997)

—, *Forgotten Survivors: Polish Christians Remember the Nazi Occupation* (Lawrence, KS, 2004)

— (ed.), *Out of the Inferno: Poles Remember the Holocaust* (Lexington, KY, 1989)

—, *The Strange Allies: The United States & Poland 1941–45* (Knoxville, TN, 1979)

K. Lundgreen-Nielsen, 'The Mayer Thesis Reconsidered: The Poles and the Paris Peace Conference', *International History Review*, 7 (1985), 68–101

—, *The Polish Problem at the Paris Peace Conference: A Study of the Policies of the Great Powers and the Poles, 1918–1919* (Odensee, 1979)

C. Macartney, *October Fifteenth: The History of Modern Hungary 1929–1945*, 2 vols. (Edinburgh, 1961)

E. McGilvray, *The Black Devil's March. A Doomed Odyssey: The 1st Polish Armoured Division, 1939–1945* (Solihull, 2003)

Col. R. Macleod & D. Kelly (eds), *The Ironside Diaries, 1937–1940* (1962)

H. Macmillan, *The Blast of War* (1967)

—, *War Diaries* (1984)

M. Macmillan, *Peacemakers* (2001)

M. McNeill, *By the Rivers of Babylon: A Story of Relief Work among the Displaced Persons of Europe* (1950)

S. Maczek, *Od Podwody do Czolga* (Edinburgh, 1961)

W. Madeja (ed.), *The Polish Corps and the Italian Campaign, 1943–1945* (Allentown, PA, 1984)

I. Maisky, *Memoirs of a Soviet Ambassador: The War 1939–43* (1967)

F. Majdalany, *Cassino: Portrait of a Battle* (1957)

J. Majka, *Generał Stanisław Maczek* (Rzeszów, 2005)

G. Malcher, *Blank Pages: Soviet Genocide Against the Polish People* (Woking, 1993)

J. Malicki & L. Zasztowt (eds), *East and West: History and Contemporary State of Eastern Studies* (Warsaw, 2009)

R. Manne, 'The British Decision for Alliance with Russia, May 1939', *Journal of Contemporary History*, 9 (1974), 3–26

E. Maresch, *Katyń 1940: The Documentary Evidence of the West's Betrayal* (Stroud, 2010)

M. Marrus, *The Unwanted: European Refugees in the Twentieth Century* (New York, 1985)

T. Martin, 'The Origins of Soviet Ethnic Cleansing', *Journal of Modern History*, 70 (1998), 813–61

V. Mastny, *Russia's Road to the Cold War: Diplomacy, Warfare, and the Politics of Communism, 1941–1945* (New York, 1979)

—, 'Stalin and the Prospects of a Separate Peace in World War II', *American Historical Review*, 77 (1972), 1365–88

W. Materski, *Armia Polska w ZSRR 1941–1942* (Warsaw, 1992)

—, *Katyń: Documents of Genocide: Documents and Materials from the Soviet Archives turned over to Poland on October 14, 1992* (Warsaw, 1993)

I. Matuszewski, *Great Britain's Obligations Towards Poland: And Some Facts about the Curzon Line* (1945)

F. Mayevski, *Fire Without Smoke: Memoirs of a Polish Partisan* (2003)

M. Mazower, *Hitler's Empire: Nazi Rule in Occupied Europe* (2008)

C. Merridale, *Ivan's War: Life and Death in the Red Army 1939–1945* (New York, 2006)

S. Mikołajczyk, *The Rape of Poland: Pattern of Soviet Aggression* (New York, 1948)

S. Miner, *Between Churchill and Stalin: The Soviet Union, Great Britain and the Origins of the Grand Alliance* (Chapel Hill, NC, 1988)

T. Modelski, *The Polish Contribution to the Ultimate Allied Victory in the Second World War* (Woking, 1986)

B. Montgomery, *Memoirs* (1958)

J. Morris, 'The Polish Terror: Spy Mania and Ethnic Cleansing in the Great Terror', *Europe-Asia Studies*, 56 (2004), 751–66

N. Naimark, *Fires of Hatred: Ethnic Cleansing in Twentieth Century Europe* (Cambridge, Mass, MA, 2001)

A. Neuman-Nowicki, *Struggle for Life During the Nazi Occupation of Poland* (Lewiston, NY, 1998)

S. Newman, *March 1939: The British Guarantee to Poland* (Oxford, 1976)

M. Ney-Krwawicz, *The Polish Resistance Home Army 1939–45* (2001)

N. Nicolson (ed.), *Harold Nicolson: Diaries and Letters 1939–45* (1970)

M. Norwid-Neugebauer, *The Defence of Poland: September 1939* (1942)

J. Nowak, *Courier from Warsaw* (1982)

L. Olson & S. Cloud, *For Your Freedom and Ours: The Kościuszko Squadron* (2004)

T. Olszański, *Kresy Kresów Stanisławów* (Warsaw, 2008)

O. O'Malley, *The Phantom Caravan* (1954)

R. Overy, *Russia's War* (1997)

A. Paczkowski, *The Spring Will Be Ours: Poland and the Poles from Occupation to Freedom* (University Park, PA, 2003)

P. Padfield, *War Beneath the Sea* (1995)

M. Parker, *Monte Cassino* (2003)

R. Parkinson, *A Day's March Nearer Home: The War History from Alamein to VE Day Based on the War Cabinet Papers* (1974)

A. Paul, *Katyń* (DeKalb, IL, 2010)

G. Paulsson, *Secret City: The Hidden Jews of Warsaw 1940–1945* (New Haven, CT, 2002)

M. Pelly, H. Yasamee & K. Hamilton (eds), *Documents on British Policy Overseas*, Series 1 [1945–1950] (1991)

J. Perrun, 'Best-Laid Plans: Guy Simonds and Operation Totalize, 7–10 August 1944', *Journal of Military History*, 67 (2003), 137–73

M. Peszke, *Battle for Warsaw, 1939–1944* (New York, 1995)

—, *Poland's Navy, 1918–1945* (New York, 1999)

—, 'Poland's Preparation for World War Two', *Military Affairs*, 43 (1979), 18–25

—, 'The Polish Armed Forces in Exile', *Polish Review*, 26 (1981), 67–113; 32 (1987), 33–69, 133–74

—, 'The Polish Government's Aid to and Liaison with Its Secret Army in Occupied Poland, 1939–1945', *Military Affairs*, 52 (1988), 197–202

—, The Polish Parachute Brigade in World War Two: A Paradigm for the Polish Military in Exile', *Military Affairs*, 48 (1984), 188–93

—, 'A Synopsis of Polish-Allied Military Agreements During World War Two', *Military Affairs*, 44 (1980), 128–34

H. Piatkowski, 'The Second Polish Corps in the Battle for Monte Cassino', *Army Quarterly*, 48 (1945), 59–60

J. Pickering, 'Tales of Friendly Fire', *Everyone's War*, no. 20 (2009), 63–5

J. Piekałkiewicz, *Cassino: Anatomy of a Battle* (1980)

—, *The Cavalry of World War II* (Harrisburg, PA, 1979)

K. Piekarski, *Escaping Hell* (Toronto, 1989)

T. Piesakowski, *The Fate of Poles in the USSR, 1939–1989* (1990)

B. Pimlott (ed.), *The Second World War Diary of Hugh Dalton 1940–45* (1986)

B.-C. Pinchuk, *Shtetl Jews under Soviet Rule: Eastern Poland on the Eve of the Holocaust* (1990)

S. Piotrowski, *Hans Frank's Diary* (Warsaw, 1961)

T. Piotrowski, *Genocide and Rescue in Wołyń: Recollections of the Ukrainian Nationalist Ethnic Cleansing Campaign Against the Poles During World War II* (Jefferson, NC, 2000)

—, *Poland's Holocaust: Ethnic Strife, Collaboration with Occupying Forces and Genocide in the Second Republic 1918–47* (Jefferson, NC, 2000)

— (ed.), *The Polish Deportees of World War II: Recollections of Removal to the Soviet Union and Dispersal Throughout the World* (Jefferson, NC, 2004)

C. Pleshakov, *Stalin's Folly: The Tragic First Ten Days of World War II on the Eastern Front* (Boston, 2005)

S. Plokhy, *Yalta: The Price of Peace* (2010)

H. Podkopacz, *Smuga życia* (Cracow, 1994)

D. Pohl, 'Hans Kruger and the Murder of the Jews in the Stanisławów Region (Galicia)', *Yad Vashem Studies*, 26 (1998), 239–65

Polish Ministry for Foreign Affairs, *Official Documents Concerning Polish-German and Polish-Soviet Relations 1933–1939 – Polish White Book* (1940)

Polish Ministry of Information, *The German Invasion of Poland – Polish Black Book* (1940)

—, *The German New Order in Poland* (1942)

—, *Polish Troops in Norway* (1943)

A. Polonsky (ed.), *The Great Powers and the Polish Question 1941–1945* (1976)

— (ed.), *'My Brother's Keeper?': Recent Polish Debates on the Holocaust* (New York, 1990)

—, *Politics in Independent Poland* (Oxford, 1972)

—, 'Stalin and the Poles 1941–7', *European History Quarterly*, 17 (1987), 453–92

— & B. Drukier (eds), *The Beginnings of Communist Rule in Poland: December 1943–June 1945* (1980)

— & J. Michlic (eds), *The Neighbors Respond: The Controversy over the Jedwabne Massacre in Poland* (Princeton, 2004)

W. Półtawska, *And I Am Afraid of My Dreams* (New York, 1989)

R. Ponichtera, 'The Military Thought of Władysław Sikorski', *Journal of Military History*, 59 (1995), 279–301

P. Potomski, *Generał Broni Stanisław Władysław Maczek, 1892–1994* (Warsaw, 2008)

A. Prażmowska, *Britain and Poland, 1939–1943: The Betrayed Ally* (Cambridge, 1995)

—, *Britain, Poland and the Eastern Front 1939* (Cambridge, 1987)

—, *Civil War in Poland 1942–1948* (Basingstoke, 2004)

—, *Poland: A Modern History* (2010)

—, 'Poland's Foreign Policy: September 1938–September 1939', *Historical Journal*, 29 (1986), 853–73

—, 'Polish Military Plans for the Defeat of Germany and the Soviet Union, 1939–41', *European History Quarterly*, 31 (2001), 601–3

M. Proudfoot, *European Refugees 1939–1952* (1957)

A. Prusin, *The Lands Between: Conflict in the East European Borderlands, 1870–1992* (Oxford, 2010)

K. Pruszyński, *Poland Fights Back* (1941)

J. Pyłat, J. Ciechanowski & A. Suchcitz (eds), *General Władysław Anders: Soldier and Leader of the Free Poles in Exile* (2008)

R. Raack, 'Stalin Fixes the Oder-Neisse Line', *Journal of Contemporary History*, 25 (1990), 467–88

—, 'Stalin's Plans for World War II', *Journal of Contemporary History*, 26 (1991), 215–27

E. Raczyński, *In Allied London* (1962)

W. Reddaway *et al.* (eds), *The Cambridge History of Poland* (Cambridge, 1951)

L. Rees, *Auschwitz* (2005)

—, *World War Two Behind Closed Doors* (2008)

A. Reid, *Borderland: A Journey Through the History of Ukraine* (1997)

J. Retinger (ed.), *All About Poland* (1940)

—, *Memoirs of an Eminence Grise* (Brighton, 1972)

D. Reynolds, 'From World War to Cold War: The Wartime Alliance and Post-War Transitions, 1941–1947', *Historical Journal*, 45 (2002), 211–27

—, W. Kimball & A. Chubarian (eds), *Allies at War: The Soviet, American and British Experience 1939–1945* (New York, 1994)

J. Reynolds, '"Lublin" versus "London" – The Party and the Underground Movement in Poland, 1944–1945', *Journal of Contemporary History*, 16 (1981), 617–48

R. Rhodes James, *Victor Cazalet: A Portrait* (1976)

A. Rieber (ed.), *Communist Studies and Transition Politics*, Special Issue, *Forced Migration in Central and Eastern Europe*, 16 (2000)

E. Ringelblum, *Notes from the Warsaw Ghetto: The Journal of Emmanuel Ringelblum* (New York, 1958)

—, *Polish-Jewish Relations during the Second World War* (Jerusalem, 1974)

H. Robbins Landon (ed.), *Wilhelm Prüller: Diary of a German Soldier* (New York, 1963)

A. Roberts, *Masters and Commanders* (2008)

G. Roberts, 'The Alliance that Failed: Moscow and the Triple Alliance Negotiations, 1939', *European History Quarterly*, 26 (1996), 383–414

K. Robertson (ed.), *War, Resistance and Intelligence* (1999)

D. Rogers & S. Williams (eds), *On the Bloody Road to Berlin: Frontline Accounts from North-West Europe and the Eastern Front, 1944–45* (Solihull, 2005)

W. Rojek & A. Suchcitz (eds), *Protokoły z posiedzeń Rady Ministrów Rzeczypospolitej Polskiej*, 8 vols. (Cracow, 1994–2007)

K. Rokossovsky, *A Soldier's Duty* (Moscow, 1985)

G. Ross (ed.), *The Foreign Office and the Kremlin: British Documents on Anglo-Soviet Relations 1941–45* (Cambridge, 1984)

—, 'Foreign Office Attitudes to the Soviet Union 1941–45', *Journal of Contemporary History*, 16 (1981), 521–40

A. Rossino, *Hitler Strikes Poland: Blitzkrieg, Ideology, and Atrocity* (Lawrence, KS, 2003)

—, 'Polish "Neighbors" and German Invaders: Anti-Jewish Violence in the Białystok District during the Opening Weeks of Operation Barbarossa', *Polin*, 16 (2003), 431–52

E. Rozek, *Allied Wartime Diplomacy* (New York, 1958)

K. Rudnicki, *The Last of the Warhorses* (1974)

P. Rutherford, *Prelude to the Final Solution: The Nazi Program for Deporting Ethnic Poles 1939–41* (Lawrence, KS, 2007)

C. Ryan, *A Bridge Too Far* (1974)

R. Ryder, *Oliver Leese* (1987)

O. Rzheshevsky (ed.), *War and Diplomacy: The Making of the Grand Alliance: Documents from Stalin's Archives* (Newark, NJ, 1995)

C. Sadler, 'Pro-Soviet Polish Americans: Oskar Lange and Russia's Friends in the Polonia, 1941–1945', *Polish Review*, 22 (1977), 25–38

W. Sagajllo, *The Man in the Middle: A Story of the Polish Resistance, 1940–45* (1984)

G. Sanford, 'The Katyń Massacre and Polish-Soviet Relations, 1941–43', *Journal of Contemporary History*, 4 (2006), 95–111

H. Sarner, *General Anders and the Soldiers of the Second Polish Corps* (Cathedral City, CA, 1997)

M. Schronek, 'Kazimierz Sosnkowski as Commander in Chief: The Government-in-Exile and Polish Strategy', *Journal of Military History*, 70 (2006), 743–80

A. Seaton, *The Russo-German War 1941–1945* (1971)

H. Sebag-Montefiore, *Enigma: The Battle for the Code* (2000)

S. Seidner, 'The Camp of National Unity: An Experiment in Domestic Consolidation', *Polish Review*, 20 (1975), 231–6

T. Sharp, 'The Origins of the "Teheran Formula" on Polish Frontiers', *Journal of Contemporary History*, 12 (1977), 381–93

B. Shephard, *The Long Road Home: The Aftermath of the Second World War* (2010)

W. Shirer, *The Rise and Fall of the Third Reich* (1964)

J. Shotwell & M. Laserson, *Poland and Russia, 1919–45* (New York, 1945)

Sikorski Institute, *Documents on Polish-Soviet Relations*, 2 vols. (1961–7)

—, *Polskie Siły Zbrojne w drugiej wojnie światowej*, 3 vols. (1950)

—, *Wykaz poległych i zmarłych żołnierzy Polskich Sił Zbrojnych na obczyźnie w latach 1939–1946* (1952)

J. Skrzynska, 'A Brief Outline of the History of Women POWs from the Polish Home Army (AK) held in Stalag Vic at Oberlangen after the Warsaw Uprising', downloaded from www.polishresistance-ak.org.

G. Slizewski, *Stracone Złudzenia: Polskie lotnictwo myśliwskie nad Francją w 1940 roku* (Koszalin, 2000)

L. Smith (ed.), *Forgotten Voices of the Holocaust* (2005)

T. Snyder, *Bloodlands: Europe Between Hitler and Stalin* (2010)

—, 'The Causes of Ukrainian-Polish Ethnic Cleansing 1943', *Past & Present*, no. 179 (2003), 197–234

—, *The Reconstruction of Nations: Poland, Ukraine, Lithuania, Belarus, 1569–1999* (New Haven, CT, 2003)

Z. Sobieski, 'Reminiscences from Lwów, 1939–1946', *Journal of Central European Affairs*, 6 (1947), 351–74

S. Sosabowski, *Freely I Served* (Nashville, TN, 1960)

M. Spoerer & J. Fleischhacker, 'Forced Laborers in Nazi Germany: Categories, Numbers, and Survivors', *Journal of Interdisciplinary History*, 33 (2002), 169–204

P. Stachura, *Poland 1918–1945* (2004)

— (ed.), *Poland Between the Wars, 1918–1939* (1998)

— (ed.), *The Poles in Britain 1940–2000: From Betrayal to Assimilation* (2004)

D. Stafford, *Britain and European Resistance* (Toronto, 1983)

—, *Endgame 1945* (2007)

K. Stasierski, *Szkolnictwo Polskie na Węgrzech w Czasie Drugiej Wojny Światowej* (Poznań, 1969)

A. Statiev, *The Soviet Counterinsurgency in the Western Borderlands* (Cambridge, 2010)

D. Stefancic (ed.), *Armies in Exile* (Boulder, CO, 2005)

Z. Steiner, *The Triumph of the Dark: European International History, 1933–1939* (Oxford, 2010)

M. Stella-Sawicki, J. Garliński & S. Mucha (eds), *First to Fight: Poland's Contribution to the Allied Victory in WWII* (2009)

M. Stenton, *Radio London and Resistance in Occupied Europe* (Oxford, 2000)

T. Stirling, D. Nalęcz & T. Dubicki (eds), *The Report of the Anglo-Polish Historical Commission on Intelligence Co-operation Between Poland and Great Britain During World War II*, 2 vols. (London and Warsaw, 2005)

M. Stoler, 'The "Second Front" and American Fear of Soviet Expansion, 1941–1943', *Military Affairs*, 39 (1975), 136–41

D. Stoltman, *Trust Me You Will Survive* (Durham, NC, 1994)

W. Strang, *At Home and Abroad* (1956)

T. Strzembosz (ed.), *Studia z dziejów okupacji sowieckiej (1939–1941): Obywatele polscy na kresach północno-wschodnich II Rzeczypospolitej pod okupacją sowiecką w latach 1939–1941* (Warsaw, 1997)

Z. Stypułkowski, *Invitation to Moscow* (1951)

W. Sukiennicki, 'The Establishment of the Soviet Regime in Eastern Poland in 1939', *Journal of Central European Affairs*, 23 (July 1963), 191–218

S. Swianiewicz *et al.*, *The Crime of Katyń: Facts and Documents* (1948)

K. Sword, 'British Reactions to the Soviet Occupation of Eastern Poland in September 1939', *Slavonic and East European Review*, 69 (1991), 81–101

—, *Deportation and Exile: Poles in the Soviet Union* (Basingstoke, 1996)

—, *The Formation of the Polish Community in Great Britain, 1939–50* (Basingstoke, 1989)

— (ed.), *Sikorski Soldier and Statesman* (1980)

— (ed.), *The Soviet Takeover of the Polish Eastern Provinces 1939–41* (Basingstoke, 1991)

—, ' "Their Prospects Will Not Be Bright": British Responses to the Problem of the Polish "Recalcitrants", 1946–49', *Journal of Contemporary History*, 21 (1986), 367–90

R. Szawłowski, *Wojna Polsko-Sowiecka 1939*, 2 vols. (Warsaw, 1986)

A. Szczepaniak (ed.), *Generał Władysław Anders: żołnierz czasu pokoju i wojny* (Opole, 2008)

Z. Szkopiak (ed.), *The Yalta Agreements* (1986)

W. Szpilman, *The Pianist* (2000)

S. Sztniewski, 'Teofil Starzyński's Activities to Recruit Polish Soldiers in Canada during the Second World', *Polish American Studies*, 63 (2006), 59–77

R. Szymczak, 'Oskar Lange, American Polonia, and the Polish-Soviet Dilemma During World War II: Making the Case for a "People's Poland" ', *Polish Review*, 40 (1995), 131–57

—, 'Oskar Lange, American Polonia, and the Polish-Soviet Dilemma During World War II: The Public Partisan as a Private Emissary', *Polish Review*, 40 (1995), 3–27

F. Taylor (ed.), *The Goebbels Diaries* (1982)

N. Tec, *Defiance* (New York, 1993)

—, *When Light Pierced the Darkness: Christian Rescue of Jews in Nazi-Occupied Poland* (Oxford, 1986)

O. Terlecki, *Generał Sikorski*, 2 vols. (Cracow, 1983)

S. Terry, *Poland's Place in Europe: General Sikorski and the Origin of the Oder-Neisse Line 1939–43* (Princeton, 1983)

J. Thakrah, 'Aspects of American and Polish Policy towards Poland from the Yalta to the Potsdam Conference 1945', *Polish Review*, 21 (1976), 143–58

P. Ther & A. Siljak (eds), *Redrawing Nations: Ethnic Cleansing in East-Central Europe, 1944–1948* (Oxford, 2001)

M. Thornton, 'The Second Polish Corps, 1943–46: Were They a Functional Mixture of Soldiers, Refugees and Social Workers?', *Journal of Slavic Military Studies*, 10 (1997), 125–37

V. Tismaneanu (ed.), *Stalinism Revisited: The Establishment of Communist Regimes in East-Central Europe* (New York, 2010)

N. Tolstoy, *Victims of Yalta* (1977)

A. Tooze, *The Wages of Destruction: The Making and Breaking of the Nazi Economy* (2007)

T. Torańska, *'Them': Stalin's Polish Puppets* (New York, 1987)

H. Trevor-Roper (ed.), *The Goebbels Diaries: The Last Days* (1978)

*Trial of the Organisers, Leaders and Members of the Polish Diversionist Organisations in the Rear of the Red Army on the Territory of Poland, Lithuania, and the Western Regions of Byelorussia and the Ukraine Heard Before the Military Collegium of the Supreme Court of the USSR – 18–21 June 1945* (London and New York, [1945])

E. Turnbull & A. Suchcitz (eds), *The Diary and Despatches of a Military Attaché in Warsaw, 1938–1939, Edward Sword* (2001)

M. Turski, *Polish Witnesses to the Shoah* (2010)

R. Urquhart, *Arnhem* (1958)

I. Valentine, *Station 43: Audley End House and SOE's Polish Section* (Stroud, 2004)

J. Walker, *Poland Alone: Britain, SOE and the Collapse of the Polish Resistance* (Stroud, 2008)

P. Wandycz, *France and her Eastern Allies* (Minneapolis, MN, 1962)

—, 'Poland's Place in Europe in the Concepts of Piłsudski and Dmowski', *East European Politics and Societies*, 4 (1990), 451–68.

—, *Polish Diplomacy 1914–45* (1988)

—, 'Secret Soviet-Polish Peace Talks in 1919', *Slavic Review*, 24 (1965), 425–49

—, *Soviet-Polish Relations 1917–21* (Cambridge, MA, 1969)

—, *The Twilight of French Eastern Alliances* (Princeton, 1988)

—, *The United States and Poland* (Cambridge, MA, 1980)

M. Wańkowicz, *Bitwa o Monte Cassino* (Warsaw, 2009)

W. Wasilewska, *Wspomnienia* (Warsaw, 1975)

A. Waskiewicz, 'The Polish Home Army and the Politics of Memory', *East European Politics and Societies*, 24 (2010), 44–58

L. Waszak, *Agreement in Principle: The Wartime Partnership of General Władysław Sikorski and Winston Churchill* (New York, 1996)

J. Węgierski, 'Kim byli "Hilary" i "Hugo" w lwowskiej Armii Krajowej i Okręgowej Delegaturze Rządu ("Wino")?', *Sowiniec*, 28 (2006), 27–34

B. Wegner (ed.), *From Peace to War: Germany, Soviet Russia and the West* (Providence, RI, 1997)

A. Werth, *Russia at War* (1964)

E. Westermann, '"Friend and Helper": German Uniformed Police Operations in Poland and the General Government, 1939–1941', *Journal of Military History*, 58 (1994), 643–62

S. Wheatcroft, 'The Scale and Nature of German and Soviet Repression and Mass Killings, 1930–45', *Europe-Asia Studies*, 48 (1996), 1319–53

J. Wieczyński (ed.), *Operation Barbarossa: The German Attack on the Soviet Union, June 22, 1941* (Salt Lake City, 1993)

S. Wiesenthal, *Justice Not Vengeance* (1999)

—, *The Murderers Among Us* (1967)

T. Wiles (ed.), *Poland Between the Wars: 1918–1939* (Bloomington, IN, 1985)

P. Wilkinson & J. Astley, *Gubbins and SOE* (1993)

D. Williamson, *Poland Betrayed: The Nazi-Soviet Invasions of 1939* (Barnsley, 2009)

P. Winter, 'Penetrating Hitler's High Command: Anglo-Polish HUMINT, 1939–1945', *War in History*, 18 (2011), 85–108

W. Wójcik, *Polish Spirit* (1996)

T. Wood & S. Jankowski, *Karski: How One Man Tried to Stop the Holocaust* (New York, 1994)

E. Woodward (ed.), *British Foreign Policy During the Second World War*, 6 vols. (1962–76)

N. Wylie (ed.), *European Neutrals and Non-Belligerents During the Second World War* (Cambridge, 2002)

M. Wyman, *DPs: Europe's Displaced Persons, 1945–1951* (Ithaca, NY, 1998)

E. Wynot, '"A Necessary Cruelty": The Emergence of Official Anti-Semitism in Poland, 1936–39', *American Historical Review*, 76 (1971), 1035–58

Z. Zajdlerowa, *The Dark Side of the Moon* (1946)

S. Zaloga & V. Madeja, *The Polish Campaign, 1939* (New York, 1985)

A. Zamoyski, *The Forgotten Few: The Polish Air Force in the Second World War* (1995)

—, *The Polish Way* (1987)

—, *Warsaw 1920: Lenin's Failed Conquest of Europe* (2008)

P. Żaroń, *Armia Andersa* (Torun, 1996)

J. Zawodny, *Death in the Forest: The Story of the Katyń Forest Massacre* (1962, 1971)

—, *Nothing But Honour: The Story of the Warsaw Uprising, 1944* (1978)

A. Zbikowski, 'Jewish Reaction to the Soviet Arrival in the Kresy in September 1939', *Polin*, 13 (2000), 62–72

S. Zochowski, *British Policy in Relation to Poland in the Second World War* (New York, 1988)

J. Zubrzycki, *Polish Immigrants in Great Britain* (The Hague, 1956)

M. Zylberberg, *A Warsaw Diary 1939–1945* (1969)

# Index